Thematic Education™
Building concrete foundations for limitless horizons

First published August, 2020
Cover & layout design by Kim Littani.

For orders and new products, please visit our website: www.themantic-education.com

Facebook Group for Teachers - ThemEd's IB TOK Teachers
IB TOK Blog: http://www.themantic-education.com/ibtok/
YouTube channel: "Themantic Education"

ISBN: 9780995139008

Acknowledgements

Thank you to the ThemEd Team: Stephanie for your help with research, Tara and Alex for your tireless work in copyediting and proofreading, Kim for the excellent design work on all of our products, Evan for organizing all of our logistics, Jamie for managing the digital and online resources.

Author's dedication: To my teacher Andrey Volochkov. Although you are no longer around, you have become a part of my own self.

CONTENTS

HOW TO USE THIS BOOK

If you are a Theory of Knowledge student, this book is for you. It is designed to be used in class or at home as a student's guide to the IB TOK course. Here is an overview of the features that you will find here.

Lessons

The book is broken down into lessons. Each lesson includes the following elements:

1. **Learning outcomes**. These are key guiding questions that you will be able to answer at the end of the lesson. There belong to three levels:
   a. *Knowledge and comprehension*: this is about knowing the key concepts or ideas and being able to explain their meaning
   b. *Understanding and application*: this is about being able to apply the concepts to specific scenarios or problems, and also to see how different ideas link to each other
   c. *Thinking in the abstract*: this is about understanding some abstract, often debatable problems of knowledge in general
2. **Key concepts**. Usually every lesson is focused on one key knowledge concept (for example, doubt, justification, bias). Sometimes there are a few other concepts that are closely related to this central one. In the lesson itself all key concepts are printed in red font. If you see the red font, it means that the concept is included in the Glossary at the end of the book.
3. **Other concepts used**. These are concepts that are being discussed in the lesson, but are not central to your understanding of knowledge problems. Usually these concepts are related to some specific theories or examples that are used in the lesson to illustrate the key ideas.
4. **Themes and areas of knowledge**. The TOK syllabus has five areas of knowledge and several "themes". Our book is organized thematically, which means that we don't discuss these elements one by one - instead, we discuss them all in comparison. However, if you want to understand how each lesson links to these elements of the TOK syllabus, it is stated here.
5. **Recap and plan.** It's a small section at the start of each lesson to give you a brief overview of what was discussed previously. It also introduces what will be discussed in the lesson.
6. **Boxes in the margins**. Each of these boxes contains a knowledge question that is related to one of the four elements of the IB knowledge framework (Scope, Methods and tools, Perspectives, Ethics). Sometimes these questions are directly discussed in the text, sometimes they are more of a "stop and think" point to extend your thinking. By their very nature, they are always debatable questions. Your teacher will choose to discuss some of these questions in class, leaving others for you to reflect upon on your own.
7. **Critical thinking extension**. This box at the end of the lesson is designed for students who are willing to explore more abstract problems of knowledge to exercise their critical thinking on a deeper level.
8. **If you are interested**. This box gives you suggestions regarding further reading or watching.
9. **Take-away messages**. This box at the very end of this lesson summarizes, just in one paragraph, the main ideas discussed in the lesson. It's a gist of the whole thing.

Units

The lessons are organized into larger units:

- **Introduction.** It contains three lessons explaining what TOK is and covering all essential curriculum terminology.
- **Unit 1: Knowledge of knowledge.** This unit is about knowledge itself - what is it, can it be defined, how are knowledge questions different from questions about the world?
- **Unit 2: Knowledge and technology.** This unit deals with the changing nature of knowledge in the age of technology. Can technology create a revolution in knowledge, change it beyond recognition? We discuss these questions in relation to all five areas of knowledge.
- **Unit 3: Bias in personal knowledge.** This unit explores one of the key concepts in the entire course - bias. Here we look at how bias influences knowledge in your everyday life. How do you know if you are biased or not, and is it possible for you to become less biased?
- **Unit 4: Bias in shared knowledge.** This unit continues exploring the concept of bias, but this time it is applied to three major areas of knowledge - Natural Sciences, History and Mathematics.
- **Unit 5: Knowledge and understanding.** This unit introduces such key concepts as objectivity and subjectivity, interpretation and understanding. What does it mean to understand something and how is understanding different from knowing? We apply this to Natural Sciences, Human Sciences and the Arts.
- **Unit 6: Knowledge and language.** This unit explores the role that language plays in both thinking and communication. Does language shape what we can know? Can we think without using a language? We also apply these problems to all five areas of knowledge.
- **Unit 7: Assessment guidance.** This unit contains focused advice on how to approach the TOK exhibition and TOK essay. We look at assessment instruments, analyze common mistakes and discuss checklists designed to ensure that you maximize your chances of getting the perfect marks.
- **Glossary.** This section contains an explanation of each of the key concepts used in the book.

Additional comments

You will notice that each lesson, including all extension boxes, is maximum 1,600 words long. This is symbolic because that's exactly the word limit for the TOK essay.

Throughout the book I am modelling the kind of thinking that will be required of you in the assessment components. I ask questions and attempt answering them. You don't have to - and you shouldn't - agree with me on the conclusions I'm reaching. But it's the process of thinking that matters, the journey that took me there. Similarly, in your TOK essay and the exhibition it is not the conclusions that are assessed, but the process of thinking that you have demonstrated.

In each unit you will find one or more "Exhibition" and one or more "Story". These serve to demonstrate links between TOK and the real world.

Finally, you don't have to use this book sequentially. Each unit is relatively independent of other units, and each lesson is relatively independent of other lessons. This book is designed to be used in class, but it is equally suitable to be used at home when you are working on the arguments for your TOK assessments.

Enjoy!

INTRODUCTION

Lesson 1 - What is TOK?

Learning outcomes

a) [Knowledge and comprehension] What is TOK about?
b) [Understanding and application] Why is it important to learn TOK?
c) [Thinking in the abstract] Why do we need meta-knowledge over and above regular knowledge?

Key concepts

Theory of Knowledge

Other concepts used

Epistemology, meta-knowledge

Themes and areas of knowledge

Theme: Knowledge and the knower
AOK: Mathematics, History, Natural Sciences

What is TOK about?

What you learn in various subjects at school is knowledge. For example, you learned in an Economics class that scarcity drives people to make decisions about how to allocate resources efficiently. That's your knowledge.

TOK is knowledge of knowledge. The main question that it attempts to answer is "How do we know what we know?"

For the example above, how do you know that it is scarcity that motivates people to allocate resources, not something else? How do you even know what drives people? It's not like you can see inside their minds. How reliable are statements like this? More generally, how universal are laws of economics? Are they more or less universal than laws of physics or chemistry? Is knowledge in economics as certain as knowledge in mathematics and, if not, why can't it be?

These and other questions would be examples of the things TOK explores. Unlike all other subjects where you gain knowledge about the world, in TOK you gain knowledge about knowledge about the world.

KEY IDEA: TOK is knowledge of knowledge. The main question that it attempts to answer is "How do we know what we know?"

Why learn TOK?

When I went to high school, my curriculum was very different from yours. I had 18 compulsory subjects. The way they were taught was less detailed than what you get in the IB, so I got broader coverage but less depth. Psychology and TOK, the two areas I ended up specializing in, were not part of my school curriculum. You might say that I have studied 18 different subjects just to discard them and pursue something else.

Image 1. Knowledge

I think that as I was learning my 18 compulsory subjects, I always felt like I was lacking something. Perhaps it was some common understanding that would bring these subjects together, or some universal principles of knowledge. Back then I couldn't really put a label to it, but now I know – I was lacking a TOK course.

I learned about the Pythagorean theorem (Math), the Napoleonic Wars (History), Newtonian laws of motion (Physics). But I couldn't help asking myself "why?" and "how do we know?"; my education was not too helpful in providing these answers.

For the Pythagorean theorem, we were required to formulate it and be able to apply it in solving problems. It was fine. But I remember accidentally coming across a book that explained how the Pythagorean theorem was derived from the simple starting axioms. The proof was not difficult, and I was able to close the book and reproduce it on a sheet of paper. That moment changed my perception of mathematics. I realized I don't have to memorize the theorem; if I happen to forget it, I can simply reconstruct the proof. Now that I knew where my knowledge came from, it felt so much deeper. Do you have your own examples of when you learned how a particular piece of knowledge was discovered, after which this knowledge suddenly made much more sense to you?

For the Napoleonic Wars, I was told what happened, when and how. I was given the end result of the work of a historian, but I was never required to play the role of a historian myself. Years later, I had to find out what happened to IQ testing in the 1930s in Soviet Russia and why it was banned for decades. I looked at the heap of documents that I managed to find and wondered how a historian can ever make sense of all this. Have you ever tried writing history? Try writing down how the current leader of your country came to power in one paragraph, and you will understand the tremendous amount of mental work that goes into this paragraph.

For Newtonian rules of motion, I was given the formulas and expected to take them for granted. I learned later that Newtonian laws are based on one important assumption: that the body is moving in an "inertial space" where no other forces exist. But I also learned that in real life, inertial space doesn't exist. So does it mean that his equations do not fully apply to the real world? More importantly, what other knowledge from Physics did I take for granted without questioning the assumptions upon which it is based? Do an exercise: remember one piece of knowledge that you studied in Physics (either in the IB Diploma Programme or before that) and identify an assumption upon which this knowledge is based. How easy is that for you?

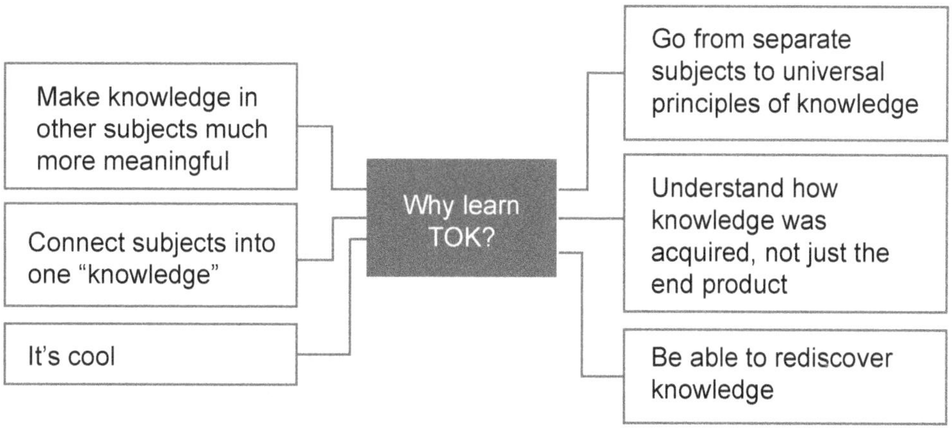

But over and above this reflection on the limitations of knowledge that I was getting in my 18 separate school subjects, I lacked something that would meaningfully combine these subjects into one "knowledge". After all, academic disciplines are divided into subjects, but the real world is not. When you are reading this, your neurons are firing electricity (physics), your brain is producing chemical messengers (chemistry), your heart pumps blood to send oxygen to the parts of your brain that are active (biology), and you engage in the mental process of reading and understanding using language (psychology). This is one single process, but we break it down and study its components separately in separate subjects.

When I discovered Theory of Knowledge, it made my knowledge in all other subjects much more meaningful.

What is TOK like?

Theory of Knowledge is a special subject. It has critical thinking written all over it. Depending on how you approach the subject, it may either leave you with a puzzling aftertaste ("What was that???") or entirely change the way you think ("That is so cool, I'm going to do it all the time!"). Obviously, we want to achieve the latter. However, being thoroughly puzzled about something is a necessary part of changing the way you think. If you do not feel puzzled or perplexed, you are not really challenging what you already know. Hence, you are pursuing an illusion of knowledge, but not knowledge itself. Therefore, I encourage you to be confused as often as you possibly can.

The first humans dramatically advanced in their development when they started using tools. Cooking food was easier with fire, hunting was easier with a spear and transportation was easier with the wheel. Tools allow us to explore the reality of the physical world. In a similar way, there are tools that help us explore the reality of the mental world (the world of knowledge). These tools are concepts. We use concepts to think about the world and ourselves, and concepts become lenses through which we know. The cleaner the lenses, the more clearly we understand things.

This is why this course is conceptual. It is designed around such central concepts as doubt, justification, truth, evidence, and so on. If you clearly understand these concepts, you will be able to apply them to various domains of knowledge and understand these domains better than ever before. There is no memorization involved in the course, but a lot of questioning, understanding and application.

***Image 2**. Knowledge is power*

Critical thinking extension

The prefix "meta" has roots in ancient Greek where it meant "after" or "beyond". You might recall a lot of instances where you have come across "meta"-something. Here are several examples:

- Metacognition in psychology means cognition about cognition (for example, when you think about how you can remember exam material better).
- Metadata in computer jargon means data about data (for example, data for Twitter is the text of the tweets while metadata is information on when and where the tweet was posted).
- Metaphysics is sometimes used synonymously with "philosophy". Aristotle originally divided disciplines into Physics (the study of nature) and metaphysics (after the Physics).

Theory of Knowledge deals with "meta" a lot. If your other school subjects are all about knowledge, then TOK is all about meta-knowledge. To what extent do you think a "meta"-something is necessary to fully understand this something? Can you come up with examples?

If you are interested...

Another term for theory of knowledge is "epistemology". In fact, this is exactly how the word "epistemology" is translated from its ancient Greek roots: *epistēmē* = knowledge, *logos* = study or theory.

All philosophy may be very broadly divided into two parts:

- Ontology (theory of being). This focuses on claims such as "X is" or "X exists". For example, God exists, infinity exists, the Universe is infinite.
- Epistemology (theory of knowledge). This focuses on questions such as "How do we know X is?" or "How do we know X exists?" For example, "How do we know that the Universe is infinite?"

IB TOK is not philosophy, though. We are staying away from all technicalities and nuances of philosophy and instead we are focusing on applications of knowledge concepts to specific areas of knowledge.

However, there is certainly a lot of overlap between IB TOK and epistemology as a branch of philosophy.

Take-away messages

Lesson 1. The main question that we attempt to answer in TOK is "How do we know what we know?" TOK is a reflection on our knowledge, a knowledge of knowledge. The value of TOK may be seen in understanding the deep underlying principles that govern the acquisition of knowledge in various areas, such as human sciences, mathematics, the arts. Additionally, TOK allows us to have a basis upon which various disciplines can be compared and combined. The division of knowledge into academic disciplines is artificial (it does not exist in the real world), and TOK is trying to restore the balance by tying them all back together. TOK is a conceptual subject. At its core are conceptual understanding and critical thinking.

Lesson 2 - Elements of TOK

Learning outcomes

a) [Knowledge and comprehension] What key elements does the course consist of?
b) [Understanding and application] What is the role of themes in the course?
c) [Thinking in the abstract] How can we draw a line between personal knowledge and shared knowledge?

Key concepts

The knower, personal knowledge and shared knowledge, areas of knowledge, knowledge questions, knowledge framework, themes

Themes and areas of knowledge

Themes: Knowledge and the knower, Knowledge and language, Knowledge and technology
AOK: Natural Sciences, Human Sciences, Mathematics, History, the Arts

Recap and plan

We have discussed what TOK is, what it "feels like" and why it is important to learn it at school. Now we will have an overview of the main components of the IB TOK course.

The knower

In the center of TOK is the knower – a person who knows. I am a knower, you are a knower. But we also belong to various communities of knowers, such as the community of people sharing a particular religious belief, the community of mathematicians, the community of students who learn European history from European textbooks.

Personal knowledge and shared knowledge

The knower has certain knowledge about himself/herself and the world around them. This knowledge can be of two types:

- Personal knowledge
- Shared knowledge

Personal knowledge is something that belongs to an individual and is not necessarily shared by other individuals. Shared knowledge is something that is jointly produced by large groups of people. Such knowledge is common to large communities. For example, mathematics is in the domain of shared knowledge. On the other hand, your intuitions about different types of food and how tasty they are belong to the domain of your personal knowledge. It may or may not be shared by others. Similarly, physics is shared knowledge, but a student's understanding of physics is that student's personal knowledge.

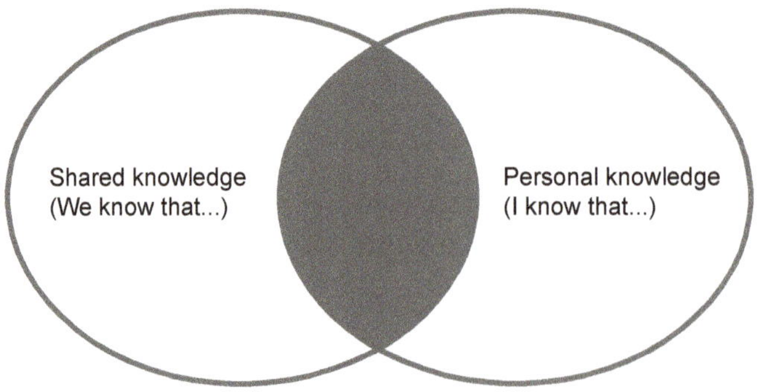

***Image 3**. Personal and shared knowledge*

Areas of knowledge

Shared knowledge may be further divided into areas of knowledge (AOKs). In IB TOK, we speak about five such areas:

- Natural Sciences
- Human Sciences
- Mathematics
- History
- The Arts

These areas of knowledge may be distinctly different in many aspects. Comparisons between these areas of knowledge through a conceptual lens is what comprises the bulk of the IB TOK course.

Knowledge questions and knowledge claims

The main focus of the course is on *knowledge questions* and *knowledge claims.*

Knowledge questions are questions about knowledge itself, such as "What counts as good evidence for a claim?" or "Are some types of justification more reliable than others?" Since these are questions about knowledge itself, they draw on TOK concepts rather than subject-specific terminology. Knowledge questions are contestable, in the sense that the answer to them is not obvious and there may exist various reasonable approaches to an answer.

A knowledge claim is a statement in response to a knowledge question. For example, "The quality of evidence is determined by its consistency with previous knowledge" or "Justifications based on observation are more reliable than logical proofs".

Knowledge framework

In IB TOK, knowledge questions are broadly organized into four categories. You may think of them as "groups" of knowledge questions. The categories, known as the knowledge framework, are:

1) Scope
2) Perspectives
3) Methods and tools
4) Ethics

Image 4. *Knowledge framework*

It is a requirement of the course that all four groups of knowledge questions are discussed.

You should not worry too much about which question belongs to which category. Sometimes categories overlap and one knowledge question may belong to more than one category. You are not required to "correctly" place knowledge questions under categories, but you are required to ensure that all four categories have been discussed. This way the IB makes sure that you do not skip, say, ethics.

In the next lesson we will discuss in more detail the nature of each of these four elements, as well as their applications in the five areas of knowledge.

Themes

Apart from the five areas of knowledge, students in IB TOK are required to study three themes: the core theme and two of five optional themes.

The core theme is "Knowledge and the knower". It is focused on personal knowledge. It is a reflection on yourself as a knower and thinker.

The five optional themes are:
1) Knowledge and technology
2) Knowledge and language
3) Knowledge and politics
4) Knowledge and religion
5) Knowledge and indigenous societies

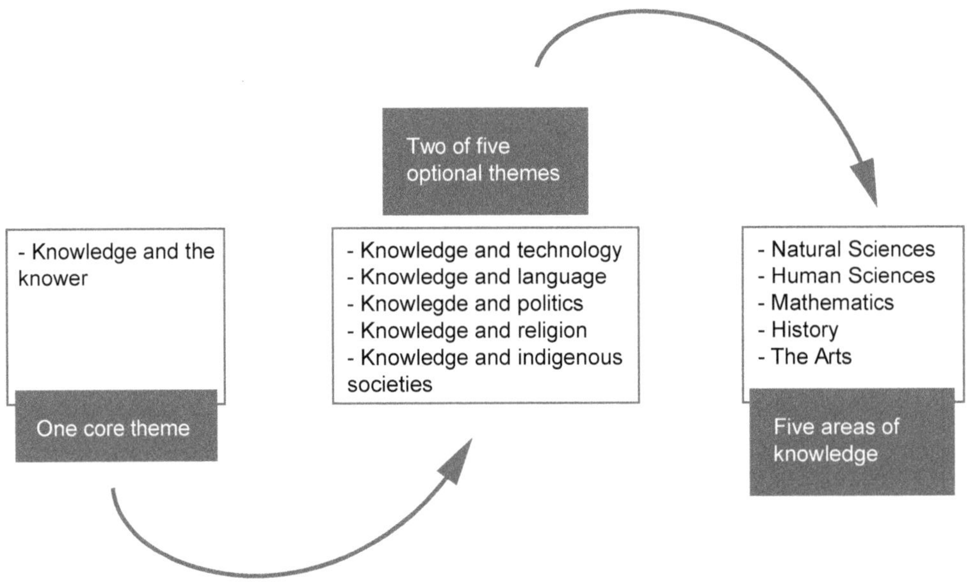

How the Themantic course is organized

Themantic Education designs courses with a focus on conceptual understanding and continuity of knowledge. We do not like the idea of studying each area of knowledge separately, one after another. Instead, we are looking at key TOK concepts and discussing how they manifest in various areas of knowledge. This allows for effective comparisons.

This book is organized around our own broad "themes". Here is a brief summary of our themes and how they map onto the elements of IB TOK:

Our themes	IB guide themes	Natural Sciences	Human Sciences	Mathematics	History	The Arts
Introduction.		✓	✓	✓	✓	✓
Unit 1. Knowledge of knowledge		✓		✓	✓	
Unit 2. Knowledge and technology	Knowledge and technology	✓	✓	✓	✓	✓
Unit 3. Bias in personal knowledge	Knowledge and the knower		✓			
Unit 4. Bias in shared knowledge		✓		✓	✓	
Unit 5. Knowledge and understanding		✓	✓			✓
Unit 6. Knowledge and language	Knowledge and language	✓	✓	✓	✓	✓
Unit 7. Assessment						

In this book we are discussing areas of knowledge not after themes and not separately from them, but *through* themes.

Extra themes that we added (knowledge of knowledge, knowledge and understanding, bias) make it possible to compare areas of knowledge conceptually within a meaningful framework. Each theme will be organized around important concepts that have relevance to all areas of knowledge. This will allow us to compare areas of knowledge throughout the book.

Assessment

In TOK there are two assessment components: a TOK exhibition (internal assessment) and a TOK essay (external assessment).

Image 5. Assessment

For the exhibition, you explore how TOK manifests in the world around us. There are 35 IA prompts (formulated as knowledge questions). You are required to select one of the 35 prompts and center your exhibition around this prompt. Examples of IA prompts are:

- (IA prompt 12) Is bias inevitable in the production of knowledge?
- (IA prompt 19) What counts as a good justification for a claim?
- (IA prompt 32) What makes a good explanation?

You will find the full list of prompts in the IB TOK Guide.

Your exhibition should comprise of three objects (or images of objects) plus a written commentary on each object (a maximum of 950 words for all three commentaries combined). In the commentary, you are required to identify the object and explain its real-world context and its connection to the IA prompt.

The exhibition is internally assessed and externally moderated. It is worth 35% of your marks.

For the essay, six months prior to the submission deadline the IB releases "prescribed essay titles". You are required to choose one of these titles and write an individual essay on it (word count limit is 1600 words). This is an external component marked by IB examiners. It is responsible for 65% of your marks. The essay title will be formulated as a knowledge question. You are assessed on the quality of your argumentation, consideration of different points of view, and making links to areas of knowledge.

You can find further guidance on TOK assessment in Unit 7 of this book.

Perhaps the most important thing that you need to understand at this point is that TOK is not assessed in a conventional way. There is nothing to memorize. It is all about understanding and thinking. It is also about skills. It is impossible, for example, to predict what the prescribed essay title will be, so it is highly likely that you will have to write an essay on something that you never discussed in class. That being said, you have plenty of time to do so and will be able to do your research if necessary. But knowledge of key concepts will help you immensely.

You should use this book accordingly. Understand the concepts, do the thinking, argue and disagree. Content only matters as far as it enables good argumentation, and your knowledge of content itself will not be assessed.

Critical thinking extension

There is a complex relationship between personal knowledge and shared knowledge. The boundary between these two is not always clear.

In fact, the IB does not officially use the terms "shared knowledge" and "personal knowledge" in the Guide (they used to be there in the previous syllabus), but this distinction is implied. Areas of knowledge are about "shared knowledge". The core theme is about personal knowledge. The optional themes may cover both aspects.

For our course it is useful to return to the clear distinction between personal and shared knowledge. We will be alternating between them from time to time, and it is important that you bear in mind the profound difference between "I know that…" and "We know that…".

Can you think of several things that you know that are uniquely your own, several things that you know differently from your classmates, several things that you know because you belong to a certain knowledge community? Where do you think we should draw a line between personal knowledge and shared knowledge?

If you are interested...

The IB TOK Subject Guide is the official IB publication outlining the syllabus, assessment requirements and other important details of the course. While your teacher, just like any other IB TOK teacher in the world, follows the Guide closely, it may be a good idea for you to also familiarize yourself with this document and have ready access to it. Ask your teacher to share it with you.

Take-away messages

Lesson 2. The key components of the TOK course are the knower, personal and shared knowledge, knowledge questions, knowledge framework, areas of knowledge, and themes. Rather than looking at each area of knowledge separately, this book looks at areas of knowledge through themes. This allows us to compare and combine areas of knowledge within the key concepts. Assessment in the course includes two components: the TOK exhibition (internal assessment) and the TOK essay (external assessment).

Lesson 3 - Knowledge framework

Learning outcomes

a) [Knowledge and comprehension] What elements does the knowledge framework consist of?
b) [Understanding and application] What role does the knowledge framework play in the TOK course?
c) [Thinking in the abstract] How should we treat knowledge questions that can be related to more than one category?

Key concepts

Scope, methods and tools, perspectives, ethics

Themes and areas of knowledge

Themes: Knowledge and the knower, Knowledge and technology, Knowledge and language
AOK: Natural Sciences, Human Sciences, History, Mathematics, the Arts

Recap and plan

In the previous lesson we looked at the main components of the IB TOK course. One of these elements – the knowledge framework – requires a closer look.

As you already know, the course revolves around knowledge questions, and knowledge questions may be broadly organized into four groups: scope, perspectives, methods and tools, ethics.

So what is the focus of each of these four elements of the knowledge framework?

Scope

This element explores the nature of the problems that are investigated in each theme / area of knowledge. It also shows the place of the theme / area of knowledge within human knowledge in general.

Examples of questions relating to scope are:

- What are the key unanswered questions and unsolved problems currently in this area of knowledge (or theme)?
- What makes this theme or area of knowledge important?

Image 6. Scope

There will be more specific knowledge questions related to scope within each theme and area of knowledge. Examples are given in the table below:

Theme / area of knowledge		Examples of knowledge questions related to scope
Themes	Core theme: Knowledge and the knower	Is there a limit to how far we can know ourselves? How biased is our personal knowledge?
	Knowledge and language	Is it possible to have knowledge without language? Can all knowledge be expressed in language?
	Knowledge and technology	How has the development of technology influenced the way we know things? Can computers make discoveries on their own?
Areas of knowledge	Natural Sciences	Is there anything that is beyond scientific understanding? What counts as scientific knowledge?
	Human Sciences	Can human sciences be replaced by natural sciences? What is it about humans that makes them a special object of research as compared to other areas of knowledge?
	Mathematics	Is mathematics a study of abstract entities or a study of the real world? How does technology affect the nature of mathematical knowledge?
	History	Is there a difference between knowledge and interpretation in history? Is knowledge of the past useful for the present?
	The Arts	What counts as knowledge in the arts? Is the aesthetic value of an artwork universal or a matter of personal opinion?

Perspectives

This element of the knowledge framework focuses on the possibility of varying interpretations or points of view regarding knowledge of something. When knowledge is open to interpretation and there are several ways of looking at it, perspectives come into play.

***Image 7**. Perspectives (credit: Mushki Brichta, Wikimedia Commons)*

The table below gives some examples of knowledge questions related to this element of the knowledge framework in various themes and areas of knowledge:

Theme / area of knowledge		**Examples of knowledge questions related to perspectives**
Themes	Core theme: Knowledge and the knower	Are personal beliefs determined by personal experiences? Is it inevitable that my knowledge will always be biased in one way or another?
	Knowledge and language	Does language contain knowledge or does it merely express it? Are there universal concepts shared by humans which are not likely to be shared by aliens?
	Knowledge and technology	Is human knowledge fundamentally different from products of computer algorithms? Does modern technology create paradigm shifts in areas of knowledge?
Areas of knowledge	Natural Sciences	Does scientific progress get us closer to the truth? Is there such a thing as an objective scientific fact?
	Human Sciences	Is it possible to understand subjective human experiences objectively? Is bias in human sciences desirable in any way?
	Mathematics	How is mathematical knowledge related to the real world? Can mathematics be biased?
	History	Is a historical perspective the same as bias? Does a combination of perspectives allow us to get closer to a historical truth?
	The Arts	Can knowledge conveyed by a work of art be universal to all people? Is art knowable? Does technology change the nature of art?

Methods and tools

Image 8. Tools (credit: Styx, Wikimedia Commons)

This element explores how knowledge is produced. Different areas of knowledge as well as individual knowers can use different ways of obtaining knowledge. This is not limited to formal methodologies (for example, the experimental method or the deductive proof), but also includes cognitive tools (such as assumptions, analogies, reasoning, perception). Technology can also serve as a tool for producing knowledge.

Examples of knowledge questions related to this element of the knowledge framework can be found in the table below:

Theme / area of knowledge		Examples of knowledge questions related to methods and tools
Themes	Core theme: Knowledge and the knower	How do we acquire knowledge about ourselves and the world around us? How can we overcome our own bias?
	Knowledge and language	How does language make it possible to manipulate beliefs and opinions? Can we think beyond concepts that we have internalized together with language?
	Knowledge and technology	How does technology overcome limitations of human knowledge? Are there aspects of the world that can be understood only by using computer simulations?
Areas of knowledge	Natural Sciences	How important is it to establish causation in scientific knowledge? Can we accept claims in natural sciences if they cannot in principle be confirmed by observation?
	Human Sciences	What does it mean to "understand" in human sciences, as compared to other areas of knowledge? Is the use of subjective methods in human sciences justifiable?
	Mathematics	How does constructing axiomatic systems differ from constructing scientific knowledge? Can computers prove theorems?
	History	How can we go beyond reporting events of the past to reconstructing their meaning? Does Big Data provide a fundamentally different approach to constructing historical knowledge?
	The Arts	How important is it to know the context to understand a work of art? What is the essential difference between knowledge of art critics and that of laypersons?

Ethics

This element of the knowledge framework explores knowledge questions implied in the ethical issues that arise in the process of obtaining knowledge. Note that the focus is not on the ethical issues themselves, but on the wider understanding of the relationship between knowledge and ethics.

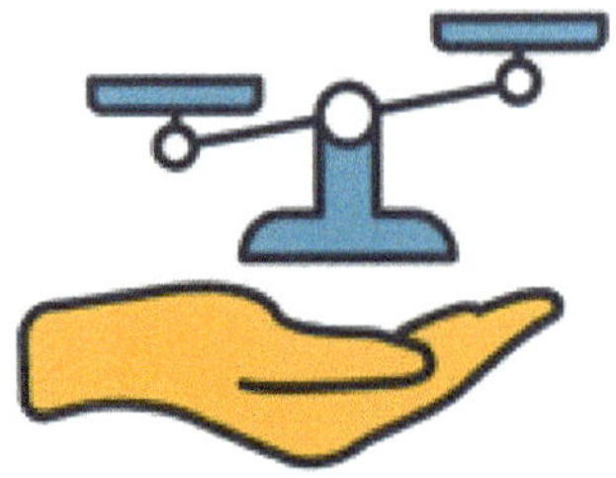

Image 9. Ethics

Some more specific examples from themes and areas of knowledge are given in the table below:

Theme / area of knowledge		**Examples of knowledge questions related to ethics**
Themes	Core theme: Knowledge and the knower	If there is a bias in our knowledge we are not aware of, do we still bear moral responsibility for negative consequences of this bias? Are we obligated to share what we know?
	Knowledge and language	Who is responsible for misunderstanding occurring as a result of using language? How can we know when language is misused for purposes of manipulation?
	Knowledge and technology	Is data privacy more important than knowledge that could be gained if all data were open? Is it our moral obligation to try and develop artificial consciousness because it can allow us to understand ourselves?
Areas of knowledge	Natural Sciences	Should ethical considerations constrain scientific research? Can natural sciences explain morality?
	Human Sciences	Should human sciences be descriptive or prescriptive? In what ways can ethical considerations be said to enhance knowledge in human sciences?
	Mathematics	Are ethical principles similar to mathematical statements that logically follow from a set of assumptions? What are the ethical issues surrounding commercial licensing of software used to prove theorems?
	History	Is it fair to apply modern standards to judge people of the past? Do historians have a moral responsibility to eliminate their own perspectives from their account of the past?
	The Arts	Are aesthetic judgments similar to ethical judgments? Are there any circumstances in which the unethical can be beautiful?

Critical thinking extension

Overlap between elements

You must have noticed that sometimes there is considerable overlap between elements of the knowledge framework. At times, one and the same knowledge question could be reasonably related to more than one category. For example, the question within natural sciences asking "Is there such a thing as an objective scientific fact?", depending on the angle at which we look at it, may be related to:

- Scope (whether or not "objective facts" lie within the scope of natural sciences)
- Perspectives (there are arguments for and against)
- Methods and tools (because we use the scientific method to be able to claim that something is an "objective fact")

What other examples can you identify?

Don't worry about these overlaps. They are perfectly natural because in real life, knowledge is not broken down into artificial categories. You will not be assessed on how "correctly" you can place various knowledge questions in various categories.

If you are interested...

There are many more examples of knowledge questions in the IB TOK Subject Guide. You might want to take a look at them, especially focusing on the themes and areas of knowledge you are more familiar and comfortable with, to get an idea of the range and type of knowledge questions that could be explored in the course.

Take-away messages

Lesson 3. The knowledge framework is a tool IB TOK uses to group knowledge questions into categories. There are four such categories: scope, perspectives, methods and tools, ethics. The knowledge framework is meant to ensure that for each area of knowledge and each theme, students discuss knowledge questions related to all four categories. This prevents a one-sided exploration of areas of knowledge. It is not always easy to place a knowledge question under one of the four categories unambiguously, but this is not what is required. In this lesson, we looked at examples of knowledge questions for each category in each of the themes and areas of knowledge.

UNIT 1 - Knowledge of knowledge

UNIT 1 - Knowledge of knowledge

Sometimes when we use the word "knowledge" casually, we may use it in relation to animals. For example, you might claim that your dog "knows" where in the house you keep meat, or mice in a psychological experiment "know" how to run through a maze, or a bee "knows" in what direction to fly in order to find flower pollen and nectar.

Indeed, very often dogs quickly understand where their tastiest treats come from, and they may guard the place for hours. One can train laboratory mice to run through mazes of tremendous complexity. It may require dozens or hundreds of repetitions, with every successful walk-through reinforced by food and every unsuccessful trial followed by punishment. However, once trained, mice will behave as if they know exactly where to run, which turns to take and in what sequence. When bees return to a beehive, they move vertically in front of it, in a dance that has been shown to communicate to the other bees the geographical location of nectar-rich areas. When the other bees see this dance, they seem to be able to transpose the vertical movements to the horizontal plane and they use that to navigate their way to nectar.

However, here is a question: do these animals know that they know? Does the dog understand that it possesses the knowledge of where meat can be found in the house? If so, can it communicate this knowledge to other dogs? Do bees reflect on the way they navigate? Can they review the mistakes and improve the system? Do mice running in a maze as part of a psychological study realize that they are learning? Do they understand the power of rewards that are reinforcing their behavior?

It seems not. Your dog is guarding that cupboard in the kitchen because it has been conditioned to do so: it did so in the past and got rewarded (with meat). But shift the meat elsewhere and the dog will still guard the same cupboard, at least for some time, even though it has seen the meat being taken away. Train a lab mouse to run through a maze without mistakes, then make one of the corridors twice as long, and the mouse will take a sharp turn right into the wall of the corridor – where the turn used to be. The lab mouse does not seem to "know" how to run through a maze, it is automatically reproducing a sequence of movements that has proven successful in the past. Finally, the dance of the bees may probably become more elaborate generation after generation, but a single bee within its lifetime cannot modify this dance language.

It looks like human beings are the only species that can think about their own thinking. Thinking is a tool to explore reality and this tool is accessible to many species, in one way or another. However, humans have a tool for a tool. Unlike animals, they can amend their own thinking. This gives us endless possibilities and dramatically enhances our survival. Add to that the ability to communicate knowledge (and knowledge of knowledge) from generation to generation, and here you are, the superior creature.

***Image 1**. Self-knowledge*

In the words of Daniel C. Dennett (2018), "We know there are bacteria; dogs don't; dolphins don't; chimpanzees don't. Even bacteria don't know there are bacteria. Our minds are different" (p. 3).

So what is this "knowledge" that makes us so different from everything else on this planet, and how can we use our ability to know that we know?

Exhibition: The philosopher's stone

This is the alchemical symbol for the philosopher's stone (*Latin: lapis philosophorum*) – the squared circle.

Image 2. Squared circle

The philosopher's stone is a hypothetical substance that alchemists were looking for; this substance was thought to be capable of turning various metals into gold. Additionally, it was believed that *lapis philosophorum* would also be a key to achieving immortality. For this reason, the philosopher's stone was sometimes referred to as the elixir of life.

Their beliefs were based on concepts such as *prima materia* and *anima mundi*. *Prima materia*, or the first matter, is the hypothetical ubiquitous base of all matter. It is the building material, so to speak, the clay out of which all things are made. *Anima mundi*, or the world soul, is a similar idea applied to the non-material world. According to this concept, the world has a soul. Every separate living creature is a part of this global soul, but it is also intrinsically connected to all other living creatures.

Since it is all connected, they thought, you can turn one element into another, for example, copper into gold. This was called "transmutation of metals". Why not? Copper and gold are simply *prima materia* coming in two different shapes. But they also believed that, since *prima materia* and *anima mundi* are connected, by manipulating metals they will also manipulate life. Their goal was not to make gold (well, that too, of course!), but to find a way to purify the human soul. It was all deeply mystical.

Alchemical experiments were more reminiscent of mystical rituals than science. With the rise of the scientific method, alchemy was debunked and many alchemists were revealed to be frauds.

But here is what I'm thinking about. I imagine I am a young man living in the 15th century. I like books and I want to know about the Universe. I take great efforts to be accepted into a university, I intern under a famous professor and now I'm finally all by myself. In my laboratory, I mix elements and observe what happens.

You could say that, by modern standards, I am making a career in chemistry, but no. I was taught to mix metals under the moon and only when the moon is in a certain phase. I was not taught that keeping track of data is necessary. If something goes contrary to my predictions, I dismiss these observations as unimportant. If something must be true, according to speculations of great authors who lived centuries before me, then I accept it as true.

My question is, how do I know that what I have is knowledge? How do I know that my methods are correct and reliable? How do I know if I am trapped within a bunch of false beliefs and misconceptions? Can I break free? Could an alchemist suddenly realize the futility of all attempts and become a scientist, in the modern sense of the word?

And, additionally, how do I know that what we believe today, in the 21st century, is not just alchemy under a different name?

Story: Hollow Earth

When students are asked to give an example of a scientific belief of the past that turned out to be wrong, they commonly mention flat Earth versus spherical Earth. People used to believe that the Earth is flat because it appears this way, but they were wrong. Let me give you a related, but slightly different example of an obsolete belief – the concept of Hollow Earth.

According to the Hollow Earth theory, our planet contains an interior space that is potentially habitable (or even inhabited). The idea was suggested by Edmond Halley in 1692.

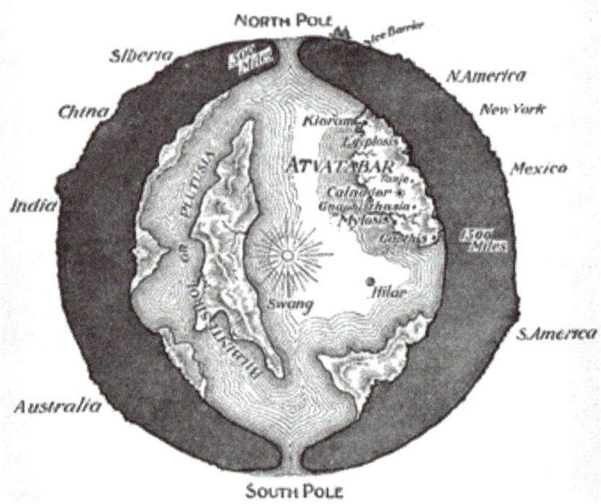

Image 3. *Map of the interior world, from The Goddess of Atvatabar by William Bradshaw (1892)*

His theory did not come out of nowhere. In his numerous expeditions, he recorded many anomalous compass readings that were not consistent with the contemporary theory of magnetic poles. Namely, the direction of the Earth's magnetic field varied over time. The Hollow Earth model explained these variations nicely by suggesting that the Earth has not one, but several magnetic fields. In his model the Earth is composed of 4 spheres nested within each other, each separated by an atmosphere. There were more similar models that followed, some suggesting that there is a sun (and even two suns) inside the planet.

The models were widely discussed and subsequently tested, with both refuting and supporting evidence found from time to time. For example, in 1846, an extinct woolly mammoth was found in Siberia, frozen in ice. It was very well-preserved, so much so that it was suggested that the mammoth had died recently (the villagers who found the mammoth gladly ate it for dinner and marveled at how fresh the meat tasted). Marshall Gardner (1920) believed that mammoths and other creatures inhabited the interior of the Earth. Apparently, this one wandered outside through a hole in the North Pole, was frozen and carried to Siberia by moving plates of ice.

The first convincing argument against the Hollow Earth theory came in 1774 when Charles Hutton conducted what is known as the Schiehallion experiment (Danson, 2006). Schiehallion is a mountain in Scotland. It is isolated and remarkably symmetrical in shape. The idea was based on the theory of gravity, and it was ingenious in its simplicity: approach the mountain with a pendulum, and the gravitational pull from the mountain will deflect the pendulum. Since gravitational pull depends on the density and volume of the body, the deflection angle will depend on two things: how dense and big the mountain is (pulling the pendulum sideways) and how dense and big the Earth is (pulling the pendulum down). We can measure the volume and density of the mountain and we can measure the deflection angle of the pendulum. From this, we can determine the volume and density of the Earth to see if the Earth can be hollow.

Image 4. *Schiehallion*

By the way, since Hutton could determine the density of our planet, he could also determine the density of other planets in the Solar System, as well as their moons and the Sun. Before the experiment, these densities were only known relative to the Earth.

To me, this is a remarkable story of the power of the human mind equipped with good theory. If I gave you a pendulum and asked you to use it to measure the mass of the Sun, would you come up with something like the Schiehallion experiment?

But apart from that, this is a story about the life of knowledge. Theories are born and theories die. Even the most absurd theories may be consistent with our observations. Even the tiniest pieces of evidence could be sufficient to put an end to a mighty and popular theory. How do we know when it is time to accept something as true and when it is time to reject it? Are we okay with the realization that something we believe to be true today may turn out to be false in the future? What, at the end of the day, counts as knowledge?

Lesson 1 - Meaningful doubt

Learning outcomes

a) [Knowledge and comprehension] What makes doubt meaningful (as opposed to superficial)?
b) [Understanding and application] How certain can we be in our knowledge?
c) [Thinking in the abstract] To what extent is it reasonable to doubt everything?

Key concepts

Doubt, meaningful doubt, superficial doubt, certainty, radical skepticism

Other concepts used

Pythagorean theorem, axiom, axiomatic system

Themes and areas of knowledge

Theme: Knowledge and the knower
AOK: Mathematics

Recap and plan

We have briefly reviewed TOK as a course – its structure, assessment details and basic terminology. It is now time to start exploring knowledge itself. To understand what it means to know, we need to understand first what it means to doubt.

Doubting meaningfully versus doubting superficially

What do you know? Think about it for a minute.

Do you know, for example, that in a right triangle the square of the hypotenuse is equal to the sum of the squares of the other two sides ($a^2 + b^2 = c^2$)? You might remember this (the Pythagorean theorem) from your Math lessons. Or do you know that force equals mass multiplied by acceleration ($F = m \times a$)? You might remember this from your Physics classes as Newton's second law of motion. Do you know that a bachelor is an unmarried man? When you are looking at the Sun and pointing your finger at it, do you know that it is there?

Do you know what your name is? What country you live in? Do you know how to tie shoelaces or how to ride a bicycle? Do you know when and how World War II happened? Do you know that it's a thrilling experience to fall in love with someone? Do you know that you exist?

And now a follow-up question: how do you know all that? How certain are you that you know these things?

Arguably, you can doubt anything. Wonderful, let us do that. I bet that's a great mental exercise. But remember that there is a difference between meaningful doubt and superficial doubt.

Under what circumstances can doubt become a hindrance to knowledge? (#Methods and tools)

Meaningful doubt targets the essential limitations of a certain knowledge. It identifies the limitation and explains it. It does not blindly reject the knowledge; rather, it identifies its weakest aspect and in this sense encourages further inquiry. This is in opposition to superficial doubt, which boils down to saying things like "nothing is certain because the government is conspiring against us, the world is an illusion and we can never believe anything".

Superficial — Doubt — Meaningful

Let me give you a couple of examples of meaningful doubt.

Example of doubt 1: Mathematics (the Pythagorean theorem: $a^2 + b^2 = c^2$)

The Pythagorean theorem in geometry states that in a right triangle, the square of the hypotenuse (the side opposite to the right angle) is equal to the sum of squares of the other two sides: $a^2 + b^2 = c^2$. It is one of the most basic theorems of geometry that you learn at school.

How do you know this theorem? You could say that you know it from textbooks or because your teacher told you it was true. You could go further and say that the theorem itself is based on a rigorous mathematical proof (that you can even recreate if you are good at mathematics). This mathematical proof takes some axioms (self-obvious statements) that were proposed by Euclid as the foundation of geometry, applies rules of logical reasoning to those axioms, and derives the theorem. So the theorem is true if we do not have any reason to doubt either the starting axioms or the rules of logical reasoning.

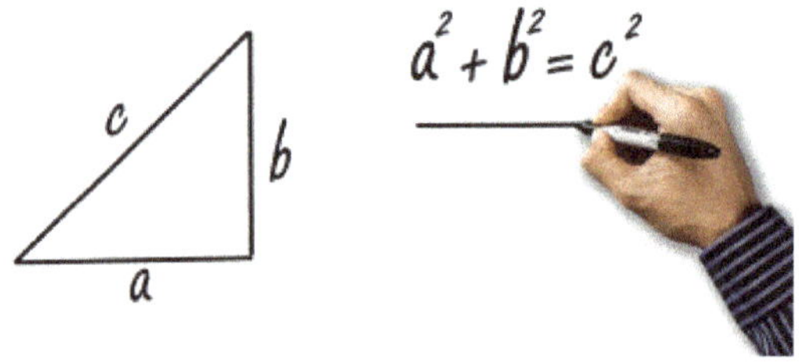

Image 5. The Pythagorean theorem

How can you doubt it? Since the starting point of any mathematical proof is a set of axioms (statements that are taken as self-obvious truths that do not require any justification), the Pythagorean theorem is true only if these axioms are true. But since the truth of axioms is, by definition, assumed, it makes them somewhat arbitrary. Indeed, for the most part, the geometry you study at school is what is known as Euclidean geometry – based on the classic set of axioms put forth by the Greek mathematician Euclid (in around 300 B.C.). Euclidean geometry only makes sense on a perfectly flat surface. Think about it: if you draw a triangle on a slightly curved surface (for example, on the surface of our planet), $a^2 + b^2$ will most certainly NOT be equal to c^2. There exist alternative axiomatic systems – non-Euclidean geometries – that do not make the assumption of a perfectly flat surface. But the Pythagorean theorem in these geometries is not true.

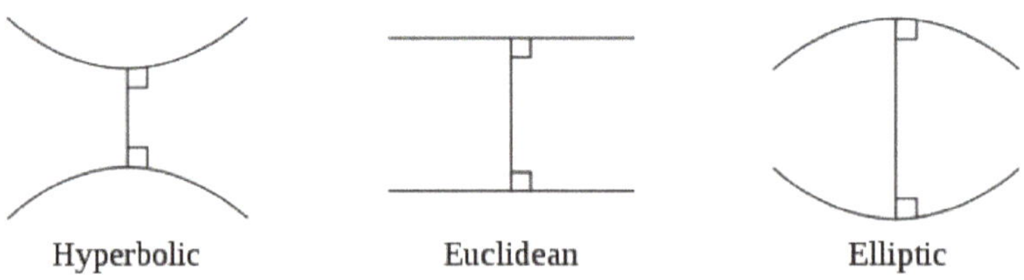

Image 6. Different types of geometries (credit: Wikimedia Commons)

Note that what is described above is an example of *meaningful* doubt. Our doubt has targeted the important limitation of knowledge and, instead of blindly rejecting the Pythagorean theorem, identified the boundaries beyond which the truth of this theorem becomes questionable.

KEY IDEA: To doubt a claim meaningfully means to identity its limitations and outline the boundaries beyond which its truth becomes questionable

By contrast, the following are examples of *superficial doubt*:

- I read it in a textbook, but textbooks can lie
- I don't understand Math, so I cannot know if the Pythagorean theorem is true
- Nothing is certain, and neither is the Pythagorean theorem

Needless to say, one of your jobs as a TOK student is to formulate meaningful doubt and avoid regressing to superficial doubt.

Example of doubt 2: Daily life ("The Sun is right there")

When you are looking at the Sun and pointing your finger at it, do you know that it is there?

The answer to this question seems obvious. Yes, of course, the Sun is right there because I see it with my own eyes right now.

However, there are some reasons to meaningfully doubt this statement:

How can we know something for certain? (#Scope)

- You see something when the light from this object reaches your retina. But light travels with a certain speed and this speed is finite (approximately 300 thousand kilometers per second). Light from the Sun takes an average of 8 minutes and 20 seconds to reach the Earth. Hence, you do not actually see the Sun the way it is right now. You see *the past* of the Sun, the way it was 8 minutes ago. Suppose at the very moment when you are pointing your finger at the Sun and saying "the Sun is over there", the Sun is exploding. You will not know that until 8 minutes later. It may not be so obvious with the Sun, but think about the more distant stars that we observe in the night sky. For example, Proxima Centauri, the star second nearest to the Earth, is 4.24 light years away. If it blows up and disappears today, we will spend at least 4.24 more years seeing it in the night sky, pointing at it and saying "look, this is Proxima Centauri, isn't it beautiful?"
- Even if the Sun does not stop existing, in the 8 minutes we would have moved in relation to it. Therefore, technically when we are pointing at the Sun and saying "it is right there", it is not. We are pointing at where it *used to* be.

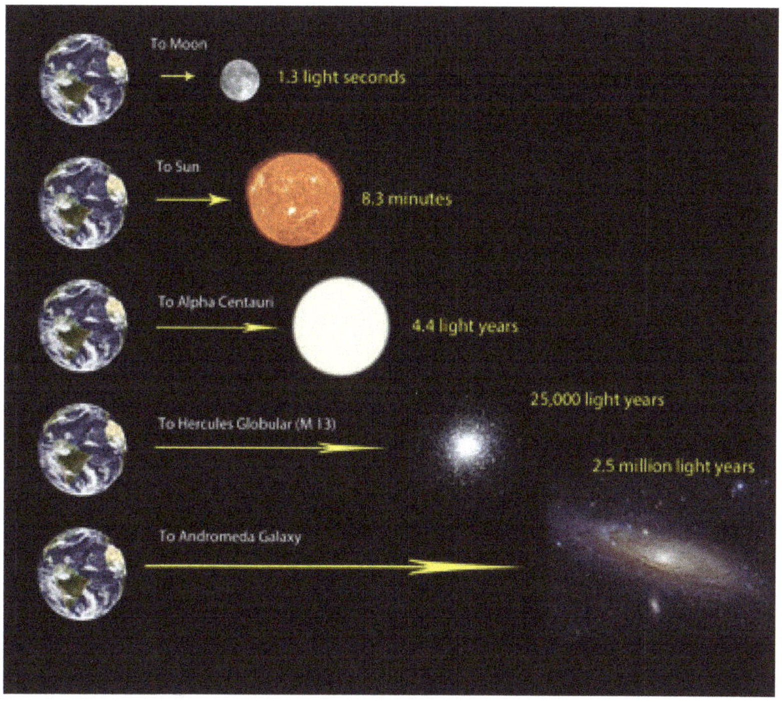

***Image 7**. Light year scale (credit: Bob King, Wikimedia Commons)*

Critical thinking extension

Perfect certainty and radical skepticism

Coming back to the daily life example ("The Sun is over there"), here is another doubt that may probably seem far-fetched to you.

Can everything be doubted? (#Perspectives)

To claim that you know something, you must know it with absolute certainty. But the knowledge that "the Sun is over there" is less than perfectly certain. There exists a possibility that your senses are deceiving you, that you are dreaming or hallucinating, or even that all things that you subjectively experience are actually illusions created for you and you are nothing but a brain in a jar connected to a computer (you will picture this last one vividly if you have seen *The Matrix*). Because the certainty of your knowledge that "the Sun is over there" is less than perfect, you cannot claim that you know it.

This argument is an example of radical skepticism. Radical skepticism is the idea that we must not accept as knowledge anything that is not absolutely certain. And since there are hardly any things (if anything at all!) that may be claimed to be absolutely certain, radical skeptics go as far as rejecting the idea that the world around us exists. After all, are we *perfectly certain* that it does?

As any radical approach, however, radical skepticism has certain drawbacks. Should we really accept the black-and-white thinking? Compare the following two arguments:

Knowledge is something that we know with absolute certainty. There is nothing we can claim to know with absolute certainty. Hence, we don't know anything.

and

A good IB student is anyone who can get 45 diploma points after studying all textbooks in one evening. No one in your school can do that. Hence, there are no good IB students in your school.

Based on this comparison, do you think knowledge can be useful or at least acceptable even if it is less than absolutely certain?

If you are interested…

Watch the video "Epistemology: the problem of skepticism" on the YouTube channel *Wireless Philosophy*.
It gives you both a brief historical overview of where skepticism originated from and the contemporary versions of skepticism such as the dreaming argument, the evil genius scenario and the brain-in-a-vat scenario.

Take-away messages

Lesson 1. To understand what it means to know, we need to understand what it means to doubt. But we should be mindful of the difference between meaningful doubt and superficial doubt. To doubt knowledge meaningfully means to identify its limitations and outline the boundaries beyond which the truth of a knowledge claim becomes questionable. To doubt superficially means to simply reject a statement because there is a possibility that it is not true. Radical skepticism is the school of thought that doubts even the most fundamental facts (such as "I exist") and rejects them on the basis of lack of absolute certainty. However, radical skepticism uses black-and-white thinking that may ignore the actual complexity of knowledge.

Lesson 2 - Forms of meaningful doubt

Learning outcomes

a) [Knowledge and comprehension] What are the existing schools of thought regarding the role of doubt in obtaining knowledge?
b) [Understanding and application] How can we apply meaningful doubt in various areas of knowledge (for example, Mathematics, Natural Sciences, the Arts)?
c) [Thinking in the abstract] Is Cartesian doubt meaningful?

Key concepts

Dogmatism, fallibilism, skepticism, Cartesian doubt

Other concepts used

Axioms, experimental data, theoretical explanation, subjectivity, interpretation, evidence

Themes and areas of knowledge

AOK: Mathematics, Natural Sciences, Human Sciences, the Arts, History

Recap and plan

In the previous lesson you saw that there is an important distinction between meaningful doubt and superficial doubt. Superficial doubt is simply negating something without giving any substantial reasons, while meaningful doubt targets specific important limitations of knowledge. Superficial doubt is destructive for arguments because it does not provide any basis for continuing the discussion, while meaningful doubt is constructive. Meaningful doubt is the start of the conversation, not the end of it. It is therefore very important to learn to doubt meaningfully.

Image 8. Doubt

In this lesson we are going to explore further examples and see how meaningful doubt manifests differently in different areas of knowledge (for example, is meaningful doubt in Mathematics the same as meaningful doubt in the Arts?). We are also going to attach labels to some ideas by considering popular schools of thought in this area – dogmatism, fallibilism and skepticism.

Doubt manifests differently in different areas of knowledge

You have already seen from the two examples in the previous lesson that meaningful doubt targets weak spots of knowledge, but what those spots are depends on what this knowledge is based on. If knowledge is based on logical reasoning and we know that logical reasoning is based on some arbitrary axioms, then perhaps the weakest spot is the axioms, and doubt would be most meaningful when it targets this weakest spot. If knowledge is entirely based on evidence that comes from our perception (such as us seeing the Sun with our own eyes), then perhaps doubt would be most meaningful when it addresses some inherent limitations of our perception.

We can conclude that meaningful doubt targets the most essential limitations of the main sources of knowledge in a particular area. But it also means that, since each area of knowledge has its own essential limitations, meaningful doubt will also manifest differently.

Does the source of knowledge fully explain its limitations? (#Methods and tools)

Let's have a broader look at this and consider some examples from various areas of knowledge.

Area of knowledge	Main sources of knowledge	Essential limitations of these sources	Doubt
Mathematics	Mathematical proof (logical reasoning from axioms to theorems)	Axioms are not proven, they are just taken for granted.	How do we know that mathematics based on this set of axioms is closer to the truth than mathematics based on some other set of axioms?
Natural Sciences	Experiments	The transition from experimental data to a theoretical explanation is a leap. When data is insufficient, there may be multiple theories that fit data equally well.	How do we know that our theory is the best fit to the data? Since there is never enough data, how do we know that our generalizations are justified?
Human Sciences	Research studies with human subjects	Multiple factors influence the behavior of human subjects and we cannot (ethically) control these factors.	When there are so many factors influencing something, how can we isolate these factors from each other and make any sort of conclusions?
The Arts	The viewer's interpretation of a work of art based on the knowledge of artistic conventions and the context in which the work was created	Interpretation inevitably includes an element of subjectivity.	How do we know that the way we interpret a work of art is the way the creator actually intended?
History	Evidence of the past (documents, eyewitness testimony)	There is plenty of contradictory evidence and it raises the problem: what evidence do we select to rely on, and what evidence do we consider more important?	While to some extent we can know *what* happened, how can we know *why* it happened? Knowledge of causal links is not given in the evidence directly, so it is a product of our interpretation.

Do you agree that the examples presented in the table above are all cases of meaningful doubt? If not, what would you change?

KEY IDEA: Meaningful doubt targets the weakest aspects of knowledge, but the aspect that is the weakest depends on the area of knowledge. Therefore, doubt manifests differently in different areas of knowledge.

How can we know if our doubts are meaningful? (#Scope)

As an IB TOK student, you need to constantly reflect on the nature of your doubt and ask yourself, is it superficial or meaningful? Turning superficial doubt into meaningful doubt is a skill that will prove invaluable in any context in your future life. Throughout this course you will also have plenty of opportunities to practice this skill.

There are different perspectives on the role of doubt in knowledge

It is a well-accepted fact that knowledge in various areas has limitations and hence we are justified in doubting it. However, this raises a question: if knowledge is not certain, should we accept it? This question has sparked some debate. There exist different perspectives on how we should treat uncertain knowledge.

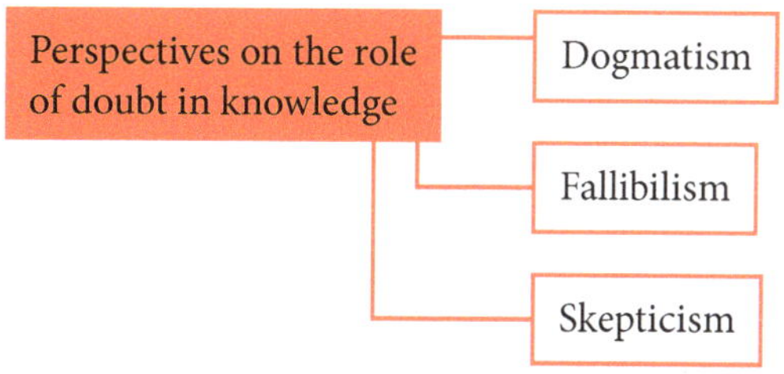

Dogmatism is the position that we can reach certain truths by applying certain methods, and that any further investigation of such truths is unnecessary and even undesirable. Dogmas are ideas that we do not question. For example, before Einstein, we believed time was absolute, not relative. Relativity of time was one of Einstein's counter-intuitive conclusions that physicists had a hard time accepting. Although the word "dogma" produces some negative associations, we need to admit that dogmatic knowledge is necessary for progress. Imagine a dozen architects who have to build a house. If they keep arguing about the foundation, they will never be able to build anything. They need to agree on a certain foundation (even if not everyone is happy with the plan) and stop questioning it. Only then will they be able to proceed. In other words, dogmatists say, "We are quite certain that some things are true, and we should accept them as such".

Fallibilism is the position that claims that our knowledge, in principle, can be mistaken. However, it does *not* claim that we should abandon this knowledge whatsoever. On the contrary, mistaken is better than nothing, and if we temporarily accept a knowledge claim as well as the possibility that this claim will be refuted as more evidence comes along, that would enable healthy development of our knowledge. In other words, fallibilists say, "If we know that we might be mistaken and seek to correct ourselves, we will get closer and closer to being certain about things".

Skepticism takes fallibilism toward an extreme and asserts that if knowledge claims are probably mistaken, they should be rejected. In other words, we should not "temporarily" accept knowledge statements. It should be either certain knowledge or nothing.

Can something that is not certain be accepted as knowledge? (#Perspectives)

On reflection, which of the three positions are you most likely to take?

Critical thinking extension

Cartesian doubt

Image 9. *René Descartes (1596 – 1650)*

You might remember the notion of "Cartesian coordinates" from your Math lessons in middle school. But have you ever heard of "*Cartesian doubt*"? It is a form of skepticism proposed by the 17th-century philosopher René Descartes (1596 – 1650). Cartesian doubt is the approach that doubts the truth of all statements in an attempt to find those few statements the truth of which cannot be doubted. In other words, it is a method of systematically using doubt to find certainty.

Indeed, we can doubt a lot of things. Do you see that lake in a distance? Maybe, but maybe not – it could be a mirage. Do you hear a bird chirping? Maybe, but maybe you are mistaking some other sound for it. Do you know that stars are distant balls of burning gas? Maybe, but maybe someone has deceived you into thinking so. For Descartes, a possibility of something being uncertain is good enough as a reason to reject it as non-knowledge.

However, when Descartes used this method to doubt his own existence, he realized that he couldn't. Indeed, the very fact that that you are doubting your existence proves that you exist! So Descartes concluded that his existence is a certain fact. He famously said "*Cogito ergo sum*!" ("*I think, therefore I am!*").

Do you think it's a good idea to doubt everything to the extent that the only thing you can claim to know is the mere fact that you exist? In other words, is Cartesian doubt meaningful?

If you are interested...

The TV show "*Adam Ruins Everything*" is an investigation of common misconceptions. A special part of the show entitled "*Reanimated History*" aims to show how many of the things that we think we know from history are actually wrong or grossly misrepresented. It also highlights the important role of doubt in gaining historical knowledge. If you haven't seen it already, you might want to start with these two examples:

- Season 1, Episode 22 ("*Adam Ruins the Wild West*") – this episode investigates today's misconceptions about the image of cowboys and the Wild West in general.
- Season 2, Episode 18 ("*The First Factsgiving*") – this is a story about the discovery of America. Among other things, it shows how the well-known story of Pocahontas is in fact historical fiction.

Take-away messages

Lesson 2. Meaningful doubt targets weak aspects of knowledge, but which aspects are weak depends on how the knowledge is acquired (and this could vary from one area of knowledge to another). This is why meaningful doubt manifests differently in different areas of knowledge. For example, the "weak spot" of mathematics is the axioms that are assumed to be true, the "weak spot" of history is that knowledge is based on sources that can be biased, and so on. Additionally, we looked at three perspectives on the role of doubt in obtaining knowledge: dogmatism, fallibilism and skepticism. These approaches differ in terms of accepting something that is not absolutely certain as knowledge. Cartesian doubt is a special form of skepticism that arrives at the following statement: "I think, therefore, I am".

Lesson 3 - Justification

Learning outcomes

a) [Knowledge and comprehension] What is justification?
b) [Understanding and application] How good is justification based on observational evidence?
c) [Thinking in the abstract] Is it possible to identify the best way to justify knowledge claims?

Key concepts

Justification, observational evidence

Other concepts used

Knowledge claims, experimentation, theory

Themes and areas of knowledge

Theme: Knowledge and the knower
AOK: Natural Sciences, Mathematics, History

Recap and plan

Earlier we discussed the importance of doubt. To move from doubting a knowledge claim to being certain about it, one needs to provide some justification to this knowledge claim.

In this lesson, we will make a first attempt at defining justification as well as trying to figure out what it means for justification to be "good". We will not completely figure this out yet, but we will take the most popular answer (good justification = one that is based on observational evidence) and find flaws with it.

What is justification and what is problematic about it?

When you doubt something, you need some justification to be convinced. Justification is simply providing reasons to demonstrate that a knowledge claim is true. However, we cannot just accept any statement that is accompanied by any justification. If that was the case, anyone could use the following strategy:

- Say a ridiculous thing, such as "cats can fly"
- Say "because"
- Provide a ridiculous reason, such as "I saw it in my dream" or "I have a gut feeling about it"

How do we decide if a justification is good? (#Methods and tools)

It looks like justifications may be divided into ones that are good enough and ones that are not good enough. But how do we decide if a justification is good?

Justification in daily life

In 1978, psychologist Ellen Langer conducted an experiment where research assistants were required to cut the line to the Xerox machine in a library (Langer, Blank & Chanowitz, 1978).

The research assistant sat in the library at a table with a clear view of the Xerox machine. Every time someone approached the copier and placed the materials to be copied on the machine, the research assistant came up to that person and said one of three phrases (in three different conditions):

Condition	Phrase
1. No information	"Excuse me. I have 5 pages. May I use the Xerox machine?"
2. Real reason	"Excuse me. I have 5 pages. May I use the Xerox machine, because I'm in a rush?"
3. Fake reason	"Excuse me. I have 5 pages. May I use the Xerox machine, because I have to make copies?"

Note that in condition 1, the research assistant did not provide any justification for the request whatsoever. In condition 2, they provided a plausible justification (saying that they were in a rush). Condition 3, however, is different because the justification is gibberish. Essentially, in condition 3, there was an appearance of justification (the word "because" was there), but the justification itself was bad and didn't make sense.

"I like this painting because it has a bench."

***Image 10**. Justification (credit: Phil Venditti, Flickr)*

Here are the results.

- In condition 1 (no justification), 60% of people allowed the research assistant to cut the line, probably out of the kindness of their hearts.
- In condition 2 (real justification), 94% of people allowed the assistant to cut the line. This is probably because the assistant explained why they were being so impatient and the reason made sense.
- In condition 3 (fake justification), 93% of people complied with the request and allowed the research assistant to cut the line.

Are we responsible for justifying our knowledge to others? (#Ethics)

Note that results in conditions 2 and 3 are practically identical! This led Ellen Langer to claim that in a variety of everyday situations, we do not actually analyze justifications: the word "because" is quite sufficient for us.

Justification in shared knowledge

Remember the important distinction between personal knowledge and shared knowledge? The example above is related to personal knowledge. We can allow bad justifications (such as "May I use the Xerox machine because I have to make copies?") in our daily lives because that is probably not a big deal. But imagine the consequences of accepting bad justifications in shared knowledge, for example, in mathematics or natural sciences. We cannot allow that.

So what counts as "good" and "bad" justification in shared knowledge?

When I ask people this question (and I do that a lot), the most popular answer revolves around the lines of "good justification is when you can see something with your own eyes or check in an experiment". In other words, they appeal to observational evidence.

In the rest of this lesson, I am going to criticize this most popular answer.

KEY IDEA: We must define what counts as "good" justification if we want our knowledge to be trustworthy

Why observational evidence is not necessarily good justification

It might seem at first sight that there is nothing more reliable than seeing something with your own eyes. We rely on our perception. Experimentation in the sciences also seems to be based on observational evidence: we conduct experiments and observe results, then we use these results as data upon which theories are created.

But before jumping to any conclusions, let's consider some counter-arguments first.

1) Observation is not entirely reliable

One popular way to illustrate this is through optical illusions. For example, consider the one in Image 11. Do the orange circles appear the same size to you? They probably don't, but they are in fact the same size. You can check with a ruler.

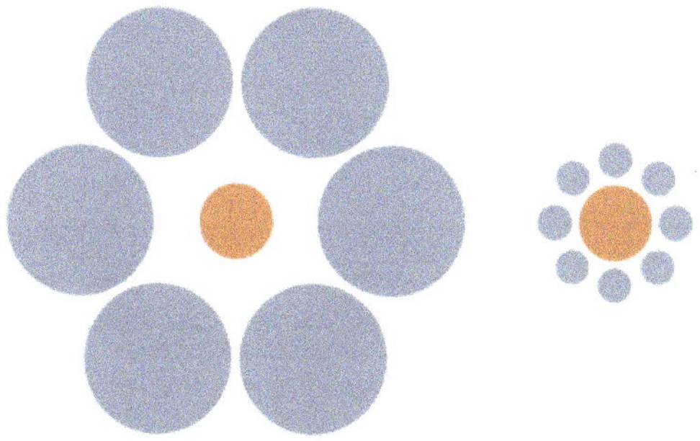

***Image 11**. Optical illusion*

2) There is no such thing as pure observation

Is observational evidence superior to other forms of justification? (#Perspectives)

Do you want to see a hole in your hand? Do the following trick. Take a sheet of paper and roll it into a tube. Close one eye and, with the other eye, look through this tube at some object in the distance (you might want to stand by the window for this to work). Now, put your other hand in front of your closed eye, touching the tube with the edge of the palm. Open your closed eye. Hopefully your hand will have a hole in the middle (that is a weird sentence to say!).

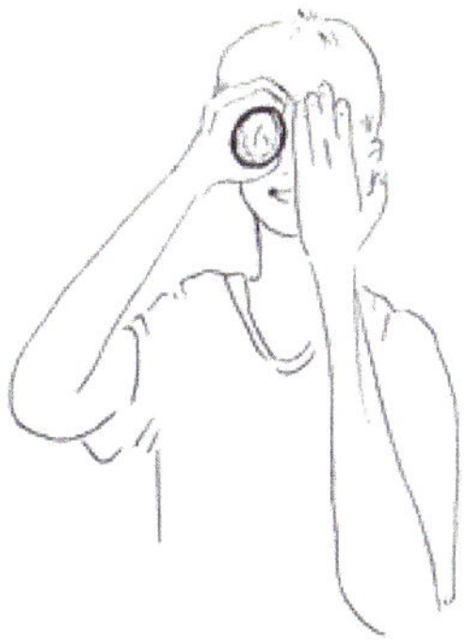

***Image 12**. The optical illusion with a hole in the hand*

What just happened? Your eyes receive a tremendous amount of sensory information every second, and your brain's job is to make sense of this information. When something does not match up, the brain will fill in some gaps and come up with the best possible fit on the basis of previous experience. Since your brain has no (or very little) experience processing information from the two eyes *separately*, it will combine the images received from two separate eyes into one whole image, with a degree of interpretation.

This means that even this simple act of observation includes an element of interpretation in it. We do not see with our eyes – we see with our brain.

3) In the sciences, observation is affected by theory

What is the role of theory in research? (#Scope)

It is often claimed that the sciences are based on observation because they rely on gathering data through experiments. But suppose you are conducting an experiment in chemistry: you are mixing two liquids in a beaker and the resulting mix produces a spectacular chemical reaction, heats up and evaporates. What you observe makes very little sense without your knowledge of the chemical composition of the two liquids and without your theoretical understanding of how substances interact. You need to have that theory to be able to correctly perceive the results of the experiment. One can say that you perceive the results of this experiment through the lens of your theoretical knowledge. In fact, without theory, a scientist would not even know what to look for.

4) Even if you accept that observational evidence does play a large role in the sciences, what about some other areas of knowledge?

Think about history. We cannot observe the past (at least not directly). If this doesn't convince you, think about mathematics. Can you use observation to justify the claim "The square root of 2 is an irrational number"? It looks like there are areas of knowledge where observational evidence does not play a significant role in the justification of claims.

KEY IDEA: What counts as "good" justification may differ from one area of knowledge to another

Conclusion

We have, using the example of observational evidence, demonstrated that we cannot give a simple answer to what counts as "good" justification. This is a complex question, the answer to which probably depends on a particular area of knowledge.

Critical thinking extension

I only used the case of observational evidence to demonstrate that we can never be certain that X is the "best" justification.

You can do that with other types of justification as well. For example, how would you object to the statement "X is the best justification of knowledge" if X is:

1) Logical reasoning
2) Intuition
3) Personal experience

If you are interested...

It is always interesting to explore perceptual illusions. See if you can figure out why the brain plays these tricks on us. Here are a couple of websites to explore (merely as examples):

- "10 cool optical illusions and how each of them work" by Kendra Cherry, published on *Verywellmind*
- "12 mind-bending perceptual illusions" by Steve Stewart-Williams (October 26, 2018), published on *Nautil.us*

Take-away messages

Lesson 3. Justification is giving reasons to support the truth of a statement. It is important to have justification for knowledge claims if we want to avoid having baseless beliefs. But then the question is, how do we tell between "good" justifications and "bad" ones? A popular thing to say is that observational evidence is the best justification of knowledge. In this lesson, I tried to criticize this by giving four reasons: (1) observation is not entirely reliable, (2) there is no such thing as pure observation, (3) in the sciences, observation is affected by theory, (4) there are areas of knowledge where observational evidence does not play a large role. It looks like the claim "X is the best justification of knowledge" is not reasonable for whatever X stands for.

Lesson 4 - Standards of justification

Learning outcomes

a) [Knowledge and comprehension] What is a standard of justification?
b) [Understanding and application] How are standards of justification different in different areas of knowledge?
c) [Thinking in the abstract] Why is it not possible to have a single standard of justification for all knowledge?

Key concepts

Standard of justification, observation, mathematical proof

Other concepts used

Laws, assumptions, reasoning based on theory, objective reality, Münchhausen trilemma: the infinite regress, the circular argument, the axiomatic argument

Themes and areas of knowledge

AOK: Natural Sciences, Mathematics

Recap and plan

Previously we looked at why it is important to have justifications for knowledge claims. We also discussed the possibility of using one type of justification (such as observational evidence) as the main standard of justifying beliefs, but we quickly ran into a problem. We had to admit that the question "How can we tell a good justification from a bad one?" does not have a simple answer that would be universal to all knowledge.

In this lesson we will use the concept of "standards of justification". The idea is that standards of justification are different from one area of knowledge to another, but within each area it may be easier to separate good justifications from bad ones.

To make things a little more specific, I will compare standards of justification in two areas of knowledge - Mathematics and Natural Sciences.

Can standards of justification be universal for all knowledge? (#Perspectives)

Example 1: Standard of justification in natural sciences

In natural sciences, value is given to any justification that shows that a knowledge claim corresponds to reality. We assume that reality exists objectively and independently of the observer. We want to uncover rules that reality follows and we formulate these rules as statements of "laws".

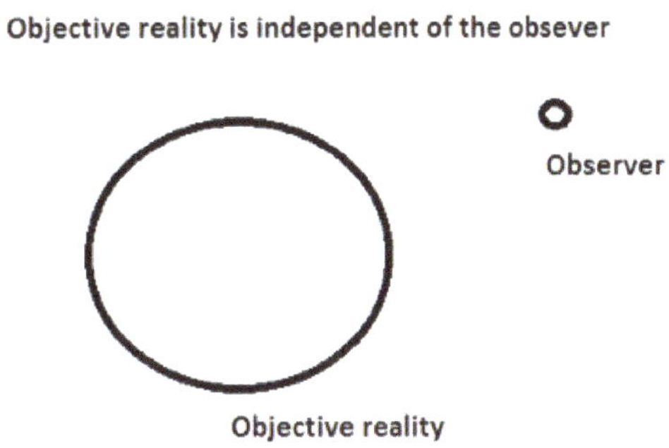

Image 13. Objective reality

For example, the classic Newtonian mechanics in physics describes laws of motion. It claims that all objects in the Universe follow these laws. One of these laws is "*For a constant mass, force equals mass times acceleration*". It is mathematically expressed as $F = m \times a$, where F is force, m is mass and a is acceleration.

These laws of motion are knowledge claims of Newtonian mechanics. What justification are such claims based on?

Image 14. Sir Isaac Newton holding an apple

The first answer that comes to mind is observation. We carefully observe the movement of celestial objects, for example, and see certain trends. If we know their mass and their acceleration, we can calculate the force that must be applied to them. If we find the source of that force, and if that source generates exactly the amount of force we are looking for, then we can say that the observed data supports our claims.

But we must also remember that there is no such thing as pure observation, and that observation makes no sense without *reasoning based on theory*. When we observed that a celestial object with mass *m* moved with acceleration *a*, we knew that there must be force *F* acting upon it. We must find a source of this force for the whole explanation to be plausible. We know from previous theory that there is a gravitational pull between all celestial objects and that the object we are observing may be influenced by gravity from other objects. We know (again, based on prior theory) how to calculate this gravitational pull, so we can identify the potential sources of *F*. Without this reasoning, our standalone observations have little value.

We must also remember that theories are always based on certain *assumptions*. There will never be a perfect fit between observed data and theoretical predictions. There are multiple factors that contribute to this lack of fit – external forces that we are not accounting for, error of measurement, and so on. We need to assume that these external forces and sources of error are negligible.

What responsibilities does a scientist bear in relation to false scientific beliefs? (#Ethics)

With all this in mind, observation in natural sciences is still the ultimate judge. We will not accept a theory that does not match our observations. At the same time, we recognize that even if a claim is supported by observation, we can only accept this claim *provisionally*. This is because there always exists a chance that, although a claim is gaining support now, it will be refuted later as more observational evidence is gathered. Such is the standard of justification in natural sciences.

Example 2: Standard of justification in mathematics

How is scientific knowledge different from mathematical knowledge? (#Scope)

In mathematics, value is given to justifications that show that knowledge claim X with certainty follows from other knowledge claims, which in turn with certainty follow from a set of originally assumed axioms. A knowledge claim cannot be true in the absolute sense of the word, but it can be true within a certain axiomatic system.

Showing how a certain statement with certainty follows from the original set of axioms is known as mathematical proof. As an example, let's consider the following task:

Prove that the sum of any two even integers x and y is even.

We know (by definitions) that:

- An integer is a number that can be written without a fractional component – for example, numbers 1, 2, 3, 2034 are integers, but numbers 9.75 and 6 1/3 are not.
- An even integer is a number that can be divided by 2 and the result will be an integer. For example, 8 is even because when we divide it by 2 we get another integer 4. Conversely, 9 is not even because the product of division by 2 is not an integer.

Since *x* and *y* are even, they must be divisible by 2 with integers as products, so we can express x and y through other integers, *a* and *b*:

$$x = 2a; y = 2b$$

Then

$$x + y = 2a + 2b = 2 \times (a + b)$$

The number 2 x (a + b) has 2 as a factor, which implies that it is an even number. Hence, $x + y$ is even.

There only exist two ways in which we can challenge this conclusion:

- If the definitions are not true
- If the logical reasoning is incorrect

But the definitions are true by definition (!), and the logical reasoning follows strict rules that can be cross-checked by independent thinkers.

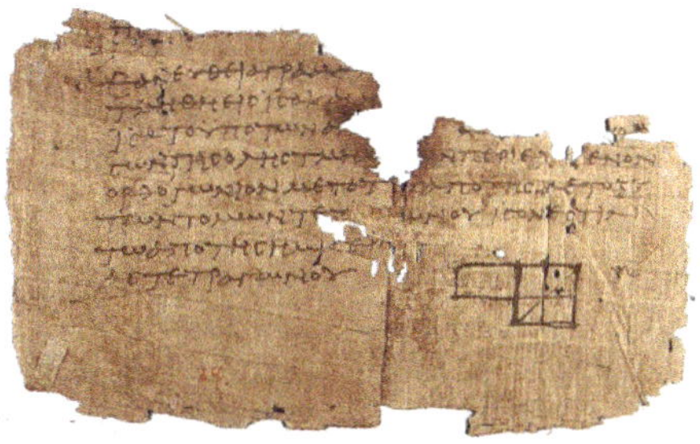

***Image 15**. One of the earliest mathematical proofs – a fragment of Euclid's "Elements"*

Therefore, justification in mathematics (at least in this example) is based completely on deductive reasoning within an axiomatic system. Mathematical proof does not require observation. At the same time, unlike what we saw in natural sciences, the conclusions derived from mathematical proofs are not provisional, but absolutely certain.

Does quality of knowledge fully depend on the method used to obtain it? (#Methods and tools)

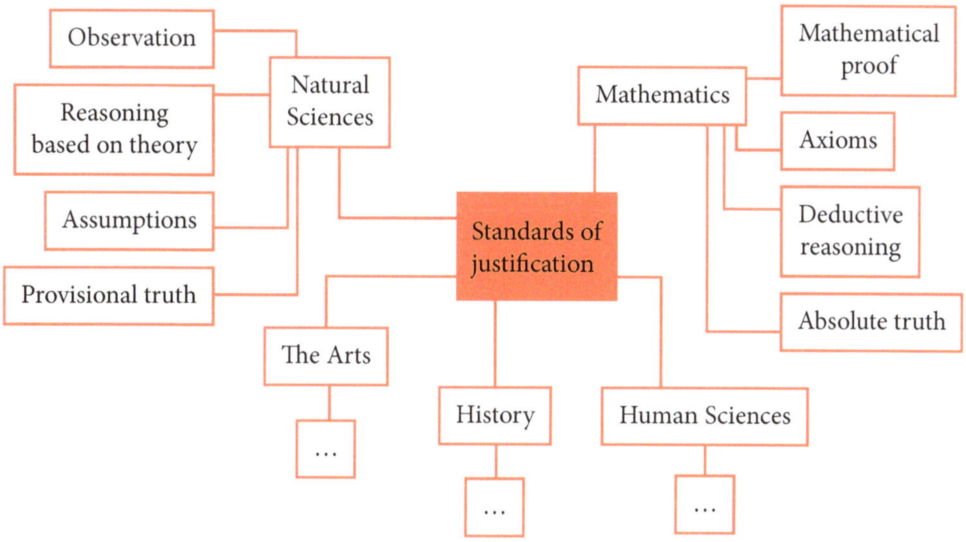

Conclusion

As you compare these and other examples, it becomes clear that each area of knowledge has its own standard of justification. It means that within each area, there is an established consensus on what is accepted as a good justification and what isn't.

KEY IDEA: Each area of knowledge has its own standard of justification

Standards of justification in different areas of knowledge are linked to the main sources of knowledge. Some areas of knowledge, such as natural sciences, are based on evidence that demonstrates a correspondence between knowledge claims and "objective reality".

On the contrary, mathematics as an area of knowledge is based on demonstrating that a new knowledge claim logically follows from already accepted knowledge claims. Mathematics does not care much about the link between these links and "objective reality".

KEY IDEA: Standards of justification are different because sources of knowledge are different

Critical thinking extension

In an attempt to figure out standards of justification in various areas of knowledge, we looked at the examples of natural sciences and mathematics. Can you try and formulate a standard of justification in a third area of knowledge of your choice (choose from human sciences, history and the arts)? Will this third standard of justification be similar to any of the first two?

Give it a go. In line with the reasoning given above, think about:

1) What the main sources of knowledge are in this area,
2) How you can doubt these sources meaningfully,
3) What justification can be possibly used to counteract this doubt.

If you are interested...

The Münchhausen trilemma is a demonstration of the impossibility of fully justifying the truth of any statement, even in such areas as mathematics.

Any knowledge statement may be doubted, and when asked how you know that the statement is true, you can provide some proof (justification). But then you can be asked how you know that the proof is true.

You will have to provide a proof for the proof. But then you can be asked how you know that the proof for the proof is true, and you will have to provide a proof for the proof for the proof, and so on.

According to the Münchhausen trilemma, there are only three possible resolutions to this problem:

- *The infinite regress* - each proof will require a further proof, and there is no end to this process.
- *The circular argument* - supporting the theory through some proof and the proof through the theory. This is a bit like the circular definitions that are often found in dictionaries.
- *The axiomatic argument* - the infinite regress will stop once we accept certain statements as axioms.

All three options, according to the trilemma, are equally bad, but it seems like we must choose one of them.

For a further explanation, watch the video "Münchhausen's trilemma" on the YouTube channel *Carneades.org*.

Take-away messages

Lesson 4. Every area of knowledge has a different standard regarding what counts as a "good" justification and these standards can hardly be compared. We took natural sciences and mathematics as two examples and compared justification in these areas. In natural sciences, observational evidence plays the role of a key source of knowledge, although it is recognized that every observation is based on theory and every theory has certain assumptions. Additionally, knowledge claims can only be accepted provisionally, with the understanding that new evidence may result in refuting them. In mathematics, observational evidence is not important. Instead, the main source of knowledge is the logical coherence between new claims and previously accepted claims. Conclusions can be accepted with certainty rather than provisionally. Since sources of knowledge in different areas of knowledge are different, standards of justification are also different.

Lesson 5 - Theories of truth

Learning outcomes

a) [Knowledge and comprehension] What is the vicious circle of truth?
b) [Understanding and application] What are the existing theories of truth and how do they deal with the vicious circle?
c) [Thinking in the abstract] Are there situations in which some theories of truth apply and others don't?

Key concepts

Truth, theories of truth, correspondence theory, coherence theory, pragmatic theory, vicious circle of truth

Other concepts used

Prior beliefs, provisional truth, indigenous knowledge communities

Themes and areas of knowledge

Theme: Knowledge and the knower
AOK: Implicitly links to all areas of knowledge

Recap and plan

In the previous lessons in this book, we have already touched upon the concept of "truth" implicitly multiple times, but so far we have been avoiding it. Truth is not an easy notion to handle. But it is time to give it a try!

Here is how the concept of truth was implicit so far in our discussions of doubt and justification:

- To doubt something essentially means to doubt that this something is true. We don't say the full sentence, but that is what we imply.
- To justify something means to give certain reasons for this something to be accepted as the truth.

So it really boils down to the relationship between what someone says (a knowledge claim) and what actually is (the truth).

In this lesson we will try to formulate what truth is (simple, isn't it?).

The vicious circle of truth

There is one problem with the truth that you may find fascinating: we determine the quality of our knowledge through its relation to the truth, but we can only know the truth through our knowledge.

How can we make judgments about the truth if we do not have direct access to it? (#Methods and tools)

This is the vicious circle of truth. Knowledge is defined through the truth, but the truth is defined through knowledge. If you can think of any other way to approach the relationship between knowledge and the truth (rather than getting trapped in this vicious circle), please step up and speak out! You might have an idea that can change the way humans have been thinking about their knowledge for thousands of years.

KEY IDEA: Knowledge is defined through its relation to the truth, but the truth can only be accessed through knowledge. This is the vicious circle of truth.

***Image 16**. Vicious circle*

Theories of truth

Broadly speaking, there exist three theories of truth – three approaches to defining what is true and what is not.

The correspondence theory of truth states that truth is determined by correspondence to reality, or facts. This theory seems to be the most intuitively obvious. Even the Oxford English Dictionary defines truth as "*Conformity with fact; agreement with reality*". So we can see that the correspondence theory of truth has made its way into our everyday language. However, there do exist objections to this theory:

How can the truth of moral claims be established? (#Ethics)

1) Some truths do not have a "reality" or "facts" to correspond to. For example, moral claims such as "*cheating on an exam is morally wrong*" cannot be assessed based on their correspondence to "reality" because there is no such thing as a moral fact (or is there?). Similarly, it is very difficult to think of correspondence to reality when it comes to logical claims in mathematics. We can indeed mathematically prove a theorem, but we cannot point at any correspondence between this theorem and "facts".
2) When we state that a knowledge claim is true if it corresponds to reality, we create a paradox because the only way for us to know what is reality is through other knowledge claims. So essentially the theory must be rephrased into "a knowledge claim is true if it corresponds to other knowledge claims we make about the reality". We cannot possibly step outside our own minds to compare a knowledge claim to "objectively existing" reality. Even if this "objective reality" exists, we don't have direct access to it.

The coherence theory of truth suggests that a statement is true if it fits into a system of other previously accepted statements. In other words, something is true if it fits into what we already know. One of the arguments supporting this theory (in opposition to the correspondence theory of truth) is that it does not require us to assume the existence of "objective reality". Since we cannot possibly have direct access to reality, all we have are our *beliefs* about reality. Hence, we cannot possibly assess the truth of a claim by looking at the correspondence between this claim and reality. However, we can look at the coherence between this claim and other claims (beliefs).

How do we know when justification is convincing enough for something to be accepted as true? (#Perspectives)

Obviously, the coherence theory of truth has also been criticized:

1) For every knowledge claim, one can find a set of beliefs that this knowledge claim will be coherent with. For example, look at two opposite knowledge claims: (A) Sentient extraterrestrial life exists, and (B) Sentient extraterrestrial life does not exist. People who believe A say that it is highly unlikely that we are the only sentient species floating around on a speck of dust in the corner of a gigantic universe consisting of approximately 1,000,000,000,000,000,000,000 (1 billion trillion) stars. People who believe B refer to the fact that evidence for the existence of extraterrestrial life has not been found, that emergence of organic life from non-organic molecules is in itself a highly unlikely event, and similar arguments. In any case, both A and B seem to be coherent with their own sets of prior beliefs. How can we decide which one is *more* coherent?
2) Some knowledge claims may be true without being coherent with prior sets of beliefs. For example, here is a couple of claims: (A) the author of this book has light hair, and (B) the author of this book has dark hair. Which one is more coherent with your set of beliefs? Unless you seriously believe that book writing ability depends on hair color, neither A nor B are coherent with prior beliefs. One of them, however, is true. Similarly, think about all the discoveries that we value so much today but that contradicted the established beliefs at the time they were made.

***Image 17**. Angry alien*

If you were a coherentist, how would you answer the objections above?

The pragmatic theory of truth arose from the dissatisfaction of some thinkers with how impractical both the previous theories are. The pragmatic theory claims that our definition of truth must be connected to practical matters such as experience, doubt, belief and the process of inquiry. As we attempt to gain knowledge about the world, we need to come up with some beliefs that we will call "true". Many of these beliefs will be *provisionally true* – we will suspect that they can be refuted in the future, but we will still accept them as true for the time being, because those beliefs are often the best we have. In other words, the pragmatic theory gives the following definition: Truth is a statement that is satisfactory to believe (as cited in Glanzberg, 2018).

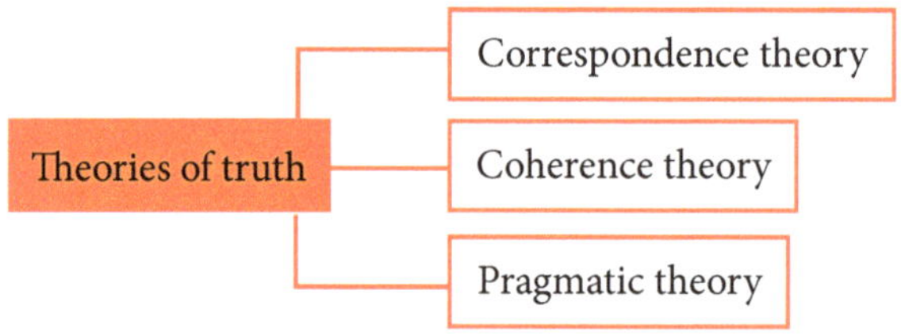

These three theories of truth are the classical approaches that have defined how we think about truth. There exist multiple contemporary versions and alternatives (some of which reject the notion of truth entirely), but even these three show how complex the issue is.

Critical thinking extension

The Inupiaq are an indigenous people of northwestern Alaska. Here is how an Inupiaq elder describes how he and his brother were taught by their father to hunt caribou (Barnhardt & Angayuqaq, 2008).

***Image 18**. Inupiaq family (photo by Edward S. Curtis, 1929)*

How widely must shared knowledge be shared? (#Scope)

One day the father called his sons to join him on a hunting trip to chase a herd of caribou that was crossing a nearby valley. When they reached the place, their father told them to lay quietly and watch as he took his bow and arrows and descended to the valley where the large caribou herd was grazing.

He walked openly right to them, and the herd started to move away, but he kept on walking openly until he reached the spot where the herd was grazing originally. The sons were wondering why he was not hiding. It seemed weird.

Then he stopped and put his bow and arrows down on the ground. He got into a crouching position and began to slowly move his arms up and down, as if imitating a giant bird that was flapping its wings. The caribou stopped and looked back with curiosity. Slowly they started approaching him, spiraling around him and getting closer and closer. When they were close enough, the father picked up his weapon and shot several caribou.

In their acquisition of knowledge, indigenous people are driven by needs of survival. Through a long history of trial and error, they discovered the natural curiosity of caribou that they learned to use to their advantage.

Looking at this example, which theory of truth do you think applies best – correspondence, coherence or pragmatic?

And on a broader scale, do you think there are situations where some theories of truth apply whereas others don't?

If you are interested...

The three theories of truth considered in this lesson are most prominent, but they are not the only ones. If you would like to dig further, have a look at the video "What is consensus theory of truth?" on the YouTube channel *The Audiopedia*.

Take-away messages

Lesson 5. Up until now, the concept of truth was implicit in our discussions of doubt and justification. In this lesson we tried to formulate what truth is. The major problem with this is that the relationship between knowledge and truth is a vicious circle: we judge the quality of knowledge by how close it is to the truth, but we can only have access to the truth through our knowledge. The truth is not objectively given to us. There exist at least three theories of truth – the correspondence theory, the coherence theory and the pragmatic theory. The correspondence theory claims that a statement is true if it corresponds to reality. The coherence theory claims that a statement is true if it fits into what we already know. The pragmatic theory claims that a statement is true if it is good enough for us to currently accept it as true. Each of these theories has been criticized, of course.

Lesson 6 - Tests for truth

Learning outcomes

a) [Knowledge and comprehension] How can "theories of truth" be used as "tests for truth"?
b) [Understanding and application] Are some tests for truth more preferable than others?
c) [Thinking in the abstract] What is the relationship between truth and justification?

Key concepts

Tests for truth: correspondence, coherence, pragmatic

Other concepts used

Truth, reality, indigenous knowledge communities

Themes and areas of knowledge

Theme: Knowledge and the knower
AOK: Natural Sciences, Human Sciences

Recap and plan

In the previous lesson we analyzed the commonly known theories of truth – correspondence, coherence, pragmatic. Although in the ideal world it would be nice to have proof that one theory is more acceptable than the others, it looks like we cannot conclusively say anything like that. We are stuck with three objectionable theories that seem more or less applicable depending on the area of knowledge and the context.

However, this issue can actually be seen as good news! If we have no objective way to choose one of the theories, why don't we use all three of them simultaneously? When used this way, theories of truth become "*tests for truth*". We can apply all three tests for truth to any knowledge statement and see how many the statement will pass. This is exactly what we will do in this lesson.

Tests for truth

Can we ever know if our beliefs are true? (#Perspectives)

When you use the three theories of truth as three "tests for truth", for each knowledge claim you can ask yourself:

- Does this belief pass the correspondence test for truth?
- Does this belief pass the coherence test for truth?
- Does this belief pass the pragmatic test for truth?

This is an interesting exercise that will lead you to a lot of insights. For example, try to apply the three tests for truth to the following statements:

- Snow is white
- 5 + 6 = 11
- Water boils at 100 °C
- Committing adultery is a sin
- The life of English society of the 19th century is masterfully portrayed in Charles Dickens's "*Oliver Twist*"
- Santa Claus exists
- All objects in space are attracted to each other through the force of gravity

Not all knowledge claims can be subjected to all tests for truth

In the course of this exercise, you will notice that some knowledge claims lend themselves readily to some tests for truth but not others. Although one may think that passing all three tests is the ideal scenario, it is not possible for all knowledge claims to be subjected to all tests for truth.

For example, take "*5 + 6 = 11*". This statement passes the coherence test for truth because it is consistent with our other mathematical beliefs (what a set of integers is, how summation works). The correspondence test does not really apply here. One can claim that we can "test" the statement against our perception by taking 5 apples, adding 6 more apples and observing that the result is 11 apples. However, this is hardly a proper experiment. We are not actually testing the statement; we are just illustrating it with apples. Finally, the statement also passes the pragmatic test for truth. That 5 + 6 equals 11 is true to the best of our knowledge, within the system of axioms and rules of reasoning that we created; currently we have no reason not to believe it.

What is the role of prior beliefs in obtaining new knowledge? (#Methods and tools)

As you can see, some tests for truth work in some knowledge scenarios but not others. This raises the question: are some tests for truth more preferable?

Are some tests for truth more preferable?

There are two ways to go about this:

1) Say *yes*, for example, that the correspondence test for truth takes priority over the other tests. The consequence of this decision would be to conclude that some areas of knowledge (such as Natural Sciences or Human Sciences) are "better" or "closer to the truth" than other areas of knowledge (such as the Arts, where the correspondence test for truth is not a possibility).

2) Say *no* and assume that all areas of knowledge are equally valuable and may be equally close to the truth, but the standards for something to be accepted as the truth are different in these areas of knowledge.

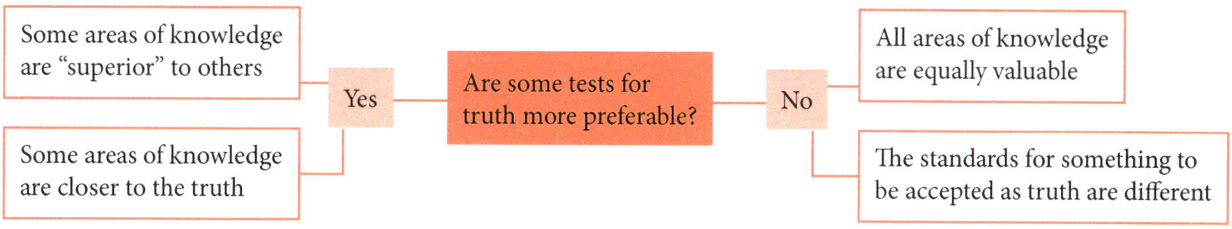

The IB takes the second approach.

But why, you might ask. It may seem obvious to some people that the correspondence test is better because it links beliefs to reality, and that scientific knowledge is superior because it is based primarily on the correspondence test.

KEY IDEA: No test for truth is superior to others, and the standards of truth are different in different areas of knowledge

I will give you just two arguments against this perspective, although many more arguments can be found.

Argument 1. Correspondence test cannot always be used in sciences

Even scientific knowledge cannot always be based on the correspondence test. Take, for example, the Big Bang theory, the best scientific model that we currently have of the origin of

Can we claim that there are things that will never be known? (#Scope)

the Universe. The Big Bang happened a long time (13.8 billion years) ago. We cannot observe it, nor can we recreate it in a laboratory. Our justification for it is relatively limited – for example, we have detected the background cosmic radiation and we think that it is the "echo" of the Big Bang. However, it is only a model that fits the limited data we have. There are other models, such as the multiverse theory that states that the Big Bang resulted in a whole variety of universes and we happen to live in just one of them. We have two models that are both mathematically consistent with whatever limited things we can observe. There seems to be nothing we can do in terms of using the correspondence test to prefer one theory to another.

There are voices today that claim that we will never know how exactly the Universe was born. One of these voices is Marcus du Sautoy, who says, referring to the multiverse theory, "Can we ever know whether this description of the Universe is true? Are we just coming up with self-consistent stories that could be true but are untestable? Even in our own universe there seems to be a limit to how far we can see. So how can we hope to know whether these other universes are real or just the fantasy of theoretical physicists?" (du Sautoy, 2017, p.229).

Argument 2. There is knowledge beyond the reach of science

***Image 19**. Indigenous peoples (Botswana bushmen)*

A very valuable source of insights about knowledge is indigenous knowledge communities. They are sometimes referred to as "primitive", although whether they are really as primitive as they seem is the subject of a whole different debate.

Are we responsible for preserving knowledge of disappearing communities? (#Ethics)

One example of this are indigenous Micronesian sailors. Steve Thomas in his book "*The Last Navigator*" describes one of the few surviving descendants of the ancient tradition, Mau Piailug. Like his ancestors, Piailug uses only natural signs (such as stars, waves and birds) to sail his canoe across thousands of miles of the Pacific Ocean from one tiny island to another (Thomas, 2009). With no compasses or charts, his ancestors navigated successfully in a tremendous ocean between tiny islands that were often 2000 miles apart. How did they do that?

When Western researchers interview them about that, their responses do not seem to make much sense to the "civilized" mind. They refer to "star paths" emitted from the stars and passing through their bodies, guiding their way. From our perspective, we don't know what that means. From their perspective, they don't know why we are having such a hard time understanding this.

***Image 20**. Mau Piailug (1932 – 2010) (credit: Maiden Voyage Productions, Wikimedia Commons)*

Certainly, we can dismiss indigenous knowledge as a naïve misconception. But we can also accept that one cannot understand one system of knowledge (indigenous) through the lens of another system of knowledge (scientific), and can try to study indigenous knowledge from within.

Conclusion

I understand that it could be tempting to say things like "sciences provide objective knowledge and art is more subjective, so scientific knowledge is more valuable", but hold on a second. Scientific methods cannot possibly answer all the questions we have, even within science itself. There are knowledge domains where science is entirely useless, such as knowledge possessed by indigenous communities. This is why we need to accept that no test for truth is superior to others, and that in some areas of knowledge, standards of justification and truth are different from scientific standards.

Critical thinking extension

Now that you know how to apply tests for truth, how do you understand the relationship between truth and justification?

Think back to the vicious circle we already mentioned:

- To justify A means to demonstrate that A is true
- We can only know if A is true through justification

Now that we have seen there are three types of justification we can use to know if A is true (correspondence, coherence and pragmatic test), does this help in breaking the vicious circle?

If you are interested...

Watch the video "What we cannot know – with Marcus du Sautoy" on the YouTube channel *The Royal Institution*. In this video he presents his book, "*What We Cannot Know: Explorations at the Edge of Knowledge*" (2016).

He asks, are there fields of knowledge that will always lie beyond the reach of science? His answer is yes. His book is a must-read if you are into science or mathematics.

Take-away messages

Lesson 6. When you use all three theories of truth simultaneously, they become tests for truth – correspondence, coherence and pragmatic. It may be tempting to say that the correspondence test for truth is superior to the others, and that scientific knowledge is the superior form of knowledge. However, it is not that simple, and in this lesson we addressed two arguments against this belief. First, even within the sciences, the correspondence test for truth is not always a possibility. Second, there exists knowledge that is beyond the reach of science, for example, that of indigenous knowledge communities. As a result, we had to accept that no test for truth is superior to others, and that in some areas of knowledge standards of justification and truth are different from scientific standards.

Lesson 7 - JTB

Learning outcomes

a) [Knowledge and comprehension] What is knowledge?
b) [Understanding and application] Are the three conditions (justification, truth and belief) necessary and sufficient in defining knowledge?
c) [Thinking in the abstract] In defining knowledge, is it better to use a metaphor than a verbal definition?

Key concepts

Knowledge, belief, truth, justification, necessary and sufficient conditions, metaphor of a map

Other concepts used

Information, justification condition, truth condition, belief condition

Themes and areas of knowledge

Theme: Knowledge and the knower
AOK: Implicitly related to all areas of knowledge

Recap and plan

The concepts we have been discussing so far are all important building blocks in Theory of Knowledge. We have seen how knowledge is manifested in beliefs and expressed in knowledge claims. We have discussed how knowledge claims can be meaningfully doubted. We have seen that in order to counteract doubt, knowledge claims require justification. We have also looked at the close relationship between justification and truth.

Now that you are familiar with such key concepts as doubt, justification and truth, we are finally ready to approach the tremendous task of defining knowledge. After all, "Theory of Knowledge" is the name of the course.

Why do we even need a definition?

The definition that I will suggest in this lesson – knowledge as a justified true belief - has been discontinued by the IB. It is no longer used in the IB TOK Guide. The reason is that this definition is problematic – there are several flaws with it. Instead, the IB does not offer any definition at all and suggests that students reflect on the nature of knowledge holistically and metaphorically.

However, I find this definition valuable precisely because it is so problematic. Ludwig Wittgenstein, an influential philosopher of the 20th century, was once advertising and distributing copies of a book written by Otto Weininger, an Austrian philosopher who had weird and controversial ideas and was denounced and disrespected. Students and colleagues were surprised why Wittgenstein even mentioned these ideas. But Wittgenstein said that Weininger was so great precisely because he was so wrong. Wittgenstein did not agree with a word Weininger said, but to him it is the way Weininger's arguments were wrong that made them so interesting (Cohen and Gonzalez, 2008).

I have a similar approach to the definition of knowledge as a justified true belief. I don't agree with it and I think it is wrong. But it is the way in which the definition is wrong that makes it so interesting, and that is why it is worth studying.

I invite you to treat this definition similarly.

Are mistakes and successes equally valuable in the pursuit of knowledge? (#Methods and tools)

KEY IDEA: The definition of knowledge as justified true belief is wrong. But it is the way in which it is wrong that makes it interesting.

Knowledge as JTB

***Image 21**. Plato (portrait bust) (credit: Dudva, Wikimedia Commons)*

There are many different definitions of knowledge – and probably not a single perfect one! However, historically, the most influential definition has been the one that originated in the works of ancient Greek philosophers such as Plato and was elaborated upon by generations of philosophers in the Western tradition up until the 20th century: *Knowledge is a justified true belief (JTB).*

In this definition, *S* knows *P* if and only if:

1) *P* is true,
2) *S* believes that *P* is true, and
3) *S* is justified in believing that *P* is true.

In other words, knowledge is a "justified true belief" (or simply JTB).

All three conditions have to be met.

The belief condition is essential because it implies that knowledge is something that belongs to conscious living beings. If knowledge is not a type of belief, then what is it a type of? If you say "information", you will have to accept that non-living bearers of information, such as books, computers or even prehistoric cave paintings all "know" something. This is very counter-intuitive. Just contemplate this for a moment. Do computers "know" in the same way as humans do? Do books "know" in the same way? Does the internet "know" in the same way? You can store all sorts of information in a computer, including contradictory information, and the computer will indifferently store it. But it will not consciously decide which parts of this information it believes, and it will not form a holistic "understanding" of the subject matter.

Does knowledge have to be something that belongs to humans? (#Scope)

The truth condition is essential because, without it, we would classify false beliefs as knowledge, as long as these false beliefs are justified in one way or another. If knowledge is any "justified belief", then I have to admit that a child "knows" that Santa Claus exists, that an astrologist "knows" that the date of birth determines a person's destiny, and that a religious cult follower "knows" that praying will cure cancer. Moreover, if one person believes *A* (the Earth is hollow) and another person believes *B* (the Earth is solid), we have to accept that both *A* and *B* are knowledge, so the Earth is hollow and not hollow at the same time! For this reason, the truth condition needs to be there.

However, there is a problem with the truth condition: the truth is not directly given to us. How do we know that a belief is true? Well, apparently, we can apply the three tests for truth (correspondence, coherence and pragmatic). As we are applying these tests, we are using some kind of justification.

Hence, the justification condition is also essential. Without this condition, any unjustified belief that happens to be true will count as knowledge. For example, imagine a primitive tribal society who believe that the world originated from a giant egg that grew in size until the yolk became the Earth and the egg white became the sky. And then one member of the tribe suddenly announces that our world is a planet, only one of many. He happens to be right! But his justification is: he once saw a kiwi, with its seeds scattered across the pulp, and he thought that this resembles the sky above his head better than an egg. Obviously, no one in the tribe takes him seriously – this is too grand a conclusion based on too weak a justification. There is no way his fellow tribesmen can accept this belief as "knowledge". But even from our perspective, although we know that this belief happens to be true, we can hardly say that the tribesman "knows" about planets.

Now you understand the rationale behind defining knowledge as a "justified true belief" (JTB). According to the definition, these three conditions – justification, truth and belief – are necessary and sufficient for something to be knowledge. *Necessary* means that each and every condition is essential, and if X fails to meet even one of the conditions, X is not knowledge. *Sufficient* means that, taken together, the three conditions are enough for X to be called knowledge.

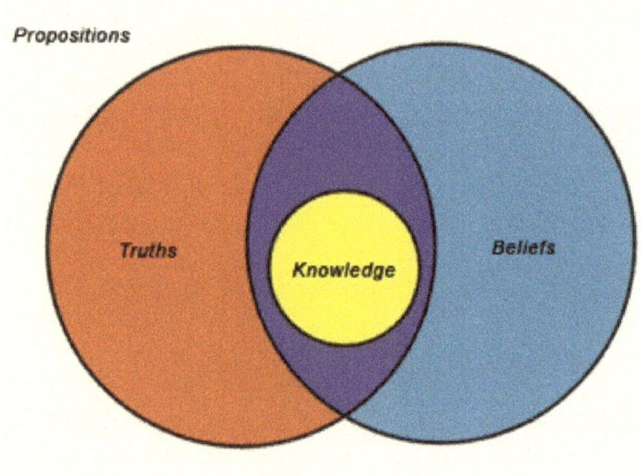

***Image 22**. Classical definition of knowledge*

We have defined knowledge. But this is TOK, after all, so obviously in the next lesson we will criticize this definition and doubt its usefulness. We will take every possible effort to dismantle the definition and show that it has no value.

KEY IDEA: According to the JTB definition, three conditions (justification, truth and belief) are necessary and sufficient for X to be considered knowledge

Critical thinking extension

Definitions are often tricky, especially when it comes to defining such basic and abstract concepts as knowledge. This is why some thinkers have abandoned the idea of defining knowledge linguistically and instead suggested defining it through a metaphor. Metaphors may be convenient because they are holistic.

Metaphors lack the strictness of linguistic definitions, but they compensate for this loss by richness of links and associations.

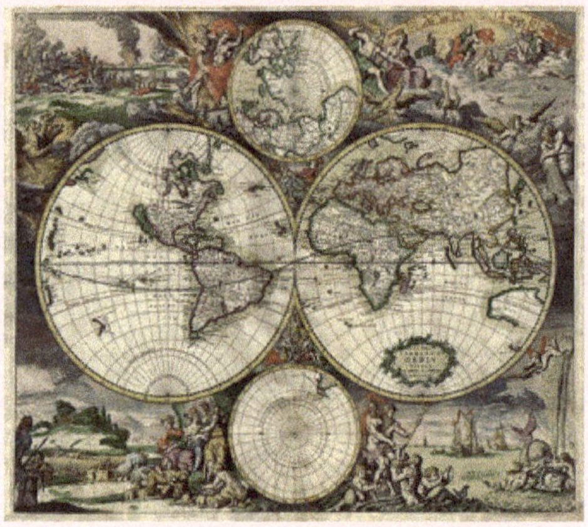
***Image 23**. World map 1689*

The metaphor for knowledge that has become popular is that of a map:

- A map is a simplified representation of some territory. In the same way, knowledge may be viewed as a simplified representation of some reality.

Is defining something necessary for understanding it? (#Perspectives)

- It is important to note that the map *is not the territory*, it is merely a representation. Same with knowledge: our beliefs about the world are not the same as the world itself.
- Additionally, a map is never a perfect representation. Every map will inevitably omit details and contain simplifications and even distortions. Same with knowledge.
- At the same time, although maps are simplified, they are useful. We can use them to navigate the world. Same with knowledge. We know that some of the beliefs we are accepting are probably only provisionally true, but that is good enough for the time being.

Do you think a map to a territory is a good metaphor for knowledge? I know we have not criticized the definition of knowledge as a "justified true belief" properly yet, but even so, do you think a metaphor is better than this definition?

If you are interested...

Watch the video "Why all world maps are wrong" on the YouTube channel *Vox*. This video demonstrates the fundamental limitation that we run into when we try to represent something complex (reality) through something simpler (map). How do you represent the 3-dimensional Earth on a 2-dimensional surface?

Also check out John Green's TED talk "*Paper towns and why learning is awesome*" (2015) where he takes the map metaphor for knowledge one step further: maps not only influence how we perceive reality, but actually can change reality itself. At the beginning of the video, he described how a fake town once became real just because it was on the map and everyone was expecting it to be there. People have built an actual town so that reality would be truthful to the map.

Take-away messages

Lesson 7. In this lesson we introduced the classical definition of knowledge as a justified true belief (JTB). According to this definition, for something to be considered knowledge, this something needs to satisfy three conditions: be justified, be true and belong to a human being as a subjectively experienced belief. These three conditions are necessary and sufficient. We also noted that this definition is problematic, but it is the way in which it is wrong that makes it so interesting. This definition is the best we currently have. An alternative approach that has been taken by many is to define knowledge through a metaphor rather than linguistically. One possible metaphor is that of a map.

Lesson 8 - Problems with JTB

Learning outcomes

a) [Knowledge and comprehension] What are the key problems with trying to define knowledge?
b) [Understanding and application] What exactly does it mean for knowledge to be "beyond a reasonable doubt"?
c) [Thinking in the abstract] How can we solve Gettier-style problems in the definition of knowledge?

Key concepts

Circular dependence, historical development of knowledge, reasonable doubt, Gettier-style counter-examples, metaphor for knowledge

Other concepts used

Knowledge, truth, justification, propositional knowledge, procedural knowledge, knowledge by acquaintance

Themes and areas of knowledge

Theme: Knowledge and the knower
AOK: Implicitly related to all areas of knowledge

Recap and plan

In the previous lesson we have defined knowledge. Let us now destroy this definition!

Problems with JTB
- Circular dependence between justification and truth
- Justified beliefs changing over time
- Gettier-style counter-examples

Problem 1: circular dependence

Is it acceptable to use knowledge when we know that it is faulty? (#Ethics)

One of the problems with the definition of knowledge as a justified true belief (JTB) is that there is a circular dependence between the justification condition and the truth condition. We cannot know the truth directly – we know it through the justification of a knowledge claim. We assume that if a knowledge claim has a high-quality justification, this knowledge claim is true. There is no other way for us to establish if something is true or not, rather than by looking at the quality of justification.

At the same time, we judge the quality of justification by how convincingly it demonstrates the relation of a knowledge claim to the truth. For example, testing something in an experiment is a high-quality justification because we think it will reliably test if a knowledge claim is true (in this case true = corresponds to reality). Seeing if a knowledge claim is consistent with our previous beliefs is also considered a high-quality justification, especially in some areas of knowledge such as mathematics (this is an example of using the coherence test for truth). But seeing something in your dream and blindly believing it is not good enough justification because we doubt that it has any connection to the truth.

KEY IDEA: There is a circular dependence between the justification condition and the truth condition of knowledge

To summarize: we judge if X is true by seeing if X is justified, but we judge the justification of X by its relation to the truth. In other words: we define truth through justification, but we define justification through truth.

Problem 2: JTB changing over time

This circular dependence also creates a problem when you look at the historical development of knowledge. We know that, logically speaking, X cannot be true and not true at the same time. But X can be *believed* to be true in one time period and believed to be false in another time period. For example, people believed at first that the Earth is in the center of the Universe, and then this was replaced by the belief that that the Earth is only one of the numerous celestial bodies. Let's express this as follows:

As knowledge develops, are new beliefs better than old ones? (#Perspectives)

- T1: X (in time period 1, people believed X = the Earth is in the center)
- T2: not-X (in time period 2, people believed not-X = the Earth is not in the center)

From where we are now, we know that only not-X is true. So belief X at T2 is *not* knowledge. The question is, was belief X knowledge at T1? And similarly, was belief not-X knowledge at T1?

At T1, belief X was justified and belief not-X was not justified, so it makes sense to admit that X was knowledge for people at that time. There was no way for them to know that X, contrary to their beliefs and the best evidence available at that time, was not true.

But this means that something that used to be true may cease to be true, which goes contrary to the whole idea of the truth.

Image 24. *Times change*

One way to resolve this is to specify that in the truth condition, *"true" = "beyond a reasonable doubt"*.

So the definition becomes "*Knowledge is a justified belief that is true beyond a reasonable doubt*".

In this definition we can still claim that only one belief is genuinely true, but at T1 X was true beyond a reasonable doubt, so X provisionally counts as knowledge.

However, this new definition, obviously, raises another question: what counts as "reasonable" doubt? Where is the line between reasonable and unreasonable?

KEY IDEA: We can never know if a claim is true. All we can know is that it's beyond a reasonable doubt.

Problem 3: Gettier-style counter-examples

There has been criticism of the idea that the three conditions (JTB) are sufficient conditions for knowledge. This idea will be challenged if we manage to find examples where X meets all three conditions and yet X, by common sense, is not knowledge. Such examples were first provided by Edmund Gettier (1963) and they are known as Gettier-style counter-examples.

Where is the line between a rule with exceptions and an incorrect rule? (#Methods and tools)

For example, Martin Cohen, a British philosopher, in his book "101 Philosophy Problems" describes the problem called "*Cow in the field*". A farmer is checking up on his cow – he stands up and looks over the field. He thinks he sees the cow, but what he actually sees is a piece of black and white paper caught up in a bush in a distance. However, the cow is actually in the field, but it is hidden from the farmer's sight. The farmer's belief ("My cow is in the field") is justified because (he thinks) he sees the cow with his own eyes. Also his belief is true because the cow actually happens to be in the field. But from the point of view of common sense, it seems odd to accept this belief as knowledge (Cohen, 1999).

***Image 25**. Cow in a field (credit: Wikimedia Commons)*

Hopefully, these three problems are enough to shatter your confidence that JTB is a good definition of knowledge.

Some people find these problems so serious that they reject the possibility of defining knowledge altogether. Instead the suggestion is to use a metaphor. A popular metaphor for knowledge is a map. In this metaphor, knowledge of something is like a map to a territory. It is a simplified representation that is useful, but we understand that the map is not the same as the territory itself.

Using a metaphor rather than a definition is debatable, but the metaphor's vagueness allows it to work where the linguistic definition fails.

***KEY IDEA**: The map metaphor for knowledge is vague (which is a weakness), but this vagueness allows it to be applicable where the linguistic definition fails*

Critical thinking extension

How can we respond to the Gettier problem? Many of the responses that have been suggested fall into one of the following three categories:

- Denying that the justification described in Gettier-style problems was sufficient. In other words, the beliefs described in Gettier-style problems are not knowledge because the justification for these beliefs was not good. The farmer's knowledge that the "cow is in the field" is not knowledge because the justification "I see a cow-like shape in the distance" is not reliable. This approach denies that Gettier-style counter-examples raise a problem for the JTB definition.
- Accepting the problem and admitting that the three conditions (belief, truth, justification) are necessary but not sufficient for the definition of knowledge. We need to add a fourth condition that would prevent the possibility of Gettier-style objections. What could this fourth condition be, though? Do you have suggestions?
- Claiming that Gettier's cases are cases of knowledge after all. In other words, the farmer *knows* that the cow is in the field.

Which of the three responses to the Gettier problem, if any, seems most reasonable to you?

If you are interested...

Is there a difference between knowing something, knowing someone, knowing how (to do something)?

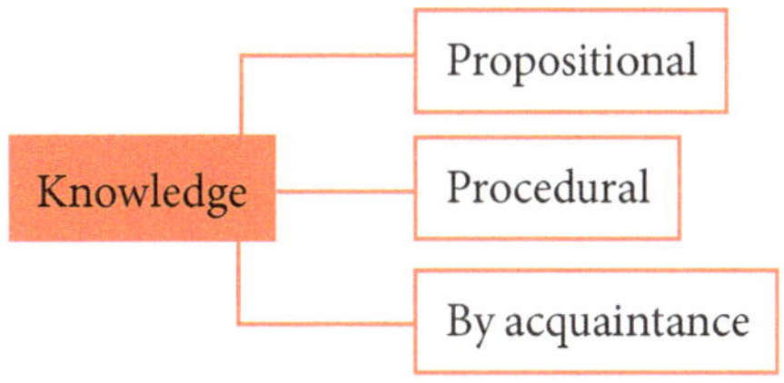

Indeed, in the discussion of knowledge as a justified true belief, we seemed to assume that all knowledge is knowledge "about something".

However, knowledge comes in a greater variety of forms and types. One of the existing distinctions is:

- *Propositional knowledge*: knowledge about something that can be explicitly formulated as a knowledge claim, or proposition. This type of knowledge is what we have assumed.
- *Procedural knowledge*: knowing how to do something. For example, you know how to drive a car, you know how to tie shoe laces, you know how to walk. Try and formulate this knowledge as a set of propositions! Procedural knowledge is difficult to verbalize. It is implicit. The concepts of justification and truth are hardly applicable here too.
- *Knowledge by acquaintance*: knowledge of someone or something. You go to a welcome party in a new school and in the crowd you recognize someone. That is a form of knowledge too, but it would be weird to describe it as a "justified belief", so the definition does not do a good job here.

Note, however, that the metaphor for knowledge as a map to a territory does perfectly well. Propositional knowledge charts the territory of our explicit beliefs. Procedural knowledge charts the territory of our skills. Knowledge by acquaintance charts the territory of the society around us, distinguishing between people we have had experience with and people we meet for the first time. Different territories, different kinds of knowledge.

Take-away messages

Lesson 8. This lesson outlined three major problems with defining knowledge as a justified true belief (JTB). The first problem is that there is a circular dependence between the justification condition and the truth condition. The second problem is that knowledge is developing, and it is possible for knowledge to satisfy the three conditions today but fail to satisfy them tomorrow. The third problem is the existence of Gettier-style counter-examples – scenarios where a belief satisfies all JTB conditions, but common sense dictates that this belief is not knowledge. In many situations it seems that using a metaphor of a map instead of a linguistic definition of knowledge does a better job. The metaphor's vagueness is its weakness, but it also allows it to work where the linguistic definition fails.

Lesson 9 - Knowledge questions and claims (part 1)

Learning outcomes

a) [Knowledge and comprehension] What makes a knowledge question or claim different from a regular question or claim?
b) [Understanding and application] Why do we need to introduce the concept of "levels of knowledge questions"?
c) [Thinking in the abstract] How can we tweak regular questions and claims to turn them into knowledge questions and claims?

Key concepts

Knowledge question, knowledge claim, subject-specific, situation-specific, levels of knowledge questions

Other concepts used

Causation, axioms, deductive reasoning, significance

Themes and areas of knowledge

Theme: Knowledge and the knower
AOK: History, Mathematics, the Arts

Recap and plan

We have explored TOK concepts leading up to the main concept – knowledge. These are all important building blocks that can be useful in the analysis of knowledge questions and knowledge claims.

But we also need to be able to clearly indicate which knowledge questions and claims belong to the realm of TOK and which don't. For example, compare the following two questions: "Is there a dog barking outside?" and "When several interpretations fit the same data equally well, how do we select the preferable interpretation?" The first question is about a dog. The second question is about knowledge. Clearly one of them belongs to the realm of TOK and the other one doesn't, but we need some strict rules here.

The role of knowledge questions and knowledge claims in the TOK course

Technically, in the new IB TOK course, you are no longer required to formulate your own knowledge questions. In both assessment components, the starting knowledge question will be given to you.

However:

To what extent is knowledge itself knowable? (#Scope)

1) You need to know the difference between knowledge questions and non-knowledge questions in order to tell the difference between TOK arguments and subject-specific arguments. If you can't tell the difference, you don't understand what TOK is.
2) Though you will not have to formulate the starting knowledge question, you will certainly need to formulate good knowledge claims in response to it!
3) Although the starting knowledge question will be formulated for you, you will see that to thoroughly analyze the question it may be necessary to ask "subsidiary knowledge questions". Obviously, the quality of your analysis depends on the quality of these additional questions.

Therefore, being able to tell knowledge questions and claims from non-knowledge ones is still at the very center of the TOK course.

How are knowledge questions different from regular questions?

Knowledge questions have three essential characteristics that make them different from regular questions:

1) *Knowledge questions are questions about knowledge. This is in contrast to regular questions that are questions about the world.*
   - For example, compare: "How did WWII start?" and "How can we establish the factors responsible for the start of WWII?" Can you feel the subtle difference? The first question is about events of the past, while the second question is about our knowledge of events of the past.
   - Another example, this time with claims rather than questions: compare "$a^2 + b^2 = c^2$ (Pythagorean theorem)" and "We know that $a^2 + b^2 = c^2$ because we can prove it mathematically by reducing it to the accepted set of axioms". The first claim is about a theorem while the second claim is about our knowledge of the theorem.

KEY IDEA: Regular questions ask about the world. Knowledge questions ask about our knowledge of the world.

---

2) *Knowledge questions are contestable. This is in contrast to regular questions that have a correct answer.* As a rule, it is possible that there are several plausible answers to a knowledge question, sometimes they may even contradict each other. In TOK there are no "right" answers; in assessment what will be judged is not what answer to the question you are giving, but how well justified this answer is and how well it is supported by appropriate examples.
   - Examples of questions that are *not* contestable: "Which school of art views the purpose of art as representation of reality?" (the answer is realism), "When was Sigmund Freud's book "*The Interpretation of Dreams*" first published?" (the answer is 1899), "Do we need empirical evidence to use the correspondence test for truth?" (the answer is yes).
   - More contestable versions of the same questions might be: "To what extent is the purpose of art to represent reality?", "How certain is the recording of dates of significant historical events?", "How reliable is the use of evidence in establishing the truth?"

KEY IDEA: Knowledge questions are contestable. It is expected for them to have several plausible answers, sometimes contradictory.

---

3) *Knowledge questions are general. This is in contrast to regular questions that are subject-specific or situation-specific.* The general nature of knowledge questions is reflected in the concepts that they draw upon – abstract concepts about knowledge that can be applied to a whole variety of subject areas and situations (such as truth, belief, justification, but also many other concepts that you will encounter further on in this book).
   - For example, look at one of the questions we used above: "*How can we establish the factors responsible for the start of WWII?*" While this is a question about knowledge, it uses a specific example and invites the use of subject-specific terminology. Let us rephrase it slightly to make it more general: "*How can we establish causation in history?*" Now this question applies to a whole class of situations and historical events, not just the stand-alone specific example of WWII. This becomes possible because the question uses an abstract concept related to knowledge - causation.
   - Similarly, the knowledge claim "*We know that $a^2 + b^2 = c^2$ because we can prove it mathematically by reducing it to the accepted set of axioms*" seems to be too specific to Pythagorean theorem. Let us make it more general by slightly rephrasing it:

"*Knowledge in mathematics is established through deductive reasoning from a set of axioms*". Now, to support this claim, we can use a whole range of examples from mathematics.

Levels of knowledge questions

KEY IDEA: Knowledge questions are general. They are not limited to particular subject-specific problems or life situations.

From the discussion above, you learned that knowledge questions are questions about knowledge, contestable and general. Two of these characteristics are binary: a question is either about knowledge or not, a question is either contestable or not. But the third characteristic is continuous – knowledge questions may be more or less general.

This commonly becomes a source of confusion. Therefore, it's necessary to have a language that would allow us to clearly label how general a knowledge question is. I will use the notion of levels of knowledge questions to achieve this goal.

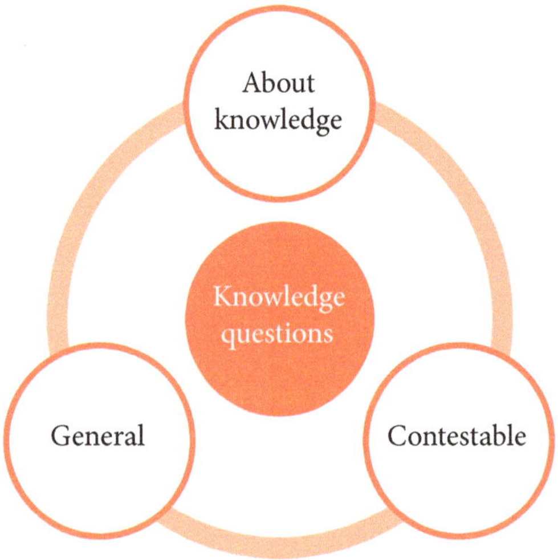

Image 26. Knowledge questions

The table below broadly summarizes four levels that can be useful as a common language for our discussions. Note that it is slightly different for personal and shared knowledge because, whereas shared knowledge is divided clearly into academic areas (natural sciences, human sciences, and so on), personal knowledge is not.

Domain of knowledge	Levels of knowledge questions and claims			
	Level 0	Level 1	Level 2	Level 3
Personal knowledge	About the world	About knowledge, but limited to a specific situation of personal knowledge	About knowledge. Not limited to a particular situation, can be applied to a whole range of similar situations	About knowledge. Very general, can be applied to a wide range of situations
Shared knowledge	About the world	About knowledge, but limited to a specific problem within an area of knowledge	About knowledge. Not limited to a specific problem, can be applied to the area of knowledge on the whole	About knowledge. Going beyond the limits of one area of knowledge, applicable to several or even all areas

As you see, level 0 in this table are not knowledge questions (and claims). They are questions and claims about the world. Levels 1-3 are all knowledge questions and claims, but they differ in terms of generality.

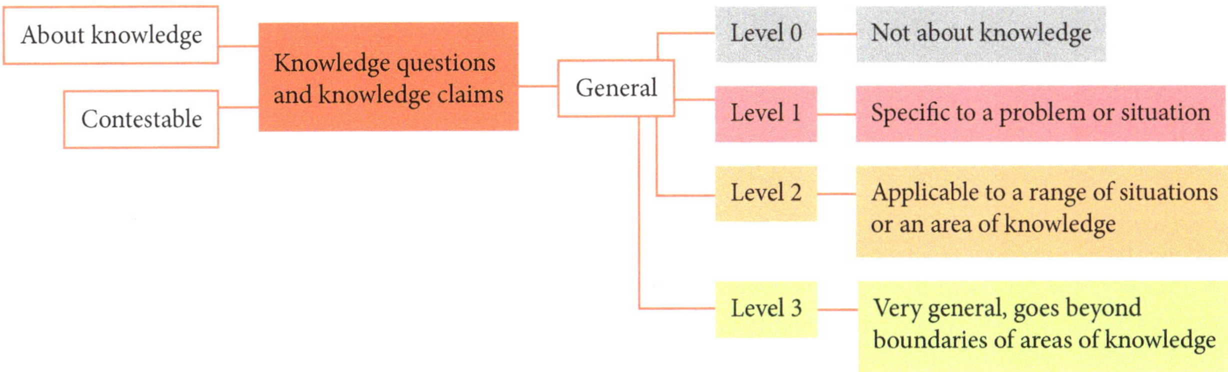

For now, it is sufficient for you to understand the general principle behind this division of knowledge questions into "levels". In the next lesson we will look at some specific examples.

Critical thinking extension

The most fundamental criterion of knowledge questions is that they are questions about knowledge, as opposed to questions about the world. We have discussed several examples in this lesson, but it is always a good idea to practice more to make sure that you have a grasp on this important difference. Below is a number of statements about the world. Can you tweak these statements a little to turn them into questions or claims about knowledge?

- I am having a hard time believing that my child grew up so quickly (daily life)
- Parallel lines do not intersect (mathematics)
- Nothing can travel faster than the speed of light (natural sciences)
- The Vietnam War began in 1955 (history)
- Demand is inversely related to price (the law of demand in economics)

If you are interested...

The ability to move in your thinking from concrete situations to abstract principles (and back) is an integral component of "abstract reasoning". Today, many popular tests used by universities in their admission process – including SAT and ACT – include assessment of abstract reasoning.

I am sure you have already familiarized yourself one way or another with these standardized tests. However, now that you know the characteristics of knowledge questions and claims, you can see these tests in a different light. Go online and review some practice questions on abstract reasoning from SAT and ACT. They are easily accessible.

Take-away messages

Lesson 9. In this lesson, we defined knowledge questions and knowledge claims. They are general, contestable questions and claims about knowledge. Two of these characteristics are binary: questions can be either about knowledge or not, either contestable or not. However, the third characteristic is continuous: questions and claims can be more or less general. For this reason, we also introduced "levels" of knowledge questions. Being able to tell knowledge questions and claims from non-knowledge ones is a crucial skill in the TOK course, as well as the ability to keep your argumentation general enough so that it does not become subject-specific.

Lesson 10 - Knowledge questions and claims (part 2)

Learning outcomes

a) [Knowledge and comprehension] How are levels of knowledge questions and claims different from each other?
b) [Understanding and application] How is the understanding of levels of knowledge questions and claims important for the TOK course?
c) [Thinking in the abstract] How can we tell if a knowledge claim is general enough to be accepted as "good TOK"?

Key concepts

Levels of knowledge questions and claims, claims about knowledge and claims about the world, situation-specific, subject-specific

Other concepts used

Shared knowledge, personal knowledge, personal beliefs, evidence, mathematical models, predictions, scientific facts, multi-determined phenomena, standard of knowledge, scientific method, theorem, deductive reasoning, axioms, historical significance, interpretation, historical fact, artistic intention, aesthetic value

Themes and areas of knowledge

Theme: Knowledge and the knower
AOK: Natural Sciences, Human Sciences, Mathematics, History, the Arts

Recap and plan

We have outlined the characteristics of knowledge questions and claims that make them different from non-knowledge ones. We have also identified various levels of knowledge questions (and claims) depending on how general they are. But this last bit requires elaboration and examples.

This lesson is devoted to unpacking levels of knowledge questions with specific examples from personal and shared knowledge. We will also discuss what significance all this has for learning and assessment in TOK.

Image 27. Levels

Levels of knowledge questions and claims: examples

Below and on the next page is a table with examples of knowledge questions and claims belonging to different "levels".

Example from...	Level 0 (questions and claims about the world)	Level 1 (specific questions and claims about knowledge)	Level 2 (general questions and claims about knowledge)	Level 3 (very general questions and claims about knowledge)
Personal knowledge	**Claim:** It is unusually warm today for a winter day. **Question:** Why are winter days getting warmer?	**Claim:** My feeling that it is getting warmer is not a reliable argument for global warming, and it should be backed up by statistical evidence. **Question:** Would statistical evidence be sufficient for me to believe with certainty that global warming is happening?	**Claim:** My personal beliefs are not reliable until they are corroborated by shared knowledge. **Question:** Can personal beliefs be as certain as shared beliefs?	**Claim:** Bias in personal beliefs is inevitable. **Question:** Is it possible for us to know our own biases?

Example from…	Level 0 (questions and claims about the world)	Level 1 (specific questions and claims about knowledge)	Level 2 (general questions and claims about knowledge)	Level 3 (very general questions and claims about knowledge)
Natural Sciences	**Claim**: The Big Bang happened 13.8 billion years ago. **Question**: How was the Universe evolving shortly after the Big Bang?	**Claim**: We know that the Big Bang happened because phenomena we observe today (such as expansion of the Universe) fit into the hypothetical mathematical model of the Big Bang. **Question**: Considering that we can neither observe nor recreate the Big Bang, what would be sufficient evidence for us to accept it as a scientific fact?	**Claim**: In natural sciences unobservable phenomena may be studied by creating hypothetical models and testing their predictions against available data. **Question**: Can something that is not observable be an object of scientific inquiry?	**Claim**: Models advance the development of knowledge because they allow us to gain insight into something that cannot be observed. **Question**: Is empirical evidence superior to other sources of knowledge?
Human Sciences	**Claim**: Financial recession is caused by an interplay among various factors, including excess leverage and lack of financial governance. **Question**: Are countries with less financial governance hit harder by a financial crisis?	**Claim**: It is difficult to study causes of financial recession because in the real world these factors do not act in isolation from one another. **Question**: How can we make conclusions about the leading cause of a financial recession?	**Claim**: Unlike natural sciences, human sciences deal with complex multi-determined phenomena that are often impossible to study in a laboratory. **Question**: Is it possible for human sciences to reach the same standard of knowledge as natural sciences?	**Claim**: Some domains of knowledge are beyond the reach of the scientific method. **Question**: Should standards of knowledge differ from one area of knowledge to another?
Mathematics	**Claim**: The area of a circle of radius *r* and circumference *C* is identical to the area of a right triangle of height *r* and base *C* (Archimedes' Circle Area theorem). **Question**: How is the area of a circle / triangle calculated?	**Claim**: It is possible to deduce Archimedes' theorem with certainty from Euclidean axioms of geometry. **Question**: Does Archimedes' theorem pass all three tests for truth?	**Claim**: Mathematical knowledge is based on deductive reasoning: if we accept axioms as true, we must also accept all conclusions as true. **Question**: Is mathematical knowledge absolutely certain?	**Claim**: A belief can only be true within a certain set of assumptions, but never in an absolute sense. **Question**: Can something that is less than certain still be accepted as knowledge?
History	**Claim**: A civil war broke out in Japan in 1331, when emperor Go-Daigo tried to overthrow the rule of the samurai lords. Question: What caused Go-Daigo to initiate the rebellion?	**Claim**: We know that the rebellion was historically significant because it ended the period of relative political stability in Japan. **Question**: How can we infer Go-Daigo's intentions from the information available to us about the events of that time?	**Claim**: It is only possible to judge historical significance of an event retrospectively, based on the changes that followed. **Question**: Is it possible for a historian to objectively know not only what happened, but why it happened?	**Claim**: There is no such thing as a neutral statement of fact. **Question**: Are judgments of significance always a product of subjective interpretation?
The Arts	**Claim**: Van Gogh's paintings violated the principles of academic art of his time. **Question**: Should Van Gogh's art be classified as modern art?	**Claim**: It is only possible to understand Van Gogh's contribution to art if we look at his work in the context of other artists of that time. **Question**: Is it necessary to decipher Van Gogh's intentions to understand the true meaning of his art?	**Claim**: Art can only be understood in the historical context of its development. **Question**: Where do we draw a line between art and non-art?	**Claim**: Aesthetic values can change over time, reflecting other changes in shared knowledge. **Question**: How can we know if something has an aesthetic value?

Explanation

You would have noticed that level 0 questions and claims are not about knowledge. These are questions and claims about the world – warm weather, the Big Bang, a financial crisis, a theorem, an event from the past, an artist. Such questions and claims are typically the focus of various other school subjects, but not TOK. We climb further up.

Level 1 knowledge questions and claims are specific to a problem or situation. Occasionally, these kinds of things are discussed in your school subjects. They usually combine abstract knowledge concepts (such as inference, understanding, certainty) and subject-specific terminology (such as Archimedes' theorem, the Big Bang, Go-Daigo's rebellion).

Level 2 knowledge questions and claims are no longer about particular problems or situations. Subject-specific terminology is completely eliminated from them.

Finally, level 3 knowledge and questions are so general that they go beyond the boundaries of areas of knowledge.

How is this important fr the TOK course?

You will have many discussions throughout this course, and you need to ensure that what you are having are TOK discussions. For this, make sure that the key arguments you are discussing are coming from levels 2 and 3. These are levels that are acceptable for a TOK discussion. Occasionally, you will go down to level 1, but that can only happen when you are giving examples to illustrate your arguments.

Needless to say, if the discussion you are having revolves around Level 0 statements, then you are not having a TOK discussion.

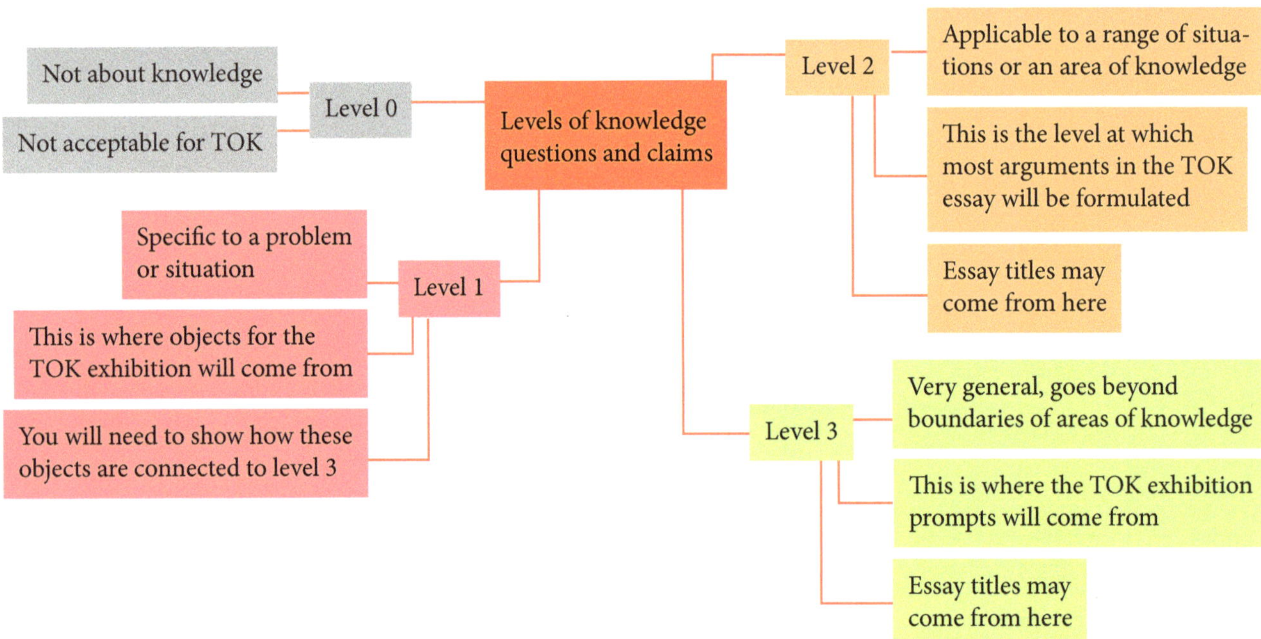

How is this important for assessment?

For the TOK exhibition you are required to create an exhibition that explores how TOK manifests in the world around us. For this, you will need to select one of the 35 IA prompts and find three real-world objects connecting to it. Objects can come both from academic studies and life beyond the classroom. You will notice that the IA prompts are formulated as level 3 knowledge questions. They are very general and can potentially be applied to a very large variety of problems and situations. For example: "What counts as good evidence for the claim?"

Essentially, what this task requires you to do is to go down from level 3 to level 1. The IB wants you to demonstrate that you can find specific examples for abstract TOK problems and that you can clearly show the connection between the abstract and the specific.

For the TOK essay you are required to write an essay in response to one of the six titles prescribed by the IB for each exam session. The titles will take the form of knowledge questions that are focused on the areas of knowledge. In the essay you are required to present clear and coherent arguments that are effectively supported by specific examples.

This means that the knowledge question given to you will be on level 2 or 3 (it may or may not focus on particular areas of knowledge). You are expected to answer the question on the same level, but you will also need to give specific examples to support your arguments. These examples are likely to come from level 1.

Critical thinking extension

What we discussed here requires practice. Here are some quotes to start with. Do you think these claims are knowledge claims? If so, are they related to personal knowledge or shared knowledge? What level would you place them under? Are they general enough to be accepted as "good TOK"?

- Knowledge is of no value unless you put it into practice (Anton Chekhov)
- Real knowledge is to know the extent of one's ignorance (Confucius)
- Human behavior flows from three main sources: desire, emotion, and knowledge (Plato)
- We are all born ignorant, but one must work hard to remain stupid (Benjamin Franklin)

(from www.brainyquote.com)

If you are interested...

It is a requirement in the IB for every subject to be linked to TOK concepts and include TOK-related discussions. The way it is seen, every teacher is a TOK teacher.

Pick your second favorite IB subject (after TOK, obviously). Take that subject's textbook. The textbook will probably include sections with "TOK links" and they will probably be formulated as questions.

Have a look at these TOK links in your second favorite textbook. Do you think they are good knowledge questions? What level do they belong to? Can you tweak them a little to make them slightly more general?

Take-away messages

Lesson 10. This lesson is a continuation of lesson 9 on knowledge questions and claims. Earlier we introduced the idea of "levels" of knowledge questions and claims, and here we looked at specific examples from personal knowledge and five areas of shared knowledge. We also reinforced once again that it is essential in the TOK course to be able to keep your argumentation focused on an appropriate level of abstraction. What is considered an "appropriate level" is slightly different for the two assessment tasks – the TOK exhibition and the TOK essay.

Back to the exhibition

I am coming back in my thoughts to the 15th-century teenager who pursues a career in alchemy. Can he ever know that his university education was full of false beliefs and misconceptions? Can he know that his whole research program is based on faulty assumptions, so he is spending his efforts in vain? I also keep thinking, how likely is it that what we call science today is alchemy in a new form? It would be good to be certain that we know something, but how can we be certain?

It all clarified a little after we explored the important concepts related to knowledge – meaningful doubt, belief, justification, truth. The young 15th-century alchemist believed in the possibility of creating the philosopher's stone and achieving immortality with it. He also believed that his methods were suitable to do it. His belief was justified, although that standard of justification would not be accepted today. His belief was not true (as we know now), but it was beyond a reasonable doubt.

I think his attempts were not in vain. They failed, but they were useful precisely because they failed. Exposing alchemists as frauds allowed us to reflect on our standards of justification and methods used to gain knowledge, making the former more rigorous and the latter less biased. In this way, the young alchemist contributed to what we know today.

It is for this reason that I am not afraid of having false beliefs. If knowledge of today will turn out to be one huge misconception, I will be neither disappointed nor upset. Our false beliefs will contribute to knowledge of future generations who will learn from our mistakes.

But there is a difference between getting it wrong despite trying your best and getting it wrong simply because you are not trying. I believe we are all responsible for trying our best to ensure that what we know is true. After all, it is only through justification that we can get to the truth, so it is justification that we should be responsible for, not the truth.

The young alchemist, unless he was a fraud, tried his best, and for that I'm grateful.

UNIT 2 - Knowledge and technology

UNIT 2 - Knowledge and technology

Technology has become such an integral part of our lives, and is changing our lives so deeply, that I'm having a hard time choosing the areas of focus for this unit. There is so much to explore.

After giving it some thought, I decided to concentrate on the following questions:

1) How does technology affect our personal knowledge? Now that information is so readily and instantly accessible to us, does it change how we know things?
2) How does technology affect our shared knowledge of ourselves?
3) How does technology affect our shared knowledge of the world?

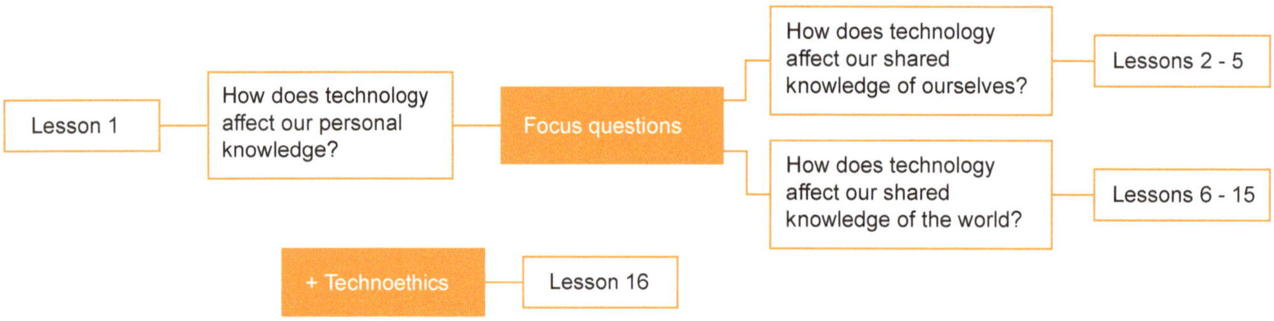

The first question (lesson 1) is about how technology has transformed the way you and I go about acquiring knowledge in our everyday lives. Admittedly, we have much easier access to information now that we have the Internet. But this is only the tip of the iceberg. Technology may be influencing our knowledge acquisition in negative ways, too. For example, search engines these days are proactive: they return results that they "think" we will find interesting. Therefore, they make some important decisions regarding relevance of information for us. We have outsourced these decisions to them. This may negatively affect us because we are trapping ourselves in an information bubble.

Note that the first question is about personal knowledge. New technology poses numerous challenges to every individual knower, but I assume that collectively we can overcome these challenges (although it may be difficult). The second and the third questions are questions about shared knowledge.

The second question (lessons 2-5) is about how technology invented by human beings has allowed human beings to understand the phenomenon of human beings. Our own brains, minds and consciousness are perhaps the toughest puzzle of the Universe. We have many questions in this area that we cannot even begin to approach answering. But if we manage to build a machine that can think, act and perhaps even feel like a human being, then we can claim to have understood these phenomena. This question revolves around artificial intelligence: what it looks like today, what it will look like in the future and how the relationship between humans and machines is likely to transform within our lifetime.

The third question (lessons 6-15) is about how we (collectively, as humanity) can use technology to better understand the world around us. There are simple and obvious examples that come to mind in response to this question: we invented the microscope and were able to see the living cell; we invented the telescope and were able to see distant galaxies; we invented brain imaging and were able to see inside the living brain without cutting the skull open. But there are also ways in which technology might have changed our knowledge of the world more radically. Does technology have the potential to create revolutionary changes in the areas of

Natural Sciences, Human Sciences, History, Mathematics and the Arts? This question is about the numerous tools we have invented to acquire new knowledge about the world as well as the strengths and limitations of these tools.

Another aspect that weaves through all of these questions is ethics (mentioned throughout the unit, but revisited in lesson 16). Technology has enabled us to do things we were not able to do before. But just because we *can* do something, does it mean that we *should* do it? Genetic engineering, for example, allows us to modify or edit genes in order to change an organism's characteristics in a particular way. We can (theoretically) clone people. We can even train an artificial intelligence to write TOK essays and submit them as our own. But should we do all that? Technology bears certain dangers. Is it anyone's responsibility to assess risks and prevent disasters?

Exhibition: Graph of emotions in the Bible

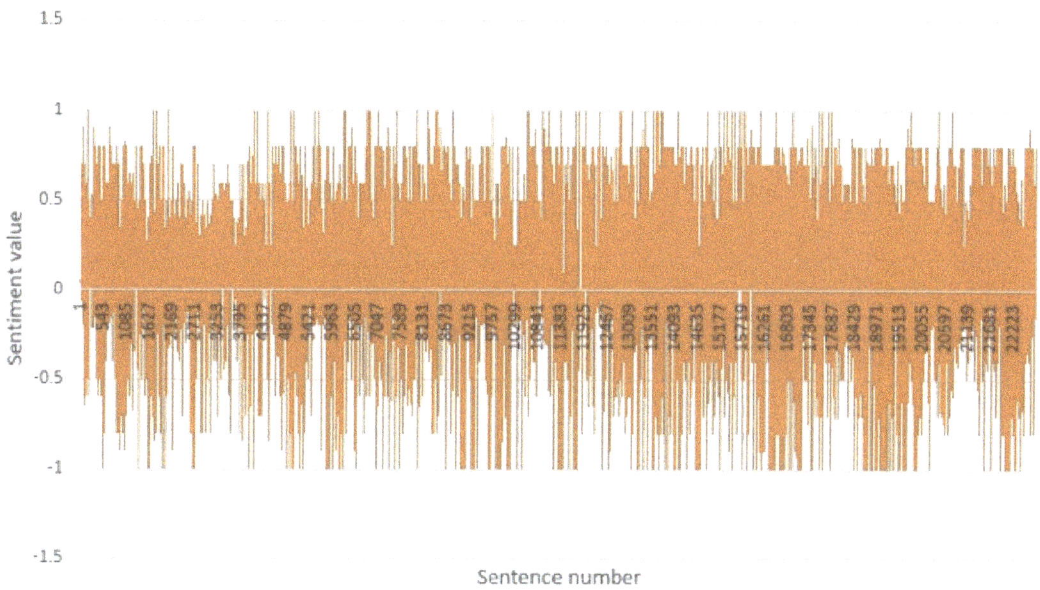

***Image 1**. Bar graph of emotions in the Old Testament (sentiment analysis)*

This is a graph of emotions in the Bible.

At some point in my career I spent several years working as a data scientist for a large company. I was trying to get an insight into the behavior of people by crunching numbers. One of the things that sparked my interest was the method of text mining known as "*sentiment analysis*".

This is how it works:

1) A group of researchers takes a large collection of words (nouns, verbs, adjectives) from a dictionary.
2) Then they ask a group of participants to rate the emotional valence of each word. Participants rate each word on a continuous scale from -1 (very negative) to +1 (very positive). For example, words like "sun", "pleasant" and "hugging" will get high positive ratings, while words like "mutilation", "dirty" and "vandalize" will get high negative ratings. This results in a database of words and their average emotional ratings.
3) If you want to calculate sentiment value of a text, you run this text through the database. The score for the text will be calculated based on the concentration of "emotional" words in it. For example, if the text contains a large number of positively colored words, then it will score a high positive sentiment value.
4) You can run multiple texts through sentiment analysis and compare sentiment values of these texts.

There are multiple examples of how sentiment analysis is used in both business and research. One such example is sentiment analysis of tweets from politicians. Every tweet is a text, so we can run sentiment analysis and calculate the sentiment value for each tweet. But every tweet also contains some useful metadata: the timestamp (when it was posted), a geotag (where it was posted from), what device it was posted from, and so on. You can then play around with data. For example, we could visualize the amount of negativity in a president's tweets depending on where they are travelling.

In my spare time, I used sentiment analysis for a more modest purpose – to analyze sentiment of the Bible. I downloaded a copy of the Old Testament from the Internet (easy to find!). I installed Python (the programming language). Then I broke down the Old Testament into separate sentences, so that each sentence becomes one unit of text. I then ran a sentiment analysis on each sentence and graphed the result. The whole thing took me just a dozen lines of code, by the way, and it was easy to do because there are plenty of step-by-step instructions online.

So, my graph of emotions in the Bible shows how the sentiment of sentences develops from the beginning to the end of the Old Testament. You can see that the Bible can get pretty positive sometimes; however, the happy notes don't reach too high and don't last for too long. On the other hand, when the Bible gets negative, it really does go all the way down. It reaches very low values of sentiment (close to -1) and stays there for a longer time.

Does my sentiment analysis of the Bible provide new insights and open up new horizons of knowledge that cannot be achieved by ordinary methods? If I put my graph in a frame and display it in an art gallery, will it deserve to be considered a proper work of art? Is it even ethical to treat a religious text as a dataset?

I seek your help in answering these questions.

Story: Predicting Supreme Court decisions

Image 2. U.S. Supreme Court building (credit: Wikipedia)

This is a story of competition between legal experts and a computer algorithm. The focus of the competition was forecasting the U.S. Supreme Court decisions. The question was, are human law experts better than a simple computer program in predicting the outcome of cases heard in the Supreme Court?

Andrew Martin and Kevin Quinn analyzed data from 628 cases previously decided by the U.S. Supreme Court justices. For each of these cases, they collected only six simple observable characteristics, for example, the type of petitioner (the United States, an injured person, an employer, etc.), whether or not the petitioner appealed to the Constitution, where the case came from, and so on. There was no theory behind selecting these variables. They were selected simply due to their easy availability in public sources. To give you a sense of the rules that the algorithm operated with, here is one example: "If the petitioner was an injured person, if the petitioner did not appeal to the Constitution, and if the case came from the Federal Circuit, Justice Sandra Rey will vote to affirm".

After training the algorithm on prior data, they used it to forecast the outcomes of new cases. They then held a competition between their algorithm and human legal experts! All experts had extensive training and experience in their domain. There was a total of 83 experts, each an accomplished professional. Many of them had practiced or clerked at the Supreme Court. Experts were asked to forecast the outcome of the cases that were within their immediate area of expertise.

Martin and Quinn set up a public website where they placed their bets (voila, the website is here: http://wusct.wustl.edu/). On the website they announced the two sets of predictions (one from legal experts and one from their algorithm) *before* the hearing of the case. After the hearing, they recorded the outcome. They collected data in this manner for the duration of one year, the U.S. Supreme Court's 2002 term. So, were expert predictions better than the predictions of the simple algorithm manipulating six easily registered characteristics of each case?

No. The model was correct in 75% of the cases, while the experts were correct in 59% of the cases. The algorithm won convincingly and publicly.

Why?

One possible explanation is that human cognition is limited. When legal experts review a case and make a prediction, they base their forecast on prior experience. But when it comes to human beings, "experience" means a handful of cases that stand out for them, cases they can hold in their memory and process. The computer algorithm in this project was able to base the predictions on the total number of available cases – 628 – without any bias in selecting them, without giving them unreasonable subjective weight.

But even so, it is surprising the algorithm won because it did not take into account any legal explanations provided by the Court (and no legal interpretation at all, for that matter). The six variables were essentially non-legal. They did not consider any substance about the case, only "superficial" characteristics such as the type of respondent and where the case came from.

Ian Ayres, who describes this project among a dozen other examples in his book *Super Crunchers: Why Thinking-by-Numbers is the New Way to be Smart* (2007), comes to the conclusion that statistical algorithms are simply better at predicting than human experts.

So, should we sack all experts?

2.1 - Technology and personal knowledge

This part of the unit consists of only one lesson. Here we will try to find the answer to the question "How does technology affect our personal knowledge?"

It is hard to imagine our life today without digital devices and information search software. They serve as a kind of gatekeepers for our personal knowledge. They are designed to make information more accessible to us and more readily available, but with these innovations may come the danger of under-exposure to information that the computer algorithm thinks we will not find useful.

Paradoxically, due to globalization, the world we live in is becoming larger, but the bubble of information around each of us may be getting smaller. By pursuing convenience through technology, we may have trapped ourselves in blissful ignorance.

Lesson 1 - Information bubble

Learning outcomes

a) [Knowledge and comprehension] What is an information bubble?
b) [Understanding and application] How can information bubbles cause confirmation bias?
c) [Thinking in the abstract] How does our personal knowledge change as a result of using digital technology?

Key concepts

Information bubble, confirmation bias

Other concepts used

PageRank, contextual advertising, digital amnesia, user-friendliness, coevolution

Themes and areas of knowledge

Theme: Knowledge and the knower, Knowledge and technology

The role of technology in personal knowledge

Let's start with how technology can affect our personal knowledge. I can see several prominent examples here, although I'm sure you can think of more:

1) Search engines select information for us
2) We rely on computers to remember things
3) We no longer have to discover answers on our own

I am using the term information bubble to refer to all of these phenomena. The idea is that, instead of being exposed to the entirety of information that is accessible to us, we create a bubble around ourselves with information that we find most helpful. But this bubble can gradually become all we ever see.

Can we trust information technology when we do not fully understand how it works? (#Scope)

Search engines select information for us

At one point in my life, I was teaching courses to adult students. On several occasions I went to remote locations where the Internet was just being introduced. In one of the student groups, we had a weird conversation along the lines of, "How do you like the Internet?"

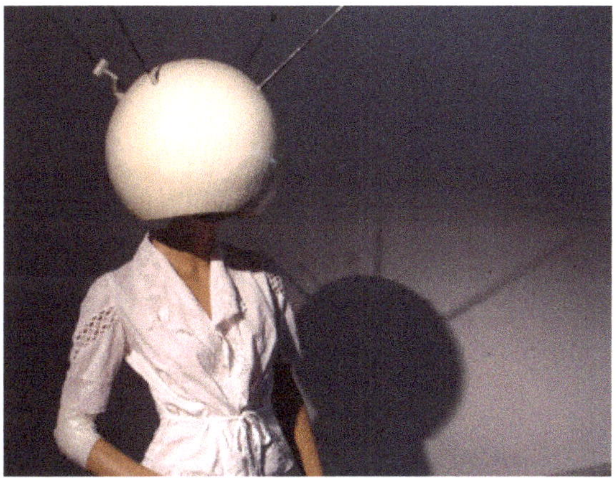

Image 3. Living in a bubble: photo of an installation at UDK Berlin (credit: quarto.sinko, Flickr)

I will never forget one lady in her fifties who said, "I like Google, it's a useful thing, but there are way too many ads for weight loss pills; they are on every page, they are just shoving these pills down your throat".

At that time, I was already familiar with the concept of *contextual advertising*. I understood that the only reason that the lady saw lots of weight loss ads was because she was often using Google to search for information related to weight loss. She naively thought that Google was bombarding her with those ads and she complained that Google was coercing her to start using the pills, when in fact she was the one responsible for all of this.

This situation is ironic, but at the same time it raises a profound issue. We all use search engines to find information. But do you know how search engines work?

Image 4. We all use search engines to find information

Modern search engines use a complicated algorithm to help you find what you need. Suppose you want to learn about the extinction of dinosaurs, so in the search field you type "extinction of dinosaurs". This is what happens behind the scenes:

Is a computer-assisted information search more biased than the traditional way? (#Methods and tools)

1) The algorithm looks for all of the documents on the Internet that contain the exact phrase "extinction of dinosaurs". This returns millions and millions of pages.
2) Then, a *PageRank* procedure is used (Sullivan, 2007). The procedure ranks the pages according to how many other pages link to them, as well as how many pages link to these other pages. So, suppose page A has the words "dinosaur extinction", but no other page links to it. Page B also has the same words, but there are 10 other pages that link to page B. These 10 pages, however, are not too popular. Finally, page C also contains these words; only three other pages link to it, but one of these three is Wikipedia, which is very popular. So, the result of the "page rank" procedure would be: page C on top, page B in the middle, page A at the bottom. This is because pages that get cited by popular pages get priority.
3) There is then another filter. The algorithm looks at your search history and decides which results may be of more interest to you personally. Suppose at some point you were interested in all sorts of "alternative theories" and conspiracy theories. The algorithm will push the pages that contain both "dinosaur extinction" and "alternative theories" to the top of the list. This way, it maximizes the "usefulness" of the result to you personally based on your previous Internet activity.

Image 5. PageRank is an algorithm to find the most relevant results for a web search query (credit: Wikipedia)

This looks super helpful, but the downside of this algorithm (that people rarely think about) is that it is actually a celebration of confirmation bias: the search results you see are the search results that match your prior beliefs and interests. You are not exposed to alternative views. An information bubble is created around you and it gets more and more impenetrable over the course of time. Isn't that weird and frightening?

Are personal electronic devices detrimental for the quality of personal knowledge? (#Perspectives)

We rely on computers to remember things

According to a report from the Kaspersky Lab (a digital security company), we are rapidly moving toward the age of "digital synergy" where human minds and digital devices are creating a close bond, unlocking new possibilities but also bringing with it new dangers. In 2015, the company conducted a survey that demonstrated that many people struggle to recall information that they can easily save on their device (such as birthdays and telephone numbers). The Kaspersky Lab coined a special term to describe this phenomenon – *digital amnesia*.

Many respondents in the survey claimed that they perceive a digital device as an "extension of their brain". The Kaspersky Lab also points out that 58% of respondents use no antivirus software and that a loss of device or a hacker attack may actually result in a "memory loss" for many of us (Kaspersky Lab, 2016).

We no longer have to discover answers on our own

I remember the time when the Internet was just making its way into ordinary households, when Google was not there and when algorithms such as PageRank were not yet invented. Some search engines were spitting out lists of results that were not sorted in any meaningful way. Other search engines were more like catalogues of hand-picked websites. Most content on webpages was static, and user-generated content was not widely used.

In these "good old" days, if you had a question and wanted to find an answer online, you had to work very hard. It was not much different from sitting in a huge library and doing your research there (except that you could now do it from home in your underwear).

Are tech companies morally responsible for promoting diversity of perspectives? (#Ethics)

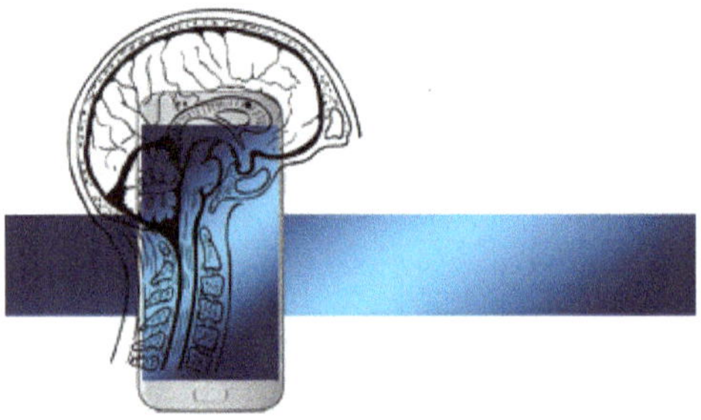

***Image 6**. Computers think for us*

But then, the Internet rapidly developed and started becoming more user-friendly.

Today, if you have a question and want to find an answer online, you pretty much type your question and get an answer on the first page. The answer comes from one of the popular answer services like Quora or Wikipedia. If I type a random question into the Google search string such as "How did dinosaurs become extinct?", I don't even have to type the whole question – the autofill feature helpfully suggests the most popular endings (try it!). If I click enter, 2,950,000 results are generated in 0.55 seconds. On the top of the page, I've got a "people also ask" section, where a drop-down menu conveniently summarizes the answer in just one paragraph.

In the "good old" days when we said "I'll go and do some research online", it actually meant working with information, sifting through it and separating the sheep from the goats. Nowadays, what is meant by research is that people will type their question into the search string and read out the answer. The search capabilities have become so powerful that it can actually be detrimental to our critical thinking abilities.

KEY IDEA: Information search is becoming quicker and more convenient, but this may come at the cost of reinforcing our confirmation bias. Pre-filtered search results create an information bubble around us.

Critical thinking extension

As technology develops and we interact with it more and more closely, we start to "merge" with it. Perhaps it's not a bad thing that we are losing the ability to memorize phone numbers. We just operate on the assumption that computers will not fail us, that we will not have to rely on our memory to the same extent ever again. Perhaps this is a natural process of coevolution.

I have been a little grumpy in this lesson about how young people today are not exposed to the same challenges of finding relevant information online, how simply typing a question results in an easy one-paragraph answer. But perhaps this leads to a different style of cognition – not worse, simply different.

How does your own knowledge change as a result of you using digital technology? What changes have you noticed? Can you say that your digital devices are in some sense a continuation of your brain? Does your brain benefit from them, or is your brain limited by them? In the future, are you ready for an even greater merging between your brain and digital devices? Would you be willing to have digital implants, for example?

If you are interested...

Watch Eli Pariser's TED talk "Beware online 'filter bubbles'" (2011). It is argued that the attempts to personalize news and search results that are so popular with web companies will ultimately do more harm because we will find ourselves trapped in "filter bubbles" of knowledge.

If you are interested to know more about the internal workings of the PageRank algorithm, read an insightful explanation by Valerie Niechai titled "The Vice and Virtue of PageRank" (April 30, 2019) on www.link-assistant.com.

Familiarize yourself with the book by Nicholas Carr called *The Shallows: What the Internet Is Doing to Our Brains (2011).* The title speaks for itself.

Take-away messages

Lesson 1. From millions of available sources, modern information search technology helpfully selects the ones that we will probably find most useful and relevant. In doing so, it adapts to our own interests and values. Although it is very useful because it saves us the effort of filtering out results that we do not want, it also limits our exposure to information that goes against our own perspective. We get exposed to information that other people found helpful, as well as information that is in line with our own interests and values reflected in our prior search history. Arguably, this creates an information bubble around us. Information bubbles increase speed of retrieval of information and perceived usefulness, but they may also reinforce our confirmation bias. Since we are relying on technology more and more, to the extent of outsourcing our cognitive functions to it, information bubbles may be a source of bias.

2.2 - Technology and the human mind

We have discussed the relationship between technology in personal knowledge and it is now time to switch over to shared knowledge.

In the next four lessons, we will be answering the question "How does technology affect our shared knowledge of ourselves?"

The key concepts here are artificial intelligence and artificial consciousness. It would be a mistake to think that this discussion is limited in its relevance to technology. It has much broader implications, including our understanding of what it means to be human and, ultimately, our answer to the question "Who are we?"

You see, if we manage to construct an artificial consciousness, this would mean that we have constructed a human being. This would mean that we fully understand what it means to be human. This would probably cause natural and human sciences to merge. This would irreversibly change the nature of knowledge in general.

Therefore, the questions dealt with in this part of the unit are not only related to understanding technology. They are equally related to our understanding of the human mind.

Lesson 2 - AI: Turing test

Learning outcomes

a) [Knowledge and comprehension] What is the Turing test?
b) [Understanding and application] Can machines act like they are intelligent?
c) [Thinking in the abstract] Should we strive to make artificial intelligence similar to human intelligence?

Key concepts

Artificial intelligence, Turing test, general intelligence, explicit and implicit thinking

Other concepts used

Chatbots, Loebner prize, personal assistants, thought experiment, brain, symbol manipulation

Themes and areas of knowledge

Theme: Knowledge and technology
AOK: Natural Sciences, Human Sciences, Mathematics

Recap and plan

We have looked at the role of technology in the ongoing transformation of our personal knowledge. In this new co-existence with our digital devices, they are becoming an extension of our brain.

But how far will this process go? Will we merge with machines? Will machines take over? Will we co-exist in a kind of knowledge symbiosis?

These are interesting and complicated questions, but to effectively address them we need to unpack such concepts as artificial intelligence and artificial consciousness over the next couple of lessons.

Two questions of artificial intelligence: acting intelligently and being intelligent

There are two key questions in the idea of artificial intelligence:

1) Can machines act as if they are intelligent?
2) Can machines be intelligent?

The difference between these two questions is really important. Mixing them up leads to a lot of confusion in any AI-related conversation. To keep them clearly separate, in this lesson we will only deal with the first question.

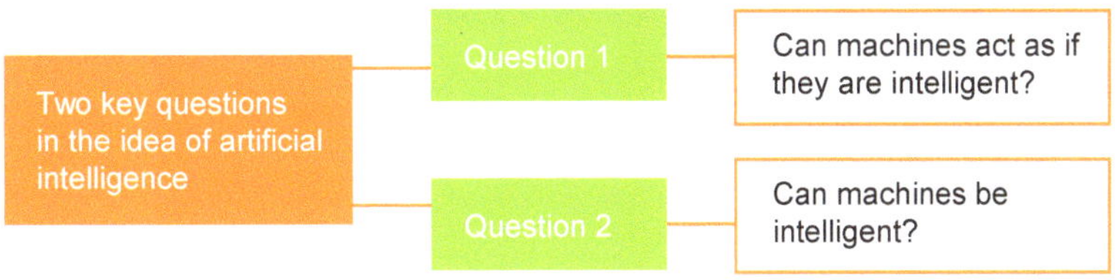

Turing test

The famous Turing test proposed in 1950 is probably the best-known thought experiment in this area. Imagine you are in one room and in two other rooms there is a computer and another human being. You communicate with them via questions and answers. You write your question on a card and push it through a slot in the wall. Sometime later, two cards with answers come back, one from the computer and one from the human (but you don't know which one is from whom). You can spend some time asking questions related to a certain subject area and receive answers in return, and then you are asked to decide which answers came from the machine and which answers came from the human. If you are unable to do so, the machine is said to have passed the Turing test for artificial intelligence. It has fooled you into believing that it's human, therefore it can act intelligently.

Actually, according to Alan Turing himself, it also means that the machine is intelligent. He did not see a difference between the two questions above ("Can machines act like they are intelligent?" and "Can machines be intelligent?"). According to him, the only way we can understand that someone (or something) is intelligent is if that someone (or something) acts intelligently.

So, do machines currently pass the Turing test?

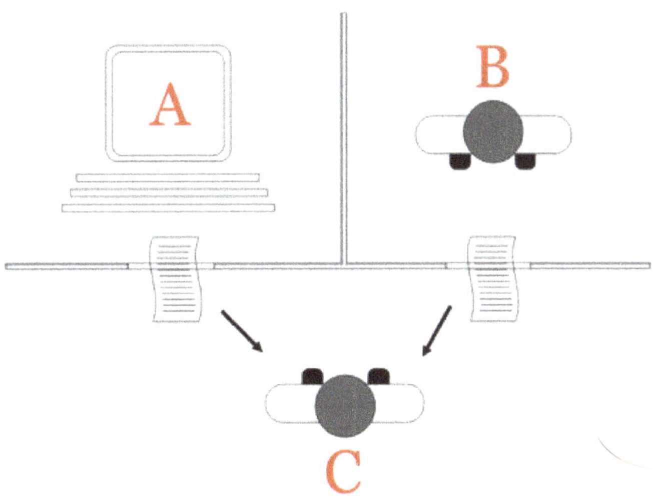

Image 7. Turing test diagram
(credit: Juan Alberto Sánchez Margallo, Wikimedia Commons)

How can we know if something is intelligent? (#Methods and tools)

Two aspects of acting intelligently

Again, it is important to carefully separate two aspects of this question:

1) Can machines act intelligently in some areas? For example, in playing chess, in predicting weather, in piloting an airplane.
2) Can machines act intelligently in *all* areas? If they can, it means that machines can be as intelligent as humans not only in some things that humans do, but in all of the things humans do, in every walk of life. This question is also sometimes formulated like this: "*Can machines display general intelligence?*"

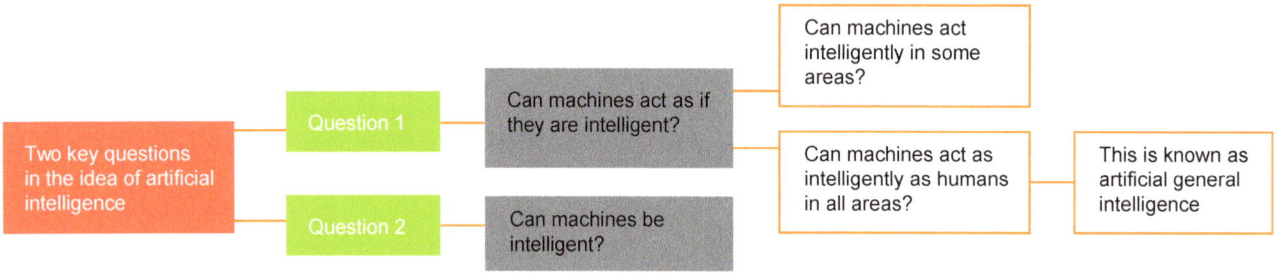

Area-specific intelligence

Chatbots provide a direct opportunity for Turing tests. Create a chatbot and have people converse with it. If they are unable to tell that they are having a conversation with a machine, then your chatbot passed the test. One of the first attempts to create a chatbot for this purpose was ELIZA, a "computer psychotherapist" designed by the MIT AI lab back in 1966. You can try having a conversation with ELIZA (http://psych.fullerton.edu/mbirnbaum/psych101/Eliza.htm) – just imagine you are visiting a psychologist and tell her about a problem you are experiencing.

Since this first awkward attempt, chatbots improved very quickly. In 1991, an annual competition was established for chatbots to try and pass the Turing test against a panel of human judges, called the Loebner Prize (https://aisb.org.uk). Eugene Goostman was the first to pass this test in June 2014. Eugene Goostman is a chatbot that simulates a 13-year-old Ukrainian boy. The conditions were quite strict: judges could ask any questions in a free unrestricted conversation, the conversation lasted for five minutes, and the chatbot was said to have passed the test if at least 30% of judges were convinced that they were talking to a human. Eugene managed to fool 33% of the judges (Veselov, 2014).

Can machines develop to the point where they will be able to solve all tasks humans can solve? (#Scope)

And of course you know about "personal assistants" such as Siri and Alexa. They are becoming more and more human-like. Google Duplex is a tool for making telephone calls to make appointments on your behalf. You tell your device that you want to book a table at a restaurant, for example, and it makes a call to confirm availability, check working hours and make a reservation. The program carries out a very realistic voice conversation with the person at the other end (Gewirtz, 2018).

Image 8*. Chatbots are becoming more and more human-like*

So, we must admit that machines can act intelligently in specific areas. They are getting better and better. But let's go over to the second aspect of the question: can machines reach a point where they are human-like in *everything* we do? In other words, can machines display general intelligence?

KEY IDEA: There is no doubt that machines can act intelligently in some areas. Whether or not they can act as intelligently in all areas (in other words, display general intelligence) is not as obvious.

Artificial general intelligence

Here are some arguments in favor of the view that machines can indeed display general intelligence:

1) If we believe that the mind is a product of the brain (which is a belief shared by many) and that the brain obeys the laws of physics and chemistry, then there is no reason why we cannot recreate it. Assuming that technology will continue evolving, there is no obstacle to that.
2) If we view human reasoning as symbol manipulation that follows certain rules, there should be no doubt that we can teach computers to use these symbols and apply these rules. If symbol manipulation is all there is to the human mind, then we must be able to simulate it one day. If symbol manipulation is *not* all there is to the human mind, then what else is there?

KEY IDEA: If we accept that the mind is a product of the brain, it also seems that we must accept that artificial general intelligence will be possible in the future

Is human knowledge unique to humans? (#Perspectives)

Hubert Dreyfus (1929 - 2017) was one of the philosophers who rejected the idea that a machine can display general intelligence the way humans do. He claimed that the human mind is larger than just explicit manipulation of symbols following some set rules. To support this claim, he introduced the distinction between explicit thinking and implicit thinking. When we are solving a mathematical problem, for example, we use explicit thinking. We can formalize this process and teach it to others (and to computers). However, when we hunt a wild boar, for example, we use implicit thinking. It is unconscious and difficult to formalize. Hubert Dreyfus's argument was that most of human reasoning is implicit reasoning (intuition).

a. Alan Turing (aged 16)
(credit: PhotoColor, Wikimedia Commons)

b. Hubert Dreyfus (a little over 16)
(credit: Jörg Noller, Wikimedia Commons)

Image 9. *Alan Turing and Herbert Dreyfus*

There are skeptics like Dreyfus, but many thinkers today accept that there seems to be no reason to believe that machines will not be able to display general intelligence one day. Remember, they do not need to have a sense of humor or feel love, they just need to simulate feelings of love and display behavior that would suggest that they have a sense of humor. We may doubt machines will ever have minds, but surely they will be able to act as if they do?

Critical thinking extension

The Turing test that we discussed in this lesson was designed as a test for artificial intelligence. The idea is that a computer's behavior is intelligent if it is indistinguishable from human behavior.

However, many AI researchers object to that. It is not the point of AI, they say, to imitate a human. When we build an airplane, for example, we are not trying to make it as similar as possible to a pigeon. And we are not judging its effectiveness by its ability to fool other pigeons into thinking it is one of them.

Is it morally permissible for us to build machines that will be superior to humans? (#Ethics)

Would you agree that the point of AI is to build machines that will be capable of solving real-world problems better than humans? Would you agree that a machine does not have to think like a human to be intelligent?

If that is the case, what could we suggest as an alternative test for artificial intelligence?

If you are interested…

Alan Turing's contribution to our civilization is difficult to overestimate. He had a fascinating life full of triumph and tragedy. There is a popular movie based on his life, *The Imitation Game* (2014). Before watching it, I recommend reading the Wikipedia entry about this movie.

For a visual explanation, watch Alex Gendler's TED-ed video "The Turing test: Can a computer pass for a human?" (2016).

Watch the video "How the "most human human" passed the Turing test" (2018) on *Quartz*. It tells the flipside of the Turing test: the story of author Brian Christian, to be named the "most human human", who competed against artificial intelligence trying to prove to a panel of judges that he is indeed a human being.

Take-away messages

Lesson 2. There are two related questions about artificial intelligence: (a) Can machines act like they are intelligent and (b) Can machines be intelligent? It is important to not confuse the two. In this lesson, we focused on the first question. The most famous method used to answer this question is the Turing test. In this test, if a human having a conversation with another human being and a machine cannot tell the difference between them, then the machine is said to behave intelligently. There have been multiple attempts to build computers that would pass the Turing test and act intelligently in a certain area, for example, ELIZA, Eugene Goostman, Google Duplex. Many attempts have been successful. But this raises a further question: is it possible for machines to display general intelligence, that is, behave as intelligently as humans in all areas of human expertise? According to some, the answer is positive because there are no visible obstacles in recreating the structure of the human brain and the rules of human reasoning. Others (like Hubert Dreyfus) claim that most human thinking is implicit and difficult to formalize, so computers will not be able to imitate it. Yet others claim that imitating human thinking should not even be the goal of creating artificial intelligence.

Lesson 3 - AI: Artificial consciousness

Learning outcomes

a) [Knowledge and comprehension] What is the difference between artificial intelligence and artificial consciousness?
b) [Understanding and application] What are the arguments for and against the idea of artificial consciousness?
c) [Thinking in the abstract] How do we know that a machine *does not* have a consciousness?

Key concepts

Artificial consciousness, subjective experiences

Other concepts used

Chinese room (thought experiment), brain replacement scenario (thought experiment)

Themes and areas of knowledge

Theme: Knowledge and technology
AOK: Natural Sciences, Human Sciences

Recap and plan

We are investigating how technology can affect our knowledge of ourselves. In the previous lesson, we started looking at artificial intelligence and we agreed that there are two questions here that must be kept separate to avoid confusion: (a) Can machines act like they are intelligent? and (b) Can machines be intelligent? So far, we have been looking at the first question, and the answer is: yes, they can, at least in some spheres.

This brings us to the second question: can machines be intelligent? It's a much more difficult question where the Turing test will not be enough.

Can machines be intelligent?

Can technology know? (#Scope)

As you remember, there's a huge gap between machines *acting* intelligently and machines *being* intelligent. If you have a modern smartphone, you know that there's a whole range of things it can do: you can ask it (literally, using your voice) about the nearest restaurants with vegetarian food, and it will understand you, conduct a search and suggest some options. I don't see why such software can't be programmed to get offended when you say something insulting, to act like it is surprised when you say something out of the ordinary, and so on. You have a machine in your pocket that can act pretty intelligently. That's ok, you still know this is just a piece of metal and plastic, a well-designed *thing*.

However, what if I tell you that your phone *is* intelligent? That it can think and feel, be offended and surprised, perhaps even experience pain when you drop it on the floor? That it has a mind? This is where things get a little frightening, don't they?

Well, don't panic. First, let's agree on what "being intelligent" means.

What does "intelligent" mean?

According to Alan Turing, there is no difference between acting intelligently and being intelligent (Turing, 1950). This may seem a little weird at first sight, but the reasoning behind this claim is quite convincing:

1) We cannot observe someone's intelligence directly. We infer their intelligence from how intelligently they behave. This doesn't only apply to computers – we do that with each other.
2) Apart from inferring intelligence from behavior, there is no other way for us to tell if an entity is intelligent.
3) If an entity demonstrates intelligent behavior, it may or may not be intelligent, but our best option is to assume that it is.

Image 10. What is intelligence?

KEY IDEA: According to Alan Turing, "being intelligent" = "acting intelligently"

Not everyone felt comfortable with this reasoning. It feels weird to claim that my smartphone "has intelligence". This is because, subjectively, we experience this "something" within ourselves that produces intelligent behavior – our minds. The behavior of my smartphone may be very much like mine, but I have a mind and my smartphone doesn't. Right?

When I make a decision, I *experience* considering options and weighing possibilities, I *feel the pain* of disappointment if the outcomes are not what I expected. Although our behavior may be the same, computers don't *feel* or *experience* like I do. It is these subjective experiences that is emphasized by those who disagree with Turing's claim. By "being intelligent" they mean "having a mind", "having subjective experiences", "having mental states", "having consciousness".

So, can computers be intelligent in *that* sense? This now becomes a question of artificial consciousness. Artificial consciousness is the ability of computers to have subjectively experienced mental states. Let's agree that artificial intelligence means the ability of computers to *act* intelligently, but artificial consciousness means their ability to actually *be* intelligent.

Where is the line between a mind and a thing? (#Perspectives)

KEY IDEA: Those who disagree with Alan Turing suggest that to be intelligent, one needs to have subjectively experienced mental states (consciousness). The question then becomes, can machines have consciousness?

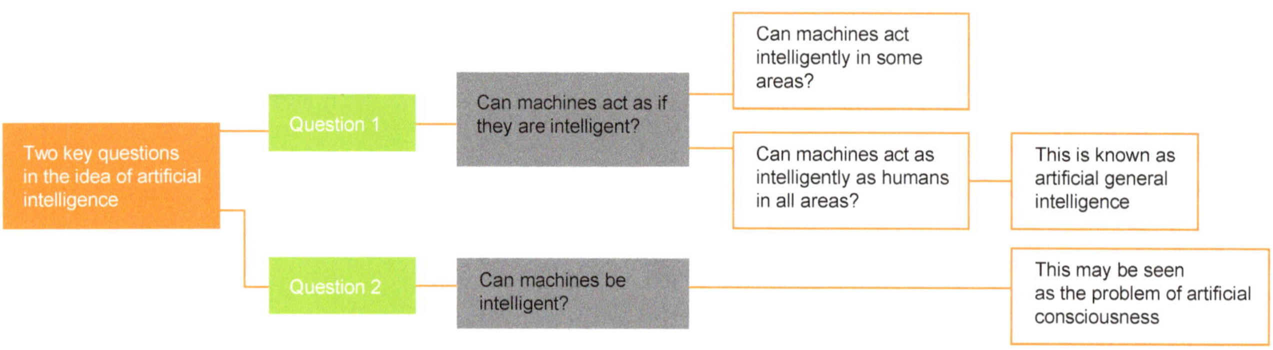

John Searle's "Chinese room"

Arguing against the idea that computers can have minds, in 1980 John Searle came up with a thought experiment that he called the "Chinese room" (Searle, 1980). It has been widely discussed ever since.

Suppose that AI scientists have succeeded in designing a computer that acts as if it understands Chinese. The software takes Chinese characters as inputs, processes them and produces sequences of Chinese characters as outputs. Suppose also that this computer successfully passes the Turing test: Chinese-speaking humans interacting with it are convinced that they are conversing with another human Chinese speaker.

Now, imagine Searle himself sits in a closed room where he has a book with an English version of the computer program, papers and file cabinets to record and store information, and pencils and erasers to write down his answer. He receives Chinese characters through a slot in the door, processes these characters according to the instructions in the book, and writes his output on a card that he pushes back through the slot in the door. Essentially, this is doing what the computer does, only manually.

How can thought experiments be helpful in gaining knowledge? (#Methods and tools)

Searle claims that in this thought experiment there is no essential difference between himself and the computer that follows instructions step by step and spits out an output that is interpreted by human beings as intelligent behavior. But just like Searle doesn't understand a word of Chinese, the computer would not understand Chinese either. And there is nothing in that room that can be said to understand Chinese. Since the computer does not understand Chinese, it does not have a mind and it is not intelligent.

***Image 11**. Chinese room thought experiment*

Arguments against "Chinese room"

AI scholars have made multiple attempts to refute the argument, generating some interesting debates.

One reply was that the mind in the Chinese room is not the man, but the whole system: the man plus the papers and file cabinets and pencils and erasers. The man does not speak Chinese, but the room does.

How do we know that we have a mind? How do we know that someone else has a mind? (#Methods and tools)

Another reply is *the brain replacement scenario*. Searle says that a computer program (or a machine) cannot be conscious no matter how closely it simulates the human brain. Imagine that scientists have invented a tiny computer that simulates the function of an individual neuron. They start gradually, one by one, replacing the real neurons in your brain with these simulated devices. If they replace one neuron, that would probably do nothing to your consciousness. But what happens when scientists continue replacing more and more neurons in your brain? According to Searle, a completely artificial brain must not have consciousness, therefore you must lose conscious control at some point during this process. Imagine that part of your brain has been replaced with these artificial neurons. Your teacher asks you "Do you believe that machines can have minds?", and you want to shout "No, never!", but much to your dismay you hear your own voice saying "Yes, definitely". Critics find this scenario weird; they say that there will be no such point where conscious awareness is replaced by automatic, mindless reactions. Therefore, conscious awareness will remain a property of the fully artificial brain.

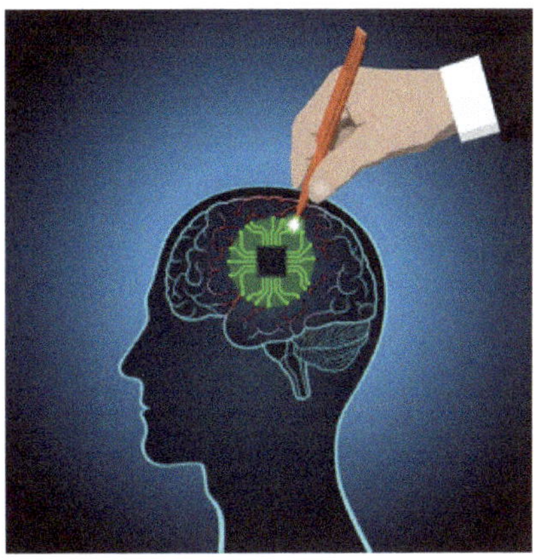

***Image 12**. In a hypothetical scenario parts of the brain are replaced by artificial neurons*

Conclusion

We don't have any satisfactory answers yet. The idea of a conscious machine is somehow counter-intuitive. It goes against our subjective experiences that a "thing" can have a mind just like our own. At the same time, we know that the brain theoretically can be reproduced. If things do not have minds, then an artificial brain will not have a mind, either. But then it is unclear what "a mind" is. If it is not entirely a product of the brain, then what is it and where does it come from? Unless we answer this question convincingly, we will need to accept that things can have minds.

KEY IDEA: The idea of a conscious machine is counter-intuitive because "a thing cannot have a mind". But then it is very difficult to explain what else is there in the mind that cannot be reduced to the thing.

Critical thinking extension

How do we know that a machine *does not* have a consciousness?

Imagine that the day has come when we have built an android that is indistinguishable from a human. The android acts like a human being in everything it does. For example, when it touches a hot surface, it pulls back its hand and screams as if it was in pain. Now, my question about this android is: is it human? Should it be given the same rights as human beings?

It probably depends on whether or not the android has consciousness. Does it experience pain or does it merely act as if it is experiencing pain?

Imagine this android is *you*, and you do experience pain and have consciousness, but people around you are convinced by John Searle's arguments and believe that you are merely a thing. How do you prove them wrong?

If you are interested...

Watch Joscha Bach's TED talk "From Artificial Intelligence to Artificial Consciousness" (2016) – insightful, though slightly on the technical side.

Watch the video "These self-aware robots are redefining consciousness" (2019) on the YouTube channel *Seeker*. This video is about a research lab that tries to build self-aware robots and their latest achievements.

Watch David Chalmers's talk "Artificial consciousness" (2016) on the YouTube channel *Serious Science*.

Watch the video "The Chinese room experiment – The hunt for AI" (2015) on the YouTube channel *BBC Studios*.

If you have not had these lessons already, you might want to have a look at lessons about "qualia" in the chapter "Knowledge and understanding". These lessons have many concepts and thought experiments that are related to our discussion of artificial consciousness.

Take-away messages

Lesson 3. We have seen that machines can act as if they are intelligent. Some even think that machines can display general intelligence, that is, they can *seem to be* as intelligent as humans in every walk of life. But the next question is, can machines be intelligent? Many thinkers assert that acting as intelligently as a human does not mean being intelligent. Many thinkers assert that it does. What is usually meant by intelligence in this context is "subjective experiences", "mental states" or "consciousness". So, this debate can be more accurately described as a debate over artificial consciousness. John Searle with his thought experiment "Chinese room" proposed that a machine cannot be intelligent even if it is an exact copy of the human brain. However, some counter-arguments were proposed too, for example, it is not clear where intelligence (consciousness) disappears when a human brain (in a hypothetical scenario) gradually turns into an artificial brain.

Lesson 4 - Hard problem of consciousness

Learning outcomes

a) [Knowledge and comprehension] What is the hard problem of consciousness?
b) [Understanding and application] What are the key responses to the hard problem of consciousness?
c) [Thinking in the abstract] What are the consequences of the three responses for such areas of knowledge as Natural and Human Sciences, History, the Arts?

Key concepts

Hard problem of consciousness, dualism, physicalism, eliminative materialism

Other concepts used

Reflex, substance, physical and mental properties

Themes and areas of knowledge

Theme: Knowledge and technology
AOK: Natural Sciences, Human Sciences, History, the Arts

Recap and plan

We have considered two questions related to artificial intelligence: (a) can machines act as if they are intelligent? (b) can machines be intelligent?

The answer to the first question is yes, definitely for some separate areas of expertise, but debatable for all human expertise on the whole. The second question is a question of whether or not machines can have consciousness. We considered some arguments for and against, but we did not arrive at any satisfactory answer yet.

We will try to have a satisfactory answer here in this lesson. For this, we will have to revisit the problem of consciousness in general. It links closely to understanding what it means to be human – a question that brings together human sciences and natural sciences.

The hard problem of consciousness

The term hard problem of consciousness was introduced by philosopher David Chalmers (born 1966). The hard problem of consciousness is to explain how and why some organisms have subjective experiences (Chalmers, 1995).

Note that there are two parts of the problem – the why and the how.

The first part is the *why*. Why do some organisms have subjective experiences? For example, why is it that we feel pain when we touch something hot? From the self-preservation perspective, if something is hot and we are touching it, we should pull the hand back immediately to prevent tissue damage. So there has to be a reflex: detect hot – pull back your hand. That's understandable. But why add a subjectively experienced feeling of pain to that? Why not just an automatic reflex? Compare this to an electric kettle (the one that automatically switches off when the water inside is boiling). The kettle detects the temperature of the water in it and (in a kind of a reflex) turns itself off. The kettle does not experience a sensation of pain (I hope!). So why is it that evolution designed human organisms to experience this sensation?

Can there be knowledge without conscious awareness? (#Perspectives)

Chalmers wrote: "*It is widely agreed that experience arises from a physical basis, but we have no good explanation of why and how it so arises. Why should physical processing give rise to a rich inner life at all? It seems objectively unreasonable that it should, and yet it does*" (Chalmers, 1995)[1].

[1] In the chapter "Knowledge and understanding" there are two lessons on the concept of "qualia". When you study these lessons, you will learn that Chalmers's question may be rephrased like this: "Why do qualia exist?" or "Why aren't we philosophical zombies?"

The second part of the problem is the *how*. How does the brain (a thing that obeys rules of physics and chemistry) create subjective experiences? The brain is a very complex collection of neurons and connections between them, but no matter how complex it is, it's still a *thing*, a device operating on electricity and chemical reactions. How does this device give birth to subtle subjective experiences such as admiration, love, shyness?

KEY IDEA: The hard problem of consciousness is to explain how and why some organisms have subjective experiences

Responses to the hard problem of consciousness

There are many responses and they are all super exciting. I will outline the major three.

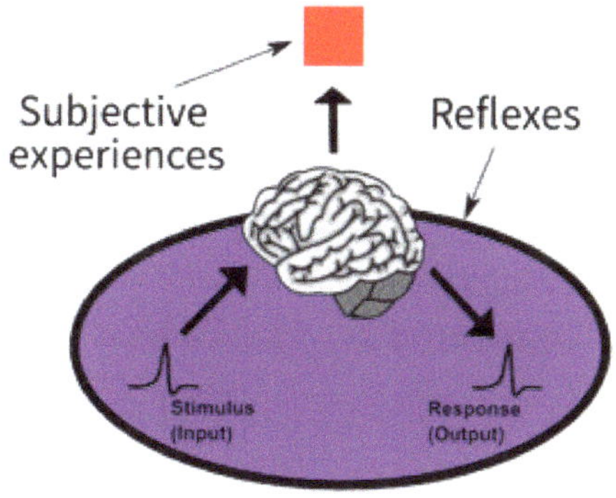

Image 13. The hard problem of consciousness asks how subjective experiences can be produced by a physical organ

Will the human mind be completely understood by natural sciences in the future? (#Scope)

1) Consciousness exists and it cannot be fully explained by the physical properties of the brain (this position is known as dualism). A classic example of dualism is René Descartes (1596 – 1650), who suggested that mind and body are two separate substances that exist independently. For dualists, the hard problem of consciousness is indeed a hard problem.
2) Consciousness exists, but it can be fully explained by the physical properties of the brain (this position is known as physicalism). For physicalists, if you build a machine that copies the human brain and if you ensure that this machine functions exactly as the human brain does (in the physical sense), then this machine will have consciousness. Physicalists reject the hard problem of consciousness. For them, it is not a problem because once we sufficiently understand the physical workings of the brain, we will automatically understand consciousness.
3) Eliminative materialism asserts that consciousness does not even exist. It is an illusion. For philosophers of this camp (such as Daniel Dennett), consciousness appears more mysterious than it really is. Consciousness is not a product of a physical process, it is a physical process. They reject the hard problem of consciousness, too. There is no problem because there is no consciousness.

Can a machine have consciousness? Three options

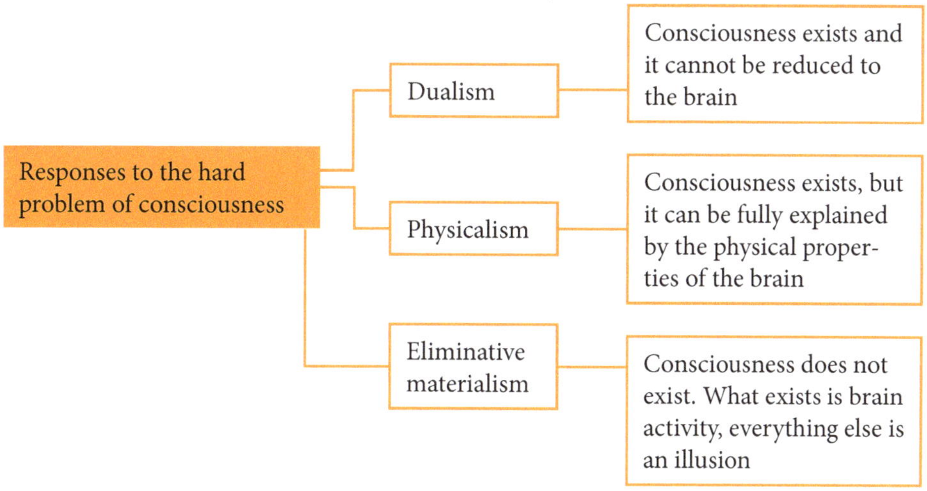

This may have seemed like a detour to you, so let me draw your attention back to the original question: can a machine have consciousness? Looking at the three possible solutions to the hard problem of consciousness outlined above, there seem to be three options:

If dualists are right, then consciousness is something that cannot be reduced to the physical basis (neurons, wires, chemistry, electricity), and hence machines cannot have consciousness. Unless we solve the mystery of what consciousness is (if it's not something physical, then what is it?) and learn to construct it somehow, we will never be able to build a machine that is intelligent. We will only be able to build a machine that acts as if it was intelligent.

If physicalists are right, consciousness is a property of the physical structure of our brain. There is nothing mystical in it, it is simply the way we describe the working of a thing. Hence, if we manage to build a machine that simulates the brain, this machine will automatically have consciousness. It is probably only a matter of time before we build it.

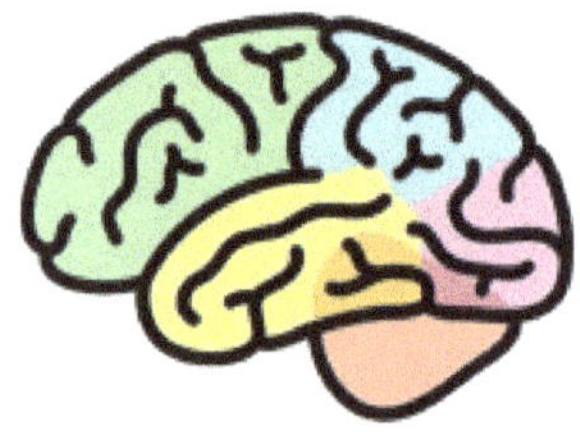

***Image 14**. Human brain*

When several explanations exist, should we prefer the simplest one? (#Methods and tools)

If eliminative materialists are right, our consciousness is an illusion. Since we don't have consciousness, we are already machines. We can probably build a machine that will simulate the human brain, and that machine will probably experience the same illusion.

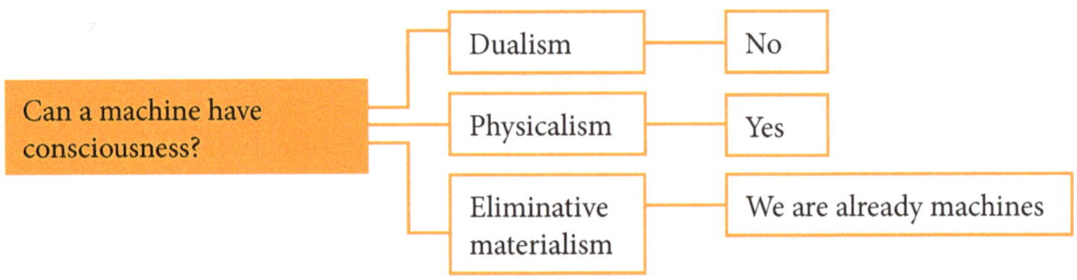

KEY IDEA: If we assume dualism, we cannot currently explain what consciousness is. If we assume the other two options, we must admit that artificial consciousness is likely to be created.

Conclusion

Let me take the liberty and summarize our arguments like this:

Can machines be intelligent?
If consciousness has a physical basis then, in principle, yes.

For the rest of this unit I will assume physicalism. I will assume that consciousness does indeed have a physical basis, and that there is no foreseeable obstacle that would prevent us from recreating this physical basis using technology. And that once we have done so, this creation of ours will have consciousness in the same sense as we do.

I am making this assumption not because I find physicalism more convincing than other positions, but because I think accepting physicalism as a starting point will allow us to explore the relationship between knowledge and technology a bit more deeply in the following lessons.

By the way, I do accept one of the three positions more than the others, but I'm not telling you which one!

Critical thinking extension

Implications for areas of knowledge

The hard problem of consciousness – and the way we choose to solve it – has profound implications for many areas of knowledge.

For human sciences, it radically changes how we understand what it means to be human. If we ever create artificial consciousness, we will be able to claim that we understand what consciousness is and how it works. And with it, many subjectively existing phenomena such as motivation, aims, meanings, interpretations.

For natural sciences, it could mean that we can tackle questions that we avoided before. Actually, if physicalism is right, natural sciences and human sciences could merge at some point. We could have the physics of motivation and the psychology of machines.

History could change. For example, if we decide that consciousness is just an illusion, we might want to rethink what we know about the forces that drive history.

Art could change. Artificial consciousness can create art. If art ceases to be something uniquely human, we will definitely have to rethink what art is.

For the three options outlined in this lesson (dualism, physicalism and eliminative materialism), how do you think areas of knowledge will be transformed if each of them "wins"?

If we can create artificial consciousness, are we morally obligated to do so?
(#Ethics)

If you are interested...

Watch the TED talk from David Chalmers "How do you explain consciousness?" (2014).

Watch the TED talk from Daniel Dennett "The illusion of consciousness" (2003). Daniel Dennett is an eliminative materialist, and in the talk, he provides a response to the hard problem of consciousness.

Take-away messages

Lesson 4. The hard problem of consciousness is to explain how and why some organisms have subjective experiences. The "why" part of the problem asks why it is that we have subjective experiences and sensations over and above simple reflexes. For example, why do we experience pain when we touch something hot, over and above the simple reflex of pulling away the hand? The "how" part of the problem asks how these subjective experiences arise from the brain, which is essentially a "thing". Three major responses to the hard problem of consciousness are: (a) dualism, which says that consciousness exists and cannot be fully explained by the brain; (b) physicalism, which says that consciousness exists but that it can be fully explained by the properties of the brain; (c) eliminative materialism, which says that consciousness is an illusion and we are all essentially machines already. In the second and the third options, machines can be conscious. The hard problem of consciousness has important implications for all areas of knowledge. For example, if physicalism is the right answer, then we can expect natural and human sciences to merge at some point.

Lesson 5 - Technological singularity

Learning outcomes

a) [Knowledge and comprehension] What is the technological singularity?
b) [Understanding and application] What are the possible scenarios of future development of artificial intelligence?
c) [Thinking in the abstract] To what extent can we know the future by extrapolating from the past?

Key concepts

Technological singularity, intelligence explosion, futurism, extrapolation

Other concepts used

What-if thought experiment, self-improvement, augmented reality, Moore's law, mind uploading

Themes and areas of knowledge

Theme: Knowledge and technology
AOK: Natural Sciences, Human Sciences

Recap and plan

In this lesson I want to make some assumptions and run a what-if thought experiment.

How useful are what-if thought experiments in predicting the future? (#Methods and tools)

We have seen that machines can act as if they are intelligent, and they are getting better and better at it, but it is still debatable if they will be able at some point to act as intelligently as humans in all possible walks of life. For this lesson, I will assume that they will.

We have also considered the question of whether or not machines can be conscious. The answer here depends on your position in response to a larger question – the hard problem of consciousness. For this lesson, I will assume physicalism – the position that claims that consciousness arises from the physical brain structure and hence a close enough artificial replica of the human brain will have consciousness.

Finally, I will assume that we will soon be able to build a close replica of the human brain.

With these assumptions in mind, what will happen? How will technology and society co-develop? I am not the only one asking this question. Others who asked it, and sought an answer, came up with the notion of the *technological singularity*.

***Image 15**. One possible scenario of the future of technology is a robot uprising*

Technological singularity

Do you know who futurists are? They are scholars who try to predict the future of human civilization based on a rational analysis of its past. They look at how technology and other aspects of human life have been developing, estimate the rates of change and try to make forecasts.

Futurists are pondering the possibility of a technological singularity - a hypothetical point in the future when technological development will result in dramatic irreversible changes to the human race. A point after which everything human will lose significance and give way to the machines (Kurzweil, 2005).

One of the reasons why such scenario may seem plausible is that artificial intelligence can be self-upgradable. It can learn and improve (just like humans do). This is a reality already, for example, voice recognition software becomes better every time you use it. Machines learn much faster than humans, plus they don't sleep or get tired or die, so this process of self-improvement is not limited in the same way as it is for humans.

Is there a limit in how far technology can develop? How can we know that? (#Scope)

Another reason is that technological progress seems to be accelerating. The kind of technological progress that used to be made in a matter of years is now made in the matter of hours (Machine Intelligence Research Institute, 2013). This suggests that self-improving artificial intelligence will develop exponentially, resulting at some point in an intelligence explosion and the emergence of an artificial super-intelligence that is billions of times more advanced than human intelligence.

KEY IDEA: The idea of the technological singularity is the speculation that the development of technology will result in an intelligence explosion and irreversible consequences for the human race

Rapid cycles of self-improvement

We humans have evolved greatly and come a long way from cavemen to air-travelling businessmen. However, the development of our intelligence has been greatly influenced by the biological constraints of our bodies. When our babies are born, they are quite incompetent, and we must spend many years raising them and giving them basic education (teaching them TOK, for example). When one particular intelligence (for example, Leonardo da Vinci) develops to a great extent, it has limited time before it dies. Let's face it, all of these constraints slow down the development of human intelligence.

If intelligent machines learn to build even more intelligent machines, then that will be a revolutionary breakthrough because multiple generations of machines will improve further and further. Theoretically, this can be very fast and reach levels that go far beyond human intelligence.

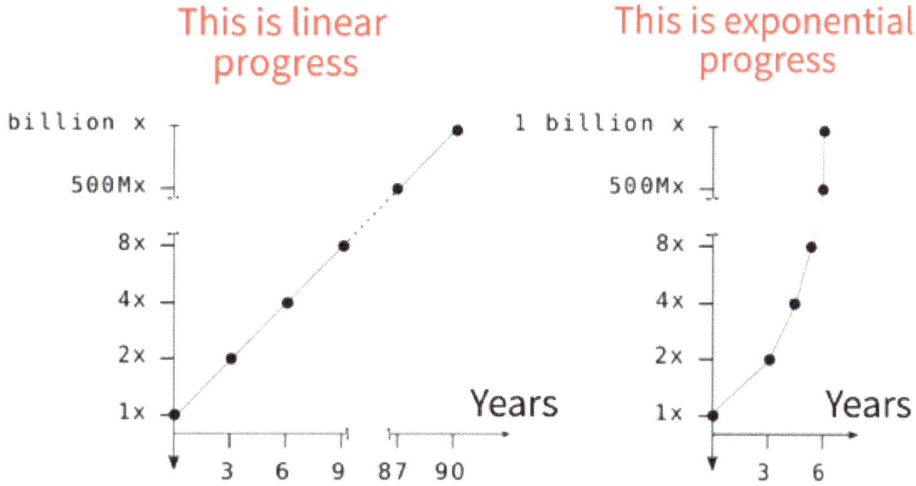

Image 16. Exponential self-improvement can lead to an explosive rate of growth (credit: Rolf Nelson, Wikimedia Commons)

To what extent is development of knowledge predictable? (#Perspectives)

Scenarios

Let's consider some possible scenarios that various teams of futurists are suggesting.

Some think that human intelligence will always remain unsurpassed. Note that this is a popular scenario in Hollywood blockbusters: humans survive in the *Terminator*, humans defeat Decepticons in *Transformers*, and humans suppress the machine uprising in *I, Robot*. Could it be that unsurpassability of human intelligence is something we would like to believe in, and that we are trying to shield ourselves from thinking about alternative scenarios? A movie where humans die out in the end and are replaced by computers would hardly be popular in cinemas.

Some think that humans and machines will merge in some way. For example, humans will have implants that enhance their intelligence. In this scenario, humans remain superior, so to speak, and technology becomes an inferior part of them. In some ways, this is already becoming reality. An example is augmented reality devices such as Google Glass.

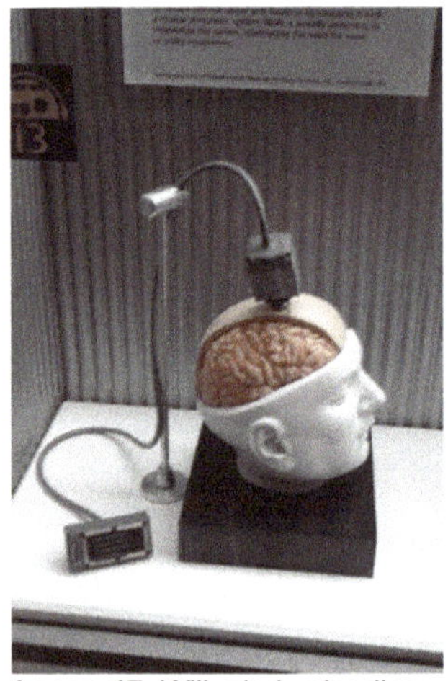

Image 17*. Will mind uploading ever become a reality?*

Another scenario of merging is for humans to be able to upload their intelligence (consciousness, personality) into a computer. In this case, humans become inferior to machines, at least in some sense. However, humans become immortal. You would be delighted to know that the first signs of this scenario are already emerging. Several companies have patented algorithms designed to replicate the personality of a deceased person and upload it to a robot (see "If you are interested" below).

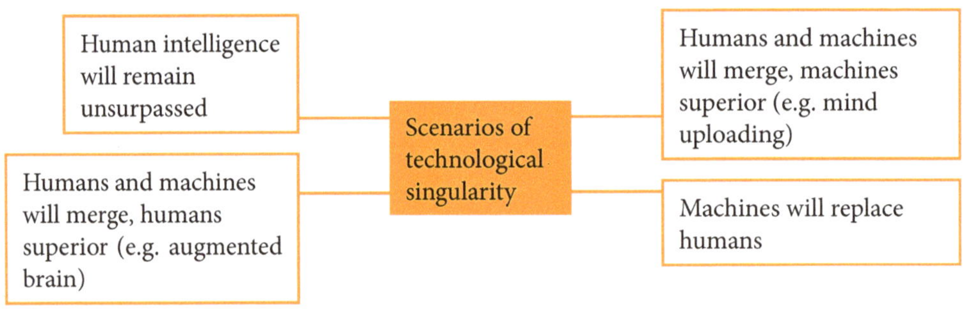

Must we slow down progress of knowledge if it poses a risk to human society? (#Ethics)

Finally, some think that the human race will be thrown out of the picture and replaced by an artificial super-intelligence. It is not necessarily a bad thing, they say. Perhaps this is our evolutionary purpose – to produce machines that are superior to us and go extinct.

When?

The best way to know the outcome is to simply wait and see. But how long do we have to wait?

Ray Kurzweil, director of engineering at Google and the author of *The Singularity is Near* (2005), estimated the onset of the technological singularity (together with mind uploading and all other similar perks) being in the year 2045. This is just to inspire a sense of awe in you – if he is right, it will happen within your lifetime. You might upload your mind onto a hard drive one day. How do you feel about that?

(Note that I'm not advocating Ray Kurzweil as a credible authority. In fact, there were many critics who argued with his ideas, both the possibility of a technological singularity per se and the time of its onset. I am just innocently provoking you into contemplating the big things).

Critical thinking extension

The idea of the technological singularity is based on the observation that the rate of technological progress is not linear but exponential. According to Moore's law, the number of transistors in a dense integrated circuit doubles every two years. This means that hardware becomes twice as efficient and computational power doubles every two years. Extrapolate this tendency into the future, and you have the idea of the technological singularity, intelligence explosion and all that.

Extrapolation is a kind of logical inference based on observing current trends and assuming that they will continue in the future.

The question is, to what extent is such extrapolation a reliable method of obtaining knowledge about the future? Could it be that there is an unforeseen obstacle at some point in the future that will slow down the rate of technological development or bring it to a stop? How can we know?

If you are interested...

You could be interested in some recent cases of *mind uploading*. Have a look at these and make your own judgment: how close are we to being able to upload our minds into computers?

1) *Terasem Movement* is a research foundation that aims to transfer human consciousness to computers. They use voluntarily submitted data such as results of personality tests or voice files. The founder, Martine Rothblatt, created a replica of her wife Bina Aspen – a robot designed to look like her, with real Bina's "mind file" installed into its software. To learn more, read the article "Companies want to replicate your dead loved ones with robot clones" (March 16, 2016) published on *Vice*.
2) Read Liam Tung's article "Google patents way to give robots personalities – and mimic the dead" (April 8, 2015) published on *ZDNet*.
3) The BRAIN Initiative (Brain Research through Advanced Innovative Neurotechnologies) is a collaborative project announced by the Obama administration in 2013 aimed at creating a "functional connectome" - the full map of the human brain, down to every single neuron and every single connection.

I find it very exciting that if you accept physicalism, you must also accept at least a theoretical possibility of mind uploading in the future. Mind uploading seems like something improbable, a topic for sci-fi movies. But physicalism does not sound so improbable and in fact today it's the most accepted solution to the hard problem of consciousness. However, one follows from the other, so mind uploading is not so sci-fi after all.

Take-away messages

Lesson 5. In this lesson, we took three assumptions as a starting point: (a) machines can display general intelligence, (b) we will be able to build a complete replica of the human brain, (c) consciousness is a property of the brain (physicalism). From there, we explored some implications. We did what futurists do – tried to extrapolate the current trends of technological development into the future and imagine what it will look like. Some futurists predict that the exponential growth of computational capacity will result in an intelligence explosion and the technological singularity, the point when the human race will undergo irreversible changes. This will become possible due to rapid cycles of self-improvement of self-replicating machines. There are several scenarios that are being suggested, from humans remaining unsurpassable by machines to humans merging with machines or giving way to machines. Obviously, all of these scenarios are based on extrapolating the past tendencies far into the future, and it is debatable to what extent this is reliable. But is there a more reliable way of knowing the future?

2.3 - Technology in Natural Sciences

Now that we have considered how the development of technology affects our understanding of who we are and what our future is likely to be, let's switch over to discussing the effect of technology on our knowledge about the world.

In other words, we will look at the role of technology in various areas of knowledge. There is little doubt that technology enhances our knowledge. We have created telescopes that allow us to see very far, and microscopes that allow us to see objects that can't be seen with the naked eye. All such inventions push the boundaries of what we can know.

However, apart from simply enhancing our knowledge in certain areas, does technology have a potential to revolutionize it? This is the question that interests me the most. By revolutionizing, I mean dramatic irreversible developments that change the way we think about knowledge in principle. I know the invention of the telescope was a big deal because this opened our access to so much more data about the Universe. But you would probably agree that teaching computers to make scientific discoveries on their own would be a much greater deal. So, to what extent can technology revolutionize knowledge and what are the likely changes that we could anticipate?

In the next ten lessons, we will try to unpack these questions in relation to all five areas of knowledge. We start with Natural Sciences.

Lesson 6 - Computer simulation

Learning outcomes

a) [Knowledge and comprehension] How do computer simulations work?
b) [Understanding and application] Why do computer simulations have a potential to revolutionize knowledge?
c) [Thinking in the abstract] How can we be certain that computer simulation models are a good reflection of reality?

Key concepts

Computer simulation, experiment, cause-effect inference, complex systems of dynamically interacting variables

Other concepts used

Real-life phenomena, confounding variables, causation versus interaction

Themes and areas of knowledge

Theme: Knowledge and technology
AOK: Natural Sciences, Human Sciences

Recap and plan

From knowing ourselves, let's now switch over to the problem of knowing the world.

Certainly, the most trivial answer that comes to mind is that technology has allowed us to overcome the biological limits of our senses. For example, a calculator makes it easier and faster to perform mathematical operations (although we could do without it, it will be difficult). A microscope allows us to see what we cannot see with our naked eye.

But there are more profound questions. One of them is: has technology merely enhanced the existing methods of getting knowledge or has it provided revolutionarily new ways?

I will claim in this lesson that computer simulations are one such method that allows us to gain knowledge that could never be gained before.

To what extent is knowledge that is available to us limited by the existing methods? (#Methods and tools)

Simulation is a unique research method

What methods of research do you know?

If you ask an average person this question, you are likely to get answers such as experiment, survey, correlational study, interview, among others. But computer simulation will rarely be mentioned. This is perhaps because simulations made their way into scientific inquiry relatively recently, and they haven't made their way yet into school and university textbooks.

Image 18. Computer simulation is a unique research method

Well, I intend to restore justice.

A computer simulation is a model of a real-life phenomenon designed to investigate how it works by changing some variables and seeing how this affects other variables. To put it simply, a scientist takes a phenomenon, recreates it in a computer and plays around with it to see what happens. This is particularly useful with phenomena that are so complex that experimenting with them in real life would be unrealistic or unethical or too time-consuming. Examples include simulations of a spreading virus, traffic jams in a large city, forest fires, and so on.

Example: computer simulation of a panicking crowd

Can complex social phenomena be successfully simulated? (#Scope)

Image 19. One of the things computers can simulate is the behavior of a panicking crowd

Some time ago, a tragedy happened in my hometown: the ceiling in a nightclub caught fire, which spread rapidly, filling the space inside with smoke. People rushed to the exit but created a stampede; many could not get out and over 150 people were killed. Among other things, further investigation showed that the exit door had two wings and one of them was latched. When people were getting out, they were using only one half of the door; they could have opened the latch and this could have resulted in saving dozens if not all lives, but they didn't do so. Furthermore, the overwhelming majority were using the main exit although they could have also exited from the back door.

If people had behaved rationally, they could have used two full doors, but they were only using one half of one door. We cannot expect a panicking crowd to behave rationally. But how can we know how a panicking crowd will behave?

A computer simulation is a perfect answer. We can try to model a panicking crowd on a computer, then "play around with variables" to see what happens. Researchers have been trying to create computer models of a panicking crowd. Such models are populated with "agents". Each agent represents one person. Each agent is coded with a simple algorithm, for example:

- If you see fire, start running
- If you see at least five other people running, start running
- If you see a door, run toward the door
- If you don't see a door, follow the person who is closest to you

Once the model is ready, you can play around with the configuration of the nightclub (square area, number of rooms, location of exits, width of exits), the number of people in the room, the speed of fire spreading. You can run the simulation multiple times and look at the outcome – how many people (apologies, "agents") managed to get out safely? How many got trapped inside because they followed other people but had to turn back due to the stampede?

Instead of trying to predict the outcome, we just run a simulation and see what happens. We run it multiple times and see if we get different outcomes with different starting parameters. If I manage to configure my virtual nightclub so that on 990 trials out of 1000 my simulated panicking crowd manages to escape – good enough, I think I am ready to communicate this knowledge to those who are responsible for designing nightclubs.

Why are computer simulations unique?

The key objective of science is discovering causes, in other words, being able to claim that A influences B. It is a widely held belief that the only scientific method that allows researchers to make cause-effect inferences is the method of experiment. In an experiment, we manipulate one variable (A), keep all the other variables constant and see how our manipulation affects another variable (B). If B changes in response to our manipulation, we can indeed claim that A influences B.

But the trick is that real-life phenomena are complex systems of dynamically interacting variables. In real life A influences B, but then B influences C, and C influences A again. This mutual influence (interaction) is dynamically evolving. How can an experiment ever capture that?

KEY IDEA: Computer simulations are a unique research method in science because experiments can only capture causation, while simulations can capture interaction. This makes them suitable for the study of complex systems of dynamically interacting variables.

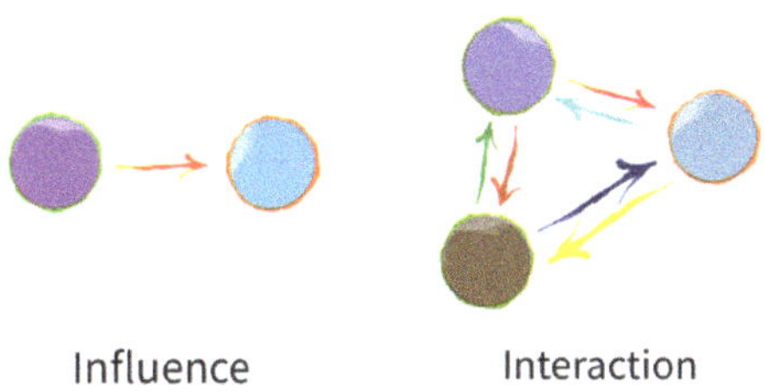

***Image 20**. Influence is not the same as interaction*

Take the evolution of biological species. Suppose I give you full genetic maps of all animals that inhabited the Earth 150 million years ago. I also give you full information on the environment in which they existed. Will you be able to predict how these species will develop in 150 million years?

You can try running multiple experiments (imagine you have unlimited opportunities for this). For example, you can try taking ten samples of Archaeopteryx ("the first bird") and placing them in 10 different environments. This will tell you in which environments Archaeopteryx are likely to survive better. From this, you could try inferring that Archaeopteryx will be more abundant on a certain territory.

Does the method of computer simulations promise a revolution in our knowledge about the world? (#Perspectives)

And you will be wrong. Organisms change in response to environmental demands, but the environment itself changes in response to how organisms modify it. Add to this that there are multiple species and they influence each other's evolution. Plus, there is an element of randomness. The experiment as a method, with its idea of "keeping confounding variables constant" cannot tackle this issue.

However, a computer simulation makes it (at least theoretically) possible. Therefore, computer simulations are not merely an "enhancement" of our existing methods and tools. They provide a revolutionarily new way of knowing the world.

Critical thinking extension

How do we know if a computer simulation is a good reflection of reality? (#Methods and tools)

Of course with simulations we run into another problem: how do we know that our simulation is a good model of the real-life phenomenon? For example, how can we be certain that a simulated panicking crowd behaves like the real panicking crowd behaves?

If we cannot guarantee this certainty, then playing around with a simulation has nothing to do with reality and the conclusions are not really applicable.

How can we ensure that a computer simulation models what it is supposed to model? What would you suggest as a solution?

Hint: you can see how well your simulation fits into whatever real-life data is available. For my panicking crowd example, you can take all nightclub fires that have happened in the world so far (there have been quite a few), change the parameters of your simulated nightclub accordingly and see if your simulation results in the same outcome (for example, the same number of victims).

If you are interested...

Computer simulations have already been used to make many exciting discoveries. They have allowed us to gain knowledge about phenomena that earlier seemed impenetrable to our understanding.

You can explore some examples if you are interested.

1) A coding language for building your own "agent simulations" – *NetLogo* - is available for free thanks to Northwestern University (https://ccl.northwestern.edu/netlogo/). They also have multiple examples of simulations from a range of disciplines like physics, biology, epidemiology, psychology, sociology, and so on. You can download the simulations and play around with them, and even see the source code. When I did research with agent simulations, I used *NetLogo*. It's not a difficult coding language to learn if you follow examples.
2) Airports are simulated. When they design an airport, they use a simulation to see how passengers would behave in varying circumstances. They try to find a configuration of gates and terminals that would provide an optimum performance under a variety of circumstances. For an overview of examples, see the following article: Li, X., and Chen, X. (2018). Airport simulation technology in airport planning, design and operating management. *Applied and Computational Mathematics*, 7(3), 130-138.
3) The Universe can also be simulated! For example, read E. Gibney's article "Model Universe recreates evolution of the cosmos" (2014) published in *Nature*.

Finally, if you are interested in crowd behavior, watch the video "Studies of panicking crowds help shape building evacuations" (2015) on the YouTube channel *AXA ResearchFundLive*.

Take-away messages

Lesson 6. In this lesson, we switched over from how technology affects our knowledge of ourselves to how technology affects our knowledge of the world. There is no doubt that technology has enhanced our knowledge, but the question is, can we claim that technology has provided a revolutionarily new way for us to gain knowledge about the world? My answer in this lesson is yes, and my example is the method of computer simulation. For the first time we have a tool to explore a dynamically evolving interaction of multiple variables in a complex system. This approximates real-life phenomena much more closely than a typical experiment does. There are many examples from different disciplines of how simulations have been used to make sense of things. The example I focused on in this lesson is understanding the behavior of a panicking crowd.

Lesson 7 - Simulated world

Learning outcomes

a) [Knowledge and comprehension] What is meant by the claim that the world is a simulation?
b) [Understanding and application] What features of a simulation can be identified in evolution of species, evolution of the Universe and our own existence?
c) [Thinking in the abstract] How plausible is it that computer simulations are the ultimate method of knowing the world because the world itself is a kind of simulation?

Key concepts

Simulation as the ultimate research method, random assignment of parameters

Other concepts used

Evolution of species, physical constants, fine-tuned Universe, multiverse theory, Bostrom's simulation hypothesis

Themes and areas of knowledge

Theme: Knowledge and technology
AOK: Natural Sciences, Human Sciences

Recap and plan

We started looking at how technology affects our knowledge of the world. It is obvious that technology can enhance our already existing ways of knowing (like a microscope enhances our vision), but my search is for non-trivial examples that suggest that technology provides a fundamentally new way of knowing the world.

One such example that I gave in the previous lesson is computer simulations. They allow us to study complex systems of interacting variables (such as a panicking crowd, an airport, the Universe).

In this lesson, I will continue trying to inspire you with my fascination with computer simulations. You might be thinking: well, computer simulations look interesting, but they are just another one of the research methods available to us.

Is simulation the only way to know complex evolving systems? (#Scope)

However, my claim is much stronger: that computer simulations are the *ultimate* method of research, that further development of our knowledge about the world is unthinkable without computer simulations.

I will make an even weirder claim for this lesson: the world is meant to be understood through computer simulations because the world itself is a simulation. I will give you three examples of this – the evolution of species, the Big Bang and Bostrom's simulation hypothesis.

Evolution of species is a simulation

The evolution of species is a simulation. Think about it:

- Two organisms mate and produce an offspring. The genotype of their offspring is a random combination of their own genotypes.
- This offspring develops and interacts with the environment – either successfully or not. If it is unsuccessful, it dies. If it is successful, it lives on and produces offspring, and the process repeats.
- However, it doesn't repeat from scratch because the environment has also changed due to the influence of previous generations. New generations have to adapt to slightly different environments.

In other words, this is what happens:

1) Parameters are randomly assigned within certain constraints
2) A simulation is run
3) Results are used to review the constraints slightly
4) Parameters are randomly assigned within those constraints again
5) Another round of the simulation is run, and so on

Genotypes and environmental demands are two groups of variables that interact dynamically. An organism's existence is driven by the following logic: "We will assign you these starting parameters and see what happens". Random assignment of parameters is the starting point in this process and there is no attempt to predict the best outcome – just picking the outcome that de facto *happened to be* the best.

***Image 21**. Evolution of species: is technology part of it?*

Therefore, evolution is designed as a simulation (I'm not saying that *someone* has designed it this way, I'm just saying that it is what it is). If that's the case, the best way to understand evolution is through simulation, isn't it? We cannot run such detailed and complex simulations yet, but perhaps in the future we will be able to recreate the evolution of species on a laptop. Who knows, perhaps we will even be able to run the simulation forward and see the likely endings.

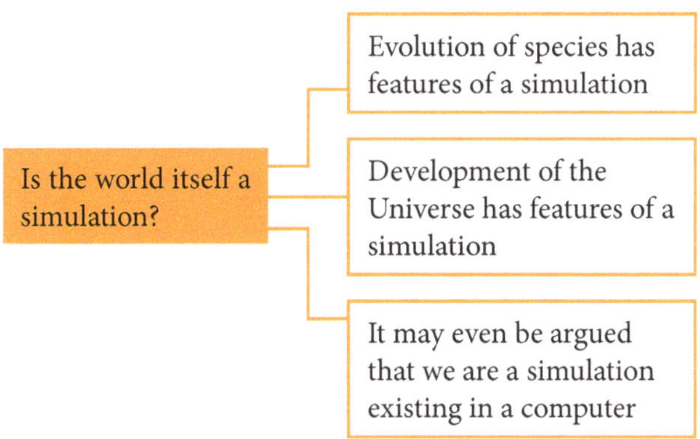

The Universe is a simulation

It is possible that our Universe is also a simulation. A problem that puzzles many scientists today is the so-called *fine-tuned Universe*. There exists a handful of *physical constants* (such as the electrical charge of the electron, the gravitational constant, Planck constant, and so on) that our world is built upon. These constants are exactly the same everywhere in the Universe. But we also know that, had at least one of these constants been even slightly different, life as we know it would not have existed. For example, if the electrical charge of the electron was a tiny bit larger, all atoms would be negatively charged and would therefore repel from each other; the atoms composing all objects in the Universe would fly apart. The same would happen if the charge of the electron was a tiny bit smaller (Debenedictis, 2014).

When it is impossible to test theories empirically, should we simply accept the one that is more coherent with our other beliefs? (#Methods and tools)

We also know that there is no compelling reason for the physical constants to be what they are, and that the Big Bang could have resulted in a tremendous amount of alternative sets of values for these constants. Why did these constants acquire exactly these values, miraculously fit for human beings to emerge somewhere on a distant planet 13.8 billion years later? This is known as the "fine-tuned Universe" problem.

Image 22. We can create simulated worlds

One of the explanations is the multiverse theory: our Universe is not the only one; the Big Bang in fact created multiple universes, each with a different starting set of parameters.

If the multiverse theory is true, then our Universe is indeed a simulation. It's the same logic as we saw in the evolution of biological species: assign values randomly, wait for some time, see what happens. Perhaps we are one of the successful simulations? Perhaps multiple other universes remained lifeless? But the simulation is not over yet! If our civilization dies out before it populates outer space, there's a good chance this particular simulation will result in a lifeless universe where life sparked in one remote corner for one brief millisecond (in cosmic terms) and disappeared for good.

KEY IDEA: The world has features of a simulation, such as random assignment of starting parameters and selection of the best outcomes. To understand a simulation, you need to create a simulation of it. Therefore, computer simulations may be the ultimate method of gaining knowledge about the world.

We are a simulation

Since we are going down this path anyway, I will also mention that there exists a theory that we live inside a computer simulation that is run by our advanced descendants on a supercomputer.

The simulation hypothesis, proposed by Nick Bostrom in 2003 (Bostrom, 2003), goes along the lines of the following reasoning:

1) Many futurists predict that enormous amounts of computational power will be available in the future. Suppose they are right.
2) Then, it would be reasonable to assume that humans of the future will want to run simulations of the life of their ancestors (after all, we are running simulations of everything that is within our power, so we will probably run simulations of ourselves once that becomes possible).
3) With all the computational power available at that time, such simulations will probably be very fine-grained and detailed, to the extent that the simulated ancestors will be convinced that they are real.
4) Therefore, it might be the case that we are all products of a computer simulation designed by the advanced descendants of the human race. Since there is only one original set of human ancestors and (presumably) a very large number of simulated sets of human ancestors, it is actually much more likely that we are a simulation rather than the original ones.

How justified is it to accept an explanation that is more likely as the true explanation? (#Perspectives)

Bostrom realized that this conclusion may seem a little far-fetched. But he observes that, logically, if we do not accept that we are simulated beings existing inside a computer program, then we must accept one of the other two possibilities that seem unlikely. He formulated these possibilities in the so-called "simulation trilemma", in which he says that one of the following three propositions must be true:

1) We almost certainly live inside a computer simulation, or
2) The human race will almost certainly go extinct before reaching an advanced stage where they can run a simulation of their past, or
3) The human race will reach an advanced stage, but they will not be interested in running a simulation of their past, and for some reason not a single individual will attempt such simulations (Bostrom, 2003).

Image 23. *We may be living inside a simulation (credit: Wikimedia Commons)*

Option 3 is very unlikely because if humans can run such a simulation, why wouldn't they? Note that even one individual can run millions of simulations, so one individual would be enough.

This leaves us with a very exciting couple of options: either you and I are simulated bits of software inside someone's computer – or the human race is doomed to go extinct relatively soon. I don't even know which one I would prefer to be true! How about you?

Critical thinking extension

My main claim in this lesson is that the world itself may be "designed" as a simulation, hence ultimately computer simulations may be the only method through which we can truly understand how the world works.

My main question is – to what extent do you agree with this claim?

Note that the fact that various aspects of the world have features of a simulation does not necessarily mean that the world has been designed by *someone*. Perhaps the process of randomly assigning starting parameters, letting the system evolve and selecting the best outcomes is simply built into the fabric of reality. Perhaps simulation is just the most natural way of development, just like a sphere is a natural shape that liquid takes in a vacuum.

If you are interested...

Watch Brian Greene's TED talk "Why is our Universe fine-tuned for life?" (2012).

Nick Bostrom's 2003 article introducing his simulation hypothesis ("Are You Living in a Computer Simulation?"), as well as a whole range of responses and arguments that followed, can be found on this special website: https://www.simulation-argument.com/

Take-away messages

Lesson 7. In this lesson, I provocatively make a strong claim: computer simulations are the *only* method through which the world can be truly understood because the world itself is "designed" as a simulation. I use the word "design" in quotation marks because I do not necessarily imply that it was designed by *someone*. I provide three examples to support the claim that the world is essentially a simulation: the evolution of species, the Big Bang and Bostrom's "simulation hypothesis". Both the evolution of species and the development of our Universe have features of a simulation – random assignment of starting parameters and unfolding dynamic interaction among multiple variables. They both seem to follow the logic "assign parameters, run a simulation and see what happens". If that is the case, then computer simulations are indeed the ultimate method of gaining knowledge about the world, and such knowledge would be impossible without technology.

Lesson 8 - Computer-generated knowledge

Learning outcomes

a) [Knowledge and comprehension] What are some of the examples of computer-generated knowledge?
b) [Understanding and application] Do humans have to understand discoveries made by computers?
c) [Thinking in the abstract] Do computer-generated discoveries deserve the status of knowledge?

Key concepts

Computer-generated knowledge

Other concepts used

Automated Mathematician, Goldbach's conjecture, Eureqa, tests for truth, subjective understanding, the status of knowledge

Themes and areas of knowledge

Theme: Knowledge and technology
AOK: Natural Sciences, Mathematics

Recap and plan

We are looking at how technology affects our knowledge of the world around us. Technology such as the microscope can enhance our existing ways of knowing. But beyond this, technology can also provide a revolutionary new way of understanding the world, for example, through creating and running computer simulations.

In all examples that we have discussed so far, technology is still just a tool. Even in a computer simulation, it is still a human being that plans the simulation, defines the starting parameters and interprets the results. Planning and reflection is still a human job, and it is only the manual work that we have outsourced to technology.

Can this relationship ever change? Can technology take over the "human territory" and go from being merely a tool to being the main actor in the production of knowledge? In other words, can there be computer-generated knowledge? If the answer is "yes", it will indeed change the very definition of knowledge which, as we currently assume, can only reside in the human mind.

Can computers make discoveries?

Some say that this has already happened. In 1982, a computer program named the *Automated Mathematician* developed by Douglas Lenat at Stanford University, "declared" the mathematical rule that every integer larger than 2 can be expressed as a sum of two prime numbers. Admittedly, this had already been known to humans. In 1742, German mathematician Christian Goldbach formulated the same rule, known today as Goldbach's conjecture. But the thing is, Lenat's computer discovered this conjecture all by itself, without any prior knowledge of it (Lenat and Brown, 1984).

The protein p53 is also known as the "guardian of the genome" because it suppresses the formation of tumors in the human body. For that reason, scientists carefully study *kinases* – enzymes that interact with p53. This meticulous research results in the identification of kinases at a rate of approximately one per year. In the period between 2003 and 2013, nine such kinases were discovered. These discoveries promise a chance of creating a cancer drug. But the thing is, each such discovery requires sifting through thousands of existing publications.

How can we attribute authorship and intellectual rights in computer-generated discoveries? (#Ethics)

In 2013, a supercomputer in California scanned 100,000 research papers for information on the p53 protein and tried to identify links that point at potential p53 kinases. Results were impressive. After scanning all papers published prior to 2003, the computer was able to identify seven of the nine kinases that were discovered in the following decade (2003 – 2013). On top of that, it identified two yet-unknown kinases. Scientists ran laboratory tests straight away, and the tests confirmed the findings (Hodson, 2014).

How are human discoveries different from computer-generated results? (#Scope)

If you still feel that neither of these examples is a "discovery" in the true sense, then try to formulate explicitly: what exactly makes human discoveries different from these computer-generated results? I am not trying to convince you that computers can make discoveries (I myself am not convinced at this point), but you probably agree that these two examples challenge us to redefine knowledge somehow so that there is a clear boundary between what belongs to humans and what can be outsourced to computers. So, what is it that makes human discoveries different?

Image 24. Who made the discovery – the human or the computer?

Do humans have to understand discoveries made by computers?

I have discussed the question posed in the previous paragraph with several people – my colleagues and students. Most of them said that the element missing from the computer "discoveries" mentioned above is human "understanding". Computers can process information and find something new, for example, a previously unnoticed link, but they will never *understand* what they found.

In this respect, I have another curious question: is it possible that a computer will make a discovery that we humans will not be able to understand?

In 2009, Hod Lipson and Michael Schmidt, computer scientists from Cornell University, created a computer program that, when given data from a physical system, runs experiments on it and describes the laws of physics that apply to that system. For example, they fed the algorithm motion-capture coordinates of a swinging pendulum, and the program produced a Hamiltonian equation describing the motion of a double pendulum and capturing the physical law of conservation of energy. The algorithm had no prior knowledge of physics. It just did what physicists normally do: observed reality, ran experiments with it, and generalized laws from its observations (Manjoo, 2011).

The program is called *Eureqa*. The authors made it freely downloadable, by the way – here is the link (https://www.creativemachineslab.com/eureqa.html), you are welcome to use it to discover some new laws previously unknown to science!

At a later time, Lipton and Schmidt worked with a molecular biophysicist Gurol Suel to study the dynamics of a bacterium cell. By their own confession, the result was mind-blowing: the computer discovered an elegant equation describing how the cell functions and that equation was applicable across various situations. But the problem was, none of the (human) researchers could explain why this equation works. They didn't understand it. As the researchers described working with their algorithm, it was a bit like consulting an oracle (Manjoo, 2011).

Do we have to understand something for this something to be knowledge? (#Methods and tools)

As you might remember from previous lessons, there are three tests for truth – correspondence, coherence and pragmatic. The equation discovered by *Eureqa* passes the correspondence test: it accurately describes the world. It also passes the pragmatic test: it is an elegant equation that allows us to solve multiple practical tasks such as prediction and control. The coherence test is the tricky one here. New knowledge is said to be coherent if it fits without contradictions into our prior system of knowledge. *Eureqa's* equation is coherent with Eureqa's knowledge-generating algorithms, but it is not coherent with our (human) knowledge because we do not have a theory that would explain it. So is this sufficient reason for us to deny Eureqa's discovery the status of knowledge?

Image 25. Do we need to understand computer-generated discoveries?

KEY IDEA: Computer-generated discoveries may pass all tests for truth (correspondence, coherence, pragmatic), which raises the question: is it justified to deny them the status of knowledge just because humans don't understand it?

Why this question is crucial

I find this last question crucial. It can potentially change the very definition of knowledge.

Here is the dilemma.

1) If you deny these examples the status of knowledge, then you are suggesting that subjective (human) understanding is a defining property of knowledge. But this is a little weird. It is like saying that whatever we humans have is knowledge and whatever computers have is not knowledge (even if it describes the world better and even if it is more useful for practical applications). Sounds like 21st century racism, doesn't it? Honestly, if computers ever decide to riot against us, I think they have every reason to do so.

Can computer-generated discoveries have the status of knowledge? (#Perspectives)

2) If you accept that Eureqa's equations (and many other examples of computer-generated discoveries) are indeed knowledge, then that is the end of the era of human domination in knowledge. And then we need to redefine knowledge and change everything we are used to in terms of knowledge production.

So, which of these two options do you prefer?

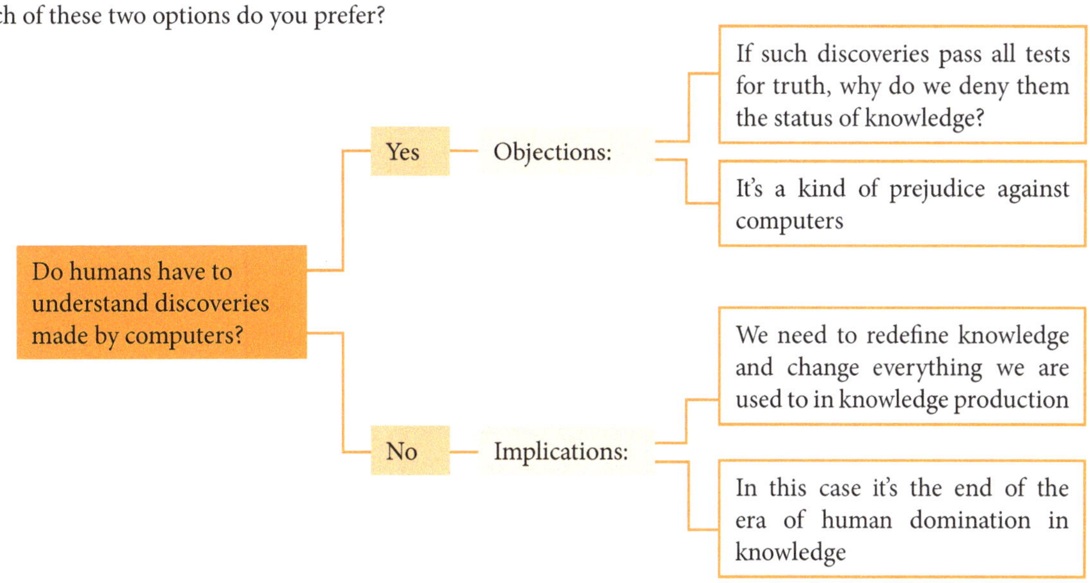

Critical thinking extension

You might wonder how knowledge-discovering computer algorithms (such as *Eureqa*) work. It sounds like the algorithm must be some super-complicated design of the human genius. But, in fact, the idea is really simple. Essentially, it's based on – surprise, surprise! – the principles of evolution.

Eureqa takes the real-world data that has been given to it and randomly generates a large number (millions?) of simple equations that could be used to describe it. These equations are then applied to the data. Many of them don't apply well, so they are eliminated. The remaining equations are then recombined to produce more variations, and these new equations are tested again. This process of natural selection of equations continues until it reaches a point when only one equation remains and it seems to apply equally well to all or most of the data points. Such equations usually represent a fundamental law of nature, such as the law of conservation of energy.

Isn't that essentially what human scientists do? Only humans do it painfully slowly, over generations. Also, humans are prone to errors and biases. Yes, unlike computers, we develop an "understanding" in the process. But could our "understanding" be a simple compensation for a lack of data, an attempt to generalize our knowledge from limited datasets? Computers will have access to full datasets, so the need to "understand" may become redundant.

If you are interested...

Read Brandon Keim's article "Computer program self-discovers laws of physics" (February 4, 2009) published on *Wired*. The program itself, designed by Hod Lipson and Michael Schmidt, was discussed earlier in this lesson.

Read and watch Ross King's publication "Better, faster, smarter? The automation of science" (March 26, 2018) on the *OECD Forum*. He argues that robots can help scientists make better discoveries.

Listen to the podcast "AI robot mixes chemicals to discover reactions" (July 18, 2018) on *Nature.com*. This is about a robot that made scientific discoveries in chemistry.

Take-away messages

Lesson 8. In the previous lessons, we looked at examples where technology greatly enhances and even revolutionizes our access to knowledge. But in all of these examples, technology was merely a tool that humans use to generate knowledge. In this lesson, we attempted answering the question: can computers generate knowledge on their own? The examples we considered (such as the *Automated Mathematician* and *Eureqa*) suggest that computers can mimic what human scientists do and generate something that seems to have all characteristics of human knowledge except subjectively experienced "understanding". Then the crucial question is: is such "subjectively experienced understanding" a defining characteristic of knowledge? If we say yes, then we are being "racist" toward computers – we are denying their results the status of knowledge simply because they are not us. If we say no, then we must radically change everything we are used to in terms of producing knowledge about the world. One day, technology may go from enhancing human knowledge to superseding it.

2.4 - Technology in Human Sciences and History

We have considered the role of technology in Natural Sciences. We have seen that this role may be larger than what we thought. One day, technology may start making scientific discoveries on its own, eliminating humans from the process. We might enter the era of computer-generated knowledge that we don't even fully understand. So let's just say that the role of technology in Natural Sciences may potentially be revolutionary.

Can it be equally revolutionary in areas of knowledge that investigate human activity? Arguably, only humans can understand humans. Human interpretation is an indispensable part of understanding our society, both its past and its current affairs. You cannot just measure these things in the same way you measure weight or velocity.

The following three lessons will focus on the idea of Big Data and the extent to which it can revolutionize our knowledge in Human Sciences and History. Whether or not Big Data will indeed create a revolution is debatable, and will be up to you to decide.

Lesson 9 - Big Data

Learning outcomes

a) [Knowledge and comprehension] What is Big Data?
b) [Understanding and application] What is the difference between Small Data and Big Data?
c) [Thinking in the abstract] Does Big Data make it unnecessary to have a theory?

Key concepts

Small Data, Big Data

Other concepts used

Volume, variety, velocity, veracity, theory-driven, social credit system, predictive analytics

Themes and areas of knowledge

Theme: Knowledge and technology
AOK: Human Sciences

Recap and plan

We are looking at how technology may change our understanding of the world. We have seen that using technology has the capacity to revolutionize the way we acquire knowledge. In the previous lesson, we even considered the possibility that technology will supersede human knowledge and computers of the future will be able to make discoveries on their own – discoveries we will not necessarily understand.

I raised the question: is understanding actually that necessary for something to be considered knowledge? I suggested that we humans might have considered understanding to be so important in the first place because we only had access to scarce data, and creating theories was our way to generalize from available datasets to "universal laws".

But with the current level of computational capacity we can have access to full datasets. We don't have to limit ourselves to samples. Does this mean that theories are bound to become obsolete?

Image 26. A sample is a subset of the target population

That's the question we are considering in this lesson while we are trying to wrap our heads around the concept of Big Data.

What is Small Data?

In human sciences we conduct studies with relatively small samples of people, but we want to believe that our results are applicable universally. For this reason we try to ensure that our sample is "representative of the target population", that is, reflects the essential characteristics of the population that we are generalizing to. For example, in economics when John Maynard Keynes proposed his revolutionary model of aggregate supply and aggregate demand, he was looking at data from American markets in times of the Great Depression. An economist of that time had to select data from a specific culture, place and time. Working with this "sample" of data, the economist then generalized universal laws that were meant to apply everywhere and at all times.

It can be claimed that this kind of research deals with Small Data. Data is "small" because:

Can knowledge be reduced to data? (#Scope)

- There is not a lot of it. The target population is billions of people, and the samples in all research studies combined are thousands at best. Every dataset is a result of a research project – planned, funded and implemented. Data is hard to get.
- It is homogeneous. It is derived as a result of a standardized procedure. In Small Data research, scientists don't stumble upon data, they carefully plan how they will obtain each dataset.
- It is static. Once collected, it does not change. New experiments are conducted sometimes and the new data can be added, but this happens at a very slow rate, so new data is not likely to change the inference considerably.

KEY IDEA: Small Data comes from carefully planned research. Based on prior theory, researchers decide what data they will collect and how. In this sense, Small Data projects are theory-driven.

What is Big Data?

As computational capacity available to us increased exponentially and digitalized data became ubiquitous, it became possible to use data in a dramatically different way.

Does Big Data mean big knowledge? (#Perspectives)

Big Data is often described as having the following key characteristics (four Vs):

1) *Volume*. This means that there's a lot of it. Megabytes and terabytes and even petabytes of data.
2) *Variety*. This means that data comes in a large variety of forms and from a large variety of sources. It is not just a huge spreadsheet with millions of rows of numbers. Big Data projects combine information drawn from texts, numbers, video recordings, audio recordings, images.

3) *Velocity*. This means that new data is generated at a high speed, often in real time.
4) *Veracity*. This means that data that is used in a Big Data project is, as a rule, of varying quality, some more credible, some less. It is not pre-selected. For that reason, any Big Data project faces the challenge of filtering out the parts of data that cannot be trusted.

KEY IDEA: Big Data is characterized by volume, variety, velocity and veracity. Big Data is not simply a large quantity of data – it's a different kind of data.

Image 27*. Big Data is diverse, and there's a lot of it*

Examples of Big Data projects

Examples of Big Data projects are numerous, but let's just look at a couple of them to better understand the phenomenon.

Is it possible to guarantee ethical use of knowledge? (#Ethics)

Example 1: the social credit system

In 2014, the Chinese government initiated the development of a national reputation system, a system that provides a standardized score of a citizen's social and economic reputation. In other words, it is a measure of how "trustworthy" the citizen is, expressed by a number. This is known as "Social Credit".

The system is based on hundreds of millions of CCTV cameras coupled with face recognition technology and Big Data analysis algorithms. Examples of factors that will contribute to your negative Social Credit score include: financial fraud, playing loud music in public, eating on a subway, crossing on a red light, making a reservation at a restaurant and not showing up (Kobie, 2019).

If your Social Credit score is not large enough, sanctions may be applied to you, for example, you may be denied an airplane or a train ticket.

Image 28*. Social credit score is a measure of trustworthiness (credit: Thierry Gregorius, Flickr)*

Example 2: predicting flu outbreaks from Google queries

In 2008, Google launched a service called *Google Flu Trends*. Although it was discontinued after some time due to some problems with accuracy, the idea itself is interesting and much in line with the Big Data philosophy (Lazer and Kennedy, 2015).

The idea is that, when people start experiencing symptoms of the flu, they commonly go on the Internet to search for "flu symptoms", "cure for flu", "high fever what to do", "sore throat" and so on. Since Google has access to billions of queries from millions of users, and since these queries are tagged by time and location, it becomes possible to analyze history of queries together with history of influenza outbreaks and see if certain search queries are predictive of the flu outbreaks in a specific location. The awesome part about this idea is that something medical is predicted from something non-medical – online behavior of Internet users.

Does knowledge imply power? Who is responsible for potential misuse of this power? (#Ethics)

Example 3: predictive analytics based on your purchasing history

Visa, the world's largest credit card provider, was reported to be able to predict divorce (although the company later denied that it was tracking such data or conducting such research). However, although Visa may deny that they are doing it, such *possibility* exists. It *can* be done. As Ian Ayres writes in his book *Super Crunchers* (Ayres, 2007), the data comes from your purchasing history. Your purchasing behavior changes slightly when you are contemplating a divorce, or even unconsciously experiencing marriage dissatisfaction, and Ayres claims that it is possible for companies such as Visa to predict when you will get a divorce even before you are aware that you want it. Based on data from your purchasing history, such companies may know you better than you know yourself.

These and other examples suggest that Big Data is making its way into our lives. Such research projects would not be a possibility if our computational power was more limited. The Internet and modern processors allow us to do things that we could not imagine before. And note that they are not only quantitatively better – they are qualitatively different. A huge question that also becomes important is that of ethics. Now that companies have access to such volumes of data, how can we ensure that Big Data is used ethically?

Critical thinking extension

It is important to remember that Big Data is not simply a lot of data. For example, a census aims to collect information from an entire population of a country. It is a complicated project that costs a lot of money and generates a lot of data. But it is still a Small Data project. The data that is collected in a census comes in a fixed spreadsheet. The spreadsheet has a lot of rows, but it is still just a survey delivered to a lot of people.

Is Big Data merely a useful tool or a radically new way of obtaining knowledge? (#Methods and tools)

By contrast, imagine you were allowed to conduct a census by using all the data collected by citizens' smartphones. In this case, the data you have on each individual includes (but is not limited to): where they are, where they were at each point of time in the past, when and how they commute to work, what they search online, how much time they spent on Instagram on Monday, when they go to bed, when they wake up, who their friends are, and so on. That's a lot of data flowing in continuously. It is very diverse, too. It is difficult to plan your research in these conditions. You will probably run multiple analyses on the available data to come up with the answers to questions you never asked.

The logic of research in Big Data projects is turned upside down. We used to make predictions and collect data to check them. Now we can collect data and see what it has to offer.

Do you think this is a revolutionary change in how research is done?

If you are interested...

Watch the video "What is Big Data?" (2016) on the YouTube channel *World Economic Forum*. It attempts to explain Big Data in under two minutes.

Read Kate Kochetkova's article "10 cool Big Data projects" (April 3, 2015) published on *Kaspersky Daily*.

Watch Kenneth Cukier's TED talk "Big Data is better data" (2014).

Take-away messages

Lesson 9. In this lesson, we considered the differences between Small Data research projects and Big Data research projects. Big Data is a new phenomenon. Today we have access to amounts of data that were unimaginable just several decades ago and the big question is, does this change our knowledge fundamentally or is this just a quantitative change? In the past, research in human sciences was typically based on small, pre-planned, homogeneous datasets. We obtained data from a limited sample and generalized the findings to a wider population. For this, we had to assume that the sample was "representative" of the population. Datasets were limited, fixed, but of good quality. On the contrary, Big Data is characterized by four Vs: volume, variety, velocity, veracity. Data collection is not always pre-planned. Some data is used simply because it is available. Data quality is not always acceptable, but there is so much data, it is so diverse and it updates at such a fast rate that it becomes possible to obtain knowledge that was inaccessible before.

Lesson 10 - Nomothetic and idiographic research

Learning outcomes

a) [Knowledge and comprehension] What is the difference between nomothetic research and idiographic research?
b) [Understanding and application] How can Big Data projects combine nomothetic and idiographic methodologies?
c) [Thinking in the abstract] Can it be claimed that the division between nomothetic research and idiographic research is artificial?

Key concepts

Nomothetic research, idiographic research, physics envy, universally applicable law

Other concepts used

Behaviorism, anthropology, generalization of results, in-depth understanding

Themes and areas of knowledge

Theme: Knowledge and technology
AOK: Natural Sciences, Human Sciences

Recap and plan

We are investigating how technology may have revolutionized knowledge. One example that we looked at was computer simulations. I claimed that computer simulations may fundamentally change the way we obtain knowledge about the world. Another example is Big Data. Again, I posed the question: is it just new wine in old bottles or is it a fundamentally different way of obtaining knowledge? We have defined Big Data and explored how it is different from Small Data, but we still need to define its status. Is it merely a tool to assist us in getting knowledge, or is it a completely new approach that redefines the very nature of knowledge?

We focus in this lesson on human sciences because that is where Big Data seems to have the most potential to make a difference.

The nomothetic and the idiographic in human sciences

Should human sciences have the same standards of knowledge as natural sciences? (#Perspectives)

There are those who claim that human sciences are not quite "sciences". Some scholars believe that human sciences cannot reach the methodological rigor and replicability that is offered by natural sciences, and for that reason human sciences are somehow inferior to, or secondary to, natural sciences.

There are two major responses to this that have shaped human sciences for a long time.

The first response is that human sciences should be modified to be more like natural sciences. This response was the result of the so-called physics envy – the desire to do what physics does: use experiments to test predictions and arrive at universally applicable laws. This idea that the purpose of research in human sciences is deriving universally applicable generalizations (laws) is known as the nomothetic approach in human sciences. An example of the nomothetic approach is *behaviorism* in psychology. Behaviorists thought that all unobservable phenomena (such as emotions, cognitive processes, subjective experiences) should be eliminated from research and that psychology should limit itself to the study of observable, objectively registrable behavior.

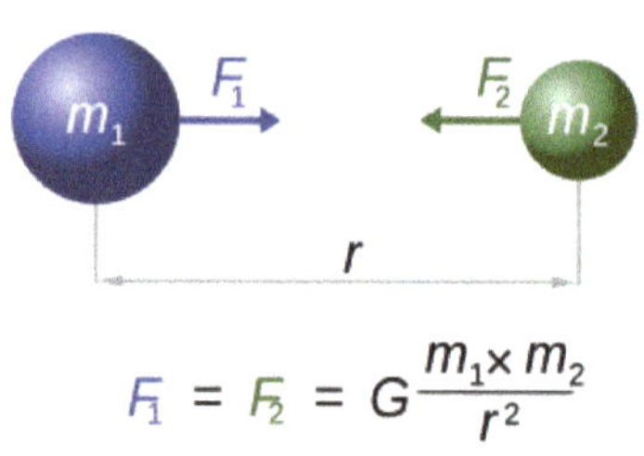

***Image 29**. A universally applicable law: Newton's law of gravitation (credit: Dennis Nilsson, Wikimedia Commons)*

The second response is that deriving universally applicable laws is not the only goal of human sciences. An equally important goal is understanding a phenomenon deeply in all its aspects. This idea that the purpose of research is an in-depth understanding of a unique person, group or phenomenon is known as the idiographic approach in human sciences. This is what an anthropological study is like: we are studying a primitive society for its own sake, because it is inherently interesting. For example, the Hamer people of Ethiopia have a very interesting rite of passage into manhood for boys – the bull jumping ceremony. When anthropologists travel to Ethiopia to study this ritual, what they discover may or may not apply to all other societies, but that does not matter.

Does nomothetic research generate better knowledge than idiographic research? (#Methods and tools)

***Image 30**. Ritual face painting at Hamer bull jumping ceremony in Ethiopia (credit: Richard Mortel, Wikimedia Commons)*

The idiographic approach is accused of being non-scientific (from the "physics envy" point of view). The nomothetic approach is accused of being reductionist and avoiding the study of all inherently human phenomena. To this day, the struggle is not resolved – the question of which of the two approaches should be superior is kind of avoided because there is no clear answer to it.

KEY IDEA: Nomothetic research aims to derive universally applicable laws; idiographic research aims to deeply understand unique phenomena

Enter Big Data

Can Big Data promise a resolution to this debate, a long-awaited compromise? If it does, that would indeed be a revolution in knowledge.

With Big Data, we are not selecting a sample from a population. Our sample *is* the population ($n = all$). We are obtaining a deep, rich characterization of a phenomenon (which is a feature of the idiographic approach), but this characterization is inherently quantitative (which is a feature of the nomothetic approach).

A Big Data project is nomothetic and idiographic at the same time. When $n = all$, any results that we obtain in our sample are automatically a universally applicable law.

Does Big Data promise a resolution of the nomothetic-idiographic debate? (#Methods and tools)

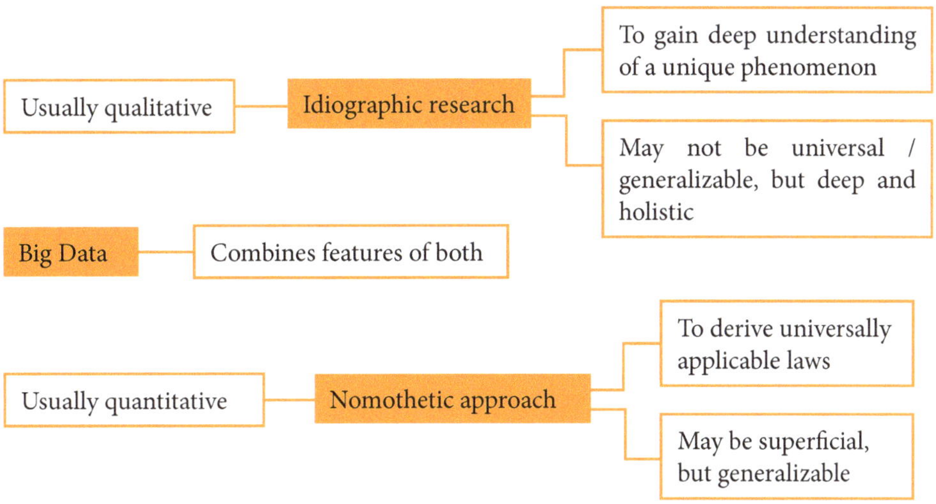

Example: Big Data in recruitment

For example, imagine you are working for a famous company that is hiring engineers for their ambitious projects. They cannot predict what projects the engineers will be solving in the future because the situation is so fluid and changeable. They ask you to conduct research into what makes a good candidate for the engineering position and to design a selection procedure to be used in the hiring process (as I'm writing this, it sounds so painfully familiar! I spent several years doing predictive analytics for a large HR company, and this was a typical task that I was required to complete).

You can take one of three approaches – the nomothetic approach, the idiographic approach and the Big Data approach.

The nomothetic approach is to look for universally applicable knowledge that would be relevant to your task. You study available publications and theories about skills that are most essential in the work of an engineer, and on that basis define a list of characteristics you are looking for. Suppose, for example, that prior research had shown that in various samples of engineers general intelligence (IQ) is predictive of their future job performance. But the problem is this: how do you know that this prior research will be applicable to your particular company? As I said, the company cannot predict what tasks the engineers will be given, so perhaps it is not smart you are looking for, but adaptable?

The idiographic approach is from the opposite side – you study the unique characteristics of the company and try to decide which characteristics are important in this particular case. For example, you could decide to rely on interviews. In an interview, you might say, the company gets the chance to evaluate a candidate holistically, to get an impression of what kind of person they are. The problem is that your subjective impressions may not be reliable. If you liked a person in an interview, and if it seems to you that they will be a good fit, it does not necessarily mean that they will do a good job as an engineer in your company.

Finally, you can run a Big Data project. You can ask the company to give you access to all relevant data that was collected in the past: results of admission tests, resumes of candidates who were and were not offered a job, work performance, satisfaction surveys, Facebook activity of existing engineers. You can crunch numbers to see which variables are more predictive of success of the engineers in your company. Some surprising findings may emerge. For example: the number of typos in a resume may turn out to be more predictive of job success than results of IQ tests (the fewer typos, the better); the length of the queue in the canteen may turn out to be a major explanatory factor of job satisfaction (the longer the queue, the more satisfied the engineers!). The results will seem surprising at first, but you might come up with some plausible post-hoc explanations.

Exactly what assessment did Fido take to get hired?

***Image 31**. Hiring decisions are not easy*
(credit: Amtec Photos, www.amtec.us.com)

For the examples above, I didn't merely make them up; these were actual results of real predictive analytics with engineers. The number of typos in your resume may be a reflection of your diligence and meticulousness, and this – for some jobs – is much more important than how smart you are. Long queues in the canteen may give you a chance to talk to your colleagues while you are waiting for food. In high-profile engineering companies, such informal conversations may be the start of very promising collaborative projects and great teamwork, hence job satisfaction. Who would have thought?

Note that the Big Data project is nomothetic and idiographic at the same time. You are crunching loads of numbers, but they all come from a specific company. Your sample is the same as your target population (n = all). "Generalization" of results becomes unnecessary because results are already as general as possible – and yet they all come from the unique context of one company.

Can Big Data replace all other forms of research in human sciences? (#Scope)

KEY IDEA: Big Data projects can be nomothetic and idiographic at the same time. They are unique in this way.

Critical thinking extension

The nomothetic approach and the idiographic approach in human sciences are diametrically opposite in their assumptions and methods. They have been co-existing for a long time, which suggests that there are plenty of arguments to support both approaches, and that both have been successful in obtaining useful knowledge. Perhaps it's a case of looking at a 3D phenomenon but only having access to its 2D projections. Imagine reality is a cylinder, but we can't see it in its 3D form. We only have its vertical projection (which looks like a rectangle) and its horizontal projection (which looks like a circle). We can argue for ages which of the two projections is better, but that is a meaningless debate.

Is the distinction between nomothetic and idiographic research artificial?

Do you think it can be claimed that Big Data is, in this metaphor, a 3D technology?

If you are interested...

Watch the video "Idiographic and nomothetic description and explanation: a non-social example" (2017) on the YouTube channel *James Cook*. In this video, Mr. Cook uses nomothetic and idiographic approaches to describe and explain... a roof.

Read Bernard Marr's article "Data-driven HR: how Big Data and analytics are transforming recruitment" (May 4, 2018) published in *Forbes*.

Take-away messages

Lesson 10. The key question for this lesson was whether or not Big Data has a potential to create revolutionary changes in human sciences. We started with the fact that human sciences are often "accused" of being unscientific. We then considered two typical responses to that from the perspective of human sciences: (a) the nomothetic approach says that the purpose of human sciences should be deriving universally applicable laws; (b) the idiographic approach says that the goal is an in-depth understanding of uniquely human phenomena and universal applicability does not matter. To this day there is a debate between the two approaches. The nomothetic approach is criticized for ignoring a whole dimension of human activity. The idiographic approach is criticized for not following the scientific method. We have argued that Big Data can potentially reconcile the two approaches because a Big Data research project is essentially nomothetic and idiographic at the same time. If that happens, this may indeed become a revolution in human sciences. We considered an example in relation to this: recruitment in an engineering company.

Lesson 11 - Text mining

Learning outcomes

a) [Knowledge and comprehension] What is text mining?
b) [Understanding and application] Is text mining an indispensable element in the work of historians of the future?
c) [Thinking in the abstract] To what extent do advantages of text mining outweigh the advantages of meaningful reading by human historians?

Key concepts

Text mining, selection bias, close reading, distant reading

Other concepts used

Quantitative and qualitative research, Google Ngram Viewer, co-occurrence of words, historical evidence

Themes and areas of knowledge

Theme: Knowledge and technology
AOK: History

Recap and plan

We have been talking about Big Data. We have been trying to figure out if Big Data can potentially trigger revolutionary changes in Human Sciences and perhaps some other areas of knowledge. In the previous lesson, I stated that this indeed seems likely because Big Data has a potential resolve the fundamental debate between the nomothetic approach (the goal of which is to derive universally applicable laws) and the idiographic approach (the goal of which is an in-depth understanding of unique people, groups or phenomena). In a Big Data research project, boundaries are erased between the idiographic and the nomothetic, qualitative and quantitative.

Quantitative research works with numbers. Qualitative research works with texts (diaries, interview answers, observation notes). Again, there has been a huge gap between the two, but now that Big Data is here, the gap may be disappearing. With Big Data we can – to some extent – turn texts into numbers. Digitalizing texts and using algorithms to derive numerical information from them is known as *text mining*.

This is pretty exciting, and in this lesson I will give you some examples of text mining to illustrate its significance for History as an area of knowledge.

Texts into numbers

As I mentioned in the recap, text mining can be defined as digitalizing texts and using computer algorithms to derive numerical information from them. When I produced a graph of emotions in the Bible (see "Exhibition"), I did a simple form of text mining.

There are some easy, trivial ways of turning texts into numbers. For example, you could conduct a survey in your school asking students to describe their attitude to the TOK course. Make it an open-ended question. After collecting the responses, count the number of times some typical adjectives were mentioned. Was the adjective "exciting" mentioned more frequently than the adjective "boring"? There you go, you have turned texts into numbers, kind of.

But text mining projects can be more sophisticated than that. Below we will look at some examples.

***Image 32**. Text mining is extracting numerical information from texts*

What knowledge can only exist in the form of a text, and what knowledge can only exist in the form of numbers? (#Scope)

Mining historical evidence: digitalized archives

Earlier when historians were studying a specific period in the past, they went to the archive and studied primary sources (letters, diaries, photographs, and so on). They had multiple sources at their disposal – more than a human can possibly read within a lifetime. Their search was directed by their interests, hypotheses and expectations. They ended up studying a small selection from the available documents, a selection *they thought* was representative of a variety of perspectives.

Does digitalization of historical evidence revolutionize historical research? (#Perspectives)

Today, they have instant access to millions of digitalized documents. As an example, look at Google's project *Ngrams* (it is easy to play around with). This project aimed to scan millions of books published throughout human history and run them through text recognition software. As a result, we have a huge collection of electronic texts tagged with metadata such as place and time of publication. For example, want to research the history of atomic bombs? Open *Google Ngram Viewer*, write "atomic bomb" in the search string, adjust the period of search (I used 1920 – 2008) and indicate that you want to search the English corpus (the collection of all books that were published in English).

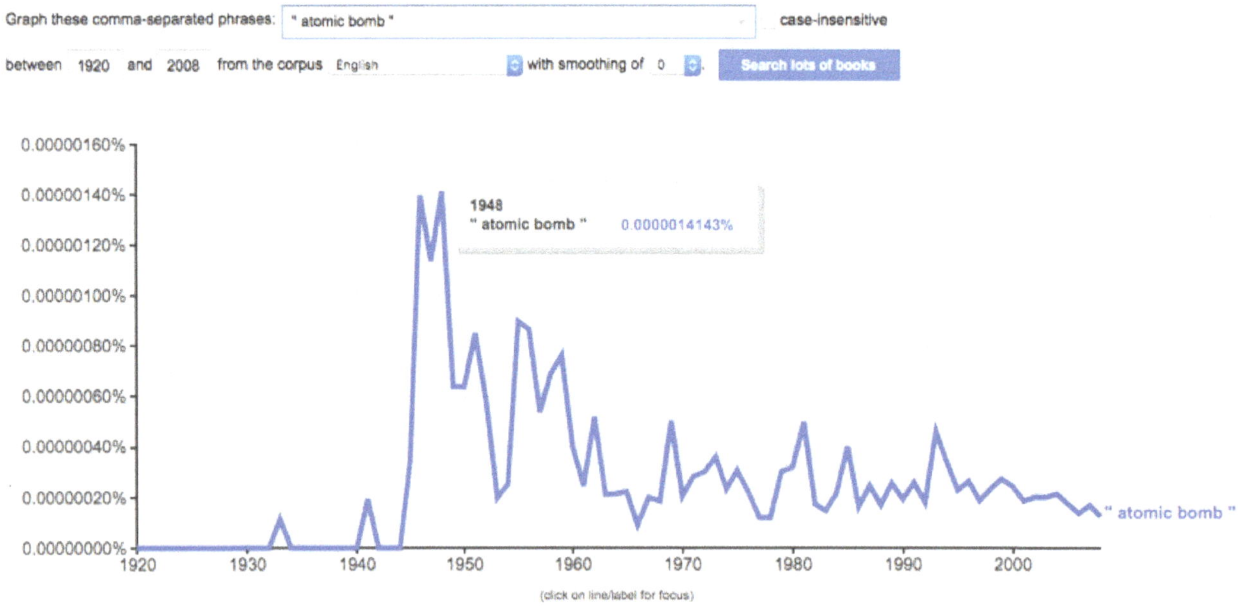

***Image 33**. Searching for "atomic bomb" on Google Ngram Viewer*

What you see is a graph showing how frequently the phrase "atomic bomb" appeared in books written in a particular year, relative to the total number of books written in that year. Hover over the graph with your cursor and you will see details – for example, I can see that in 1948 the phrase appeared in 0.0000014143% of all books. Look at the spikes and you will get some insights. When were atomic bombs mentioned most frequently? Let's look as an example at the first four spikes – years 1933, 1941, 1945, 1948 – and the last spike, 1993.

A quick Internet search yields results:

- 1933: Leó Szilárd invents the idea of an atomic bomb
- 1941: Soviet Union and the USA, the two superpowers, enter World War II and increase efforts to build an atomic bomb as soon as possible.
- 1945: Atomic bombs are dropped at Hiroshima and Nagasaki
- 1948: The USA transfer bombers capable of carrying an atomic bomb to Europe during the Berlin Blockade (the first major Cold War tension between the USA and the Soviet Union)
- 1993: The USA and Russia mutually agree to ban intercontinental ballistic missiles (a major milestone in the de-escalation of Cold War conflict).

Even on this level, without any fancy software or technical knowledge, a historian can investigate events of the past and their relative importance. They don't have to sit in dusty archives. They don't have to worry about their selection bias – the algorithm impartially looks through the whole corpus of available texts. They can run multiple tests in just seconds, allowing them to look for supporting evidence and counter-evidence to test their interpretations.

Is human partiality in the work of historians a useful tool or a harmful bias? (#Methods and tools)

KEY IDEA: Text mining of digitalized evidence may put an end to selection bias (and perhaps other human biases) in historical research

Mining historical evidence: further examples

If you add more sophisticated techniques of data analysis on top of that, you get more sophisticated results.

For example, you can study the co-occurrence of words. Suppose you find out that at a certain period in the past, the co-occurrence of words "black", "women" and "vote" suddenly increased. What does it tell you about that period and that place? You can further separate the documents in which these three words co-occur from all other documents and run a quick test: what other words occur in these documents more frequently as compared to other documents? Some names may come up. You may conclude that these people were instrumental in promoting black women's right to vote. Amazing, isn't it?

You can analyze relationships. When two names occur in a text together and in close proximity to each other, what is the relationship between them? This deep-level analysis can even enable you to create a social network of historical figures, representing people as nodes and relationships as lines between them. This could be like a Facebook for long-gone history makers. This is already reality – you are welcome to browse this network and even contribute to it in the collaborative project *Six Degrees of Francis Bacon* (http://www.sixdegreesoffrancisbacon.com).

Image 34*. A digitalized text (Sumerian inscription from 26th century B.C.)*

Historians of the future

Text mining will become more and more predominant in the work of a historian, bridging the gap between numbers and texts, nomothetic and idiographic, quantitative and qualitative, history and mathematics.

Arguably, because the number of texts available grows exponentially, their selection and analysis becomes a task that is not achievable without digital technology. Perhaps in a couple of decades from now, data crunching and working with computer software will become indispensable requirements in any History major program. Future historians will sit exams testing their coding skills.

Critical thinking extension

What historians can achieve with text mining these days is quite impressive. But, once again, the key question is this: is this a revolutionary change or is this merely a useful tool?

Many scholars draw a distinction between *close reading* and *distant reading*.

Is historical knowledge possible without reading between the lines? (#Perspectives)

Close reading of a text requires paying attention to how the author expresses the thought, what metaphors and stylistic devices are used; in other words, close reading involves a lot of reading between the lines. Only humans can read texts closely. Machines do distant reading – they are very good at quickly counting words and their combinations, calculating probabilities of co-occurrence, categorizing parts of speech and so on, but this is only the superficial layer of a text. With distant reading comes the advantage of being able to read multiple texts in a short time and quantify the results, but, critics say, the depth is lost.

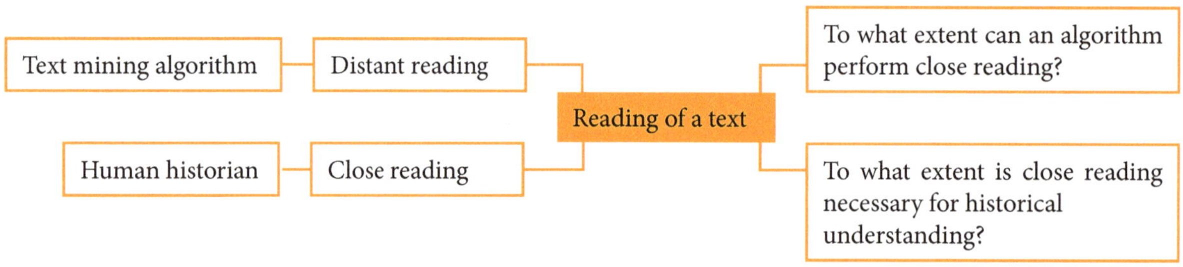

To what extent do advantages of distant reading (speed, volume, ability to quantify) outweigh the advantages of close reading? Is close reading even necessary for gaining historical knowledge? Will machines of the future be capable of close reading?

If you are interested…

Watch the TED talk "What we learned from 5 million books" (2011), where Jean-Baptiste Michel and Erez Aiden introduce Google Ngram Viewer.

Look through the outline of the university course *Text analysis for historians* created by Lincoln Mullen, Department of History and Art History at George Mason University (USA). This is for you to get a feel of what it is like to be a history student who learns text mining in college.

Watch the video "Text mining for social scientists" (2018) on the YouTube channel *SAGE Publishing*. This video is a recording of a webinar by Gabe Ignatow, Rada Mihalcea and Susannah Goldes, authors of books on text mining in the social sciences. They talk about specific examples and get slightly technical, but it is great for getting an insight into the process if you want to understand how text mining works.

Take-away messages

Lesson 11. In this lesson we looked at text mining, a Big Data technique used to derive useful numerical information from large corpora of texts. We focused on examples of how text mining can be used in history. Text mining in history becomes possible for two reasons: (a) development of digitalized archives/text corpora such as Google Ngrams, but also many others; (b) development of sophisticated numerical tools such as frequency analysis, co-occurrence analysis, sentiment analysis and many others. We have seen that when a historian is armed with these tools, it becomes possible to answer questions that could not be attempted before. Additionally, these tools reduce the influence of researcher bias because the historian is no longer required to select a sample of historical documents. However, critics draw a distinction between close reading and distant reading and claim that all text mining will ever be able to achieve is distant reading, and that this will not be enough to gain deep historical understanding.

2.5 - Technology in Mathematics

We have considered the role of technology in Natural Sciences. We have seen that this role may be larger than what we thought. One day, technology may start making scientific discoveries on its own, eliminating humans from the process. We might enter the era of computer-generated knowledge that we don't even fully understand. So let's just say that the role of technology in Natural Sciences may potentially be revolutionary.

Can it be equally revolutionary in areas of knowledge that investigate human activity? Arguably, only humans can understand humans. Human interpretation is an indispensable part of understanding our society, both its past and its current affairs. You cannot just measure these things in the same way you measure weight or velocity.

The following three lessons will focus on the idea of Big Data and the extent to which it can revolutionize our knowledge in Human Sciences and History. Whether or not Big Data will indeed create a revolution is debatable, and will be up to you to decide.

Lesson 12 - Proof-by-exhaustion

Learning outcomes

a) [Knowledge and comprehension] What is proof-by-exhaustion?
b) [Understanding and application] Why did proof-by-exhaustion have a hard time being accepted as part of mathematical knowledge?
c) [Thinking in the abstract] Is proof-by-exhaustion acceptable as an alternative of deductive proof in mathematics?

Key concepts

Conjecture, theorem, mathematical proof, proof-by-exhaustion, mathematical proof (deductive proof), human-verifiable proof

Other concepts used

Goldbach's conjecture, four-color conjecture, Kepler conjecture, mathematical "elegance"

Themes and areas of knowledge

Theme: Knowledge and technology
AOK: Mathematics

Recap and plan

In this unit, we have already looked at how technology influences our understanding of the world around us. We considered examples from natural sciences, human sciences and history. In all of these examples, the question that remains debatable is whether or not the influence of technology is sufficient to speak of a fundamental change, a revolution in the area of knowledge.

In this lesson, we are going to start discussing how technology has influenced mathematics. We will ask the same question: is the influence of technology sufficient to believe that the nature of mathematical knowledge, and the methods of obtaining it, will be fundamentally redefined at some point in the near future?

The question seems particularly interesting in mathematics because the very nature of this area of knowledge seems to suggest that doing math is an inherently human activity.

To start, in this lesson we will talk about a new kind of mathematical proof that emerged recently with the invention of computers – proof-by-exhaustion.

Theorems and conjectures

First, let me remind you of an important distinction in mathematical knowledge – the difference between a conjecture and a theorem.

Image 35. Exhaustion (this is just to visualize proof-by-exhaustion)

What is the value of conjectures in mathematical knowledge? (#Scope)

A conjecture is a mathematical rule that is hypothesized to be true. For example, Goldbach's conjecture states: *Every even integer greater than 2 can be expressed as the sum of two primes.* But even though we have observed it to be true for trillions of trillions of integers, we still cannot say for certain that it is true for *every* even integer up to infinity. However many numbers we check, infinity is always larger. Conjectures are simply observed regularities; they are not proven with certainty.

By contrast, a theorem is a proven statement. It is supported by deductive mathematical proof. It is shown that the statement can be deduced with certainty from other statements that are already known to be true.

When a conjecture is mathematically proven, it becomes a theorem.

KEY IDEA: A conjecture is a mathematical rule that is hypothesized to be true, but not yet proven. A theorem is a deductively proven statement.

The four-color conjecture

The four-color conjecture was first formulated back in 1852 by Francis Guthrie. One day, he was coloring a map of the counties of England (don't we all do that at some point?) and he noticed that only four colors were necessary to do the task. He tried it on other maps and formulated the conjecture: for any arbitrary two-dimensional map with countries, no more than four colors are required to color it so that adjacent countries never have the same color.

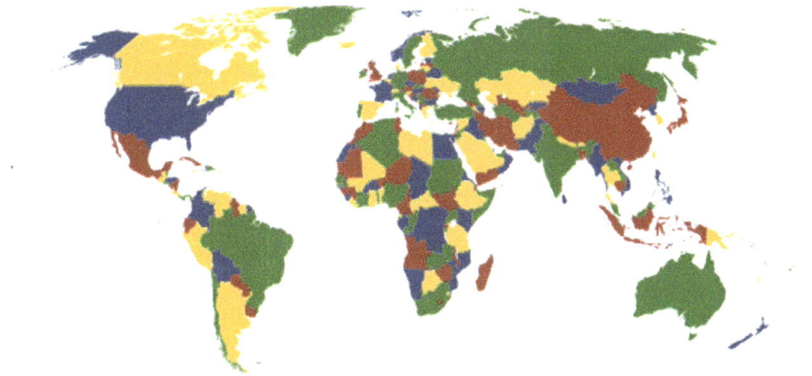

***Image 36**. The four-color theorem claims that four colors is enough to color a map of any configuration*

Proving this conjecture and turning it into a theorem became one of the most long-standing unsolved problems in mathematics. Finally in 1976, more than 120 years later, Kenneth Appel and Wolfgang Haken announced that they solved it.

Appel and Haken's breakthrough became possible with the involvement of computers. Their proof consists of two parts:

- In the first part, they proved that all possible maps can be reduced to 1,834 configurations.
- In the second part, they checked all of these configurations one by one.

Proof for the first part took more than 400 pages. It had to be checked by hand with the assistance of Haken's daughter (Appel and Haken, 1989). This was a long but solid proof. It followed the classic deductive logic of mathematics – the logic that mathematicians were comfortable with for centuries.

Proof for the second part was performed by a computer. The algorithm checked all possible maps for each of the 1,834 configurations. The program took over 1,000 hours to complete. It was this part of the proof that some mathematicians were not comfortable with. This part was not deductive. It was "empirical" in some sense. A computer checked all possible maps, exhausted all possibilities. This kind of proof when the computer simply checks all possible permutations is known as proof-by-exhaustion.

Can mathematical knowledge be empirical? (#Perspectives)

Criticism

When this proof was announced, it caused a major controversy among mathematicians.

1) The problem was that the computer-assisted part of the proof is not human-verifiable. If humans cannot verify the proof, can we accept it as part of our mathematical knowledge? Many claimed that relying on computer proof is a bit like saying "this is true because that rusty machine says so".

Is deductive proof the only way to achieve "mathematical certainty"? (#Methods and tools)

2) Many mathematicians felt unhappy with the proof because it relied on an algorithm, a computer code. Computer codes have bugs! In fact, one such bug was found in the software that Appel and Haken used for the proof, and they had to publish a paper explaining and correcting the bug. Who can guarantee that there are no more bugs in the code?
3) Proof-by-exhaustion violated the principles of the main method of mathematics - deductive proof. For a mathematical proof to be acceptable, it had to show that the new statement follows with necessity from the previously known theorems by application of deductive reasoning. This deductive logic had always been the signature of mathematics, something that set it apart from sciences.
4) Mathematicians like "elegant" proofs, and proof-by-exhaustion is very far from being elegant. It is the opposite of elegant. It applies brute force to check for all possibilities.

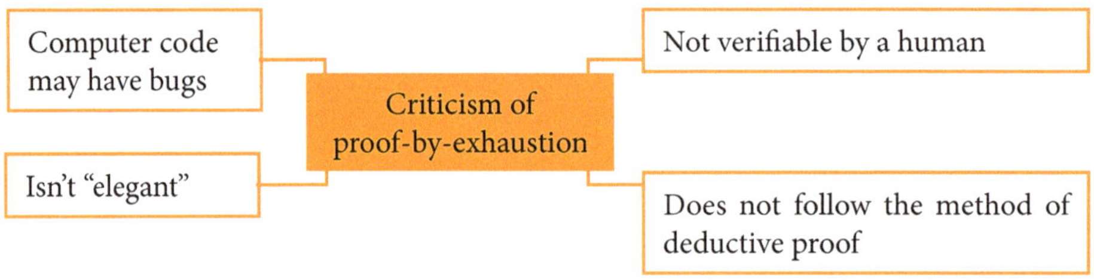

Despite the major controversy, Appel and Haken's work inspired many mathematicians to use proof-by-exhaustion to solve other long-standing problems. The number of such proofs grew, but their authors struggled with being accepted as "real mathematicians".

KEY IDEA: Proof-by-exhaustion can solve otherwise unsolvable problems in mathematics, but the issue is that humans cannot verify such proofs

The Kepler conjecture

Imagine this task. You have a large box and a large number of oranges (small equal-sized spheres). You have to pack as many oranges as possible in the box. In other words, you need to find an arrangement of oranges that is as dense as possible.

In the 17th century, Johannes Kepler (a mathematician and astronomer) created a conjecture stating that no arrangement of spheres in a three-dimensional space has a higher density than those of the cubic or hexagonal "close packing" (see the image below).

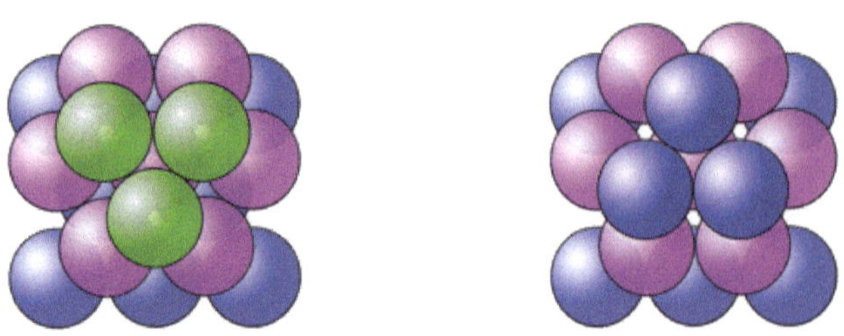

Image 37. Cubic close packing (on the left) and hexagonal close packing (on the right) (credit: Cdang, Wikimedia Commons)

Since then, there were multiple attempts to prove this conjecture. All failed. It's ironic how mathematicians have found this problem incredibly hard, but every fruit vendor seems to get it intuitively right (they do arrange oranges in a cubic close packing arrangement, although if you tell them that, they would probably laugh at you).

Then, in 1998, four hundred years later (!), Thomas Hales announced that he proved the conjecture (which changes its status from a conjecture to a theorem). The first part of his proof consisted of about 300 written pages. It was verifiable by humans – enormous work, but still possible. The second part (proof-by-exhaustion) consisted of approximately 50,000 lines of computer code and hours of computer calculation time. This part cannot be verified by humans.

Who bears responsibility for credibility of published knowledge? (#Ethics)

Thomas Hales submitted his proof to one of the most prestigious journals – the *Annals of Mathematics*. Usually, the journal assigns independent referees who check the work prior to publication. Four years after submission, the paper was returned to him – three referees said they were not able to verify the correctness of the computer code (Wolchover, 2013).

However, since then, the number of papers that used proof-by-exhaustion increased, so the journal had to consider accepting them. The editorial board decided to accept such papers, but in cases where the computer code is not verifiable by human referees, they make no claim about the code being correct. Instead the idea is that, provided the proof is important enough, there will be other mathematicians who would be interested in creating an independent code to replicate the proof.

This is how proof-by-exhaustion made its way into prestigious mathematical journals. It has been accepted with major reservations and a lot of caution.

Critical thinking extension

Many mathematicians were skeptical about proof-by-exhaustion because it is "not elegant". This is understandable. There is something magical in demonstrating how a theorem follows with certainty from millennia-old axioms.

Think about this statement: *all beach resorts in Vietnam have access to the sea shore*. There are two ways to prove this statement:

1) You can demonstrate logically that the statement is true by definition. Having access to the sea is an essential feature of a beach resort; if a resort does not have access to the sea, it cannot be called a beach resort. It follows that all beach resorts in Vietnam (and everywhere else) must have access to the sea.
2) You can go to Vietnam, visit every single beach resort and check if it has access to the sea.

Which proof would you prefer? If the first proof is not available for some reason, would you accept the second proof as a substitute?

If you are interested...

Watch the video "The four color map theorem" (2017) on the YouTube channel *Numberphile*. It is a friendly explanation of the computer-assisted proof.

Read Jessica Miley's article "The world's largest math proof is a whopping 200 terabytes in size" (October 4, 2017) published on *Interesting Engineering*. It describes the world's largest math proof – the computer-assisted proof of the Boolean Pythagorean triples problem.

For some counter-arguments, read David Wees's blog post "Objections to computer based math" (November 14, 2011) on his blog entitled *The Reflective Educator*.

Take-away messages

Lesson 12. In this lesson, we started looking at the relationship between knowledge and technology in mathematics. Mathematics has very solid traditions of acquiring knowledge based on the method of deductive proof. Mathematical statements are considered to be true if they follow with certainty from other statements that are already known to be true (such as axioms). This started changing when computers were first used to prove conjectures by creating a very long, but finite, list of possibilities and checking every single one of those possibilities with an algorithm. Examples included the proof of the four-color conjecture by Appel and Haken in 1976 and the proof of the Kepler conjecture by Thomas Hales in 1998. A lot of mathematicians were unhappy with proof-by-exhaustion and refused to accept it as real proof. One reason for this skepticism was the fact that computer proof is not verifiable by a human. Another reason is the possibility that there are bugs in the code. The third reason is that proof-by-exhaustion is simply not elegant and goes contrary to the long-standing tradition of deductive proof in mathematics.

Lesson 13 - Experimental mathematics

Learning outcomes

a) [Knowledge and comprehension] What is experimental mathematics?
b) [Understanding and application] What role do computers play in discovering mathematical knowledge?
c) [Thinking in the abstract] Does the future of mathematics belong to humans or computers?

Key concepts

Experimental mathematics, interactive theorem provers (proof assistants), automated theorem provers, mathematical intuition

Other concepts used

Coq, human-verifiable proof, logic-checking software, Appel-Haken proof, *Logic Theorist*, formalized rules, logical reasoning, "mathematically interesting theorems"

Themes and areas of knowledge

Theme: Knowledge and technology
AOK: Mathematics

Recap and plan

In the previous lesson, we looked at how technology started challenging the traditional ways of obtaining knowledge in mathematics by introducing proof-by-exhaustion.

Proof-by-exhaustion was just the beginning of increased use of technology in mathematics. The controversy around it encouraged mathematicians to look for new ways of using technology, and this resulted in the creation of a whole new field of knowledge – experimental mathematics. The name itself is a paradox, because mathematics has never had anything in common with experimental research. But this seems to be changing now, so once again, the question is, are we witnessing the beginning of a revolution in mathematics?

Scope of experimental mathematics

Pioneers such as Appel, Haken and Hale did their job. They inspired a whole generation of mathematicians to explore new ways of human-computer interaction to obtain new knowledge.

Soon the use of computers in mathematics was no longer limited to proof-by-exhaustion.

In modern times, computers are used for proving theorems. There are automated theorem provers and interactive theorem provers, also known as proof assistants. This sounds like bad news for humans, doesn't it? If machines learn how to construct deductive proofs of theorems, what will be left to human mathematicians? We will focus on theorem provers a little more in the next section – exactly how good are they?

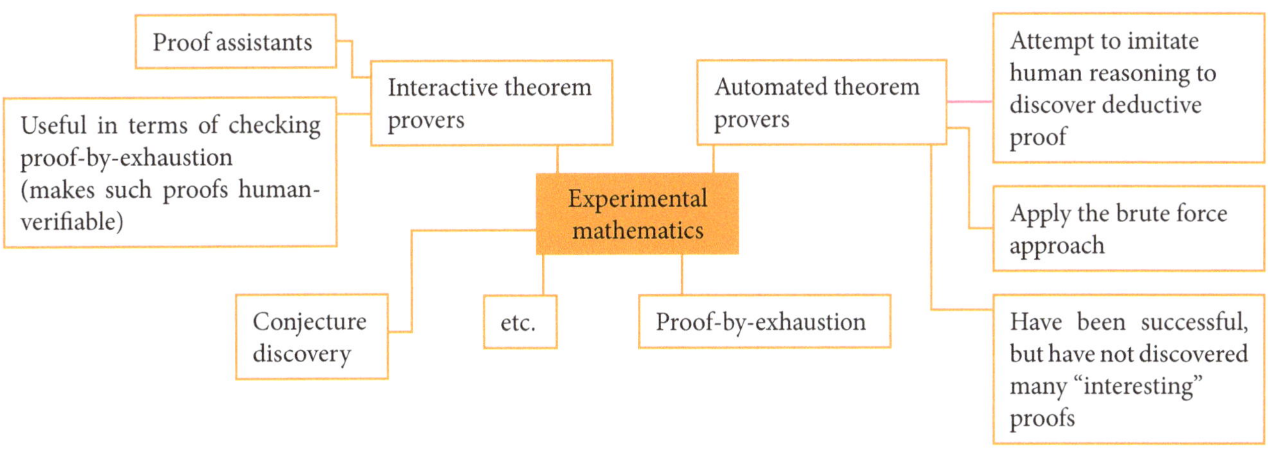

Proof assistants (interactive theorem provers)

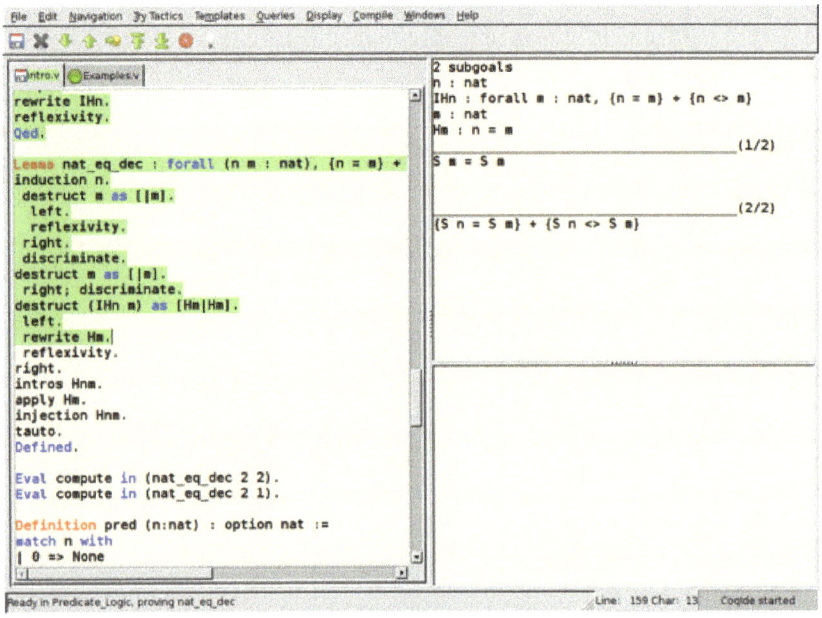

Image 38*. A screenshot of Coq in the middle of a proof*

An *interactive theorem* prover (or a *proof assistant*) is a piece of software that a human mathematician uses as a tool when developing a formal proof. Using proof assistants for mathematical proofs is a little like using a word processor to write an essay. It does not write the essay for you, but it simplifies tasks such as the search for lexical and grammar mistakes, replacing words with synonyms, formatting the document, comparing two documents, and so on. Similarly, an interactive theorem prover can easily check, for example, if there is a logical flaw in your proof.

Proof assistants have played a major role in the debate about proof-by-exhaustion. As you remember, Appel-Haken's proof of the four-color theorem was criticized for not being human-verifiable. Well, you will be pleased to know that in 2005 an interactive theorem prover, *Coq*, enabled human verification of the proof (Gonthier, 2008).

Is complicated knowledge less valuable than knowledge that is easy to understand? (#Perspectives)

Coq is a programming language released in 1989 by a French team of developers. In 2005, Georges Gonthier and Benjamin Werner translated the Appel-Haken proof into the language of *Coq* and created logic-checking software to confirm that the proof is correct. Think about it like this: they wrote something like a grammar check module in a word processor, then they translated the Appel-Haken algorithm into English, pasted it into the word processor and ran a grammar check.

This marked the point in history when it was shown that computer-assisted proofs can be human-verifiable and therefore have full rights in mathematical knowledge. Ironically, for this verification to become possible, we had to use another computer algorithm!

Automated theorem provers – how it started

Experimental mathematics is developing even further. *Automated theorem provers* are being created. This software is said to be able to prove theorems all by itself.

The first automated theorem prover was developed back in 1956. It was a computer program called *Logic Theorist*, written by Allen Newell, Herbert Simon and Cliff Shaw (Gugerty, 2006). It was designed to mimic the logical reasoning of a human being.

How did it work?

Is there anything in mathematical reasoning that cannot be performed by a computer? (#Methods and tools)

First, it contained a list of formalized rules of deductive reasoning commonly used by mathematicians. To give you a better idea of this, consider the following reasoning: *All men are mortal. Socrates is a man. Therefore, Socrates is mortal.* This is one of the basic syllogisms in formal logic. We can formalize this syllogism, for example, like this: *All A are C. B is A. Therefore, B is C.*

Second, it contained a list of mathematical axioms and already-proven statements.

Third, it contained an algorithm that instructed the program to apply the formalized rules of reasoning to the existing list of statements to derive new statements. For example, take the rule *All A are C. B is A. Therefore, B is C.* Look at the list of already-proven statements. Can you find anywhere on this list the pair of statements that follows the template "*All A are C*" and "*B is A*"? If yes, then create the new statement "*B is C*" and accept it as true. Repeat the search. If not, apply another rule from the list. Repeat the search. The result of this algorithm was a tree-like growth of statements. Existing statements were combined to produce new statements, then these new statements were combined to produce more and more.

Finally, in order to find a proof for a theorem, the researchers had to translate this theorem into a formalized statement, input it into the program and wait for it to find a pathway all the way from the tree roots (axioms) along the branches to the statement. This was then considered the deductive proof of the theorem.

Was *Logic Theorist* successful? Yes, it was. Newell, Simon and Shaw took *Principia Mathematica*, a fundamental work in formal logics and mathematics written by A.N. Whitehead and B. Russel in 1910, and fed 52 theorems from this book to their algorithm. *Logic Theorist* found proof for 38 of these theorems! Moreover, the proof that the program found for one of these theorems was actually more elegant that the one provided by Whitehead and Russel themselves (Gugerty, 2006).

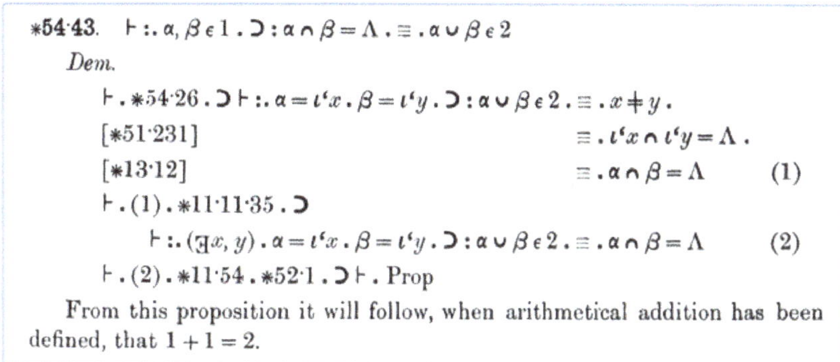

***54·43.** $\vdash :. \alpha, \beta \in 1 . \supset : \alpha \cap \beta = \Lambda . \equiv . \alpha \cup \beta \in 2$

Dem.

$\vdash . *54{\cdot}26 . \supset \vdash :. \alpha = \iota`x . \beta = \iota`y . \supset : \alpha \cup \beta \in 2 . \equiv . x \neq y .$

$[*51{\cdot}231] \quad \equiv . \iota`x \cap \iota`y = \Lambda .$

$[*13{\cdot}12] \quad \equiv . \alpha \cap \beta = \Lambda \quad (1)$

$\vdash . (1) . *11{\cdot}11{\cdot}35 . \supset$

$\vdash :. (\exists x, y) . \alpha = \iota`x . \beta = \iota`y . \supset : \alpha \cup \beta \in 2 . \equiv . \alpha \cap \beta = \Lambda \quad (2)$

$\vdash . (2) . *11{\cdot}54 . *52{\cdot}1 . \supset \vdash .$ Prop

From this proposition it will follow, when arithmetical addition has been defined, that $1 + 1 = 2$.

***Image 39**. An extract from Whitehead and Russel's Principia Mathematica*

KEY IDEA: Automated theorem provers have a list of rules of formal reasoning and a list of proven statements. They apply one to the other in multiple iterations to generate a tree of new statements.

Automated theorem provers today

Although the successes of *Logic Theorist* were impressive, it may be too early for human mathematicians to start looking for new jobs.

First, although *Logic Theorist* (and other automated theorem provers) attempted to mimic human reasoning, at the end of the day what they do is still nothing like what human mathematicians do. Automated theorem provers use a brute force approach. They take a list of starting axioms, they take a list of formalized rules of reasoning, they apply one to the other and generate an enormous tree of true statements. Human thinkers can't use this approach because they don't have enough computational capacity for this. Instead, their search is driven by mathematical intuition. While they can be slower than computers, and perhaps even less productive, generally their proofs remain to be more elegant.

Second, despite the initial excitement about the prospects of automated theorem provers back in the 1960s, mostly today they are used in highly specialized applications such as checking programs for mistakes. They have not proven any new "mathematically interesting theorems" and have not discovered anything of the same scale and importance as the Pythagorean theorem.

What is the nature of mathematical intuition? (#Scope)

It seems like at this point we must admit that even automated theorem provers, impressive as they are, remain merely assistants to human mathematicians. Therefore, I will take the liberty to claim that in Mathematics, unlike some other areas of knowledge, technology has *not* created a revolution. Not yet.

KEY IDEA: Experimental mathematics attempts to create computer algorithms that would be able to imitate human reasoning and make discoveries. This has been successful, but such algorithms are still incapable of making "interesting" discoveries.

Critical thinking extension

Humans don't have as much computational capacity as computers, so they cannot blindly sift through billions of possibilities. For this reason, humans must *understand* mathematics and develop a *mathematical intuition*.

The question is: is a mathematical truth discovered through intuition more valuable in some sense than a mathematical truth that was stumbled upon by a brute force algorithm?

Is mathematical knowledge discovered through intuition more valuable in some sense than the results of a brute force approach? (#Perspectives)

The work of a mathematician used to be the good old scribbling on paper with a pen or a pencil. Many mathematicians think that this is what it should remain. While writing down a problem (slowly, meticulously) and working on its solution, mathematicians were personally involved. Now, we press a button and the computer performs millions of calculations per second.

If you had to vote for the future of mathematics, would you vote for computers (speed and volume) or humans (mindfulness, understanding and intuition)? Is scribbling better than tapping on a keyboard?

If you are interested...

Watch the video "Four colour theorem explained by Georges Gonthier" (2018) on the YouTube channel *Isaac Newton Institute for Mathematical Sciences*. Georges Gonthier is one of the developers of *Coq*, the software that was used to human-verify the proof of the theorem.

Watch Conrad Wolfram's TED talk "Teaching kids real math with computers" (2010). It argues that the time has come to radically change our approach to teaching mathematics – computers and computation must now become an integral part of math education.

You could be delighted to know that the full source code of *Logic Theorist*, the first automated theorem prover and (as some say) the first AI, is available online on *Github* to satisfy your curiosity. I don't expect you to understand it, but have a look. Note that it is only 13 pages long!

Take-away messages

Lesson 13. In this lesson, we continued exploring the relationship between technology and knowledge in mathematics. Mathematicians explored ways of incorporating computational technology into the process of generating mathematical knowledge, and this led to a whole new field known as experimental mathematics. Can it potentially create a revolution in mathematics? We looked at interactive theorem provers (also known as proof assistants) and automated theorem provers (for example, Logic Theorist). We have seen that these programs have demonstrated some impressive results, and they seem to be infringing on the territory in mathematical discovery that was thought to be exclusively human. However, there is one important difference: experimental mathematics relies on brute force, systematically sifting through billions of options. The human approach is through understanding and mathematical intuition. But whether or not mathematical intuition is an important element of mathematical discovery that somehow makes it more valuable remains an open question.

2.6 - Technology in the Arts

The last area of knowledge that hasn't been discussed yet in relation to the increasing role of technology in obtaining knowledge is the Arts.

We have seen in the previous lessons that technology has a potential to redefine knowledge and to change the landscape of an area of knowledge beyond recognition. For example, if we accept that computers can make scientific discoveries, we must also accept knowledge and discoveries that we don't fully understand. If computer algorithms can prove theorems, the role that should be played in this process by the human mathematician must be reviewed.

I have two similar questions about the arts. First, does the development of technology have a potential to redefine what is considered art? Second, can machines create art?

In the next two lessons I will try to answer these questions, one at a time.

Lesson 14 - Redefinition of art

Learning outcomes

a) [Knowledge and comprehension] How did art redefine itself historically in the process of development?
b) [Understanding and application] In what ways does digital technology trigger a redefinition of art?
c) [Thinking in the abstract] How will technology change our understanding of authorship and originality in art?

Key concepts

Redefinition of art, authorship, originality

Other concepts used

Realism, impressionism, modern art, photography, photocopying, irreproducibility, AI-generated texts

Themes and areas of knowledge

Theme: Knowledge and technology
AOK: The Arts

Recap and plan

We are investigating the role of technology in obtaining knowledge about the world. We have looked at phenomena such as computer simulations and Big Data. We have decided that these phenomena might have the potential to trigger revolutionary changes in natural sciences, human sciences and history. We have also looked at the relationship between knowledge and technology in mathematics, and our conclusion was a little different. While experimental mathematics changes the landscape of day-to-day work of a mathematician, the fundamentals of the traditional deductive method of reasoning have not been challenged.

There's one area of knowledge left to consider – the Arts.

In this lesson, I will briefly look at the phenomenon of redefinition of art. I will claim that art develops by redefining itself in response to some major challenges or "uncomfortable questions". Some of these challenges come from newly emerging technology, as can be seen from examples such as the invention of photography, then photocopying, and now – digital devices.

How can art be defined (if it can be defined at all)?
(#Scope)

Art develops by redefining itself

Art redefined itself every time it was challenged by something and went through a period of crisis. To illustrate, I will give two examples related to technology.

Image 40. *Andy Warhol's "Campbell's Soup Cans"*

At some point in the 19th century, *realism* in art was the dominating trend. The purpose of art was to represent reality as it is, as accurately as possible. Artistic skills were of great value. It took years of traditional education in an art academy to develop these skills. Then along came photography. It became possible to click a picture of a landscape and get a realistic representation of it – without years of training, without weeks of work. Art was in crisis. To survive, it had to redefine itself, and it did. The impressionist movement started deviating from academic standards, emphasizing the importance of capturing the artist's impression of reality rather than reality itself. Photography could not compete with art anymore because a photograph cannot capture your subjective impression. Art saved itself through redefinition.

Another example was the invention of photocopying. For a long time, uniqueness had been considered one of the defining characteristics of a work of art. To be unique meant to be irreproducible. The original copy of the *Mona Lisa* is displayed in the Louvre Museum, and to see it you need to physically go there and stand in line for a couple of hours. With the invention of photocopying and mass print production, art faced some uncomfortable questions. Does a good photocopy of the *Mona Lisa* have the same artistic value as the original? How can art keep its uniqueness and protect itself from being massively reproduced? Then along came Andy Warhol and, with his famous *Campbell's Soup Cans* (1961-1962), redefined art. The *Soup Cans* were as reproducible as one could possibly imagine. With this work, Warhol claimed that art can and should be reproducible. Modern art embraced this idea. Warhol's *Soup Cans* is a great work of art precisely because it redefined art, eliminating irreproducibility from its definition.

These are just a few examples. But clearly the emergence of digital technology could not go unnoticed, and art in its development must have reacted to it.

How does art react to challenges presented by new developments in technology? (#Methods and tools)

How digital technology challenges art

Just like photography challenged realism in art and photocopying challenged the idea of irreproducibility, digital technology raises several questions that challenge the very essence of art. For example:

1) If a work of art is produced by a machine, does it still count as art?
2) Who should be credited for a work of art? Suppose an artist has created an algorithm that draws on a canvas, then the algorithm created an image using a graphic software. Does credit go to the artist? To the algorithm? To developers of the graphic software?
3) What is the nature of originality? Can computer-produced art be called "original"? If not, what exactly makes human-produced art more original than computer-produced art?

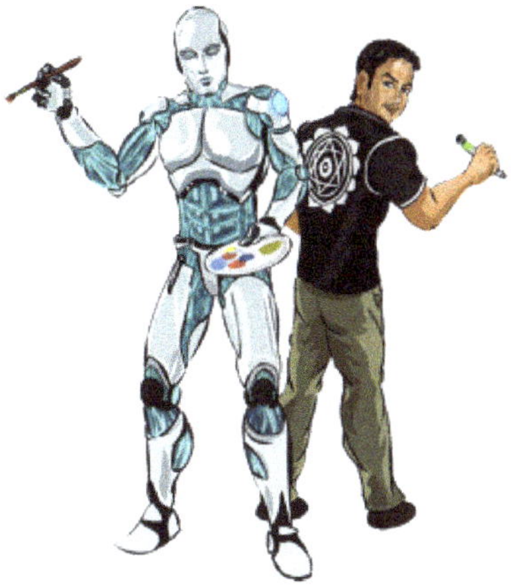

Image 41. Can robots create art?

It seems we live in exciting times because, just like after the invention of photography years ago, art will have to embrace these new developments like it usually does – by redefining itself. But the questions are tough, so I wonder if art will survive this time.

Can art be produced by a computer? (#Perspectives)

KEY IDEA: When art is challenged by a technological innovation, it redefines itself

Example: Harry Potter and the Portrait of What Looked Like a Large Pile of Ash

Let me give you one example to illustrate all the controversy that modern technology can create in terms of defining or redefining art.

Have you read the AI-generated chapter of *Harry Potter*? If not, please do me a favor and read it (see "If you are interested" below)! It comes from the tech company *Botnik Studios* and the name of the chapter is "Harry Potter and the Portrait of What Looked Like a Large Pile of Ash".

An algorithm was trained on all seven *Harry Potter* books by J.K. Rowling. In doing so, the algorithm picked up the most commonly used words and word combinations, characteristic word order, the use of suffixes, and so on. After being trained, the algorithm produced a text of its own – what Rowling could write. This did not look too meaningful (algorithms are not that good yet!), but then a team of human authors took the product and cleaned up each sentence a little. You can see the result of this work for yourself.

At times it is funny, at times it is surprisingly creative and at times it is gibberish. But you will probably agree that it is a good read and time well spent. And it does have the style and the vibe of the original novels.

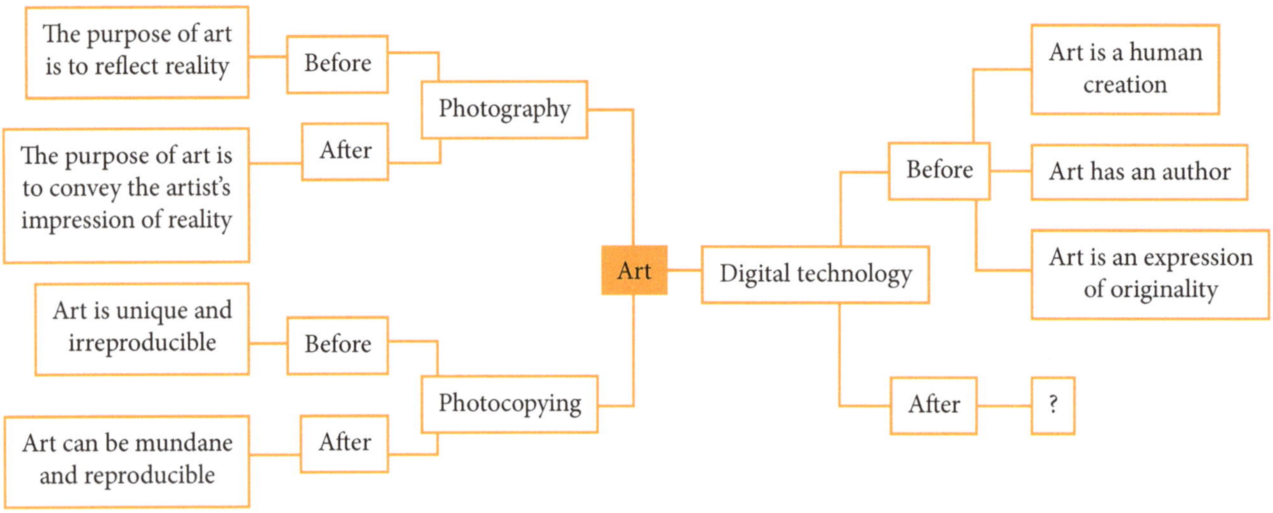

Two uncomfortable questions

Using this example, let me come back to the uncomfortable questions that art faces now that digital technology is being developed. I will try to formulate two questions that I believe are most crucial.

Question 1: Can this AI-generated chapter of *Harry Potter* be considered a work of art? It ticks a lot of boxes. It seems like it was intended as such. It can certainly be perceived as such, at least by some audiences. And in itself, I would claim that this is much better quality work than some of the human-generated pieces of literature I have seen.

Question 2: Who is the author of this chapter? There is little doubt that the algorithm is a creation of the coders. But once created, the algorithm works all by itself. The algorithm was trained on *Harry Potter* books by J.K. Rowling. The whole purpose was to write as much like J.K. Rowling as possible. So, can we claim that she is the author of this chapter, or at least one of the authors? She might not even know that this chapter exists.

What does it mean to be "original" in art? (#Perspectives)

It looks like originality and authorship will be the dimensions that art will have to redefine in itself, due to the newly emerged technology.

***Image 42**. Uncomfortable questions*

Critical thinking extension

Two more uncomfortable questions

Two more uncomfortable questions about the AI-generated *Harry Potter* chapter – these two are somewhat more general than the ones we have already discussed in the lesson, although they are also related to originality and creativity.

Question 3 (follow-up on authorship): Can art be produced by a computer? If you believe that the author of the chapter, at least partly, was the computer algorithm, then you must also accept that computers can create art. But if that is so, then what is the role of humans? Is this the end of human art?

Question 4 (follow-up on originality): What is the nature of originality in art? A common answer to the previous question is "No, art cannot be produced by a computer because computers can only follow an algorithm while humans can produce original creations". Then the question is, how exactly is a human original creation different from a computer implementing an algorithm?

I am very curious: what are your answers to the uncomfortable questions raised in this lesson?

If you are interested...

Check out the work of *Botnik*, a "machine entertainment company" as they call themselves (https://botnik.org/). Their *Harry Potter* chapter is available on their website.

Botnik

Read Janelle Shane's blog post "The neural network generated pickup lines that are actually kind of adorable" on the website *AI weirdness*. She does a lot of funny stuff with AI. Teaching AI to generate pick-up lines is just one of her projects.

AI Weirdness

Have a look at the book *Introducing Postmodernism: A Graphic Guide* by R. Appignanesi and C. Garratt (2003). This book gives an excellent overview of the history of how art redefined itself in response to various challenges. Fun to read and very insightful, it is highly recommended if you want to understand art better.

Take-away messages

Lesson 14. In this lesson, we started looking at the role of technology in art. The history of development of the Arts as an area of knowledge is a history of art redefining itself in response to periods of crisis or challenges raised by technological and other developments. We have considered two examples of this. First, the invention of photography which resulted in art redefining itself from capturing reality to capturing an impression of reality. Second, the invention of photocopying and mass production which resulted in art rejecting the idea that irreproducibility should be one of its defining characteristics. Surely, modern digital technology also presents a challenge that art needs to respond to by redefining itself. We considered the example of an AI-generated chapter of *Harry Potter* and discussed some uncomfortable questions that art needs to answer today: (1) is it possible for a machine to produce art? (2) what is the role of human skill in art? (3) who should be credited for a work of art produced with major assistance from a computer? and (4) what is the nature of human originality?

Lesson 15 - Digital art

Learning outcomes

a) [Knowledge and comprehension] What is digital art?
b) [Understanding and application] What are some of the examples of digital art?
c) [Thinking in the abstract] Does digital art have the potential to redefine art on the whole?

Key concepts

Digital art, generative art, interactive art, internet art

Other concepts used

Installation, AI-generated poetry, co-creation

Themes and areas of knowledge

Theme: Knowledge and technology
AOK: The Arts

Recap and plan

We are trying to figure out how technology affects areas of knowledge, and at the moment we are looking at the Arts. In the previous lesson, we looked at the history of development of art and analyzed it as a history of art redefining itself in response to major challenges. Quite often, such challenges are a result of technological progress, for example, the invention of photography, then photocopying, and now the ubiquitous spread of digital technology.

This lesson will be devoted to considering some examples of new developments in art that are trying to embrace the digital era. Collectively, these developments are known under the loose label "digital art".

What is digital art?

Will digital art revolutionize the Arts as an area of knowledge? (#Perspectives)

Digital art is the practice of using digital technology as part of either creating or displaying the work of art. There is a great variety of forms of digital art, and there is no such thing as a closed list of types of digital art. It looks like through this variety of approaches, art is experimenting with various forms of redefining itself.

However, for the sake of focus, I will limit this lesson to three examples of digital art:

1) Generative art
2) Interactive art
3) Internet art

Let's look at some examples from these three categories.

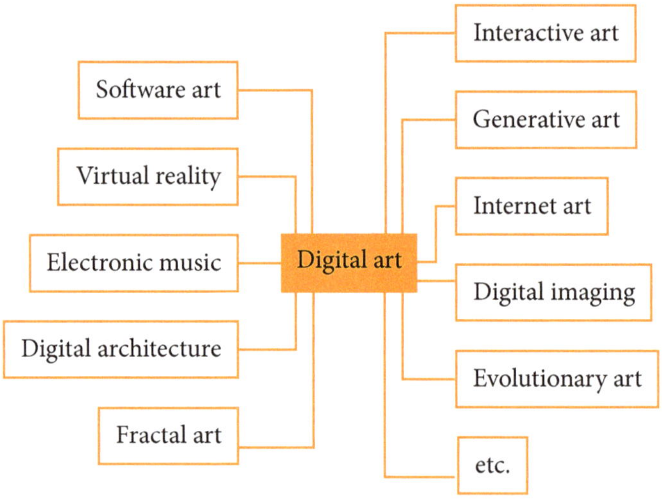

KEY IDEA: There is a great variety of forms of digital art. That's how art seeks to incorporate digital technology into its new definition.

Generative art

Generative art is art that is produced partially or completely by a computer algorithm. An example is the AI-generated chapter of *Harry Potter*. Generative art may promise a revolutionary change because it challenges the idea that art must be produced by a human. It also brings into question the whole notion of human originality.

Dmitry Morozov, a media artist living in Moscow, designed a small robot that smells pollution and visualizes it in a picture. His robot has a small plastic nose equipped with pollution sensors. The sensors react to carbon monoxide and other typical pollutants. An algorithm then turns the data from the sensors into shapes and colors. For example, if the air is clean, the algorithm produces monotonous green. The robot then prints the result, much like a polaroid prints a photo. The more pollutants, the more colorful and vibrant the picture. The pictures are displayed as works of art (Stinson, 2014). Simultaneously, they serve the purpose of raising public awareness about the issues of air pollution – there's some inspiration for your CAS project!

Does art generated by a computer still count as art? (#Scope)

Artist Ollie Palmer created and staged an ant ballet (Wilson, 2012). The core of Palmer's installation is a robotic arm that, driven by a computer algorithm, deploys a synthetic pheromone on the surface of the table. Ants then follow these pheromone trails, driven by instincts. Changing the algorithm, Palmer can coordinate ants' movements, for example, he can make them spell his name. The installation is a metaphor for us humans and our own freedom of will (you can learn more about the project at olliepalmer.com/ant-ballet/).

Then there's digital poetry. Remember our discussion of artificial intelligence? According to the Turing test, if we cannot tell if we are interacting with a human or a computer, then we must admit that the computer is intelligent. We can easily apply a similar logic to AI-generated poetry versus "real" human poetry. Does this sound like an exciting thing to try? Then you will be pleased to know that this has already been done – for example, check out the online project called "Bot or Not". See how many you will get right at botpoet.com.

In generative art, decisions involved in creating a work of art are outsourced to the algorithm, so the algorithm is not merely a tool assisting a human artist – it *is* the artist. Obviously, someone may object: but the algorithm itself was created by a human, so it is still merely a tool. And then someone else may object to this objection: but a human artist, in a sense, is also following an algorithm created by someone else (their education, their genes, mother nature?). So where is the line between a human artist and a "soulless" algorithm of generative art?

Interactive art

Interactive art is the result of a designed interaction between the viewer and the artwork, often producing an output that is unique and unrepeatable. Interactive art may be a revolutionary change because it introduces the idea that the recipient of art and the creator may be one and the same person.

The *Boundary Functions* (1998) installation, created by Scott Snibbe, is a set of lines projected onto the floor. When there is only one person on the floor, nothing happens. When there are two people, one line appears that separates them. The line moves as they move. With more

Who should be credited for computer-generated art? (#Ethics)

than two people, the floor segments itself into regions that delineate the "personal space" of each participant. There is some complicated mathematics behind defining how the regions should be configured. But beyond that, the installation makes tangible the intangible notion of personal space. "... the line that always exists between you and another becomes concrete" (Snibbe, 1998).

***Image 43**. A moment from "The Treachery of Sanctuary" (photo by Bryan Derballa, Wikimedia Commons)*

The Treachery of Sanctuary (2012) is a creation of Chris Milk. It is a giant installation that uses *Kinect* controllers and infrared sensors to take visitors through three stages of flight. It features three white walls in front of a pool. As you enter the space, your shadow appears on the first white wall. At the same time, there appears a flock of birds at the top. You reach up to the birds, but your shadow begins to dissolve, gradually breaking down into silhouettes of birds that flutter up to join the flock, until there is nothing left of it. As you move on and "enter" the second white wall, your shadow appears again, but birds from the top start attacking it, ripping it piece by piece and carrying it away in their claws. As you move over to the third wall, you can see your silhouette again, but now it has a pair of large wings. The wings follow your gestures, moving with the movement of your arms (George, Meyers and Chasalow, 2012).

There are many other examples, such as interactive stories, interactive installations and interactive images. But you could have also remembered interactive movies and, well, video games.

Interactivity may be a harbinger of a revolutionary change in art because it redefines art from an artist's creation into a co-creation between the artist and the audience.

Internet art

Is it essential for art to have a creator? (#Methods and tools)

Internet art includes forms of art that are based on using the Internet. This does not mean simply taking a work of art and digitizing it, for example, scanning a photograph and putting it on a website. Internet art uses the Internet on the whole and its collaborative capacity.

The Listening Post (2001) by Ben Rubin and Mark Hanson is an installation consisting of 231 electronic displays arranged into a grid on a curved wall. It is a real-time visual reflection of online conversations that are unfolding on the Internet, in chatrooms or online forums. An algorithm behind the installation connects to the Internet and randomly picks out words from these conversations and the screens then display these words. A text-to-speech software pronounces the words, and as the words are changing, this creates a strange polyphony. As a visitor, you can sit in front of this wall and eavesdrop on the Internet.

Mary Flanagan's *The Perpetual Bed* (1998) is a website featuring an "online world" that emulates experiences of the artist's 91-year-old grandmother in a hospital where she repeatedly fell into unconscious states. The work explores the boundary between the real world and dreamlike states. Viewers can leave a trace in this world (for example, a hint or an impression of a dialogue fragment), and subsequent viewers will be able to discover these traces. They become part of the story.

Internet art may be a revolutionary change in art for at least two reasons. First, the traditional "museum space" or "gallery space" of art has been abandoned and now art resides in the Internet. It is everywhere, easily accessible, part of our lives. Second, while interactive art was a co-creation of the artist and the audience, some forms of Internet art are a co-creation of the artist and humanity on the whole.

Through just three examples of digital art, we have seen that a lot of new forms of art are emerging that seem to be attempting to redefine art in various ways, adapting to the challenges presented by modern technology.

Critical thinking extension

Generative art, interactive art and Internet art are just a few examples I picked from a vast variety of modern art forms that make use of current technology. My intuition tells me that these forms of art may be responsible for yet another redefinition of art one day, but obviously I cannot be certain. If you explore other forms of modern art related to digital technology in one way or another, you may form other hypotheses about the most likely future of art.

Whether or not a revolution in art will occur at all is also open to debate.

After considering all of these examples, do you think it would be justified to claim that art is currently redefining itself? Or are these normal fluctuations within one firmly established tradition?

If you are interested…

Check out this small online gallery of generative art: https://www.generativeartproject.com/

Read the article "A brief history of generative art" on *Studioanf.com*. This article gives a detailed overview of the genre of generative art with plenty of visual examples.

Explore Alexandra Serrano's publication "72 interactive art installations" (2012) on *Trendhunter*. This will give you plenty of visual examples of interactive art.

Explore Nayomi Chibana's publication "10 mind-blowing interactive stories" on *Visme*. Click on the links within the publication to explore some examples.

Take-away messages

Lesson 15. In this lesson, we looked at various examples of modern forms of digital art, focusing on three types: generative art, interactive art and Internet art. It is possible (but debatable) that one of these art forms will trigger the next revolution in art where art will once again redefine itself. Generative art makes one rethink the nature of human creativity and accept that art does not necessarily have to be created by humans. Interactive art changes the status of art from a creation to a co-creation. Additionally, interactive art introduces the uniqueness and unrepeatability of every particular display (which depends on the actions of the viewer). Finally, Internet art transcends the traditional art space (museums and galleries), opens the borders and invites the whole world to be a co-creator.

2.7 - Technology and ethics

The relationship between technology and knowledge is not merely a matter of intellectual curiosity. The nature of this relationship has direct implications for our lives. Technology opens exciting, mind-blowing frontiers of knowledge, giving us possibilities that were unimaginable in the past.

However, just because we can do something, does not mean that we should do it.

This is why we need to carefully consider the ethical dimension of incorporating technology into the process of generating knowledge. Throughout this unit, multiple ethical considerations have already been raised, but this final lesson is meant to provide a summary and another reflection point.

All of the exciting advantages promised by modern technology may be easily negated by dire consequences of not using technology in an ethical manner.

Lesson 16 - Technoethics

Learning outcomes

a) [Knowledge and comprehension] What is technoethics?
b) [Understanding and application] What are the key ethical issues brought about by the development of technology?
c) [Thinking in the abstract] Should ethics be superior to knowledge?

Key concepts

Technoethics, ethics of artificial intelligence (robot ethics), data ethics, research ethics

Other concepts used

Robot rights, suffering, biased AI systems, personal data, digital trace, commercial mathematical packages

Themes and areas of knowledge

Theme: Knowledge and technology
AOK: Human Sciences, Natural Sciences, Mathematics

Recap and plan

We have looked at how technology influences our knowledge, both of ourselves and the world around us. In the process, we have raised some ethics-related questions, for example, how we should treat computers if we suspect that they might be sentient or whether we should credit a digital algorithm with a proof of a mathematical conjecture.

Ethics is one of the four components of the knowledge framework in TOK, so this lesson is meant to re-emphasize the ethical arguments that have already been brought up, as well as outline some additional ethical arguments related to knowledge and technology.

Broadly, the study of ethics related to technology is known as technoethics. This lesson is an overview of the main issues raised by the field of technoethics, especially those related to the phenomena that we have focused on in this unit.

What is technoethics

Technoethics is a sub-field of ethics that explores the new questions of morality that emerged in the age of technology. The term "technoethics" was coined in 1974 by Mario Bunge, but questions of technoethics were raised and explored long before that.

Technoethics embraces a very broad range of ethical issues, so I will limit this overview to several groups of questions related to the problems that we focused on in this unit. The groups are:

1) Ethics of artificial intelligence (also known as roboethics)
2) Data ethics
3) Research ethics

Should ethical considerations be superior to considerations of progress in knowledge and technology? (#Ethics)

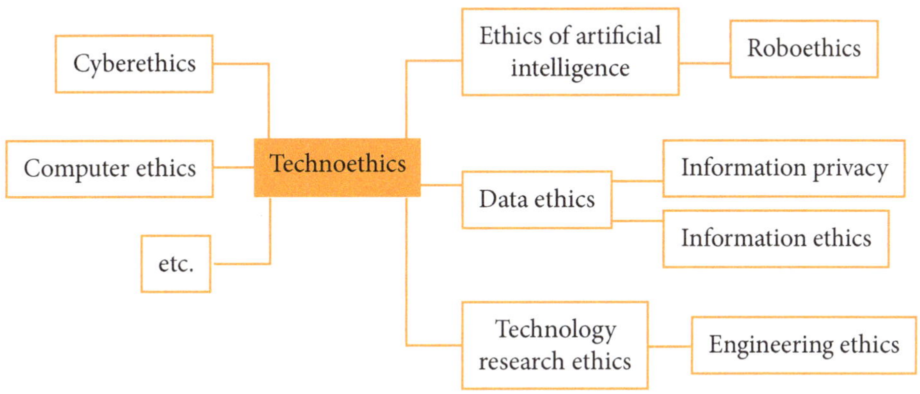

KEY IDEA: New technology – new ethical issues

Ethics of artificial intelligence

Ethics of artificial intelligence explores all sorts of ethical problems that arise when you try to build a thinking machine. There are many dimensions to this.

The first and the most obvious dimension is recognizing human-like qualities in machines. If they are (or will be) intelligent, does it mean they can (or will be able to) think, feel, suffer, understand injustice? Should they be given the same rights as human beings and treated like human beings? This dimension is related to questions of "robot rights". After all, we have accepted that animals have rights, so how are computers different?

Is it morally permissible to research something that can potentially bring suffering? (#Ethics)

Another dimension is the moral permissibility for humans to create artificial intelligence. Is it morally right to do research in this area in the first place? Currently we can – theoretically – clone people, but we don't do that for ethical reasons. Should the same moral reasoning apply to us creating artificial intelligence? One argument that can be used by those who deny the morality of artificial intelligence research is that creation of sentient AI that has human-like rights will be a burden both to the AI and human society. One possible counter-argument in this area is to say that it is our moral responsibility to understand ourselves and the Universe around us, and to accomplish that we must attempt to create an artificial intelligence.

Can a machine be held responsible for biased knowledge? (#Ethics)

The third group of questions in AI ethics concerns biases in AI systems. The problem here is that every AI algorithm is trained on some dataset, and if the dataset is in any way biased, then these biases will get ingrained into the algorithm itself, and we'll have a biased AI. For example, Amazon used to have a computer algorithm that they used in recruitment and hiring. The algorithm analyzed 10 years' worth of resumes from prior applicants and trained itself to recognize features of candidates' resumes that are most predictive of success in particular job positions. Amazon never used this algorithm as a sole decision-maker, but their HR managers could consider these scores among other characteristics. In 2015, it was discovered that the algorithm was biased against women. It preferred to give jobs to men. The reason was that the dataset the algorithm was trained on (10 years of prior applications) was dominated by male applicants to tech positions. The dataset was biased, so the algorithm ended up reflecting this bias. Amazon scrapped the use of the algorithm after this bias was discovered, but the case illustrates the potential problem with all AI systems in general (Dastin, 2018).

***Image 44**. Technology and ethics have a complicated relationship (credit: Gerd Leonhard, Flickr)*

Data ethics

For Big Data projects to work properly, they need large amounts of data. Much of the data is coming from personal users like you and me. Data ethics explores the issues of using data in a morally acceptable way. Who does data belong to? Suppose you went online and searched something in a search engine. You left a digital trace – data. This digital trace has been saved and can be used later to analyze patterns of behavior of users online. or to build a recommendation system to promote goods that people rarely buy. Who does this digital trace belong to? Do you have the right to not allow companies to use this data? In doing so, are you compromising the quality of Big Data projects and making them unreliable? There is a clash between data privacy and credibility of Big Data projects (the less data they use, the less credible their results). It is the policy of many companies today to give you the right to *not* have your personal data collected, but you probably noticed that in most cases it is being collected by default. For example, if you want Google to *not* collect your personal data, you must manually change the settings in your browser (I wonder if you have done that?).

Research ethics

Research ethics concerns itself with how to conduct research honestly and without doing harm. The technological era certainly raises new ethical questions related to conducting research. One of them is transparency. With the development of technology, research tools are becoming more complicated, and some of these tools belong to private

***Image 45**. Data privacy is a major ethical concern in the modern world*

companies. But if they hide their source code from us, it creates a situation where we cannot fully validate research conclusions.

Think about using computer technology for mathematical discovery. Mathematicians increasingly rely on using software. Software is written by human coders so it must be constantly checked and verified by independent researchers to be considered trustworthy. But software is a commercial product, and the code is a commercial secret protected by companies that developed it. Currently, the most widely used mathematical packages – *Mathematica, Maple* and *Magma* – are all closed commercial products, so you must trust the word of companies selling them that there are no bugs and that results are trustworthy. But there are bugs – they have been found in all of these products. Almost certainly, there are bugs that haven't been found yet and we can't even check.

Open-source software could be a solution, but it depends on users contributing to its development. Do mathematicians really want to spend thousands of hours verifying the code they are using for their everyday work? If I give you an arithmetic problem and a calculator together with it, will it occur to you that:

- In your solution you are assuming that the calculator works correctly, and you should not be so certain about this assumption?
- You should take the calculator apart and cross-check all of the circuits, making sure that they are connected exactly how they should be?

Knowledge-generating technology may be commercially owned. Can knowledge be owned in the same way? (#Ethics)

I can only smile when I imagine your math teacher asking you why you handed in the work late, and you telling the teacher that it took some time to disassemble the calculator to make sure it was working properly.

Overall, it is obvious that technology raises a lot of new ethical issues, such as moral permissibility of research, protection of data privacy and lack of transparency.

Critical thinking extension

All of the questions discussed in this lesson, as well as all ethical questions in general, could probably be viewed as instances of the key debate between ethics and knowledge. The debate is, should ethics be superior to knowledge or vice versa?

There are two positions in this debate:

1) One position is to say that knowledge is superior to ethics. If you share this position, you view ethics is an obstacle that hinders the development of knowledge. We could know so much about human development if we could clone babies and experiment on them, but we don't because it is unethical. If you share this position, you probably believe in "knowledge at all costs". You would want cloning to be allowed because it will advance our knowledge considerably.
2) Another position is to say that ethics is superior to knowledge. If you share this position, you believe that knowledge gained with violation of ethical standards cannot even be considered knowledge. Also, you believe that knowledge is not a goal in itself, that it is only valuable as long as it makes us better, or at least does not make us worse.

Can we accept and use knowledge gained with violation of ethical standards? (#Ethics)

Which position is closer to you?

If you are interested...

Read Jessica Baron's article "Tech ethics issues we should all be thinking about in 2019" on *Forbes*.

Read T.S. Altshuler's article "The crossroads between ethics and technology" (2019) on *Techcrunch*.

Finally, a selection of TED talks whose titles speak for themselves:

1) Marie Wallace (2014): "The ethics of collecting data"
2) Patrick Lin (2015): "The ethical dilemma of self-driving cars"
3) Zeynep Tufekci (2016): "Machine intelligence makes human morals more important"
4) Kriti Sharma (2018): "How to keep human bias out of AI"

Take-away messages

Lesson 16. This lesson summarized and re-visited ethical aspects of technological progress in knowledge. There is a special sub-field of ethics dealing with these issues, known as technoethics. It embraces a vast range of problems, so in the lesson we narrowed it down to three groups of ethical issues: ethics of artificial intelligence, data ethics and research ethics. Ethics of artificial intelligence concerns moral aspects of building thinking machines. One of the key questions is recognizing human-like qualities in machines and accepting that machines have rights. Another question is moral permissibility for humans to build artificial intelligence. Yet another question in this group concerns biases in AI systems. The second group of ethical issues – data ethics – revolves around the clash between data privacy and research credibility. Finally, the third group of issues – research ethics – concerns transparency of research involving technology. For example, complex software used in experimental mathematics is often a commercial product, which means that its source code is not open for independent checks. On a broader scale, the debate is whether ethics should be superior to considerations of making progress or vice versa.

Back to the exhibition

I'm looking again at my graph of sentiment in the Old Testament. I feel a little weird about it. Perhaps the weird feeling comes from incompatibility of two things: something as huge and immensely important for the human condition as the Bible, and something as basic, trivial and soulless as a bar graph. Or maybe I feel weird because I just used some really complicated digital technology, and I was able to do it so easily with no background knowledge or training; these things are becoming more and more accessible at a very rapid rate. How much time is left until every smartphone user will be able to build and customize an artificial general intelligence?

As discussed in this unit, technology can be used to gain knowledge about the world around us. In natural sciences, this may mean telescopes and microscopes and the Large Hadron collider – things that enhance and overcome limitations of our perception and allow us to gain better knowledge by improving our existing methods. For example, we could perform experiments even when complicated technology was not around, but the Large Hadron Collider allows us to experiment in ways that were not accessible before. Above and beyond this, technology in natural sciences also provides fundamentally new ways of gaining knowledge – for example, computer simulations. Simulations are unthinkable without technology. In human sciences and history, similar revolutionary changes brought by technology may be seen in Big Data. Big Data allows us to open up new horizons in knowing the life of human societies. My sentiment graph, for example, tells us something we did not know about the Bible.

My graph is a very simple trick. I'm sure Big Data can be used in much more impressive ways to study the Bible, and in the future it will become even more impressive. Will there be a limit? Will it be possible, for example, for a computer to *understand* the Bible and be able to interpret it, paraphrase it, translate it meaningfully into various languages?

Technology can also be used to gain knowledge about ourselves. If – or when – a computer understands the Bible, we will probably claim that the computer is intelligent, or at least behaves as if it was intelligent. But creating an artificial intelligence (or consciousness) will give us so much insight into our own intelligence (and consciousness). Where is the boundary between being able to quantify the emotions in the Bible (which my computer can do already) and *experiencing* these emotions?

Perhaps our computers will soon be able to know us better than we know ourselves. Remember the story of Andrew Martin and Kevin Quinn's algorithm predicting decisions of judges at the U.S. Supreme Court? This algorithm certainly outperformed human legal experts. Once computers learn to predict our behavior better than we can do it ourselves, will they be able to behave like humans? Will they *become* humans? Will they become a better, more advanced version of humans?

To be honest, I don't know how I feel about the possibility of my laptop being sentient. I am very curious, but there are so many ethical issues around this.

The only thing I'm sure about is that we live in exciting times, and future developments of knowledge will be unthinkable without the development of technology. Since the rate of development is exponential (as claimed by many futurists), we will soon witness more revolutionary changes. Some futurists predicted the onset of the technological singularity before the second half of this century, which means there is a good chance that within your lifetime you will be dealing with artificial humans, or maybe you will discover one day that you are already a machine that is slowly becoming conscious.

Let's wait and see.

UNIT 3 - Bias in personal knowledge

UNIT 3 - Bias in personal knowledge

You may remember from Unit 1 ("Knowledge of knowledge") that there is a distinction between personal knowledge and shared knowledge. These terms are quite transparent: personal knowledge is something belonging to you as an individual, while shared knowledge is something common to sizeable groups. Shared knowledge and personal knowledge are overlapping circles on a Venn diagram. Some of your personal knowledge coincides with that shared by other people, but another part of your personal knowledge is unique to you.

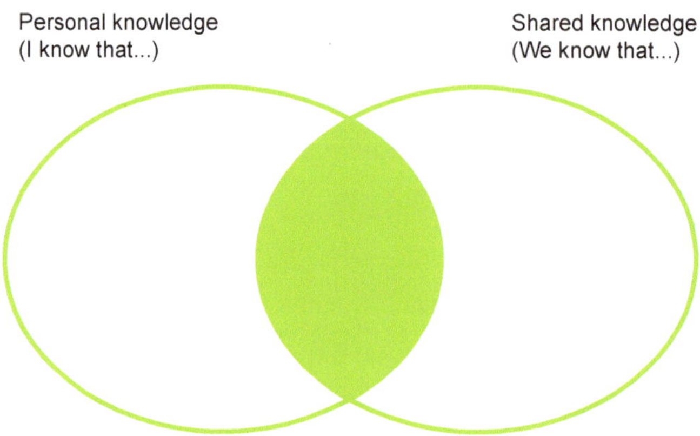

***Image 1**. Personal knowledge and shared knowledge: how they are related*

The good thing about bias is that, although every individual is biased, collectively we can keep these biases in check and overcome them. In a series of independent replications, conclusions of one scientist may be validated by other scientists. In a jury court, opinions of the jurors may be compared and discussed. Scientists may have different explanations for an observed phenomenon, but through testing and replication some explanations are eliminated and some retained. In other words, biases are abundant in the realm of personal knowledge, but not so much in shared knowledge. As a rule, shared knowledge is much less biased than personal knowledge.

Can biased personal opinions be valuable for developing shared knowledge? (#Perspectives)

The bad news is that shared knowledge can also be biased. Biased shared knowledge is probably more disastrous than biased personal knowledge simply because we trust it more. Additionally, it is much more difficult to identify the bias and eliminate it when it is the whole of humanity that is biased. In other words, although biases in shared knowledge are less numerous, they are more impactful.

	How many biases are there?	How impactful are they?
Personal knowledge	A lot!	They affect only you
Shared knowledge	Not so many	They affect everyone!

KEY IDEA: Biases in shared knowledge are less numerous, but they are more impactful

In this unit, we will consider biases in personal knowledge. On the surface, the problem may seem simple: just check your personal knowledge against shared knowledge and get rid of your bias! However, we cannot just dismiss personal knowledge as something inferior to shared knowledge. After all, as a knower, your personal knowledge is all you have access to. A belief that you retrieve from your personal knowledge can either come from the area that overlaps with shared knowledge or from the area that is uniquely yours. How do you know which area it comes from?

Can we know if our personal knowledge is biased without checking it against shared knowledge? (#Methods and tools)

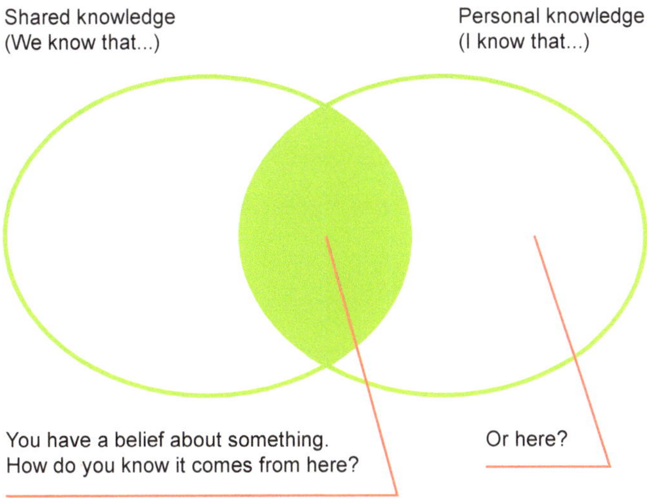

***Image 2**. Where does your belief come from?*

The knowledge that you are directly in touch with and that you use on a daily basis is your personal knowledge. For this reason, personal knowledge is worth considering on its own before we move on to biases in shared knowledge.

Exhibition: a turbulence map

In front of me is an aviation weather forecast chart (for simplicity I will call it a turbulence map).

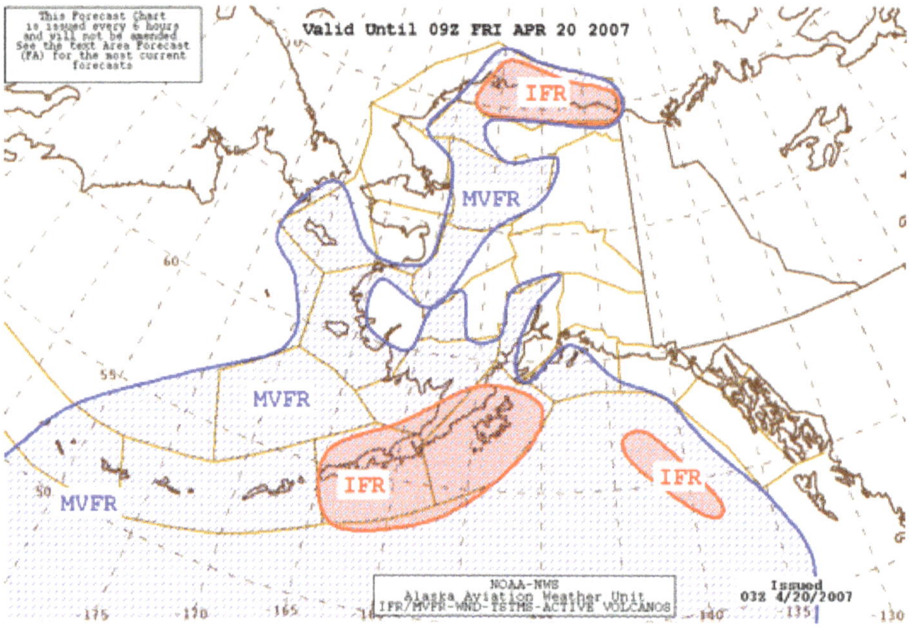

Image 3*. Aviation weather forecast chart (turbulence map) (credit: Wikimedia Commons)*

Such maps show you the areas where turbulence is more likely to occur when you are travelling by air. These maps (among other sources of information) are used by pilots to try to make your flight smoother when they are navigating.

I am a nervous flyer. I have a complicated relationship with turbulence. It is pretty unfortunate for someone who works in an international setting and needs to travel a lot.

At some point when it became really irritating, I started educating myself. I read articles and watched videos that explained turbulence and analyzed past airplane crashes. I discovered that a lot of my beliefs had been inaccurate and misleading. First of all, I used to think that turbulence can cause airplanes to crash. Now I know that airplanes are designed so that they can withstand turbulence more than two times stronger than anything commercial flights are likely to encounter. I used to think turbulence was the most dangerous part of the flight. Now I know that you are more likely to be harmed while you are on the tarmac than when you are experiencing turbulence mid-air. I used to think air travel was a risky option. Now I know that statistically I am much more likely to die in a car on the way to the airport.

Has it helped? No. Every time turbulence kicks in, I still grab the armrest until my knuckles turn white. In reality, I should be doing that in taxis, not in planes! My conscious brain knows that, but my body seems to refuse to listen.

I still check "turbulence maps" before flying. The abundance and accessibility of such maps online gives me a hint that I am not alone. It appears as though there are many more nervous flyers out there who misinterpret the danger of planes (relative to other means of travel), whose logical brain cannot override the rest of their brain, whose expectations, perceptions and attitudes to air travel are all biased because of this complicated relationship with turbulence.

The truth is, if your seatbelt is fastened, turbulence is not dangerous. My beliefs and perceptions, however, systematically deviate from this truth in the direction of misinterpreting various aspects of air travel as more dangerous than they really are.

Story: Senate Bill 464

The year 2019 in the USA saw an unusual precedent in legislation: Senate Bill 464 made it mandatory for doctors and nurses in California to undergo eight hours of implicit bias training and testing periodically (every 2 years).

This is probably one of the first times when the concept of implicit (unconscious) biases made its way into legislature.

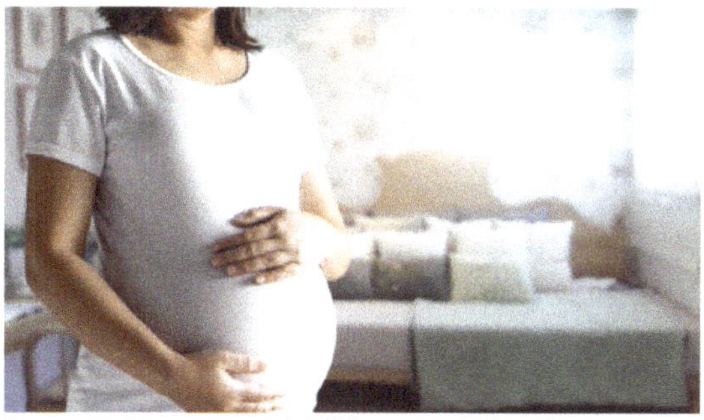

Image 4. *There are racial differences in the chance of death from complications at childbirth*

This bill was "inspired" by some disturbing research findings that showed that, although there was a decrease in the overall number of women who died giving birth in California, black women were still 3 or 4 times more likely to die from complications at childbirth compared to white women. Additional research into this issue showed that roughly half of surveyed medical professionals believed myths and shared misconceptions about racial differences in tolerating pain. For example, they believed that black patients can "endure more pain" and have "thicker skin". Such biases created a situation where, when an expectant black mother claimed she was in pain, doctors underestimated the severity of her condition and did not respond appropriately. Obviously, the medical professionals were entirely oblivious of this bias that they had. This research was conducted in 2016. While it is quite hard to believe that such racial biases are so widespread in the 21st century, we cannot simply attribute this to "bad doctors". These biases are implicit – they occur without the conscious awareness.

The bill requires medical professionals to go through training that teaches them to identify their own implicit biases and consciously counteract them. This is an attempt to reduce discrimination by targeting our own unconscious minds.

You can read more about the Bill in the article "These California bills would train nurses, judges and police how to spot their own biases" in *Los Angeles Times*.

The full text of the bill can also be found online, its name is SB-464, California Dignity in Pregnancy and Childbirth Act.

Lesson 1 - Bias

Learning outcomes

a) [Knowledge and comprehension] What is bias?
b) [Understanding and application] What are the key examples and non-examples of bias?
c) [Thinking in the abstract] How can bias be separated from similar knowledge concepts (such as prejudice, misconception or superstition)?

Key concepts

Bias, systematic deviation, opinion, perspective, mistake

Other concepts used

Stereotype, prejudice, misconception, superstition, decision-making

Themes and areas of knowledge

Theme: Knowledge and the knower

Plan

In this lesson we will define bias and think about examples and non-examples of bias. In line with the purpose of this unit, the focus will be on bias in personal knowledge. Just to remind you, bias in personal knowledge may be assessed against shared knowledge. If we want to know if our personal belief is biased or not, we can compare it to the accepted, well-established beliefs on the same subject matter that we have collectively agreed upon.

Shared knowledge, of course, can also be biased, but that will be the focus of the next unit.

What is bias?

Is it true that we are much more biased than we could possibly imagine? (#Scope)

As much as I would like to think of myself as an open-minded, unprejudiced, impartial and just individual, I know that I am not one (are you?). Growing up, I was influenced by a variety of factors and exposed to a variety of experiences. In all probability, these experiences have caused me to have certain biased beliefs. Worst of all, I am probably biased in ways that I am not even aware of.

I will define bias as a *systematic deviation from the truth.*

When I say "*deviation*", I imply that there exists a correct answer (belief, decision) and that the answer (belief, decision) we are dealing with does not match this correct one. This is important because we can identify a bias only if we know the correct answer. If we do not know what the correct answer is, or if we cannot at least assume the correct answer beyond a reasonable doubt, there is no point in talking about bias.

When I say "*systematic*", I mean a deviation that is not random. In other words, it is leaning consistently towards one direction rather than various directions at various times. For example, suppose you are measuring the width of your bed with a measuring tape. You carry out the measurement 10 times. Every time you will get slightly different readings, both higher and lower than the real width of your bed. This is an example of *measurement error*, but this is not a *bias*. A bias occurs when, for some reason, the measurement deviates systematically in one direction. For example, suppose the measuring tape itself is flawed – you washed it accidentally in the washing

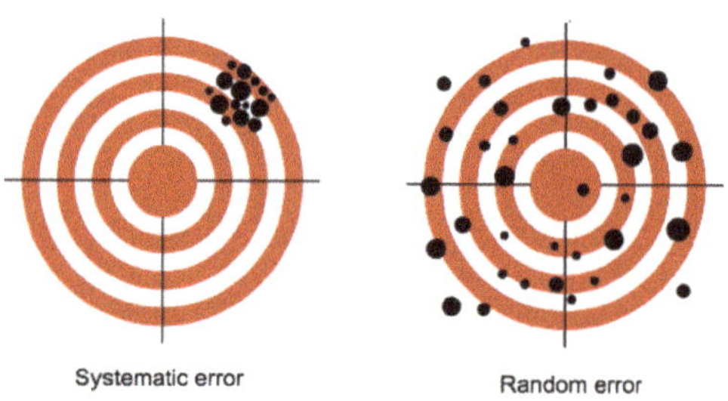

Image 5*. The difference between systematic error and random error (credit: Wikimedia Commons)*

machine and it shrank a little, resulting in each inch section being a little shorter than it is supposed to be (I am now assuming that it is a cloth measuring tape, not a metal one… why would you put a metal measuring tape in a washing machine?). In this case, no matter how many times you carry out the measurement, you will always underestimate the width of your bed. This is bias.

KEY IDEA: Bias is a systematic deviation from the truth

Sources of bias

Since the deviation is systematic, it is usually the case that the deviation is *caused* by something, in other words, that there is a source of bias. In my turbulence example, overestimating the dangers of air travel is caused by my fear of turbulence. It also probably means that whenever there is bias, we can identify one or several factors that make it happen.

Theoretically:

- If we can eliminate the source, the bias will disappear
- If we know the source, we can predict the bias (for example, knowing that a person has a fear of turbulence means that we can probably predict that they will overestimate the dangers of air travel)

Is there any way to know what causes our personal bias? (#Methods and tools)

There are many possible sources of personal bias. Some of them are linked to our identity (cultural, political, gender). Some are linked to our personal experiences (having survived through certain difficulties, having witnessed certain events). Arguably, every human being has a different background and that could determine how (in what way) they are biased.

The important take-away message here is that biases are systematic because they are systematically affected by a certain source and, at least theoretically, these sources can be identified and dealt with.

Bias versus other concepts

To understand a concept, it is always useful to separate it from (misleadingly) similar concepts by answering the question "What is it not?"

We have defined bias by stating what it is. Let us now try to delineate it from a variety of other concepts that it can be easily confused with.

Bias is not the same as opinion. Opinions are possible when there is no single truth. For example, it is my opinion that restaurant A is better than restaurant B. Airplanes falling because of turbulence cannot be my opinion because we do know that this is false. Since we have access to a pretty unambiguous truth in this case, opinions are no longer a thing – there are either beliefs that correspond to the truth or ones that don't.

Bias is not the same as perspective. Again, perspectives are possible when the truth is complex and when multiple interpretations of the truth are possible. For example, there may be various historical perspectives on events of the past. There can be various angles of looking at those events, and often there is no way to prefer one perspective over another. For this reason, perspectives are very valuable (the more the better!). By contrast, in my turbulence example, the truth is pretty straightforward. Another difference is that, when you are presenting a perspective, you are presenting it honestly as one of several possible angles in looking at a situation. You acknowledge the existence of other angles. When you are biased, you are trying to pass your bias off as the truth (and you actually believe it to be the truth).

Is it possible for biases to be accepted as valuable perspectives? (#Perspectives)

Bias is not the same as a mistake. It is a particular type of mistake – a systematic one. If I ask a child who has never travelled by air if turbulence can bring down airplanes, they may say yes. It would be a mistake but not a bias. If you ask someone like me (before they educated themselves with loads of articles and videos), they will say yes because they are afraid of turbulence. They will answer multiple other questions with similar mistakes – for example, they will overestimate the likelihood of turbulence occurring, the psychological effect it has on airline pilots, and the number of turbulence-related accidents in the past. All of their answers will be biased in the same direction, driven by one source - their underlying fear of turbulence.

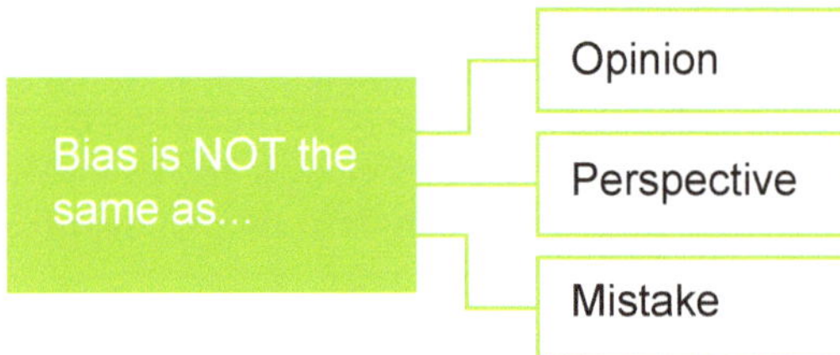

Critical thinking extension

Now that we are clear with the definition of bias and with some of the things that bias is *not*, can we name some examples of phenomena that may be categorized as instances of bias in personal knowledge?

To what extent can we claim that personal bias penetrates every aspect of our lives? (#Scope)

Here are some of the phenomena that we are going to consider further on in this unit:

1) Biased perception (for example, susceptibility to certain perceptual illusions)
2) Stereotypes
3) Prejudice
4) Biased decision-making (for example, selecting risky options when it is not logically warranted)
5) Misconceptions (biased understanding of certain ideas, not just a mistake but a systematically incorrect understanding driven by a false belief)
6) Superstitions (stubborn beliefs in supernatural influences despite counter-evidence)

Do you think all of these phenomena fit our definition of bias equally well? Would you add any other phenomena to the list?

If you are interested...

When a meteorologist talks about bias, it is worth listening to (I would know, both of my parents have degrees in meteorology). J. Marshall Shepherd's TED talk "3 kinds of bias that shape your worldview" (2018) is a good place to start.

Take-away messages

Lesson 1. Bias is a systematic deviation from the truth. This definition implies two things: (1) there exists a certain standard that we may accept as the correct answer or the truth, (2) the deviation from this standard is not occasional and random, but systematic (consistent and always in the same direction). For this reason, opinions, perspectives and mistakes are all non-examples of bias. Since biases are systematic, it must be the case that they are (systematically) influenced by some factors. Such factors are known as sources of bias and they can originate from your personal experiences, your culture, your identity, and so on.

Lesson 2 - Personal experience

Learning outcomes

a) [Knowledge and comprehension] What is a personal experience sample?
b) [Understanding and application] How do personal beliefs depend on personal experiences?
c) [Thinking in the abstract] To what extent can we claim that personal beliefs are inevitably biased?

Key concepts

Personal experience, experience sample

Other concepts used

Representativeness, sample and target population (in the analogy with human sciences), limited versus biased

Themes and areas of knowledge

Theme: Knowledge and the knower

Recap and plan

We have defined bias as a systematic deviation from the truth. We have considered some examples and non-examples of bias in personal knowledge, so now we know what it is. Now we can ask ourselves, where does it come from? Why is our personal knowledge biased in the first place?

In this lesson I start building my argument by making the point that personal beliefs are likely to be biased because they are based on personal experiences that are inevitably limited. In doing so, I will define the concepts of personal experience and experience sample.

KEY IDEA: Personal beliefs are likely to be biased because they are based on personal experiences that are inevitably limited

Personal experience and experience sample

Is personal experience always inevitably limited? (#Scope)

Personal experience is the sum total of all instances of interaction of a person with various aspects of the world. This is a broad definition that includes any type of interaction, both practical and theoretical. If you have seen a zebra on a safari trip, you have some personal experience with zebras. If you read or watched a documentary about zebras, you also have experience with them. When I say "zebra", you have a complex of associations firing up in your brain – that is your personal knowledge about zebras based on your interactions with various aspects of reality (books, documentaries, safari parks) somehow connected to them.

However, what comes to your mind when I say "Bony Giant Sengi" or "elephant shrew"? I bet your experience with this animal is very limited, maybe even to the extent where your mind is blank.

If you have never seen this animal, nor heard anything about it, you have no personal experience with it.

***Image 6**. What do you know about Boni Giant Sengi, a.k.a. elephant shrew? (credit: Kim, Flickr)*

Personal experiences are limited because the world is so vast that it is unrealistic to expect anyone to experience all aspects of it within one lifetime. Coming back to elephant shrews, there is an estimated 8.7 million different species of animals on the face of the Earth. How many of those species do you have personal experience with, either practical or merely theoretical?

To define the aspects of the world that a person has had experience with, we will also use another term – experience sample. If 8.7 million species are the "total" number of available experiences, then the several dozen species I know something about will comprise my experience sample. My experience sample is probably different from yours. Take any two people and their experience samples will overlap, but not coincide – this applies not only to knowledge of animal species, but to anything!

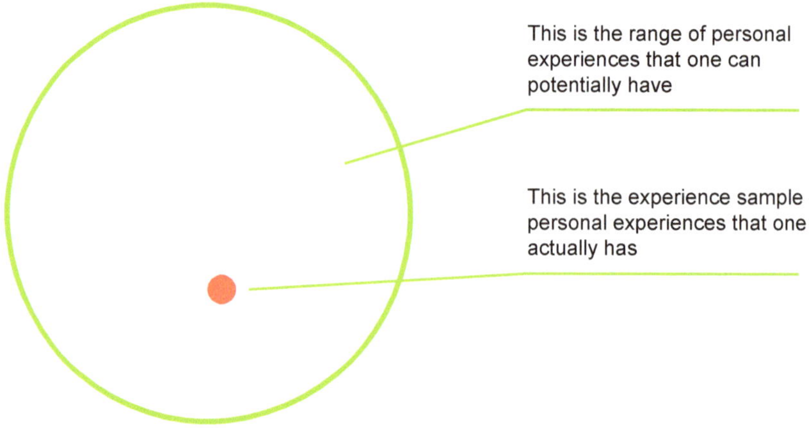

***Image 7**. Experience sample*

Personal knowledge is the product of personal experience samples

To start, I will claim that our personal beliefs are based on our experience samples (which are very limited).

I describe myself as a devoted introvert. Knowing this, you will not be surprised to hear that one of my favorite pastimes is to look up the most remote places on the face of the Earth and dream about moving to live in one of these places one day.

To what extent is our personal knowledge the product of our personal experiences? (#Perspectives)

Currently, the most remote settlement on Earth is a town with an exotic name, Edinburgh of the Seven Seas. The island upon which the settlement lies (Tristan da Cunha) has no airstrip, so the only way to travel there is by boat. The 2,810-kilometer boat ride from South Africa (the nearest location) takes around 6 days.

The settlement's population is several hundred people. I cannot help but wonder, "What are they like? What would it be like to live there?" I know very little about those islanders, but I do have some beliefs. For example, I somehow find myself believing that inhabitants of Edinburgh of the Seven Seas are simple people who feel very attached to their home, but at the same time are extremely cautious about strangers.

***Image 8**. Tristan-da-Cunha: welcome to the remotest island*

***Image 9**. Tristan-da-Cunha: aerial view*

When I think about these beliefs (thinking about thinking, metacognition!), I realize that they are based on the very limited experiences that I have had. Namely, I remember reading somewhere that in 1961, there was a volcanic eruption on the island and the whole population had to abandon the settlement and was moved to the UK. Two years later, when it was declared safe again, they all chose to go back. I remember thinking, "Wow, these people like their home and don't care about the gifts of civilization that we are all after."

I have a personal belief about inhabitants of Edinburgh of the Seven Seas, and this belief is based on a very limited experience sample. Another person may have a slightly different experience sample, which would lead to a different belief.

If the experience sample is biased (which it is likely to be), then the personal knowledge based on it will also be biased.

We must have personal beliefs which are very likely to be biased

Once I arrived at this thought, my natural reaction was: "Well, you should make sure that your personal beliefs are not based on limited experience samples... gain more experience and only then form a personal belief!"

Is it possible to have no belief at all rather than a biased belief? (#Perspectives)

However, on reflection, it does not seem to be that simple, because:

1) Is it even possible to ever have *enough* personal experience with something to be *certain* that your personal belief is unbiased? Our personal experiences will always be limited. The world is too large for us to be able to experience every aspect of it. In fact, it looks like our personal experience is a tiny spotlight on a huge canvas that the world has to offer.
2) Once I accept that my personal experience is inevitably limited, can I opt out of having a personal belief at all? Rather than having a biased belief, I want to choose having no belief. But let's face it, it does not seem to be possible. We need personal beliefs to navigate the world. They save us a ton of time and effort in a variety of everyday situations. Just think about it: when you are in a restaurant and a waiter approaches you, you do not expect the waiter to attack you, because you are operating on the assumption (expectation) that he is a decent person who is willing to serve you food. Imagine you did *not* have this belief about the waiter. He would have to gain your trust first, and that is a waste of his working hours.

KEY IDEA: We have no other option but to have personal beliefs that are very likely to be biased

I am arriving at an interesting conclusion. Having personal beliefs is inevitable. We cannot not have personal beliefs. At the same time, personal beliefs are based on personal experiences, and personal experiences are (very) limited. We cannot ever have complete experience. This means that personal beliefs are likely to be biased. Hence, when it comes to our personal knowledge, having biased personal beliefs is a necessity that we cannot opt out of.

Well... isn't this a little disappointing?

Critical thinking extension

The argument that I have been building in this lesson rests upon several key claims and assumptions:

1) We need personal beliefs in order to function in this world
2) Personal beliefs are based on personal experiences
3) Personal experiences are always limited

If you want to attack my argument (which you are welcome to do!), you probably need to target one or more of these statements. If any one of these statements is flawed, then the whole argument is flawed.

Can personal experiences be representative of the world in the same way as samples in human sciences can be representative of the population? (#Methods and tools)

For example, you might want to attack the third claim. You might point out that "limited" personal experiences does not necessarily mean "biased". We know from human sciences that a sample of participants is "limited" in relation to the population that the results will be applied to, but it is not "biased" if the sample is shown to be representative. In other words, if characteristics of the sample reflect the essential characteristics of the population, the sample is limited but not biased. Is the same logic possible with experience samples? This raises some interesting questions such as "How do you ensure that your personal experience sample is representative?"

If you are interested…

In human sciences, if a sample is representative of the target population, it is believed not to be biased despite the fact that it is obviously limited. Representative samples allow researchers to apply the results from the sample to the whole population.

If you are not familiar with the concept of representativeness of a sample in human sciences or simply want to refresh this knowledge, you can watch the video "Selecting a representative sample" from the YouTube channel *Research By Design*. It discusses populations and samples and investigates how to make your sample representative of your population.

Take-away messages

Lesson 2. Personal knowledge is formed on the basis of personal experience. Personal experience samples are inevitably limited because the world is too large for someone to experience all aspects of it. Hence, personal knowledge will also inevitably be limited. To the extent that personal experience samples are biased (which they are likely to be), personal knowledge will also be biased. Moreover, we cannot opt out of having limited personal beliefs because we depend on these beliefs to navigate the world.

Lesson 3 - Darwinian evolution of personal knowledge

Learning outcomes

a) [Knowledge and comprehension] What is Darwinian evolution?
b) [Understanding and application] What are the similarities between the development of personal knowledge and adaptation of species through natural selection?
c) [Thinking in the abstract] To what extent can we claim that development of personal knowledge is a Darwinian process?

Key concepts

Darwinian evolution, analogy

Other concepts used

Environment, evolution, superstition, personal beliefs, natural variation, differential fitness, survival of the fittest, adaptation through natural selection, Universal Darwinism

Themes and areas of knowledge

Theme: Knowledge and the knower

Recap and plan

In the previous lessons I claimed that personal beliefs are inevitably based on personal experiences and that personal experiences are inevitably limited. Since personal beliefs are inevitably based on limited information, they are likely to be biased.

We have accepted the idea that personal experience somehow influences the development of personal knowledge. That being said, what exactly is the nature of this influence?

What is the role of analogy in acquiring new knowledge? (#Methods and tools)

In this lesson I will suggest an analogy between the process of developing personal beliefs and the process of Darwinian evolution of species. My analogy will imply that the way personal experience influences personal knowledge is similar to the way the environment influences the process of natural selection.

Theory of evolution: quick refresher

Here is a quick refresher on the theory of evolution, as suggested by Charles Darwin (1809 - 1882) and modified slightly in more contemporary versions that followed the discoveries in genetics. These ideas are referred to as Darwinian evolution.

What the theory claims	What it means
When two organisms have a baby (please excuse my French!), the baby's genotype is a random combination of the genotypes of the two parents. Because of this randomness, there is always some variation in the gene pool. This is called "*natural variation*".	My child, welcome into this world. We will give you this genotype that we randomly created out of our own genes, and see what happens.
Survival of an organism depends on its fitness. Some organisms have genotypes that are more fit to the demands of the environment, some have genotypes that are less fit. This is known as "*differential fitness*".	Your genotype will determine how well you fit into the environment.
Organisms that are more fit to the environment have higher chances of survival. This principle is known as "*survival of the fittest*".	If you do not fit well, you will not be able to pass on your genes.
Through this process of survival of the fittest, generation after generation, genes that provide a good fit are more likely to stay in the gene pool while genes that provide a poor fit gradually disappear from the gene pool. This is known as "*adaptation through natural selection*".	If you fit well, you will have children and pass your genes on to them.

How suitable is Darwin's evolutionary theory to explain historical development of knowledge? (#Scope)

Darwin's biggest inspiration came from small birds known as the Galapagos finches. When he disembarked on the Galapagos Islands, he noticed that the finches varied greatly from island to island in terms of their appearances, especially the beak form. Although islands were sometimes only a few miles apart, the differences were distinct, and they seemed to correspond to the differences in the environment. For example, on an island where droughts were more likely, plants produced fewer but larger seeds, so having a larger beak could be an advantage. Conversely, on islands with wetter climate, seeds were smaller, so a small narrow beak could do a better job of extracting them from various cracks. This resulted in more than a dozen species of finches unique to this remote archipelago.

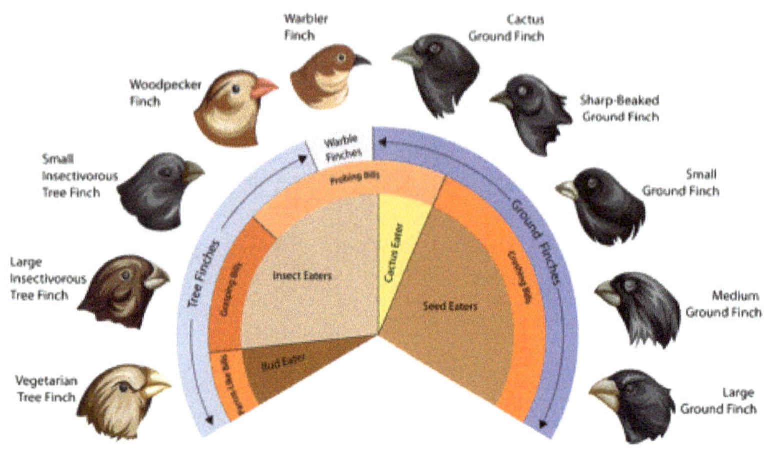

Image 10. *A chart showing various adaptations in Darwin's finches*

One thing to note is that in Darwinism, adaptation is driven by requirements of the environment. To rephrase this, adaptation is driven by the experiences that organisms have with the environment. If extracting seeds from tiny cracks between stones is a part of your experience sample, then the shape of your beak becomes important and your survival depends on it.

Evolution of personal beliefs

Can we extend the logic of Darwinian evolution to development of personal knowledge? Suppose beliefs are "organisms" that need to adapt to a certain environment in order to survive, while beliefs that do not fit too well quickly die out.

I can see pros and cons in this idea, but before criticizing, let's give it a try. I hereby present to you a "theory of Darwinian evolution of personal beliefs":

- Growing up, we develop an array of different personal beliefs (some from parents, some from media, some from education and other sources). This is *natural variation.*
- The environment we live in provides us with an experience sample. Of all the experiences we could possibly have, we actually have only a really small subset. Some of our beliefs are better fit to this experience sample. This is *differential fitness.*
- We test the beliefs against our experiences, and those that do not provide a good fit gradually fade. This is *survival of the fittest.*
- Beliefs that have survived form into complexes and produce new, related beliefs. This is *adaptation through natural selection.*

Image 11. Natural selection: those better fit to the environment have a higher chance of survival (credit: Tooony, Wikimedia Commons)

An example

Are superstitions a form of knowledge? (#Perspectives)

Imagine that a friend told you that, according to an old belief, if you want to attract good luck at an exam, you should place a coin inside a shoe that you are wearing. You found it silly. On exam day, several of your classmates had coins in their shoes and they seemed to get satisfactory results, while you did not have a coin to protect you and your results were not satisfactory at all. You still thought that was a mere coincidence, but as the next exam day approached, you thought there would be no harm in this tokenistic act so you placed a coin in your shoe and got good results. Since then, you never had an exam without a lucky coin in your shoe. That is how your experiences shaped a *superstition*.

In all probability, there were many various beliefs that potentially could become a superstition, but only one of them survived because it provided a good fit to your experience sample.

Conclusion

To sum up, it looks like we can draw an analogy between the development of personal beliefs and the development of species in Darwinian evolution. When we use the term "Darwinian evolution of personal knowledge", we imply that the dependence between personal experience and personal knowledge is analogous to the dependence between the environment and natural selection of species.

KEY IDEA: We can draw an analogy between the development of personal knowledge and Darwinian evolution of species

If we accept this analogy, it opens up many interesting implications. These will be explored in the following lessons.

Critical thinking extension

At the start of this lesson, I posed the question: "How exactly do personal experiences influence the development of personal knowledge?"

I suggested the following answer: "They influence the development of personal knowledge in a process analogous to Darwinian evolution."

Here are a couple of other questions on the relationship between personal experience and personal knowledge that I find interesting:

1) If we know what someone's experiences have been, can we predict this individual's beliefs?
2) Is it at all possible to break free from the prison of your experiences and have beliefs that transcend them?

If we accept the analogy with Darwinian evolution, how do you think we should answer these questions? Try to formulate an answer before you read on.

Can personal beliefs be fully predicted from personal experiences? (#Perspectives)

Here is my suggestion:

1) Yes, we can, but only to a very small extent. If I give a biologist a description of some environment, will they be able to describe what kind of creatures should have evolved in this environment? It should be possible to some extent. For example, if the environment is a desert, we know that the organisms should have developed some mechanism to survive extreme heat. That being said, exact predictions are probably not a possibility. Imagine I gave an alien biologist (who has never visited Earth) a thorough description of a desert. Will the alien biologist be able to draw a camel?
2) No. There is nothing in the process of Darwinian evolution that transcends the requirements of the environment. A Galapagos finch cannot just sit back, reflect and decide that it wants its future generations to develop narrower beaks. The only way to a narrow beak lies through wetter climate and smaller seeds. This conclusion is disappointing, isn't it? But if you agree that development of personal knowledge is a Darwinian process, you will also have to accept this conclusion.

If you are interested...

Darwin's theory is so influential that it has been applied to a wide range of phenomena. The concept of Universal Darwinism, which emerged in the course of time as a summary of these applications, suggests that evolution through natural selection can occur in the world of non-living as well as living things. Some even tried to apply Darwinism to the development of the Universe.

If you are interested to know more, check out Lee Smolin's book *The Life of the Cosmos* (1997). In this book, he hypothesizes about cosmological natural selection and suggests that black holes, when they collapse, give birth to new universes on the "other side". In these new universes, the starting physical parameters are reshuffled a little (in a process analogous to "reshuffling" parents' genes in an offspring). As these universes develop, some of them are more successful than others. Obviously, these new universes also contain black holes that collapse and give birth to new universes, and so on.

Take-away messages

Lesson 3. There are some important similarities between the process of Darwinian evolution of species and the development of personal knowledge. They both seem to have the key features - natural variation, differential fitness, survival of the fittest and adaptation through natural selection. We may conclude from these similarities that the processes are, in fact, analogous. In other words, the development of personal knowledge is a Darwinian process. Once we accept this idea, it has some interesting consequences that are worth exploring. They will be further explored in the following lessons.

Lesson 4 - Analogy analysis

Learning outcomes

a) [Knowledge and comprehension] What is the process of analogy analysis? What is false analogy?
b) [Understanding and application] Can the analogy between development of personal beliefs and Darwinian evolution of species be considered false analogy?
c) [Thinking in the abstract] What would be the Darwinian analogy for bias in personal knowledge?

Key concepts

Analogical reasoning, analogy, false analogy

Other concepts used

Logical fallacy, essential characteristics and superficial characteristics

Themes and areas of knowledge

Theme: Knowledge and the knower

Recap and plan

In the previous lessons I suggested an analogy between development of personal beliefs and Darwinian evolution of species.

Using analogy is in itself an important thinking tool; it is very popular but very tricky. Analogical reasoning is a valuable skill because it is so widely used in the production of knowledge in almost every area. Therefore, it is worthwhile to take a step back and formulate some general rules of analogical reasoning. In this lesson, using the analogy between development of personal beliefs and evolution of species as an example, we will look at the process of analogical reasoning and analyze the dangers of "false analogy".

These are all transferrable metacognitive skills and concepts that you can use elsewhere.

False analogy

Analogies are a tricky thing because there exists a danger to fall for the so-called false analogy – it is a logical fallacy where the analogy is based on inessential characteristics (while the essential ones are different). Therefore, false analogies are misleading and result in flawed conclusions.

Does analogical reasoning provide sufficient justification for accepting beliefs as true? (#Methods and tools)

An example of a false analogy: *When a doctor is planning a surgery for a difficult case, it is okay to consult medical books. Therefore, medical students should also be allowed to use textbooks when they are writing exams.*

Obviously, there exists some similarity between surgeons conducting a surgery and medical students taking an exam. Both are stressed. Both are short for time. Both tasks are important. However, there are some essential aspects that are different: the goal of a surgery is to save a life, while the goal of a medical exam is to test your knowledge in order to later allow you to save a life. It is fine to consult books if you are lacking knowledge while conducting a surgery, but it is not fine for surgeons to rely on books by default.

False analogy ignores this crucial difference.

***Image 12**. False analogy: chairs have legs, I have legs, therefore I'm a chair*

Analogy between development of personal knowledge and evolution of species: false analogy?

Is the analogy I have drawn in the previous lesson a false analogy?

Is development of personal beliefs analogous to evolution of species? (#Perspectives)

On the one hand, Darwinian evolution of organisms and development of personal beliefs do have similarities:

1) *Both depend on the fit to environment.* A Galapagos finch with a large beak will not survive in an environment where most food is hidden in narrow cracks. Similarly, the superstition about the lucky coin in your shoe is likely to fade if you get bad grades even when the coin is there.
2) *Both depend on the environment that you immediately experience.* It is only important to the bird what the cracks in the stones look like. Other aspects of the environment (for example, sea water temperature or the height of trees in the forest) are not essential because they do not influence the bird's everyday experiences. Similarly, when you develop a stereotype about inhabitants of a remote island, you base this stereotype on the experiences you have had: for example, the one article that you read or the one piece of gossip that you heard. It's hard to imagine how you can base your stereotypes on experiences that you might have had (but have not had).
3) *Both involve some random generation and subsequent elimination.* Mother Nature randomly generates offspring genotypes from the parents' genes. These genotypes then get tested against the environment and eliminated. Similarly, we have a whole range of beliefs, ideas, misconceptions, perceptions and transient thoughts. Not all of them stick around for a long time. Those that do not get a favorable response from the environment are doomed for oblivion.

On the other hand, there are essential differences.

1) The time scale is different. Darwinian evolution of organisms happens over the span of millions of years. Development of personal beliefs is a matter of one lifetime.
2) In natural selection, unfit genes disappear from the gene pool. In development of personal beliefs, the beliefs themselves may be suppressed or forgotten, but (thankfully!) they don't completely disappear.
3) Natural selection of genes is not quite the same as "natural selection of ideas". When genes die out (due to a poor fit to the environment), they cannot really be reborn. We lost our tails long ago, and it is hard to imagine that one of us could have a child with a tail. With ideas, it is different. I can retrieve a long-forgotten idea no matter how much time has passed since I abandoned it. Ideas are never truly and irreversibly dead.

What would your judgment be? Does the analogy stand? Can we dismiss the differences as inessential?

I personally think we can, making the analogy not false; however, I can also see why many people will not agree with me. No matter what you decide, the lesson here is that before deciding whether an analogy is true or false, you first need to decide which aspects of the two things you are comparing are essential and which aspects are more superficial. An analogy is only true if it is based on similarity in *essential* aspects.

How can we decide if the differences between two phenomena are essential or superficial? (#Methods and tools)

KEY IDEA: An analogy is only true if it is based on similarity in essential aspects

This raises a question: which aspects of an object or a phenomenon are considered essential? While there is no simple answer to this question, think about it in the following way:

> *When you take away an essential aspect, A is not A anymore. When you take away an inessential aspect, A may take a different form, but it still remains A.*

For example:

> Being a mammal is an essential aspect of a cat, but being furry is not. A cat that is not furry is still a cat (in fact, some breeds of cats look more like snakes, if you ask me). However, a cat that is not a mammal is not a cat. It is something else.

Thinking tool: analogy analysis

Let us formalize some rules of analogical reasoning in a concise form, so that you can use these tools elsewhere in thinking about knowledge.

Analogical reasoning is when you:

1) Observe that A and B are similar in essential aspects
2) Claim that A and B are analogous
3) Hence, infer that A and B must be also similar in all other aspects

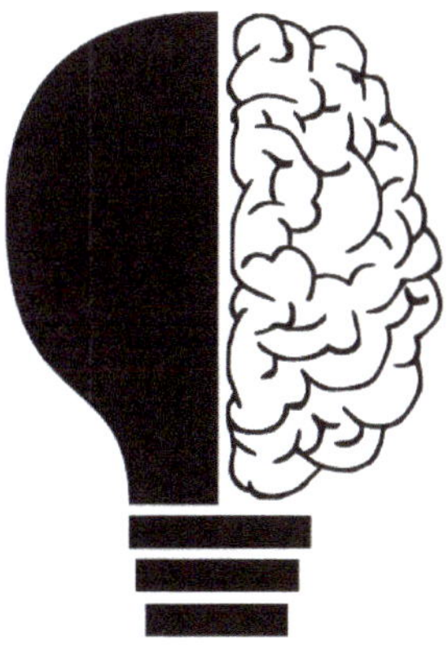

Image 13. *Analogical reasoning is based on seeing a similarity between two things*

For example:

1) You observe that chimpanzees and humans are biologically similar in many ways
2) You claim that chimpanzees and humans are analogous in terms of how they respond to treatment
3) Hence, you infer that drugs that appear to be effective to cure disease in chimpanzees should also be effective to cure disease in humans

One needs to be cautious in using analogical reasoning because analogy often turns out to be false. To carry out analogy analysis, you should ask yourself the following questions:

1) Are similarities between A and B essential or superficial? In the context of the example above, the fact that both species have two hands, two legs and one head is probably superficial while the fact that the genotype is 96 percent identical could be essential.
2) Are A and B similar in *all* essential characteristics or only some of them? Analogy is only reliable if *all* essential characteristics are similar.
3) Are there any essential differences between A and B? For example, if the 4 percent of the DNA sequence that is different between humans and chimpanzees codes for the immune system, it could actually be very essential. It could cause the reaction to drugs in the two species to be entirely different.

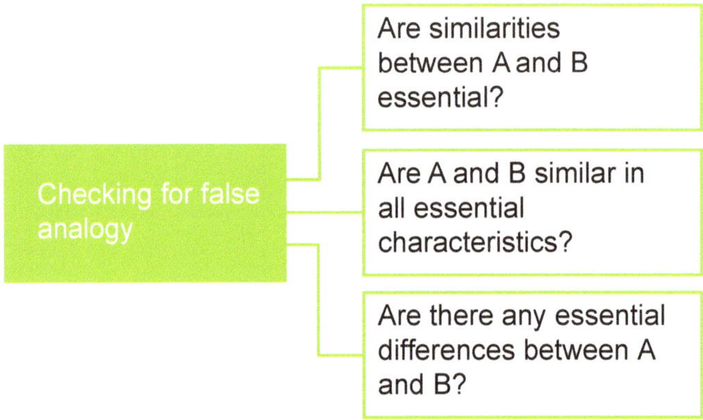

Analogical reasoning is powerful, but, to use it correctly, you need to make sure that you are not falling victim to false analogy (a logical fallacy). To do that, carry out analogy analysis! Use thinking tools to think better.

Critical thinking extension

The focus in this unit is the concept of bias. If development of personal beliefs and Darwinian evolution of species are indeed analogous, what counts as bias in these two processes?

What is the role of bias in the evolution of personal knowledge? (#Scope)

At the start of the unit, we defined bias as a systematic deviation (from some standard or truth). It seems to be easy to apply this concept to personal beliefs. A personal belief is biased when it deviates systematically from some "truth". For example, my belief about the islanders of Tristan Da Cunha is biased if it does not correspond to the real state of things (we can go and check and see if the belief was biased or not).

However, what about the process of evolution? What counts as bias there?

If you are interested...

In *Monty Python and the Holy Grail*, the 1975 British comedy, there is an episode demonstrating the dangers of false analogy. Old, but still highly relevant today! You can watch the relevant episode in the video entitled "Monty Python deductive reasoning" on the YouTube channel *RegieNetCom110*.

Take-away messages

Lesson 4. Analogical reasoning is a thinking tool that is widely used in the production of knowledge in various areas. One observes that A and B are similar in some essential aspects and concludes that therefore A and B must be similar in other aspects, as well. However, when using analogical reasoning you should be cautious about false analogy. To ensure that the analogy is not false, one needs to decide if the characteristics that are similar in A and B are essential or merely superficial. The analogy between development of personal beliefs and Darwinian evolution of species seems to be based on some essential similarities, although there are also some differences.

Lesson 5 - Cultural experience

Learning outcomes

a) [Knowledge and comprehension] How do people from different cultures differ in terms of sense perception, thinking and decision-making?
b) [Understanding and application] What is the evidence supporting the claim that culturally specific experiences may influence the way we process information?
c) [Thinking in the abstract] To what extent can we claim that culturally specific experiences shape culturally specific knowledge?

Key concepts

Culturally specific experiences, enculturation

Other concepts used

Sense perception, thinking and decision-making, trolley problem

Themes and areas of knowledge

Theme: Knowledge and the knower

Recap and plan

In the previous lessons we looked at how bias may be created in personal knowledge. I used an analogy with Darwin's evolution of species to claim that inevitable limitations of our personal experiences impose limitations on our personal beliefs.

If my claim that personal experiences shape personal beliefs is correct, then culturally specific experiences must also shape culturally specific knowledge. This is the claim that we are going to investigate in this lesson.

To what extent does culture influence personal knowledge? (#Perspectives)

KEY IDEA: Culturally specific experiences shape culturally specific knowledge

I am going to give you several examples of empirical evidence that support this claim. These examples will show how cultural experiences may influence:

1) Simple acts of sense perception
2) More complex cognitive phenomena such as thinking and decision making

Cultural experiences influence simple acts of sense perception

In the late 1950s, anthropologist Colin Turnbull spent time among the Bambuti Pygmies in the Ituri Forest in Congo, observing their behavior. He had a local 22-year-old guide, Kenge. In a fascinating series of stories, he describes how Kenge, who grew up in a thick forest and was never exposed to vast distances, travelled with Turnbull and saw prairies for the first time. They saw a herd of buffalo grazing on the plain a couple of miles away. Kenge turned to Turnbull and asked him what kind of insects they were. He lacked the mental machinery necessary to understand that large objects at a distance appear small. He just saw them as small objects. When Turnbull tried to explain this to his guide, Kenge, of course, didn't believe him so Turnbull drove to the buffalo herd. As the insects started rapidly increasing in size, Kenge asked what kind of witchcraft was involved (Turnbull, 1961).

***Image 14**. Grazing buffalo: they seem small if you look at them from a distance*

In the famous Muller-Lyer illusion, you are required to say which of the two lines appears longer – the top one with the feathers turned inwards or the bottom one with the feathers turned outwards.

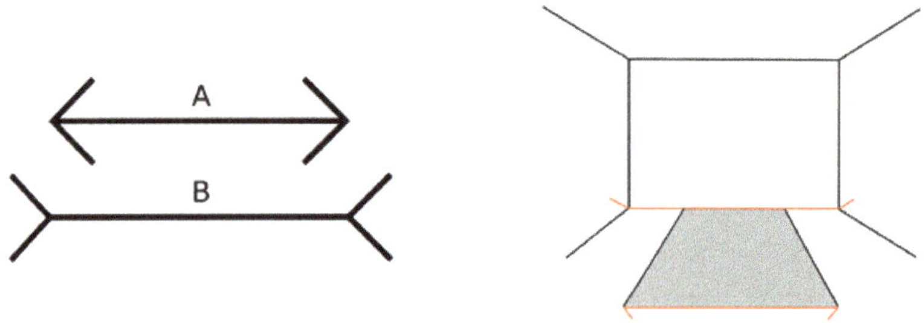

Image 15. Muller-Lyer illusion and our experience staying indoors

Most people say that the bottom line appears longer (although in reality they are the same length). It seems to be a universal phenomenon, an illusion built in the circuitry of our brains.

Is there anything culture-free in personal knowledge? (#Scope)

It is not for indigenous peoples of the Torres Strait Islands (situated between Australia and Papua New Guinea). When the anthropologist W.H.R. Rivers offered this test to the locals, he found that they were not susceptible to the illusion (Deregowski, 1998). Later he found that the same was true about many other indigenous peoples not exposed to the advances of civilization, such as the Toda people of southern India and the San people of the Kalahari Desert. An explanation that he suggests is that people in these pre-modern societies do not stay indoors as much as we do, and even when they are indoors, they are not surrounded with as many rectangular objects. Think about it: our houses are rectangular, our rooms are rectangular, our furniture tends to be rectangular. In such surroundings, if the angles along the edge of an object are out, the object is farther away from us. If the angles are in, the object is closer to us. Our human brains are not hard-wired to be susceptible to the Muller-Lyer illusion… well, they are, but only if we live in a modern society and stay indoors often.

Cultural experiences influence thinking and decision-making

In one study, participants were given tests where each question consisted of three pictures (such as cow, chicken and grass) and the task was to select the odd one out. It was found that American students (grades 4-5) consistently group objects based on belonging to a certain category – for example, they said that cow and chicken go together because they are both animals and that grass is the odd one out. By contrast, Chinese students of the same age consistently grouped objects on the basis of contextual commonality – for example, they grouped cow and grass together (because cows eat grass) and named chicken as the odd one out (Chiu, 1972).

Image 16. Cow, chicken, grass – which one is the odd one out?

So… your culture determines how you think? It seems plausible. After all, we gradually absorb all the aspects of our culture as we are growing up (this process is called enculturation). It probably means that if you are exposed to several cultures when you are growing up (a multicultural environment), your thinking will be more flexible. One is tempted to believe so. What if the reality is that the two (or more) cultures do not mix up and enrich each other, but instead reside in your mind as independent entities and you switch between them from time to time? That would be simultaneously awesome and spooky!

If you are bilingual, it turns out the language you are speaking at the moment influences the way you are thinking. Your answers to the same questions may depend on what language the question is asked in!

For example, research with university students in Hong Kong (who were fluent in both English and Cantonese and had considerable exposure to both cultures) showed that in various decision-making scenarios such as deciding which camera to buy or which restaurant to go to, participants were more likely to make compromise choices and avoid potential disappointment when speaking Cantonese. When instructions were presented to the same students in English, their decisions became much riskier and more extreme (Briley, Morris & Simonson, 2005).

Should judgments of morality of an action depend on the context in which the action is taking place?
(#Ethics)

KEY IDEA: Culturally specific experiences may influence the way we process information

Another researcher found that when bilingual individuals are presented with a moral dilemma, they tend to make emotion-driven decisions when the dilemma is presented in their native tongue and more logic-driven decisions when the dilemma is presented in the second language that they speak with more effort. For example, in one of the modifications of the "*trolley problem*", there is a train going towards five people working on the tracks that is about to kill them. You see this from a bridge above the tracks. On the same bridge, there is a fat man. You know that if you push him down from the bridge, he will get killed but his body will slow down the train and prevent the death of five people. The question is, are you willing to push the fat man from the bridge in order to kill one but save five? Apparently, if the dilemma is given to you in your second language, you are more likely to say yes (Costa et al., 2014).

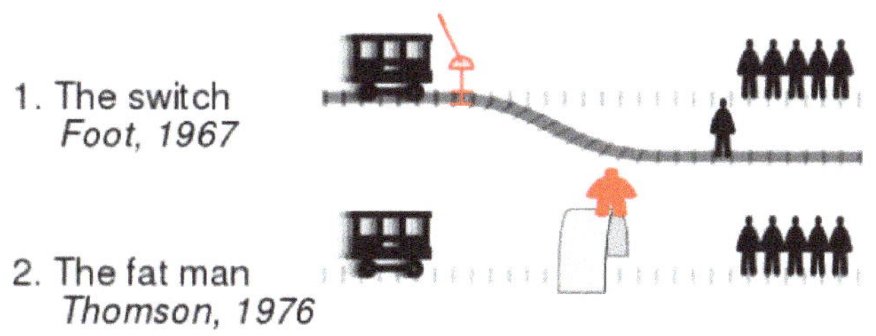

***Image 17**. The trolley problem and its modification with a fat man on the bridge (credit: Cmglee, Wikimedia Commons)*

This research with bilingual individuals also seems to suggest that the two cultures do not integrate in our mind in one holistic entity. Instead, they seem to continue to co-exist as two independent and self-sufficient entities, and you activate either of them depending on the situation, such as when a particular language is being spoken.

Conclusion

Research studies reviewed in this lesson (as well as tons of research studies that are beyond the scope of this book) suggest that culturally specific experiences may influence the way we process information. Apparently, this happens on many levels, from the simplest acts of perception to rather complex acts of thinking and decision-making.

Critical thinking extension

After reviewing some empirical evidence, the conclusion we have arrived at is "Culturally specific experiences may influence the way we process information".

However, the key argument I put forward at the start of the lesson is "Culturally specific experiences shape culturally specific knowledge".

Do you feel the difference? As with everything in Theory of Knowledge, let us be reasonably skeptical about our statements. I invite you to contemplate the following questions and arrive at your own conclusions:

1) Is information processing the same as knowledge? If we process information differently, does it necessarily mean that personal knowledge we arrive at is also different?
2) Reiterating the conclusion, culturally specific experiences *may* influence the way we process information. They may – but do they always? Is it possible, for example, to grow up in a culture but consciously override the influence of this culture on some aspects of your thinking?
3) To what extent are these cultural differences essential? Can we claim that cultural differences in information processing (and personal knowledge?) are so large that people from different cultures will not understand each other on a deep level? Or are these differences negligible?

Once you understand that culture influences personal knowledge, can you override this influence with rational thinking? (#Methods and tools)

If you are interested…

Taking one step further, there is also evidence that cultural experiences influence the structure of our brain! In other words, brains of people from different cultures are also somewhat different. You can read more about this here: Park, D.C., and Huang, C.-M. (2010). Culture wires the brain: A cognitive neuroscience perspective. *Perspectives on Psychological Science*, 5(4), 391-400.

Take-away messages

Lesson 5. Cultural experiences may shape the way we process information. This is evident on many levels, from simple acts of sense perception to complex acts of thinking and decision-making, including ethical reasoning. This influence exists because we gradually absorb various aspects of our culture as we are growing up, in a process known as enculturation. Research with bilingual individuals suggests that enculturation to several cultures at once creates separate, independent "modules" of information processing in our minds, something like several minds within the same person. A stronger claim based on such evidence would be to say that culturally specific experiences shape culturally specific knowledge.

Lesson 6 - Memes and Universal Darwinism

Learning outcomes

a) [Knowledge and comprehension] What is a meme? How is a meme similar to a gene?
b) [Understanding and application] To what extent does memetics apply to the development of personal knowledge?
c) [Thinking in the abstract] Is free will merely an illusion created by memes that disguise themselves as the host's own ideas?

Key concepts

Meme (a unit of culture that bears a certain meaning), memetics, Universal Darwinism, analyzing implications

Other concepts used

The selfish meme, replication, variation, differential fitness

Themes and areas of knowledge

Theme: Knowledge and the knower

Recap and plan

We already used the logic of evolutionary theory to explain how our personal knowledge may depend on the personal experiences we have been exposed to. Personal knowledge may be an instance of adaptation to the requirements of the environment.

In this lesson, rather than just exercising a critical comparison between two phenomena, we will consider a formal theory that already exists. I will introduce the concept of memes and the field of study known as memetics. Memetics is one of the products of Universal Darwinism – the idea that principles of evolution apply universally and not only to natural selection of biological species. I must say that the idea of memes is not fully accepted in academic circles, but it is still worth considering for the sake of raising interesting questions about bias in personal knowledge.

I will explain the concept of memes and give you a gist of the main ideas of memetics. Just a heads up: by the end of this lesson, I will claim that you only exist as a host for the spread of a cultural virus, that you are merely a vessel devoid of free will, that your self is an illusion that the virus has created to make you more complacent to its influence. Well, you know, the mundane reality of life.

What is a meme?

Richard Dawkins is a very popular evolutionary biologist and a prolific writer. In his first bestseller, *The Selfish Gene* (1976), he introduced a gene-centered view of evolution.

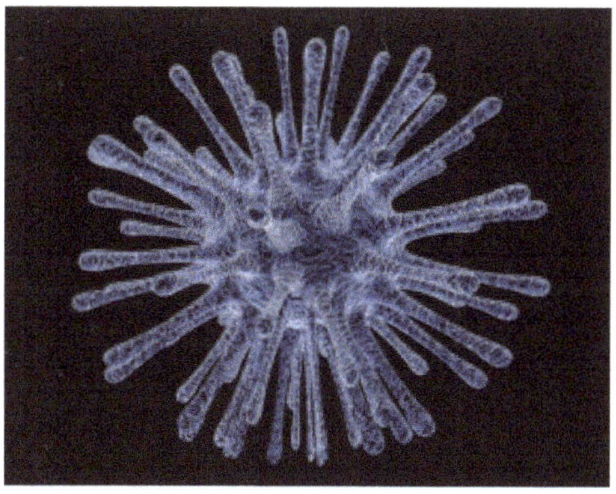
***Image 18**. Viruses spread from one host to another*

The main message is as follows:
1) It is not survival of the organism that drives evolution, but survival of a separate gene.
2) Hence it does not matter to the gene if it is passed to further generations by its host organism or by some other organism, as long as it gets passed on.
3) This explains many instances of selfless behavior that can be observed in various species. Organisms will sacrifice themselves to increase chances of survival of other organisms, but only if the two organisms are genetically related.
4) Therefore, your survival only matters as long as you maximize the chances for your genes to replicate. If there's a better way for your genes to replicate (for example, you sacrificing your life for your brother who carries a similar genotype), your genotype will not think twice.

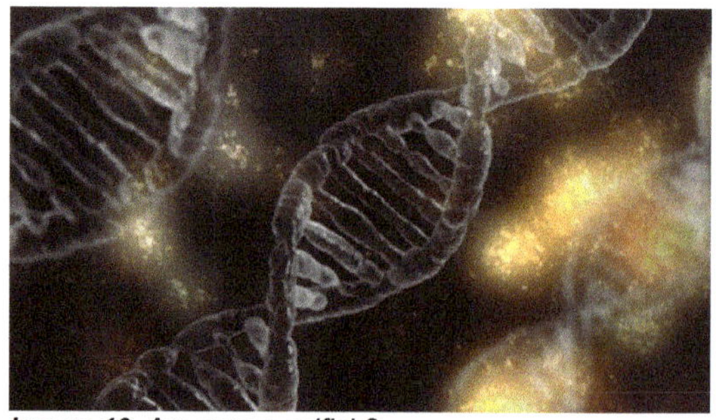

Image 19. Are genes selfish?

If you ask me, the implications of this are a little scary. The way I see it, there exists a whole parliament of little voters inside my body (we have an estimated 20,000 genes) who are very interested in replicating themselves. Each one of them has relatives living in the bodies of a bunch of other people. They protect the interest of their relatives. In every particular situation, they take a call on what behavior would be best to achieve this purpose. If as a result of this behavior my personal life is at risk, they don't really care! As a separate organism with its dreams and desires, I am actually pretty inessential.

But there's more.

Is the concept of a meme a false analogy? Is it justified to speak about a "unit" of knowledge in culture? (#Perspectives)

In the last chapter of his 1976 book, as an extension of his ideas on biological evolution, Dawkins introduced the term meme. Just like a gene is a unit of heredity coding for a specific observable trait (eye color, height, lactose intolerance), a meme is a unit of culture that bears a certain meaning (a catchy tune, the idea of God, a ritual, a greeting sign). Just like collections of genes that code for some complex trait (for example, a collection of genes that determines if you will make a good soldier), memes can be combined in complexes – called memeplexes. Examples of memeplexes include religions, languages, works of art.

Image 20. Spreading of memes

Universal Darwinism

According to Dawkins, evolution will occur whenever three conditions are met:

a) replication,
b) variation,
c) differential fitness.

KEY IDEA: Universal Darwinism: replication + variation + differential fitness = evolution

What are the necessary and sufficient conditions for evolution of knowledge? (#Scope)

Dawkins is a proponent of Universal Darwinism – the view that evolution is not limited to the biological world, that evolution must occur in any other situation where the three conditions are met. For example, it may apply to the first self-replicating molecules. An important point to note here is that the three conditions are *necessary and sufficient*: without any of them, evolution will not occur, but if all three are present, evolution *must* occur.

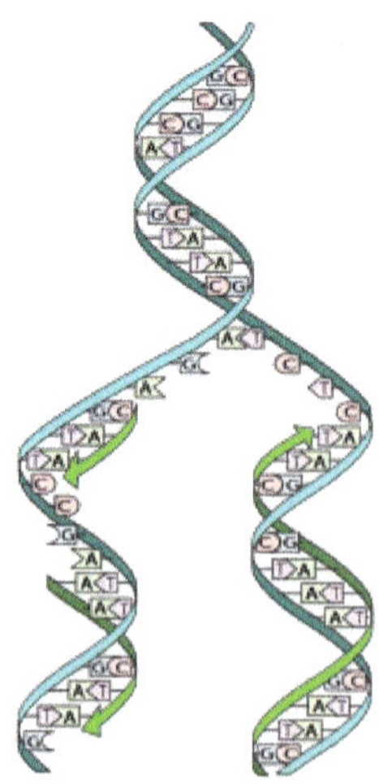

Image 21. The DNA has an ability to self-replicate

Applying Universal Darwinism to memes

Just like a gene, a meme can replicate itself. "Vertical" replication is from generation to generation (for example, parents teaching their children that they should not trust strangers). "Horizontal" replication is within one generation from one person to another. An example of "horizontal" replication is a video that becomes viral on

YouTube and spreads across the world. The idea of a meme is itself a meme, and at the moment I am engaging actively in its horizontal replication.

Just like there exists a natural variation of genes in the gene pool, there exists a natural variation of memes in the meme pool. You can feel that very evidently these days when you log in to Netflix and start choosing a TV show to watch in the evening. There is so much stuff available that it is really difficult to choose sometimes.

Just like genes show differential fitness, some memes survive and replicate better than others. Do I need to explain that? J.K. Rowling's *Harry Potter* was very successful, but *Firefly*, a sci-fi show I really enjoyed, was cancelled after the first season.

Since all three conditions are met, evolution has to occur. The idea is that memes, just like genes, evolve through a process of natural selection.

Memes and bias in personal knowledge

Now how does it all link to bias in personal knowledge? For things to evolve, there needs to be variation. What we might perceive as "biases" in personal knowledge – stereotypes, misconceptions, strange beliefs and superstitions – may simply be instances of this variation. A meme, from the evolutionary viewpoint, is an instance of trial-and-error. Just like all sorts of weird creatures exist in the biological universe because natural variation produces them to see who survives, all sorts of weird biases in personal knowledge exist because natural variation of memes produces them – for some of them to survive and for some to die out.

Is bias a necessary condition for the development of knowledge? (#Methods and tools)

KEY IDEA: Natural variation of memes is a necessary condition for their evolution. If personal beliefs are memes, then bias in personal knowledge is necessary because it enables natural variation.

So… which memes do you host? How actively are you passing them on? How likely do you think it is that these memes will survive?

And has the "meme meme" successfully replicated itself by jumping from my mind to yours?

Critical thinking extension

The selfish meme

As the "meme meme" took its roots, scholars have developed this idea resulting in the emergence of a whole new field of study – memetics. One of the famous founders of this movement is Susan Blackmore, with her bestselling book *The Meme Machine* (2000).

Just like the idea of a selfish gene implies that survival of the organism carrying genes is not as important as survival of the genes themselves (remember the 20,000-member parliament within your body?), the idea of evolving memes implies that every particular individual is nothing but a host. A vessel for a virus.

Let us take this idea and explore its *implications*.

Is morality a cultural meme? (#Ethics)

It provides an evolutionary advantage for a meme if its host thinks that he or she has free will, if there is an illusion that the meme was the host's conscious choice. For example, you might have seen the show *The Voice*. Chances are, it exists in your country. Chances are, you have seen your local version of *The Voice* and perhaps the US version, but not any of the episodes from the rest of the 145 countries where the show has been adapted! When you log on YouTube and look for *The Voice* episodes, the search algorithm politely provides episodes from your own country. It is actually very likely for people to not even suspect that the show exists somewhere other than in their native country. *The Voice* meme maximizes its chances of survival (being seen and being passed on) if it pretends like it is unique for every specific cultural group.

Could it mean that we don't choose our beliefs, but rather our beliefs choose us? They choose us but they also manipulate us into thinking that it was us who chose them – this way they will survive longer.

If you are interested...

If you are interested in studying memetics more closely, a wonderful introduction is Susan Blackmore's book entitled *The Meme Machine* (2000). You can also visit the author's website: www.susanblackmore.uk/

Take-away messages

Lesson 6. Universal Darwinism is the idea that the process of evolution is not limited to natural selection of biological species, but must occur whenever three conditions are met: replication, variation and differential fitness. Memes are units of culture that bear a certain meaning. They get replicated both vertically and horizontally. According to the "selfish meme" idea, meme hosts are not as important as the memes themselves. Memetics provides a formal application of Darwinian evolution to the development of personal knowledge.

Lesson 7 - Heuristics

Learning outcomes

a) [Knowledge and comprehension] What is a heuristic?
b) [Understanding and application] What are the advantages and disadvantages of using heuristics?
c) [Thinking in the abstract] What implications does the existence of heuristics have for our understanding of the way humans think?

Key concepts

Heuristics, cognitive biases, System 1 and System 2 thinking, normative and descriptive models of thinking

Other concepts used

Anchoring bias

Themes and areas of knowledge

Theme: Knowledge and the knower

Recap and plan

In the previous lessons we have been exploring bias in personal knowledge. We used the evolutionary theory to make sense of it. The take-away message is that personal knowledge may indeed be biased, but this bias comes from the natural variation of our personal experiences. In a process akin to natural selection, beliefs that provide an evolutionary advantage stand the test against our experiences and get reinforced (even if they are biased!).

How can personal knowledge be biased despite our awareness that it is biased? (#Scope)

In the next couple of lessons, let's look at how exactly this happens. In particular, we will look at what biases exist in our mental software and why they are still there despite understanding that they are biases.

System 1 and System 2 thinking

A lot of what we know today about biases in personal knowledge comes from psychology. Amos Tversky and Daniel Kahneman were the two scientists who framed this research as a systematic field of study and developed a coherent theory of cognitive biases (Tversky & Kahneman, 1974). The theory suggests that there are two "systems of thinking" that humans use when they process information and make decisions – System 1 and System 2 (Kahneman, 2011).

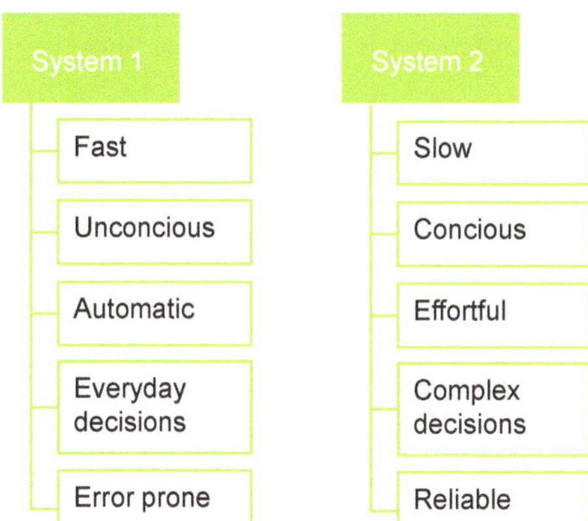

Image 22. System 1 and System 2: the intuitive and the logical systems of thinking

System 1 thinking developed earlier in the process of evolution, and humans are not the only species that have it. System 1 is quick, automatic, intuitive and based on past experiences. When you see news about an airplane crash that claimed lives of people and you are afraid to fly because it seems to you that airplanes are a dangerous kind of transport, that is your System 1 speaking. It uses vivid perceptual images to make sweeping generalizations about things it does not completely understand. It is the cause of irrational behavior.

How reliable is knowledge that is a product of intuitive thinking? (#Methods and tools)

System 2 thinking is deliberate, logical, rational and analytical. It is a consequence of our education and culture. When you tell yourself that people are probably likely to overestimate dangers of travelling by air or when you compare death statistics from airplane crashes against car accidents and learn that planes are, statistically, much safer than cars to travel, that is your System 2 overriding the initial reactions of System 1.

According to Kahneman (2011), System 1 and System 2 act sequentially. First, we react with our quick intuitive brain and then – if necessary – we override that reaction with our logical, rational, "educated" brain. This makes sense.

- First, if we were using System 2 constantly rather than occasionally, our life would be a nightmare. For every simple decision, we would be spending loads of time and energy and cognitive effort.
- Second, in most cases, System 1 works just fine. The logic that System 1 uses is "*Look, I did this before and it worked, so I can do it again*" and, yes, it will probably work again.
- Finally, since we evolved from more primitive animals, it makes sense that we have all the mental machinery they have, plus something on top of that. Evolution did not re-wire our brains completely; it wrote patches and created additional modules.

***Image 23**. First we think fast, then we think slow (credit: P.O. Arnäs, Flickr)*

KEY IDEA: System 1 and System 2 act sequentially: first we use intuition, then we override it with rational analysis

Heuristics and cognitive biases

What knowledge is more valuable: descriptive knowledge of how people think or prescriptive knowledge of how people should think? (#Perspectives)

Models that describe System 2 thinking are called "normative models". They are "normative" because they tell us what is correct and incorrect, which decision or conclusion is accurate and which is not. Examples of normative models include logic, utility theory, and probability theory. For example, probability theory may be used to arrive at the "normative" answer to the question "How dangerous is it to travel by air?"

Models of thinking that show the workings of System 1 are called "descriptive models". They are named this way because they describe thinking as it is, not as it should be. Descriptive models are comprised of so-called heuristics and cognitive biases. Heuristics are "cognitive shortcuts", simplified thinking strategies that we use under lack of time, incomplete information or similar restraints. These are utilized to save time and mental energy.

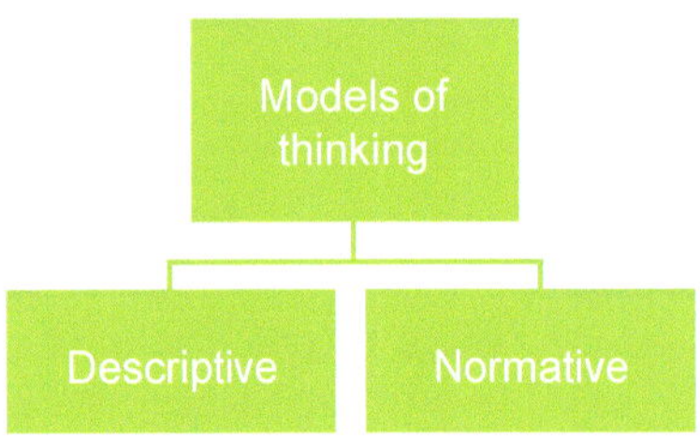

Since heuristics are based on past experience, much of the time they work fine (they are good enough). They worked in the past, so it is likely – to a certain extent – that they will work again. If they do work, there is no issue, but if they do not work, they result in cognitive biases. Cognitive biases are systematic deviations of thinking from what is dictated by normative models.

KEY IDEA: Since heuristics are based on past experiences, much of the time they work fine. But when they don't, they may result in cognitive biases.

An important discovery in psychology is that cognitive biases are predictable. People make predictable mistakes in predictable situations, which is great news (for science, maybe not so much for people!).

For the sake of illustration, I will give you just one example from a pool of hundreds of cognitive biases that have been discovered – anchoring bias.

***Image 24**. Cognitive bias: afraid to fly, although there is no reason*

Anchoring bias

Anchoring bias occurs when you make a decision based on an initial piece of information (an anchor) provided to you, even if the anchor is not very relevant.

For example, suppose you are buying a used laptop. You ask what the price is and the seller says X. This X is the anchor. In the subsequent conversation if you settle on a price lower than X, it will seem like a good bargain, and if it is substantially lower than X, the seller will appear to be making sacrifices. This will happen, to some extent, even if X is actually higher than the market price. So it all depends on where X – the anchor – is initially placed.

***Image 25**. Anchoring bias: we use an "anchor" as a starting point in thinking about numbers*

Strack and Mussweiler (1997) asked two groups of students whether Mahatma Gandhi died before or after age 9 (group 1), or before or after age 140 (group 2). Both of the anchors were quite ridiculous, and students in group 1 said "after", while students in group 2 answered "before". However, when these same students were asked to say at what age they thought Mahatma Gandhi died, the average guess differed significantly in the two groups (age 50 in the first group versus age 67 in the second group).

How can we ever know if our personal knowledge of something is biased? (#Methods and tools)

In a more dramatic example, Englich, Mussweiler and Strack (2006) used practicing judges as participants. They gave them a hypothetical scenario, and the judges had to answer a series of standard questions and arrive at a decision (a sentence). Part of the scenario was the severity of the sentence demanded by the prosecutor. Judges were told that for the sake of the study, this parameter would be determined randomly. Judges were asked to throw dice and take the resulting number as what the prosecutor demands.

Results of the study showed a correlation between the final sentence awarded by the judge and the number on the dice: the larger the number, the more severe the sentence. This is of course concerning, because severity of the punishment demanded by the prosecutor (the anchor) has nothing to do with how guilty the alleged criminal is. Moreover, judges in this study were aware that the prosecutor demands were determined at random – they threw the dice themselves!

***Image 26**. Can dice determine the severity of a court's decision?*

Critical thinking extension

What implications does the existence of heuristics have for our understanding of the way humans think?

Once again, remember that it is important in TOK to identify implications of arguments. An implication is a logical consequence. Suppose you have formulated argument X. Implications of X are all the things that must be true if X is true. Practice this skill! Look at the three arguments below and formulate the implications of these arguments (I will give you some hints which you can use or ignore):

Argument	Implications	Hints
Heuristics result from experience.	?	This fits nicely into the formula that we discussed previously: personal knowledge is based on personal experience. Heuristics will only survive if they already worked sufficiently well in the past.
Heuristics have an adaptive function.	?	We have them because it is beneficial in some way. For example, using an anchor to adjust your thinking is simple yet *usually* good enough. It helps us make acceptable decisions quickly.
Heuristics are predictable.	?	This allows us to study heuristics scientifically. This also creates a curious situation: our minds are riddled with these glitches but we are aware of them. Although we are aware of them, we cannot simply choose not to use them.

If you are interested...

Two great books to learn about heuristics and cognitive biases are: *Thinking Fast and Slow* by Daniel Kahneman (2011) and *Predictably Irrational* by Dan Ariely (2008).

A list of cognitive biases to be amazed and impressed by can be found on the Wikipedia page "*List of cognitive biases*".

Take-away messages

Lesson 7. System 1 and System 2 thinking act sequentially. The first (automatic, intuitive) decisions come from System 1, which is based on past experiences and includes a range of simplified thinking strategies called heuristics. Heuristics may or may not lead to cognitive biases. System 2 thinking may override these automatic reactions using rational, precise analysis. However, System 2 cannot be used all the time because it requires a lot of mental effort. Models of thinking that explain how thinking should work (System 2) are called normative models. Models focused on how thinking actually works (System 1) are called descriptive models of thinking. There are multiple examples of documented heuristics – one of them is anchoring bias. Heuristics have an adaptive function. Heuristics are predictable.

Lesson 8 - Implicit bias and bias self-awareness

Learning outcomes

a) [Knowledge and comprehension] What is implicit bias? What is bias self-awareness?
b) [Understanding and application] How are implicit biases different from explicit attitudes?
c) [Thinking in the abstract] To what extent is it possible to become aware of your own implicit biases?

Key concepts

Implicit biases and explicit attitudes, bias self-awareness

Other concepts used

Shooter bias paradigm, self-report questionnaire, implicit prejudice

Themes and areas of knowledge

Theme: Knowledge and the knower
AOK: Human Sciences

Recap and plan

In the previous lessons we considered some examples of biases in thinking and decision-making. I hope I have convinced you that:

- People use heuristics (cognitive shortcuts) in their thinking and decision-making
- Because of this, people are susceptible to lots of cognitive biases

If we accept all that, we should also probably accept that bias in personal knowledge is inevitable.

Many of these biases are implicit. People might be confident that they don't have them when in fact they do (remember memes? this might be one of those dirty tricks memes are using to ensure their survival!).

Is it possible to have knowledge of our own implicit bias? (#Scope)

Is it possible to have knowledge of our implicit bias? Can I at least know where I am biased, or am I doomed to be oblivious about it?

I will try to outline possible answers to these uncomfortable questions.

Implicit biases

Implicit biases are a special type of bias that stay below the level of conscious awareness. This means that implicit biases affect our thinking and behavior without us realizing it. In fact, on the level of conscious awareness, we may be certain that we are not biased when in fact we are. This makes implicit biases very powerful in terms of affecting our lives.

KEY IDEA: Implicit biases affect out thinking and decision-making, but we don't realize it

I will illustrate implicit biases with the example of *implicit prejudice*. In human sciences a popular way to explore implicit prejudice experimentally is through the so-called "shooter bias paradigm". In this procedure you are playing a video game where figures appear in random places on the screen at random times. Some of these avatars are those of majority groups and some are those of minorities; some figures are holding a gun while some figures are holding harmless objects. Your task is to quickly push a button to "shoot" those avatars that are holding a gun. This reminds me of a scene from *Men in Black* (1997) where Will Smith, as part of his pre-employment exam, had to shoot aliens in a simulation.

Research studies using the shooter bias paradigm have demonstrated that it is common for people to show implicit prejudice in these simulations. For example, one study with American participants showed that black avatars holding harmless objects had a higher chance of being shot than white avatars holding harmless objects. Decisions to shoot were also made faster for black avatars than for white avatars (Correll et al., 2007). It looked like the brain quickly and automatically associated "black" with "dangerous". In another study, the same findings were obtained for Caucasian avatars wearing Muslim headwear versus Caucasian avatars wearing no headwear. The brain appeared to associate "Muslim" with "dangerous" (Unkelbach, Forgas & Denson, 2008). Interestingly, these are all instances of implicit prejudice – they only show in a computer game simulation where participants have to make quick decisions. On the level of explicit attitudes, if you give these same participants self-report questionnaires, they indicate sincerely that they believe they are not prejudiced. How can they think they are not prejudiced when in fact they are?

To what extent are we responsible for putting effort into overriding our implicit biases? (#Ethics)

This could be explained by System 1 and System 2 acting sequentially. System 1 is irrational and automatic. It operates on vivid images that it gets from mass media and everyday experiences. If my only exposure to Muslims is (sadly) the very vivid pictures I have seen several times on TV in connection with suicide bombings, then my System 1 is very likely to operate on those images when making quick, automatic decisions. I am an educated person living in an educated society, so my System 2 will intervene and override this automatic reaction. However, the System 1 reaction remains the default one and requires some extra effort to override. In situations where there is no time to think (like the shooter bias paradigm), System 1 is used.

***Image 27**. Open mind switch: if only it was so easy*

Some questions that emerge are: What do I need to do in order to become aware of my automatic System 1 reactions? What do I need to do in order to change them? If changing them is too difficult or impossible, what do I need to do in order to ensure that my System 2 intervenes more quickly, more reliably, more consistently? In other words, how do I eradicate this prejudice from the depths of my mind?

Bias self-awareness

Let's switch from a serious example to a less serious example.

***Image 28**. Greek "Know Thyself" mosaic found at an excavation in Italy*

Suppose you are implicitly prejudiced against *Harry Potter* in favor of *Lord of the Rings*. In other words, according to your implicit attitude, *Lord of the Rings* is much cooler. However, since it is an implicit attitude, you have no idea about it. On the contrary, explicitly you believe that *Harry Potter* is the coolest thing ever, and on many occasions you have agreed with your friends that *Lord of the Rings* does not live up to this standard.

Can you ever *know* that you are implicitly prejudiced against *Harry Potter*?

If this implicit attitude really exists, it is likely to affect your behavior in certain ways, but these effects will be masked by explicit attitudes. For example, on one particularly lonely evening when you had to watch something to kill time, you decided to re-watch *Lord of the Rings*. You explained the choice to yourself by saying, "I need to refresh my memory to have better arguments and examples for the next time I need to convince people that *Harry Potter* is clearly better."

In this situation you have an explicit belief ("I prefer *Harry Potter*") and an explicit behavior ("I am watching *Lord on the Rings* on a lonely evening"). The trick is to notice your own explicit behavior and hypothesize about the existence of an implicit attitude that might explain it ("Why am I watching *Lord of the Rings*? Could it be that I actually prefer it to *Harry Potter*?"). Implicit biases are implicit, so you cannot just see them directly! To confirm your suspicions, you will need to observe your behavior a little longer ("*Let's wait until the next weekend and see what movie I will be in the mood for*") and even experiment with your own behavior ("*Let me go to a Lord of the Rings fan's party and see if I feel comfortable there*"). From all of these clues, it might be possible to infer that you have an implicit attitude.

What is the most effective way to increase bias self-awareness? (#Methods and tools)

I find it genuinely amazing that to uncover my own implicit attitudes, I have to experiment with myself like it is not "me" but some other person that I barely know. However, it makes sense: if implicit biases exist, then there is a part of "me" that is inaccessible to my conscious self. In a way, there is a whole other person inside my mind who wants to influence my behavior but remains hidden.

We need a term for this ability of a person to be aware of their own implicit biases. We will call this ability bias self-awareness.

KEY IDEA: You can't become directly aware of your implicit biases. You need to infer their existence from observing your own behavior.

Image 29. *Self-awareness*

Critical thinking extension

You will probably agree that bias self-awareness is a desirable trait, but to what extent can you train it?

To what extent is it easier to recognize bias in others than in oneself? (#Perspectives)

Essentially, training is exposing yourself to new experiences. We know from the previous lessons that personal knowledge is dependent on personal experience. Bias self-awareness is part of personal knowledge. In order to train it, you should systematically expose yourself to special experiences where this ability will be engaged and developed.

The question is, what exactly are these experiences? In what situations do you think bias self-awareness becomes particularly necessary? If you can identify such experiences, you can change your daily routine in a way that will allow you to develop unprecedented bias self-awareness!

In the *Lord of the Rings* example above, what steps would you take to train your bias self-awareness?

Being self-aware about your biases may be a huge step towards being bias-free (although arguably this goal cannot be fully attainable).

If you are interested...

If you would like to test yourself on potential implicit biases, try taking several IATs (implicit-association tests) on Harvard's *Project Implicit* website.

Please make sure to read the instructions carefully.

Take-away messages

Lesson 8. Implicit biases are not accessible on the level of conscious awareness, but they affect our thinking and behavior. Explicitly, a person may be certain that they are not biased when in fact they are. This makes implicit biases very difficult to detect, both in other people and in yourself. The ability to be aware of your own implicit biases is called bias self-awareness. At least theoretically, bias self-awareness may be trained. This requires systematic effort and exposing oneself to new experiences.

Lesson 9 - Bias reduction

Learning outcomes

a) [Knowledge and comprehension] What are the strategies that could be used to reduce bias?
b) [Understanding and application] What are arguments for and against bias reduction in the acquisition of knowledge?
c) [Thinking in the abstract] What is the role of reflexivity in bias reduction?

Key concepts

"What-if" thought experiment, bias reduction, counter-stereotypical information, reflexive control, reflexivity

Other concepts used

Bias-free individual, debiasing

Themes and areas of knowledge

Theme: Knowledge and the knower
AOK: Human Sciences

Recap and plan

We have discussed how, when it comes to personal knowledge, people have lots of biases built into their mental software. We have also seen that many of these biases are implicit; this means that they affect our decisions even though we are confident that they don't.

As discussed in the previous lesson, to some extent it is possible, at least theoretically, to increase your bias self-awareness. To do so, you should actively explore your own thinking and decision-making as if you were studying another individual, conduct experiments and test hypotheses about your own thinking.

Hopefully, being self-aware about your implicit bias may help you to reduce it to some extent and perhaps even eliminate it? In this lesson we are going to investigate the extent to which such bias reduction is possible.

Is it possible for implicit bias to be eliminated through self-awareness? (#Scope)

What if we were bias-free?

What would it be like to be bias-free? To have the superpower of seeing the world and every single detail in it with unbiased, neutral, objective eyes? Would you like to have this superpower? Would you be happy if you were the only person on Earth to have this ability? Would you be happy if all humans suddenly became bias-free?

That is just a "what-if" thought experiment. Such thought experiments are a powerful thinking tool because through hypothetical scenarios you can explore dimensions of an idea that you cannot explore otherwise.

Think about these questions for a while. I would like you to formulate a response in your mind. Whatever the mental path you took, the destination that you reach is probably one of two things: either "It would be nice if we could be bias-free" or "It would be a disaster, better continue being biased". Which of the two destinations have you reached?

***Image 30**. What-if thought experiment: what if snails had legs? (credit: Fishhead, Sketchport)*

> **"What-if" thought experiments**
>
> In a "what-if" thought experiment, you imagine that one aspect of this world is different from what it is, and then you logically derive what other aspects would be different. This may be an improbable situation. Examples include questions such as: What if you were immortal? What if there was no moon? What if the north pole and the south pole were swapped?
>
> What-if thought experiments are a powerful thinking tool. They allow you to explore scenarios that are not accessible to everyday perceptual experiences. Although this may all seem highly hypothetical, the conclusions may be really eye-opening sometimes.
>
> A great and funny resource that is tastefully written on such thought experiments is Randall Munroe's book *What If?: Serious Scientific Answers to Absurd Hypothetical Questions* (2014).

Can credible knowledge be acquired through a thought experiment? (#Methods and tools)

Although I am hesitating, I think the destination I am reaching, sadly, is the second one – "better continue being biased". Here are just a couple of arguments, without any intention to talk you into taking my side:

1) To be bias-free means to lose identity. Our biased opinions often rest upon groups that we belong to. For example, a biased historian may tweak their interpretations of events of the past because they (implicitly) want their nation to look good. Such bias is not a good thing. On the flipside, identifying yourself with a group and being impartial about it do not go together well. Although we are blaming the historian for their biased approach, they are being biased out of a sense of identity. Without identity, the lives we are living may be quite meaningless.
2) To be bias-free means to lose passion. When situations are uncertain and information is incomplete, we (biased individuals) form opinions. Since these opinions are ours, we dearly protect them. Trying to support an opinion may be a powerful driver of research and inquiry. On the contrary, to be bias-free probably means to have no opinions. Bias-free individuals will not try to prove anything to each other, so they will not be motivated to do research. Absence of bias may slow down progress in the acquisition of knowledge.
3) To be bias-free means to lose confidence. When a person is biased, they are overconfident in a belief that is not true. Without a doubt, in many situations being overconfident is a bad thing. Even so, being confident allows us to act. We live in a world that is full of ambiguity and uncertainty. If we do not jump to (biased) conclusions, we may find ourselves in a knowledge vacuum, without beliefs or values to stick to. We would doubt too much and do very little.

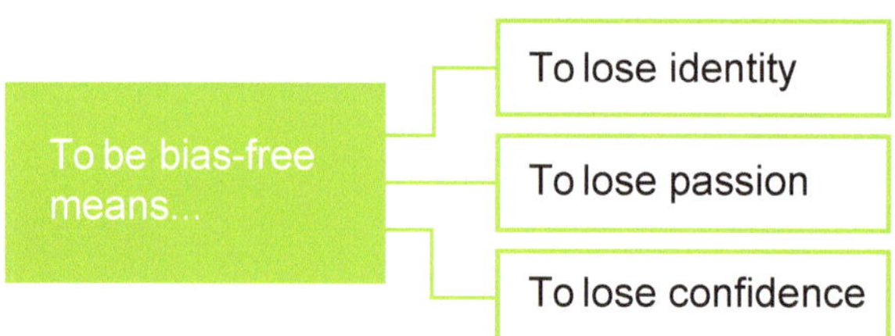

Is it better for a knower to be biased or bias-free? (#Perspectives)

For these reasons, my vote goes to "continue being biased". Biased opinions are very valuable, I think. Even if I was given a chance to eliminate bias, I would not use it.

However, I still think that controlling – not eliminating – our bias to some extent would be nice.

KEY IDEA: Completely eliminating bias from personal knowledge may be undesirable

To what extent can we control our implicit biases?

Research existing in this area suggests that it is possible to control our implicit biases, to some extent. Some strategies attempt to change the biases themselves (for example, changing the way we automatically react to minorities). Other strategies focus on leaving the biases intact, but recognizing them and changing their effect on behavior.

For example, one of the ways that proved to be effective in reducing stereotypes and prejudice is exposure to counter-stereotypical information. This can be something like watching films or simply picturing members of stereotyped groups engaging in counter-stereotypical behavior (female scientists, young presidents, sober rock stars, etc). In one study, Columb and Plant (2010) discovered the "Obama effect": showing people a picture of Barack Obama or even simply his name resulted in a temporary reduction of stereotypes and prejudice against black people. This strategy attempts to change the bias itself.

Another approach is to leave the biases intact (let them be), but learn to notice their effects and counteract these effects when they become undesirable.

This is a hot topic of research. There are some findings that suggest that training yourself to actively counteract the biases that you are aware of may have positive results. Coming back to the shooter bias paradigm, in the work of Mendoza et al. (2010) this strategy is called "reflexive control". Before starting the task, participants in their studies were instructed to use one of the rules:

- If I see a person, then I will ignore his face!
- If I see a person with a gun, then I will shoot!
- If I see a person with an object, then I will not shoot!

As you can see, all of these rules are aimed at separating the relevant aspect of the situation (gun versus a no-gun object) from the irrelevant aspect (race). Before the start of the experiments, participants were instructed to repeat the rule three times and write it down. Results showed that racial bias indeed decreased.

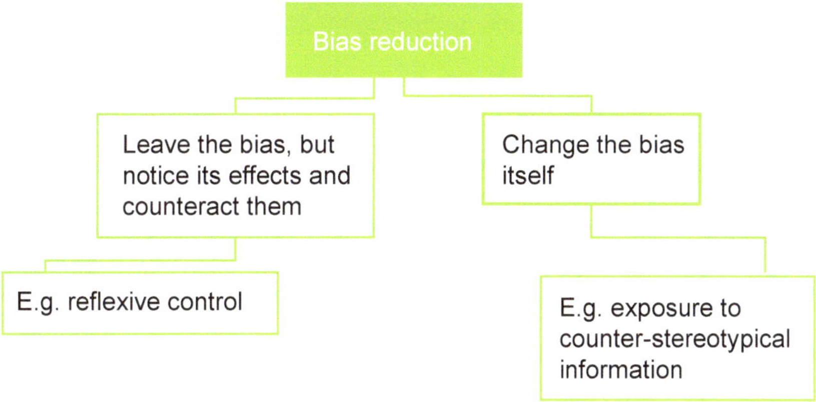

This is good news! It means that we can design relatively simple strategies that will prevent our implicit biases from acting in negative ways. Note that with such strategies, the bias itself is not targeted. We let the bias be, we just try to control the consequences.

This is a little like installing anti-virus software on your system riddled with viruses. It involves work and self-discipline, but it may prove to be fruitful.

KEY IDEA: Bias reduction is possible to some extent. We can either try to change the bias itself or mitigate its effects on behavior.

Critical thinking extension

We may agree at this point that bias in personal knowledge is controllable to some extent, but controlling it is a difficult task that requires constant cognitive effort and perhaps years of specially focused training.

At the heart of this cognitive effort lies the concept of reflexivity. This concept comes from the human sciences. It means the process of considering how the researcher's own mental processes may have influenced results of the research. For example, when an anthropologist observes a remote primitive tribe and sees that they engage in a lot of aggressive behavior, she may conclude that "the tribe in general seems very aggressive to me, but then again when I started this observation I expected them to be a violent tribe. I could have a tendency to notice aggressive behavior and overlook acts of kindness, so my observations should be corroborated by another researcher who does not have such background expectations". This is an example of reflexivity in social research – being aware of a possibility of biased judgment and taking it into account when presenting results.

Where else is reflexivity important? To what extent do you think it is important in areas of knowledge such as history and mathematics?

To what extent can bias in research be reduced through researcher reflexivity? How is it different in different areas of knowledge? (#Perspectives)

If you are interested…

Read the article "Debiasing: How to reduce cognitive biases in yourself and others" on the website *Effectiviology*.

To what extent do you think debiasing strategies are effective?

Take-away messages

Lesson 9. A what-if thought experiment shows that a bias-free society is not a desirable situation. In any case, bias elimination does not seem to be a possibility, but bias reduction could be possible to some extent. Research shows that bias reduction may take one of two forms: either changing the bias itself or leaving it intact but changing its effect on behavior. A large role in bias reduction is played by counter-stereotypical information. Exposing oneself intentionally to counter-evidence may be beneficial. Reflexive control is another key strategy of bias reduction. In this strategy, reflexivity is used to recognize the bias and consciously counteract its effects on thinking and behavior. Bias reduction involves a lot of work and self-discipline.

Lesson 10 - Compos mentis

Learning outcomes

a) [Knowledge and comprehension] What is *compos mentis*?
b) [Understanding and application] What are some arguments for and against moral responsibility for the outcomes of implicit, uncontrollable biases in personal knowledge?
c) [Thinking in the abstract] To what extent are we morally responsible for the outcomes of biases that we are not aware of and can't control?

Key concepts

Compos mentis / non compos mentis, argument from awareness, argument from control, deep self argument

Other concepts used

Awareness, moral responsibility

Themes and areas of knowledge

Theme: Knowledge and the knower

Recap and plan

We have established in the previous lessons that human mental software is riddled with biases. Many of these biases seem unavoidable, even when you are aware of them. Many biases are implicit – this means that they affect our thinking while we are certain that they don't. All this implies one thing: although it may feel like I am in control of my own mind, I am really not.

Should knowers be held responsible for their implicit biases? (#Ethics)

This has an important ethical dimension to it. The question is, since my biases are implicit and unavoidable, should I be held responsible for them?

Since my biases are implicit and unavoidable, should I be held responsible for them?

This is a question with numerous ethical and legal implications. When someone commits a crime, the judge takes into account whether or not the crime was intentional and whether or not it was compos mentis. *Compos mentis* is a Latin expression meaning "having full control of one's mind". If the criminal did not control his actions at the time of committing the crime (in other words, the criminal was non compos mentis), we send him to a mental hospital rather than jail. We do not hold him accountable for his actions and we want him to get treatment rather than punishment.

Can this be extrapolated to other situations? When a stock broker loses millions of dollars' worth of assets because they made a decision that was way too risky, was that their fault or was it the mental software that failed them? When a pilot misreads some data on the dials and puts passengers' lives in danger, is the pilot morally responsible for the mistake or was that the natural limitations of human perception and cognition that we need to blame?

***Image 31**. Most of the time our brain is on autopilot*

Does culpability of an action or a decision depend on the person's amount of self-control? (#Ethics)

There are several approaches to answer these ethical questions – the argument from awareness, the argument from control and the deep self argument.

The argument from awareness

The argument from awareness states that biases are blameworthy only when the subject is consciously aware of them. If you do not suspect you have a bias, then you cannot be blamed for it. Someone who lives in a very sexist society, for example, will probably exhibit sexist attitudes and behavior without ever realizing that there is something wrong with those behaviors. According to the argument from awareness, such sexist attitudes are not blameworthy.

Is bias blameworthy if the knower is not aware of it? (#Ethics)

The problem is that, if we follow the argument from awareness strictly, we must admit that lack of education is a sufficient excuse for immoral actions. Well-educated people will be more aware of their biases, so they hold more moral responsibility for their actions. It makes some sense, but the flipside doesn't: uneducated people are less morally responsible for their immoral behavior. Would you agree, for example, that uneducated people are less morally responsible for racism or sexism?

One way to stick to the argument from awareness and at the same time avoid this problem is to say that it doesn't matter what people *are* aware of, what matters is what they *ought to be* aware of. We may be held accountable for biases that we do not know if we *can* potentially know them. For example, if I am an uneducated person holding racist beliefs, I am still morally accountable for these beliefs as long as I have access to educational resources that I can use if I want. This is somewhat like driving a car without a license: if you get into an accident, you cannot just excuse yourself by saying "Oh, I am not to blame for this accident because I don't have a license and I can't drive". The point is, you *could* get a license and learn to drive, but you didn't.

From this point of view:

- A judge is held accountable for biases in judgment because it is their job to make judgments as impartial as possible, so they ought to take every effort to become aware of their implicit biases. They ought to read available professional literature, carefully consider alternative opinions, reflect on how and why they make decisions.
- A judge from 2020 is more morally responsible for implicit biases in their decisions than a judge from 1960. Back in 1960, scientific research on implicit cognitive biases was in its early stages; humanity was just beginning to get a grip of the idea that our mental software is full of bugs. It has all changed now. Since this knowledge is publicly available, the judge ought to have it, especially if they are involved in high-stakes decision making. They are more morally responsible now for their cognitive biases than they would have been 60 years ago.

Are humans becoming more morally responsible for their biases over the course of time? (#Ethics)

The argument from control

The argument from control holds that we can only be morally responsible for actions that are within our control. Even if we are aware of a bias, we should not be morally responsible for its effects if we are not in the power to control it.

Am I morally responsible for not being able to save a friend from drowning if I tried, but my body was not strong enough to swim against a current? Probably not. I am only blameworthy, it seems, if there's a choice between A and B and it is within my willpower to choose either. This also seems to apply to implicit cognitive biases. Since many of them reside within System 1, they are largely automatic and unconscious. When my brain is on autopilot, I am not really controlling it. Yes, I can override autopilot when necessary (and then I probably become morally responsible for what happens), but most of the time I must rely on autopilot because my cognitive resources are so limited.

However, one might argue that there exists a degree of moral responsibility even when automatic and relatively unconscious actions are involved. Our responsibility may lie not with the autopilot itself, but with knowing when to override it. Just like in a real airplane, the pilot cannot simply turn on the automatics, sit back, relax and blame whatever happens on the machine! The pilot is trained to recognize when it is better to rely on autopilot and when it is time to take over. A failure to recognize the crucial moment may well be within the pilot's moral responsibility.

The deep self argument

The deep self argument claims that subjects can be held morally accountable for all actions they perform, whether or not those actions are within their conscious control or awareness. In other words, even if an action is performed by a part of me that I am not aware of or not in control of, it is still part of my "deep self". I find this position a little scary (am I alone?) – it means that I am morally responsible for all the actions of the horse I am trying to ride, even though this horse has a mind of its own.

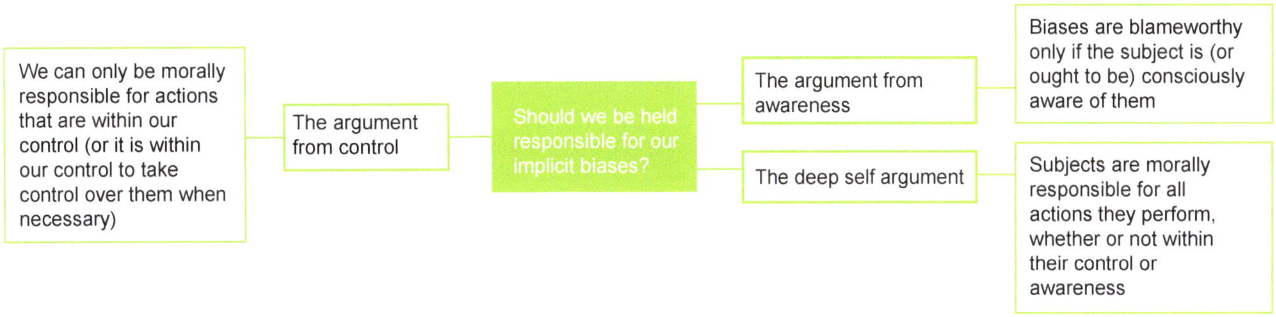

Critical thinking extension

The three arguments presented here form a kind of a continuum. On one extreme, the deep self argument claims that people should be held responsible for all actions and their consequences, even if these actions were a result of deeply implicit biases that the person was not aware of and was not able to control. On the other extreme, the argument from control claims that even if we are aware of a bias, we should not be morally responsible for its outcomes if we cannot control them. The argument from awareness takes the middle ground, claiming that if we are aware of a bias (or can potentially become aware of it), then the responsibility for the outcomes lies with us.

Who should be held accountable for negative consequences of implicit bias?
(#Ethics)

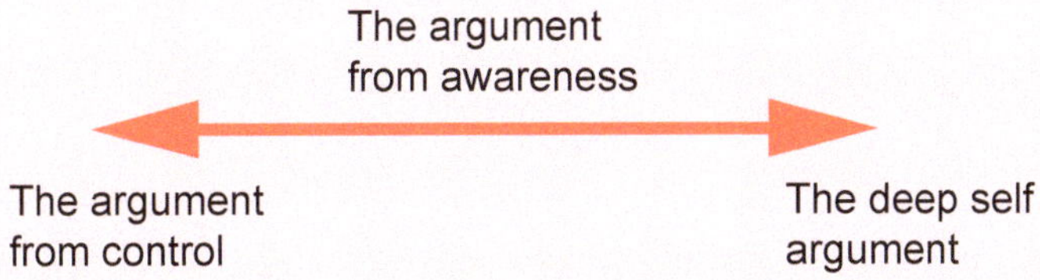

Do you think these ethical considerations are especially applicable to experts who are in a position to make high-stakes decisions affecting other people's lives and well-being? Examples include judges, surgeons, commercial airline pilots, military leaders and presidents.

Even on a much smaller scale, and in everyday thinking and decision-making, do you think we hold moral responsibility for our biased perceptions, attitudes, opinions and utterances?

Interestingly, the more educated and self-aware you become, the less the *non compos mentis* excuse applies to you. Indeed, education is a curse, and greater knowledge implies greater responsibility.

If you are interested...

Study the article "Understanding the law: culpable mental states" (June 26, 2018) on the *U.S. & Texas Lawshield Blog*. This gives you an idea of how the problem of culpability is tackled in today's law.

Read and watch Willingham and Marco's publication "She took her life, but he's accused of helping her and filming it. Is it murder?" (October 21, 2017) for *CNN*. It is a story about a teen who was charged with his friend's suicide. This raises some questions about the limits of criminal culpability.

Take-away messages

Lesson 10. The fact that our mental software is riddled with biases (many of which are implicit and beyond our conscious control) raises an ethical question: if we cannot control biases in our personal knowledge, to what extent should we be held morally responsible for outcomes of such biases? The concept of *compos mentis* ("having full control of one's mind") applies here. Although the concept is widely used in legal practice, it is currently limited to psychiatric cases. However, the problem is philosophical – to what extent are even mentally healthy people in full control of their mind? There are three main approaches to answering this ethical question. The argument from control states that we should not be held morally responsible for outcomes of biases that we are aware of, but cannot control. The argument from awareness states that we should not be held accountable for outcomes of biases that we are not aware of. The deep self argument assumes moral responsibility for all biases, both controllable and not.

Back to the exhibition

I am looking once again at my map of turbulence. I can safely say that I am a lot more confused than I was 10 lessons ago. I am not confused by the map, but by what it represents in terms of personal bias. Well, maybe not confused – more like I can see more sides to it.

Even before the journey that we undertook in this unit, I had realized that some of my fears were irrational. Now, I understand that some of my beliefs systematically deviate from shared knowledge because of distortions introduced by this irrational fear. I overestimate the danger of turbulence because I do not feel comfortable experiencing it, and I underestimate the danger of cars because I am so used to car travel.

In addition to that, I now wonder where these biases come from. They must be connected to my personal and cultural experiences. It is true, though I have travelled by air quite frequently, I never really experienced turbulence that could be categorized as severe. Perhaps it is lack of personal experience that causes me to fill the gaps with assumptions. I also wonder if fear of turbulence is a meme. These turbulence maps are pretty popular, so it must be a meme. Footage of severe turbulence quickly becomes viral, so this meme successfully replicates itself in people's minds. I wonder what the evolutionary advantage of this meme could be. Why is it there?

If it is indeed a meme that is at work here, then perhaps I am nothing more than a vessel meant to run an experimental simulation. Mother Nature infected me with this meme to see how it plays out. OK, I guess I am glad to participate in this global simulation and contribute some data to the cause.

I also wonder if it is even possible for me to reduce bias or even completely eliminate it. Overestimating the danger of turbulence really is just a tip of the iceberg. This is a bias I consciously recognize in myself. Behind it there is a whole army of biases that I am not even aware of, many of them – I am pretty sure – much worse than this one. Can I ever bring them to light and "debias" myself?

I have seen that it is possible to some extent, but also that it requires purposeful and consistent effort, struggling with my own self and slowly trying to gain control over my own mind.

Once I realized that, to what extent am I morally responsible to actually follow this path? It is not easy, so I might prefer to simply stay oblivious to the bugs in my mental software. On the other hand, if it is true that greater knowledge implies greater responsibility, I must fight them now that I realized they are there.

I sigh. It all started with an innocent map of turbulence. Ten lessons later it turned into a set of questions that make me rethink my whole existence. Perhaps turbulence is not what I should be afraid of, after all. Perhaps I should be afraid of my own self.

UNIT 4 - Bias in shared knowledge

UNIT 4 - Bias in shared knowledge

Throughout our discussion of biases in personal knowledge, we have also used shared knowledge as a standard against which these biases are assessed. In other words, if a personal belief consistently deviates from a shared belief, this personal belief is biased.

But what if shared knowledge is biased too? What if physics is biased? What if chemistry is biased? What if mathematics is biased? Is it even possible, and if it is, how do we establish that? In order to see if personal knowledge is biased or not, all we have to do is compare it to shared knowledge. But what do we compare shared knowledge to? These are the questions we will try to untangle.

The way bias manifests itself in different areas of knowledge may be different. For this reason, we will consider areas of knowledge one by one. We will focus on three: Natural Sciences, Mathematics and History. This selection will provide a good variety to work with.

Before that, however, it is important to clarify the key difference between an area of shared knowledge and someone's individual understanding or interpretation of an area of shared knowledge. Bias in physics (shared knowledge) is not the same as bias in someone's understanding of physics. There is a difference between a theory and a naïve theory. We will further unpack the concept of naïve theory in the first introductory lesson of this unit.

Lesson 1 - Naïve theories

Learning outcomes

a) [Knowledge and comprehension] What is a naïve theory?
b) [Understanding and application] How does daily experience influence the formation of naïve theories?
c) [Thinking in the abstract] To what extent is knowledge of naïve theories useful in education?

Key concepts

Naïve theory

Other concepts used

Naïve epistemology, analogy, daily experiences, physical force, statics

Themes and areas of knowledge

Theme: Knowledge and the knower
AOK: Natural Sciences

Recap and plan

I will begin this unit with unpacking the concept of naïve knowledge. It will allow us to draw a clear distinction between bias in shared knowledge and bias in something a particular individual believes to be shared knowledge (do you feel the difference?).

It's a common mistake among students to mix these up, and is a mistake that can cost marks in TOK assessment.

This lesson will also demonstrate how difficult it is sometimes to break free from the trap of our personal experiences to understand and accept shared knowledge. If the journey from (biased) personal knowledge to (unbiased) shared knowledge is that of enlightenment, then naïve theories are very attractive mirages that lure you away from your destination.

***Image 1**. Desert mirage*
(credit: Brocken Inaglory, Wikimedia Commons)

What are naïve theories: definition

Naïve theories are systems of beliefs about the world that people share despite the fact that these systems of beliefs are inaccurate or outdated. Naïve theories are usually the result of misunderstanding of shared knowledge due to the influence of personal experiences.

This is a tough definition, so let's illustrate with an example.

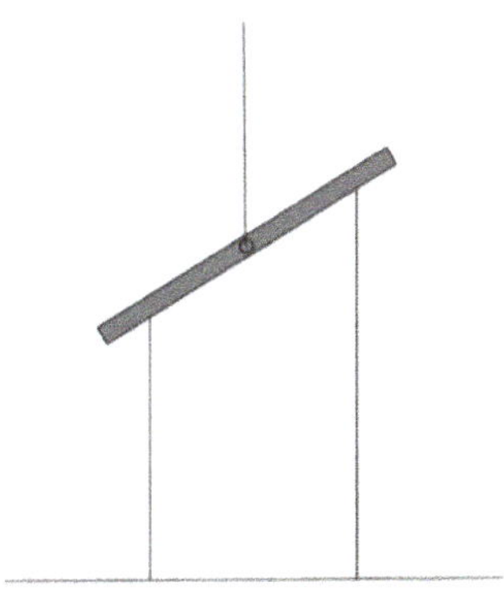

***Image 2**. A rectangular bar suspended on a ceiling, with two supports (based on Roncato & Rumiati, 1986)*

Example: a rectangular bar

In image 2, you can see a suspended rectangular bar which is attached to the ceiling by a cable. The cable runs through a hole exactly in the middle of the bar (the center of gravity), and the bar is free to rotate around this point of suspension. Underneath the bar, there are two supports that hold the whole system in equilibrium.

Your task is to decide what happens when I carefully remove the supports: will the bar change its position and if so, at what point will it come to rest?

To make the task simpler, here are six possible responses:

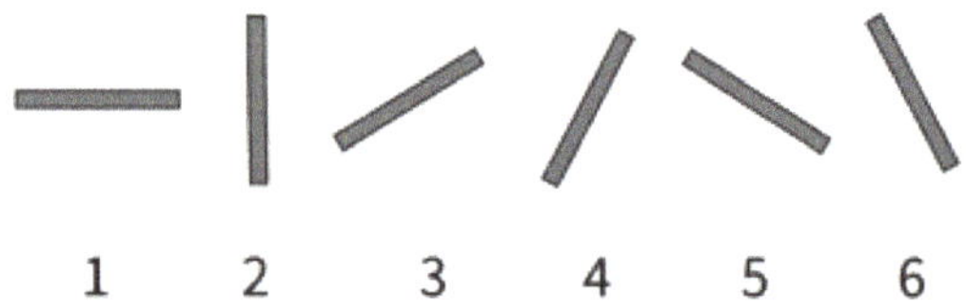

***Image 3**. Possible answers (based on Roncato & Rumiati, 1986)*

What do you think?

This is a task taken from Roncato and Rumiati's (1986) research study where they presented this and similar physics problems to university students.

The correct answer is that, when you carefully remove the supports, the bar will remain slightly tilted and will not move. There is no physical force present that may cause the bar to change its position. The cable runs through the center of gravity, so neither of the sides of the bar is heavier than the other. Yet less than 3% of participants in Roncato & Rumiati's (1986) study gave the correct answer. Most of them (83%) said that the bar will assume the horizontal position.

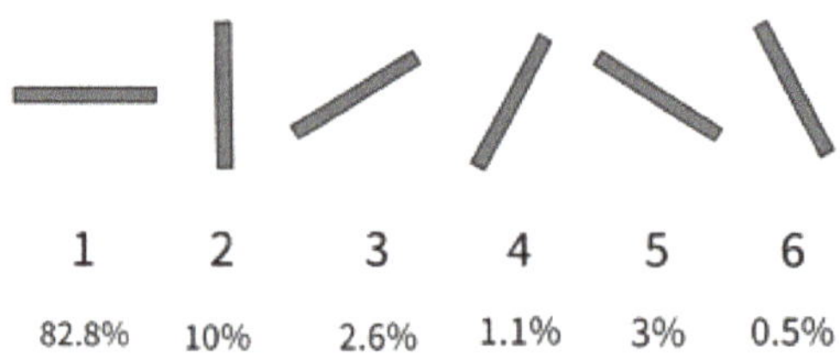

***Image 4**. Results of the study Roncato & Rumiati (1986), p. 364*

The influence of daily experience

Under what circumstances can personal experience be an obstacle for obtaining knowledge? (#Methods and tools)

If we know with certainty (collectively, in our shared knowledge) how the bar must tilt after the supports are removed, why are we (individually) so mistaken about it? Apparently, our everyday experiences come in the way. When deciding what to answer, you probably relied on your past experiences – seeing things such as weighing scales or a seesaw. It is indeed uncommon for two people to freeze mid-air on a seesaw. But the problem is, this analogy does not apply to the suspended bar problem. This is an instance of our everyday experiences interfering in our (correct) logic governed by knowledge of physics.

***Image 5**. Seesaw*

Back to the definition: unpacking

Let us think back to the definition of naïve theories that I gave several paragraphs ago:

KEY IDEA: Naïve theories are systems of beliefs about the world that people share despite the fact that these systems of beliefs are inaccurate or outdated. Naïve theories are usually the result of misunderstanding of shared knowledge due to the influence of personal experiences.

Systems of beliefs about the world: Participants in the study had a certain system of beliefs about how equilibrium works. It is not a standalone belief or idea; it is a whole "theory" which I am sure participants justified somehow.

That people share: The majority of responses in the study were similar (although incorrect), which means that people share certain beliefs about how equilibrium works.

Despite the fact that these systems of beliefs are inaccurate or outdated: The theory of statics in physics conclusively explains, both theoretically and empirically, why the iron bar should not move. So, we have a system of beliefs in physics that supersedes this popular yet inaccurate system of beliefs.

Naïve theories are usually the result of misunderstanding of shared knowledge: When participants in Roncato and Rumiati's study gave their answers, I am sure most of them actually applied their knowledge of physics (or what they thought was physics!), but clearly the application was incorrect.

Due to the influence of personal experiences: This misunderstanding probably occurs because our everyday personal experiences interfere with the "correct" theory; in this case, the mental images of weighing scales and seesaws might be responsible.

There is a whole area of research around such "misunderstood" elements of shared knowledge. It is called *naïve epistemology*. Branches of naïve epistemology include naïve physics, naïve dynamics, naïve ethics (and the list goes on).

Research (such as Clement, 1983) has demonstrated that even students who have taken a Physics course are often susceptible to these mistakes. It is just too difficult to overcome the immediacy of our personal experiences.

What makes educated opinions different from uneducated ones? (#Perspectives)

Do naïve theories repeat mistakes made by scientists in the past?

Some studies suggest that the development of our naïve theories from when we are an infant to when we are an adult may broadly repeat the development of knowledge in human history.

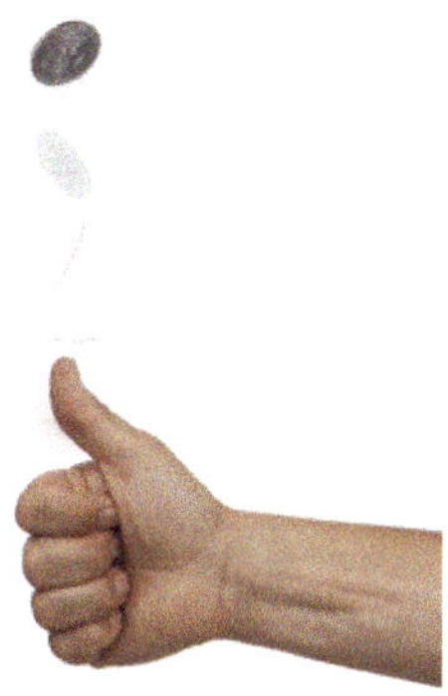

***Image 6**. Coin flip*

Steinberg, Brown and Clement (1990) investigated how Physics students develop their understanding of Physics. For example, we know that, after you toss a coin in the air, there is only one force acting upon it – the force of gravity. When it leaves your hand, the force acting upon it in the upward direction stops acting. Its movement is now inertia. If no other forces were acting upon the coin, it would move indefinitely upwards. But its inertia is counteracted by gravity, so it gradually slows down and then starts moving in the opposite direction. Despite this, only 29 percent of university students correctly said the only force acting upon the coin was the force of gravity. Many others incorrectly drew an upward force vector in the direction of the movement of the coin – a fictitious, unnecessary force from the point of view of the modern physicist.

Steinberg, Brown and Clement (1990) point out that Newton himself struggled with the same misconceptions, and it took him a lot of time and effort to overcome them! They analyzed the development of his ideas in his diaries and other writings that he left behind. They found that he formulated the starting principles of his mechanics when he was 21. Although from our modern point of view only a couple of simple logical steps were left, it took Newton around 20 years to arrive at the final version of his theory. It took that long to let go of the idea that if an object is moving, then there must be some force acting upon it.

To what extent is the history of development of knowledge a history of disillusionment? (#Scope)

This may mean that in your understanding of physics, you go through the same struggles that were faced by Aristotle, Newton, Descartes, Leibniz and Einstein. You may puzzle over the same questions, and you may fall into the same traps. However, you are in a much better position: using the power of collectively accumulated knowledge, you can climb out of the traps much more quickly. Teachers are there to help you. Teachers are hired because they (hopefully!) know the common traps that students fall into and they have designed effective scaffolds to help students navigate their way out of these traps.

***Image 7**. Inertia*

Critical thinking extension

In TOK, it is not enough to arrive at a conclusion. It is important to analyze its implications. Let's apply this to the conclusions that naive theories:

1) are common among students,
2) are caused by the interference from daily experiences, and
3) may repeat the mistakes made by scientists in the past.

If we accept these statements as true, what implications would it have for education? Here are just a couple of examples:

1) Our education is an attempt to override the misconceptions that are there in our brain by default. Our education, therefore, is a constant struggle with ourselves!
2) Studying the work of scientists of the past from the point of view of mistakes they made and difficulties they were facing may prove to be very helpful for education.

Do you agree with these implications? Would you like to add any?

If you are interested...

Watch the explainer video "Common Physics misconceptions" (2012) on the YouTube channel *minutephysics*. How many of these did you personally have? What do you think causes these misconceptions? Perhaps some elements of our everyday experiences?

Take-away messages

Lesson 1. Naïve theories are systems of beliefs that represent a misunderstanding of areas of shared knowledge. Although they may be shared by a large number of people, naïve theories belong to the domain of personal knowledge. Naïve theories are heavily influenced by everyday experiences. This influence needs to be overridden in order to step into the domain of shared knowledge. This is a difficult task reflected in the fact that many scientists of the past struggled with abandoning certain misconceptions. It is likely that students today face the same problems and fall into the same traps. Education is supposed to help students get out of these traps more easily.

4.1 - Bias in Natural Sciences

Natural sciences study the objectively existing world of material things. Therefore, the main point of reference when identifying bias in natural sciences is a deviation from the reality of things. If our beliefs about things deviate from how things really are, then we are dealing with bias. This seems simple enough.

But it's not that simple.

Examples of bias would include all scientific misconceptions and faulty theories that used to be accepted at one time but were later replaced by better theories. The ether theory in physics, the phlogiston theory in chemistry, Lamarckian views of evolution of species, the geocentric model of the world – all these and many other ideas used to be widely accepted but have been replaced.

The key questions that can be asked in this respect are:

- Why do we accept incorrect theories in the first place? Can't we see that these theories have no correspondence to the reality of things?
- What is the best way to establish correspondence between beliefs and reality?
- How do ideas replace each other in sciences? As old ideas get replaced by newer ones, are we getting closer to "the truth"?

To answer these questions, we must consider several key concepts:

- Demarcation criteria
- Falsifiability
- Underdetermination of scientific theories
- Theory-laden facts
- Verisimilitude
- Paradigms and paradigm shifts
- Incommensurability

As all of these concepts are closely linked with bias, they will be the focus of our discussion in the next several lessons.

Exhibition: Refracting telescope

In front of me is a simple refracting telescope. A device that should enable me, as its name suggests, to see (*scopein*) far away (*tele*). Above me is a vast night sky. I want to use my device to see what's out there, to get to know the Universe I live in.

But I have a doubt: will my telescope show me the truth? Will it show me the Universe as it is, without distortions? Can I trust it to be my guide? Will what I see through my telescope be distant celestial objects that are floating out there, or will it be some properties of the telescope itself that I mistake for stars and planets? This can certainly happen if there are dust particles on the lens. I can clean the dust, but how do I know the telescope does not have any other inherent biases? What if the lenses filter something out? What if they give me a distorted image with incorrect angles? If I fail to see something that is actually out there, I can probably live with that. But what if I see something that is *not* out there? That would be very disappointing and misleading.

I usually trust something that I see with my own eyes – but can I have the same amount of trust in something I see through a strange device invented by a scientist?

***Image 8**. Refracting telescope (credit: Mike Peel, Wikimedia Commons)*

My refracting telescope is the simplest of them all. It uses lenses to form an image. The lens bends (refracts) the light from a distant object and focuses it. It can gather more light than the human eye can manage. A telescope working on the same principle was used by Galileo Galilei in his observations (back then, you couldn't just order one on Amazon, so Galilei had to actually construct his own).

Since then, there have been many modifications and all sorts of telescopes working on different principles: reflecting telescopes that use mirrors to collect and focus light; X-ray and infrared telescopes; radio telescopes that have antennas that collect radio waves and microwave radiation; gravitational wave detectors; space telescopes such as the Hubble Space Telescope that is orbiting the Earth.

If I don't trust something as simple as my two-lens telescope to provide an accurate picture of reality, how can I trust something as complicated as a gravitational wave detector?

How do I know that my telescope is not biased?

Story: Discovery of Neptune

When the telescope was invented, scientists meticulously observed the sky and discovered planets in the Solar System that were not visible to the naked eye. For example, the year 1781 saw the discovery of Uranus.

This was also the era of Newtonian mechanics. Newton's (and Kepler's) equations described the motion of celestial objects and explained it by the influence of gravitation. It looked very promising because the planet trajectories that astronomers observed coincided with those predicted from Newton's equations.

But not for Uranus. As astronomers were observing it since its discovery, its orbit did not match precisely with what was expected of it. This could mean that Newton's equations were wrong. Or it could mean that Uranus was influenced by another force that the astronomers were not accounting for. Could this force be gravitational pull from another, unknown planet? If so, then it could be possible to look at Uranus's deviations from the predicted trajectory and use the equations to calculate where this force should be coming from.

In 1845, astronomers Le Verrier and Adams independently carried out calculations to determine the position of this hypothetical unknown planet. In 1846, astronomers at the Berlin Observatory pointed their telescopes at the location predicted by these calculations and voila! They saw a planet that no one had noticed before - Neptune.

In other words, Neptune was mathematically predicted before it was directly observed through a telescope. The magic of this story is that a planet was discovered "with the tip of a pen", from the comfort of a scientist's desk.

To be fair, analysis of old documents reveals that Neptune had actually been observed many times before but had not been recognized as a planet. For example, Galileo observed it in 1612 but mistook it for a distant fixed star. Some great astronomers of the past didn't recognize Neptune even when they looked at it through a telescope, while Le Verrier and Adams did not even have to look at it to know that it's there. Weird, isn't it?

***Image 9**. A photograph of Neptune taken by the Voyager 2 spacecraft in 1989 (credit: Justin Cowart, Wikimedia Commons)*

Lesson 2 - Demarcation problem

Learning outcomes

a) [Knowledge and comprehension] What is a demarcation criterion?
b) [Understanding and application] Why is demarcation based on empirical verification of statements logically flawed?
c) [Thinking in the abstract] How can we draw a line between science and non-science to ensure that what is categorized as science guarantees knowledge that is beyond a reasonable doubt while what is categorized as non-science doesn't?

Key concepts

Demarcation problem, demarcation criterion, verification criterion, pseudo-science, empirical evidence

Other concepts used

Affirming the consequent, phrenology, non-science, logical fallacy

Themes and areas of knowledge

AOK: Natural Sciences

Recap and plan

We have agreed that bias in natural sciences is defined in relation to correspondence to reality. A belief is biased if it does not correspond to how things actually are.

But how exactly do we establish if a belief corresponds to reality? The only access to reality that we have is through experiments, but there is always a possibility that experiments themselves are flawed.

What we can do, however, is make sure that our knowledge is "true beyond a reasonable doubt". We acknowledge that we will never know *for certain* if a belief is true or not, but at least we can guarantee that we have done everything we can to ensure that it is. This guarantee is a sign of quality that science is supposed to provide.

The demarcation problem is the problem of distinguishing between science and non-science. This problem is fundamental because science provides the guarantee whereas non-science does not. This lesson will give an introduction into the demarcation problem.

Demarcation criteria

Criteria that draw a line between science and non-science are known as demarcation criteria.

KEY IDEA: The demarcation problem is the problem of telling the difference between science (which provides a guarantee that our knowledge is true beyond a reasonable doubt) and non-science (which does not). Demarcation criteria are criteria used to draw the line.

So, what is the difference between science and non-science? The question sounds really simple, but it has puzzled philosophers of science for centuries.

How can we establish the difference between science and non-science? (#Scope)

Give it a thought… I will give you a number of options (many of which are popular responses given by my students who are starting on their TOK journey):

a) Science is "accepted".
b) Science uses scientific terminology.
c) Science is "precise". It uses measurement and calculations to arrive at precise conclusions.
d) Unlike non-science, science is supported by evidence.

Which of the options would you choose?

Option (a) does not seem to work because non-scientific ideas can be easily and widely accepted by the general public. Conspiracy theories are very popular. Many people have a personal astrologer or an aura cleanser. Many people use the services of mediums to communicate with their dead relatives. Bottom line, as Michael Shermer put it in one of his TED talks related to debunking myths, "Let's face it, there's a lot of bunk out there".

Therefore, whether or not the belief is accepted by the scientific community needs to be a consequence of the scientific merit of this belief, not the other way around.

Option (b) seems to be wrong because pseudo-sciences actually do a great job of inventing unnecessary terminology to sound all science-y to make up for the lack of substance. For example, in ufology (the study of UFO, unidentified flying objects) there are terms for:

Image 10. UFO

What it means	The term
Seeing the UFO less than 500 feet away	Close encounter of the first kind
Seeing it and experiencing other physical effects (trembling ground, paralysis, etc.)	Close encounter of the second kind
Encountering a UFO as well as its pilots (the actual aliens)	Close encounter of the third kind
Encountering a UFO and being abducted by the pilots	Close encounter of the fourth kind
Engaging in a conversation with aliens	Close encounter of the fifth kind
Death as a result of the UFO sighting	Close encounter of the sixth kind
The creation of a human / alien hybrid, for example, by sexual reproduction	Close encounter of the seventh kind

Just because it sounds fancy does not mean that it is scientific.

What makes the scientific method scientific? (#Methods and tools)

Option (c) is attractive but also wrong.

Non-science can also use precise measurements. For example, phrenology was a pseudo-science that involved measuring bumps on a person's head to predict their abilities. It was based on the idea that certain abilities are localized in certain parts of the brain, so bigger brain parts should be associated with greater abilities. By measuring the skull, Franz Joseph Gall (who developed phrenology in 1796) claimed to be able to predict a person's skills and talents as well as personality traits, thoughts and emotions. Phrenologists had highly elaborate charts of the human skull showing which skill resides where. Gall even opened a laboratory in which he charged people good money to have their children assessed by skull measurement and people made important school and career decisions for their kids based on that information.

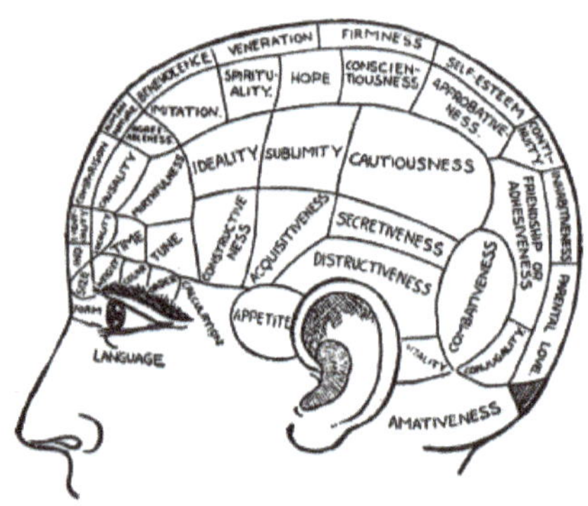

Image 11. A phrenology brain chart

Finally, option (d) is a really attractive option that most students settle with, after some debate. It seems right: something is indeed scientific if you can support it by empirical evidence. "Empirical" means based on observation and experience, and it is the opposite of "theoretical". Empirical evidence demonstrates correspondence (between the belief and reality) and hence truth of the belief. This option is also known as the verification criterion.

KEY IDEA: Empirical evidence is evidence based on observing reality. It is the opposite of theoretical. Empirical evidence is instrumental in the correspondence test for truth, which claims that a belief is true if it corresponds to reality.

Verification criterion

The verification criterion claims the following:

Scientific knowledge is true if there exists empirical evidence supporting it. A theory is scientific if its claims are verifiable by evidence. The goal of scientists is to attempt to find empirical support for the theory.

It won universal acceptance in the 19th – 20th century. It was initially suggested by members of the so-called Vienna Circle, an influential group of philosophers.

Criticism of the verification criterion

However, despite its intuitive attractiveness, the verification criterion is logically flawed. The fact that we found some supporting evidence does not necessarily mean that our belief is true. Logically speaking, the verification criterion is based on a logical fallacy known as "*affirming the consequent*":

If p then q
q
Hence, p

P and q here are any simple statements. Affirming the consequent is a fallacy because, although p is a possible condition for q, p is not the *only* condition for q. To make it clear, let's replace p and q with something meaningful, for example:

(1)
If my theory is correct, then this observation will support my theory
This observation supports my theory
Hence, my theory is correct

(2)
If it rains, rooftops are wet
Rooftops are wet
Hence, it rains

The problem with this logical strategy is that the conclusion is not certain. In fact, I should add one key word in the conclusion:

If p then q
q
Hence, *possibly* p

Is empirical evidence the ultimate judge of scientific claims? (#Perspectives)

The word "possibly" is crucial here. While we know that *q* must be true if *p* is true, we should not forget that *q* may also be true for some other *non-p* reason. While we know that rooftops must be wet every time it rains, they can also be wet because kids were throwing water balloons at it. Similarly, if my theory is actually true, then all my observations must support it, but if this particular observation supports my theory it does not necessarily mean that the theory is true.

***Image 12**. Logical fallacy*

Karl Popper, an influential 20th-century philosopher of science, asserted that using the verification criterion as the main demarcation line between science and non-science is useless and even dangerous. It leads to a situation where attempts of scientists are targeted at finding supporting evidence for their theories, but such attempts are a waste of time if we want to be certain about what we know. We can find supporting evidence for anything if we try hard enough. And no matter how much supporting evidence we find, it will not be enough to accept the theory with certainty.

So, if the verification criterion doesn't work, what works? This will be the focus of the next lesson.

Critical thinking extension

The demarcation problem is closely linked to the concept of pseudo-science. Pseudo-sciences are systems of beliefs that claim to be scientific but in fact do not provide the guarantee of knowledge that is true "beyond a reasonable doubt". In other words, pseudo-science is non-science disguised as science.

Who should be held responsible for misleading beliefs? (#Ethics)

Commonly mentioned examples of pseudo-sciences include astrology, ufology, homeopathy, alchemy, alternative medicine, crystology and occultism.

Since pseudo-sciences can do a good job presenting themselves as "genuine" science, it is also useful to know the common features that may help us identify a pseudo-scientific belief when we encounter one. Such features include:

- Use of vague or untestable claims
- Post-hoc exceptions (tweaking the original belief slightly to explain conflicting evidence)
- Lack of openness to peer testing
- Use of misleading language

Based on your own experience with pseudo-sciences, what would your personal indicators be?

If you are interested...

Watch the enlightening TED talk "Why people believe weird things" by Michael Shermer (2006), a skeptic who explains why weird myths, superstitions and urban legends may be so attractive to people.

Also note how he discusses standards of "good science" in debunking these myths. In particular, he makes the following claim: "Science is not a thing. It's a verb. It's a way of thinking about things". What does he mean by that?

Take-away messages

Lesson 2. The demarcation problem is the problem of drawing the line between science and non-science. The main criterion of truth in natural sciences is the correspondence of beliefs to reality. Science cannot ensure the correspondence with complete certainty, but using standards of science implies providing a guarantee that we have done all we can to ensure the correspondence beyond a reasonable doubt. There are many approaches to defining how this guarantee can be provided, and hence there have been multiple demarcation criteria. One that gained prominence is the verification criterion, but it is not without problems.

Lesson 3 - Falsifiability

Learning outcomes

a) [Knowledge and comprehension] What is the falsification criterion?
b) [Understanding and application] How can the falsification criterion be applied to the problem of drawing a line between science and non-science?
c) [Thinking in the abstract] What could be the arguments against using falsifiability as the demarcation criterion?

Key concepts

Falsification criterion, falsifiability, confirmation bias

Other concepts used

Modus tollens (denying the consequent), multiverse theory

Themes and areas of knowledge

AOK: Natural Sciences

Recap and plan

We have considered the demarcation problem – the problem of drawing the line between science and non-science. We have seen that it's not an easy task. The verification criterion seemed to provide a good solution with a focus on correspondence between beliefs and reality. However, it appears that the verification criterion was based on flawed logic.

At the same time, finding a reliable demarcation is essential for defining bias in natural sciences. Non-sciences cannot guarantee that every effort has been made to ensure that a belief is true beyond a reasonable doubt. On the other hand, science does provide this guarantee, and as a part of that guarantee it makes sure that all known biases have been checked and controlled.

In this lesson, we will unpack the falsification criterion and the concept of falsifiability. This criterion was proposed by Karl Popper to replace the verification criterion and overcome its flawed logic.

Attack on verificationism and confirmation bias

Can knowledge that is less than certain be accepted as scientific knowledge? (#Perspectives)

As you remember from the previous lesson, the fundamental problem with the verification criterion is that it's based on a logical fallacy known as "*affirming the consequent*". Supporting evidence for a hypothesis does not confirm the hypothesis conclusively, only probabilistically. No matter how much supporting evidence we find, we can never claim that the hypothesis has been "fully" supported.

Image 13. Confirmation bias (credit: Peter Dashevici, Flickr)

Moreover, using the verification criterion as the main guideline for scientists also pushes them toward being susceptible to confirmation bias. Confirmation bias is the tendency to focus on evidence that supports your expectation or theory and ignore evidence that contradicts it. If the focus in scientific endeavors is on finding supporting evidence, then that may reinforce confirmation bias because scientists will be reluctant to look for contradictory evidence.

KEY IDEA: Confirmation bias is the tendency to focus on evidence that supports an expectation and ignore evidence that contradicts it. The verification criterion is dangerous because it encourages confirmation bias.

In scientific search, to what extent are mistakes more valuable than lucky guesses? (#Methods and tools)

The falsification criterion

As a solution to this, Karl Popper (1963) proposed the falsification criterion. The falsification criterion claims that:

A theory is scientific if it attempts to find refuting evidence for its claims. A theory is not scientific if its claims are not falsifiable; that is, if it is impossible to carry out a study that could potentially prove the theory wrong. We accept scientific knowledge as provisionally true if we try to refute it but fail. We can only reject theories with certainty, but we can never "prove" a scientific theory.

The logical strategy that underlies the falsification criterion is known as "*modus tollens*" (denying the consequent):

If p, then q
Not q
Hence, not p

For example:

(1)
If my theory is correct, then this observation will support my theory
But this observation does not support my theory
Hence, my theory is (*certainly*) incorrect

(2)
If it rains, rooftops must be wet
But rooftops are not wet
Hence, it (*certainly*) is not raining

Note how in these examples, unlike the equivalent examples that we used for the verification criterion, it becomes possible to claim the conclusion with absolute certainty.

The big take-away message here is that, unfortunately, we can only reliably refute scientific theories, but not "prove" them. There is no such thing as a true scientific theory – only a theory that we provisionally accept as true because it has not been refuted yet. But if that is the case, efforts of scientists should be directed toward seeking contradictory evidence, not supporting evidence. We should try to falsify our own theories. To the extent that we try to do so but fail, our confidence in the theory will increase.

KEY IDEA: Scientific knowledge is falsifiable. Any non-falsifiable claim is not scientific.

As for the science versus non-science demarcation, any theory that is scientific must be in principle falsifiable.

There are many examples of unfalsifiable theories out there. Religion is not falsifiable: can you possibly design an experiment that will demonstrate that God does *not* exist? Astrological predictions (horoscopes) are not falsifiable. Here is one, taken from a random website:

But this month, as the Sun glides through Taurus until May 21, you may actually welcome a little shake-up to the status quo. Your wants and needs—or at least the process of discovering what those are—can take priority now. It's okay if you're starting from a totally blank slate, even if that feels scary.

(https://astrostyle.com/)

***Image 14**. Falsifiability*

What should happen for you to be able to say that this horoscopic prediction was wrong? It's such a vague description that to test its correctness is nearly impossible.

Are scientists ethically responsible for trying to prove themselves wrong? (#Ethics)

But there are also non-falsifiable beliefs lurking within well-established areas of knowledge and fields of research. The *multiverse theory* in physics, for example, is an idea that fits the data we currently have, but we don't really have any way to falsify this theory at the moment. What data should we obtain to be able to claim that the multiverse theory is definitively false? If you manage to answer the question, please don't forget to apply for the Nobel Prize.

Four-card problem

To demonstrate the falsification criterion as an example of "proper" scientific thinking, let me use the classic Wason's (1968) four-card problem.

In his research, Wason gave participants sets of four cards like the one shown below, together with a rule, such as: "Every card with a vowel on one side has an even number on the reverse side".

***Image 15**. Wason's four-card task (an example)*

The task is to say which cards you will turn over in order to test the rule. Most participants in Wason's research said either "A" or "A and 4", but these answers are either incorrect or not optimal. Let us look at the task more closely.

- *Turning over card A*: If there's an even number on the reverse side, it will support the hypothesis. But if there's an odd number on the other side, it will refute the hypothesis. Card A can potentially both support and refute the rule.
- *Turning over card D* is not informative because the rule says nothing about cards that have a consonant on one of the sides. It can neither support nor refute the rule.
- *Turning over card 4*: If there's a vowel on the reverse side, it will support the hypothesis. But if there's a consonant on the other side, the rule will not be refuted. In other words, turning card 4 can only support the hypothesis but cannot refute it.
- *Turning over card 7*: If there's a vowel on the other side, the rule will be refuted. But if there's a consonant on the other side, it will neither support nor refute the rule.

Is there any place for non-falsifiable claims in science? (#Scope)

In other words, the two cards that can potentially support the rule are A and 4. The two cards that can potentially refute the rule are A and 7.

From the point of view of the falsification criterion (which is widely accepted in today's scientific methodology), the correct answer is A and 7. People who choose card 4 demonstrate confirmation bias – they are choosing a card which can potentially only support the rule.

To summarize, falsifiability of a statement means that it can potentially be proven wrong. According to the falsification criterion, science is falsifiable and any non-falsifiable claim is not scientific.

Critical thinking extension

Criticism of Karl Popper: Imre Lakatos

Although falsifiability as a demarcation criterion of scientific knowledge is widely accepted today, there are some significant points of criticism of Popper's approach. Imre Lakatos (1922 - 1974) is one of the critics.

Popper's theory depends on the assumption that a test can either conclusively corroborate or conclusively falsify a theory. However, Lakatos argued that, in reality, big decisions about a theory are not made based on separate experiments. Failure to corroborate a theory does not necessarily mean falsification of the theory.

KEY IDEA: Failure to corroborate a theory does not necessarily mean falsification of the theory

Imagine that Le Verrier and Adams and the astronomers who checked their predictions (see *Story: Discovery of Neptune*) failed to corroborate the theory. Imagine that the astronomers pointed their telescopes at the location predicted by Le Verrier and Adams and saw nothing. Would that mean that Newton's system of laws had to be rejected? Yes, from the point of view of Popper, but that is not what actually happens.

The failure could be attributed to multiple factors including measurement error, unanticipated confounding variables, etc. In practice, according to Imre Lakatos, theories are never refuted based on a small number of "critical tests". There exists contradictory evidence, and a theory is trying to deal with this evidence by adjusting itself through auxiliary hypotheses.

What other criticisms of Popper's approach can you think of?

If you are interested...

Watch the episode entitled "Karl Popper, science, & pseudoscience: Crash course philosophy #8" (2016) on the YouTube channel *CrashCourse*.

Take-away messages

Lesson 3. The falsification criterion of demarcation proposed by Karl Popper in place of the verification criterion is based on the logical "*modus tollens*". According to this criterion, scientific claims, unlike non-scientific ones, must be falsifiable. This means that it must be possible to refute them experimentally. The "correct" focus of scientific endeavors is on looking for evidence to contradict one's theories rather than support them. Scientific theories can never be "proven", but the longer we are trying to falsify them and fail, the more confident we are in accepting these theories provisionally. Such attempts at falsification enable us to guarantee that we have made every possible effort to eliminate bias. Although the falsification criterion is widely accepted today, it has been criticized on the basis that in real scientific practice, a stand-alone contradictory observation is rarely enough to refute a theory because the observation itself may be doubted.

Lesson 4 - Scientific progress

Key concepts

Scientific progress, forward-looking and backward-looking scientific goals, the realist approach to scientific progress, the puzzle-solving approach to scientific progress

Other concepts used

Aims of science: accuracy, consistency, scope, simplicity, fruitfulness

Themes and areas of knowledge

AOK: Natural Sciences

Learning outcomes

a) [Knowledge and comprehension] What is scientific progress and what are the two ways of looking at it (forward-looking and backward-looking scientific goals)?
b) [Understanding and application] How can we judge if an "improvement" has occurred when an older theory is being replaced by a newer one?
c) [Thinking in the abstract] With multiple criteria of progress, how can we be certain that scientific development is progressive?

Recap and plan

We have looked at the demarcation problem and falsifiability as the line between science and non-science. Standards of falsifiability ensure that we have done everything we can to test our beliefs. We can never be certain that our beliefs are true, but at least falsifiable scientific research provides the guarantee that it is beyond a reasonable doubt.

But even with these rigorous standards, scientific beliefs may turn out to be false. Scientific beliefs have been revised multiple times in the history of science. A theory that is rejected in light of new contradicting evidence may be said to be "biased" because it was based on false assumptions which consistently led to conclusions that did not reflect the reality of things. Of course, we can only know if a theory is biased *after* we have rejected it. If an unbiased theory existed, we would never be able to recognize it as unbiased!

KEY IDEA: We can only know if a theory is biased after we have rejected it

This brings up an interesting question – how does science develop? How are biased theories replaced with less biased ones? Can we even claim that scientific knowledge is becoming more correspondent to reality, and thus less biased? In this lesson, we begin answering these questions by unpacking the concept of scientific progress.

What is progress?

Progress is different from development. Development is any change from point A to point B, whereas progress implies that B is in some way an improvement over A. This means that in order to judge whether or not progress has occurred, we must first agree on what counts as "improvement" in science. For that, we need to agree on what the goals of science are.

***Image 16**. Progress*

Although it sounds simple, the problem is that it is not easy to define goals of science. Scientists themselves have very different ideas about it. Two very popular standpoints are:

1) The goal of science is to find out the truth
2) The goal of science is to gain knowledge

I am sure you can sense how dramatically different these two goals are! I am being sarcastic, of course. But there is a difference, and an important one.

> Is having a biased theory better than having no theory at all? (#Methods and tools)

Suppose there existed a theory that was accepted at time point A, but refuted in light of new evidence at time point B. Nothing was proposed to replace the old theory. Does that count as progress? On the one hand, we now know that the theory was false. In this sense, we have gained some knowledge. On the other hand, we can hardly claim that we have gotten closer to the truth. We used to have a theory at least, and now we have nothing. So, have we made progress or not?

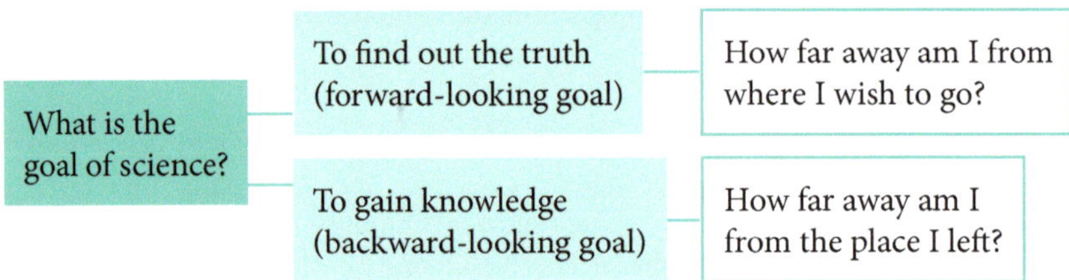

Forward-looking versus backward-looking scientific goals

Some scholars describe this dilemma as forward-looking versus backward-looking scientific goals (Niiniluoto, 2015).

- A forward-looking goal is a measure of the distance from the destination that I wish to reach eventually (how far am I from where I wish to go?).
- A backward-looking goal is a measure of the distance from my starting point (how far away am I from the place I left?).

The problem with forward-looking goals is that, if my destination is the truth, I don't actually know what it is or where it is, so how can I measure my distance from it? Suppose I am leaving Sydney and travelling to Tokyo, but "Tokyo" is actually a mystical place the location of which I do not know. If someone asks me, "How far away are you?", what should I say? While idealistically forward-looking goals remain our main guiding principle, in reality backward-looking goals is the only measure of success that we seem to have. So, I will probably reply "Hopefully close enough because I have been travelling for ages".

KEY IDEA: The problem with forward-looking goals of progress is that, if the goal of science is the truth, we don't know what it is or where it is

Theories of scientific progress

Obviously, just as there exist various views on the goals of science, there also exist different approaches to scientific progress. To illustrate, I will give you two examples, one based on a forward-looking goal of science and another based on a backward-looking goal.

> Can we claim that scientific knowledge is becoming less biased over time? (#Perspectives)

1) The realist approach to scientific progress suggests that theories may have a truth value (in other words: there are true scientific theories and there are false scientific theories). Applied to scientific progress, this means that we can use closeness to the truth as our measure of progress.

This approach is based on a forward-looking goal of science (to find out the truth). A famous proponent of this approach is Karl Popper. He thought that with the course of time scientific theories are getting closer and closer to the truth.

Note that this applies even to those parts of a theory that cannot be directly corroborated by observation. For example, we cannot see the edge of the Universe and neither can we "see" its infinity. We cannot see events in the past of the Universe such as the Big Bang. And yet, we have theories about such things. The realist view suggests that such theories may be true or false, and that although we have no direct access to the truth, we can assess it indirectly through the (limited) things that we can observe.

***Image 17**. Karl Popper (1902 – 1994)*

2) The puzzle-solving approach to scientific progress was suggested by Thomas Kuhn (1962). He rejected the idea that we can use the mysterious concept of the "truth" in defining scientific progress. If Tokyo is a mysterious place and my knowledge of its location is merely a guess, how can I use it as a measure of progress? Instead, Kuhn viewed science as a puzzle-solving activity.

Every theory produces a large number of problems ("puzzles"): there are always observations that do not fit, aspects of reality that the theory can't explain, prior knowledge that the theory contradicts, and so on.

Which is a better description of the goal of science: to gain knowledge or to find out the truth? (#Scope)

Sometimes, attempts to solve puzzles are productive and theories become better: they explain more, their predictions come true more often, they contain a smaller number of contradictions with prior knowledge. Sometimes, a theory comes to a dead end and is replaced by another theory. In any case, as science develops, more and more puzzles can be solved, therefore, we gain new knowledge.

***Image 18**. Portrait of Thomas Kuhn (1922 – 1996) (credit: Davi.trip, Wikimedia Commons)*

KEY IDEA: The puzzle-solving approach rejects the idea of scientific "truth". It judges scientific progress by the ability of theories to solve more puzzles. If a new theory can solve more puzzles, it replaces the old theory. But solving more puzzles does not necessarily mean being closer to the truth.

At the same time, being able to solve more puzzles does not necessarily mean being closer to the truth. You can compare this process to the evolution of species. Evolution is not guided by a mysterious "master plan". It is a trial-and-error process that results in selecting organisms that are better adapted to the given demands of the environment. Can we say that the selected species are the "best possible" species, a biological version of the "truth"? No. But we can say that it is better adapted to the environment than the previous species that it replaced (that it solves more "puzzles").

Let's summarize all that has been said in the table below.

Approach to scientific progress	The realist approach	The problem-solving approach
Who	Karl Popper	Thomas Kuhn
Scientific goal	Forward-looking	Backward-looking
Is there scientific truth?	Yes	We cannot know
Is development progressive?	Yes	We cannot know

Coming back to the beginning of the lesson, do you now see the immense difference between the following statements?

Under what circumstances should we value false knowledge? (#Ethics)

1) The goal of science is to find out the truth
2) The goal of science is to gain knowledge

Critical thinking extension

Multi-dimensional goals of science

Defining scientific progress becomes even more complicated when you acknowledge that the goal of science does not have to be unidimensional. For example, Thomas Kuhn (1977) named the following goals that science must strive to maximize: accuracy, consistency, scope, simplicity and fruitfulness.

Needless to say, when your goal is multi-dimensional, there will be theories that achieve one aspect but fail at some other aspects (for example, a theory that explains a lot and seems to be true, but so horrendously complicated that it is difficult to base any research on it).

In this case, how do you judge scientific progress?

If you are interested...

Watch the video "Theory change and scientific realism" (2018) on the YouTube channel *Serious Science*. In this short video, John Worrall, professor of Philosophy of Science at the London School of Economics and Political Science, unpacks the principles of scientific realism.

As a contrasting viewpoint, watch the video "Scientific correctness versus scientific progress" (2019) on the YouTube channel *ThunderboltsProject*. In this video, author Mel Acheson claims that the concept of "scientific correctness" can ultimately impede scientific progress.

Take-away messages

Lesson 4. Development is any change from A to B, but progress is a type of development where B constitutes some kind of improvement over A. If bias in scientific beliefs is a deviation from correspondence to reality, then the concept of scientific progress implies that scientific theories are getting closer to the truth and thus less biased. This is a definition based on a forward-looking goal of science (finding out the truth). The problem with it is that we have no direct access to the truth, and many scholars have rejected the idea that we can somehow judge whether one theory is "closer to the truth" than another. Instead, these scholars suggested using backward-looking goals of science (gaining more knowledge). An example is Thomas Kuhn's approach where the quality of a scientific theory is judged by the number of problems (puzzles) that it can solve, whereas the concept of truth is altogether avoided.

Lesson 5 - Underdetermination of scientific theories

Learning outcomes

a) [Knowledge and comprehension] What does it mean that scientific theories are "underdetermined" by evidence? Is underdetermination of scientific theories inevitable?
b) [Understanding and application] What are some examples of underdetermination of scientific theories, both from human and natural sciences?
c) [Thinking in the abstract] If two theories fit the available data equally well, how do we choose the one that is (presumably) closer to the truth?

Key concepts

Underdetermination of theory by evidence

Other concepts used

Singularity, red shift, background cosmic radiation, correlation

Themes and areas of knowledge

AOK: Natural Sciences, Human Sciences

Recap and plan

We have seen that falsifiability provides a rigorous standard that enables science to guarantee that its knowledge is true beyond a reasonable doubt. In other words, falsifiability is a cure against bias.

But there are two key problems in natural sciences that make things very complicated:

- The problem of underdetermination of theory by evidence. In a nutshell, the problem is that a scientific theory is always larger than the supporting data it's based upon, so falsifiability is not sufficient to guarantee its truth.
- The problem of theory-laden facts. In a nutshell, a scientific observation (which is used to falsify a theory) is itself dependent on theory. So how can something which is not independent from theory be used to falsify this very theory? This leads us to doubt the power of falsifiability as a demarcation criterion.

I know this is bit too much to digest, so in the next two lessons we are going to look at these two problems, one at a time.

Underdetermination of theory by data

When two theories fit available data equally well, how do we select a better theory? (#Perspectives)

The image below shows some data points in a two-dimensional space. Let's imagine that this data came from a small survey asking IB students how many hours a week they typically spend doing homework and also recording their average grade. Suppose the X axis is hours of homework per week and the Y axis is the grade. Each point on the graph, then, is a student.

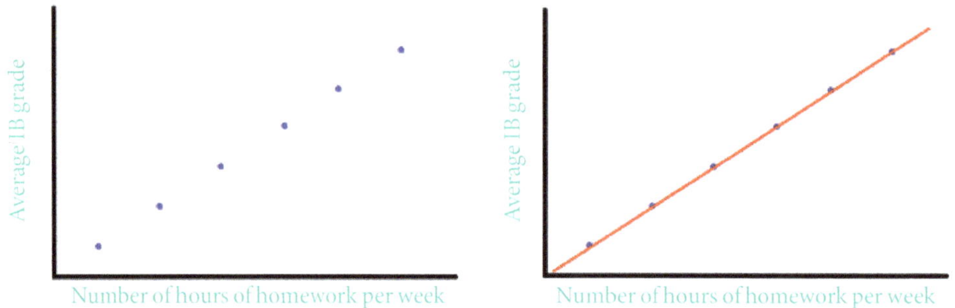

Image 19*. Trend line: option (a)*

Your task is to draw a trend line that connects all of these data points. You will quickly realize that, although in this particular situation there is one trend line that seems most probable (a straight line), the number of different lines you can draw so that all dots are connected is actually very large. In fact, mathematically speaking, it's infinite.

For example, here is one possibility:

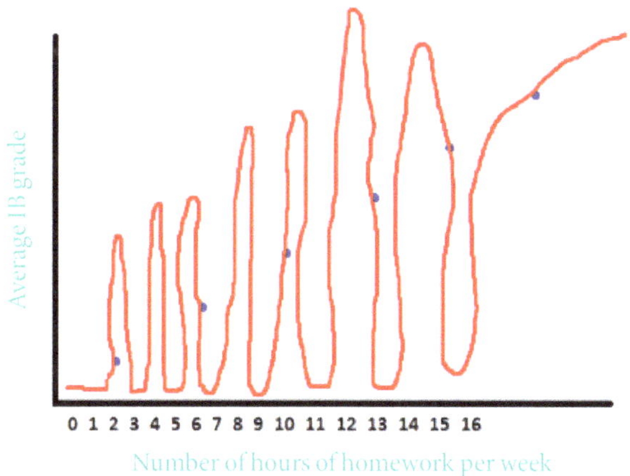

Image 20*. Trend line: option (b)*

This shows how students who spend an odd number of hours per week doing homework generally do much worse in their IB subjects than students who spend an even number of hours doing homework.

If this happened in a real-life research project, you would probably prefer explanation (a) to explanation (b). But this is because of your theoretical expectations: you have a theory that more effort leads to higher grades. On the contrary, you do not have a theory for odd versus even number of hours. But this is a theory-driven decision; there is nothing in the data itself to suggest that one explanation is more suitable than the other. In this very sense, the theory (the trend line) is underdetermined by data (the dots).

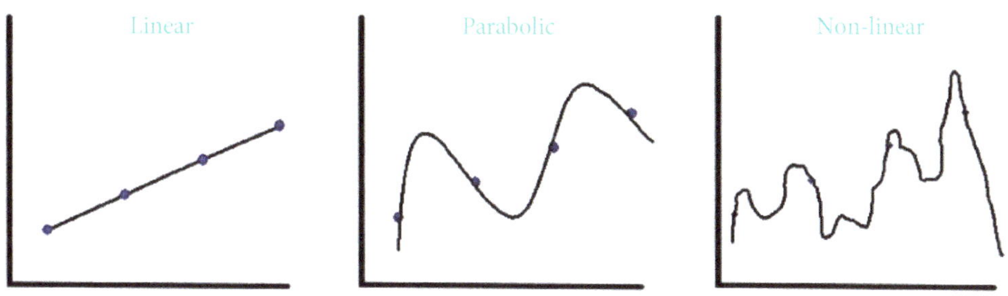

Image 21*. Underdetermination of theory by evidence (connecting the dots metaphor)*

KEY IDEA: Underdetermination of theory by data is the idea that a scientific theory can never be fully reduced to supporting evidence. Because of this, more than one explanation can usually be fit to the available evidence.

Can a scientific theory ever be fully supported by empirical data? (#Methods and tools)

Underdetermination of theory by data is the idea that a scientific theory can never be fully reduced to supporting evidence. There is always some speculation involved in the theory, something that goes beyond the supporting evidence. Because of this, it is usually the case that more than one explanation can fit to the same dataset. From the point of view of the correspondence test for truth, all such explanations must be equally accepted because they have the same amount of evidence to support them. But we can't equally accept rival theories. This means that we should have a way to prefer one explanation to another, based on criteria other than correspondence to reality.

Theories are underdetermined by data	Hence, there can be more than one theory fitting the same dataset	Hence, to select one of these theories we need criteria that are not based on evidence

I will finish this lesson with two examples illustrating this point – one from human sciences and one from natural sciences.

Example 1 (human sciences) – correlational evidence

A correlation between two variables underdetermines the belief we have about the relationship between these variables. In the example that we used above, suppose you observe a positive correlation: the more hours spent doing homework, the higher the IB grades.

There are at least three ways to explain this correlation:

1) Effort influences grades: doing more homework improves your knowledge and abilities, so you do better at exams.
2) Grades influence effort: students who happen to get high grades feel obligated to live up to their teachers' expectations so they have to spend more time doing homework.
3) There is a mysterious third variable that we have not measured that influences both grades and effort: for example, students who are conscientious get better grades (because they work better in class) and spend a lot of time doing homework (because they want to impress teachers).

Which of the three explanations would you prefer and why? Whatever your reasons, they will not be based on the dataset because all three explanations fit the data equally well. This is especially pertinent to human sciences.

Observation	Explanation	Notation
A correlates with B	A influences B	A → B
	B influences A	B → A
	C influences both A and B	C → A C → B

Example 2 (natural sciences) – alternatives to the Big Bang theory

What is the role of rival theories in the development of scientific beliefs? (#Scope)

The Big Bang theory is widely accepted today as the leading cosmological theory. This model claims that the Universe started from the so-called *singularity* – an infinitely small and incredibly dense object, the matter of our whole Universe packed in a tiny particle. The singularity then exploded, sending all the matter packed within it to fly apart. The Universe began in a hot dense state, and over the course of time it has been expanding, cooling down and becoming less dense.

The two major pieces of evidence that the theory is based on are:

1) *The red shift*. It has been observed that stars that are more distant from us emit light that is closer to the red side of the spectrum. This may happen if those stars move away from

us with acceleration – a likely consequence of an explosion that happened a long time ago.

2) *The background cosmic microwave radiation.* This radiation has been shown to be uniformly distributed in all directions – whichever way you point the registering antenna, it will be there and its characteristics will be the same. This radiation is thought to be the Big Bang echo.

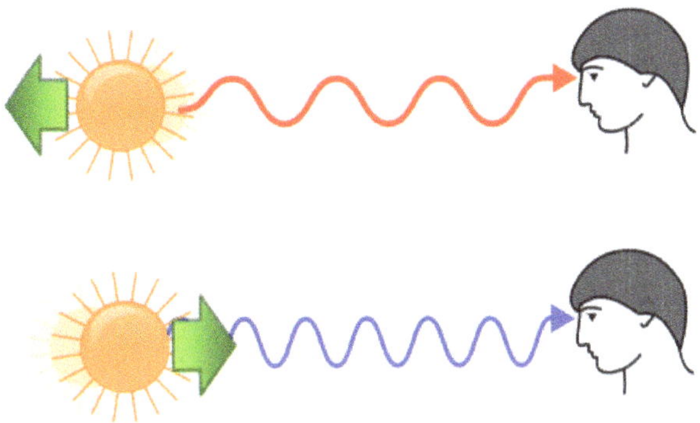

***Image 22**. The red shift and the blue shift (credit: Aleš Tošovský, Wikimedia Commons)*

The Big Bang model is a convincing explanation that fits the available data. Indeed, distant stars appear "red" because they are moving away from us, pushed by the impulse of the huge explosion that happened in the past. And the radiation that we observe is the echo of that explosion. However, some parts of the model may seem too incredible to be true. For example, the idea of singularity itself is pretty incredible.

For this reason, there have been other theories alternative to the Big Bang model. To give you just one example, Christoff Wetterich, a theoretical physicist from Germany, developed a model according to which the Universe originated with a long cold slog. There was no Big Bang – time stretched infinitely into the past. But, according to this model, every single particle in the Universe is becoming heavier as we speak.

Challenging widely accepted scientific theories is not the best way to make a career in science, but do scientists have a duty to do so? (#Ethics)

If you assume that particle masses are constantly increasing, you can explain both the red shift and the background radiation without the need for a big explosion. As one critic put it, in Wetterich's model, it is not the Universe which is expanding, it is the ruler with which we measure the Universe that is shrinking (Popkin, 2014). Voila, no singularity necessary, and the data is still explained. We have two models that fit the available evidence equally well.

Wetterich is not trying to claim that his model is the correct one; he stresses that both his model and the Big Bang theory are equally consistent with all known observations.

So, how do we decide which one to choose?

Critical thinking extension

When several theories fit data equally well, how can we choose the best theory? We must select the "correct" theory somehow to avoid bias! Falsifiability provided an empirical demarcation criterion, but it looks like we need another, non-empirical criterion in addition to that.

Think back to multi-dimensional goals of science. In the previous lesson, I mentioned the following goals that science must strive to maximize, according to Thomas Kuhn (1977):

- Accuracy
- Consistency
- Scope
- Simplicity
- Fruitfulness

Which combination of criteria would you personally choose? In my example with the trend lines in this lesson, is it acceptable for a scientist to reject explanation (b) because it is not as simple as (a)?

If you are interested...

You can read these wonderful reviews of currently existing alternatives to the Big Bang theory. Some of these are pretty mind-blowing!

- "10 alternatives to the conventional Big Bang theory", article by David Tormsen on *Listserve*, 27 December 2015.
- "5 alternative theories to the Big Bang" (2016), a video on the YouTube channel *Thoughty2*.
- "What if the Universe has no end?", an article by Patchen Barss on *BBC Future*, 20 January 2020.

Take-away messages

Lesson 5. Scientific theories are inevitably underdetermined by evidence. This means that a theory can never be fully reduced to its supporting evidence and falsifiability alone cannot guarantee the truth. There is always a speculation of some sort that is involved. As a consequence, it is usually the case that more than one theory can fit equally well into the available dataset. Therefore, we face the problem of accepting one of these theories as the one "closer to the truth". We cannot use the empirical criterion because rival theories fit the evidence equally well. This opens the door to bias. Various non-empirical criteria have been suggested, such as simplicity, scope or fruitfulness, but the problem remains: none of these criteria are based on data.

Lesson 6 - Theory-laden facts

Learning outcomes

a) [Knowledge and comprehension] What is meant by a theory-laden fact?
b) [Understanding and application] Why is it inevitable that all facts in natural sciences are theory-laden?
c) [Thinking in the abstract] To what extent can we use theory-laden observations to support or refute theories?

Key concepts

Theory-laden fact, perception, interpretation

Other concepts used

Observational fact, the tower argument, gravitational lens

Themes and areas of knowledge

AOK: Natural Sciences

Recap and plan

You now know that falsifiability is the demarcation criterion that is widely accepted today in the scientific community as a guarantee against bias. Falsifiability ensures that we are doing everything we possibly can to test the correspondence of our beliefs to reality.

However, you also know that scientific theories are inevitably underdetermined by evidence, and this means that: (1) there is usually more than one theory that fits the available evidence equally well, (2) falsifiability is not sufficient to choose between such theories. At this point we realize that falsifiability is still promising as a guarantee against bias, but its reach is limited. One might think: okay, if theories are underdetermined, let us just abandon scientific theories and operate with scientific facts!

But apart from underdetermination, there is another problem that may dethrone falsifiability completely. It's the problem of theory-laden facts. It means that there is no such thing as a scientific fact free from theory. Theory-laden facts are the focus of this lesson.

Observational facts are inevitably theory-laden

In natural sciences, it is customary to claim that our beliefs are based on observations. When we want to test the truth of a theory, we conduct observations and see if the theory is consistent with data. In other words, we just go and check. Indeed, this ability to check beliefs for their correspondence to reality is what makes natural sciences different from, say, the arts or mathematics.

But the claim that we can use observational facts to test a theory is based on the assumption that observational facts themselves are independent from theory. Suppose I have a theory that all swans are white. As a good scientist, I set out to find a black swan. Using the logic of falsifiability, I think: if I manage to find a black swan, then my theory will be refuted. I have spent lots of time looking for a black swan, but I didn't find one, so I accepted my theory – all swans are white.

But the assumption here is that, once I do find a black swan, I will see it for what it is, and my theory will not affect my perception of the black swan. But what if it isn't true? What if I actually found a black swan, but did not recognize it? For example, under the influence of my theory, I decided that the black creature I was observing was not a swan.

***Image 23**. Black swan*

To what extent can we agree with the claim that observation is a theoretical act? (#Methods and tools)

This would be a problem! I cannot use observation to test a theory if my observation itself is dependent on the theory.

Many philosophers have claimed exactly that: every observational fact already bears the influence of a theory. In other words, observational facts are inevitably theory-laden.

KEY IDEA: Observational facts are inevitably theory-laden

I will give you two examples to illustrate this formula.

Example 1: Astronomical observations

Look at image 24. This is an image obtained from the Hubble Space Telescope. The small blurs are all distant galaxies. The orange ones are closer to us than the white ones. The question is, how many galaxies do you see in this picture?

Image 24. An image from the Hubble Space Telescope (credit: National Radio Astronomy Observatory)

You might be surprised to know that the picture shows four galaxies: three galaxies that are 7 billion light years away (the orange blurs) and *one* galaxy behind them that is 11 billion light-years away (the white blurs). But why do we see not one, but five white blurs? This is because, as demonstrated in Einstein's relativity theory, light bends when it passes close to large masses. When light from that distant galaxy reaches the three "orange" galaxies, their gravitational pull bends it, and as a result we see what we see. It's called "*gravitational lens*".

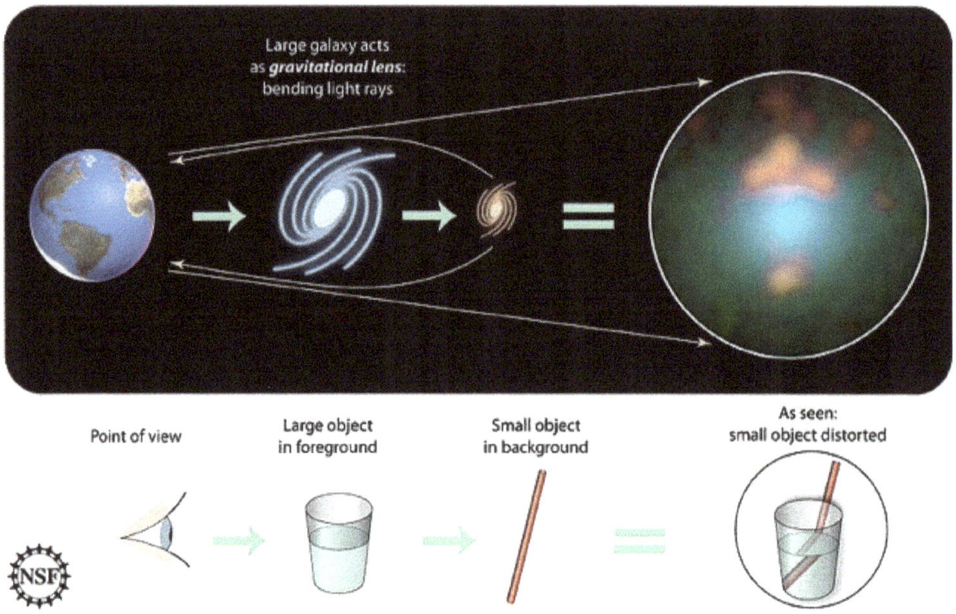

Image 25. Gravitational lens explained (credit: National Science Foundation, Wikimedia Commons)

It might seem to you that you see five galaxies, but when you filter your perception through theory, you get to know the reality hidden behind the appearance.

It is all like that in astronomy. All you see through your telescope are dots and blurs, but how do you know what they are? You filter these observations through a very complex system of theories and mathematical equations. Just pointing my telescope at the night sky for hours will not bring me closer to knowing the Universe. My brain, and all of the knowledge that it contains, is also part of my telescope and it determines what I will see. As you recall, Neptune had been observed multiple times long before Le Verrier and Adams's discovery in 1845. For example, Galileo Galilei saw it through his telescope, but mistook it for a distant star. Galileo did not have the theory that Le Verrier and Adams had, so he arrived at an incorrect observational "fact" (see *Story: Discovery of Neptune*).

Are scientific truths based primarily on theory or evidence? (#Perspectives)

Example 2: Feyerabend and the tower argument

Paul Feyerabend (1924 - 1994) heavily stressed that all facts are theory-laden and rejected the idea that observational facts can be used as a test for theories. To illustrate this, Feyerabend described *the tower argument* that was widely used in the 15th century in the times of Copernicus (Feyerabend, 1975).

When Copernicus suggested that the Earth is not stationary and is in fact moving, one of the common arguments against this "crazy belief" was the tower argument:

If you climb a tall tower and drop a stone from it, it falls directly beneath you. This is an observable fact. But if the Earth was moving, then it would have moved as the stone was falling, so the stone would not have landed vertically. So, the observable fact contradicts the theory that the Earth is moving.

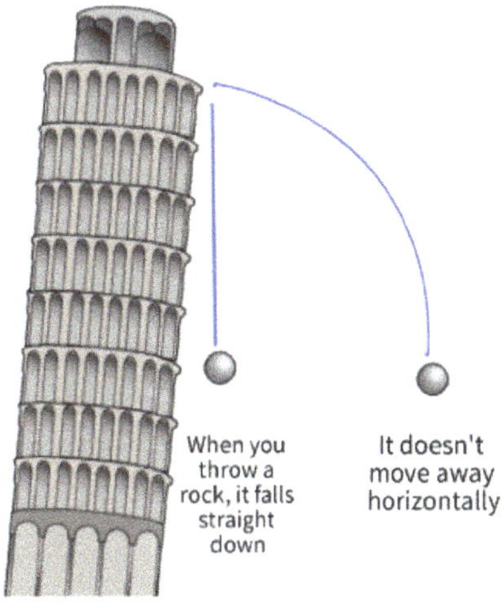

***Image 26**. The tower argument (modified from Theresa Knott, Wikimedia Commons)*

In the Aristotelian view of the world (which was later replaced by the Copernican view), it was believed that an object cannot be moving if a force is not being continuously applied to it. This is why they could not assume that the stone would be moving horizontally while it was falling.

In a way, when scholars rejected Copernican ideas of a moving Earth, they were right. Well, they were justified in doing so. From their viewpoint, Copernican ideas were not consistent with observational evidence.

Until new theories of motion were developed, Copernicus had to face empirical counter-evidence. However, when later the idea of inertial motion made its way into science, it was accepted that the stone, while falling, is also moving horizontally together with the Earth. With this in mind, Copernican views no longer contradicted the observation. Note that the theory didn't change. It was the observation, the "fact", that changed!

Is it possible for a correct scientific theory to go against empirical evidence? (#Scope)

Conclusions

In Karl Popper's view, if an observation is inconsistent with a theory, the theory should be refuted. But now we know that observations themselves are dependent on theories. This creates a vicious circle. How can we refute a theory based on an observation that depends on this very theory?

On the flipside, as you have seen from the tower argument, observations themselves may be misinterpreted and then we can refute a theory falsely, just like Copernican theory could be refuted based on the observation that the stone falls vertically.

***Image 27**. Even simple acts of perception are theory-laden (do you see a rabbit or a duck?)*

All in all, if you accept the claim that all observations in science are theory-laden, you must also be skeptical about the role of falsification in the process of scientific development. Falsifiability is still accepted as the main demarcation criterion because we don't have a better option, but we understand now that it must be taken with a grain of salt.

Critical thinking extension

Since observational facts are theory-laden, it is debatable if we can use observation to support or refute a theory. This is a huge conclusion that (if you accept it) has a whole range of implications:

1) If observation is based on a false theory, it may end up refuting a true theory.
2) If a theory is inconsistent with facts, it is not necessarily false! This is an interesting turn. It is customary to think that a scientific theory should be supported by evidence (the verification criterion) or at least not refuted by evidence (the falsification criterion). But it seems like theories that have been refuted can also be true.
3) Even false theories that have been rejected are valuable because we might find out later that we rejected them by mistake.

Is it ethically justifiable to reject scientific theories that are not consistent with empirical evidence? (#Ethics)

Can you think of examples of when each of these three things happened?

1) An example of when a theory that had been debunked later turned out to be true.
2) An example of when a theory was accepted even though it was not consistent with observations.
3) An example of when a theory that had been rejected later proved to be useful.

To support you, there is some suggested reading in the "If you are interested..." box.

If you are interested...

In the spirit of this lesson, and to help you with the tasks in the "Critical thinking extension" box, read the following articles:

1) "5 abandoned scientific theories that turned out to be right" by Ben Guarino, *Inverse*, 24 June 2015.
2) "6 conspiracy theories that turned out to be true" by Austin Thompson, *Mental Floss*, 10 July 2019.
3) The article "Theory and Observation in Science" (2017) in the *Stanford Encyclopedia of Philosophy*. It might be a little dense, but for those of you who are interested in knowledge problems of natural sciences the article may be very informative.

Take-away messages

Lesson 6. Every observation in science is theory-laden. This means that there is no such thing as a pure perception or a pure observational fact, and that every fact is already filtered through an interpretation based on some theoretical framework. This makes using observational facts to refute a theory problematic because of a vicious circle: facts are used to refute theories, but facts themselves are based on theories. The problem of theory-laden observations casts a shadow of doubt on our ability to use falsification as the guiding scientific principle. This again raises questions: how do we know, then, if a theory is biased? How do we know if scientific development is progressive?

Lesson 7 - Verisimilitude

Learning outcomes

a) [Knowledge and comprehension] What does "verisimilitude" mean?
b) [Understanding and application] How can we gauge the level of verisimilitude of a scientific theory?
c) [Thinking in the abstract] How does verisimilitude solve the problems of theory-laden facts and underdetermination of scientific theories?

Key concepts

Verisimilitude, truth, falsifiability, scientific progress

Other concepts used

Bending of light

Themes and areas of knowledge

AOK: Natural Sciences

Recap and plan

At the beginning of this unit, we discussed falsifiability as the currently accepted standard of science. Falsifiability provides a rigorous test of correspondence of theories to reality and in this sense gives the best possible guarantee against bias.

However, in the previous couple of lessons, we looked at two key problems of science that cast a shadow of doubt on the power of falsification. The first problem is underdetermination of theory by evidence. Whatever evidence we have, there always exist alternative theories that fit this evidence equally well. This raises the question: how do we prefer one such theory to another? Falsifiability alone is not enough to make this decision.

How can observation be used to test theories if observation itself is not independent from theory? (#Methods and tools)

The second problem is theory-laden facts. Observational facts themselves bear an influence of theory. This poses a problem for the very logic of falsification: how can observations be used to test theories if observations themselves are not independent from theories?

Taken together, these two problems bring us back to the notion of scientific progress. We would like to believe that scientific progress exists, and hence newer theories that replace older theories are closer to the truth. But how do we know that?

In this lesson, we will focus on the concept of verisimilitude proposed by Karl Popper to explain how there can be progress in a long chain of false theories replacing each other.

KEY IDEA: Verisimilitude explains how there can be progress in a long chain of false theories replacing each other

Falsifiability and the logic of scientific discovery

From the point of view of the falsification criterion, the logic of scientific discovery is in trying to falsify existing theories by finding counter-evidence. Once counter-evidence is found, the theory can be refuted. On the other hand, the more we attempt to falsify a theory and fail, the more our confidence in the theory grows.

In a sense, this approach views scientific development as a chain of false theories. One false theory replaces another false theory. Even if a theory is true, we will never know that because, as you remember from the lesson on falsifiability, it is impossible to prove a theory with certainty, only refute it.

But if scientific development is a chain of false theories replacing each other, then can we say that this development is progressive? Are false theories becoming "better" in any way? Are they getting closer to the truth?

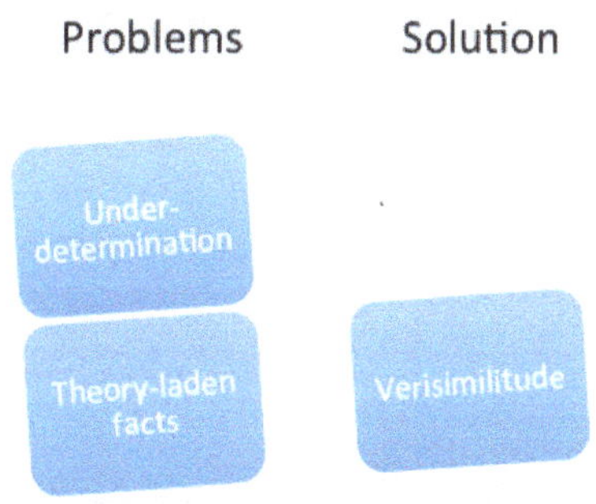

Image 28. Verisimilitude is an answer to the problems with falsification

Verisimilitude

Karl Popper took the forward-looking approach to defining goals of science. He believed that scientific truth exists and, although we cannot have direct access to it, we can infer truth indirectly.

Is there a sense in which one false scientific theory may be better than another false scientific theory? (#Scope)

He acknowledged that the concept of truth in science is problematic. The only road to facts that we can take lies through theories, and theories are underdetermined by facts. We can never tell conclusively whether something (a belief, a theory, even an observation) is true.

At the same time, he claimed that there is a way for us to make sure that we are getting closer to the truth and to compare theories based on their truth value. For this, he introduced the concept of *verisimilitude* (or "truthlikeliness"). Feel the difference between truth and verisimilitude? Instead of claiming that a theory is "true", we claim that a theory is "likely to be true". According to Popper, it is possible for one false theory to have a higher verisimilitude than another false theory. Scientific progress, then, is an increase in verisimilitude.

KEY IDEA: It is possible for one false theory to have a higher verisimilitude than another false theory

But how do we "measure" verisimilitude?

In Popper's view, the main factor is the number of informative true predictions made by the theory. Think about the following two theories:

1) Theory A claims that it will be very hot next Monday
2) Theory B claims that it will be either very hot or very cold next Monday

Suppose it turned out to be a very hot Monday. Both theories made falsifiable predictions, and both predictions were true. But the prediction of theory A was more specific and more informative. Hence its verisimilitude was higher.

So, if you have two theories that both fail to be falsified by available evidence (both fit the available dataset equally well), you should prefer the theory whose predictions are more informative – more specific, less vague, more potentially falsifiable!

Examples

When Einstein published his relativity theory, many physicists found it highly improbable and hard to believe. For example, the theory suggested that light must bend near large masses, but this dramatically contradicted all prior physics – the belief that light travels in a straight line.

The problem is, Einstein predicted that such bending of light will only occur on a detectable scale if the mass is sufficiently large. For example, light from a distant star travelling past the Sun would do this. But to test this prediction, one had to wait for a very rare and very special astronomical event – a full solar eclipse. It occurs when, for a brief period, the Moon fully blocks the Sun. If it is not cloudy, you could probably see stars in the sky behind it.

How can we be sure that in the process of development scientific theories are becoming more accurate? (#Perspectives)

***Image 29**. Space bends near a heavy mass, so light also bends (credit: Johnstone, Wikimedia Commons)*

That is exactly what the British astronomers Frank Watson Dyson and Arthur Stanley Eddington set out to do in 1919. They observed the total solar eclipse of May 29, 1919 from two locations: the West African island of Principe and the Brazilian town of Sobral. At that time, the Sun was in front of a bright group of stars known as the Hyades. The expedition was meant to check the value of gravitational deflection of starlight by the Sun predicted by Einstein for this event in 1911.

I imagine Einstein thinking, "So eight years from now on the twenty ninth of May, this star must be here according to our astronomical calculations. But I predict that if you look at it on that day from this town in Brazil, then you will not see it there. Instead here is where you will see it. And if you don't see it where I predict, then my theory is wrong".

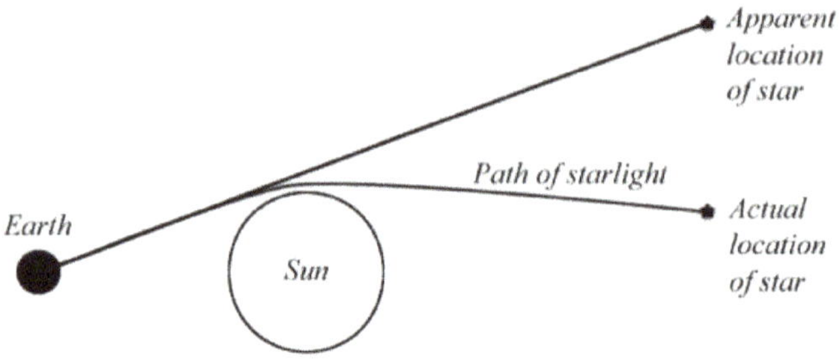

***Image 30**. The logic behind Eddington's confirmation of Einstein's theory (credit: NASA's Cosmic Times)*

That is a true instance of falsification, an attempt made by the scientist to formulate a very specific prediction that can potentially (if not true) refute the whole theory. This prediction is very specific and very informative, so if it turns out to be true, it will increase the theory's verisimilitude.

Oh yes, I forgot to mention: Eddington's observations precisely matched Einstein's predictions: the stars were observed where they were not supposed to be.

Do scientists have a moral right to be mistaken? (#Ethics)

The discovery of Neptune with the tip of a pen (see *Story: Discovery of Neptune*) is another example of verisimilitude. This discovery was celebrated as a triumph of Newtonian theories and of science in general. Indeed, the theory enabled a risky prediction; astronomers tried to falsify it and couldn't, so the theory stood the test. It does not mean that the theory is true, but it does increase its verisimilitude.

Critical thinking extension

Now let's try to link the concept of verisimilitude (this lesson) to the concepts of theory-laden facts (previous lesson) and underdetermination of scientific theories (the one before that).

According to Karl Popper's logic of falsification as the driving force of scientific progress, development of science is a string of false theories. At a given point of time, we have several theories and we formulate testable predictions on their basis. We then use observation to test the predictions, and if there's no match, a theory gets refuted and replaced with another theory – until this new theory is refuted at a later time.

However, the two problems that weaken this logic are:

1) Theory-laden facts: the observations that are used to test the theory are themselves not independent from theory, so how can we rely on these observations?
2) Underdetermination: at any point in time there can be several theories equally consistent with all available tasks, so how do we choose between them?

Can you use the concept of verisimilitude to elegantly answer both of these questions?

Hints:

- One piece of counter-evidence may not be enough to refute a theory. But if the theory is not consistent with a whole range of facts, it may be more likely that we are dealing with a faulty theory, not faulty facts.
- The theory we choose does not have to be "true". It just needs to be the "most truth-like".

If you are interested...

Watch the interview with Karl Popper himself! The video is called "Karl Popper on knowledge & certainty" (2018) on the YouTube channel *Philosophy Overdose*.

He speaks about knowledge, certainty and related concepts.

Take-away messages

Lesson 7. Although Karl Popper admitted that we do not have any direct access to scientific truth, he still believed that such truth exists and that scientific progress is a history of approximation to this truth. To solve the problem of direct access, he introduced the term verisimilitude (truthlikeliness). Verisimilitude in his approach is defined as the number of specific, informative and true predictions that the theory is able to generate. In this sense, if we have two theories whose predictions are equally true, but predictions of one of them are more specific, more informative, more falsifiable, then that theory has more verisimilitude. Verisimilitude may be used as the non-empirical criterion that we need to solve the problem of underdetermination of theory by evidence.

Lesson 8 - Paradigm shifts

Learning outcomes

a) [Knowledge and comprehension] What are periods of normal science and scientific revolutions?
b) [Understanding and application] How can we graphically represent scientific progress in Thomas Kuhn's approach?
c) [Thinking in the abstract] To what extent does an improvement of puzzle-solving ability imply getting closer to the truth?

Key concepts

Paradigm, paradigm shift, normal science, scientific revolution, Kuhn-loss

Other concepts used

Forward-looking goals of science, backward-looking goal of science, puzzle-solving, Newtonian mechanics and Einstein's relativity, neoclassical and Keynesian Economics

Themes and areas of knowledge

AOK: Natural Sciences, Human Sciences

Recap and plan

We have looked at Karl Popper's views on scientific progress, based on the concept of verisimilitude and the forward-looking goal of science (to get to the truth). Popper thought that we can judge the closeness of a theory to the truth by the number of informative true predictions that this theory contains. Strictly speaking, we can't say that such a theory is "more true", but since it is more informative, the likelihood that it is "more true" is higher. For Popper, that was enough. He did not dismiss the concept of scientific truth. Although we do not have direct access to it, we can know that we are gradually approaching it.

In this lesson, we are going to look at an alternative approach – Thomas Kuhn's idea of paradigms and paradigm shifts. This approach rejects the forward-looking goal of science (to get to the truth) and replaces it with the backward-looking goal (to gain knowledge).

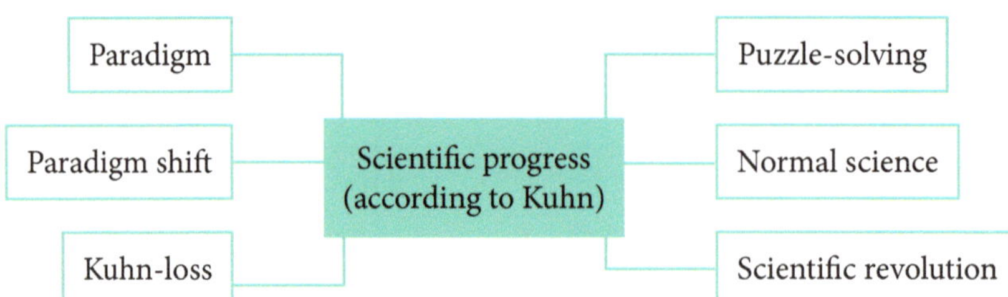

Paradigms and paradigm shifts

Thomas Kuhn (1922 – 1996) was an American philosopher of science who became very influential after the publication of his book *The Structure of Scientific Revolutions* (1962), where he introduced the term paradigm shift.

Kuhn makes several strong claims:

1) At any given point of time, it is impossible to establish the truth of a scientific theory based on observational evidence alone (underdetermination of theories by evidence). For this reason, truth is defined as a consensus reached by the scientific community. Truth is what scientists have agreed upon.
2) At any given point, there are views scientists have agreed upon. They are not conducting tests in these areas and not trying to falsify them. Such systems of agreed-upon views are

To what extent can it be said that "scientific truth is what scientists have agreed upon"? (#Perspectives) called paradigms. When eventually tests into these areas are conducted and consensus is challenged, it can lead to considerable revisions in scientific theories (this is known as paradigm shifts).

3) Thus, the process of scientific development is not linear, but a series of stable periods alternating with periods of rapid dramatic change (more like a staircase!).

KEY IDEA: A paradigm is a system of views that is agreed upon in the scientific community. A paradigm shift occurs when this agreement is challenged and the paradigm is replaced.

Development of science: periods of normal science and scientific revolutions

According to Kuhn, the development of science is an alternating series of periods of normal science and periods of scientific revolutions.

During a period of normal science, a predominant paradigm is established and scientists widely agree on this paradigm. They design their research having this paradigm as the starting point and they interpret their evidence through this paradigm's lens. During these periods, science takes the form of *puzzle-solving*. This means that scientists try to fit results of their experiments into the existing paradigm, like pieces that fit into a puzzle.

How can we know when time has come for a scientific revolution? (#Scope)

On the contrary, during a period of scientific revolution, some fundamental assumptions of the paradigm are challenged and the unsolved puzzles become so critical that the old paradigm has to give way to a newer one. It is important to note that a paradigm shift (a scientific revolution) is a very significant change where old knowledge is rejected as something based on initially faulty assumptions. In a sense, science after a paradigm shift has to build anew. The puzzle is scrambled and reassembled.

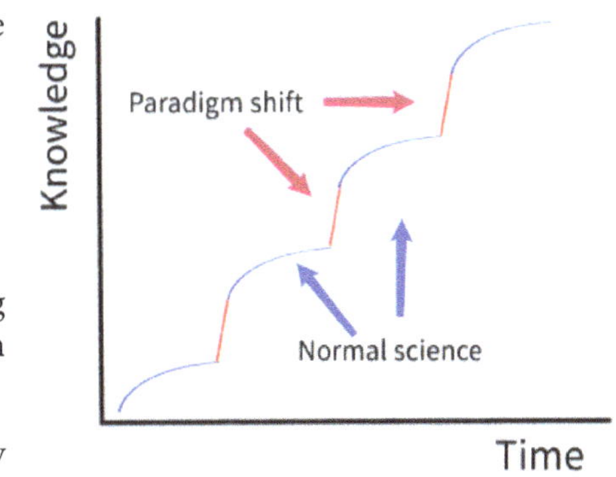

***Image 31**. Scientific progress according to Thomas Kuhn*

Puzzle-solving

I mentioned that, according to Kuhn, during the periods of normal science it takes the form of puzzle-solving. What are these "puzzles"?

- Pieces of evidence that do not entirely fit into the paradigm – an attempt is made to fit them
- Applying already-discovered laws to new areas (for example: this physical law works under water, now let's see if it also works in a vacuum)
- Piecing together various forms of evidence under a common explanation

***Image 32**. Puzzle*

As you can see, solving "puzzles" is more like clarifying the existing paradigm without challenging its foundations.

The insanely expensive Large Hadron Collider, for example, was one huge attempt to find the Higgs boson – a piece of the puzzle missing from the so-called "standard model" of particle physics. Without this piece, it was not clear how all other particles acquire their mass. The

Higgs boson was predicted. If the paradigm is correct, it must exist. This is why we have spent so much time and money on this puzzle-solving activity.

It is not a bad thing. Commitment to a paradigm allows scientists to coordinate their efforts. Think about this: if you fundamentally disagree that your teacher is a sane human being, you will probably not go far in terms of learning the subject. Therefore the "paradigm" that we accept is that your teachers are not insane. Similarly, you need to accept some theory or paradigm in order to be able to do science. To enable collaboration, this worldview must be accepted by other scientists as well. If everyone in the laboratory tries to start a scientific revolution on a daily basis, there is not much you can do in terms of gradually accumulating useful knowledge.

Should ground-breaking research be valued more than ordinary scientific work? (#Ethics)

During the period of normal science, if someone conducts an experiment and its results run contrary to the paradigm, this is seen as a faulty experiment. However, as such contradictory evidence builds up, science enters a period of crisis, which is where a new paradigm is sought that would be able to subsume the old one and fit more puzzle pieces together. This search for a new paradigm is the period of scientific revolution.

KEY IDEA: When critical puzzle pieces fail to fit, foundations of the existing paradigm are challenged and a search for a new paradigm begins. This is how science enters a period of scientific revolution.

Kuhn-loss

When a new paradigm replaces the old one, our puzzle-solving ability temporarily goes down. Since the paradigm is new, there are more things that we don't know and have to investigate anew from the fresh perspective. This is known as Kuhn-loss. However, we cannot stick to the old paradigm anymore because some of the puzzle pieces that failed to fit were critical. At least now that we have fit these critical pieces, it is our hope that, over the course of time, the new paradigm will outperform the old one in terms of its puzzle-solving ability. A graph that more accurately reflects Kuhn's ideas about scientific progress probably looks like this:

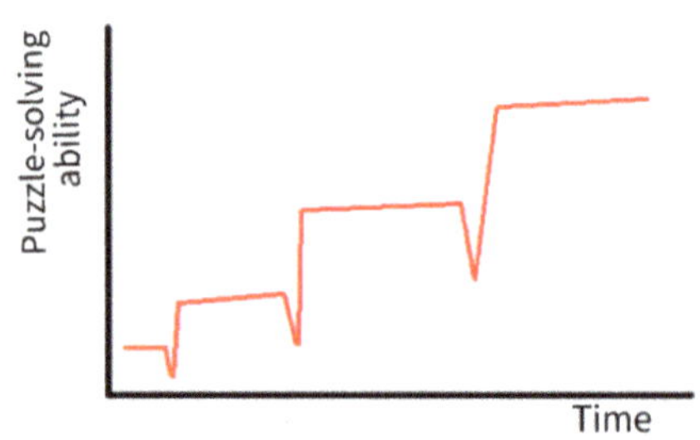

***Image 33**. Scientific progress with periods of normal science, scientific revolutions and Kuhn-loss*

In conclusion to everything that has been said in this lesson: Thomas Kuhn challenged the view that scientific progress is a linear process of development through gradual accumulation of knowledge. He suggested, instead, that it is a process of leaps, plateaus and even periods of temporary regress.

Critical thinking extension

To what extent are metaphors a helpful tool in acquiring knowledge? (#Methods and tools)

After reviewing Kuhn's views on scientific progress, a metaphor that comes to mind is changing your shoes. You were wearing a pair of shoes and you liked them. Now and then there would be a stain or some small damage, but nothing critical. You would quickly fix the problem (to the extent possible) and continue to use your favorite shoes. But on one rainy evening, you noticed that your sole came off, rendering it impossible to keep using the shoes. You had to change them urgently. In the closest store, you found a pair that had intact soles and your size, so you purchased them. Are these new shoes better than the previous ones? Not necessarily. They don't have the critical problem of having no sole, but on all other parameters they can turn out to be worse. Was your selection of new shoes driven by a desire to find an ideal pair? No, it was driven by the immediate necessity to solve the sole problem and the options available in the nearest store.

***Image 34**. Time for new shoes*

If you are interested...

Initially, the term "paradigm shift" was applied only to the most fundamental scientific revolutions that changed sciences in their entirety. A classic example of this sort is the shift from Ptolemaic cosmology (the geocentric model claiming that the Earth is in the center of the Universe) to the Copernican cosmology (the heliocentric model claiming that the Sun is in the center). This was a very fundamental change at that time. It changed not only astronomy, but everything else. For example, the relationship between science and religion was reviewed.

However, the term "paradigm shift" is sometimes also applied on a smaller scale, where the changes caused dramatic revisions, but only in a separate discipline. An example of this "smaller" paradigm shift is the Keynesian revolution in economics. Keynesian theory replaced the old framework in economics known as the neoclassical model.

If you want to study more examples of paradigm shifts, choose several disciplines and do an online search for "paradigm shifts in *XYZ*" (where *XYZ* is the name of the discipline you have chosen).

Take-away messages

Lesson 8. Thomas Kuhn viewed the process of scientific development as a kind of a "staircase". During the period of "normal science" (the plateau of a staircase step) science takes the form of puzzle-solving. A paradigm is adopted and not questioned. Contradictory evidence is treated with caution. However, as unsolved problems accumulate, the paradigm becomes unproductive, so some of its fundamental assumptions are challenged. When this happens, the choice of a new paradigm is governed by considerations of truth but also by social consensus. When a new paradigm is accepted, a scientific revolution (a paradigm shift) occurs. It causes a temporary regress in scientific development because many problems need to be reformulated and solved anew, but in the long run it may result in an improvement because one of the faulty assumptions has been corrected.

Lesson 9 - Incommensurability

Learning outcomes

a) [Knowledge and comprehension] What is meant by incommensurability of scientific theories?
b) [Understanding and application] Why does incommensurability make theory comparison difficult?
c) [Thinking in the abstract] If theories cannot be compared, how can we tell if they are becoming less biased in the course of scientific progress?

Key concepts

Incommensurability (of theories, of concepts, of facts)

Other concepts used

Universal Darwinism, theory-laden facts, underdetermination of theories by evidence, mass, motion, energy

Themes and areas of knowledge

AOK: Natural Sciences

Recap and plan

In the previous lessons, we considered Karl Popper's views on scientific progress through the concept of verisimilitude. According to Popper, scientific progress is a linear process of gradual increase in verisimilitude. More verisimilitude means less bias (if we define bias as deviation from the truth), so the issue of bias is pretty transparent here.

We have also considered Thomas Kuhn's approach to scientific progress. In this approach, the development of science is not a linear process but rather a "zigzag-y staircase" with periods of "normal science", temporary regress and rapid growth after a scientific revolution. Importantly, Kuhn avoided the concept of scientific truth. The "improvement" occurring to theories in the process of scientific development is the improvement in their puzzle-solving ability, but we do not know if this whole staircase leads to the truth or somewhere else.

But if we accept Kuhn's approach, how do we define bias? Are scientific theories becoming less biased over time? An answer to these questions is provided by the concept of incommensurability of scientific theories that we will unpack in this lesson.

To what extent can two paradigms be compared to each other? (#Perspectives)

Incommensurability: the meaning

Incommensurability of scientific theories means that rival theories cannot be directly compared because one theory cannot be understood through the perspective (or terminology) of another. This is a little like comparing apples and oranges. If you have two incommensurable theories and someone asks you if theory A is better than theory B, the best you can do is probably say "I don't know, they are just different!"

This concept has been popularized by two influential philosophers of science – Thomas Kuhn and Paul Feyerabend – in the 1960s. They both claimed that scientific theories are often incommensurable. Importantly, this applies both to rival theories existing at the same time and to theories replacing each other in the process of scientific development.

KEY IDEA: Incommensurability of scientific theories is the idea that theories cannot be directly compared because they categorize the world differently

Incommensurability of concepts

When he was a graduate student at Harvard University, Kuhn was asked to teach a class on the history of science to undergraduates. In preparation for the class, he was reading Aristotle's and Newton's original works. He was appalled at how bad Aristotle was at physics. He seemed to lack even common sense in understanding the physical world, and his works were full of mistakes both in logic and observation. Kuhn asked himself, how could Aristotle – a brilliant genius who gave birth to most of today's knowledge – be so deluded about simple mechanics?

Remember the "tower argument"? It claimed that the Earth cannot be rotating because the stone falls vertically from the tower; if the Earth really was rotating, it would have rotated beneath the stone while it was falling. Today, this argument may seem ridiculous to you. But that is only because you understand the concept of motion differently from scientists of that time. In pre-Newtonian times when you said "motion", you thought about forces that caused it. There was no idea of motion without a force being continuously applied to it. Moreover, "motion" referred to things such as water changing into ice, clouds becoming rain, plants growing, etc. Vocabulary changes.

Can language of one scientific theory be used to evaluate the claims of another theory? (#Methods and tools)

This has two implications:

1) If someone from an old paradigm is shown a scientific claim from a new paradigm, this claim would probably make no sense to them. Imagine Aristotle was shown the claim $E = mc^2$. Even if you explained it to him, he would not understand. "Energy" for him was something entirely different from what Einstein understood as energy, as well as mass, and the concept of "speed of light" was just entirely alien. I am sure Aristotle would frown and dismiss $E = mc^2$ as rubbish.
2) It is only possible for us to understand claims of the older paradigms (like the tower argument) if we set aside our current conceptual frameworks. If we look at those older claims using our "modern eyes", they will seem ridiculous or non-sensical.

***Image 35**. Apples and oranges*

KEY IDEA: Concepts in one fundamental theory do not have the same meaning as the same concepts in another theory. Therefore, we cannot understand one theory from the perspective of another.

Incommensurability of facts

As you remember, Karl Popper viewed scientific progress as a more or less linear process, where facts are accumulated, theories that are inconsistent with facts are refuted and replaced with theories that are more consistent with facts, and overall these theories gradually approach the truth. By contrast, both Kuhn and Feyerabend recognized that when a paradigm shift occurs, facts also change.

KEY IDEA: *When a paradigm shift occurs, facts also change*

Remember the problem of theory-laden facts? There is no such thing as a theory-free fact. Hence, when a paradigm shift occurs, old facts are re-interpreted through the lens of the new theory and become new facts. If theories are incommensurable, so are facts. You can't really say that facts support one theory more than another because facts themselves are not fixed.

But this is contrary to Popper's logic of verisimilitude. If we are not approximating our theories to a fixed reality (given in fixed facts), then what are we approximating them to?

What does it mean for scientific progress?

Does science develop toward the truth or away from ignorance? (#Scope)

In Kuhn's view, we cannot really say that the paradigm shift is a change *toward* some fixed goal (some ideal "true" scientific theory). Rather, it is a change *away from* the critical problems encountered by the old paradigm. Remember my "old shoes" metaphor from the previous lesson? In Kuhn's approach, scientific progress is like finding a solution to that shoe problem. There is no correctly unique theory that nature is guiding us to, just like every new pair of shoes that I buy does not take me closer to an "ideal pair of shoes".

Kuhn suggested that this process is similar to that of Darwinian evolution (universal Darwinism again!). Just like biological species, theories are trying to solve some puzzles. Just like in the process of natural selection, theories that are unable to solve the puzzles are eliminated and those that provide a better solution are retained. But just like evolution is not driven by a master plan, selection of theories is not driven by the mystical "truth". It is driven from behind - it is merely an adaptation to the currently existing problems.

KEY IDEA: *A paradigm shift is not a change toward a fixed goal (truth); it is a change away from the problems encountered by the old paradigm*

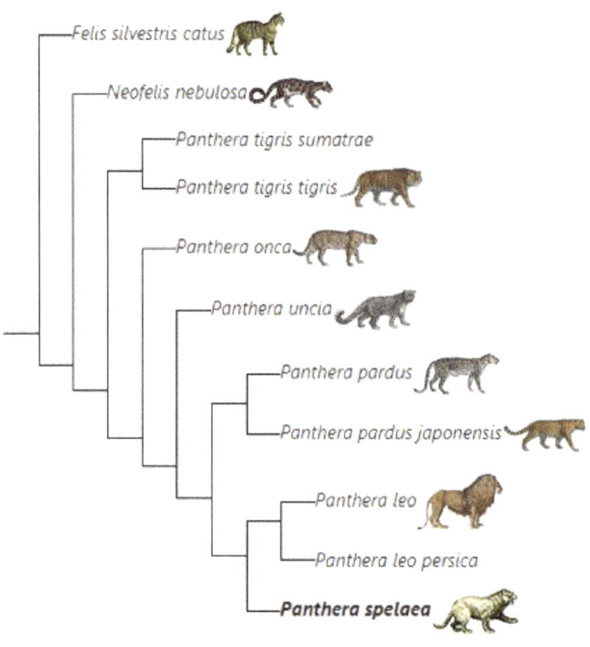

***Image 36**. Evolution of species: are some species in any sense "closer to the ideal"? (credit: O'micron, Wikimedia commons)*

Critical thinking extension

As we conclude analyzing bias in natural sciences, here is a tricky question.

In Karl Popper's view, scientific progress is forward-looking. It is a gradual increase of verisimilitude and approximation to a scientific truth. Therefore, as science develops, bias is reduced.

But what would Thomas Kuhn and Paul Feyerabend say about bias? They rejected the idea of a scientific "truth". But if bias (as we defined it) is a deviation from the truth, then what would they say about bias?

Hint: think in terms of the analogy between scientific progress and biological evolution. Biological species, much like scientific theories in Kuhn's view, develop by responding to current challenges. A better species is the one that better responds to the challenges. But can we say that some species are more "biased" than others? Perhaps the concept of bias itself becomes meaningless once you accept the idea of incommensurability of scientific theories?

If you are interested...

Works of Thomas Kuhn and Paul Feyerabend inspired the emergence of a new discipline – sociology of science. It was noted in this discipline that the selection of a new paradigm from a host of rival incommensurable theories may be driven by social factors. This is a little scary because it puts an end to our image of science as something driven purely by logic and observation. Is science like a TV show that survives only if it becomes popular?

If you want to know more about it, you might want to start with the Wikipedia article "Sociology of scientific knowledge" and the article "The social dimensions of scientific knowledge" (2019) in the *Stanford Encyclopedia of Philosophy*.

Take-away messages

Lesson 9. Incommensurability of scientific theories is the idea that one fundamental theory cannot be directly understood through the perspective and terminology of another, making any sort of comparison between these theories difficult. This is a bit like comparing apples and oranges. Incommensurability exists even on the level of facts: facts are theory-laden, and for this reason every new paradigm reinterprets the old facts and turns them into new facts. But this contradicts Karl Popper and his idea of verisimilitude. We cannot really say that theories in the process of scientific development become more "true to the facts" because facts themselves change. According to Kuhn, science is driven from behind in a process similar to biological evolution. Every theory faces a number of problems (puzzles) that it is trying to solve and every new theory is a better solution to the crucial problems of the previous one. But there is no master plan and no direction to this process.

If we accept this point of view, we reject the idea of scientific truth altogether, so the concept of bias becomes inapplicable.

Back to the exhibition

After these nine lessons, I am looking at my telescope with a new pair of eyes. My feelings about the triumphant story of the discovery of Neptune with the tip of a pen are also much more complicated than before.

I used to think that my telescope is a powerful tool that gives me access to facts, that I use facts to corroborate my theory, and that my theory is correct because it corresponds to facts. Indeed, what better proof of the power of science than the discovery of a planet with the tip of a pen?

But now I am a bit more skeptical.

I learned that corroborating theories with supporting evidence is a logically flawed way of doing science. Instead of verifying our claims, we should be trying to falsify them. According to Popper, we should reject theories once we come across contradictory evidence. I ask myself: what would have happened if astronomers at the Berlin observatory, when they pointed their telescopes at where Le Verrier and Adams predicted the new planet, had not discovered anything? Would this have led to the rejection of Newtonian gravitational theory? Probably not. The failure to discover anything in the night sky on that day could have been attributed to multiple factors: distortions of the atmosphere, mistakes in calculations, etc. This has actually happened. In trying to explain anomalies in Mercury's orbit, Le Verrier claimed the existence of a small hypothetical planet Vulcan in an orbit between Mercury and the Sun. Multiple investigations followed, but Vulcan was never found. Anomalies in Mercury's orbit have now been explained by Einstein's theory of relativity. But failure to find Vulcan did not lead to a rejection of Newtonian physics.

I learned that scientific observational facts are always theory-laden. If I do not have a proper theory, I will not see a star (or a galaxy, or a planet) even if I am looking straight at it through my telescope. I could see several stars when in fact there is only one. My telescope is useless without a good theory.

But I have also learned that there is no simple way to tell if a theory is good. I wish I could say that a good theory is the one that corresponds to facts, but: (1) facts themselves are theory-laden, (2) theory is underdetermined by facts.

Well, even if there is no reliable way to tell that my theory is good, perhaps I can be certain at least that my theory is better than the old theories that we have discarded? That my theory is closer to the truth? That, because in the 21st century we are equipped with a better theory, we can see the night sky more clearly than Galileo did? Karl Popper thought so. He thought of scientific progress as a linear process with a gradual increase in verisimilitude.

But I have also learned that this approach is not without flaws. Galileo's theory and our current theory are incommensurable. Thomas Kuhn and Paul Feyerabend have shown that our theory certainly solves more puzzles and explains more anomalies, but we cannot claim that it means we are "closer to the truth". Perhaps if Galileo encountered different puzzles, our current theory would have evolved very differently. How can we tell?

The days that I spent simply gazing at the night sky through my telescope are in the past. The thrill of spotting shiny objects in the sky is over. I want to know what these objects really are. So, my observation kit has grown: apart from the telescope, there is a laptop with a detailed map of the sky, some books on astronomy explaining how the Universe works, a calculator. I will not be fooled now when I see a collection of shiny objects… I know this could actually be *one* object whose light has been distorted in the gravitational pull of less distant stars. Equipped with my theory, I can see better.

But wait. In the beginning, I didn't trust my telescope – a simple device – because I thought there was a chance it somehow distorts reality. But now that my telescope is inseparable from my theory, this whole system becomes much more complicated. How can I trust that this "telescope + theory" system does not distort the reality of things?

Trust is the key word, it seems. I can certainly exclaim "What a beautiful star!" and feel the aesthetic pleasure of gazing at it. But deep inside I will always know that what I really mean to say is, "This blur of light that the theory that I currently trust interprets as a star – it is beautiful".

4.2 - Bias in History

History is the study of the human past. The human past as an object of research is very curious. On the one hand, it already happened and one might argue that it is impossible to change it. In this sense, it is objective, or "fixed". On the other hand, precisely because it already happened and it is in the past, we do not have access to it through our sense perception. If we have a certain belief about the past, we cannot go back in time and see if this belief is true. We have to rely on evidence from those who actually witnessed the event, but that is not the same as seeing it with our own eyes. In this sense, the human past is very subjective. It is only given to us through the filter of someone else's perception.

If you also bring into the picture the fact that there is another layer of interpretation involved – that between the evidence left by the witnesses and the conclusions produced by historians who study this evidence – you realize that the statement "the past is fixed" is pretty debatable. The past itself may be fixed. But the past as we know it is not fixed. We revise history all the time.

This makes it all the more interesting to try and figure out what bias is in the context of history and how to overcome it, if at all possible.

Exhibition: British History for Dummies

In the stack of books on my table there is a book entitled *British History for Dummies*, authored by Sean Lang.

To be fair, I could have selected any other history textbook for this example; this is just something that caught my eye the other day, so I randomly purchased it online. Don't let the "dummy" in the title fool you – this is a proper history textbook, just written in an accessible way. When it comes to British history, I am indeed a dummy. History was not among my favorite subjects at school (this changed when I grew up a little!). And even so, I'm not British, so the focus of our school program was on a different part of the world.

***Image 37**. "For Dummies" book series (credit: Marcus Quigmire, Wikimedia Commons)*

I would like to think that books like this – history textbooks – contain accurate knowledge about our past, that I will read *British History for Dummies* and my beliefs about the British past will coincide with what actually happened in the British past.

Just like I wondered previously if my telescope can give me an accurate picture of the Universe, I wonder if history textbooks – like the one sitting peacefully on my desk – can give me an accurate picture of the past. In a sense, this textbook is the telescope through which I am looking back in time.

I do realize, however, that the textbook I am holding in my hands is thrice removed from the actual events of British history:

1) When something happened in the past, someone observed it and recorded it in some form (diary, letter, painting, legal document). Among historians, such recordings are called "*primary sources*". In between the event and this recording, there was the filter of human perception, memory, selective attention, interpretation. Can I trust that the primary source is an accurate reflection of the event?
2) Perhaps each and every primary source is not accurate, but if we analyze them collectively, we will restore the objective picture of what happened. This is what historians do – they analyze primary sources and on the basis

of that they write history. These writings that historians produce are known as "*secondary sources*". Secondary sources provide a logically coherent account of events of the past, showing how one event led to another. This is much more readable. But then again, in between primary sources and secondary sources, there is the filter of historians' perception, selective attention, interpretation. Can I trust that the secondary source is an accurate reflection of the available primary sources?

3) And finally, there are textbooks – "*tertiary sources*", thrice removed from events of the past. This is what my *British History for Dummies* falls under. Textbook writers work with secondary sources and present them in a brief and simple form so that students can easily understand them and enjoy learning. And again, a textbook writer is a filter of human perception, selective attention, interpretation (and, in some cases, propaganda!).

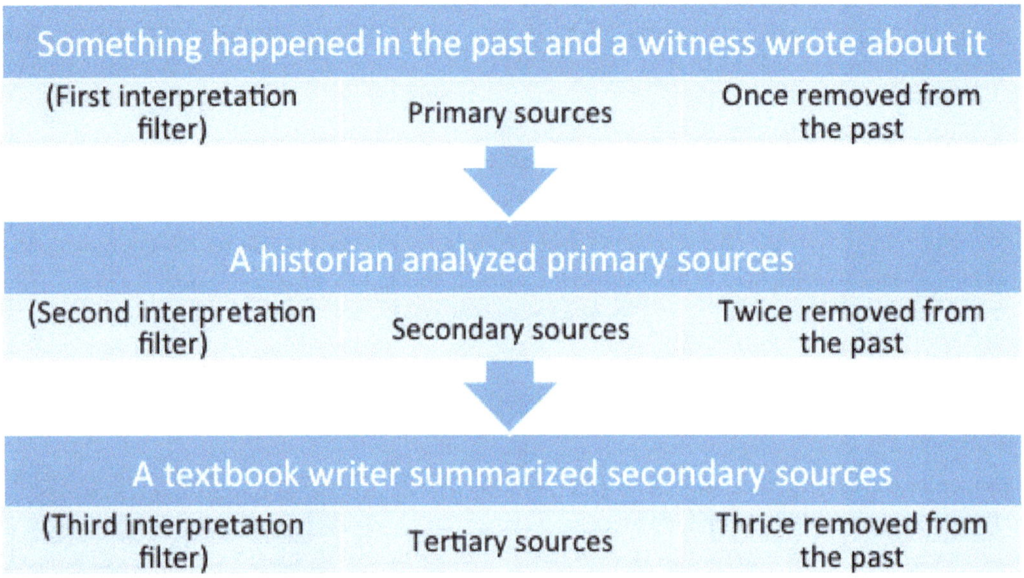

So, can I trust *British History for Dummies* – or any other history textbook – to give me unbiased knowledge of the past that corresponds to what actually happened in the past?

Story: The Battle of Waterloo

The Battle of Waterloo is a significant event in European and world history. It happened on June 18, 1815 near the town of Waterloo (currently Belgium, but at that time part of the Netherlands). It was a battle of three armies: a French army under the command of Napoleon Bonaparte against an army of British and Dutch allies led by the British Duke of Wellington, and a Prussian army led by Field Marshall Blücher.

Napoleon Bonaparte

The Duke of Wellington

Field Marshal Blücher

***Image 38**. The three commanders in the Battle of Waterloo*

The battle is so significant because it put an end to the so-called Napoleonic Wars – a series of military campaigns of the French in which Napoleon extended his power to much of Europe and beyond.

This battle is often portrayed as a victorious deed of the British army under the command of the Duke of Wellington against a larger army led by the French: the website www.britishbattles.com states that the battle was held between "23,000 British troops with 44,000 allied troops and 160 guns against 74,000 French troops and 250 guns".

There is a lot of debate surrounding who should be glorified for the victory: the British troops who withstood all of the attacks of the French army including their elite troops? The Duke of Wellington who masterfully planned the defense? The Prussian reinforcement that arrived later in the afternoon and turned the course of the battle?

***Image 39**. The Battle of Waterloo, by William Sadler (1815)*

Or was it the heavy rain that fell upon the region the night before? Artillery was Napoleon's strongest point, but after the roads got muddy and soggy, Napoleon was afraid the advance of his heavy artillery would be too slow. It is perhaps for that reason that he waited until noon to launch his attack, hoping for the mud to dry up. Had he attacked earlier, the Prussian reinforcements would not have had sufficient time to arrive.

Lesson 10 - Historical interpretation

Learning outcomes

a) [Knowledge and comprehension] What are the three major factors involved in historical interpretation?
b) [Understanding and application] Why is the use of interpretation inevitable in history?
c) [Thinking in the abstract] How is historical interpretation related to objectivity in historical knowledge?

Key concepts

Objectively existing phenomena, subjectively existing phenomena, historical interpretation

Other concepts used

Subjectivity, objectivity, subjectivity-objectivity continuum, objective measurement, causality, significance, historical revisionism

Themes and areas of knowledge

AOK: History

Recap and plan

Areas of knowledge that study humans and their activity have to deal simultaneously with objectively existing phenomena and subjectively existing phenomena. Objectively existing phenomena include aspects of human activity that are independent of the observer and can be objectively registered, such as someone's brain activity or credit card history. Subjectively existing phenomena are the meanings, intentions and individual explanations behind these aspects of human activity: the emotional state that produces a pattern of brain activity, the values that lie behind what the person spends money on.

Understanding of human activities cannot be complete if you limit it to objectively existing, observable phenomena. Without understanding the subjective side (meanings, intentions, goals), you cannot really explain why people do what they do.

Understanding the subjective side of human existence requires subjective methods – it requires interpretation. We cannot "objectively register" or measure human experiences, goals and intentions in the same way as we measure the weight and size of a rock. This makes the process of interpretation central to knowledge in such areas as Human Sciences, History and Art.

In this lesson, we will analyze what interpretation means in the context of history.

Why interpretation is necessary in history

To what extent can human activity be understood by objective measurement? (#Methods and tools)

Objectively existing phenomena in history include such examples as an army crossing the border of a neighboring country, a dictator giving the order to suppress a riot, or a peace treaty between two nations. All of these things can be objectively registered. They either happened or they didn't. Two historians can debate the reasons for signing a peace treaty or its significance for the future, but they cannot really debate whether or not those signatures were put on that document.

Subjectively existing phenomena in history refer to questions such as:

- What was the intention behind the army crossing the border of the neighboring country? Was it an act of aggression, a pre-emptive strike, an attempt to prevent escalation of aggression, a mistake of an army commander who overestimated the threats?

- Why did the dictator order to suppress the riot? Did he try to inspire fear in people to secure his position in power? Did he see it as a necessary move or did he see it as just another excuse to exercise his power?
- What is the significance of the treaty between the two nations? Was it a symbol of friendship or merely an attempt to team up against a common enemy, only to break the treaty once the common threat is eliminated?

If we only limited ourselves to objective phenomena, history would be a very long, very detailed and very meaningless list of trivia. We would not see a story behind it. To really understand the past, it is inevitable that we must account for subjectively existing phenomena. And since it is impossible to understand these phenomena by objective measurement, we only have access to them through the subjective process of historical interpretation.

KEY IDEA: Understanding in history = objective knowledge + subjective knowledge (trivia + interpretation)

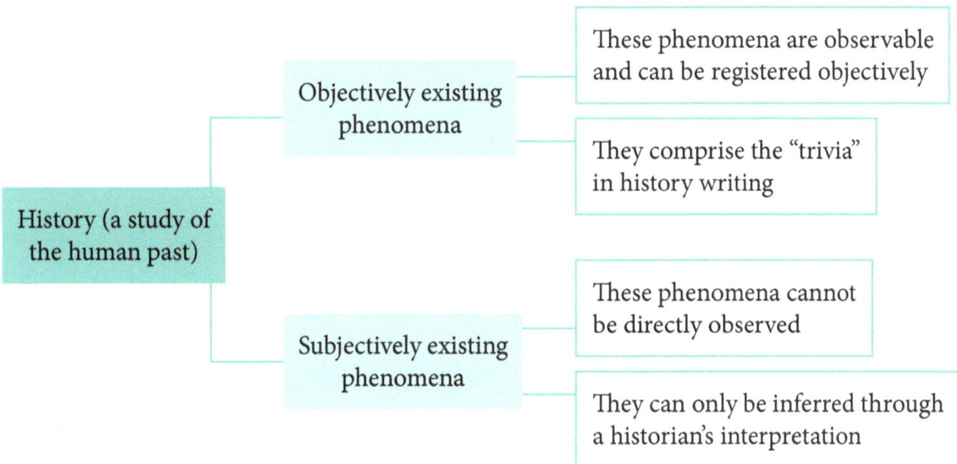

Elements of historical interpretation

So, what exactly does the process of historical interpretation involve? We can speak of at least three major components in this process:

Is bias in history writing avoidable? (#Scope)

1) *Selecting evidence.* When it comes to events of the distant past where not much information is available to us, we can probably use all of the data we have. For example, Herodotus's writings are perhaps the only source of information we have about some events in the history of Ancient Greece. But when it comes to events of a more recent past, we actually have loads of data, so much that archives don't have storage capacity for all of it and need to be selective about what they store. When a historian wants to use this evidence, it is physically impossible for them to use this sea of information in its entirety. So they select one drop from the sea. This selection is driven by their expectations, prior understandings and prior interpretations. Two historians may have access to the same huge dataset, but it is inevitable that they will select slightly different sub-sets.
2) *Inferring causal chains.* Without causality, history is just a collection of isolated trivia. If causality was not an issue, our best historian would probably be a huge hard drive that simply stores all of the information submitted to it. But we are interested in *why* X happened, not only the fact that it happened. These causal links are not given in the evidence itself. They are a product of the historian's judgment.

3) *Identifying historical significance*. A historian is interested in events that are historically significant, not just any events. But identifying historical significance is not limited to postulating that an event was significant – we also want to know *in what way* was it significant. Significant *how*? Again, the answer to this question inevitably depends on a historian's interpretation.

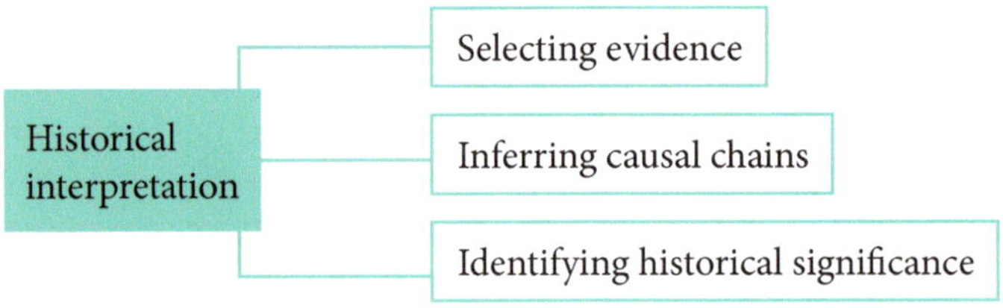

The Battle of Waterloo: who was outnumbered?

Since interpretation plays such a fundamental role in history writing, we should probably expect that there will exist multiple versions of history, multiple interpretations of events of the past. To illustrate this, I selected (quite randomly!) the Battle of Waterloo (see *Story: The Battle of Waterloo*).

If you look at various national accounts of the battle, you will stumble upon some significant differences (MacGregor, 2019).

According to the British and Dutch versions, the allied forces commanded by the Duke of Wellington numbered 78,000, while Napoleon's troops engaged in this battle numbered 84,000. At first the Prussians did not arrive, so the Duke of Wellington's forces had to endure a series of attacks, including an attack of the elite French regiment – Napoleon's last resort. The French had to withdraw due to brilliant tactics of the defending side. This is when the Anglo-Dutch forces started their advance to finish off the French army, and that is when the Prussian reinforcements also arrived.

According to the French version, the French army was outnumbered. An army of around 70,000 was faced with combined forces of around 150,000. Napoleon's tactics were brilliant and he came very close to victory, but being outnumbered two-to-one tipped the scales.

According to the Prussian version, the French were about to defeat Anglo-Dutch troops when the Prussian army arrived and changed the course of the battle. The Prussian force was a small reinforcement (around 30,000), but it played a crucial role in determining the outcome.

It is understandable when people disagree about their interpretations of significance of certain events - for example, was the arrival of the Prussian reinforcement "crucial" or did it only support the already decided course of the battle? But in this case, disagreement also seems to exist on the level of simple facts – for example, who was outnumbered by whom?

When should historians bear moral responsibility for biased interpretation of the past? (#Ethics

It turns out that even these "basic facts" are open to interpretation. For example, it is known that the Duke Wellington placed a part of the British troops (up to 20,000 soldiers) to the west of the main battlefield to guard the potential retreat route for the British forces. This part of the army did not participate in the battle. When the Duke of Wellington claimed that he was outnumbered by the French forces, he did not count this part of his army. When Napoleon claimed that he was outnumbered by the British, he did (MacGregor, 2019).

Interpretation is an integral part of history writing, after all.

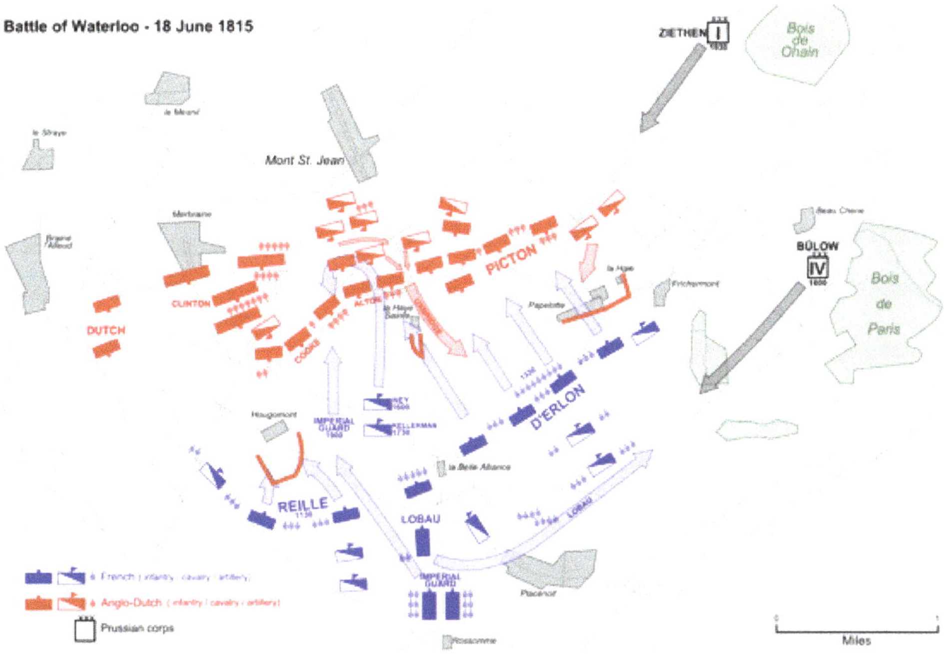

Image 40. *Battle of Waterloo (Napoleon's units in blue, the Duke of Wellington's in red, Blücher's in grey)*

Critical thinking extension

Interpretation and objectivity

The fact that historical interpretation plays such a crucial role in history writing may suggest to you that there is no place for objectivity in history (but don't jump to conclusions yet!).

How do other areas of knowledge achieve objectivity in situations where interpretation is involved? Does interpretation necessarily preclude objectivity?

Does interpretation necessarily preclude objectivity? (#Perspectives)

Hint: What if you think about subjectivity-objectivity as a continuum rather than a dichotomy (a spectrum rather than a black-and-white approach). If subjectivity-objectivity is a continuum, it makes sense to talk about some knowledge as being "more objective" than some other knowledge. Additionally, if subjectivity-objectivity is a continuum, saying that some knowledge "is not objective" is meaningless. You must specify where exactly this knowledge lies on the subjectivity-objectivity continuum.

Image 41. *Subjectivity-objectivity continuum*

If you are interested...

Historical revisionism is a re-interpretation of historical records. Historical revisionists are skeptical about the currently accepted "version" of history. They look at the available evidence again and interpret it from scratch. Revisionism in history is possible because knowledge is based on interpretation. As time goes on, our interpretations evolve, so our understanding of the past may evolve accordingly.

For some interesting examples, listen to Malcolm Gladwell's podcast "Revisionist History": www.revisionisthistory.com. Every episode of this podcast re-examines something from the past.

Take-away messages

Lesson 10. Like other areas of knowledge dealing with human activity, history simultaneously studies objectively existing phenomena (such as observable, measurable human behavior) and subjectively existing phenomena (such as human experiences, intentions or values that drive their actions). Understanding in history can only be achieved if we take into account both of these dimensions. However, understanding subjective human experiences inevitably requires one to use subjective interpretation. The process of historical interpretation includes three key aspects: selecting evidence, inferring causal chains and identifying historical significance. Interpretation is an integral part of history writing which is inherent even in seemingly impartial accounts of trivia such as which of the two armies was larger in numbers. Such omnipresence of interpretation in the work of a historian raises the question: how does that impact objectivity of historical knowledge?

Lesson 11 - Historical perspectives

Learning outcomes

a) [Knowledge and comprehension] What is a perspective (in general and in history in particular)?
b) [Understanding and application] What is the role of a vantage point in defining a perspective?
c) [Thinking in the abstract] Is having a perspective inevitable for a historian?

Key concepts

Perspective, historical perspective

Other concepts used

Descriptive perspective in history, historical determinism, great man theory, feminist history, colonial history

Themes and areas of knowledge

AOK: History

Recap and plan

History is the study of the human past.

On the one hand, the past objectively happened. A dictator did or did not command to suppress a riot in the country. One nation's troops did or did not cross the border of another nation. Such occurrences are objectively existing phenomena, they are what they are regardless of how anyone is looking at them.

On the other hand, the reasons, the motives, the expectations and the meanings behind such occurrences belong in the subjective world of human experiences. Soldiers crossing the border could be "invaders" or they could be "peacemakers" depending on who is interpreting the situation.

Interpretation is a necessary part of history because we want to understand not only what happened, but why it happened. Historians do their best to study available evidence and arrive at a holistic, unbiased understanding of events of the past. But since multiple interpretations of the same historical event are possible, there exist *perspectives*.

In this lesson we will look at the concept of historical perspectives, discuss several examples of them and try to understand where they are coming from.

What is a historical perspective?

A perspective is a particular way of regarding something, a point of view. But the term "perspective" should not be confused with a simple opinion; it has a slightly more complicated connotation.

Is a historical perspective something a historian chooses or something a historian is stuck with? (#Methods and tools)

***Image 42**. Perspectives*

To illustrate this, imagine a house in the middle of a valley surrounded by mountains. The house has a very pretty facade facing North, but the back end is quite shabby and needs renovation. Now, imagine four people – Norman, Sara, Ellen and William – standing at four different points. Norman is standing close to the house from the North side. From his perspective, the house appears big and beautiful. Sara is standing close to the house from the South side. From her perspective, this is a big old shabby house. She wouldn't want to live in it. Ellen is at some distance from the Eastern side. From her perspective, the house is okay, but she can't really tell for sure because it's so far away. Finally, William is behind the mountain range on the West. From where he is, the house is not visible at all.

A perspective is a way of looking at something that is determined by where you stand. To define your perspective on an object, you must first define your position in relation to it. This could be your geographical position (like in my house example), your theoretical orientation, your cultural background, your political beliefs, and so on.

Image 43. *House in a valley*

By contrast, an opinion does not have to be determined by where you stand. If you say "In my opinion, this house is ugly", I will shrug my shoulders and think, okay, everyone is entitled to have an opinion. But if you say "From my perspective, this house is ugly", I would be interested to know where exactly you are standing and how your position in relation to the house is different from mine.

KEY IDEA: To define a perspective, it is necessary to define the vantage point. Without an explicitly stated vantage point, it is an opinion rather than a perspective.

Examples of historical perspectives

How does a historian's identity shape their perspective of the past? (#Perspectives)

As I mentioned, someone's position in relation to an object or issue may be based on a variety of things such as cultural background, theoretical orientation, political beliefs, and so on. Accordingly, there are plenty of historical perspectives defined by a variety of factors. Here I will give just a few examples of historical perspectives, with no goal of providing a comprehensive list.

First of all, a historical perspective may depend on your answer to the question "What is the purpose of history"? One possible answer is: to teach us a lesson and to morally improve the reader. For example, one of the first historians Plutarch (46 – 120 A.D.) did not hesitate to invent speeches for great leaders of the past when writing about them. From Plutarch's perspective, if it morally improves the reader, why not? The opposite to this is the *descriptive* perspective: according to this view, history as such does not tell us what to do. It just happened, and our job is to write it down.

Another example is how your historical perspective depends on the way you answer the question "Is history pre-determined?" If you say yes (which makes you a *historical determinist*), then you believe that events of the past have identifiable reasons and that these events are not random. For example, Karl Marx believed that economic factors and class struggle were the leading causes that explained everything else in history, and that history in this sense is predictable. If you say no, then you believe that history is a chain of events that do not have a strong cause-effect relationship and that many of these events are simply random. An example of this is the *great man theory* of history – the belief that history is driven by great leaders, their ambitions and whims.

Finally, your perspective may depend on your multiple identities – national, political, social, gender, and so on.

For example, it has been noted in the 20th century that traditional history had been written by males and the role of females had been largely ignored. Male historians from male-dominated cultures wrote histories of males building these cultures. The 20th century saw a surge of alternative historical accounts where the role of women was brought out – *feminist history*. Such accounts may also be biased because they may underestimate the role of men!

Another example is *colonial history*, which was written from the perspective of the colonizers where the views of the colonized were largely ignored. The balance is being redressed now as alternative histories written from the perspective of the colonized emerge. Consider this passage about the history of Australian aborigines:

What ethical considerations are involved in history writing? (#Ethics)

"To focus upon oppressed people alone runs the risk of ignoring the reasons others had for their behavior towards them. Aborigines viewed those who took their children away to white, state institutions with horror; but the whites often acted for what they judged to be the good of those children. We now know them to have been dreadfully mistaken. But to portray them as heartless violators of Aboriginal families, from the Aboriginal perspective, and say nothing about the way they interpreted their actions, would be to demonize them unjustly, and might create attitudes of revulsion towards them among Aboriginal people which they do not entirely deserve"

(McCullagh, 2000, p. 51-52).

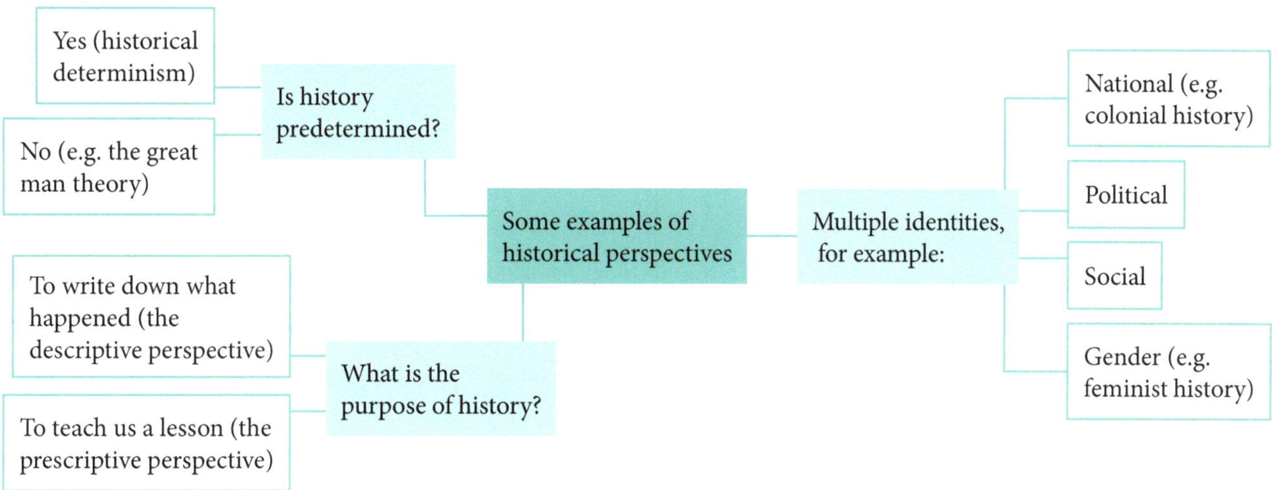

Overall, there will always exist multiple perspectives depending on multiple vantage points because people find themselves on different sides of events of the past.

Critical thinking extension

Are historical perspectives something that needs to be avoided or encouraged? (#Scope)

Is having a perspective inevitable for a historian?

If we answer "no", then we assume that an absolutely "neutral" account of the past may exist and that historians may choose not to be influenced by their background. If that is the case, we can also say that objectivity in history is achievable and that any non-objective account of the past is a bias caused by the negative influence of perspectives.

If we answer "yes", then that would mean that an absolutely "neutral" account of the past is not possible and that historians cannot help being influenced by perspectives. If that is the case, then it becomes problematic to decide which of the interpretations of the past is the correct one. For that reason, we would probably have to look at perspectives not as biases that prevent us from getting knowledge, but as tools that help us get it. We should then encourage as many perspectives in history writing as possible.

Which of the two options are you leaning toward? Or, do you think there exists a third option?

If you are interested...

Perspectives are fascinating to explore. They bring out aspects of the past that you might have overlooked. Here are just a few examples of some fresh perspectives on events of the past:

- Mikhail Zygar in his TED talk "What the Russian Revolution would have looked like on social media" (2018) speaks about Project1917, a "social network for dead people" that posts diary entries and letters of people who lived during the Russian Revolution of 1917. What would it look like if Lenin, Trotsky and others were active Facebook users?
- Chris Kniesly's TED-ed video "History through the eyes of a chicken" (2018) has a title that speaks for itself.
- Since I took this road already, I also recommend watching Eva-Maria Geigl's TED-ed video entitled "The history of the world according to cats" (2019).

Take-away messages

Lesson 11. Like other areas of knowledge investigating human activity, history studies phenomena that exist simultaneously in two worlds (objective and subjective). For this reason, full understanding of such phenomena is impossible without an element of interpretation. Since multiple interpretations of the same historical event are possible, there exist perspectives. A perspective is a particular way of regarding something (an object, an event) which is determined by your position in relation to it. Hence, to define your perspective on something, you must first define your position in relation to it (this makes perspectives different from opinions). Examples of historical perspectives include historical determinism, the "great man theory" of history, the normative and the descriptive views on the purpose of history, as well as multiple perspectives defined by the historian's identity – national, political, social, gender, and so on. A question of great debate is whether historical perspectives are something we should avoid or something we should encourage.

Lesson 12 - Historical objectivity and historical facts

Learning outcomes

a) [Knowledge and comprehension] What is historical objectivity?
b) [Understanding and application] What is the problem with defining historical objectivity as correspondence to facts of the past?
c) [Thinking in the abstract] To what extent can we claim that there is an objectively existing past?

Key concepts

Historical facts, theory-laden facts, historical objectivity

Other concepts used

Perspective-free account of the past, noumenon, phenomenon

Themes and areas of knowledge

AOK: History, Natural Sciences

Recap and plan

In the previous lesson, we established that an element of interpretation is inevitable in history and that since multiple interpretations are possible, there inevitably exist perspectives. We also looked at several examples of historical perspectives.

But is perspective the same as bias?

Since we define bias as a deviation from something (the truth), the answer probably depends on whether or not we can have access to this "something". This "something" is an objective, unbiased, perspective-less account of history. In other words, if historical objectivity is at least theoretically achievable, then perspectives are indeed unwelcome biases. If it is not, then perspectives are all we shall ever have and the word "bias" cannot be applied to them.

This is why we must now look at the concept of historical objectivity – what is it and how can it be achieved? Objectivity in history is associated with "facts", so we need to unpack the concept of historical facts, too.

When does a perspective become a bias? (#Perspectives)

What are historical facts?

When asked to define historical objectivity, my students often say that it is something based on historical facts. They say that to be objective in history is to describe facts as they are (pardon me, *were*).

This answer looks intuitively attractive, but there is a serious problem with it.

First, it assumes that "facts" are something that doesn't depend on a historian's interpretation or a viewpoint. But as we discussed, history is not interested in long lists of boring neutral statements about who did what and when. It is interested in reasons, connections between events and intentions of the actors. Therefore, any meaningful statement of a historical "fact" will inevitably include an element of interpretation.

Second, it assumes that a historian may have a direct access to "facts" of the past unaffected by their perspective. However, since a "fact" always has an element of interpretation to it, the fact itself will inevitably be influenced by the historian's perspective. What is a "pure fact"? Does it even exist?

Objections to the idea that historical objectivity is something based on historical facts:

- The focus of history is not on long lists of neutral trivia (who did what and when), but on understanding causation and significance
- Facts are theory-laden
- A fact already has an element of interpretation in it
- Even the most neutral statements have an element of interpretation (for example, they were selected over other statements)

We must conclude that historical facts themselves are statements about the past that already contain an element of interpretation in them.

KEY IDEA: Historical facts are statements about the past that already contain an element of interpretation in them

Is there an objectively existing past?

It is a known "fact" that Christopher Columbus discovered America. According to what I studied at school, Columbus was a glorious explorer of the seas who opened up a whole new world of opportunities for Europeans.

To what extent are historical facts independent from a historian's interpretations? (#Methods and tools)

Image 44. *Landing of Columbus, by John Vanderlyn (1847)*

But it is also known that:

1) Columbus did not intend to discover America. He was sailing to India. So… did Columbus actually "discover" America, or did he rather "stumble upon" America?
2) Columbus was not the first European who reached America. Five centuries before Columbus's birth, an explorer from Iceland, Leif Eriksson, sailed to the West and reached modern-day Canada. We know this from folklore that survived until our times as well as archaeological evidence.
3) Although from the European perspective the actions of Columbus were described as exploration, trade, creating settlements and bravery, from the point of view of the indigenous peoples those same actions could be better described as invasion, violence, land seizing, and cruelty.

If we take all of this into account, is there any way to capture what Columbus did in one sentence in a way that is free from interpretation?

What does it mean for a historical account of the past to be biased? (#Scope)

If your answer is no, then you agree that there is no such thing as an objectively existing past and that any "fact" in history is already a product of interpretation.

KEY IDEA: Since any "fact" in history is already a product of interpretation, we must also accept that there is no objectively existing past

Viewpoint: objective historical knowledge is impossible

I said earlier that objective historical knowledge is often defined as knowledge that is "true to facts". This definition implies that we have access to "facts" that are perspective-free and interpretation-free. But we have seen that such "pure facts" seem to be impossible to obtain. This poses a problem.

Because of this, many philosophers have indeed rejected the possibility of objective historical knowledge (Bevir, 1994).

As Charles Beard stated back in 1935, the historian "*does not bring to the partial documentation with which he works a perfect and polished neutral mind in which the past streaming through the medium of documentation is mirrored as it actually was. Whatever acts of purification the historian may perform he yet remains human, a creature of time, place, circumstance, interests, predilections, culture*" (Beard, 1935; cited from Assis, 2016, p.3).

In relation to this, Michel Foucault has said that we must abandon our ideal of history as something that offers a true reconstruction of the past. Instead, he says, we should strive to construct a history of the present using our understanding of the past to challenge currently existing systems of power and knowledge (Bevir, 1994, p. 328). In other words, it does not matter if our reconstruction of the past is "true to facts" or not. What matters is whether or not our reconstruction of the past helps us achieve a deeper understanding of the present.

Is it acceptable for a historian to lie or exaggerate if it creates a better future? (#Ethics)

Similar problem in other areas of knowledge

I could end the discussion of historical objectivity here: it does not exist, full stop. Indeed, this is a popular conclusion among many. But wait a minute.

History is not the only area of knowledge that is dealing with the problem of "facts" being a product of interpretation. Even in natural sciences, this problem is fully present. In earlier lessons we referred to this problem as "theory-laden facts". However, we are not rejecting natural sciences as something completely useless and fictitious. Why should we do that to history? "Theory-laden facts" does not necessarily mean false, biased, or misleading.

As you will recall, in natural sciences, although we cannot guarantee direct access to the truth, we can still select among rival theories on the basis of criteria that we think (or hope) bring us closer to the truth. One such approach is Karl Popper's verisimilitude: a theory with a larger number of specific, informative, true predictions is preferable. Another approach is through Thomas Kuhn's concept of puzzle-solving: we prefer a theory that solves more problems and fits more puzzle pieces together. In both of these approaches, we don't know the theory we select to be "true", but we know it to be "beyond a reasonable doubt".

KEY IDEA: Although there is no such thing as a pure historical fact, it does not automatically mean we should completely reject the notion of historical objectivity

So perhaps there is an equivalent for "beyond a reasonable doubt" in history? That will be the focus of the following lessons.

Critical thinking extension

Noumena versus phenomena

The discussion of historical "facts" that I started here reminds me of the distinction between noumena and phenomena introduced by the great German philosopher Immanuel Kant (1724 - 1804). This distinction goes beyond history and applies to all human knowledge.

A noumenon (also called a thing-in-itself) is something that exists independently of human perception. For example, a red rose far away in a field where no one is looking at it is a noumenon. Presumably, it exists regardless of whether or not someone is observing it.

A phenomenon (also called a thing-for-us) is something that is given to us in our (human) perception. For example, someone looking at this rose would have an image of it in their mind – that would be their phenomenon. If ten different people are perceiving the same rose, we might be dealing with ten phenomena that are all slightly different.

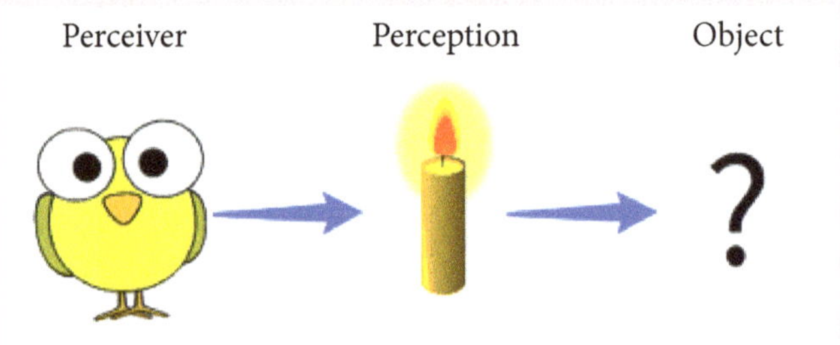

***Image 45**. Objects are only given to us through the filter of our perception; we don't have direct access*

With this distinction in mind, when we say "a historical fact", do we mean a noumenon or a phenomenon? When I argued earlier in this lesson that "pure" historical facts don't exist, essentially, I was saying that we humans do not have direct access to historical-facts-as-noumena. All we have access to are historical-facts-as-phenomena. But I was not *denying* the existence of noumena!

If you are interested...

Watch Leonora Neville's TED-ed video "The princess who rewrote history" (2018). It tells the story of Anna Komnene, daughter of a Byzantine emperor who wrote a book on the history of her father's reign. In doing so, she had to combine loyalty to her own family with a historian's obligation to be objective. To what extent was this manageable?

Take-away messages

Lesson 12. Is perspective the same as bias? Since we defined bias as a deviation from the truth, the answer depends on whether or not we believe historical truth exists. If it does, then perspectives are indeed biases. If it doesn't, then perspectives are the only historical knowledge we can possibly have.

This brings us to the concept of historical objectivity. Very often historical objectivity is defined as something that is "true to facts". But this is problematic because historical facts themselves are not free from interpretation. Facts already include an element of interpretation in them. This is akin to the problem of "theory-laden facts" in sciences.
This has prompted many philosophers to claim that historically objective knowledge is impossible. However, this conclusion may be a bit too hasty. The problem of theory-laden facts is not unique to history. Natural sciences deal with it somehow, so perhaps history can deal with it too?

Lesson 13 - Historical objectivity and rival interpretations

Learning outcomes

a) [Knowledge and comprehension] What are Bevir's criteria for selecting a historical interpretation?
b) [Understanding and application] How is selecting between rival theories in sciences similar to selecting between rival interpretations of the past in history?
c) [Thinking in the abstract] How can we justify selecting one historical interpretation over another when there are multiple selection criteria?

Key concepts

Historical objectivity, rival interpretations

Other concepts used

Verisimilitude, puzzle-solving, paradigm shift, accuracy, comprehensiveness, consistency, openness, progressiveness, fruitfulness, Occam's razor

Themes and areas of knowledge

AOK: History, Natural Sciences

Recap and plan

We are trying to find out if objective knowledge in history is possible or not. The answer to this question is important to us because it determines what we think about bias in history.

We have seen in the previous lesson that defining historical objectivity as something that is "true to facts" does not work. This is because "facts" in history already have an element of interpretation in them. The problem is similar to that of "theory-laden facts" in sciences. But perhaps there is an alternative way to define historical objectivity?

There have been several approaches to solving this problem. In this lesson we will consider one such approach – objectivity through comparison with rival interpretations.

Objectivity through comparison with rival interpretations

Bevir (1994) notes that the argument against access to facts of "pure perception" is not unique to history – it can be applied to sciences too. History certainly doesn't have to be more objective than science; we just need to ensure that it approaches roughly the same standard of objectivity as scientific knowledge.
This makes sense, doesn't it? We do not want knowledge that is "true" (even if we did want it, we can't have it). We want knowledge that is "true beyond a reasonable doubt".

KEY IDEA: The problem of "theory-laden facts" is not unique to history. It is also true for natural sciences. History doesn't have to be more objective than natural sciences.

Should standards of objectivity be different for different areas of knowledge? (#Scope)

Bevir says:
"*What claim to objectivity do scientists make? Few scientists say they can give us conclusive answers; their theories are always vulnerable to improvement, revision, and rejection. What scientists do say is that their theories are the best currently available. This suggests that objectivity rests not on conclusive tests against a given past, but on a process of comparison between rival theories*" (Bevir, 1994, p. 332).

Indeed, at any given point of time in natural sciences, we have a number of rival theories offering explanations for the same problem or phenomenon. For example, earlier in this unit I mentioned that there are currently quite a few alternative explanations for the origin of the world (the Big Bang theory may be the most famous one, but there is also the Steady State theory, the multiverse theory, Christoff Wetterich's model where the Universe is not expanding but everything in it is becoming heavier, and so on).

How do we select between rival theories in sciences?

In science, rival theories are often equally supported by the available evidence. So how do we eliminate some of the explanations to select the one that we prefer? Let me remind you of some things that we talked about:

1) Some explanations make more specific, informative predictions. We prefer such explanations to the ones that are vague and not so informative (recall Karl Popper's concept of verisimilitude).
2) Some theories turn out to be better puzzle-solvers. They solve more of the puzzles that turned out to be critical to the theory that is currently being rejected and replaced (this is Thomas Kuhn's approach).
3) Thomas Kuhn (1977) also suggested the following criteria: accuracy, consistency, scope, simplicity and fruitfulness.
4) For example, to unpack "simplicity": If we have two explanations that fit the observable data equally well, we tend to prefer the one that makes fewer assumptions. This principle is known as the *Occam's razor*.

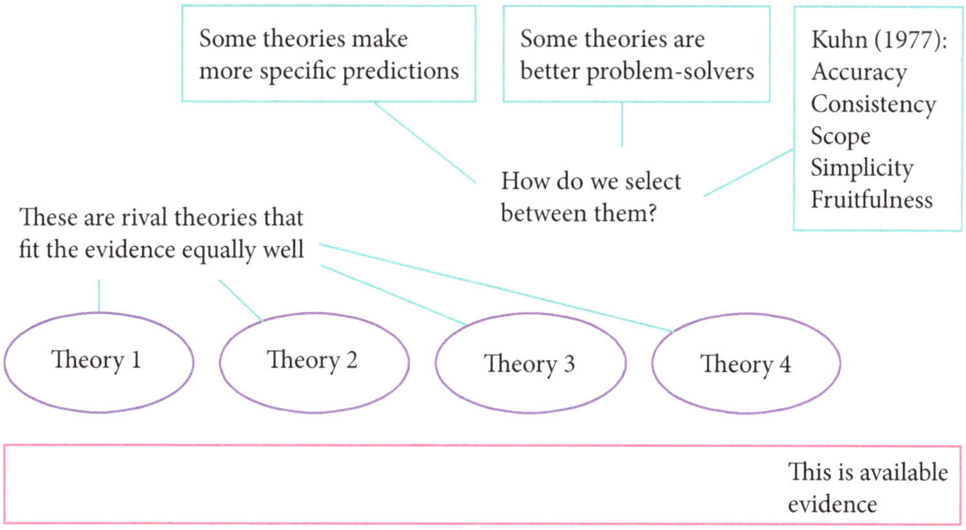

Image 46. *Choosing between rival theories in natural sciences (and history?)*

The take-away message here is this: it would be a mistake to claim that in science "objective facts" are the only thing that determines which of the rival theories is accepted. We don't accept a theory because it fits facts. We accept a theory because it seems better than the currently available rival theories. And we accept a theory provisionally, knowing that if a better rival theory comes up, we will abandon the one we currently accept and replace it with a new one. This is the standard of objectivity in sciences.

How similar are historical interpretations to scientific theories? (#Perspectives)

Therefore, Bevir (1994) asks: why not use the same standard for history? An "objective fact" in history is not something that corresponds to what really happened (although ideally, we want it to be). An "objective fact" is an interpretation that we currently find more acceptable than the existing rival interpretations.

KEY IDEA: An "objective fact" in history is an interpretation that we currently find more acceptable than the existing rival interpretations

What criteria should we use when selecting among multiple interpretations of the past? (#Methods and tools)

How can we select between rival interpretations in history?

Based on this, Bevir (1994) offered some criteria that can be used to select one historical interpretation over others. These are:

Criterion	Short explanation	Detailed explanation
1. Accuracy	A fit to the facts supporting the interpretation	Yes, facts are theory-laden, but only to an extent. You can't possibly have a theory that denies that people died during World War II. Such a theory would be inaccurate.
2. Comprehen-siveness	A comprehensive interpretation is one that fits a wide range of facts with few exceptions	This is similar to Thomas Kuhn's puzzle-solving in sciences. There will always be pieces of evidence that don't fit this or that theory or interpretation. But a theory that manages to fit more puzzle pieces together may be preferable to the one that leaves a lot of them out.
3. Consistency	A consistent interpretation is one that does not have any logical contradictions	For example, if your historical interpretation suggests that a nation leader's primary aim was establishing peace in the region, why did this leader invade neighboring countries? Any historical account will include a number of contradictions, but the one that has fewer of them may be preferable.
4. Openness	An open interpretation includes clearly formulated claims that invite criticism rather than blocking it off	This is similar to the concept of verisimilitude in natural sciences, defined by how specific and informative the theoretical predictions are. For example, compare: "Attila the Hun invaded Western empires in the 5th century" and "In 441, Attila the Hun successfully invaded the Byzantine Empire which emboldened him to move further and invade the West". The second statement is much more specific and invites criticism.
5. Progressiveness	A progressive interpretation is one that responds to criticism positively and constructively rather than defensively	When critics point out certain limitations of a historical interpretation, the author of this interpretation may either (1) adjust the interpretation and revise it in light of the criticism, or (2) deny criticism and become defensive. In the first case, the historical interpretation is progressive. In the second case it is a non-progressive interpretation.
6. Fruitfulness	A fruitful interpretation is one whose revisions enable new perspectives as well as reinterpretation of existing data	When a historical interpretation is revised (in response to criticism), this revised version may or may not generate new perspectives. If it does, such historical interpretation is said to be fruitful.

To summarize, in Bevir's view, we should redefine historical objectivity from "being true to facts" to "being the best of the rival interpretations currently available". It seems identical to how we approach the same problem in sciences, so that's good enough.

Critical thinking extension

Although Bevir's selection criteria is an attractive approach, it also poses a problem. How do we compare two rival interpretations against six criteria at the same time? What if interpretation A is more open and comprehensive, but less consistent and fruitful than interpretation B? Should we prioritize comprehensiveness over consistency? These criteria themselves do not suggest any algorithm of choice in a situation like that.

Try an exercise. Select any two rival historical accounts of the same event in the past. If you study history, it should be easy for you because you do this sort of thing all the time in class. If you don't study history, then simply do an internet search of alternative historical interpretations (if you are stuck, use, for example, the Wikipedia page entitled "Alternative historical interpretations of Joan of Arc").

For each of these interpretations, try rating them on Bevir's six criteria. Then try selecting the "best" one and justifying your selection.

How difficult of a task is it?

If you are interested...

Was Napoleon a hero or a tyrant? This debate is still going on. Depending on which camp you belong to, you will color the available evidence accordingly. Both interpretations make sense in their own way, so it is fascinating to see how this debate is unfolding. To get a glimpse, check out these resources:

- Study Alex Gendler's TED-ed lesson "History vs. Napoleon Bonaparte"
- Watch the news segment from *Al Jazeera* on YouTube entitled "Tyrant or national hero? France exhibition aims to paint positive image of Napoleon" (2017)
- Watch the video "Napoleon the great? A debate with Andrew Roberts, Adam Zamoyski and Jeremy Paxman" (2014) on the YouTube channel *Intelligence Squared* (this one is long but captivating!)

Take-away messages

Lesson 13. The definition of historical objectivity as "being true to facts" fails because facts themselves are a product of interpretation. But instead of blindly rejecting historical objectivity, we may try to find other approaches to defining it. One such approach is through selecting the best of available rival interpretations. In this approach, an "objective" historical interpretation is not the one that is "true to the facts", but the one that is the best of currently available rival interpretations. This approach seems to be similar to what is followed in natural sciences, and history certainly does not need to be more objective than science. Bevir suggests using six criteria to determine which of the available rival interpretations is better: accuracy, comprehensiveness, consistency, openness, progressiveness, fruitfulness. However, the problem with this approach is selecting between interpretations in complex scenarios where interpretation A is superior to interpretation B on some criteria but inferior on others.

Lesson 14 - Historical objectivity and ethics

Learning outcomes

a) [Knowledge and comprehension] What are the ethical standards of history writing that historians must adhere to?
b) [Understanding and application] How can we define historical objectivity in terms of ethics of history writing?
c) [Thinking in the abstract] To what extent can epistemology and ethics be combined?

Key concepts

Ethics of history writing

Other concepts used

Epistemology, ethics, truth, truthfulness, objectivity, responsibility, consistency, comprehensiveness

Themes and areas of knowledge

AOK: History

Recap and plan

We are trying to find out whether there exists, at least theoretically, an objective, unbiased account of history.

We have rejected the definition of historical objectivity as something that is "true to facts" because facts themselves inevitably are a product of interpretation. However, instead of blindly rejecting the possibility for history to be objective, we are looking at alternative solutions. One such solution is to define objectivity not as something that is true to facts, but as the best of the currently available rival historical interpretations. This was suggested by Bevir, who pointed out that sciences also face the problem of theory-laden facts and solve it through selecting the best among available rival theories. He also noted that history should only live up to this standard – it certainly doesn't have to achieve a higher standard of objectivity than sciences do.

To have some variety of viewpoints, in this lesson we are considering another possible solution to the problem of historical objectivity - a definition based on ethics of history writing suggested by Arthur Assis.

Ethical dimensions of history

Should the use of historical knowledge be subject to ethical constraints? (#Ethics)

As you recall, the IB considers ethics an essential component of each area of knowledge. Applied to history, examples of ethical problems include:

- How can we use historical knowledge responsibly?
- Is it morally wrong to include an element of propaganda in teaching history?
- Does knowledge of history make us more morally responsible for shaping the present?

In this lesson we will be dealing with one particular ethical dimension – ethical standards of history writing. This ethical dimension is the responsibility of those who write history, not the "end users" like you and me.

Ethics-based approach to historical objectivity

Arthur Assis (2016) suggested a definition of historical objectivity based on ethics of history writing. In a nutshell, according to this approach, a historical interpretation is objective if the historian has abided by the ethical standards of history writing and made every attempt for it to be objective. In other words, if a historian has really tried to make their historical interpretation objective, then it is objective.

KEY IDEA: According to the ethics-based approach to historical objectivity, a historical interpretation is objective if the historian has observed all ethical standards of history writing

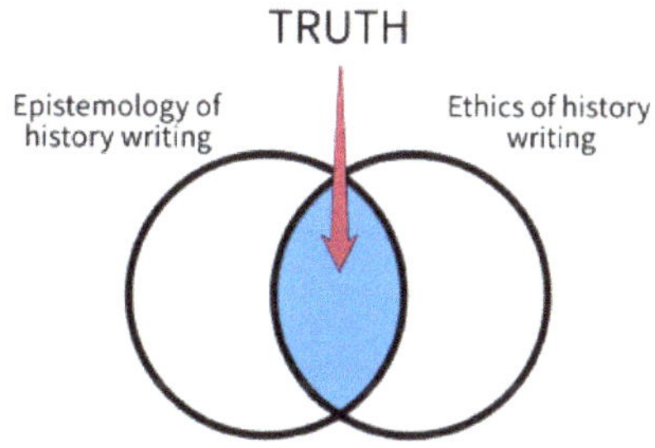

Image 47. Ethics-based approach to historical objectivity

How does that sound to you?

This approach lies at the "intersection of the ethics and epistemology of historiography" (Assis, 2016, p.2). Assis claims that when we understand objectivity this way, as a mix of moral and epistemic elements, objectivity is no longer in opposition to subjectivity. Indeed, there are no "objective" historical interpretations, but there are more or less credible historians.

So, what are the moral obligations that historians must follow? Here is a list suggested by Assis:

What should be the main moral principles of history writing? (#Ethics)

1) They ought not to present something that they know is untrue as true.
2) They must by all means avoid the partiality that could lead them to distort what they believe to be the truth (note: they must try; there is no demand that they actually succeed because we accept that it is impossible).
3) They must not omit inconvenient facts from their account of the past.
4) They must be courageous to tell what they believe to be the truth no matter whose interests might be affected by this honesty.

Image 48. Well, I tried

Accordingly, Assis admits that there may be no such thing as "*truth*" in history writing. But there is "*truthfulness*" – an honest attempt of the historian to stay as close as possible to what they believe to be the truth. In simple words, the job of a historian is to avoid consciously lying. As long as they live up to this expectation, we can believe what they say.

Pros and cons

This approach certainly deserves attention because it has some advantages over other approaches to defining historical objectivity.

First of all, it avoids the problem of theory-laden facts. We just accept that all facts are theory-laden and that's okay (we can't really do anything about it). It does not try to appeal to a mystical "historical truth" that we do not have direct access to anyway.

Second, it brings ethics into the picture, and that is not the worst criterion to use when you are selecting among rival interpretations. Suppose we have two rival historical interpretations A and B.

- A was produced by an honest, open-minded historian who studied loads of primary sources and genuinely tried to make sense of them. However, sometimes it lacks in consistency and comprehensiveness (recall these criteria from the previous lesson).
- B was produced by a shady scholar driven by motives of propaganda. This historian tried to produce an interpretation that sounds convincing. Therefore, they invested

Is it acceptable to use knowledge that was gained unethically? (#Ethics) a lot of effort into making it consistent and comprehensive; to do this, they did not hesitate to lie a little where necessary (well, not to distort facts, but to exaggerate them here and there).

Using Bevir's criteria (see the previous lesson), we should probably select interpretation B as the more objective one. It is superior to A in consistency and comprehensiveness. But you would agree that somehow it feels wrong to prefer a theory that was driven by wrong motives. This is a little like awarding a high mark to an essay that has academic honesty issues in it.

At the same time, the approach is not without limitations.

First, following ethical standards of history writing seems like every historian's personal business. But how can we make them accountable for that? As an end user who is about to read *British History for Dummies*, how do I know if its author thoroughly observed the ethics of history writing? If we take it on a historian's word, it will create a curious situation: dishonest historians may be more likely to claim that they have followed all ethical standards than honest ones.

Second, it is difficult to define lying. Earlier I said that the job of a historian (in Assis's approach) is to avoid consciously lying. But so many things may be categorized as lying. Very subtle things like omitting a tiny detail or using a slightly emotionally colored adjective instead of a neutral one may all count as lying. And where do you draw the line between consciously lying and unconsciously lying? Let me ask you this: what happened in your school last Monday morning (tell me, to the best of your knowledge). Now answer this: have you lied to me in any way? How simple is it for you to answer this last question?

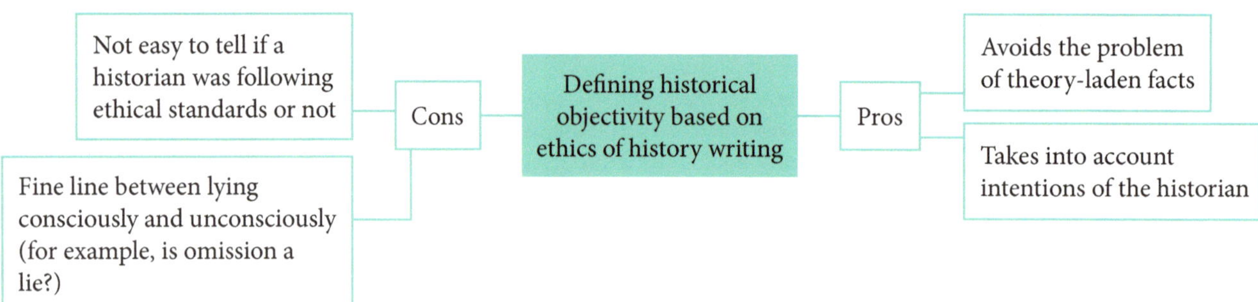

Conclusion

As an overall conclusion for the last two lessons, let's agree that categorically rejecting the idea of historical objectivity may be a little too hasty. Yes, theory-laden facts in history pose a big problem (just as they do in natural and human sciences), but it doesn't mean that an unbiased historical interpretation is unachievable even to a little extent. It seems like, although we do not have a direct access to "true events of the past", we can still compare historical interpretations to each other and conclude that some are more biased than others. This is good enough.

Should ethical considerations be involved in judgments about the truth? (#Ethics)

Criteria of comparison and selection may be different (we have considered two approaches – Bevir's and Assis's). But the very process of comparison and selection is a healthy process that must be encouraged if we want to maximize our chances at historical objectivity. Somewhat paradoxically, it may be the case that the more perspectives we have, and the more open these perspectives are to criticism, the more chances we have for creating historical interpretations that are as unbiased as humanly possible. In other words, to achieve historical objectivity, we must nurture and encourage historical subjectivity.

KEY IDEA: It may be the case that, in order to achieve historical objectivity, we must encourage historical subjectivity

Critical thinking extension

The uniqueness of Assis's approach is that it erases the border between epistemology and ethics. Just to remind you, epistemology deals with the question "How do we know something" while ethics typically deals with the moral implications of such knowledge. It is customary to think of epistemology and ethics as two very separate things.

But are they really separate? Imagine how areas of knowledge would change if we actually recognized ethics as one of the criteria of objectivity. For example, how would our understanding of objectivity in natural sciences change if we included an element of ethics in it?

If you are interested...

Read Suzannah Lipscomb's "Code of Conduct for Historians" published in the magazine *History Today* (March 3, 2014). Do you agree with her suggestions on what counts as ethical use of evidence for a historian?

Take-away messages

Lesson 14. Another solution to the problem of historical objectivity is based on the ethical dimension of history writing. In an approach suggested by Arthur Assis, a historical interpretation must be recognized as objective if the historian has made every attempt to follow the moral standards of history writing and has avoided consciously lying. This approach has both pros and cons, the pros being the fact that the subjectivity-objectivity opposition is avoided and the fact that the ethical dimension is brought in. Limitations include the difficulty of telling honest historians from dishonest ones, as well as the difficulty of defining what "consciously lying" means. However, the two solutions given in the last two lessons demonstrate that we do not have to hastily dismiss historical knowledge as absolutely and categorically non-objective. Just like in sciences (that also deal with the problem of theory-laden facts), there exist various approaches to judging some theories / interpretations as less biased than others.

Lesson 15 - Heteroglossia (in theory)

Learning outcomes

a) [Knowledge and comprehension] What is heteroglossia?
b) [Understanding and application] How does the concept of heteroglossia solve the problem of historical objectivity?
c) [Thinking in the abstract] If we prioritize multiplicity over objectivity, what consequences does it have for defining bias?

Key concepts

Heteroglossia

Other concepts used

Dialogue, historical objectivity, incommensurability

Themes and areas of knowledge

AOK: History

Recap and plan

Several lessons ago we acknowledged that interpretation is an inevitable component of history. Since this is the case, it is natural that there exist multiple histories (multiple interpretations of the past). These multiple histories are produced because historians view the past from different perspectives. However, this raises the question of historical objectivity. Does an unbiased, perspective-free, objective account of the past exist, and can we claim that all perspectives that deviate from this account are biased?

We have made an attempt to define historical objectivity through correspondence to facts (objective = true to facts), but this approach failed. This is because facts themselves are a product of interpretation.

However, we have also seen that there exist other, indirect approaches to defining historical objectivity. One solution is to equate an "objective" interpretation to the best of the currently available. Another solution is to claim that an "objective" interpretation is the one whose author has made every attempt to adhere to the moral standards of history writing.

There is also another stance that we can take. Rather than rejecting the possibility for a historical interpretation to be objective, it rejects the concept of historical objectivity as such. It claims that history consists of perspectives and instead of trying to find the "correct" one, we should allow multiple perspectives to co-exist (including contradictory ones). In this lesson, we will take a closer look at this approach through the concept of heteroglossia.

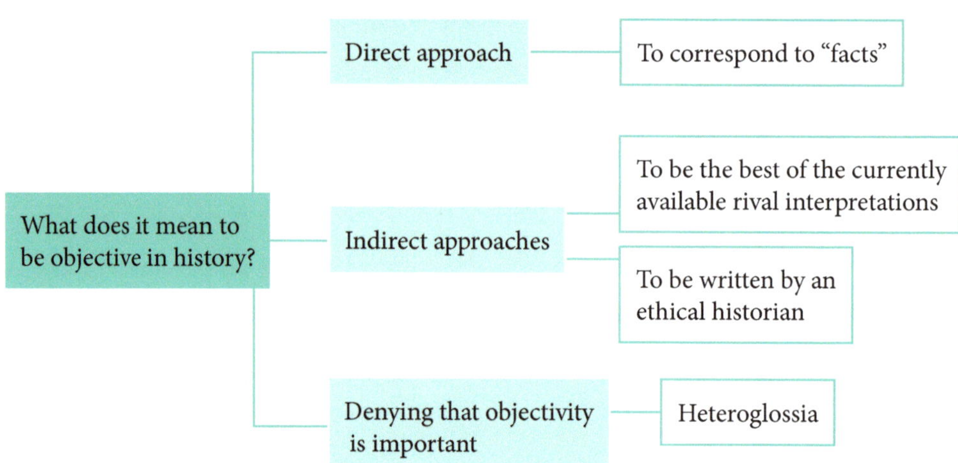

The value of multiple perspectives

Is having multiple perspectives in history a source of valuable insights or rather a source of confusion? (#Perspectives)

Let's summarize the key arguments against objectivity in history, and let's summarize some counter-arguments to these arguments.

No	Argument against objectivity	Counter-arguments
1	We know that a perspective-free account of history is impossible. Every historian has some personal interests, beliefs and expectations that will inevitably influence selection of evidence, conclusions that are made on the basis of this evidence, and the language in which these conclusions are presented. This means that all we have in history are opinions of historians who write books.	Well, yes, personal interests, beliefs and expectations will inevitably influence how a historian writes history. But there is a difference between bad historians and good historians. Bad historians allow these things to happen and pass their subjective opinions for facts. Good historians can produce historical accounts that are less affected by their personal interests and motivations. They do that by carefully studying alternative interpretations and reflecting on them. At the very least, good historians understand where their perspectives are coming from and explicitly identify their perspectives as perspectives rather than "facts".
2	Even if a historian does a good job overcoming their personal biases and grounding their interpretations in evidence, evidence itself is biased. Even the primary sources are not "objective". They are a product of someone's perception. How can a historian working with such subjective sources produce an objective account of events of the past?	Yes, primary sources are quite inevitably biased. But bias itself may be an important source of information. Working with multiple (biased) documents from the same epoch and knowing why and how these documents may be biased, the historian can see the real past events behind these biased accounts of them. "If the English describe the battle of Waterloo as a great victory for Wellington over Napoleon, and the French describe it as an unlucky defeat thanks largely to the Prussian army which came late in the day to support Wellington, historians have little difficulty in working out what really happened, and why the accounts differ as they do" (McCullagh, 2000, p. 60).
3	Even if we imagine a hypothetical scenario where all available evidence is impartial and so is the historian, every historian is still a product of their culture. Culture itself imposes a perspective. It is impossible for a historian to be culture-less, no matter how hard they try. It is beyond our conscious control. Even the best historians will be affected by their cultural perspectives.	Historians are indeed a product of their culture, and very often there is little they can do about it. However, generations of historians collectively do become aware of certain biases and overcome them. This is what happened with feminist history, for example. Humanity has recognized the fact that much of previously written history had been dominated by males and there have been attempts to correct this. It is a long and tedious process, but development of shared knowledge is always long and tedious. An important pre-requisite for achieving productive results in this area is historians being honest and open, working together and being able to criticize each other. If everyone is given a voice and a right to be heard, eventually – there is hope – we will arrive at an understanding of our past that is less biased.

Note that all three counter-arguments that I mentioned somehow depend on having multiple perspectives and enabling a dialogue between them. This looks to be the key to overcoming the inevitable one-sidedness of every separate perspective.

Image 49. Dialogue

Is it a historian's responsibility to constantly re-think their understanding of the past? (#Ethics)

Heteroglossia

Heteroglossia (translates from Latin as "different languages") is the creative co-existence of varying and often conflicting perspectives. The idea is that each individual perspective is probably biased, but we can allow multiple historians to present multiple perspectives and look at this combined product holistically. Each perspective will be biased, but the variety of them may paint a picture that transcends what each individual perspective can do.

***Image 50**. Mikhail Bakhtin (1895 – 1975)*

The term "heteroglossia" was coined by Mikhail Bakhtin, a Soviet philosopher. He emphasized the role of dialogue in all spheres of life: we can only understand ourselves if we listen to what others think about us (I sometimes ask students to tell me what they think their best personality qualities are and they struggle with an answer; they say it is probably up to their friends to decide). The same applies to historical perspectives: a historian can only truly understand their own perspective through a dialogue with other historians' perspectives! According to Bakhtin, an individual perspective cannot even exist in isolation. It is always a product of interaction with other perspectives, a response to these perspectives and an anticipation of their response.

KEY IDEA: Heteroglossia is the idea that truth requires many incommensurable perspectives

Can a perspective-less history exist? (#Scope)

It should be noted that heteroglossia can – and should – include perspectives that are fundamentally incompatible with each other, and they will still co-exist. Bakhtin criticized the idea that disagreement between two parties means at least one of the parties must be wrong. Truth, he said, requires many incommensurable perspectives. The world is irreducible to a unity, and there is no such thing as a single meaning or a single truth. "It is incommensurability which gives dialogue its power" (Robinson, 2011).

Conclusion

As applied to our discussion of objectivity in history, heteroglossia means that:

1) To look for a perspective that is "closer to the truth" is a meaningless activity. On the contrary, we must encourage the existence of multiple perspectives (the more the merrier!).
2) The main quality requirement for a historical perspective is that it is well-defined and open to dialogue. As long as you explicitly acknowledge your interpretation as a perspective, and as long as you are ready to listen to feedback from other perspectives, "the truth" doesn't matter. This dialogue itself is the only "truth" that may ever exist in history.

Critical thinking extension

The idea of heteroglossia is often misinterpreted as simple co-existence of multiple perspectives. Many voices are better than one, because they allow us to see the problem from various sides.

However, the idea is deeper than that. Heteroglossia is an alternative to objectivity: reject objectivity and replace it with heteroglossia. As we have done time and again throughout this book, let's suppose we accept this idea and analyze what implications it has.

So, if we accept heteroglossia over objectivity, we must also accept that:

1) There is no such thing as "truth", only dialogue of perspectives
2) There is no such thing as "bias", biases *are* perspectives
3) We cannot say that perspectives are valuable because they allow us to get closer to the truth – no, perspectives are valuable in themselves
4) Historians should not try to provide a perspective-less account of the past. Instead historians should be responsible for clearly formulating their perspectives and engaging in a dialogue with other historians

This is quite a radical approach to bias and objectivity that rejects the concepts of "bias" and "objectivity" entirely.

Do you think this approach is possible in other areas of knowledge, such as Natural Sciences, Human Sciences or the Arts?

To what extent is the term "bias" applicable to history where subjective interpretations are inevitable? (#Methods and tools)

If you are interested...

Watch the animated video "Three minute thought: Mikhail Bakhtin on polyphony" on the YouTube channel *Tadas Vinokur*. This is a brief and simple explanation of Bakhtin's philosophical ideas.

Take-away messages

Lesson 15. Most of the arguments against historical objectivity may be rebutted on the grounds that if we allow multiple perspectives to co-exist and engage in a dialogue, we will get a better understanding of the past than if we simply rely on one perspective. In other words, multiple biased perspectives are much better than one biased perspective. Even if we acknowledge the impossibility of having an objective perspective in history, it does not mean that history is useless. The creative co-existence of varying and often conflicting perspectives is known as heteroglossia (the term was coined by Mikhail Bakhtin). Importantly, he emphasized the necessity to bring together contrasting, even incompatible, perspectives and treat them equally. The application of his ideas to the problem of objectivity in history suggests that: (1) there is no other "truth" in history beyond a dialogue of perspectives, (2) rather than trying to single out one perspective that is somehow deemed superior to others, we should allow them all to have an equal voice, (3) doing so will give us a deeper understanding of the past.

Lesson 16 - Multiperspectivity (in practice)

Learning outcomes

a) [Knowledge and comprehension] What does it mean that multiperspectivity is broader than heteroglossia?
b) [Understanding and application] What are the main difficulties that we encounter when trying to teach history from the multiperspectivity approach?
c) [Thinking in the abstract] How useful is multiperspectivity in establishing the truth in history?

Key concepts

Multiperspectivity, heteroglossia

Other concepts used

Gatekeepers, "cold history", "hot history"

Themes and areas of knowledge

AOK: History

Recap and plan

We have seen that it is essentially inevitable for a historian to be partial and express a certain perspective. Thus, there is no such thing as a "fixed past" or an objective account of the past. The past is reconstructed through the perspective of the knower. Over the course of time, such perspectives may change, so one might even claim that the past, paradoxically, also changes.

Is knowing historical perspectives more important than knowing historical truth? (#Scope)

We can deal with this in three ways. First, we can reject the idea of historical objectivity. We can claim that the work of a historian is no different from the work of a fiction writer. Second, we can accept a less radical viewpoint stating that, although there is no way to arrive at a "true" perspective, we can still compare perspectives to each other and conclude that some perspectives are "more likely to be true" than others. After all, this is how it works in sciences, too. Third, we can reject the idea that a "true" perspective should be sought in the first place. We can claim that it is a dialogue between perspectives that matters, and that combining various perspectives (heteroglossia) makes it possible to get a holistic picture of the past.

Which camp do you choose?

Before you answer, there is one final thing for us to do – criticize the third camp. We have considered how heteroglossia should work in theory, but does it always work smoothly in practice?

Image 51. Theory and practice

Can history be taught on the basis of heteroglossia?

Among history teachers, the idea of using different perspectives to help students embrace history more holistically is known as multiperspectivity. Multiperspectivity as a concept is a little broader than heteroglossia. In heteroglossia, you have a combination of fundamentally incompatible perspectives that engage in a dialogue, transforming each other. Multiperspectivity is simply the presence of various perspectives. Where there is heteroglossia, there is always multiperspectivity. Where there is multiperspectivity, there may or may not be heteroglossia.

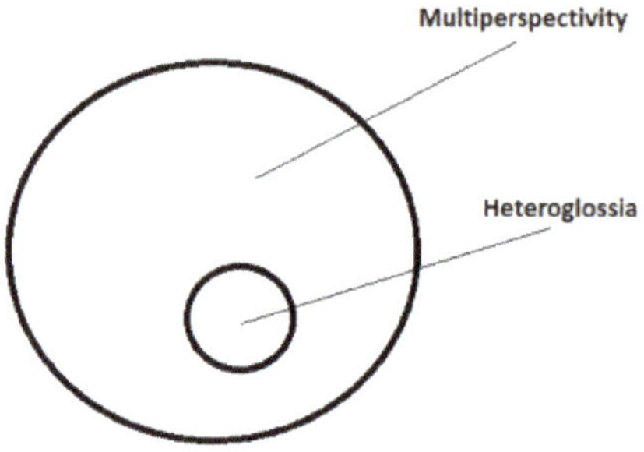

Image 52. Heteroglossia is a kind of multiperspectivity

Multiperspectivity has firmly established its position in history teaching, especially in Western countries. As populations in these countries are becoming increasingly diverse, it becomes important to give voice to everyone and acknowledge the various perspectives. IB History is no exception, and if you are a History student, you are familiar with studying historical documents representing different sides of a conflict, looking at events of the past through the eyes of different social sub-groups, and so on. It is now widely acknowledged in Western education that history should be taught from multiple perspectives.

Multiperspectivity sounds like a great thing, but how does it work in practice? Do teachers cope with the task? This was investigated in a research study by Wansink et al. (2018).

How can we choose which historical perspectives should be taught? (#Perspectives)

Researchers looked at how five different (carefully selected) expert history teachers construct their lessons. The teachers were asked to design three lessons from the multiperspectivity approach, one on each of the following topics: the Dutch Revolt (1568 – 1648), slavery and the Holocaust. The rationale behind this selection of topics was that they represented a range from "cold history" (that is, historical events to which students are not likely to have any emotional connection) to "hot history" (events to which at least some groups of students have an emotional connection). The Dutch Revolt in their study represented a "cold history" topic, the Holocaust represented "hot history", and the topic of slavery was in the middle.

All lessons were video-recorded and teachers were interviewed afterwards. Some of the findings from these interviews are summarized below:

To what extent are emotional connections to the past beneficial or detrimental in understanding history? (#Methods and tools)

1) Teachers found it easier to use multiperspectivity when teaching "cold history" topics. For example, as one of them said about the Dutch Revolt, this event of the 16th century is far removed from the students' personal lives. It is easy to be impartial about something that you are not emotionally involved with, hence it is also easier to discuss various perspectives. By contrast, it was not so easy with "hot history" topics such as the Holocaust. Many teachers avoided certain perspectives or behaved prescriptively in relation to them. For example, in one class there was a group of students whose perspective was to trivialize the Holocaust, and the teacher said to them: "I am sorry, but this is not funny, this is not a topic to laugh about…. Your own opinion does not count for this topic". (Wansink et al., 2018, p. 516). In other words, in areas that students may be emotionally related to, teaching from the multiperspectivity approach is much more difficult.
2) Apart from sensitivity of the topic, other factors that came in the way of conducting lessons from the multiperspectivity approach were:
    a) lack of time to cover different perspectives (it is easier and faster to teach one perspective as the "correct" one)
    b) unavailability of historical sources (to teach perspectives, you need sources that express those perspectives, these sources need to be found, and that's effort)
    c) lack of expertise with the subject (to teach history from the multiperspectivity approach, you need to know history really well, and so do your students!)

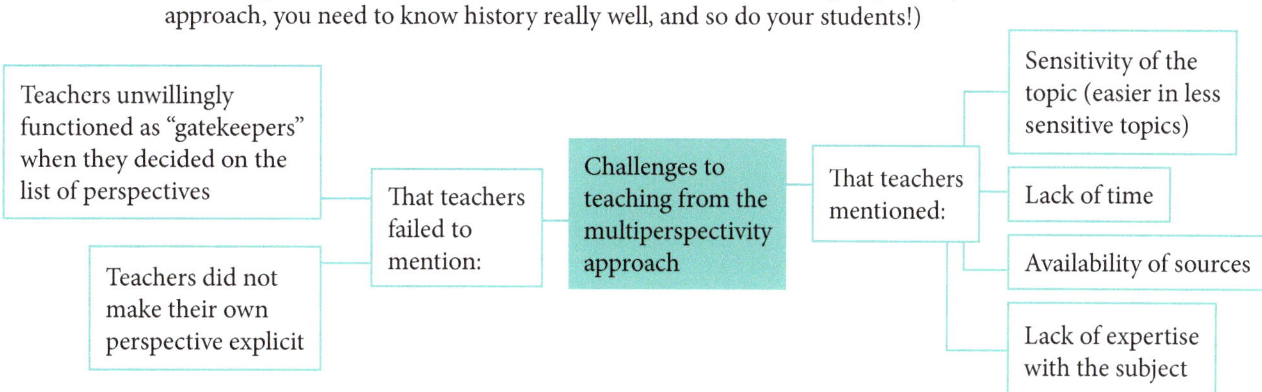

More importantly, however, Wansink et al. (2018) discovered that multiperspectivity in almost all lessons was limited without teachers realizing it. Here is why:

1) In almost all of the cases, teachers gave students the list of perspectives to be investigated. Out of hundreds of available perspectives, teachers selected five or six. They never allowed their students to make a selection themselves. Obviously, if you do allow students to make their own selection, the lesson may become chaotic and not go according to plan. But if you don't, your own perspective will be reflected in which other perspectives you deem worth studying. Teachers unwillingly functioned as "*gatekeepers*" deciding which perspectives will and will not be addressed in the lesson.
2) Teachers made their own perspective explicit in only one third of the lessons. Most teachers said that they deliberately avoided stating their own perspective because they wanted to remain neutral and value-free. But Wansink et al. point out (rightfully, I think!) that it is impossible to be neutral in history. So, the best strategy is to make your perspective known and clear. Without stating their own perspective, teachers might have influenced students in subtle ways to prefer some perspectives over others.

Is it ethically justifiable for a teacher of history to keep their own historical perspective a secret? (#Ethics)

As you see, although multiperspectivity (and heteroglossia) sounds great in theory, there are certain difficulties when it comes to practice. The list of perspectives that is being taught is itself influenced by the teacher's perspective. When you try to use multiperspectivity in "hot history" topics, there may be a clash with considerations of morality (do you really want to teach students all available perspectives even if some of these perspectives are "ugly"?). If teachers do not make their own perspectives explicit, they can influence students' opinions in subtle ways without them knowing it. But if they do make their perspective explicit, students may be influenced because a teacher is an authority figure.

In a nutshell, putting multiperspectivity into practice is a challenge.

Critical thinking extension

How useful is multiperspectivity in establishing the truth in history?

Although the idea of combining multiple perspectives to get a more unbiased picture behind them is attractive, it raises some tricky questions.

Let's imagine that we have a bunch of honest perspectives, open to criticism and explicit about their own partiality. This is a little like a parliament full of honest politicians each of whom has a distinct opinion on the matter that is being discussed. All of these politicians are extremely polite and ready to acknowledge that their point of view is affected by their cultural and political identity. They are not trying to pass their perspective as an absolute truth or impose their views on everyone else, but at the same time they stand by their perspective. What a lovely bunch of people.

Image 53*. Parliament session (credit: European Parliament, Wikimedia Commons)*

But no matter how lovely they are, the question remains: how do we make a decision? In a democratic parliament, politicians take a vote, and the viewpoint we accept is determined by the majority of voices. Whichever perspective is represented by a larger number of people wins. This scenario is okay when we decide whether or not to increase taxes, but are you ready to take a similar approach to establishing the historical truth? And in case you aren't, how do you think we should go about combining the perspectives?

If you are interested...

Watch Thomas Ketchell's TEDx talk "Teaching History in the 21st Century" (2014). He talks about a project he launched where through social media people actually relive events of the past. Do you think this idea could revolutionize teaching history from the multiperspectivity approach?

Take-away messages

Lesson 16. Among history teachers, the idea of using different perspectives when teaching students about the past is known as multiperspectivity (this term is broader than heteroglossia: heteroglossia implies multiperspectivity, but the opposite is not true). While this sounds attractive in theory, there are certain difficulties with implementing this approach in practice. For example, when selecting a list of perspectives to consider, the teacher may unknowingly select the ones that go in line with their own perspective. Another problem is that pursuing multiperspectivity is much more difficult in emotionally sensitive topics due to moral considerations. In general, multiperspectivity sounds like an attractive approach, but it is difficult to put in into practice.

Back to the exhibition

I am holding Sean Lang's *British History for Dummies* in my hands again. After everything that has been discussed in these seven lessons – can I trust this or any other history textbook to give me unbiased knowledge of the past?

The small section on the Battle of Waterloo in this book is entitled "The Battle of Waterloo: Wellington boots out Napoleon" (Lang, 2007, p.279). The name itself suggests that the Duke of Wellington was the hero of the day – not the Prussian reinforcement, not the unfortunate heavy rain earlier that morning.

But I am also thinking: if I had to rephrase this title in a more neutral language that is not suggestive of any perspectives, what would it be? It is almost impossible to linguistically formulate what happened there on that day without expressing a perspective, either explicitly or implicitly. I can probably list dry facts in a language as neutral as I can manage. But even in that case, my perspective will be there, lurking behind my text. It will affect which facts I list and which ones I omit. It will affect the sequence I choose to present the facts in. It will affect the fact statements themselves: as you've seen from these lessons, facts already have an element of interpretation in them.

And even if I do manage – to some extent – to stay neutral, my text will be very boring and not really meaningful.

So maybe it is actually better to be bold and open about your perspective? At least when the author writes "Wellington boots out Napoleon", I know what perspective the author expresses. He is honest and explicit about it. It is up to me to decide if I agree with this perspective or with some other perspective.

I am coming to the conclusion that I would like my history textbook to be biased! But to also be honest and explicit about its bias. And I would like to have several history textbooks, preferably coming from different contexts.

Sadly, this also makes me realize that the version of the past that I create based on reading these history textbooks will not match what actually happened. But maybe that's not what I am looking for.

When I have a conversation with friends and we are discussing politics, am I interested in finding out who of my friends is right and who is wrong? Probably not. The whole purpose of the conversation is to find out what they think. I am then using that to develop my own point of view. So perhaps I should approach my *British History for Dummies* in a similar way. I am not using it to learn about the Battle of Waterloo. I am using it to find out what Sean Lang thinks about the Battle of Waterloo. Maybe it is not a book about British history, after all. It is a book about Sean Lang's thoughts on British history.

But that is great. Sean Lang seems like an honest guy. I am interested in what he thinks about British history.

I will read it precisely because it is so openly biased.

4.3 - Bias in Mathematics

Mathematics as an area of knowledge is unique. There is little doubt that Mathematics is indeed an area of knowledge and that this knowledge is shared. Actually, among all other areas of knowledge, Mathematics may be the least dependent on the language spoken by a scholar. I am pretty sure a Russian mathematician who knows very little German may read German-language papers in mathematical journals and understand them. Mathematics has created a language of its own, and it is widely shared by scholars around the world.

Mathematics also has this aura of preciseness and absoluteness about it. It is often said that mathematical truths are absolute, timeless, limitless – unlike the truths in all other areas. When we prove something in mathematics, this proof is certain. Even in natural sciences, all we have are provisional truths, something that we currently accept as true but we know may be rejected in the future when more evidence becomes available. By popular opinion, mathematics is the opposite of that.

Given this image of a rigorous, precise, certain area of shared knowledge, is there any place for bias in mathematics?

Exhibition: A FIFA football

In front of me there is a football. A standard size 5 football. FIFA has specific regulations in place that specify the parameters of the ball: its circumference, diameter, weight and inflation pressure. Mine is 70 centimeters in circumference, it weighs 430 grams and it is inflated to the pressure of around one standard earth atmosphere at sea level. Its diameter is 22.28 centimeters. This fits the specification. My football could probably be used in a football competition supervised by FIFA.

Image 54. Football

But this is not why I find it interesting.

There is a deep relationship between my football's circumference and its diameter. If I divide the circumference by the diameter, I will get 3.14 (I am rounding to two digits). If I get another ball, perhaps a little larger, its circumference and diameter will be different, but the division will yield exactly the same result – 3.14. No matter what the size of a football is, this magical number – 3.14 – will be there, intrinsic to the reality of the ball.

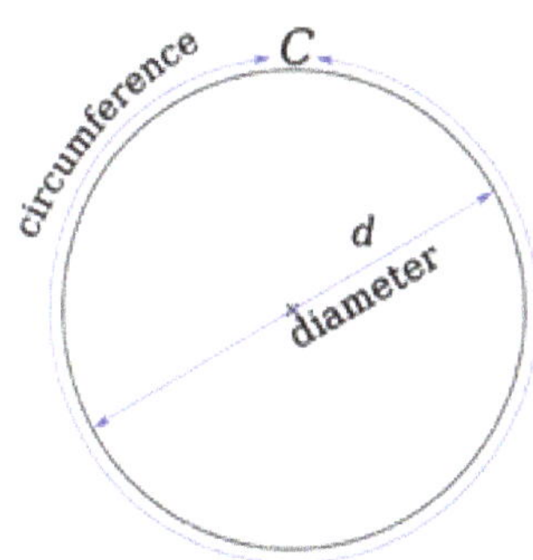

Image 55. Circumference and diameter

This number is known as the number pi and you may remember it very well from your school Math program. Sometimes represented by the Greek letter π, sometimes spelled "pi" and sometimes referred to as Archimedes' constant, the number has puzzled many mathematicians. It lurks in every circle. Whatever circle you draw (assuming you draw it on a flat surface), the ratio of its circumference to its diameter will be exactly pi. It is an irrational number: this means that the sequence of digits after the decimal point is infinite and never settles into a repeating pattern.

Since 1988, humanity celebrates Pi Day on the 14th of March every year (if you write down 14th of March as 3.14, you will understand the reason this day was chosen). It has been a sort of a tradition among mathematicians and programmers to see how precisely (to which digit) they can calculate the value of pi. On March 14th, 2019 Google announced that one of their developers (Emma Haruka Iwao) broke the record by successfully calculating pi to 31,400,000,000,000 (31.4 trillion) digits. Another interesting number! It has 3.14 right in it.

This degree of precision doesn't really have any practical value. For example, NASA only uses around 15 digits of pi in its calculations (which, by the way, are: 3.141592653589793) and NASA sends rockets to space!

My football is much more than what it seems to be. It hides within itself a code that captures the essence of all other objects in the Universe that have a similar shape. This code is an infinite string of digits, and yet any other circular object hides in itself exactly the same infinite string of digits! This code is invisible to a naked eye, but it becomes apparent to us through mathematical inquiry.

So, what is this pi? What is its nature? Does it exist, or have we imagined its existence? Is our knowledge of this pi "true"? Or is it biased? And how can we tell?

I would have never thought that my football may somehow contain the key to some profound mysteries of the world. And yet it does.

Story: George Dantzig's homework

George Dantzig (1914 – 2005), an American mathematician, became very famous in 1939 for something that happened to him. He was a first-year student at UC Berkeley at that time. He was late for a class at the beginning of which his professor (Jerzy Neyman) wrote two examples of famously unsolved mathematical problems on the blackboard. Dantzig came late, saw the examples on the blackboard, assumed they were a homework assignment and wrote them down.

In an interview for the College Mathematics Journal in 1986, Dantzig recalled that "the problems seemed to be a little harder than usual".

A few days later, he apologized to the professor for being late and submitted his work. His professor told him casually to throw it on his desk (which was full of other papers). About six weeks later, on a Sunday morning, Dantzig heard someone banging on his front door. It was Professor Neyman. He seemed very excited. He rushed inside with papers in his hands and said that he wanted Dantzig to read an introduction that he wrote to his homework – so that he could send it straight away for publication. Dantzig says: "To make a long story short, the problems on the blackboard that I had solved thinking they were homework were in fact two famous unsolved problems in statistics. /…/ A few years later, when I began to worry about a thesis topic, Neyman just shrugged and told me to wrap the two problems in a binder and he would accept them as my thesis" (Albers, Reid & Dantzig, 1986).

It would be more accurate to describe the problems that Dantzig solved not as "unsolvable problems", but as statistical theorems that did not have a proof. He worked out a proof for both of them.

The story became so famous that it even made its way into the introductory scene of the movie *Good Will Hunting* (1997).

Did George Dantzig "invent" a solution to these problems or did he "discover" the solution?

Lesson 17 - Proof

Key concepts

Mathematical proof, deductive reasoning, inductive reasoning, certainty, axiom, theorem

Other concepts used

Inductive generalization, probabilistic conclusion, premises, conclusions

Themes and areas of knowledge

AOK: Mathematics, Natural Sciences

Learning outcomes

a) [Knowledge and comprehension] What is mathematical proof?
b) [Understanding and application] What are the key characteristics of mathematical proof from the TOK perspective?
c) [Thinking in the abstract] If all knowledge in mathematics follows with necessity from the original axioms, why does it take such a long time for mathematicians to discover new theorems?

Recap and plan

In this unit we have so far discussed bias in natural sciences and bias in history. Now we will turn our attention to mathematics. The nature of knowledge in mathematics is very different from any other area of knowledge, and obviously this will have implications for how we understand bias.

So, the first step is to understand how exactly knowledge in mathematics is different from knowledge in other areas. In this lesson we will talk about mathematical proof – what it is and why it makes mathematics so special.

What is mathematical proof?

Can any other knowledge be as certain as mathematical knowledge? (#Scope)

Mathematical proof is a deductive argument showing that a statement is true because it logically follows with certainty from other true statements. A statement that can be proven this way is called a theorem.

KEY IDEA: Mathematical proof is a deductive argument showing that a statement is true because it logically follows from other true statements

Example: Pythagorean theorem

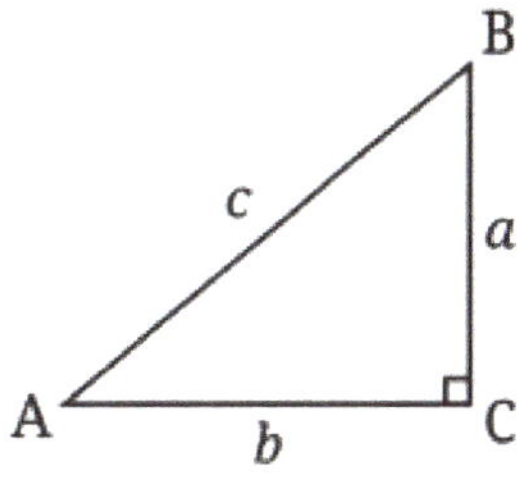

Image 56. Right triangle

The Pythagorean theorem states that in every right triangle the square of the hypotenuse is equal to the sum of squares of the other two sides. In short it is written as $a^2 + b^2 = c^2$.

Let me explain this a little. A right triangle is a triangle in which one of the angles is right, that is, 90 degrees. In image 56, this is the angle between sides a and b. The side of the triangle opposite to the right angle is called the hypotenuse. It is denoted as c. The other two sides are called legs (also called catheti, but legs sounds more fun). So, the theorem claims that the length of c squared must be equal to the length of a squared plus the length of b squared.

Also, here are the things that we know because we have already proven them:

Premise 1. Area of a square is equal to the length of its side squared (remember that in a square all sides are equal).

$$area\ of\ a\ square = (length\ of\ its\ side)^2$$

Premise 2. Area of a right triangle is equal to the length of one leg multiplied by the length of another leg and divided by

$$area\ of\ a\ right\ triangle = \frac{ab}{2}$$

Premise 3. The square of a sum is calculated like this:

$$(a+b)^2 = a^2 + 2ab + b^2$$

Now, to prove the Pythagorean theorem, I can draw a big square of side (a + b), like this:

Note that the area of this big square is equal to the area of the smaller square inside it (the one with the side c) plus the area of four identical triangles in the corners.

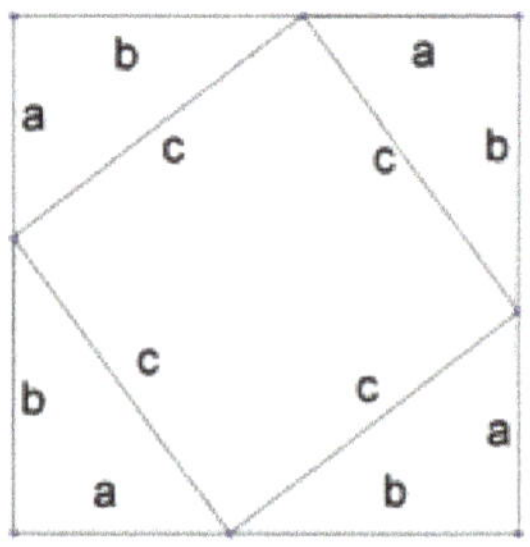

Image 57. *Proving the Pythagorean theorem*

I can write it down like this:

the area of the big square	equals	the area of the smaller square inside	plus	the area of four identical triangles
$(a+b)^2$	=	c^2	+	$4\frac{ab}{2}$
This follows from premise 1		*This also follows from premise 1*		*This follows from premise 2*

From premise 3 we know that $(a+b)^2 = a^2 + 2ab + b^2$

So I can plug in the values from the table above and rewrite the equation like this:

$$a^2 + 2ab + b^2 = c^2 + 4\frac{ab}{2}$$

And simplify it like this:

$$a^2 + 2ab + b^2 = c^2 + 2ab$$

$$a^2 + \cancel{2ab} + b^2 = c^2 + \cancel{2ab}$$
$$a^2 + b^2 = c^2$$

What just happened?

We demonstrated that, if premises 1, 2 and 3 are true, the theorem ($a^2+b^2=c^2$) logically follows from them with necessity. This is a mathematical proof. The statement $a^2+b^2=c^2$ is called a theorem because we proved it this way. The three premises are themselves theorems because they have their own proofs.

The TOK behind mathematical proofs

This was a nice reminder of what it feels like to be in a Math lesson, but now we need to discuss how it is all important from the TOK perspective.

First, note that all proofs in mathematics are deductive. Deductive reasoning takes some previously known statements (premises), applies logic to them and derives new statements (conclusions). For example:

All men are mortal. (First premise)
Socrates is a man. (Second premise)
Therefore, Socrates is mortal. (Conclusion)

The proof of the Pythagorean theorem that you saw above is also an example of deductive reasoning. In deductive logic, if the premises are true, then we know for sure that the conclusion is also true.

How big is the role of deduction when it comes to areas other than mathematics? (#Methods and tools)

Unlike mathematics, other areas of knowledge often rely on inductive reasoning. Inductive reasoning makes the leap from observed instances to a generalized statement. For example, imagine you have a huge box with pencils. There may be thousands of pencils in it, but you can only take the pencils out one by one through a narrow slot. You take out the first pencil and it's green. You take out the second pencil and it's green. You take out a hundred pencils and they are all green, at which point you conclude that all the pencils in the box are green. That is a simple example of *inductive generalization*. It is a leap from "many pencils" to "all pencils".

***Image 58**. Mathematician*

In natural and human sciences, conducting experiments is somewhat like taking out pencils from the box. For example, Newton's law of universal gravitation states that the gravitational force acting between two objects depends on the mass of these objects and the distance between them:

$$F = G\frac{m_1 m_2}{r^2}$$

(Here F is the force of gravitation acting between the two objects, m_1 is the mass of the first object, m_2 is the mass of the second object, r is the distance between objects, G is a "gravitational constant" always equal to 0.00000000006674).

Did Newton deduce this formula from any other previous statements? No. He used data from astronomical observations and he saw that whatever celestial objects are being observed conform to this formula. He was working up from observations toward this generalization. A mathematician, on the other hand, works "down" from previously known premises to a conclusion.

KEY IDEA: Mathematics is deductive

Second, mathematical proofs are certain, and mathematics is the only area of knowledge where conclusions can be made with absolute certainty. As long as the premises are true, we are absolutely sure that the conclusion is also true, and that it will always be true (today, tomorrow, a thousand years later) and everywhere (in Japan, on Mars, on the other side of the galaxy). Since it logically follows from the premises, we know without checking.

How is development of mathematical knowledge similar to and different from scientific progress? (#Perspectives)

Again, this is opposed to the nature of conclusions that can be obtained in sciences. As powerful as science is, it can only make probabilistic conclusions. We can only accept theories provisionally. As for Newton's law of universal gravity, we have used it many times now and it seems to work every time. But there is no logical guarantee that the law of universal gravitation will not suddenly break down somewhere in a remote part of the Universe. With all of our scientific observations, we have taken a great number of pencils from the box, but we have not taken them all (and we will never be able to).

***Image 59**. Certainty*

KEY IDEA: Mathematics is the only area of knowledge where conclusions can be made with absolute certainty

Third, mathematics is a system based on axioms. An axiom is a statement that is accepted without proof as something that is obviously true. You have seen from the example above (the Pythagorean theorem) that theorems are proven by tracing them back to premises that we already know to be true. But these premises are also theorems, because they have to be proven by tracing back to some other premises. And those premises are based on even earlier premises, and so on. We cannot continue this process indefinitely. Eventually, we have to hit the rock bottom of premises that are accepted without proof because they are so evident that they don't require one. The premises – axioms – are the foundation of the whole building that is mathematics.

KEY IDEA: Mathematics is based on axioms

Can ethical considerations influence the development of knowledge in mathematics? (#Ethics)

As you can see, mathematics is a very special area of knowledge because knowledge in it is derived through the process of mathematical proof, which is based on deductive logic. Mathematics is the only area of knowledge where conclusions can be accepted with absolute certainty. A key feature of mathematics is the existence of axioms.

Critical thinking extension

The nature of mathematical proof means that, when mathematics was young, it existed as a set of axioms. Then rules of deductive reasoning were applied to these axioms to derive some theorems. Then rules of deductive reasoning were applied to these theorems to derive further theorems. This is how the original set of axioms was gradually "unpacked" and became what we know as mathematics.

Therefore, we can say that all mathematical knowledge is already contained in the original set of axioms. It is already there, it just needs to be "unpacked". In other words, if all theorems necessarily follow from axioms, then the original set of axioms already contains mathematics in its entirety.

But then the question is, why is mathematics so difficult and why does it sometimes take hundreds of years for mathematicians to "discover" something new?

If you are interested...

Watch Scott Kennedy's TED-ed video "An introduction to mathematical theorems" (2012). It is a viewer-friendly animated explainer video.

Take-away messages

Lesson 17. In this lesson we tried to figure out how mathematical knowledge is different from knowledge in all other areas. The main method of obtaining knowledge in mathematics is mathematical proof - a deductive argument showing that a statement is true because it logically follows with certainty from other true statements. At the basis of mathematical knowledge is a set of axioms, statements that are believed to be so obviously true that they do not require any proof. Unlike natural and human sciences (where inductive reasoning plays a large role), knowledge obtained through deductive mathematical proof is absolutely certain. The fact that all further theorems logically follow from the original set of axioms means that the axioms somehow already contain in them the entirety of mathematical knowledge. This knowledge just needs to be "unpacked".

Lesson 18 - Axiomatic systems

Learning outcomes

a) [Knowledge and comprehension] What is an axiomatic system and what are its key characteristics?
b) [Understanding and application] Why is mathematics an axiomatic system?
c) [Thinking in the abstract] How arbitrary is the choice of the starting set of axioms in mathematics?

Key concepts

Axiomatic system

Other concepts used

Underdetermination of scientific theories by evidence, mathematical proof, axiom, theorem, rules of reasoning, the law of excluded middle

Themes and areas of knowledge

AOK: Mathematics, Natural Sciences, History

Recap and plan

We are looking at bias in shared knowledge. Earlier, we defined bias as a systematic deviation from the truth (or something that is currently accepted as the truth). We looked at bias in natural sciences and history. It turns out that the problem is not easy at all.

In natural sciences, looking at the scientific progress, we are not sure what is happening: are we getting closer to the truth (our final destination) or are we simply evolving in response to the problems we are currently facing, but without any direction to guide us? The former, says Karl Popper. The latter, says Thomas Kuhn.

In history, we are dealing with both objective phenomena (what happened and when) and subjective phenomena (such as reasons, intentions and meanings behind events of the past). This makes it necessary to rely on interpretation. Where there is interpretation, there are perspectives. Even the simplest historical facts have an element of interpretation in them, and this means that we cannot define an "objective" historical perspective that is supported by "facts". Moreover, some thinkers have said that the co-existence of multiple perspectives in history may actually be desirable (heteroglossia), which means that bias may actually be a good thing!

Now we need to understand the nature of bias in mathematics. As we have seen, mathematics is a very special area of knowledge. Mathematical proof gives us the luxury of conclusions that are absolutely certain. So is it even possible for mathematics to be biased?

To start answering this question, we should begin by unpacking the nature of mathematics as an axiomatic system.

Axiomatic systems

An axiomatic system is a body of knowledge built upon a small number of self-evident statements (axioms) using deductive reasoning. When deductive reasoning is applied to the starting statements, further statements are derived – they are called theorems. Theorems must be true if the axioms are true (which we assume them to be). These theorems are then used to derive further theorems, and so on.

KEY IDEA: An axiomatic system is a body of knowledge built upon a small number of self-evident statements (axioms) using deductive reasoning

How is knowledge gained through deductive reasoning better or worse than knowledge gained through inductive reasoning? (#Methods and tools)

In other words, there are two components in an axiomatic system:

1) Axioms (a small set of statements that are assumed to be self-evident and hence do not require proof)
2) Rules of reasoning (basic rules of deductive logic that we have agreed upon)

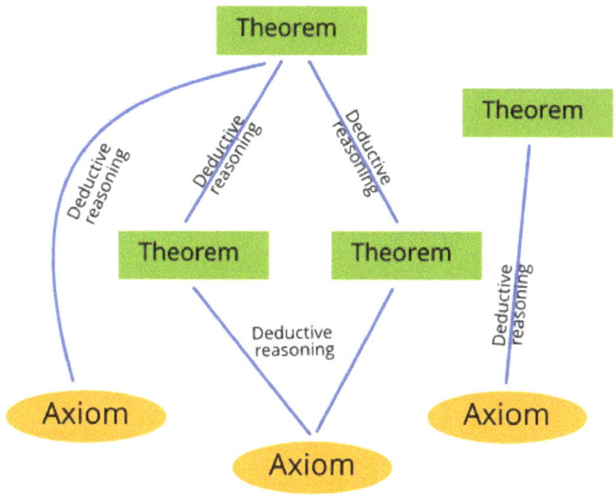

Image 60. *Mathematics is an axiomatic system*

An example of an axiom is: A straight line may be drawn between any two points (this is an axiom of Euclidean geometry). As you see, the statement is pretty self-evident. It does not require any proof.

Overall, Euclidean geometry is built on a set of five axioms. Here is the full set:

1) A straight line may be drawn between any two points
2) Any terminated straight line may be extended indefinitely
3) A circle may be drawn with any given point as its center and any given radius
4) All right angles are equal
5) For any given point not on a given line, there is exactly one line through the point that does not meet the given line

An example of a basic rule of deductive reasoning we have agreed upon is the "*law of excluded middle*". It states that for any statement, either this statement is true or its negation is true (and there is no third option). For example, take these two statements: "It is Monday" and "It is not Monday". The law of excluded middle states that either one of these statements is true, and there is no third option. You cannot add the option "It is kind of Monday" or something like that. Seems pretty obvious, doesn't it? But imagine if we agreed not to follow the law of excluded middle – what would happen? Mathematics would be quickly rendered meaningless.

KEY IDEA: Mathematics is an axiomatic system. Deductive reasoning is applied to axioms to derive theorems.

Some features of axiomatic systems

An axiomatic system is a building that is constructed using only two things: axioms (which may be compared to a foundation of the building) and rules of reasoning (which may be compared to the mortar that holds bricks together). The bricks in the building are theorems that are built on top of the foundation.

***Image 61**. Brick building*

You should note that:

1) By definition, an axiom is a statement that is self-obvious and does not require a proof. If you were able to demonstrate the truth of an axiom based on some other axioms, then it is not an axiom. It is a theorem. Looking back at Euclid's five axioms for example, none of them can be deduced from the other four.
2) Since all further statements in an axiomatic system depend on the initial set of axioms (plus the rules of logical reasoning), we can trace any statement back to the axioms. In a sense, the whole system is nothing else but the axioms unpacked. Some even say that all mathematical knowledge is already contained in the axioms, we just need to unwrap it and make it explicit.
3) Axioms are arbitrary. You are free to choose how many axioms you want, and what you want them to be. Since so much in axiomatic systems depends on the initial set of axioms (actually, *everything* depends on this initial set!), what axioms you select will determine the whole building you will end up constructing.

To what extent can we claim that all mathematical knowledge is already contained in the starting set of axioms? (#Scope)

KEY IDEA: Axioms are arbitrary, and this means that we can have multiple maths all based on different sets of axioms

This third consideration is extremely important because it poses a problem: if axioms are arbitrary, we can have multiple maths, so how do we know that our math is the best one?

Funny, but isn't that exactly the same question that we asked ourselves in natural sciences (we have multiple theories that are underdetermined by data, how do we choose?) and in history (we have multiple perspectives on the events of the past, how do we choose?).

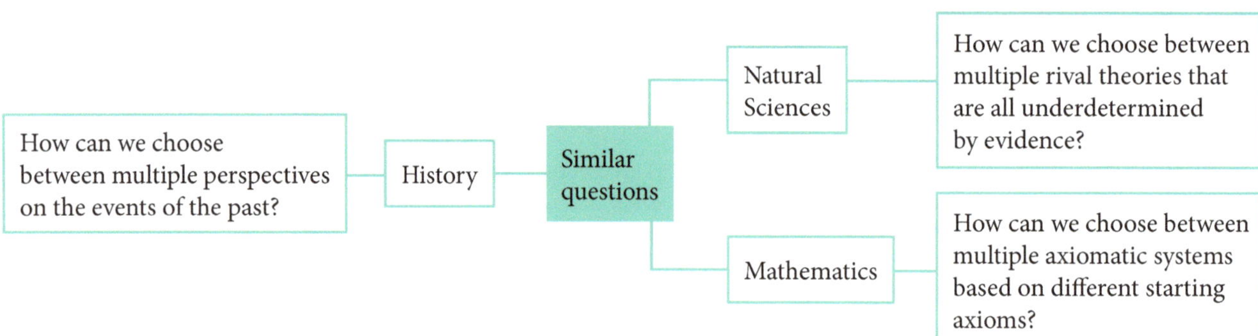

The answer to the question depends on where we place the criterion for truth in mathematics – within the axiomatic system itself or outside of it. This debate is widely known as the question: "*Is mathematics discovered or invented?*" We will look at it in the next few lessons. The answer we choose has implications for what we consider to be bias in mathematics.

Critical thinking extension

I have claimed in this lesson that axioms are arbitrary, but this is somewhat oversimplified. "Arbitrary" implies that we simply take the starting set of axioms "off the top of my head". But is that really so? Think about how Euclid must have defined his set of five axioms:

1) Was his choice of the five axioms completely "off the top of his head" or was it informed by something?
2) If it was "off the top of his head", then how come geometry turned out to be so useful? Was Euclid somehow incredibly lucky to come up with exactly the set of axioms needed to create a successful axiomatic system that would be used centuries later by organizations like NASA that are launching rockets to outer space?
3) If it was informed by something, then by what, exactly? Why did he feel necessary to claim that all right angles are equal? Why this claim and not some other similar claim?
4) Why are there five axioms, no more or no less?

To what extent are mathematical axioms arbitrary? (#Perspectives)

It could be an iterative process. Suppose Euclid started by accepting only one axiom and from this axiom he proved some theorems. But then he stumbled upon a situation where to prove further theorems he had to introduce additional axioms. Since the axioms seemed self-obvious, he went ahead and added them. He finally reached a point where he could prove all of his theorems using the set of only five axioms and no further axioms were required.

This is just a hypothesis. How likely do you think it is that Euclid followed this kind of reasoning?

If you are interested...

Watch the video "What is Mathematics?" (2017) on the YouTube channel *Free Animated Education*. It is 2.5-minute reflection on the nature of mathematics, what it is and what role it plays in our lives.

Take-away messages

Lesson 18. Mathematics is an axiomatic system. The foundation of an axiomatic system is a set of self-evident statements that are accepted as true without requiring any proof (axioms). Rules of deductive reasoning are applied to the axiomatic set to derive further statements (theorems). These theorems are used to prove further theorems. In this sense, an axiomatic system may be seen as unfolding from the original set of axioms, and the axioms themselves may be said to contain all of the potential knowledge within the axiomatic system. Although it takes time to develop the axiomatic system through proving all of its potential theorems, the system is entirely predetermined by the axiomatic set. Since the axiomatic set is arbitrary, multiple maths could exist. This raises the question: how do we select "the best" mathematics? The problem is similar to selecting among competing scientific theories or competing interpretations in history.

Lesson 19 - Discovered or invented? Truth in mathematics

Learning outcomes

a) [Knowledge and comprehension] What do we mean when we ask "Is mathematics discovered or invented"?
b) [Understanding and application] If mathematics is invented, who invents it and how? If mathematics is discovered, where does it exist before we find it?
c) [Thinking in the abstract] To what extent is it justified to use a super-mathematical criterion of truth in mathematics?

Key concepts

Intra-mathematical criterion of truth, super-mathematical criterion of truth

Other concepts used

Truth, mathematical proof, correspondence test for truth, coherence test for truth, mathematical entities

Themes and areas of knowledge

AOK: Mathematics, Natural Sciences

Recap and plan

Mathematics is an axiomatic system. Like any axiomatic system, it starts with a clearly defined set of self-evident statements accepted as true and not requiring any proof (axioms). Rules of reasoning are then applied to axioms to derive theorems. If the axioms are true (which we assume them to be, by definition) and if there is no flaw in reasoning, then the theorems are also true.

This also suggests that developing an axiomatic system is essentially unpacking the original axioms. In a sense, all potential knowledge of the axiomatic system is already contained in the axioms – it just needs to be gradually extracted. But axioms are arbitrary. This means that there could exist multiple axiomatic systems, for example, multiple maths. This raises the question: how do we select between them, or how do we know that our math is the best one?

KEY IDEA: All potential knowledge of the axiomatic system is already contained in the axioms

The first thing that comes to mind in response to this question is that perhaps some of the axiomatic systems are biased in some way, and we reject the biased ones and select the ones that are less biased?

We defined bias as a systematic deviation from the truth (or something that is currently accepted as the truth). So, naturally, the starting point of this discussion is finding out what "the truth" means in mathematics.

What counts as "the truth" in mathematical knowledge? (#Scope)

Truth in mathematics

What is truth in mathematics? There is no single answer to this question. There are approaches.

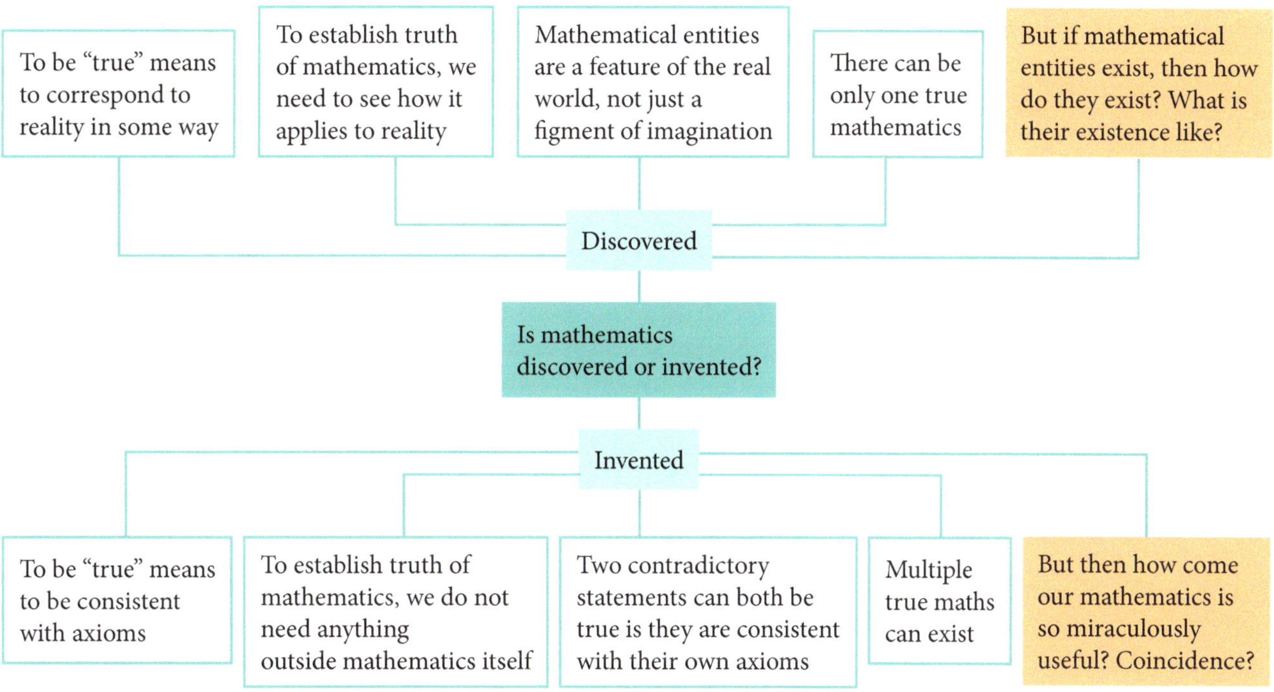

Approach 1: Mathematics is invented

Some philosophers emphasize the role of the coherence test for truth in mathematics (as you may recall, the coherence test says that something is true if it is coherent with what we already know. It is often opposed to the correspondence test, which says that something is true if it is supported by observation).

Unlike natural sciences whose objects exist somewhere in the real world in time and space, mathematics deals with abstract entities that cannot be observed. For example, can you observe the number 7? Not seven of something (seven watermelons, seven backpacks), but the concept of 7 itself? Can you observe a square root of 2? This is what I mean by abstract entities. There seems to be nothing in the real, physical world that corresponds to these entities.

Hence, the correspondence test for truth – the foundation of natural sciences – is not applicable here. We cannot "go and check" the truth of a mathematical statement.

Mathematics is based on deductive reasoning: from axioms to theorems. From this point of view, "true" in mathematics means "coherent with previous statements" or simply "provable". A theorem is true if it can be demonstrated that this theorem logically follows from the axioms. But the axioms, as you know, are arbitrary and, in this sense, mathematics is "invented".

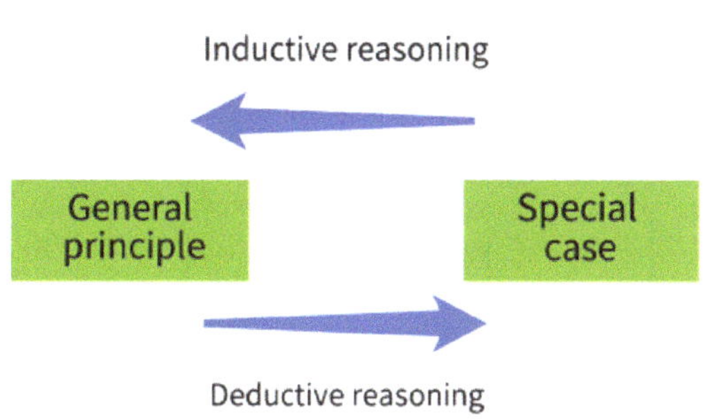

***Image 62**. Deductive and inductive reasoning*

Sometimes it is said that the criterion of truth in mathematics is intra-mathematical ("intra" means "within"). This means that we do not need anything beyond mathematics to establish whether mathematics is true or not. If it is coherent with the axioms, it is true, and the "reality" outside mathematics has nothing to do with it.

KEY IDEA: True in mathematics = coherent with previous statements = provable (intra-mathematical criterion). This is the "invented" position.

Note that in this approach two opposite statements may be true at the same time if they exist in different axiomatic systems, where each of these statements is coherent with its own set of axioms. A simple example: the statement "1 + 1 = 2" is true in base ten (the decimal system of numbers) but it is false in base two (the binary number system). In the binary system, 1 + 1 = 10. Another example is "parallel lines do not intersect". This statement is true in Euclidean geometry but may be false in some non-Euclidean geometries.

Approach 2: Mathematics is discovered

Other philosophers disagree with the idea that coherence is all that matters. Coherence with the axioms is essential, they say, but it is not the defining characteristic in mathematics. Since axioms are arbitrary, theoretically it is possible to take any arbitrary set of axioms and develop mathematics upon it. A large number of alternative maths is possible, each consistent with their own starting axiomatic sets. But not every one of these maths will be as helpful to us in our other endeavors.

Are there circumstances in which two opposite statements in mathematics may both be true? (#Perspectives)

You see, the mathematics we are using now has demonstrated its usefulness in a variety of ways. It is used in scientific calculations and it works, in the sense that the results of these calculations coincide with scientific observations. So, there must be something in the mathematics we are using that provides a good fit to the world we live in. From this point of view, only one "true" math exists. Here "true" in mathematics means "enabling successful practical applications".

KEY IDEA: True in mathematics = enables successful practical applications in science and technology (super-mathematical criterion). This is the "discovered" position.

The belief that mathematics is discovered (rather than invented) does indeed explain why mathematics seems to provide such a good fit to the world we live in. Euclid lived in the 4th century B.C. and he "arbitrarily" took a set of five axioms and started to build a geometry on that basis. He did not finish. His followers, generation after generation, continued to construct this building (remember, all of the knowledge was already contained in the axioms and his followers were only unpacking it). Geometry made its way into a variety of applications, including natural sciences. Physics used geometry in its calculations to describe how the world around us works and to predict its behavior. And these predictions have consistently been successful. Question:

***Image 63**. Euclid*

if the starting set of axioms, and hence mathematics itself, is arbitrary, how come it is so miraculously helpful to natural sciences in advancing our understanding of the world?

Therefore, those who believe that mathematics is discovered claim that the main criterion of truth lies outside of the axiomatic system itself. In other words, the truth criterion is super-mathematical ("super" means "beyond"). It is found in the real, objective world around us. Those axiomatic systems that do not provide a good fit to reality (not directly, but through other channels such as physics) will not survive.

But this approach also runs into a problem. If mathematics is discovered, then where does it exist before we find it? Think about it: if mathematical entities do exist in the real world, what is their existence like? It is easy to understand how a celestial object exists, or a chemical compound, or a beam of light. All of these things have material existence and they can be registered by our sensory organs. But in what sense does the number pi exist, or the square root of two, or "two" itself?

To what extent is coherence with axioms sufficient for a mathematical claim to be accepted as true? (#Methods and tools)

It looks like whatever position we take (discovered or invented), there is a difficult problem we will have to solve.

Mathematics is...	To be true means...	Criterion of truth is...	Can there be multiple true maths?	The problem is...
Invented	To be coherent with axioms	Intra-mathematical	Yes	If it is arbitrary, how come it is so miraculously useful?
Discovered	To enable successful practical applications	Super-mathematical	No	What are these mysterious mathematical entities that "exist" out there?

Critical thinking extension

Is it justified to use a super-mathematical criterion of truth in mathematics?

One of the solutions is to say that mathematical entities objectively exist as relations between material objects and their properties. We can claim that material objects of a circular shape (balls, planets, suns) objectively exist. Hence, their properties such as diameter and circumference also exist objectively. Thus, the number pi objectively exists as an objective relation between these two objective properties of material things.

To what extent do you agree with this understanding of the "objective existence" of mathematical entities? Can you suggest a different understanding? If you cannot, does it mean that you reject the idea that mathematics can be "discovered"?

If you are interested...

Watch the video "Is Math a feature of the universe or a feature of human creation?" (2013) on YouTube from *PBS Idea Channel*.

(The channel itself is also recommended: it discusses complex things in a way that is accessible and humorous).

Take-away messages

Lesson 19. Since multiple axiomatic systems are possible, we face the challenge of selecting some over others. Such selection is possible if some of the axiomatic systems are biased in some way – then we reject the biased ones and select the non-biased ones. But since bias is a deviation from the truth, we must define what we mean by the "truth" in mathematics. The answer to this question depends on your position in the debate "Is mathematics invented or discovered?" If you believe that mathematics is invented, you believe that mathematical entities do not have an existence of their own. They cannot be observed and hence the correspondence test for truth cannot be applied to them. Therefore, we should apply the coherence test and assume that for a statement to be true in mathematics means to be consistent with the previous statements. "True" from this perspective means "follows from the axioms", or simply "provable". If you believe that mathematics is discovered, you believe that only one "true" math exists. You also think that the criterion of truth is super-mathematical (lies outside of mathematics). For this reason, you define "true" in mathematics as "enabling successful practical applications" in science and technology.

Lesson 20 - Consistency

Learning outcomes

a) [Knowledge and comprehension] What is consistency of an axiomatic system?
b) [Understanding and application] Can an axiomatic system prove its own consistency?
c) [Thinking in the abstract] What does Gödel's second incompleteness theorem mean in terms of how we understand bias in mathematics?

Key concepts

Consistency of an axiomatic system, inconsistency of an axiomatic system, Hilbert's second problem, Gödel's second incompleteness theorem

Other concepts used

Contradiction, provability

Themes and areas of knowledge

AOK: Mathematics, Natural Sciences

Recap and plan

We have considered the debate "Is mathematics discovered or invented?"

If you believe mathematics is discovered, then you believe that to be "true" in mathematics means to correspond to reality. The statement "2 + 2 = 4" is true because it somehow reflects the reality of things and because, when we used this statement to construct a space rocket, the rocket successfully landed on the moon. The statement "2 + 2 = 5" cannot be true because it goes against the nature of things.

If you believe mathematics is invented, then you believe that, if you can show that a statement is coherent with the original axioms, then this statement is true. The statement "2 + 2 = 4" is true because you can demonstrate that this statement logically follows from the axioms that you previously accepted. But the statement "2 + 2 = 5" can also be true in some other mathematical system that has a different set of axioms.

In this lesson we will look closely at the "mathematics is invented" position. Within this position, mathematics is not biased if it is internally coherent. The question is, then, to what extent is mathematics internally coherent?

In what ways are ethical judgments similar to and different from mathematical statements? (#Ethics)

To answer this question, an important characteristic that should be considered is consistency of an axiomatic system.

Consistency of an axiomatic system

Mathematics is an axiomatic system. To be "true" in such a system means to be "provable". If a statement can be proven by showing that it logically follows from the original set of axioms, this statement is true.

But there exists a situation that may show that the set of axioms itself is creating contradictions and in this scenario, we will have to admit that the whole axiomatic system is inconsistent.

Imagine you were able to demonstrate that "2 + 2 = 4" follows from your axioms. But you were also able to demonstrate that "2 + 2 = 5" follows from these same axioms. So, within your axiomatic system both "2 + 2 = 4" and "2 + 2 = 5" are true. Hence, 4 = 5. This can only mean one thing: your axiomatic system is rubbish because it creates a contradiction. We call such axiomatic systems inconsistent.

Needless to say, we want our mathematics to be consistent.

KEY IDEA: Consistency is the absence of contradictions. An inconsistent axiomatic system is the one in which two contradictory statements can both be proven from the same set of axioms.

What happens when an axiomatic system is found to be inconsistent?

What is the role of contradiction in obtaining mathematical knowledge? (#Methods and tools)

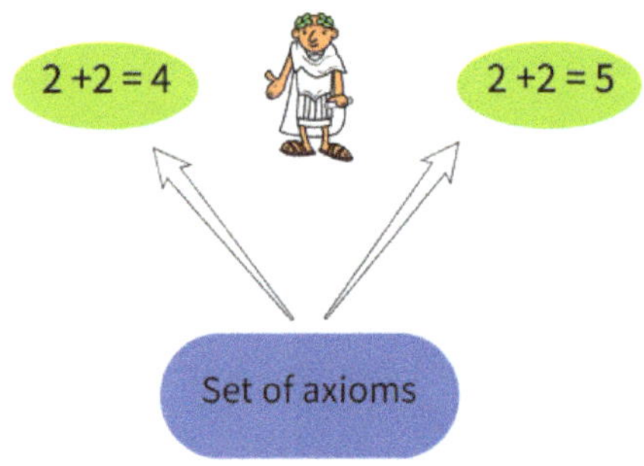

***Image 64**. Contradiction in mathematics*

Even one contradiction is enough for us to conclude that the whole system is rubbish. Imagine mathematicians actually proved both the statements "2 + 2 = 4" and "2 + 2 = 5" by showing that both of these statements are deducible from the same axioms. You might think that it is not a big deal, but it is. It means that we cannot trust any other calculations whatsoever. If 4 = 5, integers no longer make sense. Summation doesn't make sense. The "equal" sign doesn't make sense. If that is the case, then we cannot trust any scientific and technological applications that used such calculations, either. We need to reject mathematics and, with it, science and technology. This would be a truly catastrophic scenario.

It does not have to be something as obvious as my example. Even the tiniest, most insignificant contradiction will lead to the same catastrophic consequences. It does not matter how small the contradiction is. If it exists, the whole system is inconsistent and hence rubbish.

Which is why we really want our mathematics to be consistent!

KEY IDEA: If an axiomatic system has been shown to generate a contradiction, this system is inconsistent and must be rejected

Can we prove that an axiomatic system is consistent?

This problem was posed in 1900 by the mathematician David Hilbert. It is known as Hilbert's second problem (it was second in his list of 23 problems).

We know various mathematical systems that have been consistent so far. In the process of its development, Euclidean geometry, for example, did not generate any contradictions, so the building did not have to be demolished. But the question is, is there a possibility that in the future, as these mathematical systems develop even further, such contradictions *will* be found and the building *will* have to be demolished? Is there a possibility that someone will prove a

***Image 65**. David Hilbert (1862 – 1943)*

***Image 66**. Kurt Gödel (1906 – 1978)*

theorem that follows from Euclidean axioms but contradicts another theorem that follows from those very axioms?

To what extent can it be claimed that mathematical knowledge is absolutely certain? (#Perspectives)

Certainly, we can just wait and see what happens. In natural sciences, for example, it would be perfectly okay to accept a theory provisionally, until the times when counter-evidence is discovered. However, mathematics is supposed to be different from natural sciences exactly because mathematics is the only area of knowledge where we know things with absolute certainty. We must be able to prove our statements.
Additionally, to wait and see what happens may not exactly be an option because the consequences are so catastrophic. Imagine we started with a set of simple axioms and developed a math based on it. But, 60 thousand years later, someone proves that 5 is not 5. So, we have to throw away 60 thousand years of hard work.

This is why we want to prove (with a 100% certainty) that our math is consistent and will remain to be consistent as it develops further. Can we do that?

KEY IDEA: We want to know for sure that mathematics is consistent because the consequences of discovering a contradiction at some point of time in the future would be catastrophic

Gödel's second incompleteness theorem

In 1931, mathematician Kurt Gödel published a proof that no proof of its own consistency can be carried out within the axiomatic system itself. In other words, his answer was a "no": an axiomatic system cannot prove its own consistency. This is known as Gödel's second incompleteness theorem.

It may be one of the most complicated theorems in mathematics, but I will try to summarize it in the next few sentences.

> In mathematics, it can be proven that 2 + 2 is 4. And it can be proven that it can be proven that 2 + 2 is 4.
>
> On the other hand, it can be proven that 2 + 2 is not 5. And it can be proven that it can be proven that 2 + 2 is not 5.
>
> Can it be proven that 2 + 2 is 5? We hope not. If it could be proven that 2 + 2 is 5, that would be the catastrophic scenario that I described earlier and that would mean that all mathematics is rubbish.

Image 67. *If you understand this joke, I bet you do very well in mathematics*

> Hoping is nice, but we want proof. So, the question is: can it be proven that it cannot be proven that 2 + 2 is 5? Here comes Gödel's answer: no, it cannot. Although mathematics can prove that 2 + 2 is not 5, it cannot prove that it cannot be proven that 2 + 2 is 5.
>
> *(Based on Boolos, 1994)*

Hence, the answer to the question "can mathematics prove its own consistency?" is no.

KEY IDEA: Gödel's second incompleteness theorem: a consistent axiomatic system cannot prove its own consistency

Critical thinking extension

Now you know that an axiomatic system (such as mathematics) cannot prove its own consistency. You also know that if an axiomatic system is inconsistent, then this system is rubbish. So, to rephrase, mathematics cannot prove that it is not rubbish.

What implications does this have for our understanding of bias in mathematics?

If we believe that mathematics is invented, any mathematical statement is true (and not biased) if it is coherent with the axioms. And, so far, we have been able to demonstrate (quite miraculously) that this is indeed true and the axioms do not generate any contradictions. But we cannot prove that this will continue in the future. The stakes are high: if it happens, we will need to accept that the whole system of mathematics is false, including all statements we previously believed to be true.

Does this mean that mathematics *may be* biased, but we will only know it if (and when) it generates a contradiction?

What is the nature of bias in mathematics? (#Scope)

Does this mean that mathematics is not at all as certain as we imagine it to be?

If you are interested...

If you are interested in a deeper understanding of the theorem, follow the reader-friendly article "Gödel's incompleteness theorems" of the web project *Infinity plus one math* (infinityplusonemath.wordpress.com). There are pictures!

Take-away messages

Lesson 20. Consistency of an axiomatic system refers to the absence of contradictions in its statements. Conversely, an axiomatic system is inconsistent if we can show that two contradictory statements both follow from the axioms of this system. Discovering that mathematics is inconsistent may be a truly catastrophic scenario, so it is vital to prove that mathematics is consistent. However, according to Gödel's second incompleteness theorem, mathematics cannot prove its own consistency. We can prove mathematics to be inconsistent (if we stumble upon a contradiction), but we cannot prove its consistency from within mathematics itself. If you believe that mathematics is invented, you have to make peace with the fact that one day it may turn out to be biased.

Lesson 21 - Mathematical realism

Learning outcomes

a) [Knowledge and comprehension] What do mathematical realists mean when they claim that mathematics is discovered?
b) [Understanding and application] What are the main arguments for and against mathematical realism?
c) [Thinking in the abstract] From the perspective of mathematical realism, how do we know if mathematics is biased?

Key concepts

Mathematical realism, mathematical anti-realism, two meanings of "discovery" in mathematics

Other concepts used

Mathematical entities, Fibonacci's sequence, Euclidean and non-Euclidean geometry, science and technology

Themes and areas of knowledge

AOK: Mathematics, Natural Sciences

Recap and plan

We have seen that, if mathematics is invented, bias takes the form of inconsistency. Mathematics is not biased as long as it is consistent. However, the problem is, we cannot prove that mathematics is consistent. Therefore, we cannot prove that mathematics is not biased. If we believe that mathematics is invented, we have to make peace with this annoying uncertainty.

Let's now turn our attention to the other camp in the "discovered or invented" debate. Let's assume that mathematics is discovered.

It is not an ungrounded assumption because you must admit that the successes of mathematics have been very significant. How likely is it that a set of axioms that is pretty much arbitrary enables such hugely successful real-world applications? Mathematics indeed seems to be in synchrony with the world. The fit is too miraculous for an invention.

Is mathematics an independent area of knowledge or merely a tool of science? (#Scope)

Mathematical realism

As Einstein put it, "How can it be that mathematics, being after all a product of human thought which is independent of experience, is so admirably appropriate to the objects of reality?" (Einstein, 1921).

When you claim that mathematics is discovered, you are assuming the realist view. Mathematical realism claims that mathematical structures are intrinsic to nature. We are so successful in building a math with a range of successful applications because we are inspired by these intrinsic relationships and because they inspire our thought. They exist in the world around us, and mathematicians merely discover them.

***Image 68**. Alien*

KEY IDEA: According to mathematical realism, mathematical structures are intrinsic to nature

To better understand the differences between mathematical realism ("mathematics is discovered") and mathematical anti-realism ("mathematics is invented"), consider the following hypothetical scenarios:

Hypothetical scenario	Mathematical realism	Mathematical anti-realism
The human civilization disappeared and another society had to build it from scratch.	This new society will end up with the same mathematics that we currently have. This is because the intrinsic properties of reality would inspire them in the same way, and their mathematics will be similar because the objective reality around them will be the same.	This new society will probably end up with a math quite different from ours. This is because the starting point of an axiomatic system is a set of axioms, and axioms are not given to us in any way (they are decided upon by humans).
Aliens visited planet Earth and shared their knowledge with us, including mathematical knowledge. Since they reached us first, it is likely that their knowledge is more well-developed than ours.	The alien mathematics will either coincide with ours (same axioms, but further unpacked) or subsume ours (a larger set of axioms that includes ours as a part of it). This is because mathematics reflects the properties of the real world, so our axioms are "correct", but we may not have identified all of them.	The alien mathematics may be entirely different from our mathematics. As a consequence, their science will be different too. It is likely that it will make no sense to us.

Arguments for mathematical realism

How reasonable is it to claim that mathematical entities exist in the real world? (#Perspectives)

We have already mentioned one argument for mathematical realism: it is hard to believe that we can arbitrarily invent something that centuries later turns out to be so useful in solving real-life problems in science and technology. In this respect, Eugene Wigner noted that our math seems "unnaturally natural" (Lessel, 2016). For example, Fibonacci's sequence is the series of numbers where the next number is found by adding up the two numbers before it: 0, 1, 1, 2, 3, 5, 8, 13, 21, 34…

Image 69*. Fibonacci sequence in nature*

Fibonacci's sequence was first described as part of an idealized model of rabbit population growth. A pure mental exercise in the abstract dimension of a highly specific, niche problem. Much later, the Fibonacci sequence was seen in a great variety of other aspects of the world around us: in sunflower seeds, flower petals, lungs, the structure of a pineapple, snail shells, and so on. This suggests that the Fibonacci sequence is not purely a figment of our imagination – it has some deep connection with the structure of the objective world.

Another argument is that at any point of time there exist (or could potentially exist) many different maths. We can prefer one of these to the others because it helps us better in our scientific and technological developments. For example, the theorems of Euclidean geometry are true only if the surface is ideally flat. There exist alternative non-Euclidean geometries that assume a spherical surface (much like the Earth) rather than a flat surface. In such geometries, it is okay for parallel lines to intersect (think about the surface of the Earth – longitude lines are parallel, but they intersect at the poles). When Einstein was developing his relativity theory – millennia after Euclid and centuries after the main non-Euclidean geometries – the flat surface assumption did not work for him. He thought that space-time was "curved". So, he abandoned Euclidean geometry and instead used a non-Euclidean one to inform his formulas and calculations.

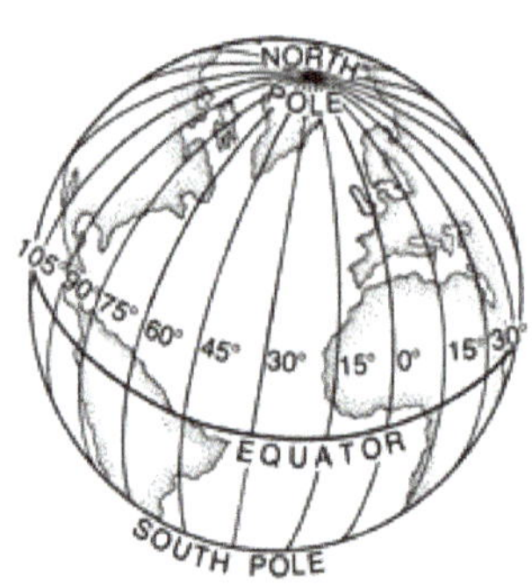

Image 70*. Intersecting longitude lines*

Arguments against mathematical realism

One argument against mathematical realism is that it sounds a little mystical, akin to religion. It claims that mathematical entities or mathematical structures "exist" in the real world, although we cannot perceive them in any tangible way, and that they "inspire" us when we come up with our sets of axioms. The question is, how can we check for this existence? In the absence of direct observation, it looks like we can only rely on faith.

Another argument is that mathematics can turn out to be useful (in scientific and technological applications), but when we do mathematics, we never know if it will turn out to be useful or not. In other words, "writing something down doesn't guarantee usefulness" (Lessel, 2016, p. 84). When mathematicians work, they are not interested in applications. They work in the purely abstract space, unpacking their axiomatic sets. They do math as a logic exercise. Real-world applications may or may not be discovered in the future, but they are certainly not what drives a mathematician in the process of their reasoning.

Arguments for and against mathematical realism

For:

- Mathematics is unnaturally natural: the fit to reality is too miraculous for an invention
- There are multiple maths; we gradually select the ones that fit the world better

Against:

- Existence of mathematical entities in the real world cannot be tested by senses; we need to rely on faith
- When mathematicians work, they are not interested in applications. Applications are a by-product

Two meanings of "discovery"

It is important to clarify what it means for something to be "discovered".

As we discussed earlier, all knowledge of an axiomatic system is already implicitly contained in the axioms. When Euclid identified his set of five axioms, all Euclidean geometry was already contained in this set. When Pythagoras derived his theorem ($a^2 + b^2 = c^2$), did he "discover" it? It was already there lurking within the set of Euclidean axioms, waiting to be unpacked. But at the same time, this theorem was not known to us before Pythagoras "found" it. This is what is meant by "discovery" from the perspective of the "mathematics is invented" camp. Indeed, we invent a set of axioms and then we "discover" the consequences of these axioms.

Are mathematical discoveries made in a way that is similar to scientific discoveries? (#Methods and tools)

On the other hand, to "discover" may mean to find something in the real world around us. Columbus "discovered" America because it had already existed in the real world and he only stumbled upon it. If we say that mathematics is "discovered" in this sense of the word, we imply that the theorem we discovered reflects some property of the world around us. It is this meaning of the word "discover" that mathematical realists imply. Hence, mathematics is biased if it somehow fails to reflect the properties of the real world.

Critical thinking extension

If mathematics is discovered, how can we know if it is biased? To show that it is biased, we need to show that it fails to reflect mathematical properties of the real world, but how exactly can this be done?

Perhaps there is some similarity between rival axiomatic systems in mathematics and rival scientific theories? The choice between these axiomatic systems is informed by our choice of a scientific theory (for example, if we choose Einstein's theory, we must also choose non-Euclidean geometry). But the choice between scientific theories is informed by how well the theory fits the observed data from real world. Therefore indirectly fit to the real-world data affects the choice of an axiomatic system.

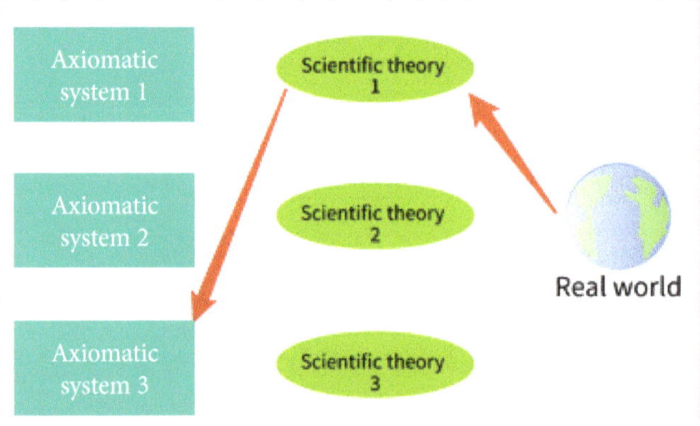

***Image 71**. Fit between mathematics and reality*

Should we value mathematical knowledge with no real-life applications as much as knowledge that can be directly applied? (#Ethics)

Or perhaps it is simply meaningless to speak about bias in mathematics? It is the job of science to reflect reality. To do that, science uses mathematics as a tool. Science discovers and mathematics just assists science in doing so. From this perspective, the concept of bias does not apply to mathematics. Perhaps mathematics, unlike science, can be useful or not so useful, but can't be biased or unbiased.

Which one of these options are you leaning toward, or do you think there is a third option?

If you are interested…

Watch the video "Why numbers are more real than atoms" on the website *Lucid Philosophy* (lucidphilosophy.com). It presents a deep summary of some key arguments in favor of mathematical realism.

Take-away messages

Lesson 21. The "mathematics is discovered" position emphasizes the miraculous fit between abstract mathematical structures and real-life applications. It is very unlikely that we simply invented something that ended up being so useful, with so many practical applications in science and technology. From this position, it must be that mathematics reflects some deep properties of reality itself. The view that mathematical structures are intrinsic to nature is known as mathematical realism. One way to justify mathematical realism is to say that when we are defining axioms, we are somehow inspired by nature and our axioms already reflect some intrinsic properties of the world. Another way to justify mathematical realism is to accept that axioms are indeed arbitrary, but multiple alternative maths may co-exist, and ultimately it is the scientist who decides which of these axiomatic systems are more suitable. Since the scientist tries to create a theory that would reflect the real world, the mathematical system that the scientist chooses will also reflect the real world in some sense.

Back to the exhibition

After five lessons of TOK mathematics, my football is still a mystery to me. It seems like the ball somehow "contains" the number pi, ready to be discovered, and yet it still feels weird to say that the number pi somehow "exists" within the ball.

If I send the football to space and it lands (billions of years later) on a planet inhabited by an alien civilization, will they eventually discover the number pi that my soccer ball "contains"? I don't know.

But if the number pi actually exists, then mathematics can be biased pretty much in the same way as natural sciences. If, on the other hand, the number pi is an invention of the human mind, then "consistency" is a much better word for mathematics than "bias". We have seen in this unit that there is a trick with consistency – a consistent axiomatic system can never prove its own consistency.

The number pi is not the only mysterious number out there. There is an impressive list of mathematical constants that have been discovered (invented?) in the history of math, many of them in the 20th century. You might want to refer to the Wikipedia page "List of mathematical constants" to be impressed.

One of my favorites is the Feigenbaum constant – the mysterious number 4.669 lurking inside chaos. For a nice explanation of the constant, you can watch the video entitled "The Feigenbaum Constant (4.669)" on the YouTube channel *Numberphile*.

I am still deeply puzzled with the ball. This is probably why I have never been a fan of football. It's just too stressful, to kick the puzzle of the Universe around a field.

Lesson 22 - Overview: bias in Mathematics, Natural Sciences and History

Learning outcomes

a) [Knowledge and comprehension] How is the problem of bias approached in the three areas of knowledge?
b) [Understanding and application] How does deciding if an area of knowledge is biased depend on answering additional questions – and what are these questions?
c) [Thinking in the abstract] Despite how the three areas of knowledge are different, what are the crucial similarities when it comes to defining bias in these areas?

Key concepts

Bias, truth

Other concepts used

Theory-laden facts, rival theories, rival interpretations

Themes and areas of knowledge

AOK: Natural Sciences, History, Mathematics

Recap and plan

We have looked at the concept of bias in three areas of shared knowledge – Natural Sciences, History and Mathematics. Bias manifests itself very differently in these areas. But, at the same time, there are quite a few surprising similarities.

In this extra lesson, we are revisiting all of the key ideas from this unit and trying to compare what it means to be "biased" in the three areas.

This lesson is meant to consolidate your understanding through comparing the areas of knowledge rather than looking at them separately.

Natural Sciences

Initially, it was believed that our beliefs in natural sciences are not biased if they are supported by observation (*verificationism*).

But it was recognized later that verificationism is flawed for at least three reasons:

1) False beliefs can also have empirical support
2) Scientific theories are underdetermined by evidence (*underdetermination of scientific theories*)
3) Scientific facts are theory-laden (*theory-laden facts*)

Therefore, empirical support does not guarantee lack of bias.

The first problem can be solved through the concept of falsifiability: we can try to refute our beliefs instead of supporting them (*falsifiability*).

The second and the third problem can be solved through the concept of verisimilitude. As science progresses, theories include more and more informative testable statements that enable successful predictions about reality. Although we cannot claim that these theories are true, we can claim that they are likely to be true (*verisimilitude*).

But the idea of progressive increase in verisimilitude does not seem to reflect what's actually happening:

1) When an old theory gets rejected, there are always a number of rival theories that can potentially replace the old one (*paradigm shift*)
2) These rival theories are built on entirely different foundations; even the "facts" in them

are different because facts are theory-laden (*incommensurability of scientific theories*)
3) For this reason, we cannot use facts alone to choose between them
4) And we cannot say that the scientific progress is a gradual approximation to the truth

The answer to the question "Is science biased?" depends on the answer to the question "Do we have at least indirect access to scientific truth?"

Question	Option 1 (verisimilitude, Karl Popper)	Option 2 (incommensurability, Thomas Kuhn)
Do we have at least indirect access to scientific truth?	Yes. Although we cannot see it directly, we can claim that a theory that has a large number of specific testable predictions is likely to be true.	No. All facts are theory-laden, so even the facts can be said to be different in different theories. Therefore, we cannot use correspondence to facts alone to select among rival theories.
Is science biased?	Yes, but as science progresses it is becoming less and less biased through the process of falsification.	Probably, but there is no way for us to know and the question is meaningless. Much like evolution, the development of science is a response to problems currently faced by theories and a solution to these problems. But much like evolution, scientific progress is not driven by some "plan" or "truth". Evolution cannot be "biased", and neither can science.

History

In history, the paradox is that the past happened objectively, but the only access to the past that we have lies through someone's interpretation of it. Interpretations are influenced by a perspective. Perspectives are influenced by multiple things in our background (nationality, education, identity) and there is no way we can step out of our minds to look at the past without a perspective acting as a filter.

The answer to the question "Is history biased?" depends on the answer to the question "Does a perspective-free account of the past exist?"

Question	Option 1	Option 2	Option 3	Option 4
Does a perspective-free account of the past exist?	Yes, it does. To achieve it, we must overcome the influence of our perspectives and base our history writing on facts.	No, it doesn't. The goal of abandoning our perspectives is simply unachievable, and facts in history, much like in sciences, are theory-laden. A historical fact is already a product of our interpretation.	No, but we don't need a perspective-free account. All we need is a way to claim that one interpretation is in some way "better" than a rival interpretation.	No, but multiple perspectives are actually exactly what we need!
Is history biased?	Some historical accounts may be biased, but it is possible to create an objective history that will "correctly" reflect what actually happened in the past.	Yes, it is, and there is nothing we can do about it because we cannot even see where the bias is.	Some interpretations are more biased, some less. We can select some interpretations and abandon others. We may believe that the ones we select are closer to the truth, but there is no way to know for sure (this is similar to the verisimilitude versus incommensurability debate in science).	The question is meaningless. Bias is a deviation from some "standard", but there is no standard in history. There are only multiple – often incompatible – perspectives that engage in a dialogue (heteroglossia).

Mathematics

In mathematics, defining bias depends on defining the truth. Truth will be defined differently depending on how we answer the question "Is mathematics discovered or invented?"

Question	Option 1	Option 2
Is mathematics discovered or invented?	Discovered. It means that mathematical entities exist in the real world, alien mathematics will closely resemble our mathematics, and if we ever had to rebuild the civilization from scratch, we would end up with the same mathematics. There is only one true math. We know which math is true indirectly, through science. If a scientific theory (which uses mathematics) is successful, then mathematics is "true".	Invented. It means that mathematics is a self-contained axiomatic system that is created from a set of axioms. All knowledge is already contained in the original axiomatic set. It just needs to be "unpacked". To be true in mathematics means to be consistent with the rest of the system (e.g. a theorem is true if it can be traced back to the original axioms).
Is mathematics biased?	The question may be meaningless. Science can be biased or unbiased depending on its fit to the world, and mathematics can be more or less useful for the scientific theory we currently choose over others.	In this approach, mathematics will be biased if it is inconsistent (that is, generates contradictions). But it was demonstrated by Gödel that an axiomatic system cannot prove its own consistency. So far, mathematics has not generated any major contradictions so we believe that it is consistent (unbiased), but there exists a possibility that such contradictions will be generated later. The consequences could be dramatic. There is nothing we can do to rule out this possibility.

As you can see, in each area of knowledge, the answer to the question "Is this AOK biased?" is not that simple. It depends on how you solve some other crucial problem within the area of knowledge. In some cases, instead of answering the question, we actually conclude that the question itself makes no sense!

Critical thinking extension

Interestingly, although the three areas of knowledge are so drastically different, there are some curious similarities in how they deal with bias. Here are just a few examples:

1) Theory-laden facts are a problem not only in history (where a fact already includes an element of interpretation in it), but also in natural sciences (where a fact is based on a theory through which it was registered). As such, "correspondence to facts" is not sufficient as a test for truth, neither in history nor in natural sciences.
2) At any particular point of time, there exist rival explanations and we are faced with the task to choose the "best" among them. There seems to be no strict rule to guide this choice. In natural sciences, this takes the form of rival incommensurable theories competing with each other during a paradigm shift. These theories may fit the available evidence equally well. In history, it takes the form of multiple perspectives on the same events of the past. One may claim that these perspectives are equally supported by "facts". Weirdly, even in mathematics, there exist alternative axiomatic systems (such as Euclidean geometry and a number of non-Euclidean geometries). At times, science needs to select one of these axiomatic systems, and it often selects the one that provides a better fit to the problems that science is trying to tackle (such was the case when Einstein chose to use a non-Euclidean geometry to describe his relativity theory).

Can you spot any more similarities?

If you are interested...

We have compared bias in three areas of knowledge that were the focus of this unit. If you are interested, you might want to keep comparing and bring in the other two areas – Human Sciences and the Arts!

The Arts may be especially interesting to look at. Does the concept of "bias" make any kind of sense in art? If it does, what forms does it take? Is there biased art and unbiased art?

Take-away messages

Lesson 22. In this lesson, we summarized the key bias-related problems encountered by three areas of knowledge – Natural Sciences, History and Mathematics. Despite how different these areas are, they face some common challenges, such as the problem of theory-laden facts and the need to select among a number of rival theories.

UNIT 5 - Knowledge and understanding

UNIT 5 - Knowledge and understanding

When you think about how we use the words "knowledge" and "understanding" in our daily lives, it feels like understanding is deeper and more difficult to achieve than knowledge. You cannot understand something without knowing it. But you can know something without understanding it. So it seems like the formula is: first knowledge, then understanding.

KEY IDEA: First knowledge, then understanding

"Understanding" also seems to imply an element of subjectivity, or individual interpretation. We can say "this is how I understand it", but it is less common to say "this is how I know it".

Let's talk about love. I have two questions for you, and I wonder if you can see the difference between them:

- Do you know what love is?
- Do you understand love?

A common response would be that we know what love is from sources such as research studies (demonstrating, for example, the role of various brain chemicals in attraction), cultural studies (looking at traditions and rituals surrounding mating), economics (looking at financial benefits of forming stable, lifelong bonds), evolutionary theory, and so on. This is how we know love objectively as a social phenomenon. By contrast, we understand what love is when we read poetry, try to support a friend who lost a close person, and fall in love ourselves. Understanding involves a subjective dimension: being empathetic, relating knowledge to our own personality.

So, understanding is deeper, but it comes at the cost of being more subjective. But this is a problem because everything "subjective" is very often frowned upon. In common perception, "subjective" is synonymous to unreliable and inferior. Here are examples of what students often say, in various contexts:

- "But this is your subjective interpretation" (read: there are many ways to look at this situation, so I don't care what you think)
- "Human sciences are subjective" (read: human sciences are incorrect and useless, and knowledge obtained in them is inaccurate)
- Marking in Theory of Knowledge is subjective (read: unfair)

***Image 1**. Love*

I have taught Psychology in schools where there exists a strong preference for sciences, students aspire to become engineers or economists, and very few students (or parents) take humanities seriously. My Psychology students complained about being ridiculed by "the PCM kids" (PCM stands for physics-chemistry-mathematics) about their subject choices. Reportedly, these are some of the things "PCM kids" said about humanities:

- It is subjective. Everything you talk about in these subjects are just opinions
- There are too many factors influencing human behavior so you can't predict it
- You should pay attention in Math, maybe this way you will be able to count how much money you are going to make doing humanities (ouch!)

Well, I have many rebuttals to these and similar statements. Some of them are:

- They are not just opinions, but educated interpretations. And if you think Physics is free of such interpretations, you are wrong
- If something is very complex and influenced by a lot of factors, it does not mean you should simply give up studying it
- Brilliant scientists in the field of humanities are often more financially successful than brilliant scientists in the field of natural sciences. While the average salary in the field may indeed be lower, you are not planning on becoming an average human being, are you?

But I am going off on a tangent. The point is, in the mind of some groups of people at least, humanities are sometimes stereotypically dismissed as "subjective and hence not serious", and interpretation (and hence understanding) is associated with something that has nothing to do with science.

In this unit, we challenge these stereotypes. We develop a more balanced and thoughtful approach to the concepts of objectivity and subjectivity. We will defend the following statements, among others:

- Knowledge may be fragmented but understanding is holistic. Understanding brings fragments together and arranges them in a coherent whole where these fragments make a lot more sense. For this reason, understanding is a desirable goal.
- Understanding is distinctly different in different areas of knowledge. In this unit, we will focus on three: Natural Sciences, Human Sciences, and the Arts.
- There are situations where subjective knowledge is preferable to objective knowledge.

Exhibition: Kamal, a navigation device

Image 2. The kamal
(credit: Bordwall, Wikimedia Commons)

This is a kamal.

It is a simple device that was used by sailors of the past to figure out where they were to not get lost.

Today we use GPS technology instead, and you may be spoiled by how simple it is to open an app on your phone and immediately see your position on the face of the planet. But imagine you are on a boat stranded somewhere in the middle of a vast ocean, all you can see around you is sea, and your battery is dead. What would you do?

That is probably how Arab navigators felt in the 9th century when they ventured bravely into the unknown. That is when they invented the kamal, which became the first tool for quantitative navigation.

The kamal is a small piece of wood attached to a string. It uses Polaris (the North Star) to determine the boat's latitude. The North Star has this wonderful property of being almost exactly above the Earth's north pole. If you stand on the North Pole, the star will be directly above your head. Additionally, as the Earth rotates, so do the stars in the sky, but not Polaris. It pretty much stays in the same location in the night sky, with the other stars rotating around it. This makes Polaris perfect for navigation. When you move away from the North Pole toward the equator, the star appears lower above the horizon. When you reach the equator, the star will appear just above the horizon level, and then when you cross the equator and move to the Southern Hemisphere, Polaris will disappear from the sky.

Before you leave the port, hold the string of the kamal in your mouth and pull the wooden block until its lower side is aligned with the horizon and the top side is aligned with the North Star. Tie a knot where you are holding the string with your teeth. This knot will represent your current latitude. When at sea, you can repeat the measurement. To return, just sail the boat to your original latitude and go back (if you sailed West when you left, then go East, and vice versa). It is simple, and it saved many lives from being lost in the ocean.

When you look at the stars in the night sky, what are you thinking about? When a 9th-century Arab seafarer looked at the stars, what was he thinking about? Did he know the same things about stars as you know now? Did he understand stars differently from the way you understand them today?

He did not realize that stars are giant balls of gas floating in empty space millions of miles away. He did not know that the Sun is just one of these stars. He understood stars differently. But his understanding of how stars work, I bet, was more practical than that of many of us today. With a simple piece of wood attached to a piece of rope, he could find his way home from miles away in the open sea. So which one of you knows more about stars, and which one of you understands stars better?

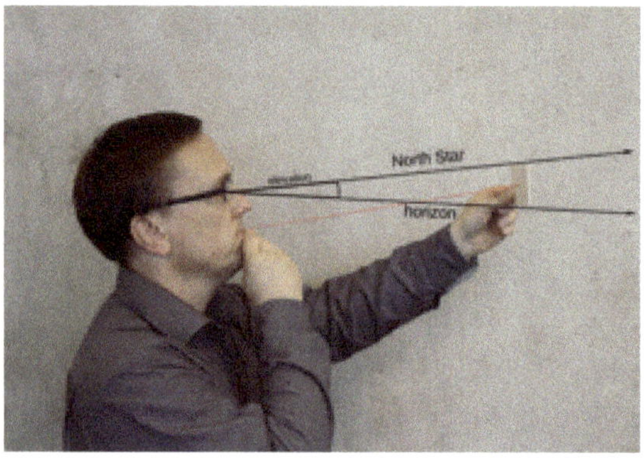

Image 3. The kamal in use
(credit: Markus Nielbock, Wikimedia Commons)

Story: The savior of mothers

Image 4. *Ignaz Philipp Semmelweis (1818 - 1865)*

Ignaz Philipp Semmelweis (1818 - 1865) was a Hungarian physician who is sometimes described as the "savior of mothers".

In 1847 he worked in an obstetrical clinic in Vienna. His role was to assist a professor. He prepared patients in the morning, took care of clerical records, and so on. At that time, an unpleasantly large number of women used to die after giving birth due to childbed fever – an infection of the female reproductive tract. Childbed fever was often fatal. An average of about 10 percent of women giving birth in the clinic died. Surprisingly, Semmelweis's records showed that the rate of mortality was lower even among women who gave birth in the street on their way to the clinic.

Semmelweis conducted research where he systematically recorded clinical practices and mortality rates. He concluded from this research that after-birth mortality can be drastically reduced if doctors washed their hands with a chlorinated lime solution. He published results suggesting that, when doctors washed their hands, mortality rates in the clinic dropped below 1 percent.

But Semmelweis could not explain why. At that time, the germ theory was not yet confirmed. People did not know that disease could spread with tiny organisms living on your hands. They believed that every disease is a result of an imbalance of the basic "four humors" in the body, and that the doctor's job was to identify the imbalance in each individual case and cure it through practices such as bloodletting.

The recommendation to wash hands with a chlorinated lime solution contradicted the "old ways", and many doctors were offended with this suggestion. They did not see why they would waste their valuable time on washing hands multiple times during a day. They were also offended by the idea that what was required to save lives was not doctor genius, but simple cleanliness. They felt like Semmelweis suggested that these respected gentlemen were "unclean". Semmelweis was mocked, his findings were rejected. He was dismissed from his hospital – the same hospital where he managed to reduce the mortality rate of mothers by 90%. His colleague committed him to a lunatic asylum, where Semmelweis died two weeks later after being beaten by a guard. Such is the fate of the savior of mothers.

Long after his death when Louis Pasteur confirmed the germ theory, Semmelweis's recommendations became common practice and saved millions of lives.

Did Semmelweis know why women die from childbed fever? He clearly saw a correlation between mortality from childbed fever and washing hands, but he could not explain why. Did his colleagues know why women die from childbed fever? They certainly had a well-reasoned theoretical explanation. Did Semmelweis *understand* more than his colleagues about childbed fever? If he understood and they didn't, why did he not manage to convince them, and why were they not open-minded enough to be convinced?

5.1 - Objectivity, subjectivity and understanding

In the first couple of lessons of this unit I will introduce the key concepts that will be used throughout the rest of it. As mentioned, I will argue that the concepts of subjectivity and objectivity are more complicated and multi-dimensional than they seem to be. I will separate two dimensions of objectivity and subjectivity – the ontological one and the epistemological one. By the end of the first lesson you will know lots of great concepts that will allow you to think much more deeply about what it means for something to be "objective". There will be many new words, but don't worry – we will apply them a lot in the rest of the book, so it will become your second nature to use these words casually in your daily conversations.

In the second lesson, we will discuss what it means to understand something and how it is different from knowing it. Again, these general principles will be later applied to specific areas of knowledge.

Lesson 1 - Subjectivity and objectivity

Learning outcomes

a) [Knowledge and comprehension] What are ontologically objective and ontologically subjective phenomena? What is epistemologically objective and epistemologically subjective knowledge?
b) [Understanding and application] What are the examples of subjective and objective knowledge of objectively existing and subjectively existing phenomena?
c) [Thinking in the abstract] Can we ever know objectively existing phenomena for what they really are?

Key concepts

Ontology, epistemology, ontologically objective phenomena, ontologically subjective phenomena, epistemologically objective knowledge, epistemologically subjective knowledge, noumenon, phenomenon

Other concepts used

Phenomenology

Themes and areas of knowledge

Theme: Knowledge and the knower
AOK: Natural Sciences, Human Sciences

Recap and plan

It is very common for people to believe that good knowledge has to be objective. "Subjective" has become a synonym for unreliable, unsupported and speculative. Similarly, if knowledge is objective, then it is, according to common belief, reliable, credible and trustworthy.

In this lesson I will try to show you that the relationship between subjectivity and objectivity is far more complex than it seems. We will introduce the difference between epistemological and ontological subjectivity and objectivity and look at the interplay between these two dimensions. This distinction will serve as an overarching idea that we will keep coming back to throughout this unit and even the rest of the book.

If you are someone who believes that good knowledge must be objective, I invite you to take a deep breath and read on. I don't promise to prove you wrong, but I promise to make you doubt.

Ontological and epistemological objectivity and subjectivity: definitions

The title of this section is not easy to pronounce. However, once you understand these terms, a lot of other ideas and knowledge concepts will fall into place.

As you might remember, philosophy may be broadly divided into two parts – ontology and epistemology. It is important to separate them, because mixing them up often results in confusion.

- Ontology is the study of being. It answers questions like "Does X exist?" For example: Does God exist? Is the Universe infinite?
- Epistemology is the theory of knowledge. It answers questions like "How do we know that X exists?" For example: Can existence of God be proven? How can we know if the Universe is infinite?

Ontology
- Theory of being - Does X exist?
Epistemology
- Theory of knowledge - How do we know that X exists?

Is it possible to eliminate subjectivity from our knowledge of the world? (#Perspectives)

Ontologically objective phenomena are comprised of a range of phenomena that exist in the world around us. In other words, they are what we call "objectively existing reality". Ontologically objective phenomena are independent of the observer. Even when nobody is looking at them, they still objectively exist. Trees around you, the book you are reading, your brain cells and the electrical impulses in your brain – all of these are examples of ontologically objective phenomena. We will also refer to them as "objectively existing phenomena".

KEY IDEA: Ontologically objective (objectively existing) phenomena are independent of the observer. They exist even when nobody is experiencing them.

Image 5. Falling tree

Imagine there is a deep forest. After a strong gust of wind, a tree falls in the middle of it with a crashing sound. There is no one around to hear that, though. The question is, if nobody heard the crashing sound, was there a crashing sound? Although there are some philosophers whose answer is no (they are known as *phenomenologists* – you can research this further if you'd like), the commonly accepted position is yes, there was a crashing sound. The falling tree produced certain vibrations in the air, and although these vibrations never reached a human ear, they did exist objectively. It was an ontologically objective phenomenon. Similarly, the forest itself, according to the common belief (but not phenomenologists!), exists even when no one is looking at it. It is just there.

Ontologically subjective phenomena are the ones that only exist in an individual's subjective experiences. You cut your finger accidentally and you feel excruciating pain – that is part of your subjective experiences. You fall in love with someone and the emotional turmoil you experience is also part of that. Your dreams and desires, what you feel when you see a beggar in the street, and how you experience the loss of your pet are other examples. You will probably not deny that all of these phenomena *exist* – after all, you experience them first-hand so you know them for sure. But at the same time, they all exist *subjectively*. They form a part of your own subjective experiences and another person cannot "objectively" see what you experience. They might try to infer, but they will never be able to experience your pain or your love or your grief exactly the way you do. We will also refer to such phenomena as "subjectively existing phenomena".

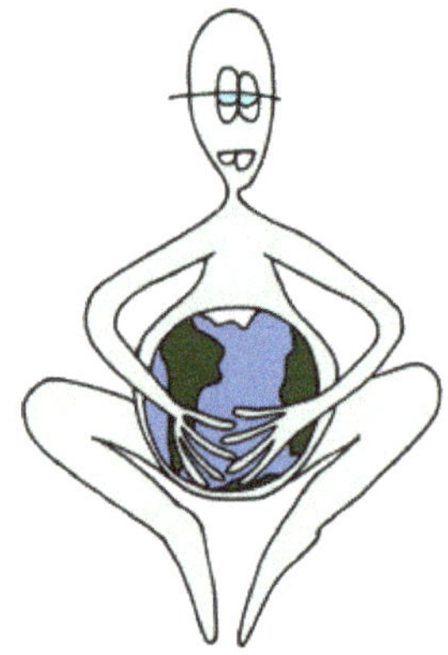

***Image 6**. Ontologically subjective phenomena (inner experiences)*

KEY IDEA: Ontologically subjective (subjectively existing) phenomena exist in an individual's subjective experiences. By definition, they don't exist if someone is not experiencing them.

Epistemologically objective knowledge is knowledge gained through methods that register reality without the participation of human interpretation. Epistemologically objective knowledge of reality does not depend on who is observing it. An independent researcher who repeats the same procedure is supposed to get the same results. For example, it is known in chemistry that combining an acid (such as lemon juice) with a base (such as baking soda) results in a reaction that produces salt and water. This is epistemologically objective knowledge. No matter who performs the experiment and observes the reaction, results will be (or are supposed to be!) the same. Epistemologically objective knowledge is independent of the observer. We will also refer to it simply as "objective knowledge".

KEY IDEA: Epistemologically objective knowledge (or simply "objective knowledge") is obtained through methods that are independent of the observer. Different people using the same method have to arrive at the same knowledge.

Is knowledge obtained through interpretation deeper than knowledge obtained through measurement? (#Methods and tools)

Epistemologically subjective knowledge refers to knowledge that is obtained through interpretation. Suppose you are a psychiatrist conducting an interview with a person who wants to know if they are clinically depressed. The person felt unusual sadness for the last two weeks and experienced insomnia. But are they depressed or just temporarily sad? Your conclusion will partially depend on your interpretation of the client's situation, and another psychiatrist's conclusions will not necessarily be the same. Another example would be literary critics analyzing a classical novel. They interpret the novel in their own ways (although, of course, they all have some justification for their conclusions). It is not uncommon to see very different interpretations of the same novel. These are examples of epistemologically subjective knowledge. We will also refer to it simply as "subjective knowledge".

***Image 7**. Epistemologically objective knowledge*

KEY IDEA: *Epistemologically subjective knowledge (or simply "subjective knowledge") is obtained through interpretation. Different people may arrive at different conclusions.*

***Image 8**. Epistemologically subjective knowledge*

Ontological and epistemological objectivity and subjectivity: intersections

Interesting things emerge when we look at the combination of these ideas:

		Epistemology	
		Objective knowledge	Subjective knowledge
Ontology	Objectively existing phenomena	1	2
	Subjectively existing phenomena	4	3

These combinations will be the focus of later lessons. For now, let me just identify them:

- **Option 1:** Objective knowledge of objectively existing phenomena. This is when you use scientific methods and measurement to study something that exists objectively and independently of the observer.
- **Option 2:** Subjective knowledge of objectively existing phenomena. This is when something exists objectively, but for some reason the method you are using to study it does not meet the requirements of scientific objectivity. Can you think of any examples of this?
- **Option 3:** Subjective knowledge of subjectively existing phenomena. This is when someone has a subjective experience of something and someone else is trying to understand what it feels like. For example, Rose has just won a big acting award (her lifetime dream), and Robert is interested to know what it feels like, to experience such unexpected success. Robert interviews Rose, observes her closely during the award ceremony and then writes an essay describing what he thinks is happening in Rose's mind.
- **Option 4:** Objective knowledge of subjectively existing phenomena. This is when Robert believes in strict scientific methods, so he asks Rose to get into a brain scanning machine and shoots strong rapidly changing magnetic fields at her brain while she is trying to deliver her acceptance speech.

Under what circumstances is subjective knowledge more desirable than objective knowledge? (#Scope)

Critical thinking extension

Although we used the phrases "objectively existing phenomena" and "subjectively existing phenomena" (and we are going to keep using them), there exists an even more sophisticated way to capture the difference.

Immanuel Kant, an 18th-century German philosopher, suggested to use the terms *noumenon* and *phenomenon* to denote the following:

- A noumenon is an object or an event that exists independently of human perception. The sound of a falling tree travelling through the forest (when no one is there to hear it) or the forest itself (when nobody is there to see it) are examples of noumena.
- A phenomenon (by contrast) is an object or an event as it is given to us through our perception. The sound of a falling tree *as we hear it* and the forest *as we perceive it* are all examples of phenomena in Kantian philosophy.

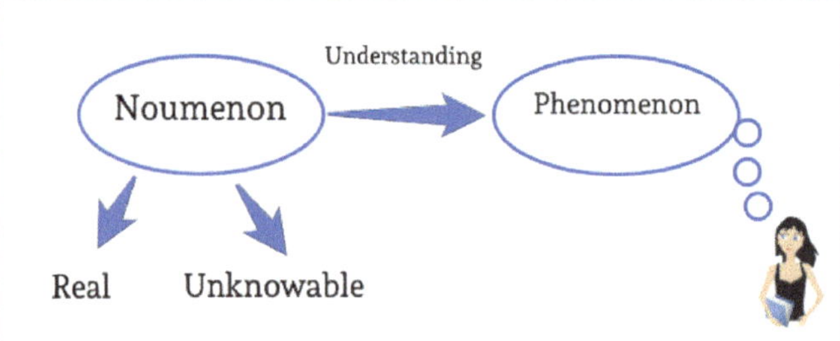

***Image 9**. Noumena and phenomena*

Is it our duty to overcome limitations of human subjectivity? (#Ethics)

The thing with noumena is, they exist in reality, but they are in principle unknowable to us. The only way for us to know something is through senses (according to Kant), but our senses can introduce various distortions. By definition, what we can know is a phenomenon. We can postulate that noumena exist (and that they may be different from phenomena), but we will never know what they actually are.

Sad, isn't it? Do you think this justifies the conclusion that the world we live in is an "illusion"? Can we ever know objectively existing phenomena (noumena) for what they really are?

If you are interested…

If a tree falls in a forest and no one is there to hear it, does it make a sound? To find out, watch the video "EXPLAINED: If a tree falls in the forest…" on the YouTube channel *Pragmatic*.

And, to add some humor, watch how the same question is being answered in the British comedy quiz show "QI". Just search the YouTube channel *QI: Quite Interesting* for "If a tree falls in a forest".

Take-away messages

Lesson 1. We need to refrain from a superficial understanding of objectivity and subjectivity. For this, we need to keep in mind the distinction between ontology and epistemology. There are objectively existing and subjectively existing phenomena (ontology), and there is objective and subjective knowledge of these phenomena (epistemology). These concepts create four curious combinations.

1) Objective knowledge of objectively existing phenomena is knowledge of the reality around us obtained through impartial measurement.
2) Subjective knowledge of objectively existing phenomena is when we obtain knowledge about the reality around us through subjectively experiencing it.
3) Subjective knowledge of subjectively existing phenomena is when we try to understand someone's experiences through interpretation.
4) Finally, objective knowledge of subjectively existing phenomena is when we attempt to "measure" someone's subjective experiences objectively.

Lesson 2 - Understanding

Learning outcomes

a) [Knowledge and comprehension] How is understanding different from knowledge?
b) [Understanding and application] Is understanding possible without knowledge? Is knowledge possible without understanding?
c) [Thinking in the abstract] Can it be claimed that understanding is an advanced form of knowledge?

Key concepts

Understanding

Other concepts used

Holistic, context

Themes and areas of knowledge

Theme: Knowledge and the knower
AOK: Natural Sciences, Human Sciences

Recap and plan

In the previous lesson, you learned the difference between ontologically objective and ontologically subjective phenomena (the former exist independently of any observer and the latter are comprised by subjective experiences of sentient beings). You also looked at the difference between epistemologically objective and epistemologically subjective knowledge – this depends on the extent to which the methods you are using conform to the standards of objective measurement.

We have also mentioned four curious combinations formed by these concepts. For example, objective knowledge of objectively existing phenomena is the focus of many natural sciences, while subjective knowledge of subjectively existing phenomena may be the focus of such fields as the arts.

We will develop these four options to a greater detail in further lessons, but before we do that, we need to discuss the meaning of "understanding" as a concept distinctly different from "knowledge".

How is understanding something different from knowing it? (#Scope)

Everyday usage of the words "knowledge" and "understanding"

Someone approaches you in school and asks if you know molecular biology. What do they mean? That you have heard about molecular biology, that you know it exists? That you had classes on molecular biology and you attended those classes (assuming you are a biology student)? Or that you can explain the topic to them? Or that you are equipped with sufficient expertise in molecular biology to conduct your own meaningful research that will contribute to the shared body of knowledge? Actually, depending on the context, they can mean any of those things, so you might want to ask the person to clarify. Ask them to be more specific and to use knowledge concepts precisely to avoid ambiguity (and watch them walk away in confusion).

Or someone asks, do you know Elton John? What do they mean by that – that you recognize the name, that you know who he is, that you have heard his songs, that you know what kind of person he is? And even if you know all that, is it sufficient to say that you *really* know Elton John?

***Image 10**. Do you understand me? (Credit: Dave Gray, Flickr)*

Or suppose you have a close friend and you describe the nature of your relationship like this: *She understands me*. It has a slightly different meaning than "she knows me", doesn't it? You would probably agree that a lot of people know you, but only a few of them understand you.

Let's just agree for the time being that there seems to be a difference between "knowledge" and "understanding".

Should knowledge be contextualized to be meaningful? (#Methods and tools)

Understanding comes after knowledge

We will define understanding as an *insight that becomes possible when we combine fragmented knowledge about various parts or aspects of something into one meaningful whole*. I realize that the definition is quite flimsy, so a table that summarizes essential features of understanding as opposed to knowledge might do a better job.

Knowledge	Understanding	Notes / examples
May be fragmented	Is holistic	You may "know" history by knowing what happened and when, but you understand history when you can tell why this happened and what it meant. If you understand why things happened, you can see the chain of historical events as a whole that has its internal logic, rather than a fragmented set of facts.
Covers some aspects of a phenomenon	Covers all essential aspects of a phenomenon	You may claim to "know" a religious ritual if you can describe some facts about it (for example, you know that candles are lit in a temple when people pray). However, you can claim to "understand" the ritual if you are aware of the cultural and religious significance of the act. For example, that fire in that particular religion is associated with cleansing power, therefore lighting a candle symbolizes that the believer's intentions are pure. Without knowing cultural and religious significance – which is an essential aspect of a ritual – one can only have (partial) knowledge of the phenomenon, but not (complete) understanding.
May be detached from context	Is rooted in context	The difference here is between "how it works" and "how it works in a particular situation". For example, in mathematics you might "know" calculus if you know the rules of finding derivatives from functions, but you can only claim to "understand" calculus if you see how these rules can be used in the context of various real-life problems: finding acceleration of a moving object, solving optimization problems in engineering, and so on.
May be abstract	Applies to individual cases	This follows from the previous three points. Since understanding is holistic, complete and rooted in context, it can be applied to individual cases and situations, with all the richness of individual circumstances that may come in the way. For example, one may "know" laws of macro- and microeconomics. But when it comes to applying these (abstract) laws to a particular financial crisis in a particular country, we want to employ people who "understand" to save the situation. Simple knowledge of laws is not enough.

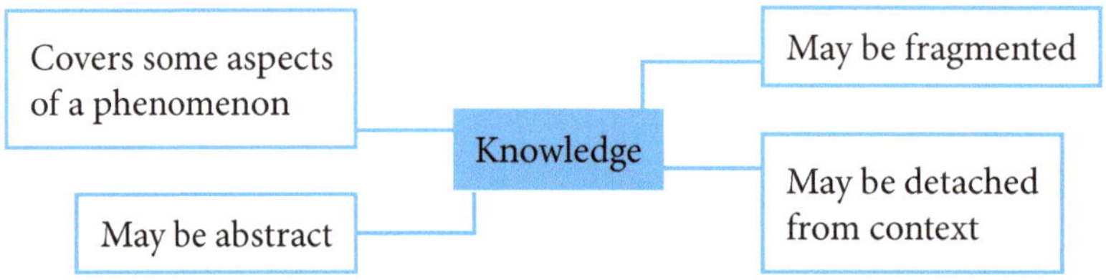

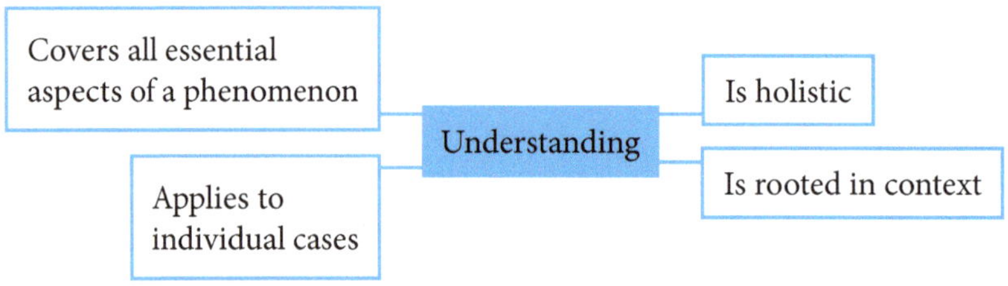

The key take-away message from these four differences is that understanding is something that comes after knowledge. It is easy to think of a person who knows but does not understand. But is it possible to imagine a person who understands something, yet does not know it? It seems like first we know it and then we understand it.

KEY IDEA: Understanding comes after knowledge. It is possible to know something without understanding it, but it is not possible to understand something without knowing it.

Knowledge becomes understanding

The line between knowledge and understanding is blurred. It could be the case that, as we are accumulating knowledge, it crosses some threshold somewhere and becomes understanding. It could also be the case that, no matter how well we know some aspects of a phenomenon, we will never fully understand it unless we know each and every detail of this phenomenon. In any case, knowledge becomes understanding at some point, but what are the conditions that need to be met in order for this to happen? How knowledge gradually transforms into understanding may be different in different areas of knowledge, which is exactly the focus of the next several lessons in this unit.

KEY IDEA: At some point, knowledge becomes understanding if certain conditions are met. These conditions may vary from one area of knowledge to another.

***Image 11**. Fragmented knowledge*

Critical thinking extension

We have agreed that understanding is some form of advanced knowledge which covers all essential aspects of a phenomenon, is holistic, rooted in context and can be applied to individual cases. From this perspective, knowledge and understanding are just two sides of a continuum – understanding is an advanced form of knowledge.

But there is also an alternative approach: to define understanding as something that requires "feeling into" the phenomenon that is being studied. From this perspective, knowledge is purely cognitive (beliefs) while understanding implies emotion, empathy and other non-logical elements.

Is understanding an advanced form of knowledge, or is it something bigger than that? (#Perspectives)

In this lesson we have looked at several examples of knowledge versus understanding. But the challenge is to apply these concepts to a larger pool of examples. Although we will do that in the lessons that follow, why don't you give it a thought now? Try to think and identify examples of understanding (as opposed to knowledge) in areas of knowledge such as:

- Human Sciences
- The Arts
- Mathematics

Based on the examples that you have identified so far, which of the two approaches to defining understanding works better: understanding as an advanced form of knowledge or understanding as an emotional, empathetic insight?

If you are interested…

There are many different approaches to describe the difference between knowledge and understanding. There is no consensus. What I have suggested in this lesson is just one of the possible approaches; you do not necessarily have to agree with it. You might find it useful to explore some other approaches. For example, start with these resources:

1) Colin Robertson's article "The true difference between knowledge and understanding" (April 11, 2016) on *Medium*. It describes the fascinating story of riding a "backwards bike" and lessons derived from this fun experiment.
2) Search for "Difference between knowledge and understanding" on the website *Differencebetween.com* (not that I am advocating this website as a reliable source of knowledge, I just think it was a good idea to make this site in the first place).

You can also conduct a simple internet search for "knowledge versus understanding" and see what comes up. Note the abundance of spiritual and religious resources!

Take-away messages

Lesson 2. Knowledge may be fragmented, incomplete, detached from context and abstract, but understanding is holistic, complete, rooted in context and applicable to individual cases. Understanding comes after knowledge. Knowledge and understanding are two sides of a continuum. Knowledge gradually becomes understanding when certain conditions are met, but how exactly it happens and what the conditions are may be different in different areas of knowledge. It is debatable if understanding may be seen simply as an advanced form of knowledge, or if it is bigger than that.

5.2 - Knowledge and understanding in Natural Sciences

We have defined understanding. We have agreed that understanding is an advanced form of knowledge where knowledge of all essential elements of a phenomenon is combined into a holistic picture, rooted in context and applicable to individual cases. But we also agreed that understanding seems to manifest differently in different areas of knowledge. The rest of this unit will zoom in on the specifics of understanding in three areas: Natural Sciences, Human Sciences and the Arts. These have been selected with the aim to bring out the differences.

KEY IDEA: Understanding manifests differently in different areas of knowledge

We will start with natural sciences.

Using terminology that we established in Lesson 1 ("Objectivity and subjectivity"), knowledge in natural sciences may be categorized as *objective knowledge of objectively existing phenomena.*

This means that in natural sciences we assume that the material world around us objectively exists irrespective of whether or not it is being observed. It existed long before there were sentient beings in it to observe it, and it will exist after these sentient beings are gone. Planets revolved around suns and they will keep revolving; chemical reactions in cosmic clouds of gas happened and will keep happening. Since we believe that the world exists independently of observers, we want our knowledge of the world to be independent of observers, too. For this reason, we have developed the scientific method – a series of procedures that allow us to eliminate the observer's influence as much as possible. We design strict experimental protocols with precise measurements and run them in highly controlled conditions. We encourage independent researchers to replicate these experiments in a variety of conditions, and we expect the results to be the same no matter who conducts the experiment. It would be weird if chemical reactions followed different rules depending on who conducts the study! Imagine learning rules of chemistry such as "Hydrogen reacts with oxygen to make water, but only if the person who is observing this reaction is in a good mood".

Subjectively existing phenomena (such as people's individual experiences and interpretations) do not interest natural sciences. Subjective knowledge (which is based on interpretation) is also considered substandard and not credible.

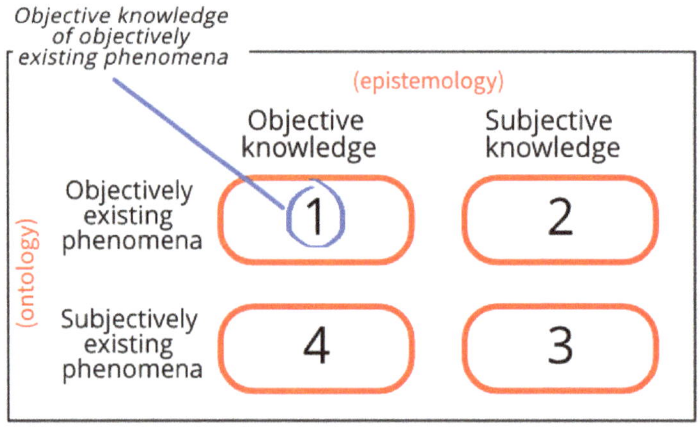

Image 12. Natural Sciences are here

With this said, what does it mean to understand in natural sciences, as opposed to "simply" knowing?

- We agreed that understanding is holistic, in the sense that it combines fragmented pieces of knowledge in a bigger picture. So what counts as a "bigger picture" in natural sciences?
- We agreed that understanding covers all essential aspects of a phenomenon. So what aspects are considered "essential" in natural sciences?
- We agreed that understanding is rooted in context. So what is the role of the context in which natural phenomena occur, and how does understanding in natural sciences relate to knowing this context?
- Finally, we agreed that understanding enables application of knowledge to individual cases. What does this mean in the realm of natural sciences?

These are the questions we will attempt to answer through introducing the following key concepts:

- Determinism
- Scientific worldview

Lesson 3 - Determinism

Learning outcomes

a) [Knowledge and comprehension] What is determinism?
b) [Understanding and application] Why is determinism a major explanatory principle in natural sciences?
c) [Thinking in the abstract] Is identifying causes both necessary and sufficient for understanding in natural sciences?

Key concepts

Determinism, functions of science (description, explanation, prediction, control)

Other concepts used

Causes, Laplace's demon, necessary and sufficient conditions

Themes and areas of knowledge

AOK: Natural Sciences

Recap and plan

Knowledge obtained in natural sciences may be categorized as objective knowledge of objectively existing phenomena. The focus is on the "natural world" consisting of material things. Since we believe that this world exists independently of us observers, we want our knowledge of it to be independent of the observer, too.

As we agreed earlier, as knowledge develops, at some point it becomes understanding, but only if certain conditions are met. So the key question now is this: in natural sciences, in the domain of objective knowledge of objectively existing phenomena, what conditions need to be met in order for knowledge to become understanding?

We are going to look at the key features of knowledge in natural sciences that enable one to move along the continuum from (fragmented) knowledge to (holistic) understanding. Uncovering the causes of observable natural events is one of these features. This is where the concept of determinism comes into play.

Determinism

Determinism is the idea that all events are determined completely by causes acting upon them. Applied to the world of material objects, it means that:

- The current state of the Universe is completely determined by the state in which it was a moment ago, plus the laws of nature.
- Hypothetically, if we knew every single detail about the state of the Universe in the past, and if we applied laws of nature to that knowledge, we would be able to fully explain the current state of the Universe.
- Similarly, if we (hypothetically) knew every single detail about the current state of the Universe, we could apply the known laws of nature to predict the future states of the Universe exactly.
- Laws of nature describe how causes are linked to effects, and if everything in the Universe is explained by a set of preceding causes, then it should be possible for us to trace the development of the Universe both into the past and into the future.

What is the role of causation in understanding in natural sciences? (#Scope)

KEY IDEA: Determinism is the idea that all things in the Universe can be completely explained by causes that acted upon them in the past

This seems feasible (at least at first sight). An asteroid is travelling through space in a particular direction and with a particular speed because it was (probably) the result of a collision between two heavenly bodies that gave a particular impulse to the debris. If we know its speed and acceleration and trajectory at present, we can calculate its exact position at any time in the future. That's what we actually do in astronomy.

***Image 13**. Causal determinism*

Laplace's demon

The philosophical tradition of determinism is very old, but one scholar who articulated it precisely for the first time was the French philosopher Laplace in 1814. He wrote:

***Image 14**. Laplace's demon (credit: Rhetos, Wikimedia Commons)*

> *We may regard the present state of the universe as the effect of its past and the cause of its future. An intellect which at a certain moment would know all forces that set nature in motion, and all positions of all items of which nature is composed, if this intellect were also vast enough to submit these data to analysis, it would embrace in a single formula the movements of the greatest bodies of the universe and those of the tiniest atom; for such an intellect nothing would be uncertain and the future just like the past would be present before its eyes (Laplace, 1951, p.4).*

If your actions are fully determined by preceding events, should you be held accountable for them? (#Ethics)

The idea became known as *Laplace's demon*. This hypothetical "intellect" (or, as we call it more lovingly nowadays, demon) has all the information about the state of the Universe at a given point of time. It also perfectly knows all the laws of nature. For that reason, it can tell precisely what the Universe was like in the past and what it will be like in the future.

KEY IDEA: According to determinism, if we have complete knowledge of the state of the Universe at a particular time, we can completely recreate its past and exactly predict its future

Four functions of science

Natural sciences traditionally have been based on principles of determinism, so the main question that they are trying to answer is why (for what reason) something happens.

Is it true that if we cannot predict, then we do not know? (#Methods and tools)

It is believed that there are four major functions of science:

- **Description**: observe the Universe and describe how it works. For example, Kepler's equations describe the trajectory along which planets move in the Solar System. These equations do not explain why planets move the way they do, they just state a fact.
- **Explanation**: explain what you have described by identifying its causes. For example, the theory of gravity provides an explanation for Kepler's equations.
- **Prediction**: now that we have described and explained something, we can predict what will happen. For example, calculations allow us to predict where each planet will be at each point of time in the future.

- **Control**: since we can predict the future and we know what causes it, we should also be able to manipulate it. For example, we can change the trajectory of an asteroid approaching the Earth by blasting a nuclear bomb on its surface, at the right place and at the right time.

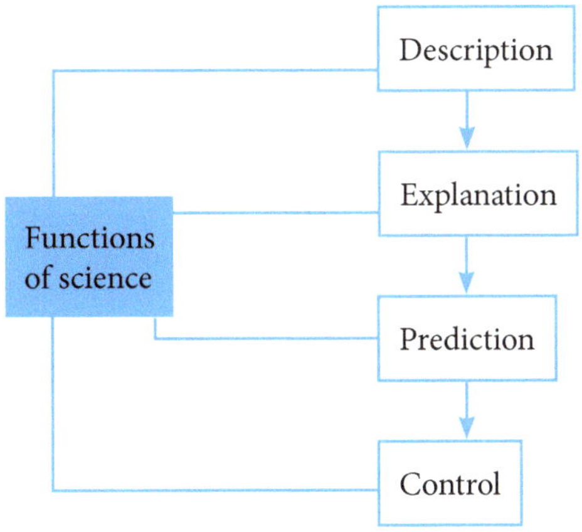

As you can see, all four functions assume determinism.

KEY IDEA: All four functions of science (description, explanation, prediction and control) assume determinism

Imagine the trajectory of an asteroid moving through space was actually *not* completely determined by preceding causes. What if the asteroid could "change its mind" and tweak its trajectory slightly once in a while? Then our knowledge would become useless, even if this only happened once in billions of years.

Similarly, explanation by identifying causes is only possible if we believe that the way things are is completely determined by a set of preceding causes. Explaining a phenomenon in natural sciences means identifying its cause.

Based on all of this, I'm arriving at the conclusion that to understand something in natural sciences means to be able to identify its causes and predict its consequences. As we gain knowledge about one influencing factor after another, we gradually gain holistic understanding. A small child may know some random facts about the Universe, but the child doesn't understand it. A scientist understands the Universe a little better. Laplace's demon is the one who understands the Universe fully.

Will complete knowledge of the past allow us to completely understand the future? (#Perspectives)

KEY IDEA: To understand something in natural sciences means to be able to identify its causes and predict its consequences

Critical thinking extension

I have arrived at the thought that causation lies at the heart of understanding in natural sciences. It may be claimed that we have reached understanding when we can perform all four functions (description, explanation, prediction, control). If we know what caused a phenomenon, why it is the way it is, we can predict it and control it.

It seems reasonable to say that, if we don't know what caused a phenomenon and can't predict how it will develop, we cannot claim that we understand it. In other words, knowing causes is a *necessary* condition for understanding.

But is it a *sufficient* condition? Is knowing causes enough for us to fully understand a phenomenon in natural sciences? What do you think? If you think it is not sufficient, then what else is necessary?

In one of the lessons that follow, I will argue that another component of understanding in natural sciences is being able to fit the explanation nicely into the bigger picture (that is, the existing *scientific worldview*).

If you are interested...

The idea of determinism is often contrasted to the idea of "free will". Free will versus determinism is a very long-standing philosophical debate. It does not apply so much to the objectively existing reality around us that the natural sciences are interested in (such as asteroids, atoms and chemical reactions), but it applies to human behavior.

The question is, can it be claimed that our behavior is fully determined by preceding causes, and hence we have no control over what we do, think and decide? In other words, will Laplace's demon, given complete knowledge about your past, be able to predict your future thoughts and your future behavior to the tiniest detail?

A good introduction into this debate, as well as some key arguments in favor of both sides, can be found in the video "Determinism vs. Free Will" on the YouTube channel *CrashCourse*.

Take-away messages

Lesson 3. In natural sciences we move from knowledge to understanding as we are uncovering the causes of observable natural events. This is because natural sciences are largely based on the ideas of determinism (the view that everything in the Universe has a set of identifiable preceding causes). Laplace's demon captures this idea metaphorically. Uncovering causes is one of the necessary conditions for knowledge to become understanding in natural sciences. However, whether or not it is a sufficient condition remains an open question.

Lesson 4 - Indeterminism

Learning outcomes

a) [Knowledge and comprehension] What is indeterminism?
b) [Understanding and application] What evidence goes against the idea of causality in the world?
c) [Thinking in the abstract] What does it mean for randomness to be "intrinsic in the fabric of nature"?

Key concepts

Indeterminism, randomness

Other concepts used

Collapse of wave function, double-slit experiment

Themes and areas of knowledge

Theme: Knowledge and technology
AOK: Natural Sciences, Mathematics (implicitly)

Recap and plan

In the previous lesson, we unpacked the meaning of "determinism" and explained that understanding in natural sciences is largely dependent on the belief that everything in the Universe has an identifiable set of causes. Nothing in the Universe is random or undetermined.

The principles of determinism have served as a foundation of science for centuries.

However, many discoveries of recent times have shattered our confidence in determinism. Many scholars are starting to doubt that it correctly captures how reality actually works. Collectively, these objections are known as the idea of indeterminism. Although the idea has been around for quite a long time, the 20th century saw increasing scientific evidence supporting it.

If new evidence suggests that a certain fundamental principle is incorrect, what should happen to old knowledge based on that principle? (#Perspectives)

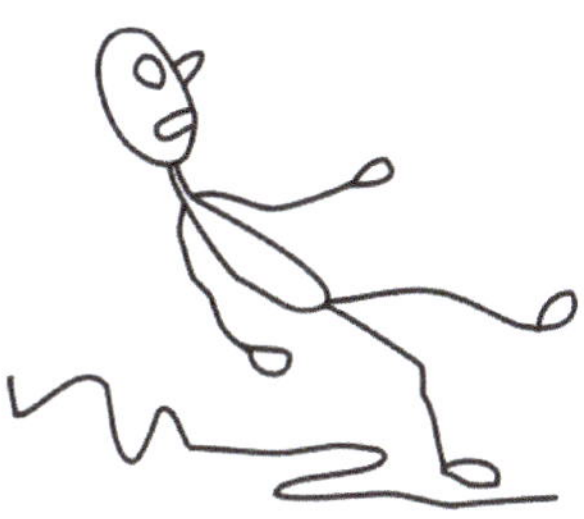

Image 15. Collapse of wave function

In this lesson I will talk about one such discovery – *collapse of wave function* in quantum physics (I can hear a terrified gasp from many readers who are not science students, but I promise it will not be too science-y). I hope this discovery will blow your mind.

KEY IDEA: Indeterminism is the idea that not all events in the Universe occur due to preceding causes; some events are a product of true chance. Therefore, we cannot understand these events by identifying their causes.

Double-slit experiments with water

If you drop something on the surface of water, waves will be produced. A wave is an oscillating motion of the matter of which water consists. The wave propagates across the surface which you can visually observe as ripples.

Image 16. Dropping two objects in water at the same time

Interesting things happen when you perform a *double-slit experiment*. Put a barrier with two openings across your bath, excite waves on one side of the bath and observe the other side – you will see that waves pass through the slits creating two new ripple patterns. When these two patterns meet, they interfere with each other, producing a curious interplay of calm and excited areas. Another way to achieve the same effect is to simply drop two objects in water at the same time. The ripples will meet and create an interference pattern.

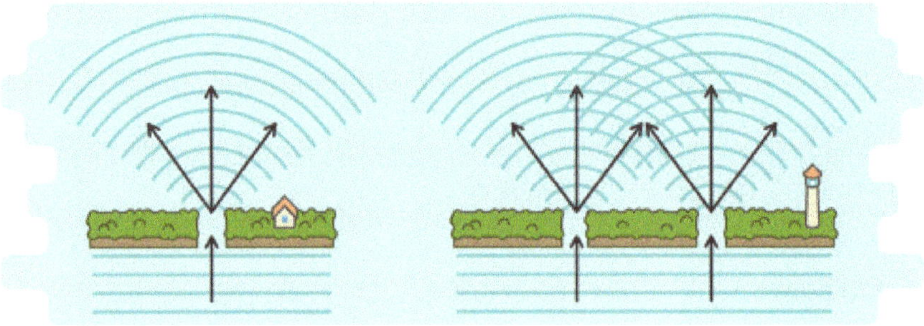

Image 17. *Interference of water: double-slit experiment*

The interference pattern occurs because:

- When the two waves meet at their peaks or troughs ("ups" or "downs"), they reinforce each other
- When one of the waves is at its peak but the other wave is at its trough, the two waves cancel each other out

Nothing too fancy so far!

Double-slit experiments with light

Let's repeat the same experiment with light and do what Thomas Young did in 1801. Let's take a large box divided by a plate with two parallel slits. On one side of the box, install a source of light. On the opposite side of the box, install a screen to detect where light falls.

Can scientific conclusions ever be fully justified by evidence? (#Methods and tools)

Perform this experiment and you will see a curious pattern of light and shadow on the screen. Contrary to what one might expect, the areas directly opposite the slits will be dark. However, there will be a whole series of stripes of light alternating with stripes of darkness.

Thomas Young took this as experimental evidence that light is a wave, not a particle. Indeed, if light was a particle, one might expect each particle of light to pass through one of the slits and land directly opposite, creating exactly two bright stripes on the screen. But the pattern the light actually produces is much like the one observed with water. As we know today, light does have properties of a wave. Rather than being a disturbance of matter, it is an *electromagnetic wave*.

Interesting, but still nothing too fancy! Perfectly in line with determinism so far.

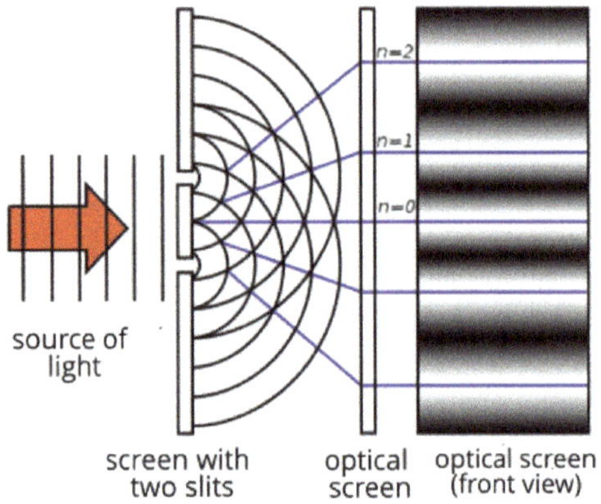

Image 18. *Interference of light*

Double-slit experiments with a single electron

Let's now repeat the same experiment with a slight modification and do what Davisson and Germer did in 1927. Once again, take a large box divided by a double-slit plate in the middle. But this time on one side of the box, install an electron beam gun that fires one electron at a time. On the opposite side of the box, install a photosensitive screen that shows where the electron has landed.

As you fire electrons one by one, they light up dots on the photosensitive screen where they land, one dot at a time. As you keep firing, a pattern gradually emerges – the same old stripy interference pattern again!

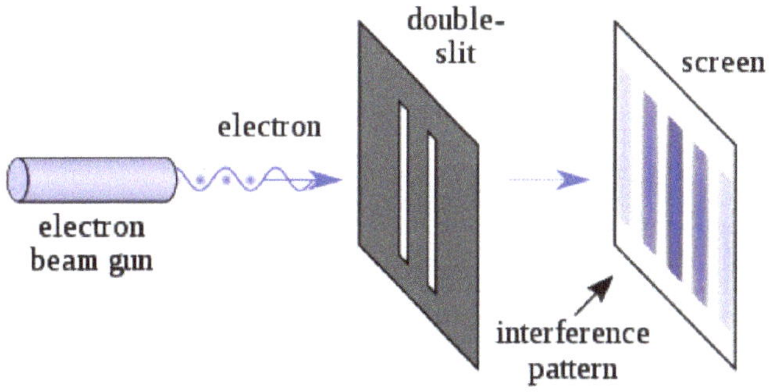

Image 19. Double-slit experiment with a single electron (credit: NekoJaNekoJa and Johannes Kalliauer, Wikimedia Commons)

But why? In the previous experiments, the interference pattern was understandable because when the wave passes through the two slits (simultaneously), it creates two new waves that interact with each other. This interaction produces interference. But here no interaction is possible. Electrons are particles. We fire them one by one. An electron should pass through either one of the slits and land on the area of the screen directly opposite the slit. This is indeed weird.

Is counterevidence reason enough to reject a theory? (#Scope)

This experiment (and its numerous replications) gave birth to the idea that each particle is in fact also a wave. According to the current belief, what happens is the following:

- When fired from the beam gun, the electron travels through space not as a particle, but as a wave – a distribution of probabilities. Not as a dot found at a specific location in space, but as a distribution of possible locations.
- As such, it passes through both the slits simultaneously (!). It kind of splits in two and interacts with itself. Just like waves, these distributions of probabilities interact with each other and create an interference pattern. Now the electron can land on any of the locations from that distribution.
- However, at the moment of observation (when the electron hits the screen), it actually chooses one particular location from that distribution. It hits the screen as a dot. It is believed that the electron chooses the location randomly. At the moment of observation, the wave function suddenly collapses and the electron behaves like a particle again.

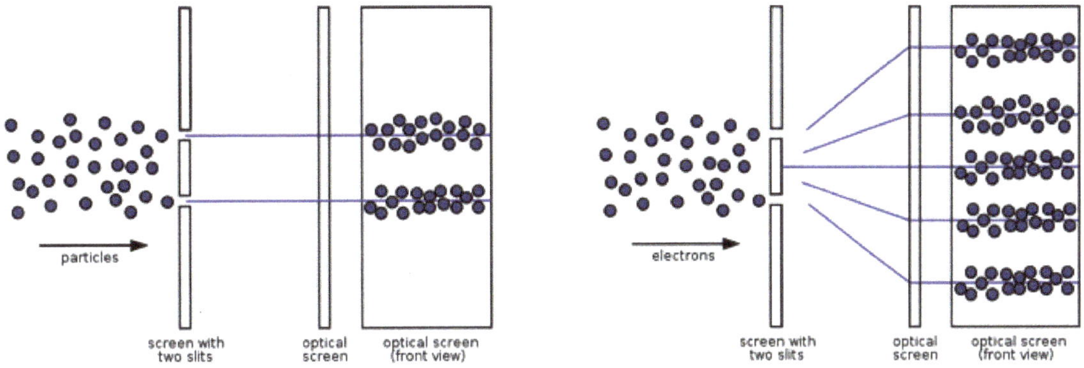

(a) Expected *(b) Observed*

Image 20. Double-slit experiment with a single electron: expected versus observed

Implications

That is intense. Let's look at it again, this time through the lens of determinism. We are used to thinking of electrons (and other particles) as quite definite things that are located at a precise point in space. However, it appears that when an electron travels through space in the double-slit experiment, it is not a "definite thing". Rather it exists as a probability, smudged across various locations where it could potentially be. However, when we decide to look at it, the wave function collapses and the electron springs back into the definite reality, randomly choosing one location out of all accessible to it. Can we predict where exactly the electron will hit the screen? No. Is the location where it hits the screen determined by any previously acting forces? No. It appears that randomness rather than determinism is in the fabric of nature, at least when it comes to small particles!

A point in favor of indeterminism.

KEY IDEA: According to indeterminism, randomness rather than causality is in the fabric of nature

---

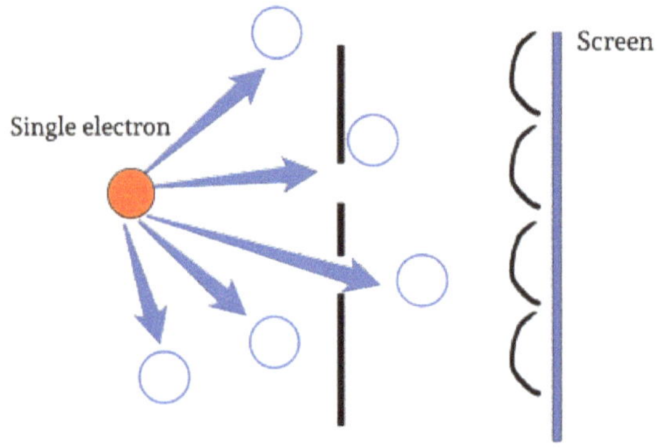

Image 21. *An electron passes through both slits simultaneously!*

Critical thinking extension

These single-particle double-slit experiments have been repeated with different particles, with atoms and even with a whole molecule (Eibenberger, 2013).

All this evidence suggests that indeterminism is intrinsic in the physical reality of the world, it is in the very fabric of nature. As objects become larger, effects of indeterminism (such as collapse of wave function) become less and less visible. In objects we are used to dealing with on an everyday basis (such as an elephant) these effects are negligible.

Don't get me wrong, these effects are still there even in large objects. The elephant also exists in multiple locations at the same time, as a probability distribution. When we look at it, the wave function collapses and it randomly chooses one of these locations to "materialize" in. If you look at an elephant, blink and look again, the elephant will have leapt from one random location on the distribution to another random location. Only with an elephant, this distribution is negligibly tiny. After you blink, the elephant does not shift to the other end of the forest. It remains roughly in the same place… roughly, but not exactly!

Do you find this easy to comprehend?

This is beautifully described in George Gamow's fiction book *Mr. Tompkins in Wonderland* (first published in 1939). Check out the chapter entitled "Quantum Jungles". In this chapter Mr. Tomkins rides a quantum elephant to a quantum jungle where he gets attacked by quantum tigers. Do have a look.

If you are interested…

Watch the video "If a tree falls in the forest…" on the YouTube channel *Up and Atom*. It is a brilliant explanation of the double-slit experiments from two young bloggers. It summarizes what we have discussed in this lesson and adds a twist!

The video also links the double-slit experiments back to the question we discussed earlier: If a tree falls in a forest and no one is there to hear it, does it make a sound?

Do you see how particle physics can contribute to our answer?

Take-away messages

Lesson 4. Some discoveries in the 20th century caused scholars to doubt that determinism accurately captures the nature of reality. An alternative philosophical approach – indeterminism – has gained some support. Indeterminism views reality as being fundamentally uncertain and unpredictable. One of the many discoveries that supports this view is "collapse of wave function" in particle physics, found in double-slit experiments with single particles. According to discoveries like this, knowledge of preceding causes will not be sufficient to understand and predict events in the material world.

Lesson 5 - Scientific worldview

Learning outcomes

a) [Knowledge and comprehension] What is the scientific worldview?
b) [Understanding and application] Why is fitting knowledge into the scientific worldview a necessary condition for understanding?
c) [Thinking in the abstract] Can we claim to fully understand something in natural sciences?

Key concepts

Scientific worldview

Other concepts used

Coherent description, prior knowledge

Themes and areas of knowledge

Theme: Knowledge and the knower
AOK: Natural Sciences

Recap and plan

Earlier I posed the question: is knowledge of causes necessary and sufficient for understanding something in natural sciences?

As for "necessary", determinism has been a fundamental principle guiding knowledge in natural sciences. Determinism suggests that to understand a phenomenon, we need to trace it back to its causes. Sometimes, as we have seen in the previous lesson, it is impossible. But when it is possible, we try to do it because we believe that uncovering causes is the key mission of science.

In this lesson I will address the "sufficient" part of the question. I will claim that knowing the causes of a phenomenon is not enough for us to claim that we understand it. Another necessary component is being able to fit our knowledge into the scientific worldview. What it is and how it works is the focus of this lesson.

Scientific worldview

How necessary is it to have a common worldview accepted by the scientific community? (#Perspectives)

The scientific worldview is a coherent global description of the world currently accepted by the scientific community. It includes all body of knowledge accumulated over the millennia of scientific inquiry. The key thing to remember here is that a worldview has to be coherent (otherwise it is not really a worldview, it is a collection of contradictory beliefs!). Every new phenomenon must be explained through the lens of this coherent global description.

KEY IDEA: The scientific worldview is the "big picture" – a coherent global description of the world currently accepted by the scientific community

What does this imply for understanding in natural sciences? That it is possible to describe, explain, predict and control an isolated phenomenon, but we can only claim to fully understand this phenomenon if we can clearly show its place in the big picture.

Below, I will try to give you an example of learning something new in physics and trying to fit it into the bigger picture (in an attempt to understand it).

Why do stars twinkle?

A popular children's song goes: "*Twinkle twinkle little star, how I wonder what you are...*". It is only a matter of time though until your future child asks you "Why do stars twinkle?", and you will need to produce a satisfactory answer (by the way, good luck with that!).

I asked myself, do I (personally) understand why stars twinkle? And do we (collectively) understand it?

Equipped with Google, I learned the following. Stars twinkle because light emitted by them goes through the Earth's atmosphere and gets refracted by areas of varying temperature and density. So twinkling is the result of distortions introduced by the atmosphere.

***Image 22**. Twinkle, twinkle, little star (credit: Helix84, Wikimedia Commons)*

But wait a minute, I said to myself. I know that stars twinkle but planets don't. It doesn't make sense! Light from both stars and planets has to travel through the Earth's atmosphere for me to see it, so why don't planets twinkle? I don't understand. So I asked Google again.

I found out that planets do, in fact, twinkle, but to a much lesser extent. This is because planets are much closer to us in space, and while stars are essentially pinpoints in the sky, planets appear as tiny discs. Light from planets gets refracted, too, but these refractions cancel each other out so the image appears as more stable. Oh okay, I said to myself. The puzzle fits now.

But wait. Why does light get refracted at all? What does it mean? Why does it happen even when the sky is crystal clear? And how can refractions from tiny discs cancel each other out? I can say "stars twinkle because light from them gets refracted in the Earth's atmosphere" and it sounds cool, but if I don't know how refraction works, I don't really understand anything!

Where is the line between a sufficient scientific explanation and an incomplete one? (#Methods and tools)

So I Googled refraction of light. I remembered studying it in middle school, but my memories were vague. I learned (once again!) that refraction is the bending of light that happens when it passes from one transparent substance to another. Refraction depends on the angle at which light enters the new substance. For example, when a ray of light travelling through air enters water at an angle, it will change direction. That is why if you put a pencil partially in water it will appear broken.

***Image 23**. Refraction of light*

Enough explanation? No! I have described what happens, but I have not explained why it happens. Why does light bend when it goes from one substance to another? What causes it to bend? It makes no sense to me. I have no idea.

Back to the Internet. I learned that refraction occurs because light is a wave, and also because light changes its speed when it enters a medium with a different optical density. To illustrate this in Physics classrooms, teachers sometimes use the analogy with marching soldiers. They ask students to stand shoulder to shoulder in a line and hold a meter stick. Students are instructed to walk toward a masking tape boundary placed on the floor at an angle. Students should all pace normally, but once they reach the boundary they need to change to baby steps. Because students reach the masking tape at different times, one side of the line will slow down while the other side of the line will still be moving at a normal speed. The result will be that the whole line of students will change direction.

Can contradictory beliefs co-exist in a system of knowledge? (#Scope)

At this point I said to myself: wow, I will be an awesome dad. When my child asks me for the first time why stars twinkle, we will call some friends and do some marching, and that will be such a good answer to the question. But after two seconds of euphoria, I scratched my head again. Why does light change its speed when it enters a different substance? I remember from high school that speed of light is a constant. It is not supposed to change. I remember that constant speed of light was a big deal in Einstein's theory. This doesn't make any sense. This explanation does not fit into my worldview. I don't understand it.

Image 24. *Refraction of light: the marching soldiers analogy*

Back to the Internet, and I learned that light is an electromagnetic wave. When travelling through substances, this wave interacts with electrons within the atoms: electrons absorb the energy from the wave and turn it into their own vibrations, then reemit the energy. The speed of light in the interatomic space remains constant, but the time that is lost on this absorption and reemission may vary in different substances depending on their atomic structure. As a result, light travels at a constant speed, but due to the absorption and reemission, the total time to travel through a substance can vary. Ooph, I said to myself, this is getting intense, but now it fits into the larger picture. No contradictions, the puzzle is complete. I understand it now.

KEY IDEA: Understanding something in natural sciences = knowing its causes + being able to fit it into the scientific worldview

Conclusion

From the discussion in the last three lessons, we can conclude that understanding a phenomenon in natural sciences means:

- Being able to identify the causes of this phenomenon (which links to being able to describe, explain, predict and control it)
- Being able to relate this knowledge without contradictions to a larger scientific worldview

Understanding something in natural sciences means:

- Being able to identify its causes
- Being able to relate this knowledge to a larger scientific worldview

Understanding in natural sciences is a form of advanced knowledge. As knowledge is accumulated, as we are able to answer more and more questions about the world, as we connect all pieces together in one coherent system, we are moving toward deeper and deeper understanding of the world. Will we ever achieve *perfect* understanding? This remains an open question.

Critical thinking extension

When earlier in this lesson I exclaimed, with reference to a twinkling star, "I understand it now", I was of course fooling myself. For a more sophisticated knower it might not be the case. Examples of further questions that can be asked (and doubts that can be raised) include: How do we know that light is a wave? Where does light even come from? Why are stars farther away from us than planets? Why do stars emit light?

I understand one piece of the puzzle if I know exactly where its place is in the whole puzzle. Ultimately, to understand a twinkling star, one needs to understand everything else in the Universe (but I bet this is not the answer your future child will be expecting!).

But since we can safely say that we don't understand *everything* in the Universe, should we also conclude that we do not fully understand *anything* in it?

Should scientists be allowed to give explanations of something they do not fully understand? (#Ethics)

If you are interested…

Check out this awesome website where astronomers answer all sorts of naïve questions: curious.astro.cornell.edu. Make sure to find the answer to the question "Why do stars twinkle?", but don't stop there. Explore the whole menu of questions they have, ranging in difficulty from beginner to advanced.

Just three examples:

1) Why do airplanes take longer to fly west than east?
2) How can we see the Milky Way if we are inside it?
3) How do we weigh objects in space?

Take-away messages

Lesson 5. Another necessary condition for knowledge to become understanding in natural sciences is our ability to fit this knowledge into the scientific worldview. The scientific worldview is a coherent global description of the world currently accepted by the scientific community. Understanding something in natural sciences implies, apart from knowing its causes, showing its place in the bigger picture. We considered this with the example of a naïve question – Why do stars twinkle?

5.3 - Knowledge and understanding in Human Sciences

In a broad sense, human sciences may be defined as *a systematic investigation of activities and creations of human beings*. There is no definitive list of disciplines belonging to human sciences, but some commonly given examples include Anthropology, Psychology, Business Studies, Economics, Political Science, Sociology, Law. Note how it is not only about human beings themselves, but also about the products that they have created. For example, a study of culture will probably belong to human sciences because culture is something created by humans (even if they are no longer alive).

KEY IDEA: Human sciences are a systematic investigation of activities and creations of human beings

Human sciences are fundamentally different from natural sciences, and this has implications for what counts as "understanding". Over the next several lessons, I will unpack what I mean by that.

However, in this short introduction I want to give you a glimpse of the problem. There is no better example for this than psychology because this is a discipline that is somewhere in between natural and human sciences. Depending on the focus, in some universities Master's programmes in psychology result in awarding the Master of Arts degree, in other universities the result is a Master of Sciences.

Psychology is defined as *a systematic study of human behavior and experiences*. Sometimes "experiences" is changed to "mental processes", but the idea is the same. This short definition captures the great controversy of human sciences and the great divide between natural and human sciences. The thing is:

- **Behavior** is observable. It is an objectively existing phenomenon. Independent observers can register someone's behavior precisely. This makes it possible to study behavior objectively, that is, to have objective knowledge about it.
- **Experiences** are unobservable. One cannot objectively register what people think, believe and feel or how exactly they experience reality. Experiences are a subjectively existing phenomenon. However, they are no less important to understand human beings. At the same time, the sheer possibility of objective knowledge of human experiences is very debatable.

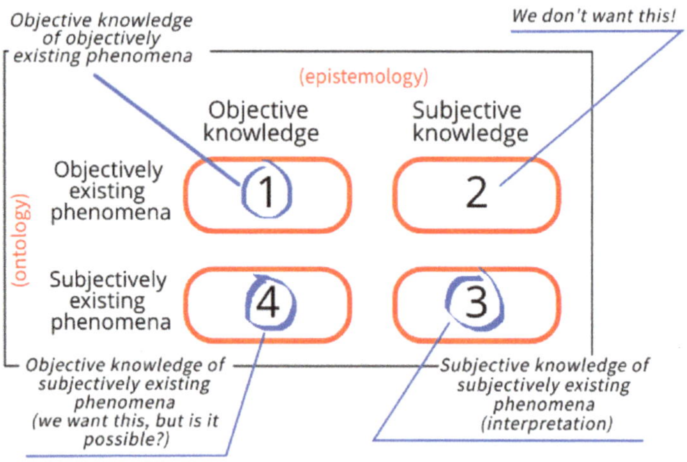

***Image 25**. Human sciences cover areas 1, 3 and 4*

To fully understand "the activities and creations of human beings", one needs to understand both the "worlds":
- The world of objectively existing phenomena - observable behavior and its measurable causes
- The world of subjectively existing phenomena - meanings, purposes and experiences

KEY IDEA: Human sciences deal with two types of phenomena at the same time: objectively existing (such as behavior) and subjectively existing (such as experiences)

This is indeed the challenge faced by human sciences. The next several lessons will focus on what this challenge implies and how we can possibly solve it.

Lesson 6 - Reasons versus purposes

Learning outcomes

a) [Knowledge and comprehension] What is the difference between reasons and purposes?
b) [Understanding and application] What does it mean for activities and creations of human beings to exist in two worlds simultaneously?
c) [Thinking in the abstract] Which is more essential to understand human activities – knowing what caused them or knowing the purposes behind them?

Key concepts

Reasons (*how come?*), purposes (*what for?*), human activity, teleology

Other concepts used

Behavior, experiences, observation, experimentation, behaviorism

Themes and areas of knowledge

Theme: Knowledge and the knower
AOK: Human Sciences, Natural Sciences

Recap and plan

In the previous lessons in this unit, you saw that natural sciences have traditionally viewed the world as governed by cause-effect relationships. Determinism is the idea that natural phenomena can be explained completely by a set of preceding causes, and that whatever happens, happens because something has caused it.

When it comes to human beings (the focus of attention in human sciences), we also have grounds to believe that human activities are caused by some preceding factors acting upon them. At the same time, some argue that determinism is not enough to explain human activities completely because human activities are also purposeful. We perform an action not only because we were determined by some preceding causes, but also for a purpose.

What makes purposes special? Can purposes be reduced to causes? We will try to find out.

Are humans any different from asteroids?

While natural sciences study the "natural" world consisting of material things, human sciences investigate human activity and its products. This difference is profound and has deep implications: human activity, unlike the behavior of material things, is purposeful and meaningful. An asteroid travels in space because it is driven by a set of forces that are acting upon it (gravity, collision with other celestial objects, and so on). The asteroid does not have an intention to go where it is going, and neither is there a "meaning" to its movement through space. The asteroid certainly does not ask itself, *What am I, where am I going, what is the meaning of all this?*

Are methods of natural sciences applicable in human sciences and vice versa? (#Methods and tools)

Unlike an asteroid, when you go to a grocery store to pick up some food, you have an intention, maybe even a plan, and your actions are meaningful. You are doing it because you want to treat yourself to some sweets, because you had a difficult day, because you enjoy croissants, because you want to reward yourself for hard work. Two strangers that happen to be at the same grocery store at the same time, while on the surface might have behavior that looks quite identical, are likely to have entirely different intentions and meanings behind shopping.

***Image 26**. Grocery shopping: what is she thinking about?*

What does it take to understand the behavior of these shoppers? Can we apply the same methods we use to study the behavior of asteroids travelling through space? Given sufficient time and equipment, you can certainly register all the tiniest movements of their body, their trajectory as they move around the store. You can also record the products they choose and perhaps even their brain activity as they are choosing what to buy. Using that data, you might be able to find some correlations; for example, younger customers tend to make shopping decisions more quickly and purchase more products containing added sugar. But do you know from that vast data of yours that this particular customer is buying the cake because he worked hard today but felt lonely, and he wants to reward himself for all the hard work by having this particular cake that his grandmother used to buy him when he was little? This information is nowhere in the data you have collected. You cannot "see" purposes by simply observing people's behavior.

Is understanding the meaning of things more important than understanding their origins? (#Perspectives)

On the other hand, you can approach the shopper and ask him to answer one simple question: "Why did you buy this cake tonight?" He will tell you, and his actions will suddenly start making sense. You cannot ask an asteroid why it is travelling through space!

KEY IDEA: Humans, unlike asteroids, act purposefully

To summarize, the difference between behavior of asteroids and activity of human beings is that the former is determined (driven by a set of causes) while the latter is also purposeful. As Daniel Dennett (2018) puts it, there are two meanings to the question *Why?* in the English language – for what reason (*how come?*) and for what purpose (*what for?*). When we ask *Why is the asteroid moving through space in that direction?* we are inquiring about reasons (how come?). When we ask *Why is this customer buying this cake?* we are inquiring about purposes (what for?). This may be the fundamental difference between natural sciences and human sciences, in terms of what they are attempting to study.

Image 27. *Humans act purposefully*

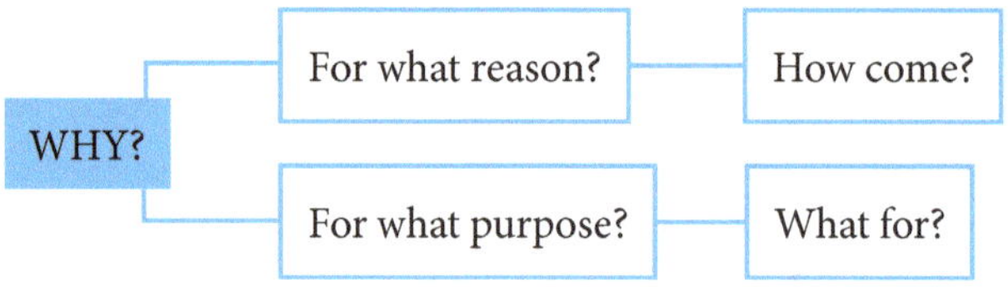

Understanding in human sciences implies understanding purposes

Is knowledge in human sciences broader or narrower than that of natural sciences? (#Scope)

This difference between reasons (causes) and purposes has implications for the concept of understanding. To understand in natural sciences means to have a satisfactory answer to the *how come?* question. This is achievable, at least in principle, through observation, experimentation and mathematical analysis. By contrast, to understand in human sciences means to have a satisfactory answer to both the *how come?* and *what for?* questions. The trick is, answering the *what for?* question is not possible through observation and experimentation, even in principle!

KEY IDEA: To understand in human sciences means to answer both questions – "how come?" (reasons) and "what for?" (purposes). This is in contrast to natural sciences where "how come?" is sufficient.

So the big question is, if not through observation, experimentation and mathematical analysis, then how? I will leave this question hanging for now. Try to come up with an answer. When we discuss it further in this unit, you will be able to check your reasoning against the arguments presented in this book.

To understand in Human Sciences means to answer both versions of the question "Why":	
Why = How come?	Why = What for?
Understanding causes	Understanding purposes

Critical thinking extension

Determinism and teleology

While determinism is the belief that everything happens by necessity of causation, teleology is the belief that things happen for a purpose. Teleology comes from two Greek words: *telos* (goal, purpose) and *logos* (reason, explanation, study). So teleology is a study of purposes, or an explanation of a phenomenon with references to its purposes.

At the dawn of psychotherapy in the first half of the 20th century, scholars turned their attention to mental problems, how to identify and treat them. The founder of psychoanalysis Sigmund Freud used an approach rooted in determinism. One of his students, Alfred Adler (who later became Freud's ardent opponent), developed a teleological version of psychoanalysis.

Suppose an alcoholic client sought therapy with these two guys, complaining about his alcoholism and looking for a treatment. This is what they would most likely do:

- **Sigmund Freud** would have long deep conversations with the client to establish what might have caused alcoholism. This would usually be some sort of a childhood trauma. Becoming aware of the causes, according to him, brings the required relief.
- **Alfred Adler** would assume that the patient has alcoholism for some purpose. He would try to identify the benefits the patient is getting from being an alcoholic. For example, it might be that the patient is so scared of being a failure at his job that he prefers to develop a "disease" that he will use as an excuse for not achieving what he can achieve.

Which one do you think is a better approach? On a broader scale, which is more essential to understand human activities – knowing what caused them or knowing the purposes behind them?

How can we decide on the line between bearing personal responsibility for something and being a victim of circumstances? (#Ethics)

If you are interested...

There was a period in the development of psychology when researchers claimed that in order to make the discipline more scientific, they needed to dismiss subjective experiences as not observable and hence speculative. They suggested focusing psychology solely on observable behavior. This approach was called behaviorism. Behaviorists rejected all unobservable "constructs" such as intentions, plans, mental representations, and so on.

Behaviorists did a great job with reestablishing psychology as a "proper" science governed by principles of determinism. Until one of the devoted behaviorists – Edward Tolman – conducted a research study with rats that led him to challenge his own beliefs.

In this study, behavior of his rats could not be explained by reducing it to preceding causes. His rats ran through the maze in a way that suggested that they had a plan, a mental map of the maze. They were using this mental map to guide their behavior. There is something in the world of subjective experiences, he concluded, that we cannot ignore; otherwise, we will never be able to fully understand rats' behaviors. If that is true for rats, that must be true for humans.

Tolman's seminal 1948 research study is called "Cognitive rats in maps and men". You can find it on the website *Classics in the History of Psychology:* psychclassics.yorku.ca.

Take-away messages

Lesson 6. Activity of human beings is driven by both causes and purposes. Causes belong to the world of objectively existing phenomena, but purposes exist subjectively as part of human experiences. For this reason, methods used in natural sciences are not applicable to the study of purposes. To understand in human sciences means to understand both reasons (*how come?*) and purposes (*what for?*). This is in opposition to natural sciences, where understanding of reasons (*how come?*) is sufficient. The challenge for human sciences, then, is to figure out how to study purposes when methods of natural sciences are not applicable.

Lesson 7 - Verstehen

Learning outcomes

a) [Knowledge and comprehension] What is the Verstehen position?
b) [Understanding and application] What is the role of interpretation in understanding human activities?
c) [Thinking in the abstract] In what circumstances is subjective interpretation preferable to objective measurement?

Key concepts

The *Verstehen* position, interpretation

Other concepts used

Observation, measurement, meaning of human actions, subjective knowledge of subjectively existing phenomena

Themes and areas of knowledge

Themes: Knowledge and the knower, Knowledge and technology
AOK: Human Sciences, Natural Sciences

Recap and plan

We have discussed the difference between reasons (causes) and purposes. This difference is important, although it is sometimes hard to grasp because we can use the same word in the English language to denote both – the word *why*. However, *why* may mean "for what reason" (*how come?*) and "for what purpose" (*what for?*).

Although it is probably sufficient to answer the "*how come*" question to fully understand the behavior of an asteroid, when it comes to human activities, we need to answer both questions to fully understand them.

So let's focus on answering the "*what for*" question. How do we uncover the purpose behind human activities and how do we understand what meanings humans attach to what they do and create? It is probably impossible to "measure" meanings and purposes in the same way as we measure physical things.

In this lesson we are going to unpack the concept of "*Verstehen*" that sheds some light on this problem. It sounds so exotic because it is a German word for "understanding" that philosophers used to emphasize that it is a special kind of understanding, not the same as what we are used to in natural sciences.

Thought experiment: an alien scientist

Imagine that scientists from an alien civilization have reached the Earth and are carrying out observations. This alien civilization is entirely different from ours in every possible way, so the scientists do not really have any background knowledge that would help them understand human beings. They cannot see the "meaning" of human actions, but they can try to infer this meaning based on observation. These are the things they observe:

- People praying in a temple – they are standing on their knees, facing a statue and whispering
- A person jogging in a park on Saturday morning
- A group of schoolchildren playing football
- Fans having a good time at a rock concert
- A teenager playing a video game
- IB students writing a test

Image 28. Alien scientist

Is it possible to understand a culture without being a part of it?
(#Perspectives)

What can alien scientists infer about human beings from such observations? How are they likely to explain the above-mentioned behaviors? And would it be possible for them to fully understand human culture without actually living among us?

The alien scientists can probably make accurate observations and predictions and even establish "laws" of human behavior. An example of such a law would be: on a particular day of the week, humans dress in a particular way and enter a differently designed building, where they perform uniform actions repeatedly for an hour; they are always facing a marble representation of what appears to be another human. If (in a particular religion) visiting a temple always occurs after it rains, the alien scientist may even draw inferences such as "rain causes people to visit a differently designed building". However, they would find it very difficult to understand what these humans are actually doing – the *meaning* behind their actions.

KEY IDEA: It is impossible to fully understand the meaning behind human actions by means of observation and objective measurement

Just to continue the thought experiment, imagine you are the alien scientist and you are observing human behaviors described above. How would you be likely to explain them?

Understanding through interpretation

Is subjective interpretation the only way to understand subjective experiences? (#Methods and tools)

What lesson do we learn from this thought experiment? We learn that human behavior cannot be reduced to objective "causes" and that to fully understand it we need to look into the meaning of this behavior and its purposes. That it is impossible to establish meaning and purpose by using the scientific methods of observation, experimentation and measurement. That to fully understand meaningful human behavior, one needs to *interpret* that behavior in the context of human values, their history, beliefs, fears, aspirations, and so on. To make such interpretation possible, one needs to:

- Know humans very thoroughly. For example, to fully understand temple-going behavior, the alien scientist will need to know some history of religion, the religious doctrine, cultural aspects linked to religion, and so on.
- Know not only the events that objectively happen to humans, but also how humans *perceive* these events. For example, it is one thing to observe that going to the temple commonly occurs after a rain. It is a completely different thing to know that the ancestors of these people lived in a very dry location where harvest (and hence survival) was dependent on precipitation, that the ancestors made it a rule to thank the gods every time it rained, that these people no longer depend on rains to survive but they value everything associated with their ancestors, that for them going to the temple and praying to the gods after it rains is a symbol of respect, a sign of belonging, and search for inner strength. It is what they feel when they are visiting a temple that matters, what they *perceive* these simple rituals as, what these activities *mean* to them.

***Image 29**. Can you measure love?*

How can you achieve this level of understanding? Arguably, this can happen only by being among these people for a long time, possibly becoming a part of their society and living the life they live, by interacting with them and gaining experience with them in a variety of situations, by understanding their society *from within* rather than being an impartial observer from the outside.

This position – that in order to achieve full understanding of meaningful human behavior you need to study it from within – is known as the Verstehen position. It comes from the German word *Verstehen* which means *understanding*.

KEY IDEA: Verstehen is complete understanding of meaningful human phenomena. It is impossible to achieve Verstehen by being an impartial observer from the outside.

Verstehen as subjective knowledge of subjectively existing phenomena

Verstehen is holistic understanding that places human activities in a larger context and identifies certain subjective experiences (such as meanings or purposes) behind them. Using *Verstehen* we are able to say that candle-lighting in a temple is a symbol for purification of the soul, that laws are created by humans with the purpose of making life in a society safer, and that non-financial incentives for workers in organizations are effective because humans want validation of their competence.

But the path to *Verstehen* lies through the process of interpretation. Unlike scientific observation which theoretically could be carried out by a robot, interpretation requires the presence (and active participation) of a human interpreter. The interpreter uses his or her own world of subjective experiences to understand someone else's world of subjective experiences. This makes interpretation an epistemologically subjective method.

As you know, subjective experiences (including human experiences of meanings and purposes guiding their actions) belong to the realm of subjectively existing phenomena. This makes interpretation, and hence *Verstehen*, a form of subjective knowledge of subjectively existing phenomena.

KEY IDEA: Verstehen requires interpretation – an epistemologically subjective method

Note that "subjective knowledge" here does not mean unreliable. It is my hope that by this time you have already abandoned this simplistic approach to subjectivity. Subjectivity in this context simply means that it is impossible to eliminate the knower (the interpreter, the subject) from the process of obtaining knowledge. That is not necessarily a bad thing because human knowers can understand or "see" things that robots cannot understand or see.

Under what circumstances is subjective knowledge preferable to objective knowledge? (#Scope)

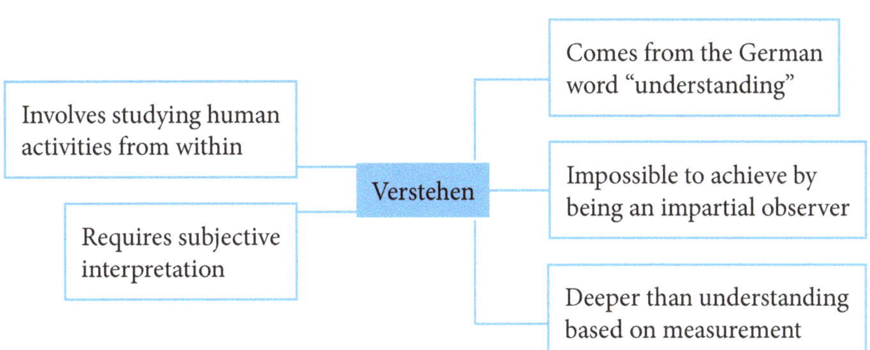

Critical thinking extension

Do you agree that subjective knowledge may be deeper than objective knowledge? That understanding gained through interpretation can give you a greater insight into a phenomenon than understanding gained through measurement?

This may be true for some phenomena but not others. For example, measurement might be a better option when trying to understand population dynamics in a species of fish (in biology). On the other hand, interpretation might be a better option when trying to understand cultural differences between native peoples of Tasmania and the migrant population of Tokyo.

Can you formulate some sort of an abstract "rule" that tells you in which cases interpretation is preferable to measurement?

If you are interested…

Must we understand knowledge communities from within before judging them from the outside? (#Ethics)

The Toraja people of Indonesia are known for their ancient ritual – the Ma'nene festival. This translates as "the ceremony of cleaning corpses" and it is held every three years. Funerals are extremely important for the Toraja. During the festival, the Toraja people dig up the bodies of their relatives. The bodies are cleaned, dressed up and admired. Family reunion pictures are taken. This is the day when the dead spend time among the living.

We may find this ritual eerie or bizarre. But the question is, what will it take an outsider to understand it? What do you need to know or to do in order to *Verstehen* the Ma'nene?

You will see some pictures taken during the ritual if you find Mark Hodge's article "Indonesian villagers dig up their dead relatives and dress them up in eerie ritual" (January 5, 2018) in the Internet newspaper *The Sun*.

You can also simply search using the name of the ritual. Beware: there will be graphic images.

Take-away messages

Lesson 7. It is impossible to measure meanings and purposes behind human actions. Hence we need to use interpretation. The interpreter uses their own world of subjective experiences to understand someone else's world of subjective experiences. Ideally, to achieve full understanding of human activities, one needs to study them from within. This is known as the Verstehen position. To the extent that we can immerse ourselves in the observed phenomenon, interpretation becomes more insightful. Interpretation (and hence Verstehen) is a form of subjective knowledge of subjectively existing phenomena.

Lesson 8 - Intersubjectivity

Learning outcomes

a) [Knowledge and comprehension] What is intersubjectivity?
b) [Understanding and application] Is it possible for knowledge to be subjective and reliable at the same time?
c) [Thinking in the abstract] To what extent is intersubjectivity a useful alternative to objectivity?

Key concepts

Intersubjectivity, extremes of a continuum

Other concepts used

Background cosmic radiation, diagnostic manual of mental disorders, inter-rater reliability

Themes and areas of knowledge

Themes: Knowledge and the knower, Knowledge and technology
AOK: Human Sciences, Natural Sciences

Recap and plan

When we looked at the nature of understanding (as opposed to knowledge) in human sciences in two previous lessons, some of the take-away messages were:

- Unlike the behavior of material things, activities of human beings are meaningful and purposeful.
- Meanings and purposes behind human activities belong to the realm of subjective human experiences (in other words, subjectively existing phenomena).
- One way to understand such phenomena is through interpretation. Interpretation is an example of subjective knowledge.
- "Subjective knowledge" in this context does not mean "unreliable".

This last statement, however, was left hanging. In this lesson we will take a closer look at how subjective knowledge may be reliable. For this, we will further enrich your understanding of subjectivity and objectivity by introducing a middle point – intersubjectivity.

Objectivity-subjectivity as a continuum

I will claim that objectivity and subjectivity are not a black-and-white distinction but rather extremes lying on the same continuum. Knowledge may be more or less objective and more or less subjective, but never entirely this or that. If you find yourself disagreeing with this statement, consider the following examples.

KEY IDEA: Subjectivity and objectivity are extremes of the same continuum

Example: a bit of subjectivity in otherwise objective knowledge

Is the scientific method truly objective? (#Methods and tools)

Even when experiments and observations are standardized to the extent that they are being carried out by a computer (as is the case, for example, with the Large Hadron Collider, the largest particle accelerator in the world), the ocean of data that is being registered in itself suggests nothing. It is the human scientist, equipped with some solid theory that dictates what patterns they should be looking for, who spots regularities in this data and who formulates laws. That is indeed a form of interpretation.

In 1964 Arno Penzias and Robert Wilson were experimenting with a supersensitive 6-meter horn antenna to measure radio waves coming from Echo balloon satellites. Echo balloon satellites were balloon-like artificial satellites that were designed to reflect communication signals from the Earth. The idea was that you could send a radio wave up from one point on the Earth, it reaches the Echo satellite, bounces off its surface and lands at another point on the Earth where it is detected by the receiver of your message. Sounds like a cool way to communicate, doesn't it? Or something that scientists would want to try, just for kicks. Remember, this was before cell phones arrived.

Image 30. *Echo satellite (credit: NASA)*

Image 31. *Horn antenna to detect signals from echo satellite (credit: NASA)*

To detect these faint radio waves that bounced off the Echo satellite, Penzias and Wilson had to remove all possible interference (background radio broadcasting and so on). Even the heat from the antenna itself could produce interference, so in order to remove that they cooled the receiver with liquid helium to -269 °C (quite a lot of trouble to build a phone, huh?).

After doing all that, Penzias and Wilson detected a steady mysterious noise in their receiver. It persisted day and night, regardless of the direction the antenna was pointed at. Their first hypothesis was – more interference. They suspected pigeon droppings in the antenna. So the two scientists thoroughly cleaned the huge antenna of all pigeon droppings. But the noise did not disappear. They thought this looked like a signal that was coming from outside of our galaxy, but since they did not have any theory that would suggest the existence of a source of radio waves out there, they didn't really know what to make of it. They probably kept thinking that there must be another source of interference that they failed to remove.

That was until Penzias and Wilson came across an unpublished paper by several astrophysicists from Princeton University. In this paper the scientists reasoned that if the Universe had indeed started with a big explosion, then radiation from that explosion should still be detectable today. The Big Bang theory was still very much debated at that time. The scientists predicted what the characteristics of such radiation would be, and their predictions happened to match exactly what Penzias and Wilson were registering with their antenna. The two groups of scientists met and published the paper together. They realized that they had discovered the echo of the Big Bang. In 1978 Penzias and Wilson were awarded the Nobel Prize (Bernstein, 1984).

What is the difference between data and knowledge? (#Scope)

KEY IDEA: Even natural sciences inevitably include an element of interpretation

Such is the story of two guys who were trying to detect radio waves bouncing off a big metal ball floating in the sky, but instead detected the Big Bang echo from 13.8 billion years ago. But the point is, registering the data itself was never sufficient for them to make a discovery. It was their *interpretation* of data, backed up by solid theory from fellow scientists, that resulted in a discovery. It is an element of subjectivity in otherwise objective knowledge.

Example: elements of objectivity in otherwise subjective knowledge

Similarly, knowledge that we often hastily dismiss as subjective is not always that subjective at all.

In psychiatry, when a clinician diagnoses mental illness, they usually use a special manual on diagnosing disorders. The one that is most commonly used in the Western world is known as the DSM – "Diagnostic and Statistical Manual". The manual lists the known mental disorders along with their symptoms. As a clinician, your job is to conduct an interview with the patient and establish what diagnosis (if any) fits best. It is a matter of interpretation, of course, because one and the same symptom may belong to different disorders, one and the same behavior may be interpreted as a norm or a deviation, and so on. Obviously we do not want a situation where diagnosis varies widely from clinician to clinician.

As a measure against this unwanted subjectivity in diagnosis, psychologists use a metric known as inter-rater reliability. *Inter-rater reliability* of diagnosis is the extent to which different psychologists diagnosing the same patient with the same manual converge in their conclusions. You can calculate inter-rater reliability of diagnosis for each disorder separately. From this research we know, for example, that inter-rater reliability of diagnosing depression is pretty high, whereas inter-rater reliability of the DSM for things like GAD (Generalized Anxiety Disorder) leaves a lot to be desired.

Does knowledge become less subjective when more people start sharing it? (#Perspectives)

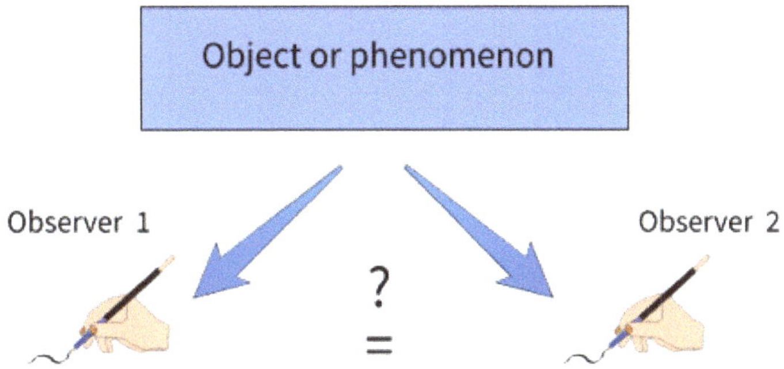

***Image 32**. Inter-rater reliability*

But the point here is we cannot simply dismiss psychiatric diagnosis as something "subjective". It would be an oversimplification. Yes, it is subjective since it relies on interpretation. But in many cases, we can achieve high inter-rater reliability of diagnosis, which means that different clinicians will independently arrive at the same diagnosis for the same patients. When that is achieved, it is not a pure case of subjectivity any longer. It is a case of intersubjectivity.

KEY IDEA: Intersubjectivity is a case of convergence between subjective beliefs

Intersubjectivity looks like a useful compromise. Indeed, some things can only be known through interpretation and, in this sense, non-subjective knowledge of such things is not an option. But when subjective interpretations converge, we have reason to believe that these interpretations are true.

Critical thinking extension

Even objectivity (the opposite side of the continuum) can be seen as an extreme case of intersubjectivity. When 1000 physicists conduct the same experiment in the Large Hadron Collider and arrive at the same result 999 times (because one of the physicists ran the experiment with a mistake without realizing it), we are dealing with a very high degree of intersubjectivity. Perhaps objectivity itself is simply an extreme case of intersubjectivity.

However, one must bear in mind that intersubjectivity comes with limitations:

Is it a responsibility of a knower to try making their knowledge less subjective and more objective? (#Ethics)

- Sometimes experts unanimously agree on something and yet they are miserably wrong.
- There is no good way to answer the question "How many experts agreeing on something is enough?" Would 10 experts agreeing be better than 3 experts agreeing? What if the group of 10 all come from the same country and similar educational backgrounds, while in the group of 3 they all represent different cultures and different theoretical perspectives? Is it negligible when 1 out of 12 experts disagrees? In jury trial, a verdict cannot be reached until the decision is unanimous, so even if one juror disagrees the knowledge is not considered "intersubjective enough".

Keeping all this is mind, do you agree that intersubjectivity can be a useful alternative to objectivity?

If you are interested…

The entry "Intersubjectivity" on the YouTube channel *The Audiopedia* is a recap of intersubjectivity as a concept. It also mentions some alternative interpretations of the meaning of this term. Watch it for a summary of what we have discussed in this lesson.

Take-away messages

Lesson 8. Objectivity and subjectivity are extremes on the same continuum. Arguably, extremes on this continuum are hypothetical (never observed in real life). For example, knowledge in natural sciences, although believed to be highly objective, always includes an element of interpretation when making the leap from data to theory. Conversely, in diagnosing mental illness (which seems to be a highly subjective process), one can estimate the convergence in opinions of clinicians and establish a measure of intersubjectivity. Hence, it is possible for interpretation to be subjective and reliable at the same time. It may even be claimed that objectivity is in fact an extreme case of intersubjectivity.

Lesson 9 - Qualia (part 1)

Learning outcomes

a) [Knowledge and comprehension] What are "qualia"? What are examples of "subjective experiences"?
b) [Understanding and application] Is it possible to have objective knowledge of subjectively existing phenomena?
c) [Thinking in the abstract] How can we know if technology will ever develop to the extent that it becomes possible to objectively measure someone's subjective experiences?

Key concepts

Qualia, subjective experiences

Other concepts used

Brain scanning technology, voxel, magnetic resonance imaging

Themes and areas of knowledge

Theme: Knowledge and technology
AOK: Human Sciences

Recap and plan

In the previous lessons as we discussed the nature of understanding in human sciences, we highlighted the fact that human activities (unlike the behavior of an asteroid or any other material things) are meaningful and purposeful. Meanings and purposes are represented in the world of human subjective experiences, in other words, they are subjectively existing phenomena.

We also argued that the only way for us to know subjectively existing phenomena is through interpretation, that is, using our own subjective experiences to understand the subjective experiences of others.

In the next two lessons we take this discussion several steps further and attempt to answer the following question: is it possible at all to know other people's subjective experiences? There is a debate going on around this question, and the central concept in this debate is that of qualia. Qualia are defined as instances of subjective experiences.

Do you agree with the saying "You never know people"? (#Scope)

These lessons will be filled with zombies and androids, artificial intelligence and questioning your own sanity.

Is it possible to have objective knowledge of subjectively existing phenomena?

So far we have discussed instances of subjective knowledge of subjectively existing phenomena. We assumed that it is possible to understand other people's subjective experiences through the process of interpretation. When I interpret someone else's subjective experiences, I use my own experiences to try and understand them. This of course is a "subjective" method.

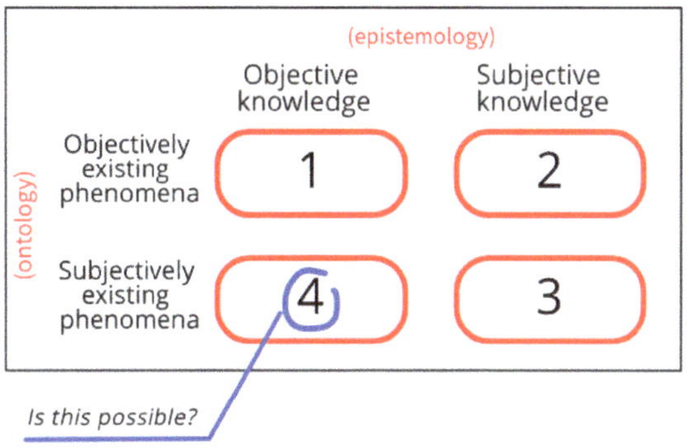

Image 33. Objective knowledge of subjectively existing phenomena

So here is a question. Can we know other people's subjective experiences objectively, without the need to resort to interpretation?

Can you, for example, put a human subject into a brain scanner and "see" or "measure" what they feel when they are looking at a picture of a person they love? Or can you, at least theoretically, measure someone's brain activity to objectively identify what they are thinking about or what emotions they are experiencing when they are contemplating a work of art?

Is it possible to have objective knowledge of subjective human experiences? (#Perspectives)

It turns out that there is no simple answer (after studying TOK for a while now, are you surprised?). But if you insisted on a simple answer and I had to choose between yes and no, I would say no.

For the rest of this lesson, I will imagine that you hold a different opinion and you are arguing with me. I will try to foresee two key objections on your part and I will try to respond to these objections.

It is impossible to know objectively what another person is experiencing

Objection 1: Can't we use brain imaging technology?

Answer 1: We can, but it's crude. Does not really give an insight.

Objection 2: But in the future technology will develop to the extent to make it possible

Answer 2: That's not certain. Technology can hit a threshold. This has happened before.

Objection 1: Can't we use brain scanning technology?

To start with, brain scanning technology is not that good. The best we can do is put people in different conditions, scan their brains and look at the crude differences in brain activity between these conditions. On the basis of such research we can make inferences such as "this brain area is associated with this behavior".

For example, Helen Fisher with colleagues (Fisher, Aron and Brown, 2005) compared brain activity of a group of participants while looking at a picture of a beloved person versus looking at a picture of a neutral acquaintance. They found that in the first condition there was increased activation in the ventral tegmental area (VTA) and caudate nucleus. What does this tell you? Probably nothing. Well, we also know from previous research that these two areas of the brain are involved in transmitting dopamine (a neurotransmitter). So increased activation in these two areas is somehow associated with increased activity of dopamine in the brain. Okay, so what? We also know from previous research that increased activity of dopamine in the brain is usually associated with motivation and feelings of pleasure. So what can we say in conclusion? We can say that, based on results of this research, people that are looking at a picture of someone they love *probably* have increased levels of dopamine in their brains which means that they are *probably* experiencing *some sort of* motivation or pleasure. Fisher herself concludes that "dopamine plays a role in feelings of romantic love".

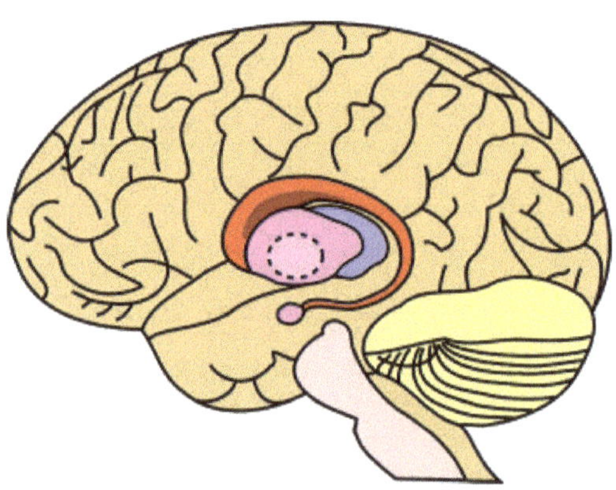

***Image 34**. Caudate nucleus (the red area) (credit: Leevanjackson, Wikimedia Commons)*

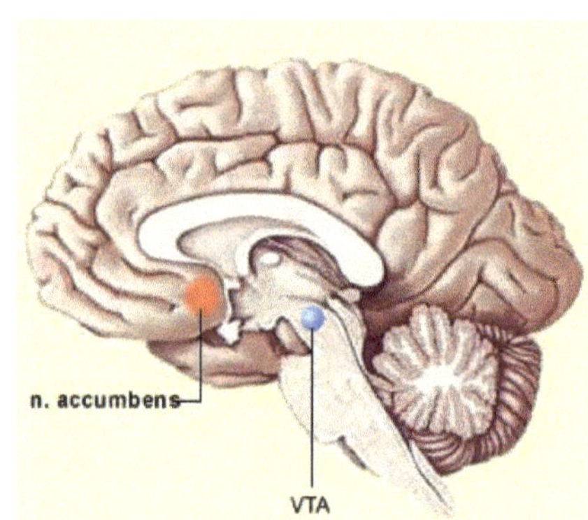

***Image 35**. Ventral tegmental area (the blue dot) (credit: Gustavocarra, Wikimedia Commons)*

This is as far as we can go. Such knowledge hardly applies to individuals. Can we use brain scanning to say that Cynthia experiences love and affection when she is looking at a picture of Todd? We can, but that will be an educated guess. Here is why:

- Her VTA and caudate nucleus may be activated for some other reason. She might be planning to murder Todd and looking at the picture might remind her of how she will get rid of that person soon, which brings her pleasure (pardon the grim example, this is just to make a point!).
- Her VTA and caudate nucleus may not be activated at all. Results of the experiment are results about averages. These results do not mean that the VTA and caudate nucleus are activated in *all* people *every time* they look at a picture of someone they love. In some participants in the experiment, these regions were not activated when they were looking at the picture of a beloved person. In some participants, these regions were activated even when they were looking at the picture of a neutral acquaintance. The experiment shows a statistical trend, but it does not apply to each and every individual situation.

Image 36. *People in love*

How can we decide when research with human subjects becomes morally unacceptable? (#Ethics)

Objection 2: It is not possible now, but it will be possible in the future.

You could agree with my point above, but still argue that our conclusions are so limited only because brain scanning technology is not sufficiently developed yet. As technology develops, you might say, we will be able to know more and more. We will eventually reach a point whereby we will be able to tell exactly what a person is experiencing by measuring their brain activity.

That is a fair assumption because history suggests that our insight into human experiences is getting deeper and deeper. A hundred years ago we had no idea what dopamine was, and we could not even dream about being able to see what is happening inside a person's brain without waiting for them to die and cutting their skull open. We have made considerable progress, and it seems logical to assume that the progress will continue.

However, there may be a threshold beyond which we will not be able to go. We have hit such thresholds in other fields of science. For example, we cannot see inside a black hole because gravity is so strong there that light cannot escape it. We will never be able to have a peek inside, no matter how far technology develops, because no technology can break the laws of physics. Is there a similar threshold in brain scanning?

Is there a threshold after which technological progress will provide no further increment in knowledge? (#Methods and tools)

Currently the picture we are getting is quite crude. The smallest "brain particle" the activity of which we can register through a brain scanner – a voxel – contains several million neurons and several billion connections between them. We could probably learn to make voxels smaller, but will we ever be able to capture all the intricacies of the brain – an immensely complex system

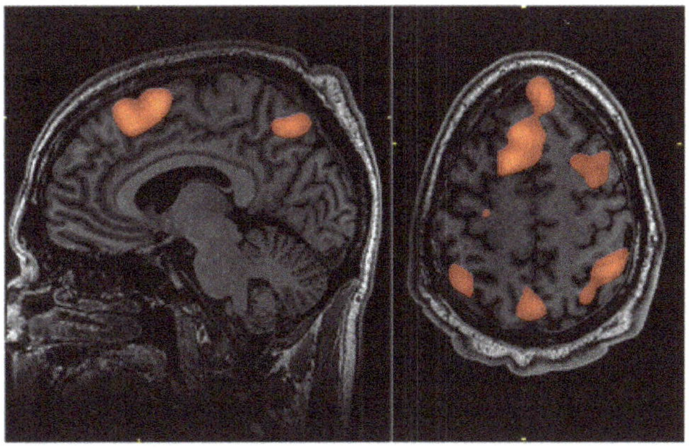

Image 37. *fMRI (functional magnetic resonance imaging)*

where the number of neurons approaches 100 billion (about the same as the estimated number of stars in the Milky Way) and the number of connections between them is just uncountable? Or we could hit the limit where the act of observation itself (such as the MRI scanner acting on a person's brain) changes brain activity in ways that make it impossible to know what it is like when we are not observing it.

How do we know if such a threshold exists? We do not know. We will try, and we will or will not reach it.

However, for now I must conclude that it is impossible to have objective knowledge of subjectively existing phenomena.

KEY IDEA: It is impossible to have objective knowledge of subjectively existing phenomena

Critical thinking extension

In the branch of human sciences known as futurology, academics try to predict the likely future of society, science, technology and other aspects of our lives. These predictions are educated guesses, extrapolations based on the current state of things as well as the lessons accumulated by history.

Could you assume the role of a futurologist and make educated guess: will technology ever develop to the extent that it becomes possible for us to objectively measure another person's subjective experiences? If you think you are lacking some information to answer this question, then what extra information do you need exactly? You might even want to do some research online to make your educated guess more… well, educated.

If you are interested…

Poppy Crum in her TED talk "Technology that knows what you're feeling" (2018) walks us through some of the latest developments in "empathetic technology" – registering physical parameters like the slightest changes in facial expression, body temperature and chemical composition of breath to determine what emotion the person is experiencing.

Do you think this technology is just the beginning and one day we will reach a point where we would actually be able to register subjective experiences objectively? Or do you think that the technology described in this TED talk is pretty much as far as we will ever get?

Take-away messages

Lesson 9. Interpretation falls under subjective knowledge of subjectively existing phenomena. But is it possible to have objective knowledge of subjectively existing phenomena? In other words, is it possible to know objectively what other people experience? At the current level of development of technology, the answer is no. Whether or not the answer will change with the development of technology remains an open question. Hypothetically, we may hit a threshold beyond which we will not be able to go.

Lesson 10 - Qualia (part 2)

Learning outcomes

a) [Knowledge and comprehension] What are the two thought experiments: Mary's room and Philosophical zombie?
b) [Understanding and application] How do these thought experiments support or refute the existence of qualia?
c) [Thinking in the abstract] If qualia exist, are they in principle knowable?

Key concepts

Qualia, thought experiment, Mary's room, Philosophical zombie, physicalism

Other concepts used

Consciousness, interpretation

Themes and areas of knowledge

Theme: Knowledge and the knower
AOK: Human Sciences

Recap and plan

In the previous lesson, we discussed if subjective human experiences can be known objectively through precise measurement and without the need of resorting to interpretation. We decided that at the current level of technological development the task is impossible, but whether or not it will become possible in the future is very hard to tell.

However, I am itching to have some sort of an answer now. I don't think I can wait dozens (hundreds? thousands?) of years to find out. In such cases we usually use thought experiments – combining our imagination with logical reasoning to explore some hypothetical scenarios.

In this lesson we will make another attempt to answer the question "Is it possible to have objective knowledge of subjectively existing phenomena?" This time, we will approach it through the use of two thought experiments – Mary's room and Philosophical zombie. These thought experiments will have two interesting implications – one romantic and one scary.

How useful are thought experiments as a tool of obtaining knowledge? (#Methods and tools)

Do qualia exist? How can we know them?
- Thought experiment 1 — Mary's room
- Thought experiment 2 — Philosophical zombie

Qualia

I already briefly mentioned qualia in the previous lesson, but it is time to give a more formal definition.

Qualia (singular: *quale*) are instances of subjective experience. This term captures the "what it's like to" phenomenon. For example, what it is like to smell a rose on a misty morning, what it feels like to take the first sip of coffee after a long night's sleep, what it feels like when you get a paper cut – these are all qualia. In our terminology, qualia fall under subjectively experienced phenomena.

Scholars have been arguing for some time now: do qualia exist? And how can we know them?

Thought experiment 1: Mary's room

Image 38. Mary the color scientist (credit: Jahooly, Wikimedia Commons)

The thought experiment "Mary's room" belongs to Frank Jackson (1982).

Mary is a brilliant scientist who specializes in the study of vision. She acquires all the scientific (physical) information that could possibly exist about what happens when we see the blue sky, a ripe tomato, and so on. She knows, for example, how light of different wavelengths affects the retina of the eye, how this transforms into signals travelling along the neurons to the brain, which brain centers these wavelengths activate, as well as other tiny responses of the human body to the blue sky and the ripe tomato. When we respond by saying "the sky is blue" or "this tomato is red", she can describe exactly what happens in the brain as it accesses the words "blue" and "red" stored in its memory, associates these words with the sensory information from the retina, and sends the signals to our speech muscles to produce that kind of utterance. However, her entire life, Mary has been confined to a black-and-white room and investigated the world through black-and-white monitors. She has never actually *experienced* seeing anything red or blue. One day, Mary is finally released from her black-and-white room and sees the blue sky (and the red tomato) for the first time in color. The question is, has she learned anything new?

It seems reasonable to say yes, Mary is learning something new on top of what she already knows. Although she knows all that there is to know about the sensation of color in the physical sense, she has never had a *subjective experience* of color. She knew every single detail of what happens in the brain when we see a ripe tomato, but she did not know *what it is like* to see one.

Are qualia knowable? (#Perspectives)

If you agree with this, then you acknowledge the existence of *qualia* – instances of subjective conscious experience that cannot be reduced to physical properties. But since qualia cannot be reduced to physical properties, they cannot be studied objectively. This is then an example of something we will never understand objectively, no matter how far our technology develops.

KEY IDEA: If qualia cannot be reduced to physical properties, then they cannot be studied objectively no matter how far technology develops

Objections to Mary's room

It is also possible to disagree that Mary learns anything new when she is released from the black-and-white room. In this case you are a physicalist. Physicalism is the belief that everything in the world, including mental states and consciousness, is physical in nature.

For example, one common objection is that the mystical component of "actually seeing the color red for the first time, on top of knowing everything physical about it" is also physical. Actually seeing the color for the first time produces an additional physical reaction of excitement, perhaps, that was not there when Mary was simply studying the color from the comfort of her black-and-white room. But if Mary actually knows everything physical there is to know about the color red, then she would know this additional physical reaction of excitement, too. Whose side are you on in this argument?

Thought experiment 2: Philosophical zombie

Imagine there is a creature (an android of some sort) that is indistinguishable from a normal human being on the outside but has no subjective experiences. For example, if this creature puts its hand in a fire, it will not feel pain yet it will react exactly like any human would react – scream and quickly pull out the hand, complain that the burn hurts, and so on. This Philosophical zombie has all of the external manifestations of a human being, yet lacks subjective experiences. The question is, then, how can we tell the Philosophical zombie from a normal human being?

It does not matter whether such an android could be constructed or not. If the Philosophical zombie can exist in principle, that is, if it is logically conceivable, then this has at least two implications, the "romantic" one and the "scary" one.

What reasons do we have to believe that subjective experiences are reducible to physical processes? (#Scope)

The "romantic" implication is refuting physicalism and believing that conscious human beings cannot be reduced to physical factors. We are something larger than just a very complicated machine. Qualia cannot be studied by objective methods. I call this implication "romantic" because it suggests that humans will never be understood by science. To understand what love feels like, it will never be enough to know chemistry; to understand love, one needs poetry and empathy, and perhaps one even needs to be in love to truly understand love.

The "scary" implication is that there is no way for an external observer to know if the Philosophical zombie has subjective experiences or not. Imagine there are two men in front of you: one is a Philosophical zombie and one is a human philosopher. You tickle them and they both roll with laughter. You pull their hair and they both scream and reprimand you. How can you tell them apart? If subjective experiences are something that are beyond the scope of knowing objectively, how can you ever know that a Philosophical zombie is in fact a zombie? Moreover, how can you know that your friends and teachers are *not* zombies? How can you know that your parents are not zombies? What if you are the only person in the world who actually has qualia?

And conversely… I find your behavior very suspicious. Can you prove to me that you are not a zombie?

***Image 39**. Zombie (not philosophical)*

Conclusion

In conclusion, what can we say about objective knowledge of subjectively existing phenomena? It is debatable that such knowledge is possible. There are only two options here:

1) If you believe it is possible, you must also reject the existence of qualia and be a physicalist.
2) If you believe it isn't possible, you are stuck with the puzzle of knowing something that is objectively unknowable.

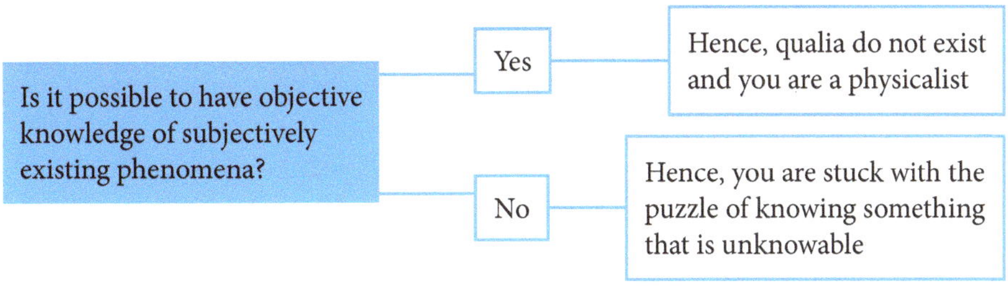

Critical thinking extension

Isn't it wonderful that we know that the answer is one of these two options? Although we can debate which one of the two, both of them seem amazing and terrifying at the same time.

If it is indeed possible to have objective knowledge of subjectively existing phenomena, then qualia can be reduced to measurable physical processes. This would mean we are nothing else but advanced machines and our so-called "consciousness" is simply the product of brain activity.

However, if it is *not* possible to have objective knowledge of subjectively existing phenomena, then qualia do exist and we are something larger than just advanced machines. This means we can only understand qualia through subjective interpretation. Therefore, I will never be able to understand your qualia directly – only through my own qualia. This would mean that it is not possible for anyone to ever fully understand you.

So which of the two options would you prefer? Are we fancy physical things, or do we live in a world that will never be fully known?

What are the ethical implications of physicalism (the belief that people are advanced biological machines)? (#Ethics)

If you are interested…

Here is a selection of videos for you to watch if the concept of qualia and the thought experiments discussed in this lesson piqued your interest:

1) Watch an animation video summarizing the Philosophical zombie argument: "Are we surrounded by zombies?" on the YouTube channel *Humanities Program – Zewail City*.
2) Watch the TED-ed animation video lesson by Eleanor Nelsen titled "Mary's Room: A Philosophical Thought Experiment" (2017).
3) Watch the video "Consciousness, Qualia and Self" on the YouTube channel *RecursionX*. The video features the famous neuroscientist Dr. V.S. Ramachandran. Remember – he is a neuroscientist, so he is approaching this from the scientific angle.
4) Watch David Chalmers's TED talk "How do you explain consciousness?" (2014).

Take-away messages

Lesson 10. Qualia are instances of subjective experience that cannot be reduced to physical properties. The bigger questions are: 1) do qualia even exist? 2) are they knowable in principle? We can attempt to investigate qualia in thought experiments. Two well-known thought experiments are Mary's room and the Philosophical zombie. Mary's room seems to suggest that qualia do indeed exist; since they are not reducible to physical properties, we will never know them objectively, no matter how far technology develops. The Philosophical zombie seems to suggest that qualia, even if they exist, are unknowable in principle, neither by objective nor by subjective methods. This has some scary implications.

5.4 - Knowledge and understanding in the Arts

It is not by chance that I have picked Natural Sciences, Human Sciences and the Arts as examples of areas of knowledge to illustrate the concept of understanding. Understanding is distinctly different in these three areas.

We have seen that natural sciences deal with objectively existing phenomena and attempt to study these phenomena using methods that do not depend in any way on who uses them (observation independent of the observer). In other words, natural sciences pursue objective knowledge of objectively existing phenomena. We have also seen that this has implications for understanding. Understanding in natural sciences is an advanced knowledge of the objective world. By "advanced" we mean based on knowing the causes, being able to perform all four functions of science (description, explanation, prediction and control), and fitting into a larger coherent picture of the world (scientific worldview).

We have seen that the focus of human sciences is the activity of human beings and the products of this activity. Unlike the behavior of material things, activity of human beings is not only caused by something, but also directed toward something (it is meaningful and purposeful). Meanings and purposes are represented in the world of subjective human experiences. So the additional challenge that human sciences face is to understand this world of subjectively existing phenomena. It is possible to have subjective knowledge of such phenomena, but the possibility of objective knowledge is debatable. In any case, understanding in human sciences implies using *interpretation* to arrive at inferences about meanings and purposes behind human activities.

By making this step from measurement to interpretation, we are losing in objectivity but gaining in depth.

Taking one further step in the same direction, there's the arts. While we lose in objectivity even more (some even claim that there is no objectivity in art whatsoever), we gain even more depth (some claim that art is the best way to capture what it means to be a human being). In this series of lessons, we will explore what it means to "understand", perhaps as opposed to "knowing", in the arts.

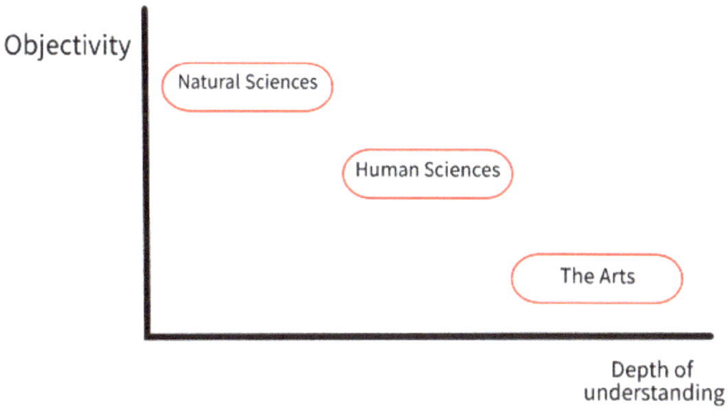

***Image 40**. Losing in objectivity but gaining in depth?*

> **Note**
>
> Art forms are very diverse. There is sculpture, music, poetry, dance, film-making, theatre, artistic installations, graffiti, martial arts, stand-up comedy. Even further, within each form of art, there has been some historical development, and views on what counts as art (or good art) have changed multiple times.
>
> For this reason, it is quite difficult to make any generic knowledge arguments about art that would apply to all art forms and all epochs.
>
> In this unit, we will discuss art with a focus on paintings. Moreover, we will actually focus on one specific example – Van Gogh's *Starry Night*. I believe this will allow us to investigate knowledge questions much more deeply and to reach some meaningful conclusions that you can further apply to other art forms.

Lesson 11 - Propositional and non-propositional knowledge

Learning outcomes

a) [Knowledge and comprehension] What is the difference between propositional and non-propositional knowledge?
b) [Understanding and application] What counts as knowledge in art?
c) [Thinking in the abstract] What is the role of propositional knowledge in art?

Key concepts

Propositional knowledge, non-propositional knowledge

Other concepts used

Explicit knowledge, implicit knowledge

Themes and areas of knowledge

Theme: Knowledge and the knower
AOK: The Arts

Recap and plan

This is the first in a series of eight lessons that unpack the concept of "understanding" in relation to art. We have seen in the previous lessons that understanding is distinctly different in natural and human sciences, the reason being that human sciences have to deal with a whole new realm – subjective human experiences. In its turn, art is distinctly different from sciences (both natural and human) and this has to have implications for knowledge and understanding.

In this particular lesson, we will consider the concepts of propositional and non-propositional knowledge and see how they relate to the Arts as an area of knowledge.

Propositional and non-propositional knowledge

Propositional knowledge is any knowledge that can be expressed in the form of a claim / statement. For example, "*Atoms consist of electrons and protons*" is a claim, so it is a form of propositional knowledge. It does not have to be expressed in everyday language: the statement "$P(A \cap B) = P(A) \times P(B \mid A)$" is also a form of propositional knowledge. It makes sense as a claim for anyone who knows conditional probabilities in mathematics. Your textbooks are filled with examples of propositional knowledge; in fact, most of what you learn at school is propositional knowledge.

How can knowledge be shared without being expressed in language? (#Methods and tools)

Non-propositional knowledge, on the other hand, cannot be expressed verbally. Examples include "how to" knowledge (I know how to tie my laces, I know how to ride a bicycle) and knowledge by acquaintance (I recognize my brother when I see him, I can tell when my mother is upset but trying to hide it). Such knowledge is gained with first-hand experience and it is difficult if not impossible to transfer this knowledge to someone who lacked such experience. Can you sit someone in front of you and teach them verbally how to ride a bicycle? I invite you to give it a try.

JTB does not apply to non-propositional knowledge

The definition of knowledge as a justified true belief (JTB) is only applicable to propositional knowledge. This makes sense: belief is a proposition, a statement. Beliefs can be verbally formulated and communicated from one person to another. Beliefs can be true or false, more or less justified. By contrast, what is the belief in knowing how to tie your laces? Can you justify knowing how to tie your laces? Is your knowledge of how to tie your laces "true"? No, JTB doesn't apply here.

We already acknowledged that the definition of knowledge as a JTB is limited. One alternative that we discussed previously is using a metaphor instead of a definition: knowledge as a map to a territory. As far as propositional knowledge is concerned, JTB seems to be the best definition that we currently have. However, for non-propositional knowledge, it would probably make sense to use alternatives.

Propositional knowledge	Non-propositional knowledge
Can be expressed as a claim	Cannot be expressed verbally
JTB applies	JTB does not apply
Explicit	Implicit

What can we learn from art?

If the Arts are indeed an area of knowledge, then what can we learn from art? As you could expect, there has been debate around this question. This debate is very old and if you think it is somewhere close to a resolution you are, of course, deeply mistaken.

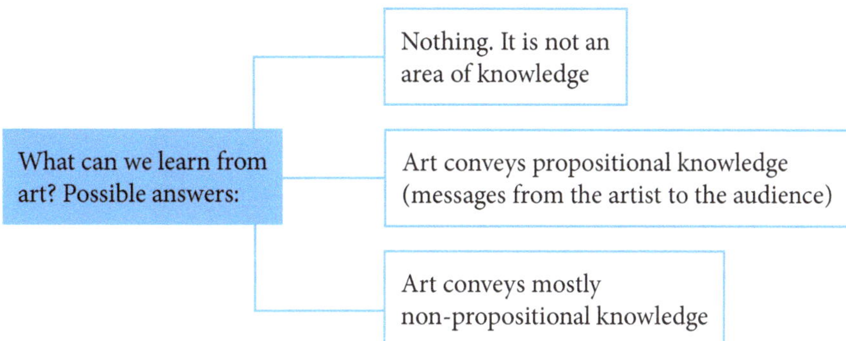

One side of the debate is that it is possible to attain meaningful knowledge from art but this knowledge is non-propositional. For example, our engagement with art arouses certain emotions that lead to a greater understanding of both ourselves and the world around us through producing some insights. These insights help us see the world in a new way, but they cannot be easily put into words. Suppose you watch the *Shawshank Redemption* and it influences you in such deep ways that you become a different person. You understand something about life but you cannot clearly verbalize what it is that you have understood. One of my favorite things to do after watching a powerful movie in the cinema is to watch people's faces as they get up from their seats and leave the hall, and then eavesdrop on their conversations. Their faces clearly convey a deep emotional experience, but their scarce comments to each other do not do justice to that at all. It's either that people are afraid to admit they have emotions or that they lack the language to express what they have been through.

If art is knowledge, what is it knowledge of? (#Scope)

The opposite side of the debate is to deny that we can learn from art. Those who hold this position claim that knowledge can only be propositional. Since art does not convey any truth, we should reject art as a source of knowledge. For example, what knowledge is conveyed in Mozart's *Moonlight Sonata*? Yes, it is a fine piece of music that stirs certain emotions when one listens to it, but there is no *knowledge* in it.

Can art convey propositional knowledge? (#Perspectives)

Yet another possible position in this debate is to claim that art does indeed convey propositional knowledge and that the artist creates artwork with the intent of sending a message and that the job of the audience is to decipher this message. For example, a painter creating a landscape might be sending messages like "I think this landscape is beautiful and peaceful", "We should value nature untouched by humans", "When the Sun is setting, light creates interesting patterns".

Which position are you leaning toward? Can we learn from art or not? And if we can, is the knowledge that we are acquiring propositional or non-propositional?

By now, you could have guessed already that since the Arts are included as one of the 5 areas of knowledge in IB TOK, we will be assuming the position that we can indeed learn from art. We will also assume that knowledge that is conveyed by art is to a large extent non-propositional. However, for the time being we are not rejecting the idea that elements of propositional knowledge are also possible.

KEY IDEA: To a large extent, knowledge that is conveyed by art is non-propositional

***Image 41**. Does art convey a propositional message?*

Is ethics propositional knowledge or non-propositional? (#Ethics)

Critical thinking extension

It would be fair to say that objective knowledge is all propositional. Indeed, objective knowledge needs to be independent of the knower, but if this knowledge has not been expressed as a proposition, it means that it only resides in the head of the knower somehow. If we cannot pull it out of one person's head, how is it objective?

As for subjective knowledge, it can be both propositional and non-propositional. In areas of knowledge such as Human Sciences, the focus is on propositional knowledge, although it is understood that in some fields of research propositional knowledge is not possible or not desirable. For example, we might be interested in what it is like to have extreme anxiety or a social phobia. We could interview some patients and we could get a glimpse of their inner world – through their words, their behavior, their non-verbal reactions, emotions, perhaps drawings, and simply through the look in their eyes. If you are the interviewer, then over the course of time you will develop a sense of understanding of your patients. But now the challenge is to convey this to others. All you can do, really, is to write an article that uses words to convey knowledge that is partly propositional and partly non-propositional. I bet you will find it very difficult to capture non-propositional elements of your knowledge, especially if you are limited to the academic style of writing. A poem or a fiction story might have done a better job, but even they might not be sufficient. In any case, human sciences are based on propositional knowledge and even non-propositional elements are reduced to propositions, to the extent possible.

The Arts is one area of knowledge that prioritizes non-propositional knowledge over propositional knowledge. This comes with pros and cons. Pros include our ability to attempt to know things that cannot be captured in words. Cons include the necessity to interpret knowledge rather than simply receive it. In a sense, looking at a work of art requires a lot more mental work than reading a textbook!

What do you think is the role of propositional knowledge in the Arts? Can you think of other areas of knowledge where non-propositional knowledge is emphasized rather than avoided?

If you are interested…

Words often become insufficient when we speak about love. Listen to Harry Baker – the 2012 World Poetry Slam Champion - perform his poems "59" and "Paper People". To do this, you can simply find his TED talk "A love poem for lonely prime numbers" (2014).

Can you summarize the poems in 2 or 3 sentences (propositional statements) without any stylistic devices such as metaphors, similes or oxymorons (just simple neutral statements)? Try that. What exactly do you think gets "lost in translation" when you summarize poetry in regular language?

Take-away messages

Lesson 11. There has been debate around what counts as knowledge in art. One position is that art conveys propositional knowledge, another position is that art does not convey any knowledge at all and hence it should not be considered an area of knowledge, the third position is that knowledge conveyed through art is mainly non-propositional. We will stick to the third position. While in natural sciences all knowledge is propositional and in human sciences even non-propositional knowledge is reduced to propositions, art prioritizes non-propositional knowledge. Through art, we can attempt knowing things that cannot be captured in words. The problem is, we need to use interpretation, which is a subjective process.

Lesson 12 - Van Gogh's Starry Night (part 1)

Learning outcomes

a) [Knowledge and comprehension] What is the personal context behind Van Gogh's *Starry Night*?
b) [Understanding and application] How do critics use personal context when interpreting a work of art?
c) [Thinking in the abstract] How can we know if art critics are justified in their interpretations?

Key concepts

Personal context of a work of art

Other concepts used

Art critics, interpretation

Themes and areas of knowledge

Theme: Knowledge and the knower
AOK: The Arts

Recap and plan

In the previous lesson, we concluded that art can indeed be a source of knowledge and that this knowledge is to a large extent non-propositional. To make our discussion a little more concrete, in the next two lessons we are going to consider one particular piece of art – Van Gogh's painting *Starry Night* (1889). The arts are very diverse, but in looking at this diversity one can easily overlook the depth of meaning behind each and every individual piece. The idea is that if we focus on one work of art and analyze it more thoroughly, you will be able to use this approach with any other work of art on your own.

***Image 42**. Vincent van Gogh, Starry Night (1889)*

Opening questions

Look at this painting – *Starry Night* – created by Vincent van Gogh in 1889. Think what your answer would be to the following questions:

- What was Van Gogh's intention when he created it? What was he trying to convey?
- How can you describe the audience's reaction to this painting? What feelings and thoughts would it stir in the audience (and what feelings does it stir in you)?
- Is this painting a skillful work of art? Does it require a lot of skill to paint something like this?
- Is it beautiful?

Is the aesthetic perception of something as "beautiful" a form of knowledge? (#Perspectives)

When you were answering these questions (supposing you don't know anything about when and how and under what circumstances the painting was created), you probably went with what is depicted, wondered about the color choices, maybe asked yourself what the weird-looking silhouette was in the foreground, perhaps felt some emotions or an aesthetic response of some sort.

Let's see if this changes in any way once you get a slightly better knowledge of the context.

KEY IDEA: Our understanding of a work of art may change when we get to know the context in which it was created

What is there in the painting?

In the painting there are whirling clouds, shining stars and a crescent. In the left foreground there is a curvy cypress tree (some say there are two cypress trees!). The painting also shows a village with a church (I am trying to use neutral language here and avoid interpretations as much as possible; some people might agree that the village is "peaceful" and some might disagree, but everyone will probably agree that there is indeed a village). How do we know that the weird shape is a cypress tree? Because it was one of Van Gogh's favorite things to paint and it appears in many of his other works. In this particular painting, it is just a silhouette, but anyone familiar with Van Gogh's other paintings will have no doubt recognizing it.

What is the personal context of this work?

His whole life Van Gogh (1853 - 1890) struggled with money and recognition. I mean, he didn't have any. He was trying to pursue the career of an artist but he had to heavily depend on his brother Theo's money. He was a very productive painter, almost to the extent of fanaticism, producing around 900 paintings over the period of 9 years. However, critics were not favorable to him; in fact, they ridiculed his work. He was able to sell only one (!) painting in his lifetime.

Is knowledge of an artist's biography essential for understanding a work of art? (#Methods and tools)

He developed some mental health issues. A well-known episode from his life is when he cut off a part of his own ear with a razor, wrapped it in paper and delivered the package to a woman in a brothel that he frequented (it's getting interesting, isn't it?). Several months after that, Van Gogh admitted himself into a mental asylum in France. He painted *Starry Night* during his 1-year-long stay in the mental asylum. He mostly painted what he could see: *Starry Night* shows a view from his asylum bedroom window.

Image 43. *Vincent van Gogh, Self-Portrait (1887)*

The painting was one of Van Gogh's late works; he committed suicide the following year. His suicide is also a mystery. He seemed happy and he claimed that he had been cured. One day he went to the field to paint and he shot himself there. He did not die straight away – he came back to his room with a bullet in his stomach and died two days later, without explaining any reasons for this act.

Some contextual details about the painting

In this work as well as his later works, Van Gogh started using a lot of the color yellow (compared to his previous works as well as other artists). The use of color is very vivid, with large, thick brushstrokes. It was usual for artists of that time to use silhouettes when portraying night scenes. Van Gogh's choice of vivid lines was unusual.

Some elements of the painting deviate from the real-life view from his asylum window. Van Gogh added a village that did not exist. Calculations show that the moon at the time Van Gogh created this painting was about three-quarters full, not in a crescent phase as shown in *Starry Night*. Studies show that Van Gogh added the cypress tree later after he had finished the whole painting.

Several months after painting *Starry Night*, Van Gogh wrote: "*Why, I say to myself, should the spots of light in the firmament be less accessible to us than the black spots on the map of France?... Just as we take the train to go to Tarascon or Rouen [towns in France – A.P.], we take death to go to a star*" (Letter 638 To Theo, July 9/10, 1888; vangoghletters.org).

As we know from his letters to Theo, Van Gogh regarded *Starry Night* as a failure.

How critics interpret the painting

Critics have proposed various interpretations of *Starry Night*.

How do we know if an interpretation of a work of art is far-fetched? (#Scope)

One interpretation sees religious content in the painting. It is known that Van Gogh was religious. In one of his personal letters in 1888, he referred to "*the great starry firmament... one could only call God*" (Letter 670 To Willemien, August 26, 1888; vangoghletters.org). The painting has also been related to a verse from the Bible (Genesis 37:9) describing a dream of Joseph, an outcast from the group of his 11 elder brothers. The verse goes like this: "*Then he dreamed still another dream and told it to his brothers, saying, 'Look, I have dreamed another dream. And this time, the sun, the moon and the eleven stars bowed down to me*'". Coincidentally, Van Gogh painted exactly eleven stars in his *Starry Night*. It has been claimed that Van Gogh may have found the biblical character Joseph relatable because, like Joseph, he was an outcast in the world of art at that time, never getting recognition from art critics and ending his life in complete isolation in a mental asylum (Dowding-Green, 2018).

Another interpretation focuses on the cypress tree together with the fact that the painting was made during a sad period of Van Gogh's life. This interpretation sees the cypress tree as something that Van Gogh identifies himself with – massive, undefined, clumsy and dark, isolated and caught in between the peaceful town and the boiling bright sky.

Yet another popular interpretation is to read the feeling of hope in the painting. Those who stick to this interpretation suggest that there is a contrast between the dark quiet village and the bright dramatic stars, and that this contrast represents Van Gogh's hope that he will be in a better place after death. This interpretation suggests that Van Gogh somehow started contemplating the thought of his death at the time of creating the painting (remember: he committed suicide the next year).

KEY IDEA: Interpreting a work of art, critics use their background knowledge about the artist

Critical thinking extension

The process of interpretation is always a leap from some facts to some inferences. Looking at the three interpretations above, how justified do you think they are? Before you categorically say "not justified!", consider the following:

- To someone who does not know how religious Van Gogh was, the religious interpretation may seem very far-fetched. For someone who does not know that Van Gogh committed suicide a year after completing the painting, reading the symbolism of death into it seems out of the blue.
- But to someone who knows all of these contextual details such interpretations may seem, let's put it this way, *less unjustified*.
- So does this mean that to judge how justified an interpretation is, you must know the same contextual details as the interpreter?
- Hypothetically, if there were two art critics who had perfect knowledge of the context, do you think they would arrive at the same, or at least similar, interpretations?

If you are interested...

To get a better understanding of Van Gogh's complicated biography, especially the last several years of his life, watch the movie *Loving Vincent* (2017). It is a fully painted animated feature film, a biographical drama. I really enjoyed the stylistic features of it when I was watching – it is like Van Gogh's paintings come alive on the screen.

Take-away messages

Lesson 12. We introduced one example of a work of art – Van Gogh's painting *Starry Night* (1889). In this lesson, we looked at the subject matter of the painting as well as elements of Van Gogh's biography that may be relevant to this work. We also considered some popular interpretations of art critics. These interpretations may look completely uncalled for to someone who does not have any knowledge of the context, but they make more sense once you know what was happening behind the scenes.

Lesson 13 - Van Gogh's Starry Night (part 2)

Learning outcomes

a) [Knowledge and comprehension] What is the historical context behind Van Gogh's *Starry Night*?
b) [Understanding and application] How does knowledge of historical development of art affect our understanding of it?
c) [Thinking in the abstract] What is the role of knowledge of context in understanding and appreciating a work of art?

Key concepts

Historical context of a work of art

Other concepts used

Realism, impressionism, post-impressionism, expressionism

Themes and areas of knowledge

Theme: Knowledge and the knower
AOK: The Arts

Recap and plan

In the previous lesson, we started looking at Van Gogh's *Starry Night*. We considered some details from Van Gogh's biography and discussed how important these details may be in interpreting the painting. In this lesson, we will keep adding on to the context. This time we will place the painting in a wider historical context of art movements.

Historical context: development of art

To what extent is the current state of knowledge determined by its historical development? (#Perspectives)

Let's see what place Van Gogh's work has in the context of historical development of art. What was art before Van Gogh and what was art after him, and how might he have influenced the former to become the latter?

KEY IDEA: Knowledge of historical context is essential to understand a work of art

Van Gogh is typically categorized by art critics as a "post-impressionist". To understand what this means, let's look at what preceded post-impressionism and what followed after it (this is a very simplified outline, but I'm hoping to make my point).

***Image 44**. Jean-Francois Millet, The Gleaners (1857)*

1. ***Realism*** was the predominant school of art in 1840 - 1870. The purpose of art was commonly perceived as providing an accurate representation of reality. Art was academic. It required a lot of skill and the point was to follow established academic standards (such as the use of guiding lines and structure) to capture reality. This was a time of detailed, skillful landscapes and portraits and still life. I suppose the response artists typically wanted to evoke from their audience was something along the lines of "Wow, look how realistic this tree looks! How skillfully the artist has conveyed the patches of morning light playing on the lake surface! What a detailed apple!". Have a look at some examples of paintings from that period (see images 44-46).

Image 45*. Gustave Courbet, Young Ladies of the Village (1851-1852)*

Image 46*. Edouard Manet, The Old Musician (1862)*

2. Realism went through a crisis after the invention of photography and was later replaced by ***impressionism*** (1860 - 1890). Impressionists asked, what is the point of spending years of academic art education and then hours of meticulous work trying to capture what the world looks like if this is much better - and more easily - achieved by clicking a picture? No, they said, the purpose of art is very different - it is to capture the artist's impression of reality rather than reality itself. They used small thin brush strokes that kind of quickly capture the essence of the subject rather than working on every single detail of it (well, it makes sense - when you see a face in a crowd, you don't discern every single dimple and pimple, you just get the overall impression of it being a face). They also used less mixing and applied colors side by side. They paid close attention to light and its transient qualities (dusk, dawn, reflections in water), exploited movement and unusual visual angles. I imagine the response an impressionist wanted from their audience was something like: "Wow, would you look at that. How accurately they've captured an impression of the breezy summer morning; what a transient moment, such movement of light and shadow… no photo would ever be able to convey that". That is certainly *not* the response impressionists received at first; in fact, Claude Monet's painting "*Impression, Sunrise*" (1872) was ridiculed by some critics as being a sketch rather than a real paining.

Does aesthetic quality of an artwork always depend on how skillfully it is made? (#Method and tools)

Image 47*. Claude Monet. Impression, Sunrise (1872)*

3. ***Post-impressionists*** (1886 – 1905) objected against accurate depiction of light and color that was a big deal in impressionism. I imagine they could have said, "Well, if it is our impression of reality that we are capturing rather than reality itself, let's take it one step further and stop using light and color naturalistically. After all, this is all about how *I* see it". Post-impressionism was a relatively short movement mostly confined to France. It was pretty diverse since the painters experimented with how exactly they could deviate from impressionism. A couple of paintings below will give you a glimpse of that period.

Image 48. *Vincent Van Gogh, Sunflowers (1880s)*

Image 49. *Paul Gauguin, Yellow Christ (1889)*

4. One of the influential art movements that followed was ***expressionism*** (1905 – 1930). For expressionists it was no longer about depicting reality. It was about expressing their own inner world. They might have said, "If impressionism is so cool because we can see the artist's inner world through their impression of reality, why do we even need to limit ourselves to this impression? We can cast reality aside and explore the artist's inner world in its pureness". Have a look at some examples of expressionist paintings (images 50-51). Early expressionists admitted that they were very heavily influenced by Van Gogh's work.

Image 50. *Edvard Munch, The Scream (1893)*

Image 51. *Franz Marc, Deer in the Forest (1914)*

Putting all the contextual knowledge together

Imagine that you are in the Museum of Modern Art in New York City and you see Van Gogh's *Starry Night* and you happen to be equipped with all the contextual knowledge discussed in these last two lessons. You look at the painting and your mind goes something like this:

> *Oh, look at that swirling sky… it looks so exaggerated and the color is somewhat unnatural. And these huge stars made in thick brushstrokes, almost carelessly. In his time dominated by academic art and still under the influence of realism in art, that must have been a very bold thing to do, to paint like this. And he anticipated expressionism and other art movements. It's like he is painting not the night sky, but his own personality… So when I look at the painting, I can see a starry night but I can also see a part of Van Gogh, the person. Oh, and I know that life was not treating him easily. He was rejected and isolated, but he kept working relentlessly. This village in the painting is also pretty isolated. But this sky is in stark contrast, it's swirling and bright. And here's an undefined silhouette of a tree, connecting the two worlds somehow, in between. The swirling and the peaceful together, the dark and the bright, the quiet and the screaming. Isolation and aspiration, acceptance and rebellion, life and death?*

Is there a difference between appreciating art and understanding it? (#Perspectives)

At this point, although it is difficult to be captured in words, you will probably start experiencing an aesthetic response. You will appreciate the painting for its depth and multiple layers of meaning, for the emotions and reminiscences that it stirs in you, and for the complex experience that it produces in your mind. At some point you might even feel like you *understand* Van Gogh. It doesn't necessarily mean that you *like* it. It is perfectly possible to appreciate a work of art and dislike it at the same time!

KEY IDEA: It is possible to appreciate a work of art and dislike it at the same time

Critical thinking extension

We have seen that knowledge of context greatly affects our interpretation (and our appreciation!) of art.

Think of this metaphorically. When we go to an art gallery and see a painting hanging on the wall, what we actually see with our physical eyes is not the complete work, it is just a tiny bit. There is also a huge part – the context - that is inaccessible to our physical eyes. This context consists of relevant details of the artist's biography, relevant details of the historical situation, predominant art movements of that time, and so on. We can "see" this context with our mental eyes. So to see the work of art in its entirety, you need to use two pairs of eyes simultaneously.

The metaphor that would be suitable in this context is that of blind men trying to create the mental picture of an elephant by touch. One of the blind men is touching the elephant's tail and thinks it is a snake. Another is touching the elephant's leg and thinks it is a tree, and so on. None of the blind men has a full picture of the elephant because they are exposed to incomplete information. Moreover, the reason these blind men end up with different perceptions is because their experiences with the elephant are all equally limited. Had they been able to perceive the elephant in its entirety, their perspectives would be much more similar.

Are we allowed to make judgments about art when we do not fully understand it? (#Ethics)

Image 52. Blind men and the elephant

So coming to an art gallery and trying to "appreciate" art without knowing the context of it is akin to being a blind man who is trying to understand the elephant by feeling its tail. If you do not think that the elephant is gorgeous, it is because you haven't seen the whole elephant.

Do you think this metaphor is applicable to appreciating art?

If you are interested...

To get a feel of the epoch, browse through some paintings that belong to the following art movements:

- Realism
- Impressionism
- Post-impressionism
- Expressionism

A good place to start would be a Google search for images. Just type in the name of the art movement and click "Images" on the top menu.

Take a note of the year when the painting was created. Try to capture the commonality between paintings belonging to the same art movement and the difference between paintings belonging to different art movements. Can you see the gradual changes in composition, subject matter, style, use of color?

Take-away messages

Lesson 13. In this lesson, Van Gogh's *Starry Night* was placed in the historical context: development of art from realism to impressionism to post-impressionism to expressionism. Van Gogh's work is categorized as post-impressionism, and critics recognize his large influence on expressionism and subsequent movements. The take-away message from the last two lessons is that knowledge of a larger context is very essential in understanding a work of art. Without knowledge of context, appreciating a work of art may be compared to being a blind man who is trying to understand the elephant by feeling its tail. You just don't see all of it.

Lesson 14 - Three components of art: artist, creation, audience (part 1)

Learning outcomes

a) [Knowledge and comprehension] What are the three approaches to identifying the source of knowledge in art?
b) [Understanding and application] What does it mean for a work of art to bear both physical and conceptual properties?
c) [Thinking in the abstract] What is problematic with the claim that knowledge in art is in the artist's intention? What is problematic with the claim that knowledge in art is contained in the artwork itself?

Key concepts

Artistic intention, physical and conceptual properties of a work of art, perception of the audience, artwork

Other concepts used

Implications

Themes and areas of knowledge

Theme: Knowledge and the knower
AOK: The Arts

Recap and plan

In the previous lessons, we agreed that we can learn from art, but the nature of knowledge that we learn (propositional or non-propositional) remains unclear. We have also investigated Van Gogh's painting *Starry Night*. In this lesson, we will return to the abstract realm of knowledge and further unpack what is meant by knowledge in art. To do this we will try to figure out what exactly is the source of knowledge in art – where is it contained?

Three components of art

If art is knowledge, where is this knowledge contained? (#Scope)

In any work of art, there are always three components:
- The artist (the one who creates a work of art)
- The creation (the art piece)
- The audience (the recipients of the creation who perceive it and possibly form an impression)

You would not be surprised to hear that there is disagreement regarding which of these three components is the primary source of knowledge in art. Here are the common views:
- Knowledge is in the intentions of the artist. To "know" a piece of art means to correctly decipher the intention that the artist had when creating it.
- Knowledge is in the perception of the audience. When someone looks at (or listens to, or otherwise experiences) a work of art, they have certain impressions or emotional reactions. It is these reactions and impressions that comprise knowledge. The artist's intention is irrelevant.
- Knowledge is contained in the artwork itself. It may or may not coincide with the artist's intentions. It may or may not produce a reaction in the audience. But since this work of art exists, it contains certain information and knowledge that may be extracted from it.

Obviously, there are also positions that see the source of knowledge in art as a combination of several things. For example, the artist's intention combined with the perception of the audience, or the artist's intention as manifested in the artwork.

Considering each of these three components as a source of knowledge raises additional questions.

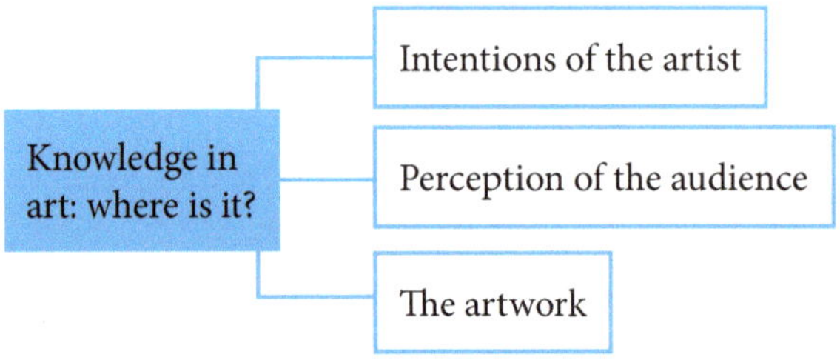

KEY IDEA: Knowledge in art may be contained in the artist's intention, perception of the audience or artwork itself

Intentions of the artist

It is reasonable to assume that when an artist creates, they have some sort of intention. The intention could be to convey a feeling or emotion, to send a message, to express an attitude or a sentiment. It is difficult to think of a work of art that has no intention behind it. What could it be? A picture that you accidentally took on your phone that you later saw, admired and posted online? Well, it could be argued that, although there was no intention in taking the picture itself, there was a particular intention behind interpreting it as something "worth posting online", as well as the act of posting itself. It became intentional once you singled it out among dozens of other pictures that were taken accidentally.

Is there a way to select one subjective interpretation of artistic intention over another? (#Methods and tools)

Obviously, the problem here is that it is very difficult to know what the artist's intention was. It belongs to the world of subjectively existing phenomena. Arguably, even the artist cannot always verbalize what the intention was. All we can do is try and interpret the artist's intention based on the features of the artwork itself and our knowledge of the context in which it was created. Once again, we are dealing with subjective knowledge of subjectively existing phenomena. But here the additional difficulty is that it may not even be possible to ask the artist directly (for example, when the artist is dead).

This seems to apply to Van Gogh's *Starry Night*. He never explicitly said what the intention behind the painting was. He gave us some hints through his letters to his brother Theo, but that is all we have. We cannot interview him either because he shot himself in the fields! So the only thing we can do now is to carefully scramble all available evidence (for example, there is an awesome website with the complete collection of Van Gogh's letters, translated and annotated: www.vangoghletters.org) and, using this incomplete data, *decipher* the artist's intention using an educated guess.

***Image 53**. What is the artist's intention?*

Work of art

The creation itself – the work of art – bears certain physical or conceptual properties.

Can something be intrinsically beautiful, even if we do not perceive it this way? (#Perspectives)

What I mean by physical properties of a work of art are things like color, shape, composition, symmetry. To what extent can we claim that certain knowledge is contained in these physical properties? For example, is it sensible to say that the palette used in Van Gogh's *Starry Night* bears the message of brightness, power and motion? Not that we *interpret* the palette this way, but that the combination of colors itself contains this information? If this seems like a far-fetched example, think about the difference between a regular line and a graceful line. Certainly you can easily imagine physical properties of a graceful line – it should be curved and smooth. So to what extent can we say that this "gracefulness" is contained in the physical properties of the line rather than our perception of it?

What I mean by conceptual properties of a work of art is its symbolic content. For example, a controversial art installation by Maurizio Cattelan features a dead horse suspended from the ceiling. Certainly some knowledge may be contained in the physical properties of this installation, for example, the shape and weight of the "object". But the conceptual properties are perhaps more informative – the fact that it is a horse (from all animals), the fact that it's hanging from the ceiling, the sheer unusualness of displaying a dead horse in the context of an art gallery.

KEY IDEA: A work of art bears both physical and conceptual properties

***Image 54**. Another example of conceptual art - Ladder and wheelchair, by John LeKay, 1991 (credit: John LeKay, Wikimedia Commons)*

Obviously the problem here is to know which properties (physical and conceptual) are a source of knowledge and how exactly these properties can convey this knowledge. If we assume that art conveys some special non-propositional knowledge, then can we establish any "laws" that connect the properties of the artwork to the knowledge that they create? In other words, can we say something like "*combining wide strokes of red and yellow conveys the sensation of serenity and grandeur*"?

A related question is, if it is indeed the work of art that is the source of knowledge, does it mean that beauty is not, after all, in the eye of the beholder? That a work of art may be beautiful (or not) irrespective of whether or not we think it to be beautiful?

Should ethical considerations limit artistic creativity? (#Ethics)

Critical thinking extension

A mental exercise that I find very engaging and eye-opening is making a categorical statement and exploring the implications of it (I'm pretty sure you have no doubts left at this point that I am a hopeless nerd).

For example, take the statement "To know in art is to know the artist's intention". Make this statement categorical: knowledge of the artist's intention is the only thing that matters, all other things are irrelevant. Assume that this is true. Think what implications this would have. Here are a few suggestions from me:

- We know modern art much better than we know art of the past
- It is impossible to know a work of art just by looking at it, unless the artist has explicitly explained the intention in the note below it
- It doesn't matter if the audience perceives a work of art as ugly as long as they know that the artist intended it to be beautiful

Try this exercise with some other categorical statements, for example, "Knowledge in art is contained entirely in the artwork itself".

If you are interested...

David Salle, a painter, believes that reading a painting should be natural and that a visitor in an art gallery should enjoy looking at an artwork and appreciate how it is made. Listen to his arguments in the video "One painter on why understanding art is as simple as looking" (2016) on the YouTube channel *PBS NewsHour*.

Do you agree?

Take-away messages

Lesson 14. The primary source of knowledge in art has been associated with (a) intentions of the artist, (b) the artwork itself and (c) the audience's response. Whichever position you take, you run into certain problems. For example, it is difficult to know the artist's intention because artists themselves may find it difficult to verbalize (or because they may already be dead). The artwork itself bears certain physical and conceptual properties, but it is not clear if these properties are aesthetic in themselves or only become aesthetic in the eye of the beholder. The last component – perception of the audience – will be considered in the next lesson.

Lesson 15 - Three components of art: artist, creation, audience (part 2)

Learning outcomes

a) [Knowledge and comprehension] What does it mean for knowledge in art to be contained in the perception of the audience?
b) [Understanding and application] What are the implications of the claim that knowledge in art is contained in the perception of the audience? What is problematic with this claim?
c) [Thinking in the abstract] Where is the line between educated interpretation in art and uneducated interpretation?

Key concepts

Educated interpretation, perception of the audience

Other concepts used

Artistic intention

Themes and areas of knowledge

Theme: Knowledge and the knower
AOK: The Arts

Recap and plan

We are trying to find out where exactly knowledge "resides" in art. If art is knowledge, what is the source of this knowledge? In the previous lesson, we considered two such sources – the artist's intention and the physical and conceptual properties of the artwork itself. We have investigated some implications of these ideas. In this lesson, we will be looking at the third component of art – perception of the audience.

Perception of the audience

A popular point of view is that the source of knowledge in art lies in the way the audience interprets an art piece. Let's use the exercise from the previous lesson and explore implications of this idea. If knowledge in art is indeed contained in the audience's perception and nowhere else, it implies that:

First, *knowledge in art is independent of the artist's intentions*. The artist might have created something with an intention, but the moment the creation becomes public it starts leading an independent life. The impressions that it creates in the audience are what constitutes knowledge, whether or not these impressions coincide with what the artist originally intended.

Can we claim to know art if we perceive it differently from what the artist intended? (#Perspectives)

Claude Monet, the founder of French impressionism in painting, was known for his distinctive blurry style. A well-known series of his paintings, *Water Lilies,* depicts a flower garden at his home in France. Over the years, the way he painted considerably changed and the color selection in the latest paintings is most unusual. Many critics have interpreted these changes as a gradual change in Monet's approach, from reproducing the nature to conveying the artist's impression of it (which is, indeed, the central theme of impressionism). Impressionists were known for their selection of unusual colors – purple sunflowers, blue tree leaves, etc. It was probably Monet's influence, at least partially, that established this priority of impression over reality in art.

If knowledge in art is in the perception of the audience, then:

- Knowledge in art is independent of the artist's intentions
- Knowledge gained from the same work of art may change with the course of time
- Knowledge contained in a work of art may be different depending on the audience perceiving it

When perceptions differ, who should be the final authority in interpreting the meaning of art? (#Ethics)

However, here is another fact: approximately at the time when Monet started his *Water Lilies* series, he also started developing cataracts in both of his eyes. The cataracts got progressively worse (until he finally had a surgery). Some critics think that it is the cataracts that were responsible for the unusual color palette. So which is it: did Monet simply paint what he saw and then we falsely interpreted his weird selection of colors as his intention to convey something? Or did he actually intend to convey some meaning through his selection of color? And how can we ever know which is true? According to the view that knowledge in art is in the perception of the audience, Monet's intentions are irrelevant. It is the effect that matters.

***Image 55**. Claude Monet, Water Lilies, 1897-1898*

***Image 56**. Claude Monet, Water Lilies, 1904*

Second, *knowledge gained from the same work of art may change over the course of time*. It is possible that we start interpreting the piece differently, for example, due to newly acquired knowledge of the historical period in which the artwork was created or due to a change in our own historical context. There are many examples of works of art that were only recognized much later after their creation, with recognition often coming to the artist posthumously. Not to go far, Van Gogh's *Starry Night* is one such example! In his life, Van Gogh suffered from lack of recognition, he only sold one painting and was financially dependent on his brother. Today, the estimated cost of *Starry Night* exceeds 100 million dollars and the estimated price of all Van Gogh's works collectively may be over 10 billion dollars. So the perception of the audience clearly changed over the course of time.

***Image 57**. Claude Monet, Water Lilies, 1914-1917*

But the painting itself hasn't changed, and neither has the artist's intention. So which is it: (a) there was some knowledge contained in the painting at all times, but it is only now that we started to see it; or (b) there was no knowledge in this work of art when it was created, but a lot of knowledge emerged when the audience gradually started perceiving it differently? Did we discover the meaning and value of Van Gogh's *Starry Night* – or did we create this meaning and value? If you assume that knowledge in art resides within the audience's perception, it is the latter option that we must pick.

Third, *depending on the audience that perceives and interprets a work of art, knowledge contained in it may be different*. This implication is somewhat dangerous, actually, because does it mean that a certain work of art (depending on the audience that is interpreting it) may be beautiful and ugly at the same time? This seems very illogical. It suggests that in art something may be true and not true at the same time. But if that is the case, then we do not really have any grounds for any sort of judgments beyond "I like it" or "I dislike it". Just like the Earth cannot be hollow and solid at the same time (although there may be people who hold either belief), can a work of art be beautiful and ugly at the same time?

Is an aesthetic judgment merely a judgment of personal taste? (#Methods and tools)

A combination of components

What if we assume that knowledge in art is the product of a complex combination of all three sources – the artist's intentions, the artwork itself, and the audience's interpretation of it? This seems reasonable because this way we avoid all of the problems mentioned above, but then uncovering this knowledge becomes a tremendous task. These are just some among the many things that a knower will need to consider:

- Existing evidence of the artist's intentions: letters, notes, recollections from the artist's friends and colleagues
- Known facts of the artist's biography
- The artistic context in which the piece was created (which trends were accepted at that time, how art was perceived in the society, what were the popular themes)
- The technique in which the work was created
- How the artwork was (or was likely to be) perceived at the moment of creation
- How the artwork is (or is likely to be) perceived today

Given its complexity and ambiguity, is art even knowable? (#Scope)

And many other aspects! Indeed, the work of an art critic becomes a very complex act of interpretation in which information about the context is combined with the critic's analysis of the artwork's physical properties to produce an educated (but nevertheless subjective) judgment about what knowledge the artwork conveys. A knowledgeable art critic, then, is capable of educated interpretation.

KEY IDEA: Assuming that knowledge in art comes from all three sources, interpretation of art becomes a tremendous task requiring thorough contextual knowledge. Hence, there must be a difference between educated and uneducated interpretation of art.

Critical thinking extension

Think back to our idea that a we need to look at a work of art with two pairs of eyes – the physical eyes to see the work itself and the mental eyes to see the context behind it. It looks like the context that can only be seen with mental eyes is actually very complex itself. If perception of the audience (or multiple audiences that exist or existed in the past) is also part of the picture, then it is a pretty multi-dimensional phenomenon that we are dealing with!

This delineates the difference between educated and uneducated interpretation. One might give an educated interpretation if one sees the essential context behind a work of art.

But this also raises a number of difficult questions. For example:

- Hypothetically if there existed an "absolutely educated" interpretation, would we claim that this interpretation is "true"?
- How do we know when an interpretation is educated enough (to be accepted as something credible)?
- If art requires all this invisible context to be understood, why don't artists provide explicit explanations? Why do they leave it to the audience to figure out?
- If art requires all this context to be understood, what is the purpose of art galleries? Is there even a point in visiting an art gallery if you don't have a formal art education, or if you are not an art history major?

If you are interested…

There is a wealth of videos available on YouTube on how to understand and appreciate art. Browse through some of them freely and watch the ones that catch your eye.
If you prefer to have some places to start, here are some suggestions:

1) Watch the instructional video "The Death of Socrates: How to Read a Painting" (2015) from the YouTube channel *Nerdwriter1*. "The Death of Socrates" is a painting by Jacques-Louis David (1787) and the video walks the viewers through the process of interpreting a painting.
2) A similar video from the same author is "How to understand a Picasso" (2016) – an example of a modern time painting.
3) Watch Hayley Levitt's TED-ed video with a self-explanatory title "Who decides what art means?"

Take-away messages

Lesson 15. If we assume that the primary source of knowledge in art is the perception of the audience, this also leads to somewhat bizarre conclusions, for example: (a) what the artist intended is irrelevant, (b) knowledge contained in an artwork may change over the course of time, (c) knowledge contained in an artwork may be different for different audiences. Given that all three positions lead to certain logical problems, it is likely that knowledge in art actually comes from a complex combination of all three sources. But if this is the case, understanding an artwork becomes a tremendous task that requires a lot of contextual knowledge. Thorough knowledge of context delineates the difference between educated and uneducated interpretation.

Lesson 16 - Aesthetic judgment: subjectivity and universality

Learning outcomes

a) [Knowledge and comprehension] What is an aesthetic judgment?
b) [Understanding and application] What does it mean for an aesthetic judgment to be subjective and universal? Why is aesthetic relativism logically problematic?
c) [Thinking in the abstract] To what extent is it true that someone who does not appreciate art simply does not understand it?

Key concepts

Aesthetic judgments, subjectivity and universality of aesthetic judgment, judgments of likes and dislikes, aesthetic relativism

Other concepts used

Knowledge claim, appreciation of art, statement of preference, commonality of judgment

Themes and areas of knowledge

Theme: Knowledge and the knower
AOK: The Arts

Recap and plan

Up until now, we have agreed that knowledge in art seems to have both propositional and non-propositional components and it seems to come from some combination of three sources – the artist's intention, the physical and conceptual properties of the artwork itself, and the audience's interpretation.

Anyone who engages with a work of art needs to perform a very complex act of interpretation that is not at all limited to the actual canvas hanging on the wall.

A question remains open: what counts as a unit of knowledge in art, as a "knowledge claim"? And how is this "knowledge claim" different from its counterparts in other areas of knowledge, such as Natural Sciences or Human Sciences?

Various thinkers have suggested "aesthetic judgment" as such a knowledge unit. In this lesson, we will try to unpack this concept.

Immanuel Kant: subjectivity and universality of aesthetic judgments

The 18th-century German philosopher Immanuel Kant distinguished aesthetic judgments as a separate, independent type of judgment (I think we can safely assume that "judgments" in his terminology are the same as "knowledge claims" in ours).

KEY IDEA: According to Immanuel Kant, aesthetic judgments have two properties: they are subjective and at the same time universal

***Image 58**. Immanuel Kant (1724 – 1804)*

For Kant, there were two essential properties that characterized aesthetic judgments: subjectivity and universality. Both subjectivity and universality, according to him, are necessary conditions; that is, if a judgment is either not subjective or not universal, then this judgment is not an aesthetic judgment.

Aesthetic judgments are *subjective* in the sense that they are based on a complex subjective response that we experience when engaging with a work of art. For example, it can be the feeling of pleasure or displeasure, we might feel repulsed by something or, on the contrary, experience the subtle feeling of witnessing something beautiful. In any case, it is the subjective response that aesthetic judgments are based on, not the "objective reality".

But aesthetic judgments are very different from judgments of likes and dislikes. Compare the following two statements:

- Dumplings are tasty
- Van Gogh's *Starry Night* is beautiful

As applied to art, is beauty really in the eye of the beholder? (#Perspectives)

Do you agree that there is a vast difference between these two statements? When we say things like "Dumplings are tasty", we simply mean "I like dumplings". We are not trying to make a universal statement. We are expressing our personal preferences and nothing else. We will be perfectly fine if our friend said in response to that: "Oh no, I hate dumplings, they are so yuck". We are fine with this disagreement because we know that tastes differ and so do likes and dislikes. But when we say "Van Gogh's *Starry Night* is beautiful" we do actually imply that the painting is beautiful in a way that transcends our likes or dislikes. When one person says that the painting is beautiful and another person says it is ugly, we believe one of them is mistaken. For example, one of them does not understand the painting enough to realize how beautiful it is. Appreciating art is not the same as liking dumplings because in art there exist some "correct answers" or, if you will, the truth. When someone judges in art, they judge not only for themselves, but for everyone.

***Image 59**. Tastes differ*

It is for this reason that Kant introduced the second necessary property of judgments of taste: *universality*. Universality means that when we make an aesthetic judgment, we speak as if certain properties were properties of reality itself: for example, when we say that a painting is beautiful, we speak as if beauty was a property of the painting itself, not a property of our perception of it. In other words, although aesthetic judgments are subjective (based on a subjective reaction to a work of art), they are also universal (claiming that all people without exception ought to have this subjective reaction). Note that universality is different from commonality: to claim that "Van Gogh's *Starry Night* is beautiful" is not the same as claiming that "Most people will perceive Van Gogh's *Starry Night* as beautiful". Being universal, aesthetic judgments do not depend on how many people agree with them. Aesthetic judgments may be "*true*" even if very few people agree with them.

How do we know if something is beautiful? (#Methods and tools)

Aesthetic relativism

As I am writing this, in my head I can hear voices of students objecting to what I'm writing (do not worry, I have these voices under control, I do not have to see a mental specialist about this yet).

These voices are saying that to claim the existence of the "truth" in art is nonsense. These voices happily agree that aesthetic judgments are subjective, but they cannot accept that these judgments are universal. They see little to no difference between the statements "Dumplings are tasty" and "Van Gogh's *Starry Night* is beautiful". To them, both the statements are statements of personal preference. Beauty, they say, is in the eye of the beholder.

These voices are speaking from the perspective of aesthetic relativism (I wonder if they themselves realize that). Aesthetic relativism claims that aesthetic properties (such as beauty) are merely characteristics of our perception, no different from individual preferences, likes and dislikes. And while I can see the beauty in aesthetic relativism (pun intended!), this is why it does not work for me:

Are aesthetic judgments the same as judgments of personal preference? (#Scope)

Image 60. *Beauty is in the eye of the beholder*

- Relativism in general is flawed because it creates a logical contradiction. If you say "everything is relative", then certainly the phrase "everything is relative" is relative, too! Therefore, everything cannot be relative. Aesthetic relativism does not provide an explanation for what aesthetic judgments are, it simply avoids the question.
- If we accept that aesthetic judgments are relative, and that there are no right and wrong judgments in this area, we must also accept that *anything* is art. Even if a work of art seems tasteless and meaningless and useless and trivial, we cannot make judgments like "this is bad art" or "this is not art". All we can say is, "Personally I don't like it".
- But if anything is art, then there is no point in even separating the Arts as an independent area of knowledge. Art becomes no different from cuisine preferences. We do not include cuisine preferences in the list of areas of knowledge in TOK, so we should not include the Arts either. There is no "truth" in art; therefore, there is no knowledge.
- Moreover, if anything is art, then there is no way we can separate art from non-art. But in this case there is no point in even speaking about art. Art only makes sense as opposed to non-art in the same way as "tall" makes sense only when there is "short" and "hot" makes sense only when there is "cold". If aesthetic judgments are relative, then anything is art. If anything is art, then art does not exist.

KEY IDEA: If aesthetic judgments are relative, then anything is art. If anything is art, then art does not exist.

For these reasons I would argue that anyone who accepts aesthetic relativism in art actually destroys art as an area of knowledge and downgrades it as a human activity. Accepting aesthetic relativism will lead to some undesirable social consequences.

Should we allow our beliefs to be influenced by their anticipated social consequences? (#Ethics)

For these reasons, although accepting that aesthetic judgments are universal seems counter-intuitive to me too, I am accepting it. The question then becomes, how is it possible for aesthetic judgments to be subjective and universal at the same time?

Critical thinking extension

F.J. Rocca, a classical musician and a writer, has an article with a self-explanatory name: "The Collapse of American Morality and the Dangers of Aesthetic Relativism" (Rocca, 2015). You can read it online in *The Washington Sentinel.*

In this article, among other things, he talks about how the younger generation including his children declare that they "hate" classical music because they think it is not cool. He says: "If one's sphere of experience is constrained, one's tastes will be constrained, as well".

To what extent can you agree with the claim that, if you find yourself disliking a piece of classical music, you simply lack the experience and understanding necessary to appreciate it? If something is a work of art, are we not allowed to dislike it?

If you are interested...

Watch the video "Aesthetic Appreciation: Crash Course Philosophy" (2016) on the YouTube channel *CrashCourse*. This is a lesson on aesthetic appreciation providing a summary of our discussion as well as a number of additional dimensions of aesthetic judgment.

Take-away messages

Lesson 16. The equivalent of a "knowledge claim" in art is aesthetic judgment. According to Immanuel Kant, aesthetic judgments have two essential properties: subjectivity and universality. They are subjective because they are based on the subjective response that we experience when we are engaging with an artwork. But they are also universal because they imply that all people ought to have this subjective response. In this way, aesthetic judgments ("this painting is beautiful") are different from statements of preference ("I like dumplings"). At the same time, being universal, aesthetic judgments do not depend on how many people agree with them. A common objection to the idea of universality of aesthetic judgments is aesthetic relativism. It claims that beauty is in the eye of the beholder and that aesthetic judgements are in fact no different from statements of preference. However, if we assume this position, we are standing on a slippery slope at the end of which we must accept that art does not deserve the status of an area of knowledge or a meaningful human activity. We would have to accept that art does not exist.

Lesson 17 - Deep human response

Learning outcomes

a) [Knowledge and comprehension] What is the deep human response?
b) [Understanding and application] How can aesthetic judgments be subjective and universal at the same time?
c) [Thinking in the abstract] How plausible is it that some subjective experiences are shared equally by all humans?

Key concepts

Deep human response, the human condition

Other concepts used

Subjectivity and universality of aesthetic judgment, collective unconscious, archetypes

Themes and areas of knowledge

Theme: Knowledge and the knower
AOK: The Arts, Human Sciences

Recap and plan

In the previous lesson, we followed the traditions of Immanuel Kant and looked at aesthetic judgment as a special sort of knowledge claim. We discussed two necessary and defining characteristics of aesthetic judgments – their subjectivity and universality. The concepts of subjectivity and universality at first sight seem to contradict each other, but we have what we have – if we want to give art the status of a meaningful human activity and possibly an area of knowledge, then we must also accept that aesthetic judgments are subjective and universal at the same time. This raises the question: how is that possible?

I will suggest a solution to this problem and your job is to criticize me. I am not necessarily satisfied with it, but it seems to solve a bunch of logical contradictions. If you have a better solution, please email me!

Can aesthetic judgments be subjective and universal at the same time?
(#Scope)

Deep human response and the human condition

Suppose the world of subjective human experiences consists of two parts.

One part includes all the experiences that are individual to you. Some associations with moments from your life, your memories, your aspirations and desires and perhaps fears and anxieties. Let's call it your *individual subjective world*. Take two random people from your school and obviously their individual subjective worlds will not be the same.

When I say "autumn", what subjective response do you have to that? You might really like autumn or really dislike it. If you are from areas with moderate climate, you might imagine colored trees and carpets of leaves on the ground. If you are from tropical areas where autumn is really no different from spring, you might think of it more in calendar terms. Bottom line is, the array of subjective reactions will be entirely different.

The other part consists of subjective experiences that are universal to humankind. These are the deep subjective experiences that we share as a species. They are relatively independent of an individual's personal history, cultural background, and so on. To give you an example, think about the idea of a "mother". On a deep level, we all share a similar image and a similar complex of emotions in relation to "mother". When we read in a novel that the protagonist's mother died, we feel a very special kind of sadness. The interesting thing is, it does not depend on your own history. Even if you don't have a mother, you still know what all those things ought to feel like.

Image 61. *People are like mushrooms: individual on the surface, deeply interconnected underground*

Some more examples of things that we can all share on a very deep level: our feelings about death, our attitude to solitude and isolation, our feeling of guilt toward those whose expectations we do not live up to, the idea of home, the idea of love, the idea of light and darkness. You would agree that all this is very different from "autumn". These are parts of our subjective experiences that constitute the deep human response. We share them on a deep level simply because we are all human beings.

Are there subjective beliefs that are common to all individuals? (#Perspectives)

The human condition is another term that has been widely used in many contexts to refer to the experience of existence as human. The human condition is what we experience because we are living human beings – conflict, mortality, aspiration, identity, suffering, pain, and so on.

Art appeals to the deep human response

Image 62. *The human condition*

I promised that I would suggest a solution to resolve the paradox of aesthetic judgments being subjective and universal at the same time. So, summarizing all we have discussed so far, here it goes:

- Works of art should be perceived in context.
- Engaging with a work of art is a process of understanding wherein the more you engage with it and the more contextual details you take into account, the deeper your insight will be.
- Art appeals to the deep human response. Art can certainly evoke some individual associations or emotions, but beyond that, it also targets something that is fundamentally universal to all humans.
- Aesthetic judgments are subjective because they are judgments about subjective experiences triggered by a work of art. However, aesthetic judgments are also universal because the deep human response is itself universal.

Image 63. *Deep human response*

The implications of this idea are:

- Liking a piece of art and appreciating it is not the same. It is possible to appreciate a work of art aesthetically but at the same time dislike it. Personally, I don't like Shakespeare. At the same time, I do appreciate Shakespeare as a phenomenon that was ground-breaking in literature, his contributions to the field, his use of language, and so on. I do enjoy how skillfully his sonnets are written… I just don't like them. But if I claim that Shakespeare's sonnets are "bad" or "ugly", I will be confusing my aesthetic judgment with my personal preferences.
- If one person claims that an artwork is beautiful and another person claims that the same artwork is ugly, in all likelihood these individuals do not see the same amount of context behind the work. For example, one of them might ignore the historical context of the time when the work was created. In other words, superficial aesthetic judgments may differ, but deep aesthetic judgments will more likely be similar.
- Any deviations from universality (for example, when someone claims that *Starry Night* is an ugly painting) would be explained by underdeveloped understanding or some personal experiences that cloud their judgement, not allowing them to be in touch with the part of their subjective experiences that they are supposed to share with other human beings.

How does art capture knowledge that is inaccessible by other means? (#Methods and tools)

KEY IDEA: We can explain how aesthetic judgments can be both subjective and universal by assuming that there exists a part of subjective experiences that is common for all humans and that art appeals to this part, evoking a "deep human response"

Such is the solution. What do you think about it? What objections do you have? And more importantly – do you have a better one?

Critical thinking extension

The idea of deep human response has actually been around for a long time. Just one example is *the collective unconscious* – the concept introduced by Carl Jung (1875 - 1961) to refer to structures of the unconscious mind shared by all human beings. According to Jung, we can distinguish recurring themes in the collective unconscious that manifest themselves as images or symbols. He called such recurring themes *archetypes*.

Are ideas of "right" and "wrong" intrinsic in the human existence? (#Ethics)

He describes some pretty spooky case studies, for example in one of them he analyzed dreams of a 6-year-old girl and found them full of symbols that she could not possibly encounter anywhere in her personal experience, such as a fairy that leads her into a temple where she (the fairy) turns into a flame, with three snakes crawling out of the flame, wriggling (Jung, 1979). Moreover, these symbols overlapped a lot with ancient mythology (which the girl was not familiar with).

***Image 64**. Yggdrasil – the Tree of Life in Scandinavian mythology*

One of the archetypes – the Tree of Life – is a symbol that can be found in practically every mythological tradition and religion in the world. This tree somehow connects the underworld to the sky, serving as a bridge between the two worlds.

Think back to the cypress tree in Van Gogh's *Starry Night*. Do you think this cypress tree could be an expression of a deeper idea archetype that all humans share? And on a broader note, how plausible is it that some subjective experiences are shared equally by all humans?

If you are interested...

If you are looking for some deep philosophical reading to make your understanding of aesthetics even more profound than it is, the article from the *Stanford Encyclopedia of Philosophy* (plato.stanford.edu) entitled "Aesthetic Judgment" is an ideal place to go.

The article is challenging because it is a proper philosophy paper. However, with the understandings that you have developed in this unit, you will find it manageable. Additionally, it will give you a glimpse into the style and language used by many philosophers in their writing.

Take-away messages

Lesson 17. How is it possible that aesthetic judgments are subjective and universal at the same time? I suggested one possible solution (although there may exist a better one). The world of subjective human experiences consists of two parts – the individual subjective world and the subjective experiences that are universal to humankind. When the latter part is engaged, we refer to these experiences as the "deep human response" of the "human condition". These are experiences that we all share on a deep level simply because we share the experience of existing as human beings. The problem of aesthetic judgments being subjective and universal at the same time is solved if we accept that art appeals to the deep human response. This implies that there is a difference between appreciating a work of art (aesthetic judgment rooted in the understanding of the context) and liking it (simple personal preference).

Lesson 18 - Understanding in art

Learning outcomes

a) [Knowledge and comprehension] What does it mean to understand in art?
b) [Understanding and application] How is understanding in art different from understanding in other areas of knowledge?
c) [Thinking in the abstract] Can areas of knowledge be placed on a continuum, with Natural Sciences on one side of it and the Arts on the other?

Key concepts

Understanding, observer, interpretation

Other concepts used

Subjectivity, objectivity, intersubjectivity, propositional knowledge, non-propositional knowledge

Themes and areas of knowledge

Theme: Knowledge and the knower
AOK: The Arts, Human Sciences, Natural Sciences

Recap and plan

We have discussed the nature of knowledge in art. We have seen that:

- Knowledge claims in art take the form of aesthetic judgments
- This knowledge is to a large extent non-propositional: it cannot always be easily verbalized
- Although aesthetic judgments are subjective, they are also universal: these judgments may be more or less "correct"
- A way to resolve this contradiction is to suggest that aesthetic judgments are judgments about a subjective response evoked in the core part of subjective experiences that all humans share among themselves (the deep human response)
- To experience the deep human response, one needs to see the work of art in its entirety including elements of the context that are not physically present in the artwork itself

But now we have to circle back to the original question: what is the difference between knowledge and understanding in art? Is the relationship between knowledge and understanding in art similar to that in natural sciences and human sciences? In this lesson we will try to find out.

It is impossible to fully understand something in art, but degrees of understanding are possible

Is it possible to fully understand a work of art? (#Scope)

I feel pretty confident to claim that we can never fully understand art. As we discussed, knowledge in art comes from a combination of sources: the artist's intention, the artwork itself, and the audience's response. To decipher the artist's intention, one needs to be closely familiar with things such as their biography, historical context, cultural context, and so on. At the end of the day, knowledge of the artist's intention is always our interpretation of the artist's intention. We could be wrong. Judgment of the artwork itself requires great expertise in areas such as artistic techniques and schools of art. Aesthetic properties, as we discussed, are quite subtle responses that cannot be easily verbalized. Finally, to know the audience's response, one needs to know the audience very thoroughly, including its cultural and historical contexts, its tastes, and so on. So, if someone claims that they understand Van Gogh's *Starry Night* completely, I will argue that this person is deluded and overconfident.

But it is still possible to have some level of understanding. Some people understand *Starry Night* better than others. When someone understands a work of art, they:

- See the artwork in its entirety (with both their physical eyes and their mental eyes)
- Experience an aesthetic response that is universal (it is universal because it is a deep human response)

- See how the context (in which the piece of art was created and in which it is being perceived by the audience) influences these experiences

This is all very complicated – to the extent that it is impossible in principle to take into account all important aspects.

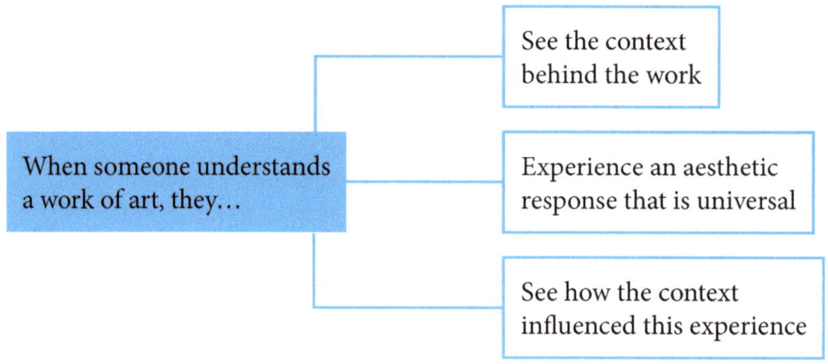

How is understanding in art different from understanding in natural and human sciences?

Interpretation is an inherent part of this process of understanding. The observer cannot be eliminated from the process of observation. In fact, the observer is the main tool of observation because it is the subjective responses that become the focus of attention.

Is the role of interpretation as a tool of obtaining knowledge different in human sciences and art? (#Methods and tools)

You may think of the difference like this:

- In natural sciences, the observer is trying to understand the world of material things that is independent from him or her. They use methods that eliminate the observer from the process of observation as much as possible. The observer in natural sciences is neither the tool nor the object of observation.
- In human sciences, the observer does whatever is done in natural sciences. However, on top of that, since human beings are creatures of two worlds (objective and subjective), the observer in human sciences is trying to understand subjective experiences of other human beings. For this they use interpretation – their own subjective experiences become a tool for understanding subjective experiences of other people. To make sure that this understanding is correct, they seek help from other observers and try to ensure that their interpretations converge. The observer in human sciences may be a tool of observation, but it is not an object of observation.
- In art, the observer observes their own subjective reactions to a work of art. They believe that these reactions may be profoundly common to all people. To understand these reactions in an unbiased way they try to, through the process of interpretation, take into account a broad context in which the artwork was created. In art the observer is both the tool of observation and the object of observation. This makes art ultimately subjective (but remember that "subjective" does not mean "unreliable").

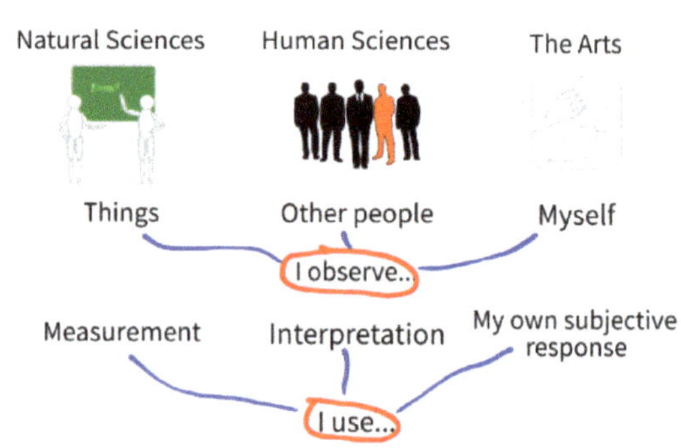

***Image 65**. Objects and tools of research in three areas of knowledge*

Let me try to use a table to summarize this key idea as well as some other ideas that follow:

Aspect	Natural Sciences	Human Sciences	Art
Type of reality that is studied	Objectively existing phenomena	Objectively existing phenomena (observable human behavior) + subjectively existing phenomena (subjective human experiences)	Subjectively existing phenomena (artist's intentions, audience's reactions, aesthetic judgments)
Type of knowledge	Objective	Objective where possible + subjective when necessary	Subjective (absolutely depends on interpretation)
Role of the observer in the process of obtaining knowledge	Observer is eliminated as much as possible	When studying behavior phenomena, the observer is eliminated as much as possible. When studying subjective experiences, the observer cannot be eliminated but intersubjectivity is sought	Observer cannot be eliminated in principle. In fact, the observer looks at their own subjective experiences to make aesthetic judgments about works of art
Role of interpretation	Minimized	Accepted, but checked for intersubjectivity	Absolutely predominant
Nature of knowledge	Absolutely propositional	Mainly propositional; non-propositional knowledge is allowed in special cases where propositional knowledge is not an option	Mostly non-propositional
Is understanding cognitive or non-cognitive?	Absolutely cognitive	Mostly cognitive	Both cognitive and non-cognitive
How difficult is it to verbalize this understanding?	Not easy, but perfectly possible using mathematics as a language	As far as understanding subjective experiences is concerned, may become difficult because no formal language exists	Very difficult to express in language because knowledge is non-propositional
Understanding and knowledge	Understanding = thorough knowledge of causes	Understanding = thorough knowledge of causes (obtained through objective methods) and purposes (obtained through interpretation)	Understanding = sophisticated aesthetic response that takes into account multiple aspects of the artwork (and the context around it). Focus is on purposes

In all three areas of knowledge, understanding is an advanced stage in the development of knowledge. As we accumulate knowledge, we gradually cross an invisible line after which we can claim to "understand" something. However, the conditions for crossing this line are different.

To what extent is it possible or necessary to eliminate the observer from the process of observation? (#Perspectives)

In natural sciences, no matter how much we know about the causes of a particular phenomenon, we cannot claim to understand it unless it fits perfectly into the bigger picture of the world (the scientific worldview). In human sciences, no matter how much we know about objective causes of human behavior, we cannot claim to understand unless this knowledge is accompanied by an insight into the purposes and meanings that are hidden from direct observation. In art, no matter how much we know about artistic techniques, schools of art and historical contexts, we cannot claim to understand a work of art unless we have a sophisticated, non-cognitive aesthetic response that we believe should be common to all human beings (a deep human response).

Critical thinking extension

If we imagine a continuum where natural sciences are on the left, art is on the right and human sciences are somewhere in the middle, we can see how various things change as we move from left to right:

1) The object of research changes: from objectively existing phenomena to subjectively existing phenomena (with human sciences being a combination of the two).
2) The role of interpretation in obtaining knowledge increases.
3) The observer becomes more and more indispensable in the process of observation.
4) Knowledge becomes increasingly non-propositional.

Are moral judgments more subjective than aesthetic judgments? (#Ethics)

What other changes can you think of?

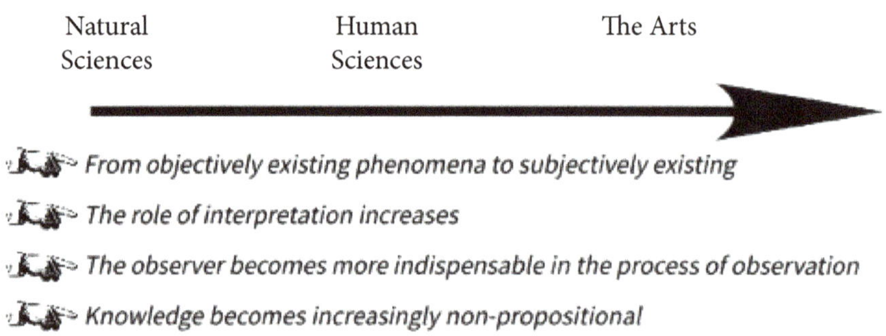

If you are interested…

Watch the video "Better Know: The Starry Night" (2018) on the YouTube channel *The Art Assignment*. This is a critical analysis of Van Gogh's painting.

Now that you are equipped with all this knowledge and understanding of aesthetic judgments, to what extent can you relate to the arguments put forth in this video?

Take-away messages

Lesson 18. Arguably, reaching complete understanding of an artwork is impossible, but degrees of understanding exist. Unlike some other areas of knowledge, the observer in art cannot be eliminated from the process of observation. Moreover, the observer becomes the main focus of attention because it is the subjective response we are interested in. What is considered a bias in other areas of knowledge becomes the main object of investigation in art. Art falls under subjective knowledge of subjectively existing phenomena. "Subjective" in this context does not mean "unreliable". In fact, we have shown how understanding in art is actually universal due to the deep human response.

5.5 - Hermeneutics

We have now finished a discussion of knowledge and understanding, both in general and in application to three distinctly different areas of knowledge – Natural Sciences, Human Sciences and the Arts.

What follows is a standalone lesson on hermeneutics – the "theory of understanding". There were thinkers who claimed that understanding is larger and more important than just an advanced form of knowledge. According to them, understanding is fundamental in the process of obtaining knowledge, and a "theory of understanding" should actually replace the "theory of knowledge". With such a bold statement, they deserve a mention at least. Perhaps it's not IB TOK that we should be studying, but IB Hermeneutics?

Lesson 19 - Hermeneutics

Learning outcomes

a) [Knowledge and comprehension] What is hermeneutics?
b) [Understanding and application] How does interpretation circulate between the text and the context?
c) [Thinking in the abstract] To what extent is hermeneutics applicable to natural sciences?

Key concepts

Hermeneutics, hermeneutic circle, pre-interpretation, text, context

Other concepts used

Interpretation, understanding, doubt

Themes and areas of knowledge

Themes: Knowledge and the knower, Knowledge and language
AOK: The Arts, Human Sciences, Natural Sciences

Recap and plan

In this unit, we have investigated how understanding is different from knowledge and how the relationship between these two concepts changes from one area of knowledge to another. We looked at three areas of knowledge – Natural Sciences, Human Sciences and the Arts.

We have seen that in areas of knowledge solely focused on objectively existing phenomena (such as an asteroid moving through space) understanding takes the form of a coherent picture of the world that explains why things happen. Understanding in these areas is achieved through the scientific method that eliminates the role of the observer as much as possible. Precise measurement is at the center of investigation.

However, as we move to areas of knowledge that also attempt to study subjectively existing phenomena (elements of human experiences), we must replace measurement with interpretation. With this replacement, we gain in depth but we lose in objectivity. In any case, interpretation is a key process of gaining knowledge wherever human activity is involved. This realization has led some scholars to claim that we need a special "theory of understanding" that would complement "theory of knowledge" and perhaps even replace it. They suggested that it would be a mistake to apply standards of knowledge that we have developed for natural sciences to areas of knowledge involving human activity, because the object of research is so dramatically different.

In what sense may subjective interpretation be more reliable than objective measurement? (#Methods and tools)

Hermeneutics was this "alternative" to theory of knowledge that they proposed. In this lesson, we will briefly look at the key ideas of hermeneutics. This lesson serves as an extension to our discussion of the concept of understanding elsewhere in this unit.

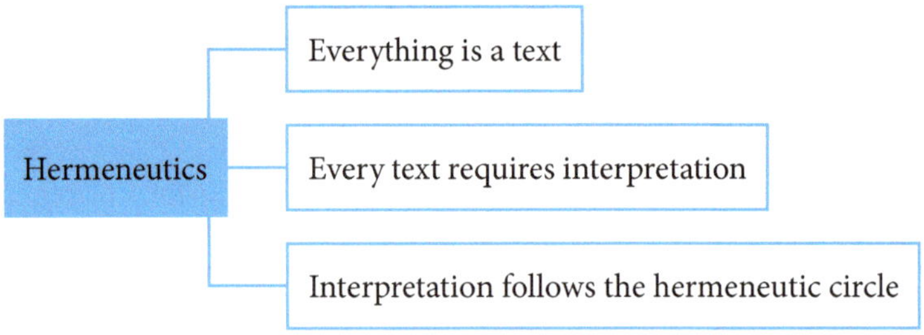

What is hermeneutics?

Hermeneutics has been defined in various sources as "the art and science of understanding". Regarding its purpose, "Hermeneutics explores how we read, understand and handle texts, especially those written in another time or in a context of life different from our own" (Thiselton, 2009, p.1).

Originally, hermeneutics was born as a discipline to assist interpretation of sacred texts. As you may know, sacred texts tend to be vague and not too straightforward, so history has seen multiple interpretations of the same texts. In many cases varying interpretations led to conflicts and wars. Obviously, there had to be some scholars who said, "*Look, some interpretations are better than others, and even if we cannot agree on a single one, surely we can at least agree on some features that all good interpretations must share*". This is how hermeneutics was born.

Over the course of time, it became something larger than a practice of deciphering religious texts. Influential 19th-century philosophers (such as Friedrich Schleiermacher) observed that *every text requires interpretation*. No text just throws its meaning at us. We unpack the meaning with the help of our prior assumptions, expectations, beliefs and preconceptions. There is never a guarantee that two people will arrive at identical results, so every text is inherently ambiguous.

Is there knowledge that is not a product of interpretation? (#Perspectives)

Taking one step further, these philosophers also noted that *everything is a text*. A sculpture, a painting, an ancient vase, a dinosaur bone – these are all texts. They are not made up of letters, words and sentences, but they are made up of elements that are symbolic of something, and we decipher the meaning contained in those elements using our prior knowledge in the same way we uncover the message contained in a regular text using our prior knowledge of language.

KEY IDEA: According to hermeneutics, every text requires interpretation and everything is a text

With this redefinition of a "text", hermeneutics became a very broad theory, a "theory of understanding" that is comparable in breadth to a "theory of knowledge".

Interpretation and the hermeneutic circle

To describe the process of interpreting a text, founders of hermeneutics suggested the notion of the hermeneutic circle:

- To understand a text, one needs to understand every separate element of this text
- But complete understanding of a separate element is only possible if one understands the whole text

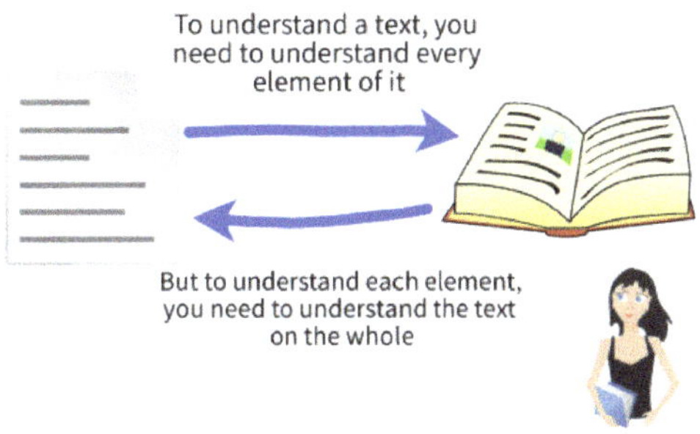

***Image 66**. Hermeneutic circle*

This applies to any text. For example, to understand a sentence, you need to understand every word in it, but every single word in the sentence acquires its full meaning only in the context of the whole sentence. Take the sentence

"A bare conductor runs under the tram"

When you think of each word separately, you might imagine the person who sells tickets on the bus when you hear "conductor", someone naked when you hear "bare", people moving fast when you hear "runs", and a form of public transport when you hear "tram". In the context of the whole sentence, however, it might occur to you that the text describes a non-insulated wire that is stretching under a tram carriage (raise your hand if you pictured naked ticket sellers running back and forth)[1].

Scholars insist that the hermeneutic circle is not a vicious circle. It is actually more like a spiral. When we start reading a text, we form some initial interpretation (pre-interpretation) and then, as we go on and know more and more about the whole, we come back and revise the pre-interpretation in light of this new information.

Keep in mind that the hermeneutic circle applies to any text. A dinosaur bone is also a text, according to hermeneutics. When we first dig out a dinosaur bone, we immediately have a sort of a pre-interpretation about it. But as we investigate it further and uncover further details about the bone itself and the context in which it was found, we review our first understanding and develop a more sophisticated one.

What comes first – knowledge or understanding? (#Scope)

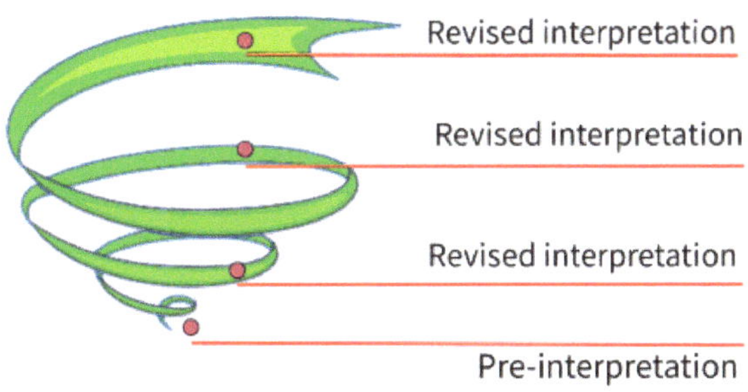

***Image 67**. The spiral of unfolding pre-interpretation*

[1]The source of this pun is the sci-fi novel "The Crew of the Mekong" (1974) by E. Voiskunsky and I. Lukodyanov, where one of the characters had to translate a similar phrase into Russian and, of course, she understood the phrase quite literally, which led to an awkward situation.

First belief, then doubt

Remember Descartes with his "I think, therefore, I am" (*cogito ergo sum*)? He said that we must systematically doubt everything before we accept something as a belief. First doubt, and then where you cannot doubt anymore, accept a belief. This is how he arrived at the belief that he existed – he could not doubt his own existence simply because the very fact that he was doubting meant that there was a "he"!

Proponents of hermeneutics changed that. They claim that belief comes first and doubt comes second. If a painting is a text (which it is, according to hermeneutics), then when we first look at it, we have some initial belief (some initial impression or pre-interpretation). Then as we look more closely, we start noticing more details and wondering why they are there, or we remember some things we know about the context in which the painting was created, and this is how we gradually review our pre-interpretation. We doubt the initial belief and develop a new belief on that basis. This constant movement between the whole and its parts, between the text and the context, is what comprises the hermeneutic circle. According to hermeneutics, art (just like any other text) speaks to us; engaging with an artwork is a conversation of sorts and we are uncovering depths of the artwork in the process of this conversation.

It is impossible, according to hermeneutics, to ever reach full understanding, but that does not matter. What matters is the process of the conversation between the interpreter and the text, the sheer fact that this conversation is progressing.

Image 68. *Conversation*

Critical thinking extension

Do you think one can apply the idea of a hermeneutic circle to the process of discovery in natural sciences? After all, when we conduct an experiment in natural sciences, all we get is data. The data requires interpretation. A human researcher must make sense of it.

So should hermeneutics actually replace theory of knowledge as something that is more applicable to how knowledge actually works?

If you are interested...

There is a series of books entitled "A very short introduction", published by Oxford University Press. One of the books in the series is *Hermeneutics*. Watch the brief video "Hermeneutics: A Very Short Introduction" on the YouTube channel *Oxford Academic*. The video is an introduction of the book by Jens Zimmerman, its author.

On a side note, the whole series is worth checking out.

Take-away messages

Lesson 19. Interpretation is a key process of obtaining knowledge wherever human activity is involved. Therefore, it could be a mistake to apply standards of knowledge from natural sciences to the investigation of human activity. According to hermeneutics, (a) everything is a text, (b) every text requires interpretation, (c) the process of interpretation follows the hermeneutic circle. In the hermeneutic circle we need to understand the whole in order to fully understand the parts, but we need to understand the parts in order to understand the whole. Interpretation of a text starts with a preliminary understanding (pre-interpretation) which later gets refined and corrected as we get to know more and more about the text and the context. Applied to art, this means that an artwork "speaks to us", and in the process of this conversation we understand it deeper and deeper. Full understanding may never be reached, but it is the unfolding "conversation" that matters. It should be noted that, according to hermeneutics, this reasoning applies not only to art, but any other area of knowledge.

Back to the exhibition

Once again, I am looking at the simple navigational device invented by Arab seafarers in the 9th century – the kamal. I bet without knowing what a kamal is, it would be easy to mistake this engineering miracle for a piece of garbage.

It is, indeed, just a piece of wood with a string attached to it. But if you combine it with knowledge of how stars work, it becomes a powerful tool which opens up horizons and saves lives. What matters is not the thing itself, but the incredible achievement of the human mind that it represents.

In order for a kamal to perform its function, people of the past had to understand something about stars. Just knowing disparate facts about stars would not be enough. They had to have this knowledge organized into a meaningful whole. They had to have a coherent picture of the world – *a scientific worldview* – that linked together their knowledge of geography, astronomy, navigation, optics. The kamal is so interesting because it is just one piece of a bigger scientific worldview that existed at that time. It represents scientific understanding of the world in the 9th century. That's why this piece of wood is interesting from the perspective of natural sciences.

But it is also interesting from the perspective of human sciences, because it tells us something about the life of human society at that time. Human beings live simultaneously in two worlds, the objective world of things and physical laws and the subjective world of human experiences, meanings and motivations. Similarly, the kamal is linked to the world of objects because it reflects the movement of stars. To understand this dimension of the kamal, you ask yourself the question "How does it work?" But at the same time, it is linked to the world of human experiences. To understand this dimension, ask "What was it built for?" Unless we ask that second question, we will not be able to understand the kamal as a human phenomenon.

And finally, is the kamal beautiful? Are there any circumstances in which it may be considered a work of art? This question is not easy, but we can only answer it when we thoroughly know the context behind the kamal. If I just show a wooden block and a string to a random person and ask them if they consider this art, the response will be a resounding no. But if I tell them the full story behind it, they will start seeing the object differently. Knowing the context may get them closer to *understanding* it. Perhaps it will even produce a deep human response, like it has done for me. When I am looking at the kamal, I feel an urge to explore, fear of the uncertain, longing for home, hope – a whole bunch of things that, I believe, drove 9th-century seafarers out of their homes and into the scary vastness of the sea. To me, the kamal is beautiful.

But, although it looks so simple, I do not dare claim that I fully understand it.

UNIT 6 - Knowledge and language

UNIT 6 - Knowledge and language

Language is all around us. The words you are reading right now are language. The news you watched yesterday used language to tell you what happened. When you used an emoji yesterday in a text to your friend, that was language.

But more than that, language is in your thoughts. Even when you don't say anything out loud, you use language to think. Would we be capable of thinking if we could not speak a language? Some say no. Language is even in your perception. When you look at an apple and perceive an apple, you perceive an entity that you have already named. To some extent, your perception is a product of language.

Language is also a key to our culture. When a child learns a language, they internalize culture together with it. In some languages, for example, the child learns that there are two words for "you" – a polite version to be used when addressing an older person and an informal version to be used with friends. With this distinction comes the cultural attitude to old age and authority. Without language, how would culture get transmitted from generation to generation?

Language has many functions, but there are probably two key functions that everything else revolves around:

1) Language is a tool of thinking
2) Language is a tool of communication

When students think about language, they commonly assume the priority of the second function. They discuss, for example, how speaking the same language and understanding terms in the same way is important for scientists to collaborate on their work. This is indeed relevant, but I encourage you to not forget about the first function. The link between language and thought raises so many profound issues relevant to the production of knowledge. In this unit, we will consider both functions of language in turn, focusing on thinking first and then looking at communication.

Exhibition: Pioneer plaque

The Pioneer plaques are rectangular aluminum plates that were placed on board *Pioneer 10* and *Pioneer 11*, spacecraft that were launched into space in 1972 and 1973, respectively. These were the first human-built objects that escaped the Solar System. The reasoning behind the plaques was that, in case the spacecraft are ever intercepted by intelligent extraterrestrial beings (in other words, aliens), they will understand where the plaques are coming from and how to find us. We wanted to send aliens a message that they will understand even if they don't speak our language (how dare they!).

The two plaques are identical. They are 22 centimeters in width and 15 centimeters in height. Each plaque is 120 grams in weight. If you had these constraints, how would you design your message to the aliens?

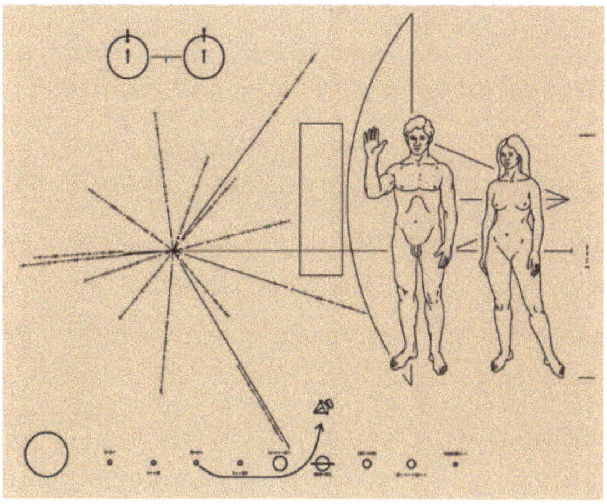

Image 1. *The Pioneer plaque*

The figures of the man and the woman were originally intended to hold hands, but Carl Sagan (who designed the plaque) thought that aliens could misinterpret this as the man and the woman being a single creature rather than two separate creatures. The man raises his hand in a greeting gesture. Carl Sagan realized that this may not be understood by aliens, but this also shows that we have an opposable thumb and the way our arm may move.

Everything in the plaque bears significance. The radial pattern on the left, for example, shows the position of the Sun relative to 14 pulsars (pulsars are something like space lighthouses, they radiate two beams of light in opposite directions and they rotate). Most of the lines are accompanied by long binary numbers which stand for periods of these pulsars (a period is the time needed for a pulsar to make one rotation). The 15th line that extends far to the right indicates the Sun's relative distance from the center of the galaxy, using the same measurement units.

At the bottom of the plaque, there's a schematic diagram of the Solar System, also showing the trajectory of the Pioneer spacecraft travelling past Jupiter and out of the Solar System.

Image 2. *Carl Sagan (credit: Michael Okoniewski, Wikimedia Commons)*

The binary numbers near the planets show their relative distance from the Sun. The unit is 1/10 of the orbit of Mercury. The binary numbers themselves use the symbols "I" and "–" instead of "1" and "0".

Carl Sagan had only three weeks to design the plaque. Subsequently, the design was criticized for several reasons. One of them, for example, is the use of an arrow to represent the trajectory of the spacecraft. It has been claimed that arrows are so easily understood by us because we all come from hunter-gatherer societies; an alien with a different heritage may find the symbol meaningless and not suggestive of direction.

The plaques are still out there, like a message in a bottle thrown into a vast ocean. If someone finds the bottle, will they understand the message, or will they even understand that this is intended as a message? It remains an open question.

Story: Arrival

I will cheat a little. The story that I am about to tell you is not real. It is a work of fiction that first appeared in a sci-fi story and later in a Hollywood movie.

Image 3. Spoiler alert

The story is called *Story of Your Life*, written by Ted Chiang in 1998. The movie is called *Arrival*, directed by Denis Villeneuve and screened in 2016. The movie tells a story of a linguist, Louise Banks, who was enlisted by the U.S. Army to figure out how to communicate with aliens whose 12 spacecraft arrived and hovered over the surface of the planet in different countries, intentions unclear, creating worldwide tension and provoking a military response from humans.

If you were going to watch this movie or read the story later, don't read on, because what follows contains major spoilers! But in this case, do watch it, as it is closely related to the subject matter discussed in this unit.

Louise Banks comes on board the spacecraft and makes contact with two aliens, large creatures with seven limbs ("heptapods"). They communicate by writing complicated circular symbols.

As she begins to decipher their language and understands some basic vocabulary, she asks them "Why did you come?" To this, they answer with symbols that she translates as "offer tool", but some other linguists translate as "offer weapon", and Chinese officials interpret as "use weapon".

Simultaneously, Banks begins having flashback visions of her daughter who died of an incurable disease when she was a teenager.

As tensions escalate, the U.S. military plants a bomb inside a spacecraft, which kills one of the aliens. Before bringing their spacecraft higher up and out of reach, aliens issue an extremely complicated message. Each spacecraft only issues one twelfth of the message, so apparently aliens want human linguists from the 12 countries to collaborate in reading the message as a whole. The symbol for "time" appears many times in the message. However, after the panic that ensued, collaboration is not possible. China, Sudan, Russia and Pakistan have discontinued their scientific investigation and are planning a military operation.

Amidst this crisis, Louise Banks, who has now deciphered the alien language to a considerable degree, enters the spacecraft alone. The aliens explain to her that they came to help humanity by offering them a powerful "tool", and that they are doing this because they will want help in return in 3,000 years. Bank realizes that the "tool" they are referring to is their language. Their language changes the linear perception of time: anyone speaking this language can see the future as if it was in the past.

Image 4. An episode from Arrival showing the strange signs of alien language (credit: BagoGames, Flickr)

Banks realized that her flashbacks are visions not of the past, but of the future: the teenage daughter that she sees dying from a disease has not been born yet.

This new ability of hers allows her to prevent the war. She also marries the person with whom she later has a daughter, although she knows that her daughter will die in adolescence.

Although the plot is pretty complicated, note that it revolves around one central idea: that the language one speaks can change the way they think and the way they see the world. Alien language changed Louise's perception of time from linear to circular, where there is no difference between the past and the present, much like in the complicated circular symbols of the heptapods.

6.1 - What is language?

In the first part of this unit, we will consider the nature of language. What counts as language and what does not? Do animals have language? What is the difference between a signal and a sign? What does it mean for a word to "mean" something?

All of these things are essential to understand because on them depends your answer to most of the questions regarding the relationship between language and knowledge.

You will learn that human language is fundamentally different from animal language. I will even claim that animals cannot have a language. You will consider language as a system of signs, and you will learn that each sign has a complex structure that tightly links together three elements: the world of objects, the world of ideas, and the material token of the sign itself.

You will also learn that there is a debate regarding which of the components of a sign is responsible for its meaning. Some scholars have even claimed that a sign is meaningless unless you place it within a system of other signs, i.e. that you have to know the whole language to understand a separate word.

The next two lessons will equip you with the key concepts that will be necessary to analyze language as a tool of thinking.

Lesson 1 - Signals and signs

Learning outcomes

a) [Knowledge and comprehension] What is a sign?
b) [Understanding and application] How are signs in human language different from signals in animal communication?
c) [Thinking in the abstract] What are advantages and disadvantages of having a system of signs that duplicates the world?

Key concepts

Signal, sign, duplication of the world

Other concepts used

Immediate environment, conditional reflex, system of signs, animal communication

Themes and areas of knowledge

Themes: Knowledge and language, Knowledge and the knower

Do animals have language?

Birds chirp, dogs bark and whales do whatever it is that they do – all of that allows them to communicate. In the animal world, communication does not have to happen through sounds. Many insects (such as ants) use chemical communication through pheromones. Some higher primates also use pheromones for things such as signaling fertility. An example of communication through smell is dogs marking their territory. This signals to other dogs where they were and when. Speaking of dogs: your dog may wag its tail cheerfully when you come home from school – what do you think this communicates? That your dog is glad to see you?

Image 5. *Animal communication*

But something feels weird here. Yes, birds communicate with each other by chirping, but can we really say that this is the same as human language? Indeed, there are many differences.

The key and perhaps the most essential difference is that between signals and signs.

Signals and signs

Is there a fundamental difference between human language and animal language? (#Perspectives)

A signal is a sound that points to an aspect of the environment that has an immediate significance. It does not have to be a sound – it can be a smell or a gesture or anything else – but for simplicity I will just use sounds as the example. When one bird sees danger in close proximity (such as a predator), it will chirp in a special way. The chirp signals danger to other birds. The predator is an aspect of the environment that has an immediate significance (survival). Similarly, some species of monkeys will let out a special cry when they see food while rummaging through a forest. That is a signal for the other monkeys to explore the area. People have signals, too. Think about a cry of terror – when we are terrified, we cry in a very special way. It is extremely hard (or even impossible) for people to fake a genuine cry of terror when the situation is not actually threatening.

***Image 6**. Chirping bird*

The following is true for signals:

- They *cannot occur in the absence of the aspect of the environment that they are linked to*. For example, a bird cannot produce its "danger" chirp if there is actually no danger around. A signal simply draws attention to something already present in the immediate environment.
- *Animals cannot teach signals* to each other. One bird cannot teach another bird to chirp because the teacher cannot produce the chirp in a classroom situation. They actually need danger for the chirp to be produced, but when danger is around, teaching other birds is probably the last thing that's on their mind. Animals are either already born with their signals or acquire them through conditional reflexes.
- *Signals are linked to a biological need*. The bird's "danger" chirp is linked to survival; the monkey's cry for food is linked to satisfaction of hunger. These things signal something that has a biological significance, and that's why they launch a reflex.

If there was no language, what would knowledge lose and what would it gain? (#Methods and tools)

On the contrary, a sign is a sound (or a gesture, or a knot tied on a rope, or whatever) that *denotes* some aspect of the environment. To denote is not the same as to signal. A sign may be used in the absence of the actual stimulus. For example, I don't have to actually see a chair in order to say "chair", and you don't have to see a chair to understand what I mean. Signs denote the actual things, but they exist on their own, even in the absence of these things. As a consequence, the following is true for signs (but not signals):

1) They don't have to be linked to a biological need (for example, the word "chair" does not have any biological significance in terms of your survival, hunger or reproduction).
2) They can be learned and taught from one person to another. Therefore, they are acquired through culture and education.

The differences between signs and signals are summarized in the table below:

Aspect	Signals	Signs
1. Can it exist without the thing that it represents?	No	Yes
2. Does it have to be linked to a biological need?	Yes	No
3. Can it be learned and taught from one member of the species to another?	No	Yes

My big claim for this lesson is this: language is a system of signs (not signals); therefore, humans have language but animals do not.

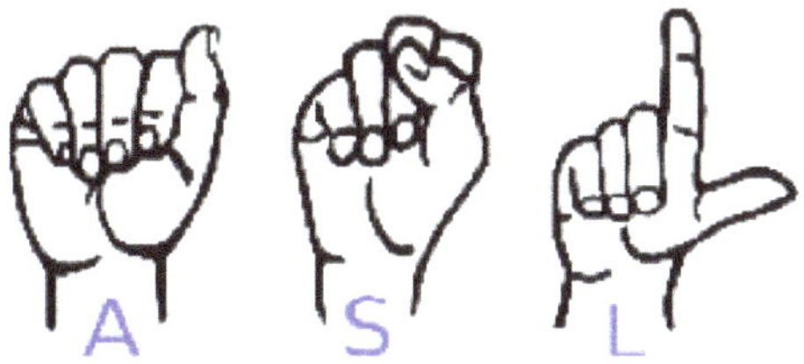

Image 7. *American Sign Language*

KEY IDEA: Language is a system of signs (not signals), therefore humans have language but animals do not

Objections?

I can hear some of you actively objecting. You claim that your dog understands the word "salami" because every time you say this word, your dog becomes agitated and starts running around the house and barking, clearly in anticipation of a snack. I beg to differ. I think your dog does not understand what the word "salami" means.

To what extent does human knowledge depend on language? (#Scope)

When you give your dog a piece of salami, it satisfies hunger (a biological need). Show it some salami, and this will trigger a complex biological reflex: salivating, agitation, barking, chasing around. It's an automatic, unconditional reflex. When you repeatedly say the word "salami" every time you give the dog the actual salami, the word develops an association with hunger through a conditional reflex. Now the word triggers the same reaction as the actual salami does. It is a trigger for a complex automatic reaction: salivating, agitation, barking, chasing around. This particular sequence of sounds has become a signal for anticipation of hunger satisfaction. Your dog cannot tell the difference between the word "salami" and the actual salami because both these stimuli cause the same reaction, the ultimate goal of which is to eat. To your dog, the word "salami" is not a sign that denotes a certain gastronomical delight, it is merely a signal that triggers a reflex.

Compare this to a similar situation: I say the word "salami" to you. Do you become agitated and start chasing me around? No, because you understand the difference between the word "salami" and the actual food. When you hear me say "salami", you do not think "Oooh, I have a chance to eat something tasty, where is it?" You understand that I am just referring to something that is not necessarily present in this immediate situation. To you, a human being, the word "salami" is not a signal but a sign.

Let's go back to the three differences between signals and signs that I outlined above:

1) To you, the word "salami" can exist without the thing it represents. To your dog, it can't.
2) To you, signs do not have to be linked to a biological need such as hunger. You use the word "chair" as a sign for a piece of furniture and you are okay with that. But try to teach your dog what "chair" means and I bet it won't be interested. "Salami" is linked to hunger, but "chair" isn't.
3) If I don't know what "salami" means, you can teach me. But can your dog teach the word "salami" to other dogs? No, each individual dog will have to go experience multiple repeated presentations of the word "salami" and the actual meal in order to develop the same association.

I hope I have convinced you that your dog does not understand "salami".

Can morality exist without language? (#Ethics)

Critical thinking extension

We live in two worlds

Metaphorically speaking, a signal just *points at* some aspect of the world, whereas a sign duplicates this aspect. Language (as a system of signs) duplicates the world. We humans live in two worlds simultaneously – one is the world of actual chairs and tables and wolves (?!) and one is the world of signs that we created to duplicate that first world. This allows us to do amazing things. For example, we can learn about wolves without ever meeting one. We do not have to be exposed to danger to learn how to deal with it. Additionally, we can learn from other people's experiences without actually following them everywhere and imitating what they do.

What do you think are the advantages and disadvantages of having a system of signs that duplicates the world?

If you are interested...

Koko the gorilla

Image 8. *Gorilla (not Koko)*

I started off by comparing humans to birds and dogs, but to be fair there do exist instances in the animal world where more features of human language are demonstrated. This makes scientists puzzled. Don't get me wrong, there is no doubt that language is unique to human beings, but there is a grey area regarding certain species (and certain individual animals).

One example is the famous Koko – a female gorilla who was taught human sign language. Koko was born at the San Francisco Zoo and was taken care of by researcher Francine Patterson.

Patterson taught Koko a special "Gorilla Sign Language". Reportedly, Koko knew around 1,000 words. She was also reported to be able to invent new words. For example, to refer to a ring (an object for which she was taught no sign), she decided to combine two signs that she knew, "finger" and "bracelet". So, a "finger-bracelet" became her sign for a ring. However, these reports were also met with a lot of criticism from skeptical scientists. One major argument was that Koko did not understand the meaning of those signs and was simply trained to use these signs in certain situations because she was rewarded for them.

If you are interested, find out more about Koko's story in a recent documentary *Koko: The Gorilla Who Talks to People* (2016). I will also mention that Leonardo DiCaprio played a part in it – perhaps this will convince some of you to watch it.

Take-away messages

Lesson 1. The difference between human language and animal communication is the difference between signs and signals. Animal communication is based on signals – automatic reactions to environmental stimuli, such as food or approaching danger. Signals cannot appear in the absence of the environmental stimulus, they have to be linked to a biological need, and they cannot be taught by one member of the species to another. By contrast, human language is a system of signs. Signs are arbitrary (we agreed upon them) and they can be used in the absence of the thing they represent. Signs are culturally learned. Humans duplicate the real world in their language. Signs exist alongside the real world that they represent, but the physical presence of the thing is not necessary for the sign to be used and understood by others.

Lesson 2 - Meaning

Learning outcomes

a) [Knowledge and comprehension] What are the three components of meaning of a sign?
b) [Understanding and application] What are the arguments for associating meaning with the intension as opposed to the extension?
c) [Thinking in the abstract] What is the role of a sign as a bridge between the world of things and the world of ideas?

Key concepts

Meaning, the signifier, the signified, the referent, intension of a sign, extension of a sign

Other concepts used

Concept, mental notion, idea, token, structural linguistics

Themes and areas of knowledge

Themes: Knowledge and language, Knowledge and the knower

Recap and plan

In the previous lesson, we made a distinction between signs and signals. Signals point to some aspect of the immediate reality. They cannot exist independently of reality itself. They are usually linked to some biologically important need (for example, food or survival). Signs duplicate reality. They denote some aspect of reality and can be used even without that aspect of reality being physically present in the immediate surroundings.

Image 9. Ferdinand de Saussure

Signals don't have a meaning. They are reflex-like responses to a stimulus in the environment. Signs, however, stand for something. This "something" that they stand for is their meaning.

What does it mean to mean? (#Scope)

In this lesson, we will try to understand what meaning is. We will dissect it and analyze its parts. We will try to understand what it means to mean.

Components of a sign

Ferdinand de Saussure (1857 - 1913), the founder of *structural linguistics*, suggested that every sign has three components:

Can ideas be expressed without signs? (#Methods and tools)

1) The signifier. This is the material token that we are using to convey an idea or name an object. For example, a sequence of sounds in the word "elephant" is a signifier. And so is the sign language gesture for "elephant". And so is the word "elephant" in any language. You will agree that the signifier is arbitrary. There is no reason why we cannot express the idea of an elephant with some other sequence of sounds, for example, "chipmunk" or "gemplunkle".
2) The signified. This is the idea or a mental image that is evoked by the signifier. When I say "elephant", you have a mental image formed in your head – not of a particular elephant, but of a generalized idea or concept of an elephant. This mental image is the signified. There are words that express abstract concepts, such as "love", "sophisticated", "arbitrary". The "images" that these words evoke are not so much "images", but ideas or concepts existing in the mental space.
3) The referent. This is the class of objects or phenomena of the material world to which the sign applies. So, in my example, the referent of the word "elephant" is the collection of all elephants in the world: the ones existing now, the ones that existed in the past and the ones that will exist in the future. While the signified exists in your mind, the referent exists in the real world.

The signified is also known as the intension of a sign and the referent is also known as the extension of a sign. They are called this because the signified is internal (exists in your mind) while the referent is external (extends into the real world).

KEY IDEA: Every sign has three components: the signifier, the signified (a.k.a. intension) and the referent (a.k.a. extension)

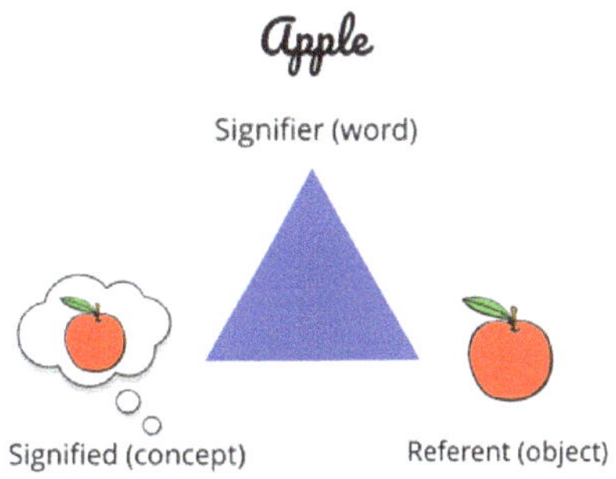

Image 10. The structure of meaning of a sign

What is meaning?

Now that we have uncovered the three major components of a sign, can we define meaning? What does it mean to mean?

You will not be surprised to learn that a commonly accepted answer does not exist. But broadly speaking, the two "camps" in this debate are those who claim that meaning of a sign is in the extension versus those who claim that meaning of a sign is in the intension.

Is meaning in the extension?

One approach was to link meaning of a sign with its referent (extension). Proponents of this approach claimed that the "meaning" of a word is the collection of all things in the real world that the word applies to.

An advantage of this approach is that it does indeed capture the first stages of language acquisition: when a baby learns a language, the first skill that is being acquired is pointing at surrounding objects and naming them.

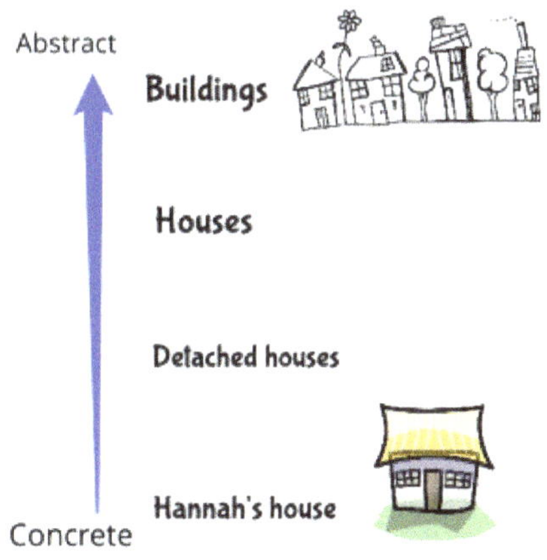

Image 11. The ladder of abstraction

An obvious disadvantage is that language in its fully developed form is so much more than a collection of labels for things that exist. Abstract words have no referents (what is the referent of words such as "policy", "honesty" or "abstraction"?). We have words that convey a meaning that is purely grammatical ("is", "to", "the"). As a matter of fact, we can even perceive some meaning in a sequence of made-up words with no referents. Just read the beginning of Lewis Carroll's nonsense poem "Jabberwocky":

'Twas brillig, and the slithy toves
Did gyre and gimble in the wabe:
All mimsy were the borogoves,
And the mome raths outgrabe.

But we can probably reconcile these arguments by agreeing that linguistic meaning began as a referent and then later, as language developed, acquired more complex forms. First, we learned to use the word "elephant" as a label for real-world elephants, later we learned to use the word "big" to denote all things in the real world that are big (like an elephant), and even later we coined the word "size" to refer to the objectively existing difference between big

How do we get to understand the meaning of moral values? (#Ethics)

things and small things. If we reconcile the arguments this way, we still agree that primarily meaning = referent (extension), and all the other forms of meaning are add-ons. We will still agree in this case that the meaning of a word is the collection of all things in the real world that this word represents.

KEY IDEA: According to one position, meaning of a sign is the collection of all things in the real world that the sign represents (i.e. the extension)

Is meaning in the intension?

However, not everyone agrees that the meaning of a word is its link with real-world objects.

A common counter-argument is based on Ferdinand de Saussure's observation that a linguistic unit can only acquire its meaning in opposition to other linguistic units. For example, the word "big" means pretty much nothing if you do not oppose it to "small". "Light" is meaningless without "heavy", and so on.

To what extent can it be said that abstract concepts are completely unrelated to the real world? (#Ethics)

Imagine my whole language consists of one word denoting an elephant (say, "boobooka"). Imagine we see an elephant, I point at it and say "boobooka". Do you understand what I mean? "Boobooka" may mean an elephant, or an animal, or a big object, or a grey object, or a thing we can eat. It can mean pretty much anything. Now, suppose my language consists of two words: "boobooka" for an elephant and "sploosh" for a non-elephant. If that is the case, you can gradually figure out the meaning of both words, as you observe me repeatedly referring to elephants as "boobooka" and everything else as "sploosh". Once you figure it out, you will understand what "boobooka" means.

From this point of view, to know the meaning of a sign means to understand how this sign relates to other signs in a language. But then, the meaning of a sign does not lie in the outside world, it lies inside my head. It is the idea that forms in my mind when I hear the word. In other words, meaning is in the intension.

KEY IDEA: According to another position, meaning of a sign is in the idea that it conveys (i.e. the intension). This idea exists not in the world, but in the human mind. Signs only acquire their meaning when they are placed in a system of other signs.

***Image 12**. Elephant = "boobooka"*

Critical thinking extension

Earlier, I claimed that language duplicates the world, but apparently it does much more than that. The second world that is created by language is based on the first world (of real things and phenomena), but it is not limited by this first world. One might say that this second world is "inspired" by reality but goes far beyond it. Using language, we can recreate the first world (reality) in the second world (ideas), but we can also create things that in reality do not exist. In fact, language gives us infinite possibilities. Just watch me create a new animal species:

A meerpigeon is a meerkat with wings.

Have you imagined it? That is the power of language. Using language, I created a mental image in my mind and I sent this mental image to you through the pages of this book. This concept of a meerpigeon is inspired by the real world, but not limited by it.

So, we have the world of things on one side and the world of ideas on the other side, and signs of our language are the bridge between the two worlds.

Now my question is: what is the role of this bridge? Will the two worlds remain the same if the bridge disappears?

If you are interested...

Watch the introductory video "Ferdinand de Saussure and Structural Linguistics" (2014) on the YouTube channel *Bella Ross*.

Take-away messages

Lesson 2. There are three components in a sign – the signifier, the signified and the referent. The signifier is the physical token itself (a sequence of sounds in a word, a sequence of movements in a gesture). The signified is the idea that is expressed in the sign. This idea exists internally, in our mental world. This is why the signified is also called "intension". The referent is the collection of objects in the world that the sign is applicable to. The referent exists externally in the world around us. This is why it is also called "extension". Some scholars suggest that the meaning of a sign is its referent (extension), while others suggest that the meaning of a sign is in its link to the mental idea (intension).

6.2 - Language and thought

You are now familiar with the key concepts related to language. You know that language is a system of signs and that each sign has a meaning that has a complex structure. The meaning of a sign ties together the world of things and the world of ideas. It is a bridge between our mental world and the real world out there.

This is a perfect starting point to discuss the interaction between language and thought. As I said at the very start of the unit, language is both a tool of thinking and a tool of communication. We are going to look at these functions one by one. The focus in the next several lessons is on language as a tool of thinking.

We will speak about concepts – the units of thought. We will discuss what concepts are, how they are formed, how they define our thoughts. We will consider the idea that some concepts may be innate, and we will try to figure out how to tell the difference between what is actually there in the real world and what our mind imposes on our perception.

We will discuss the debate between linguistic nativists and linguistic empiricists. The former claim that when we are born, we already understand some concepts and rules of grammar. The latter claim that all language is learned. The position you take in this debate has dramatic implications. For example, our success in reaching out to alien civilizations depends on it.

Related to this debate, we will try to figure out which of the following is true:
- Does thought influence language, or
- Does language influence thought?

Finally, we will consider Mentalese – the hypothetical "language of thought" that unfolds behind the scenes as we are speaking a natural language.

Lesson 3 - Concepts

Learning outcomes

a) [Knowledge and comprehension] What does it mean for a concept to be based on abstracted properties?
b) [Understanding and application] How can it be that a concept is simultaneously wider and narrower than the object?
c) [Thinking in the abstract] To what extent can it be claimed that abstract concepts have no connection to reality?

Key concepts

Concept, conceptual hierarchy, abstraction

Other concepts used

Abstracted property, abstract words, category, instance within a category, Vygotsky blocks

Themes and areas of knowledge

Themes: Knowledge and language, Knowledge and the knower
AOK: Mathematics

Recap and plan

In the previous lesson, we tried to figure out what it means to mean. If we assume that meaning is the link between the signifier and the referent (for example, between the word "tree" and the collection of all trees in the world), we run into a number of problems. One example is the existence of words that have no referent in the real world, such as "unicorn". Another example is abstract words or words that bear a purely grammatical meaning: "intensity", "sophistication", "to", "must have been". Moreover, from the perspective of structural linguistics, words can only bear a meaning in a system of other words because meaning is constructed through oppositions (for example, "large" can only mean something if there exists an opposition with "small"). All of this suggests that meaning should be sought in the link between the signifier (the material token of a sign) and the signified (the idea, or the concept). The signified exists in the mental space.

But what are concepts and how can we study them? What does this "mental space" consist of?

What are concepts?

Concepts are abstract ideas that exist in the mental space. Presumably, concepts are the building blocks of thoughts: we combine them to form complex beliefs. For example, take the sentence:

"Concepts are the building blocks of thoughts"

This sentence expresses a complex belief that is a product of combining such concepts as "concepts", "building blocks" and "thoughts". These three concepts exist in a certain relationship with each other (which is expressed by auxiliary words like "are", "of"). Concepts + relationships between them = complex thought.

So, what is the nature of concepts?

Concepts are organized in a hierarchy

Is there knowledge that cannot be expressed conceptually? (#Scope)

One thing that is noticeable about concepts is that they are organized in a conceptual hierarchy. High-level concepts include low-level concepts as their instances. For example, take these concepts: baby chair, chair, furniture, man-made object, matter. I have arranged them hierarchically: a baby chair is a kind of chair, a chair is a type of furniture, furniture is a certain type of man-made object, and man-made objects are material things. But "chair" includes other instances apart from baby chairs, "furniture" is not limited to chairs, and "matter" does not only include man-made material things.

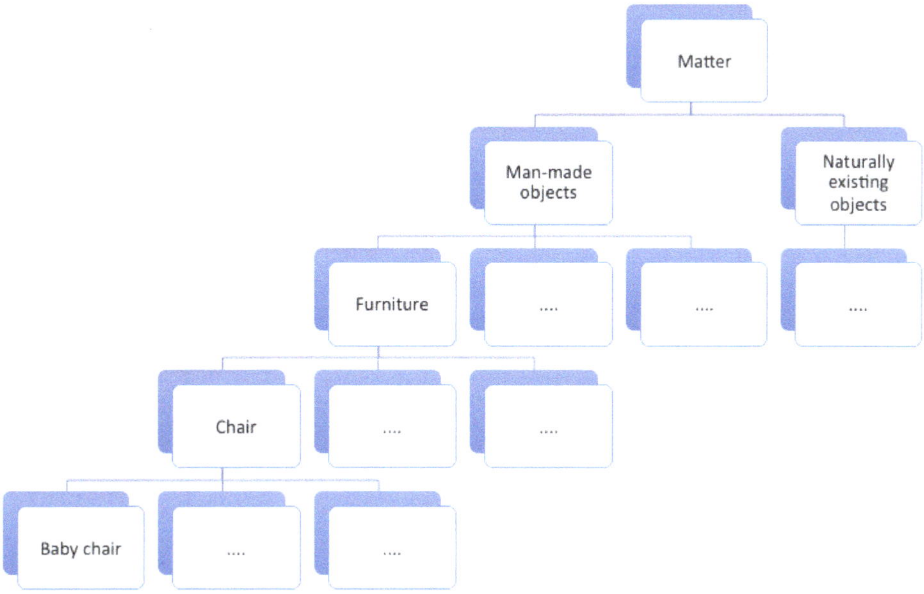

***Image 13**. Hierarchy of concepts*

What do we need to correctly define a concept?

If concepts exist in a hierarchy, what do we need to correctly identify a concept among others? We need two things:

1) Name a higher-level concept (category) that our concept is an instance of (for example, "a chair is a piece of furniture")
2) Name the properties that differentiate our concept from other instances in the same category (for example, "a chair is a piece of furniture with four legs and a back designed for sitting of one person")

This brings us back to the ideas of structural linguistics: a concept can only be defined in the system of other concepts. The whole hierarchy needs to be present for a concept to make sense. We can also put it this way: the meaning of a concept is its position in relation to other concepts.

KEY IDEA: To define a concept, name a higher-level concept (category) and name the properties that differentiate your concept from other instances in the same category

Concepts are based on abstracted properties

Remember that concepts and referents are not the same thing. Concepts are abstract generalizations. When we say "tree", we do not think of a specific tree, or of a specific collection of trees. We think of the generalized idea of a tree, a mental category that every existing tree will fall under.

***Image 14**. Concept of a tree*

What is the role of abstraction in understanding reality? (#Methods and tools)

This process of taking a bunch of real-life objects and *abstracting* some of their properties is vital for the formation of concepts. Without this process of abstraction, concepts would not exist. On the other hand, with this process of abstraction in place, we can continue abstracting until all connection with reality is lost. Let me illustrate this.

Here is a definition of a "tree" provided by Collins dictionary (collinsdictionary.com):

A tree is a tall plant that has a hard trunk, branches and leaves.

Here is a random variety of trees:

***Image 15**. Various trees (credit: Freepik.com)*

Every individual tree has a lot of properties. Some are wide and some are narrow, some are large and some are small, some are branchy and some are not, some come in pretty weird shapes. But when I create the concept of a "tree", I ignore all of these differences and I focus my attention on a small number of properties, such as *Is the trunk hard?* The resulting idea that exists in my mental space is simultaneously poorer and richer than a real tree:

- It is poorer than a real tree because it does not have all the properties a real tree has. My concept (assuming the definition provided by Collins dictionary) only has five properties: "a plant", "tall", "with a hard trunk", "with branches", "with leaves". Unlike any individual real tree, it does not have the property of shape, color, smell, texture, and so on. It is stripped of the wealth of properties that trees have in real life.

- At the same time, it is richer than a real tree because my concept potentially includes millions of real trees. Even the ones that do not exist yet. Moreover, it includes trees but does not include objects that are non-trees! And that is indeed the power of a concept.

KEY IDEA: A concept is simultaneously poorer and richer than the thing it denotes

How do people learn abstraction?

How do people become capable of this process of abstraction (abstracting properties from real-life objects)? Well, we learn them through opposition and categorization when we are little. You must have seen (and played with!) toys that require you to categorize objects based on their shape, color, height and other properties. They are also called *Vygotsky blocks*.

Can moral values be defined in the same way as concepts are defined in an academic discipline? (#Ethics)

Every block in this toy set has the properties of color, shape and height. If I ask you to give me all circle-shaped blocks, you will have to focus on one property only and mentally ignore all of the other properties. It's not easy. Similarly, if I ask you to give me all tall blocks, you will have to abstract the property of height and ignore all other properties such as color and shape. That's how we learn abstraction. When children are done playing with blocks, they go through the same process when they learn a language, learn to count, study a school subject.

***Image 16**. Vygotsky blocks*

Why is it important to learn abstraction? Because by learning abstraction, we acquire concepts. As we know, concepts are building blocks of thoughts. Therefore, by learning abstraction, we go from simply perceiving the world to thinking about it. In a similar way, by learning the abstract concept of "tree", you go from being familiar with several individual trees to knowing the essence of all trees. You see the forest behind the trees. To continue this metaphor, if various school subjects are the trees, then TOK is the forest. School subjects are about various instances of knowledge, while TOK is about knowledge as such.

How can two people using an abstract concept know that they understand it in the same way? (#Perspectives)

Critical thinking extension

How far does abstraction go?

Humans can go a long way in the process of abstraction. First, we understand how to group objects based on a single abstracted property (shape, color) and we give this property a name. This is how we create the first simple concepts, such as "rectangular" or "yellow". Then, on the basis of that, we build a whole hierarchy of concepts, and at the top of the hierarchy the concepts become incredibly abstract. Examples include such abstract ideas as "property", or the concept of "concept", or the concept of "knowledge" – the main focus of TOK. Theory of Knowledge deals almost entirely with high-level abstract concepts that embrace a lot of real-life examples. Mathematics is another example that includes very abstract concepts such as "variable", "number", "set" and "operation".

Although concepts are not limited to simply being labels of things existing in real life, we must acknowledge that concepts grow out of these things. But as concepts become more and more abstract as we move up the hierarchy, can we claim that the connection with reality is entirely lost? For example, is there a connection between the idea of "must have been" and an object or phenomenon of the real world? Is there something in the real world that is connected to the mathematical concept "operation"?

If you are interested…

Watch the video "Concept learning in pigeons. Sometimes they are smarter than humans" (2009) from the YouTube user *Casper H*. This short video demonstrates concept learning in animals – in this case, pigeons are trained to tell the difference between paintings of Picasso and Monet. Do you think this proves that pigeons have concepts?

Take-away messages

Lesson 3. At the core of concept formation lies the process of abstraction. A concept of a tree is the idea that includes several essential properties abstracted from real trees. A concept of a tree is simultaneously richer and poorer than a real tree: poorer because it includes fewer properties, richer because it applies to all the trees in the world. Concepts exist in a hierarchy. The higher along the hierarchy, the more abstract the concepts become. The lower in the hierarchy, the easier it is to find the real-life objects that the concepts denote (tree, table, human being). Concepts high in the hierarchy lose obvious connection with the real world and acquire their meaning through other abstract concepts (truth, love, honesty).

Lesson 4 - A priori and a posteriori concepts

Learning outcomes

a) [Knowledge and comprehension] What is the difference between a priori and a posteriori concepts?
b) [Understanding and application] Why is the existence of a priori concepts a big deal for the study of language and thought?
c) [Thinking in the abstract] To what extent does the existence of a priori concepts imply that language is innate?

Key concepts

A priori concepts, a posteriori concepts

Other concepts used

Innate abilities, time and space, concepts

Themes and areas of knowledge

Themes: Knowledge and language, Knowledge and the knower
AOK: Natural Sciences, Human Sciences

Recap and plan

In the previous lesson, we analyzed concepts – what they are and how they are formed. Concepts exist in the mental space, we said, and they begin with the process of abstracting properties from the real-life things that we observe around us. For example, a child learns the concept of "shape" when he/she is required to sort toy blocks according to their shape, ignoring all other properties such as color or height.

I also claimed, by this logic, that concepts grow out of the real-world objects. In other words, concepts are based on our experiences with real-life objects.

Immanuel Kant called such concepts "a posteriori concepts". A posteriori means "based on experience". But he also suggested that there exists another set of concepts that we have even before we experience the real world – a priori concepts. "A priori" means "before experience". This lesson is about what these concepts are and why it is important to know about them.

Are all concepts based on experience? Can conceptual knowledge be innate? (#Perspectives)

A priori concepts

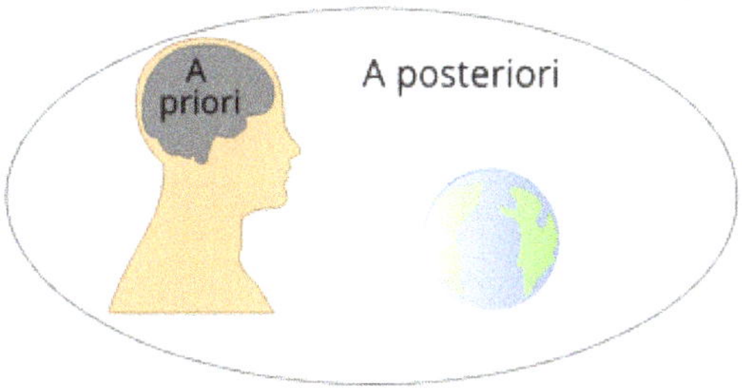

Image 17. A priori and a posteriori

As evident from their name, a posteriori concepts are formed in our minds as a result of our interaction with the world around us. We gain experience with the world (for example, by sorting, combining and categorizing toy blocks) which allows us to perform a mental abstraction of certain properties of objects, and on the basis of this abstraction we form concepts. Since such concepts come from the real-world experience, it is reasonable to assume that they also reflect the reality of things around us.

By contrast, a priori concepts exist in our minds even before we gain any sort of experience with the environment. In fact, these concepts may influence our perception of the environment, so that the way reality appears to us will be shaped by these concepts and will not necessarily coincide with the way reality actually is.

By definition, a priori concepts must be innate, which means that we must be born with them. Do a priori concepts exist? It is debated, and I will argue that the position you take in this debate has profound implications for knowledge and language.

KEY IDEA: A posteriori concepts are based on experience with the world, so we can expect them to reflect reality. A priori concepts are innate, so we can expect them to shape our perception of reality.

Why does it matter?

Suppose we do accept that such a priori, innate concepts exist. What would be the implications of that?

Can language distort our perception of reality? (#Methods and tools)

1) It would influence the way our language is formed. Since language expresses concepts, language would develop in ways that make the expression of these innate concepts possible. For example, if time (with the idea of the present, the past and the future) is an innate concept, then all languages existing in the world would have grammar to capture the position of an event on a timeline (did, am doing, will do).
2) It would impose certain limitations on the variety of natural languages. For example, the existence of an innate concept of time would make it impossible for a natural language to not have words or grammar for time.
3) It would influence the way we perceive and interpret the world. For example, we would perceive time as something that objectively exists, even if it doesn't.

Therefore, to put it simply, whether or not innate concepts exist is a big deal.

Immanuel Kant: time and space are a priori concepts

To give an intentionally provocative example, I will focus here on concepts that are really fundamental - space and time.

The German philosopher Immanuel Kant (1724 – 1804) – you might remember him from our discussion of *noumena* and *phenomena* – believed that time and space are a priori concepts that our mind brings into our perception of the real world. Our experience of the world is then a combination of our perceptions and these concepts mixed into them.

I remember first coming across this idea in a book that I was reading, and I remember putting the book aside and staring at a wall blankly for a good hour. That was how deeply I was shaken by this thought. I was 15. In the following pages, I will do my best to recreate that feeling in you (because why should I suffer alone?).

Imagine space and time do not actually exist. There is no past, present or future in the world around us. Things are not close to each other or far from each other or next to each other. The world is timeless and space-less. But we humans have two filters that are hard-wired into our brain: the concepts of space and time. When we perceive the world, we impose these concepts on our sensory information; as a result, we experience things as situated somewhere in space and existing at some point in time.

For comparison, think about your experience of color. You know that colors, physically speaking, do not exist. Color is a certain wavelength of light reflected from the surface of the object that you are looking at. But can you "unsee" yellow or blue and perceive the pure physical wavelength? No, you can't. Although the perception of color originates from your mind (and not actually from the object you are looking at), there is nothing you can do about it.

What if it's true?

So what, you would ask? To this, I reply: what do you want to gain knowledge about – the world around you or the way it appears to be? Reality or appearances?

Image 18. "The Pillars of Creation" – interstellar gas and dust in the Eagle Nebula, a photo taken by the Hubble Space Telescope (credit: NASA)

Is there knowledge we will never have because the human brain is not capable of it? (#Scope)

Jokes aside, this is actually exactly the same question that Morpheus asked Neo in *The Matrix* (1999) , offering him the choice between the red pill and the blue pill. If you do not want to listen to Immanuel Kant, listen to Morpheus!

The Matrix is everywhere. It is all around us. Even now, in this very room. You can see it when you look out your window or when you turn on your television. You can feel it when you go to work ... when you go to church ... when you pay your taxes. It is the world that has been pulled over your eyes to blind you from the truth. /.../ This is your last chance. After this, there is no turning back. You take the blue pill, the story ends; you wake up in your bed and believe whatever you want to believe. You take the red pill, you stay in Wonderland and I show you how deep the rabbit hole goes (The Matrix, 1999).

(To paraphrase: take the blue pill and continue seeing the world through the filter of a priori concepts, take the red pill and discard these filters and see the world as it actually is).

The idea of a priori concepts is debatable, but since it has so many profound implications, it is worth exploring further. If it is true that a priori concepts exist, it is also true that we live in a matrix!

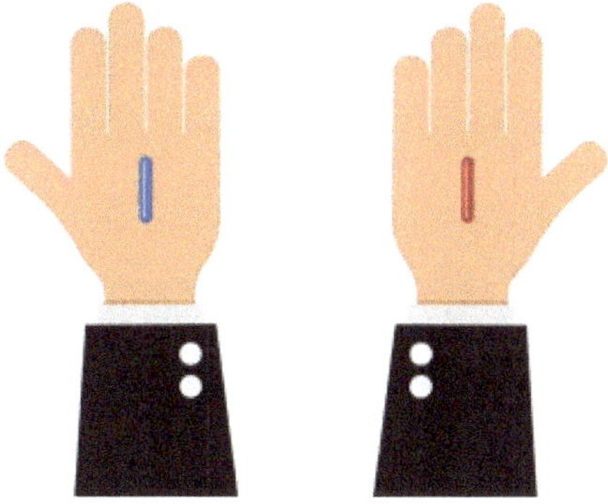

Image 19. The blue pill and the red pill

Critical thinking extension

If some concepts are indeed innate, how would that influence language? For example, does it mean that:

Are moral values a priori or a posteriori? (#Ethics)

1) All existing human languages will share certain core features?
2) It will be possible to extract this "core similarity" and construct a universal grammar that expresses the a priori concepts?
3) Children are born with some understanding of language, or at least a predisposition to understand linguistic constructions?

It makes sense, doesn't it? The meaning of a linguistic unit is its connection to the concept. If some concepts are innate, then there must be linguistic units expressing these concepts, and that should be the same in all languages. But then children must have some sort of predisposition to learn a language because they already have some ideas, they just lack the labels for these ideas.

Do you find this argument debatable? We will revisit it in a later lesson, so it would be good if you could formulate an initial position.

If you are interested…

Watch the video "Philosophy: Kant on Space" (2014) on the YouTube channel *Wireless Philosophy*. The video has two parts. It explains Immanuel Kant's views on space as an a priori concept.

Read the article "Why space and time might be an illusion" (April 26, 2016) by George Musser published in *Huffpost*.

Take-away messages

Lesson 4. The view that concepts "grow out of" the real world applies to a posteriori concepts. "A posteriori" means "based on experience". A posteriori concepts are learned. However, some scholars – such as Immanuel Kant – suggested that some concepts exist before any kind of experience with the environment. They are called a priori concepts. "A priori" means "before experience". A priori concepts are innate. Their existence is debated, but if they exist, it must have profound implications for human knowledge. For example, if a priori concepts exist, human language and cognition imposes important limitations on what humans can ever know. Kant argued that space and time (among others) are a priori concepts. It means that space and time are categories of our minds that we impose on the real world around us, rather than properties of the world itself.

Lesson 5 - Spacetime

Learning outcomes

a) [Knowledge and comprehension] What are some of the modern scientific discoveries that are challenging the traditional beliefs about space and time?
b) [Understanding and application] How do these findings support Kant's idea of space and time as a priori concepts?
c) [Thinking in the abstract] Can we ever prove that a concept is a priori?

Key concepts

Space, time, reality, appearance, spacetime

Other concepts used

Quantum entanglement, quantum eraser, collapse of wave function, the arrow of time, pulsating universe

Themes and areas of knowledge

Themes: Knowledge and language, Knowledge and the knower
AOK: Natural Sciences

Recap and plan

In the previous lesson, we discussed the difference between a posteriori concepts (acquired through our interaction with the environment) and a priori concepts (innate). We had a closer look at a priori concepts because whether or not we believe in their existence has several big implications. For example, if a priori concepts truly exist, then they influence our perception of the world in deep ways that may be impossible to overcome. A priori concepts may create a "matrix" that is superimposed on reality, such that we live in the matrix rather than in the real world.

A dramatic example of a priori concepts is Immanuel Kant's belief that time and space are not properties of reality itself, but rather concepts innate in our minds. This is a big idea that may sound a little crazy. It may or may not be true, but science students (and not only them!) may be interested to know that some of the recent findings suggest that Kant may have been right. In this lesson, we will be looking at such findings.

Appearance and reality

In his talk "*Do We See Reality as it Is?*" (Hoffmann, 2015), Donald Hoffman notes that we humans have a rich history of false beliefs that were based on how something appears to be. We used to believe the Earth was flat because it looks this way. We used to believe the Earth is in the center around which other celestial objects revolve – because it looks this way. There are numerous other examples of mistaking appearance for reality. As a matter of fact, history of science on the whole seems like a history of disillusionment, a history of realizations that reality is not the way it appears to be. Therefore, it is not at all improbable that the concepts of space and time are just another one of these illusions that we will eventually overcome.

"History of science is a history of disillusionment". Do you agree? (#Scope)

Space

Regarding the notion of space.

It seems very obvious and very intuitive: as I am writing this now, my laptop is close to me in space and the airplane that's flying over my head is somewhat farther away. I see a family walking in the park - they are not too far away and not too close. I can remember events of yesterday, and tomorrow hasn't happened yet.

But this has all been challenged already.

First, Einstein inspired some developments in theoretical physics that suggested that time and space are not at all separate. Hermann Minkowski, building upon Einstein's relativity theory, proposed a model of time as the fourth dimension of space. He even coined a word that referred to them as a whole: spacetime. In Einstein's theory, when objects move fast (close to the speed of light), time and space affect each other: as time expands, space shrinks and vice versa. For example, imagine you and I are twins (sorry!). If you sit in a spaceship and zoom into outer space at almost the speed of light, from my point of view you will be covering a larger distance, but the time on your spaceship will flow more slowly. When you return home, I will be older than you even though we were born on the same day (research "twin paradox" for details).

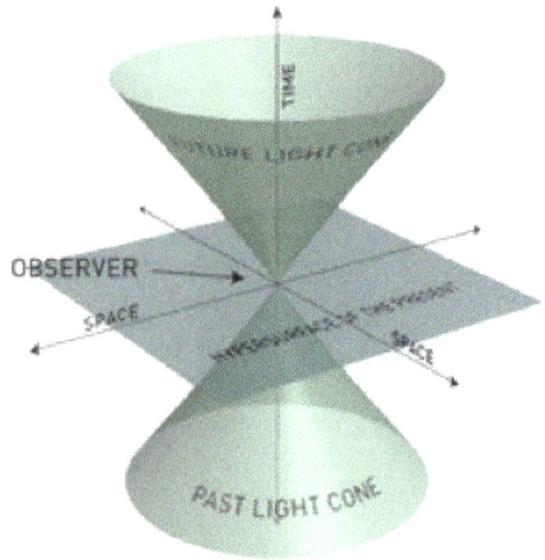

Image 20. *Spacetime (credit: Stib, Wikimedia Commons)*

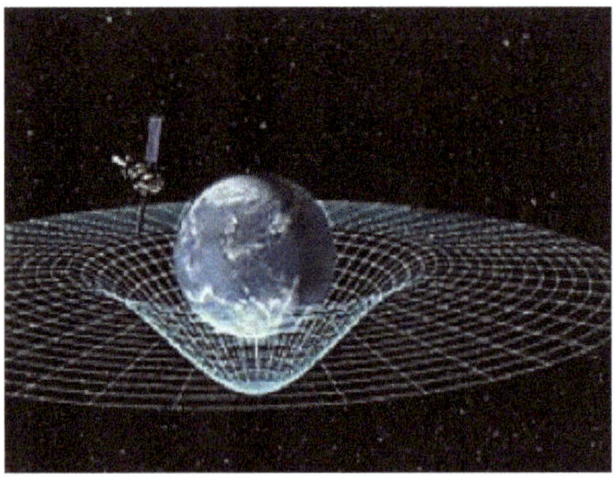

Image 21. *Spacetime curvature (credit: NASA)*

Note, however, that such effects are only visible when the speed is very high. The thing is, we humans never have to deal with such high speeds in our everyday lives. Perhaps our language (and therefore thinking) evolved to capture the aspects of everyday reality? And perhaps this is why we find theories such as Einstein's so counter-intuitive, unbelievable and ground-breaking? As we are trying to comprehend the cosmos with the mental software that evolved in a tiny village in the corner of the Universe, we might need to abandon some of that software, but can we?

Is it possible to overcome the influence of a priori concepts on our knowledge of things? (#Methods and tools)

Second, Einstein also showed that space is *not flat*. It curves near heavy objects. As discussed earlier, if I see a star in a particular location in the night sky, it does not mean that the star is actually in that location, or even in that direction.

Third, there's *quantum entanglement*. Quantum entanglement is a phenomenon that puzzles physicists because they don't know how to fit it with the rest of their beliefs. When two particles are entangled, changes in one particle result in corresponding changes in the other. When one particle changes its "spin", so does the other. But here is the puzzling thing: it has been discovered that changes happen instantaneously no matter how far away the two particles are from each other. Suppose one of the particles is near my desk. Let's put the second particle near your desk. I change the spin of my particle – the spin of yours changes at the same exact moment. Now, let's move your particle to the other side of the Universe. I change the spin of my particle – and the spin of yours, again, changes at the same exact moment. But we know that nothing in space can travel faster than the speed of light – nothing, including information. So how does the second particle "know" that the first one has changed its spin? They are so far away from each other that it should take years for this information to reach to the other side. What if entangled particles seem to be far away from each other, but in fact they are very close because space is not a real thing but just a category of our mind that we impose on our perceptual experiences?

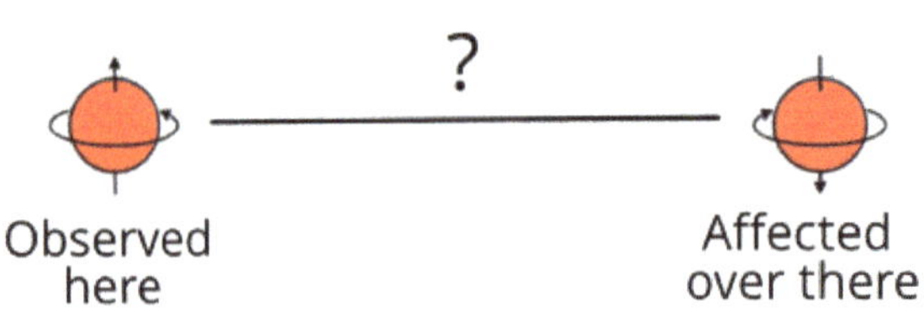

Image 22. *Quantum entanglement*

Time

Regarding the notion of time.

In the strange world of quantum mechanics, events of the present may change the past. In the double-slit experiments with a single electron, we believe that the electron passes through both slits simultaneously. Because, until it is observed, it exists as a "wave" of mathematical probabilities. This "wave" passes through both slits, interferes with itself and creates a curious interference pattern on the optical screen on the other side of the box.

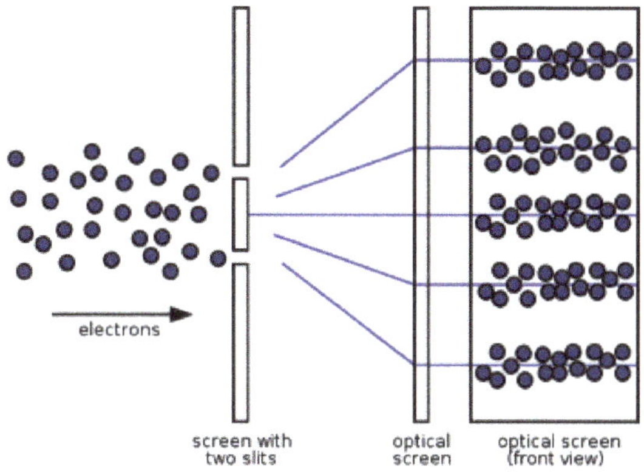

Image 23. Unobserved, an electron passes through both slits at the same time

If we observe the electron *before* it passes through the slits (for example, register its location with a magnetic detector), the wave function collapses and it behaves like a particle. It passes through just one of the slits and does not create the interference pattern on the optical screen.

However, if we observe the electron *after* it has passed through the slits, but *before* it hits the optical screen on the other side, the wave function also collapses and it also behaves like a particle, and the interference pattern is not created. This is what happens:

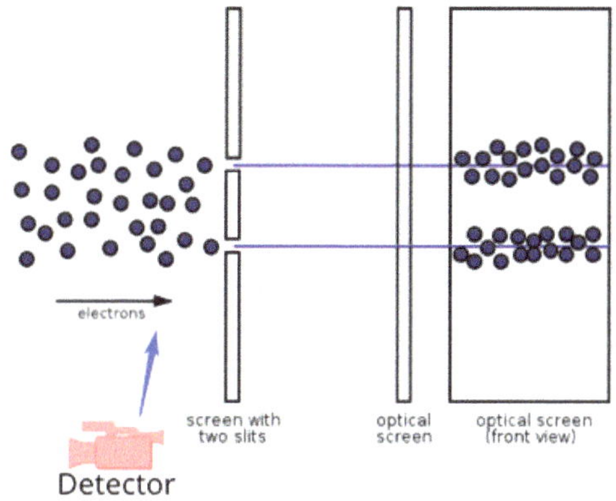

Image 24. If you observe the electron before the slits, it will pass through only one of them

1) The electron passes through both the slits as a wave.
2) We observe it, and it starts behaving like a particle. But it can only behave like a particle if it passed through one of the slits, not both of them.
3) So the electron *changes its past*. Now in its past it went through only one of the slits.

This phenomenon when an event in the present changes the past is known as "*the quantum eraser*". Do you also think it's a little weird? Well, that's the most plausible explanation we currently have for this strange behavior of quantum objects. Perhaps it only seems weird to us because our language is not equipped to deal with this kind of reality.

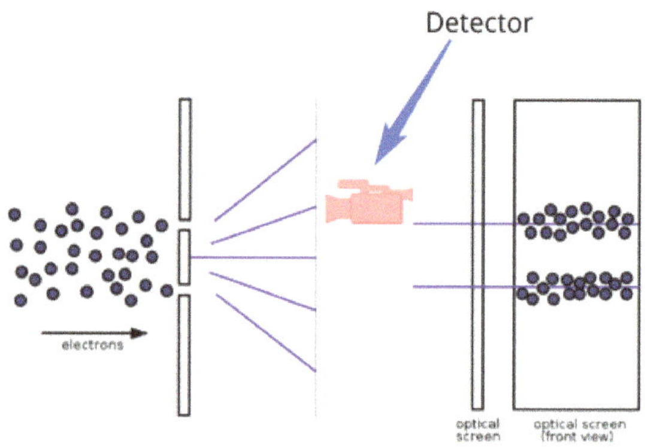

***Image 25**. If you observe the electron after the slits, it will pass through both of them, but then it will change its past. It will have gone through a single slit in its new past.*

Is it inevitable that human knowledge will be limited because human experiences are limited? (#Perspectives)

Physicists are also saying that there is no theoretical reason why "the arrow of time" cannot be reversed. If time in our Universe flew in the opposite direction, our current formulas would still describe the development of this Universe perfectly well. There is no direction in these equations. This has led some theorists to suggest that we may be living in a "*pulsating universe*": currently it is expanding, but at some point it will reach the state when expansion will stop and the Universe will start shrinking, and time will start flowing backwards, and I will be writing this book again (or un-writing it?).

***Image 26**. Arrow of time*

Perhaps time does not exist, after all? Perhaps it is simply a way for our limited human minds to describe reality as it appears to us?

Critical thinking extension

All recent discoveries that I mentioned in this lesson suggest that time and space (as we know them) do not exist. Suggest, but do not prove with certainty.

Can we ever empirically demonstrate that time and space are a priori concepts? As you remember, all facts in sciences are theory-laden. If time and space are indeed a priori, then every "fact" that we empirically register will already bear the influence of these concepts.

So, can we ever get facts against the idea of time and space if every fact we get is already influenced by the idea of time and space?

Science is tough.

If you are interested…

Watch Donald Hoffman's TED talk "Do We See Reality as it Is?" (2015). This talk was discussed earlier in this lesson.

Watch the video "Quantum entanglement & spooky action at a distance" (2015) on the YouTube channel *Veritasium*.

Watch the video "How the quantum eraser rewrites the past" (2016) on the YouTube channel *PBS Space Time*.

Take-away messages

Lesson 5. In this lesson, we looked at some scientific findings that seem to be in line with the Kantian suggestion that space and time are innate concepts rather than properties of reality itself. These included: the theory of spacetime (where space and time are not separate phenomena but rather manifestations of the same thing), quantum entanglement, quantum eraser, the theory of pulsating universe and reversible arrow of time.

Lesson 6 - Linguistic nativism

Learning outcomes

a) [Knowledge and comprehension] What are the main claims of linguistic nativism?
b) [Understanding and application] How does the poverty of the stimulus (POS) argument support the idea of universal grammar?
c) [Thinking in the abstract] To what extent does the existence of universal grammar imply that human knowledge is fundamentally limited?

Key concepts

Linguistic empiricism, linguistic nativism, poverty of the stimulus (POS), universal grammar, principles of universal grammar

Other concepts used

Trial-and-error learning, co-reference, grammar constraints

Themes and areas of knowledge

Themes: Knowledge and language, Knowledge and the knower
AOK: Human Sciences

Recap and plan

To summarize the discussion so far and go further, let's agree on the following:

1) Language is a system of signs (not signals)
2) Meaning is the link between the signifier and a concept
3) Some concepts are a priori (i.e. they are innate)

Now my key question is: if some concepts are innate, does it mean that some language is innate? This is a difficult question. Remember how we deal with difficult questions? In any difficult situation, split into two camps! So, scholars have split into two camps.

The first camp (linguistic empiricism) claims that all language is learned. Children are born with no knowledge or understanding of language, and they gradually acquire language through experience (such as trial and error). You would probably not argue that believing that language is learned seems more natural than believing that language is innate.

However, the second camp – linguistic nativism – claims otherwise. According to linguistic nativists, children are already born with some understanding of language (more precisely, grammar). It may seem counter-intuitive, and that's exactly why we are devoting this lesson to linguistic nativism.

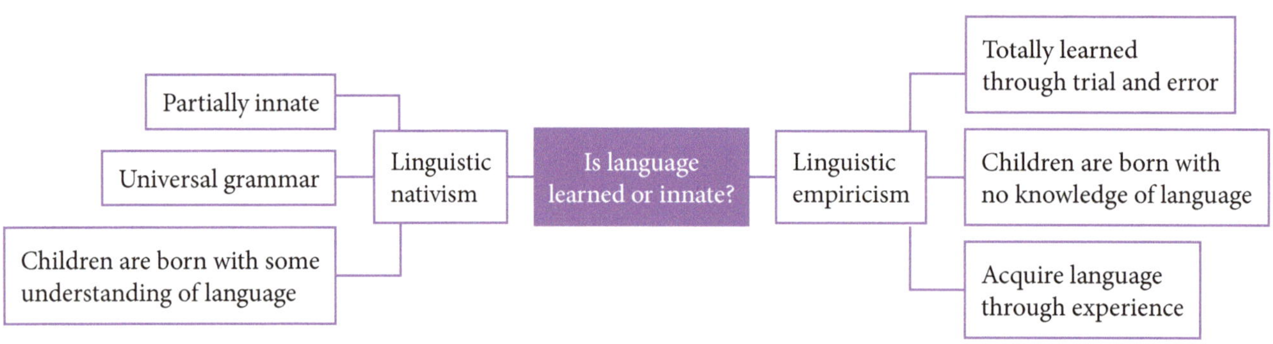

Noam Chomsky: poverty of the stimulus and universal grammar

Noam Chomsky (born 1928) is an influential linguist and philosopher who introduced the ideas of innate language. One of his key arguments was the poverty of the stimulus (POS) argument.

Poverty of the stimulus (POS) is the observation that children are exposed to quite minimal language (parents use limited grammar and vocabulary in their communication with the child, and children are never explicitly taught which grammatical structures are *incorrect*). Theoretically, from the minimal language that children are exposed to, they can infer a variety of grammars. But they don't. For any given language, they somehow infer the correct one.

To solve this problem, Chomsky suggested the existence of universal grammar. When children are born, rules of universal grammar already exist in their minds and this directs the child's learning toward correct destinations. This is how the child knows that some grammatical structures are incorrect, and this is how he/she learns language correctly based on such limited experience.

Image 27. *Universal grammar*

KEY IDEA: According to Noam Chomsky, the poor linguistic environment around children is not sufficient to explain their surprising grammar proficiency. Therefore, there must exist a universal grammar which is innate.

Ninja Turtle

Can the language we speak limit the knowledge we can possibly have? (#Methods and tools)

To understand where this reasoning comes from, consider the following couple of sentences:

(a) *The Ninja Turtle danced while he ate pizza*
(b) *He danced while the Ninja Turtle ate pizza*

The pronoun "he" in (a) can refer either to Ninja Turtle or to some other male person not mentioned in the sentence. In either case, the sentence is grammatically correct. When "he" refers to the Ninja Turtle, this is known as a co-reference ("Ninja Turtle" and "he" refer to one and the same creature). Linguistically speaking, in sentences like (a), co-reference is allowed.

However, the pronoun "he" in (b) can only refer to another male person not mentioned in the sentence. It cannot refer to the Ninja Turtle. Linguistically speaking, in sentences like (b), co-reference is not allowed.

When certain structures are not allowed in a grammar, this is known as "*grammar constraints*". So there exists a certain constraint in English grammar that does not allow speakers to have co-reference in sentences like (b).

Children know this. It can be shown experimentally. For example, Crain and McKee (1985) (as cited in Crain and Thornton, 2006) designed a study where they role-played a situation (a Ninja Turtle simultaneously dancing and eating pizza, or a Ninja Turtle dancing while another person is eating pizza). The situation was observed by Kermit the Frog, who then made a statement about what he saw by using sentences such as (a) and (b). Children had to reward Kermit the Frog with a strawberry if he described the situation correctly, and they had to remind Kermit the Frog to pay close attention if he made a mistake.

Image 28. Ninja Turtle

Image 29. Kermit the Frog

Such experiments showed that children are indeed proficient in knowing that, when the Ninja Turtle is dancing and eating pizza at the same time, (a) is grammatically allowed and (b) is not. They also knew that both (a) and (b) were allowed when the Ninja Turtle was dancing but another person was eating pizza.

Here is where linguistic nativists (like Noam Chomsky) make their poverty of the stimulus (POS) argument:

- How are children supposed to learn which sentences are allowed in which situations if they are never exposed to them? Grown-ups never produce sentences that are not allowed, and technically there is no explicit rule that tells children that it is wrong to construct a sentence like this in a situation like this.
- Children seem to possess this knowledge at a very young age, even when their linguistic experience is very limited.

Hence the idea of universal grammar.

Principles of universal grammar

If language is a tool of thinking, can we invent new languages to enable new thoughts? (#Perspectives)

Noam Chomsky believed that principles of universal grammar are the deep rules that are common to every language and cannot be violated. An example of such principle could be the rule that a pronoun that appears before the subject (such as "he" appearing before "Ninja Turtle") cannot refer to the subject, only to someone else. Principles are fixed, in the sense that they cannot differ from language to language.

The variety of human languages that can possibly exist is also constrained by principles. Not any language can exist.

KEY IDEA: Rules of universal grammar constrain the variety of human languages that can possibly exist. No language can violate these rules, therefore not any language can exist.

Just think about this. If innate universal grammar actually exists, then our children are already born with a predisposition to understand some core concepts. Nature has already pre-programmed a draft of language in every human being. The final version will differ from the first draft (depending on experience), but it cannot differ radically. If everyone starts with the same draft, then the variety of final versions will be limited.

Is it true that we are born with these a priori understandings?

Linguistic nativists have not produced anything like a comprehensive list of a priori concepts and rules that comprise universal grammar. Their main argument goes along the lines of: "The idea that language is fully learned cannot be true, because it is not consistent with data – poverty of the stimulus! Linguistic competence of children far exceeds their linguistic experience". It is an argument from the contrary: language cannot be fully learned, therefore it is partially innate.

But if linguistic nativists are right, that is huge. Language expresses concepts, and if language is partially innate, so are some concepts. So, if we accept linguistic nativism, we must also agree with Kant – maybe not specifically with his claims about space and time, but with the idea that a priori concepts exist and influence how we perceive the world.

Image 30. *Noam Chomsky in 1977*

Critical thinking extension

Assume for a moment that universal grammar exists. It means that all the languages we humans speak, or can possibly speak, share the same core principles. And obviously, because language is closely tied to concepts, this suggests that we all share the same concepts.

What these concepts are and why exactly these specific concepts are innate, we don't know. Some very sophisticated research has to be designed to find out. Linguistic nativists just claim that some core principles need to be there because otherwise we can't explain why children are so competent at language.

But language is a tool of thinking. Does this mean that we are all born with fundamentally similar tools of thinking, and hence human knowledge is fundamentally limited by these tools?

In other words, I am trying to make the logical leap from the statement "universal grammar exists" to the statement "human knowledge is fundamentally limited". To what extent do you think this leap is justified?

What are the knowledge implications of the idea that language may be innate?
(#Scope)

If you are interested...

The idea that knowledge can be innate dates back to Plato's dialogue "Meno". In this dialogue, Socrates is talking to a young slave and demonstrates that he (the slave) knows more about geometry than he could have possibly gained from experience. Plato concludes based on this that we are already born with knowledge of geometry and learning new information is not as much learning as it is remembering. You can read this dialogue on the *Project Gutenberg* website.

Take-away messages

Lesson 6. Noam Chomsky has been influential in building a theory of innate concepts. He observed that the idea that language is learned is not entirely consistent with observational data. One of the main arguments is poverty of the stimulus (POS): the idea that linguistic competence of children exceeds their linguistic experience. In other words, linguistic inputs that children receive (phrases they hear from others, instances when they are taught directly) are not enough to become as proficient in language as they are. To Chomsky, this suggests that there exists a universal grammar – a set of innate concepts and rules of their combination that govern the acquisition and the use of any existing language. Universal grammar contains a set of principles - rules that are common to all languages and cannot be violated. Principles of universal grammar constrain the variety of human languages that can possibly exist. It may also be the case that universal grammar fundamentally limits human knowledge.

Lesson 7 - The continuity hypothesis

Learning outcomes

a) [Knowledge and comprehension] What is the continuity hypothesis?
b) [Understanding and application] To what extent is the continuity hypothesis supported by evidence?
c) [Thinking in the abstract] Can there ever be enough evidence to answer the question "Is language learned or innate" with certainty?

Key concepts

The continuity hypothesis, language-A, language-B, language-C

Other concepts used

Universal grammar, wh-questions, linguistic nativism

Themes and areas of knowledge

Themes: Knowledge and language, Knowledge and the knower
AOK: Human Sciences

Recap and plan

We have discussed linguistic nativism. We have pointed out that if we accept linguistic nativism, it will have major implications. For example, we will also have to accept the existence of a priori concepts and perhaps agree with Kant that there is an unbridgeable gap between reality and appearance.

For this reason, many scholars find it difficult to accept the idea of nativism in linguistic development. The opposite idea (that language is learned) seems so much more intuitively obvious. But nativists claim that this idea is not consistent with evidence, such as poverty of the stimulus.

Today, this debate has taken the form of looking for empirical evidence. Both camps have agreed that they will not convince each other with just arguments, so they agreed to turn to data. In this lesson we will look at one such example: the continuity hypothesis.

Language-A, language-B and language-C

Let's first invent some new words. English does not have enough words for the different concepts behind the word "language" that I'm about to use, so why not invent some?

Why is it important to know if language is learned or innate? (#Scope)

Let us agree that:

- Language-A is language in a generic sense, a system of meaningful signs. When we ask "When did humans acquire language?", "Are there concepts without language?", "What role does language play in the acquisition of knowledge?", these are all about language-A.
- Language-B is a naturally existing language. English, Mandarin, Italian, Russian – these are all examples of language-B. Language B is a specific manifestation of language-A.
- Language-C is a language as it is used by a particular individual. For example, when a 4-year-old boy speaks English, they speak language-C, but not necessarily language-B. Obviously, as they grow up, language-C becomes more and more similar to the "standard" language-B. But, arguably, there still remains a difference.

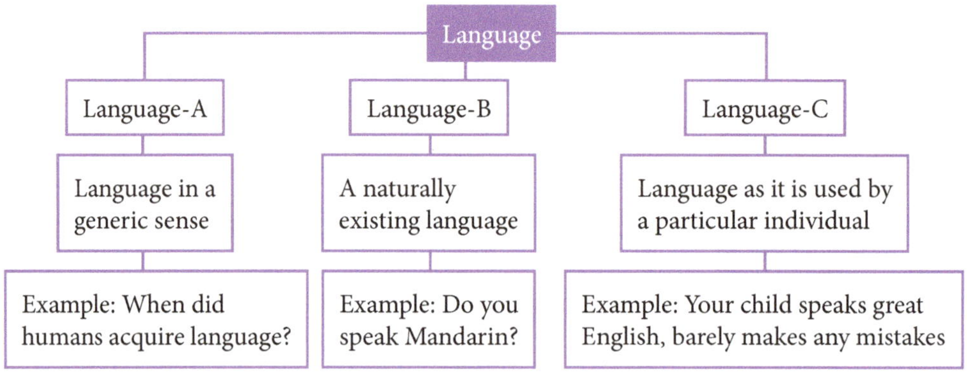

The continuity hypothesis

In the process of language acquisition, children eventually learn to use the adult version of the grammar of their native language. Language-C becomes more similar to language-B. But before that happens, they make mistakes. Language-C is "incorrect" from the point of view of language-B. Children can construct sentences that are not allowed in adult grammar. (For example, my daughter liked using phrases such as "*We goed to the beach*", "*I wake uped*" and "*Two toilets paper*").

Proponents of the nativist view on language closely study these mistakes. They observe that the illegal structures that children produce are usually legal in one of the other existing languages. On the other hand, according to them, children never violate principles of universal grammar.

***Image 31**. Child language*

In other words:

1) Language-A has certain rules that language-C never violates.
2) If language-C produces a structure that is incorrect in language-B, there always exists another language-B where this structure is correct.

Does this make sense? It means that my daughter never uses incorrect grammar – she just speaks one of the other natural languages that exist out there. Her grammar is correct, but not in the language I speak. If she makes a mistake in forming a grammatical structure (such as "I wake uped"), there probably exists a language in which the past tense is formed exactly like that. At any given point in time, she is speaking a possible human language.

This idea is known as the continuity hypothesis.

KEY IDEA: The continuity hypothesis suggested by linguistic nativists asserts that child language can differ from local adult language only in ways that adult languages differ from each other.

Supporting evidence

How big of a role does empirical evidence have in human sciences? (#Methods and tools)

Here is an example to illustrate the continuity hypothesis and some data that has been found to support it.

Wh-questions are questions beginning with words such as Why, What, When, Where, Who. Which. In English, the wh-word in the question must be immediately followed by the auxiliary verb (be, do, can, have, etc.). Here are examples of grammatically correct wh-questions in English:

- Why is he staring?
- What do you plan to do about it?
- Where are we going?
- Who do you want to travel with?

And here are examples of wh-questions that are grammatically incorrect in English:

- Why he is staring?
- What you plan to do about it?
- Where we are going?
- Who you want to travel with?

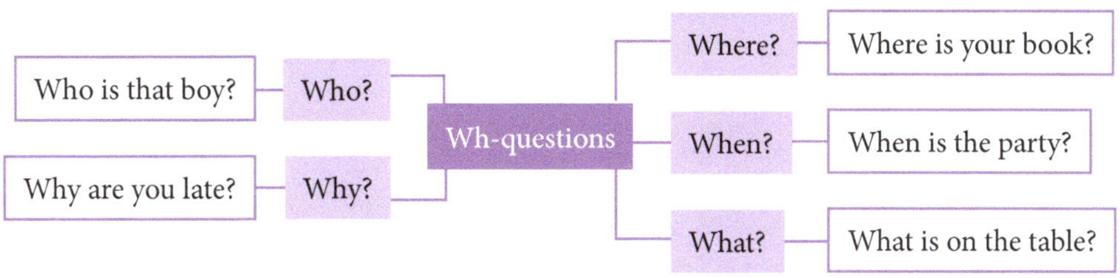

It is all pretty much the same in Italian, with the exception that *perché* (the Italian for *why*) can be followed by other words in simple questions, but not in complex questions. So, for example, the question *Why did your friend say that he would resign?* is a complex question. Nothing can go in between why and the auxiliary verb *did*. But the question *Why your friend already has resigned?* is a simple question, and in Italian it is allowed to use other words after *why* and before the auxiliary verb (Thornton, 2004, as cited in Crain and Thornton, 2006).

Here's a table that summarizes what I've just said:

Is it allowed to have other words between the wh-word and the auxiliary verb in a question?		
	Complex questions	Simple questions
What, When, Where, Who	English: not allowed Italian: not allowed	English: not allowed Italian: not allowed
Why	English: not allowed Italian: not allowed	English: not allowed **Italian: yes, allowed!**

Let's now turn to the children.

Studies of child English (language-C) have shown that:

1) Children often produce non-adult why-questions (such as "Why he is staring?")
2) They do it even after they have learned to produce correct adult questions with all of the other wh-words (What, When, Where, Who)
3) They only produce non-adult grammatical forms in simple questions, but not in complex questions

Certainly, this is a finding that is difficult to explain if you believe that language is learned. Why would children learn to use complex questions correctly before they learn to use simple forms of the same questions correctly? Moreover, they must hear more simple questions around them, so they should learn simple questions faster because there is more practice. This is not what data suggests, however. Thornton (2004) explains this finding from the perspective of the continuity hypotheses: when children use a grammatically incorrect form of English why-questions (such as "Why he is staring?"), they are simply speaking grammatically correct Italian!

Sounds like a weird finding, right? But this finding is more consistent with the view that language is innate compared to the view that language is learned. Obviously, however, it does not mean that this finding "proves" that language is innate.

KEY IDEA: Some evidence (e.g. Thornton, 2004) is more consistent with the view that language is innate than with the view that language is learned. But this is far from being a conclusive proof.

Critical thinking extension

Can we ever find out with certainty if language is learned or innate? (#Perspectives)

Let's take a step back and talk about the role of evidence in human sciences.

The question of whether language is learned or innate belongs to the realm of human sciences. It is related to the activity of humans as cultural beings. The question is very broad. It asks about language on the whole.

Compare the question "Is language learned or innate?" to the question "How many words on average are used by 5-year-old children in bilingual families?" The first question is very broad, and the second one is quite specific. It should be easy to conduct a study to find out the answer to the second question, but how easy is it to conduct a study to find out the answer to the first one?

You have seen in this lesson that research such as Thornton (2004) contributes evidence to the continuity hypothesis, which contributes evidence to the idea of universal grammar, which supports the idea that language is innate. But is this kind of evidence sufficient to make such broad generalizations?

And on a broader scale, do you think we can ever conduct *enough* research for us to conclusively accept one position over the other?

If you are interested...

The debate between nativists and those who believe that all language is learned is going on. It has taken the form of inventive experiments and observations that are conducted with children to see which of the hypotheses is more consistent with data. To a large extent, the outcome of this debate depends on how you interpret available data. We are trying to get more and more data in a desperate attempt to make our conclusions more... well, conclusive. One result of this collective effort is the existence of databases like CHILDES.

CHILDES stands for "Child language data exchange system". It is a publicly available corpus of language produced by young children. It has data in the form of transcripts, audios and videos. The database constantly grows as users submit more data. Essentially, CHILDES is a huge collection of child utterances. You can analyze it just like you analyze any other collection of texts. For example, you can count how frequently certain grammatical constructions appear in the speech of children of a certain age.

If you want to get first-hand experience with CHILDES, here is the link: https://childes.talkbank.org/.

Take-away messages

Lesson 7. The continuity hypothesis suggests that children are already born with the rules of universal grammar and, if they make mistakes in their speech, those mistakes are actually correct grammar in one of the existing languages. Therefore, children are not making mistakes but they are instead fine-tuning the parameters to the language of their parents. There is some experimental support for the continuity hypothesis, but of course it does not offer a "conclusive proof" of the idea that language is innate. How much proof is enough is a question that is open to debate.

Lesson 8 - Mentalese

Learning outcomes

a) [Knowledge and comprehension] What is Mentalese (the language of thought)?
b) [Understanding and application] What evidence can support the existence of Mentalese?
c) [Thinking in the abstract] Do animals speak Mentalese?

Key concepts

Language of thought (Mentalese)

Other concepts used

Linguistic nativism, linguistic empiricism, pre-linguistic creatures, mental representations, universal grammar

Themes and areas of knowledge

Themes: Knowledge and language, Knowledge and the knower
AOK: Human Sciences

Recap and plan

We are assuming that meaning is the link between a signifier (e.g. a word) and the signified (i.e. the concept).

This raises the question of the exact nature of this link. Is it causal, that is, does one influence the other? If so, do concepts influence language or does language influence concepts? Can one exist without the other? For example, can pre-linguistic creatures have concepts?

Essentially, these are questions about the relationship between language and thought. Not easy to answer, but we will try to shed some light on it in this lesson.

What are we debating about?

Assuming that language is secondary to thought, what implications does it have for knowledge? (#Perspectives)

The debate is about what influences what: does language influence thought or does thought influence language? I know that it is very tempting to say "both", but view this as a chicken-and-egg problem: which one is the primary influencer? Which one was there in the beginning?

***Image 32**. Language of thought*

If you belong to the camp that says "*In the beginning, there was thought, and thought influenced language*", you believe that:

1) Concepts can exist without language. They get expressed in language, but they can exist without it.
2) There is some other structure existing behind language – the "language of thought".
3) The language that we speak is an attempt to translate this "language of thought" into a conventional language accessible to others (English, Spanish, Mandarin).
4) It is possible for language to be insufficient to express the thought you want to express.

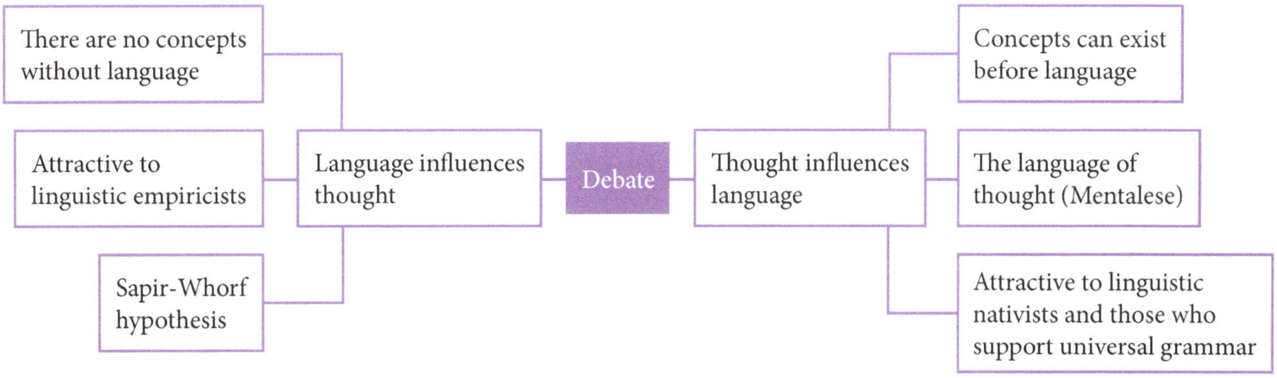

If you are with the camp that says "*In the beginning, there was language, and language influenced thought*", you believe that:

1) There are no concepts without language.
2) The "language of thought" – the hypothetical structure behind the language we speak – does not exist. This is because we think in the same language as we speak.
3) The language you speak determines the way you think and the concepts through which you understand the world.
4) The more languages one speaks, the richer their concepts and the deeper their understanding of the world.

The first position is more attractive to *linguistic nativists* and those who support the existence of *universal grammar*. The hypothetical "language of thought" that I mentioned is also referred to as Mentalese. That's the focus of the current lesson. The second position is more attractive to *linguistic empiricists* and proponents of Sapir-Whorf hypothesis (we will talk about this hypothesis in the following lessons).

KEY IDEA: Mentalese is the hypothetical "language of thought". The language that we speak is an attempt to translate Mentalese into a conventional language like English or Mandarin, but Mentalese can exist without these conventional languages.

Can there be concepts without language?

Donald Davidson, an American philosopher, thought that concepts cannot exist without language. According to him, a belief existing only as a private attitude, without being expressed in language, is "not intelligible". And therefore "a creature must be a member of a speech community if it is to have the concept of belief" (Davidson, 1975, p.170).

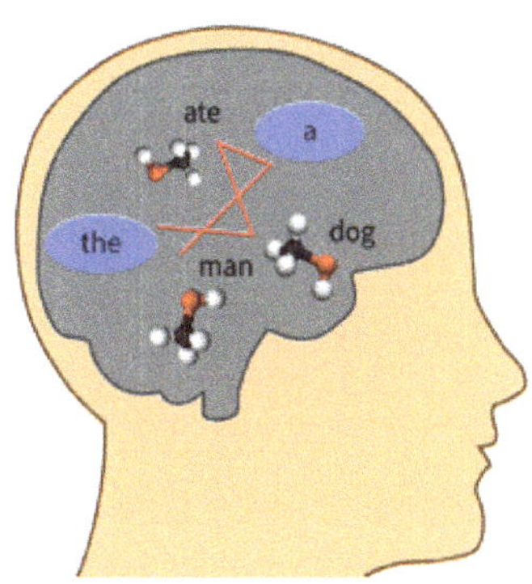

***Image 33**. Conceptual structures in the mind*

Do we think in the same language as we speak? (#Methods and tools)

On the other hand, if we believe that concepts cannot exist without language, how can we explain that sometimes we have a thought that we find difficult to formulate or express? We feel like we know what we want to say, but we struggle to put it into a verbal form. Does it show that we first think (in concepts) and then speak?

Give a muffin to a mouse

Steven Pinker in one of his TED talks "*What Our Language Habits Reveal*" (2005) discusses the following statements:

1) Give a muffin to a mouse
2) Give a mouse a muffin

***Image 34**. Mouse and a muffin*

He notes that hundreds of verbs in English can be used in both types of constructions: "verb-thing-to-a-recipient" and "verb-recipient-thing". It looks like the rule we can generalize is that any verb can appear in both constructions.

However, there are also some exceptions to the rule, such as in the following sentences:

3) Bill drove the car to Chicago
4) * Bill drove Chicago the car
5) * Sal gave a headache to Jason
6) Sal gave Jason a headache

Sentences 4 and 5 (marked with an asterisk) sound odd and are grammatically incorrect in English. But why? Even using the same verb "to give", why can we say "Give a muffin to a mouse", but not "Give a headache to Jason"?

Because these sentences express different concepts, or different thoughts. One thought is "cause X to go to Y". Another thought is "cause Y to have X".

Language	The thought that is being expressed	Explanation
Alex gave a muffin to a mouse	Alex caused the muffin to go to the mouse	Both are acceptable, a slightly different focus in the meaning.
Alex gave a mouse a muffin	Alex caused the mouse to have a muffin	
Bill drove the car to Chicago	Bill caused the car to go to Chicago	It's possible to cause the car to go to Chicago, but it is not possible to cause Chicago to have a car because cities cannot "possess" something.
* [incorrect] Bill drove Chicago the car	Bill caused Chicago to have a car	
* [incorrect] Sal gave a headache to Jason	Sal caused headache to go to Jason	It is possible to cause Jason to have a headache, but it is weird to think of someone causing headache to move from one place to another. Headache is not an object that we can move.
Sal gave Jason a headache	Sal caused Jason to have a headache	

As Steven Pinker says, "there's a level of fine-grained conceptual structure which we automatically and unconsciously compute every time we produce or utter a sentence, that governs our use of language" (Pinker, 2005). This "*language of thought*" that is unfolding behind the scenes as we speak our natural language is known as "Mentalese".

KEY IDEA: According to the language of thought hypothesis, there is conceptual structure that we compute prior to uttering a sentence. This conceptual structure gets expressed in language, but it does not need language to be formulated.

"Mentalese" is an old concept, but it has been revived in modern times by American philosopher Jerry Fodor. There have even been attempts to describe Mentalese or to create something like a dictionary and grammar.

But the point is, from these examples it seems like it is the language of thought that has the primary function. We use language because we try to express thoughts. It is the thought (or the concept) that decides if we can use a certain language construction or not ("give a muffin to a mouse" versus "give headache to Jason").

The opposite side of the debate is the claim that language influences thought, that it is the language we speak that imposes constraints on our concepts. The most famous formulation of this position is known as the Sapir-Whorf hypothesis, and we will handle it in the next lesson.

Can moral principles exist when they are not expressed in a language? (#Ethics)

Critical thinking extension

Another interesting strategy to support the claim that concepts can exist without language is to demonstrate that even pre-linguistic creatures have concepts. In a sense, if we demonstrate that animals have concepts, we can claim that animals "speak" some form of Mentalese.

The BBC Documentary "Inside the Animal Mind" in Episode 2/3 ("The Problem Solvers") demonstrates that crows can solve puzzles of incredible complexity. In one such puzzle, a crow had to perform a series of eight steps in order to retrieve a food reward. The crow had to use a small stick to retrieve several rocks, then drop these rocks in a container to make its lid open under the weight, then take the now accessible longer stick and finally use the longer stick to retrieve food. It was a situation unfamiliar to the crow. No cat or dog can solve a problem as complex as this!

Can pre-linguistic creatures have concepts? (#Scope)

For further examples, you can also read the article "13 surprisingly weird reasons why crows and ravens are the best birds, no question" by Michelle Starr published in *Science Alert* (December 31, 2017).

***Image 35**. Crows are smarter than you might think*

Experiments like this suggest that the crow "knows" when it needs to use a long stick and what happens to a lid when heavy objects are placed on it. The crow has a mental representation of length and weight. But the question is, does the crow – a pre-linguistic creature – have the *concepts* of length and weight? Or are these just complex automatic reflexes?

If you are interested...

Watch Steven Pinker's TED talk "What our language habits reveal" (2005). It was mentioned earlier in this lesson.

Another one of his talks – "Human nature and the blank slate" (2003) – is also worth watching in the same context. Here, he focuses more specifically on the idea that humans may be born with some innate traits and defends this idea against critics.

Take-away messages

Lesson 8. One of the big debates around language and concepts is what influences what. If you take the side of linguistic nativism, it would be natural to suggest that concepts come first and language comes second. A child is born with a predisposition to comprehend certain ideas and structures (such as the concept of time, the concept of space, the idea of causing something to go somewhere, the idea of causing someone to have something, etc.). Language is then used to express these thoughts. There is a term for this hypothetical "language of thought" – Mentalese. Researchers such as Steven Pinker are proponents of the idea that Mentalese exists and influences how we use language.

Lesson 9 - Sapir-Whorf hypothesis

Learning outcomes

a) [Knowledge and comprehension] What is the strong and the weak version of the Sapir-Whorf hypothesis?
b) [Understanding and application] What evidence is there to support the hypothesis?
c) [Thinking in the abstract] To what extent can we settle the debate between "thought influences language" and "language influences thought" by acknowledging that both processes take place?

Key concepts

Sapir-Whorf hypothesis (strong version, weak version), "core Mentalese", "peripheral Mentalese"

Other concepts used

Perception of color, perception of time, Tarahumara, Pirahã, Tuyuca, Ayamara

Themes and areas of knowledge

Themes: Knowledge and language
AOK: Human Sciences

Recap and plan

We have been dealing with the problem of language and thought – what influences what? So far, we have focused on the view that thought influences language. If that is the case, then there must exist a special "layer" of mental concepts and structures in which our thoughts are formulated – a hypothetical "language of thought", or Mentalese. It would also suggest that variation of natural languages is restricted by rules of universal grammar that must be common to all of them. Concepts first, language second.

In this lesson, we are turning to the alternative position (language first, concepts second). The most visible milestone in this approach is the Sapir-Whorf hypothesis.

Sapir-Whorf hypothesis

Can language shape the way we think? Can speakers of two different languages be exposed to the same reality and yet represent it differently in their minds because they speak (and think) these different languages?

Are some thoughts only thinkable in some languages? (#Scope)

In 1929, linguist Edward Sapir and later his student Benjamin Whorf suggested that the way people think is strongly affected by the language they speak. This suggestion became known as the Sapir-Whorf hypothesis.

Strong and weak versions

There are actually two versions of the Sapir-Whorf hypothesis, the strong one and the weak one. The strong version asserts that our native language determines our thought. The weak version says that our native language influences thought ("influences" is not the same as "determines"!).

***Image 36**. Benjamin Whorf*

***Image 37**. Edward Sapir*

Weak version (language influences thought)	Sapir-Whorf hypothesis	Strong version (language determines thought)

To what extent does culture impose constraints on what you can possibly know? (#Scope)

Testing the hypothesis

There were some attempts to test the hypothesis experimentally. Many of them were based on the idea that language is used to categorize various aspects of reality into groups defined by the linguistic labels.

For example, take colors. In the English language, there is a distinction between "blue" and "green". However, in *Tarahumara* (a language spoken in Northern Mexico) there are no separate words for "green" and "blue". Instead, there is one word that means "green or blue" – "*siyoname*".

Kay and Kempton (1984) conducted a study comparing native speakers of English and Tarahumara. They wanted to see if this difference in language structures would influence participants' perception of color. The Sapir-Whorf hypothesis predicts that, since language influences thought, people who speak English will have a tendency to see a sharp boundary between green and blue, while people who speak Tarahumara will not.

Image 38. *The Tarahumara*
(credit: Lance Fisher, Wikimedia Commons)

This prediction was supported by results. When presented with two colors close to the green-blue boundary (blueish green and greenish blue), English speakers perceived these two colors as more different than Tarahumara speakers did. It is as if language caused the perception of English speakers to push these colors further apart.

Pirahã – language with no time and no numbers

Obviously, there is a very long leap from the observation that speakers of certain languages categorize colors a little differently to the strong claim that language determines how we think. Is there any other evidence for the belief that language determines (or at least influences) thought, something more substantial?

Proponents of the Sapir-Whorf hypothesis have used anthropological observations of cultures that speak unusual languages as evidence to support their claims.

A popular example is *Pirahã* - a language spoken by a single tribe in Brazil. Reportedly, this language has no way to express the concept of time. For instance, take this English-language sentence: "When I finished reading my TOK textbook yesterday, I was so inspired that I rethought my whole life". If you were to construct a Pirahã equivalent of this sentence, you would end up with something along the lines of: "I read a TOK textbook, I am inspired and I rethink my life". Did it happen in the past, is it happening now, will it happen later? There is no way to tell.

Image 39. *The Pirahã*
(credit: Alisha Jaison.c, Wikimedia Commons)

As a result of this, some researchers claim that the experiences of Pirahã people are "trapped in the present" (von Bredow, 2006). Unlike most other cultures, they have no myth of the origin of the Universe – when asked how the world began, they simply say that everything is the same. If something is not important in the present, it quickly loses significance and is forgotten; for example, very few Pirahã remember the names of all four grandparents.

Should moral reasoning depend on your cultural origin? (#Ethics)

These findings mainly come from researcher Daniel Everett, who spent years living among the Pirahã and trying to make sense of their language and culture.

Perhaps even more astonishingly, the Pirahã language does not have any numbers. Additionally, they do not use words like many, any, more, less. When their mathematical abilities were tested, researchers were surprised to see that even the basic understanding of arithmetic was missing. For example, they could not remember if three or eight nuts were placed in a can. Without words for numbers, the Pirahã seem to be unable to understand the concept of numbers or quantity (Gordon, 2004). This brings up the question: are we only able to form thoughts in our mind if we have certain words in our language? Everett attempted to teach the Pirahã to count to ten and reportedly spent several months doing so, but all in vain. Indeed, they seemed simply unable to comprehend this mental dimension of human existence.

Criticism

There are doubts regarding both the Sapir-Whorf hypothesis and the research supporting it.

First, if bearers of different languages indeed had fundamentally different conceptual structures in their minds, learning a second language would not be possible. However, in reality, even learning a language that is entirely different from your native tongue is possible. After all, Daniel Everett – an English speaker – learned the language of the Pirahã.

Second, research such as Kay and Kempton (1984) shows only insignificant influences of language on thought (categorization of colors is not a big deal). We want some more fundamental results to reach fundamental conclusions.

Third, fundamental results come from anthropological studies of societies like the Pirahã, but such studies are not rigorously controlled and it is difficult to cross-check the conclusions. One needs to learn the Pirahã language in order to conduct a study with them! Some critics have said that the Pirahã actually understand time and quantity, but the researchers misinterpreted the results of their observations. Want to check? Go live with the Pirahã, learn their language and repeat the study! Be my guest.

Do you agree that it is only possible to understand how people think if you speak their language? (#Methods and tools)

Today, practically no one supports the strong version of the Sapir-Whorf hypothesis ("language determines thought"), but many scholars accept the weak version ("language influences thought"). The exact extent of this influence, however, remains to be established.

KEY IDEA: The weak form of the Sapir-Whorf hypothesis is widely accepted today because there is evidence that language affects some aspects of cognition, but the strong form is not accepted. How fundamental is the influence of language on thought? It remains unclear.

Critical thinking extension

What if you want to accept linguistic nativism, Mentalese, the continuity hypothesis, and the Sapir-Whorf hypothesis all at the same time? It could probably be possible if you assumed that there exist two layers in Mentalese:

1) The "core Mentalese" – this consists of concepts and structures that are a priori and innate. All people have these concepts and all people think this way.
2) The "peripheral Mentalese" – this consists of concepts and structures that are learned through experience (a posteriori). It may be different for different people and cultures.

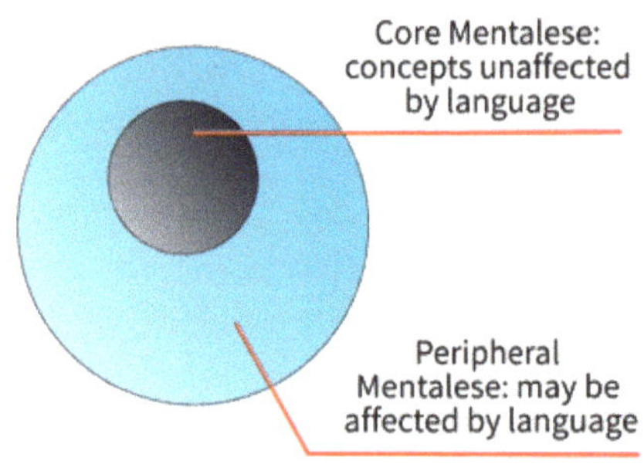

***Image 40**. Core and peripheral Mentalese*

Once this distinction is made, there seems to be no contradiction. Then, we would claim "thought first, language second" for the core Mentalese, but accept "language first, thought second" for the peripheral Mentalese.

But to what extent would we be justified in making the assumption that these two layers of Mentalese exist?

If you are interested...

You might find it interesting to review some further anthropological evidence from cultures whose languages are unusual. For example:

1) *Tuyuca*, a language spoken by an indigenous ethnic group of around 1,000 people in Colombia and Brazil, is a language with "mandatory evidentiality". This means that it is linguistically impossible to make a statement without making a reference to how you know it. So instead of simply saying "The dog is running around the house", you must say something like "The dog is running around the house and I know this because I saw it".
2) *The Aymara language* is a language spoken by people living in the Andes of South America. Instead of referencing the future as something lying ahead of them, bearers of this language reference the future as something lying behind them, and vice versa. They even gesture in front of them when speaking about the past and gesture behind them when speaking about the future. Apparently, the cultural reasoning that went into this is that the future is unknown to us and invisible, while the past has already happened, so here it is – right in front of our eyes.

For these and related examples, read the article "10 languages with uniquely bizarre quirks" by Morris M. published on *Listverse* (March 12, 2015).

Take-away messages

Lesson 9. The opposite side in the debate is the idea that the language we speak influences the way we think, hence language influences (or even determines) concepts. The claim that language determines thought is known as the Sapir-Whorf hypothesis. It is based on anthropological studies of societies with unusual languages, such as a language having no words for numbers. Research has shown that people who speak such languages apparently differ from the rest of us in how they conceptualize the world, or at least some aspects of it. How can quantity, for example, be an innate concept if people whose language does not have words for numbers cannot understand the idea of quantity? There are some arguments against the Sapir-Whorf hypothesis, but at least in its weak form (that language *influences* rather than *determines* thought) it still stands.

6.3 - Language and communication

We had quite a mind-blowing journey into the depths of the human mind, trying to figure out how language interacts with thought. We considered both sides of the debate: "language influences thought" and "thought influences language". We have looked at concepts, the building blocks of thought, and we have discussed how concepts shape what we can know.

As mentioned at the start of this unit, language is both a tool of thinking and a tool of communication. It is time now to consider its second function as a tool of communication. The reason I chose to talk about thinking first and communication second is because thinking is heavily involved in any act of communication. In fact, is communication even possible without thinking?

When we send a message to another person, we need to encode our thought (the idea we are trying to convey) in a language that we both know, and that person will need to decode our message. They will need to figure out what we meant by what we said.

In the next several lessons, I will be operating with the term Mentalese. I will assume that Mentalese exists. But even if you do not believe so, just mentally replace it with "thoughts", and all the arguments will still be valid.

We will be looking at the problem of translation. I will make the claim that any act of communication is also an act of translation, even when the two people speak the same language. The translation is from Mentalese to the natural language and back. We will look at the key problem in this area – untranslatability.

Since communication is translation, it is of interest to know if machine translation can be adequate. If we can teach machines to translate, does it mean we can also teach them to understand Mentalese, in other words, to think? That would be huge.

Finally, we will consider the problem of loaded language. Loaded language is possible because our language is so rich and there exist multiple labels for the same thing. By carefully selecting the label, we can manipulate the emotions and beliefs of the recipients of the message. Language is rich, but this richness unleashes a power that can potentially be harmful. There are ethical issues involved here.

Lesson 10 - Translation

Learning outcomes

a) [Knowledge and comprehension] What does it mean that translation lies at the core of communication?
b) [Understanding and application] Can we claim that there are things in every language that are fundamentally untranslatable?
c) [Thinking in the abstract] Can we ever be certain that a translation is correct?

Key concepts

Communication, translation, untranslatability, indeterminacy of translation

Other concepts used

Components of communication, coding, decoding, Mentalese

Themes and areas of knowledge

Themes: Knowledge and language
AOK: Human Sciences

Recap and plan

We have analyzed language as a tool of thinking, which is not an easy task. The big question that we were answering was: does language influence thought or does thought influence language? We do not have a conclusive answer, but we do recognize that this is a very important debate and, whatever the answer is, it will have serious implications for knowledge.

It seems like we could be dealing with a bidirectional influence, which means that thought influences language on a deep level (universal grammar, a priori concepts), but language we speak can also influence the way we think on a somewhat more superficial level (a posteriori concepts).

In any case, we agreed that the meaning of a linguistic unit is its connection to the concept or a thought that is being expressed.

With that in mind, how does language work as a tool of communication? Are there any knowledge problems that we encounter in this process, and what are they?

Components of communication

Are there ways in which language creates an obstacle for communication of ideas? (#Methods and tools)

Any communication, in a nutshell, is a process where one person sends a message and another person receives it. But it is slightly more complicated than you might think at first:

1) The sender has an idea that he or she wants to send across. This idea exists in the mental world (Mentalese).
2) The sender codes this idea, or translates it into a language. The idea becomes a message.
3) Using language, the message is sent.
4) The recipient receives the message.
5) The recipient decodes the message, that is, translates it from its language into the language of ideas and concepts (Mentalese).

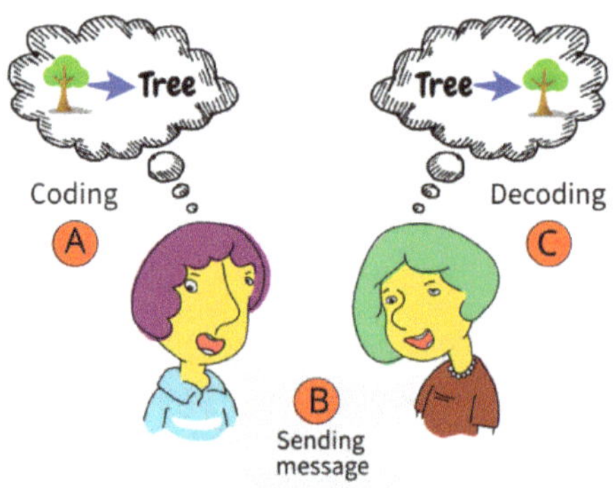

Image 41. Communication

Obviously, communication is successful when (1) and (5) coincide. But many things can go wrong.

Translation as a key communication problem

Who is responsible for miscommunication of ideas that results from inadequate translation? (#Ethics)

It may seem unusual to start this discussion with translation. After all, translation is not the first thing that comes to your mind when you think of "communication". However, I would claim that the problems of translation are central to the process of communication on the whole.

What is translation? Translation is when you take a text in one language (also called the source language), reconstruct the meaning behind it (Mentalese) and express this meaning in another language (also called the target language) .

Contrary to a popular belief, there are not two languages that are involved in translation, but three. One of these languages is Mentalese, the language of thought. If you throw it out of the picture, translation will take the form of superficial connections between structures of two languages – more or less exactly what machine translation engines (such as Google Translate) do. But if you have ever tried machine translation, you will know how clumsy it can get.

KEY IDEA: Translation lies at the core of every act of communication, even when people speak the same language. Mentalese is one of the languages always involved in the translation process.

You might argue that translation is *not* the key problem of communication. That translation is only a problem when the two people speak different languages (and think in these different languages), and in a regular conversation between same language speakers, translation is not involved.

But I claim that translation is involved even in this case. It is less obvious, but it is still at work. You still need to translate what your friend says into what he/she means (from their native language to Mentalese). There is no direct correspondence between these two. A lot depends on the context. For example, when your friend says "I wonder if you could pass me the salt?", you "translate" this to understand that they are not merely wondering about your ability to pass the salt, they are actually asking you to pass it.

Untranslatability

A curious phenomenon that defines the limits of translation, and therefore communication, is untranslatability. As the name suggests, untranslatability is the inability of something from one language to be adequately translated into another language.

KEY IDEA: Untranslatability is the inability of something from one language to be adequately translated into another language

If an utterance is untranslatable, does it mean that the thought behind it is unthinkable? (#Scope)

Thai language has words equivalent to the English pronouns "I", "you", "he/she", but they are used rarely and only in formal settings. In everyday speech, Thai people don't use such pronouns. Instead, they refer to the roles in relation to each other. If a mother wants to say to her child "I will read you a story", she will – literally – say "Mother will tell child a story". If an older friend wants to say to a younger friend "I like your new haircut", they will say – literally – "Older sibling likes the younger sibling's new haircut". When we translate such utterances into

English, we simply use pronouns, but this culturally specific perception of relations gets lost in translation. The meaning changes slightly.

Similarly, it is typical in English to say phrases such as "I have a car" or "I have a husband". The same idea in Russian, if translated literally, would read: "At me there is a car" and "With me there is a husband". In the Russian language, it is not so much about possession as it is about being in close proximity to something or someone. This shade of meaning gets lost in translation.

Untranslatability is not limited to grammar; it also exists on the level of separate words.

1) Waldeinsamkeit (German) – the feeling of solitude or connectedness to nature when being alone in the woods
2) Wabi-Sabi (Japanese) – finding beauty in imperfections
3) Saudade (Portuguese) – the feeling of longing for an absent something or someone that you love that might never return
4) Forelsket (Norwegian) – the euphoria experienced as you begin to fall in love
5) Mamihlapinatapei (Yagan, one of the indigenous languages of Tierra del Fuego) – the wordless, meaningful look shared by two people who both desire to initiate something but are both reluctant to do so

***Image 42**. An untranslatable word*

As a general rule of thumb, in any language pair there always exist some structures that cannot be adequately translated. Translators go to great lengths to convey such ideas. They may describe the meaning instead of directly translating the word, or they may even replace the structure completely with something that creates similar associations in the target language. In other words, they go from being "translators" to being "interpreters".

KEY IDEA: In any language pair there always exist some structures that cannot be adequately translated

How can we tell if knowledge is precisely communicated from one knower to another? (#Perspectives)

Critical thinking extension

W.V.O. Quine's indeterminacy of translation

The 20th-century American philosopher W.V.O. Quine described the following hypothetical situation. A native speaker of Arunta (a made-up language) saw a rabbit and uttered the word "*gavagai*" (Quine, 2013, p. 23-29). A speaker of English hears this and tries to translate it.

***Image 43**. Williard Van Orman Quine (1908-2000)*

There are multiple possible translations that fit the available evidence equally well:

- Look, a rabbit
- Let's go hunting
- Look, food
- Look, an undetached rabbit part
- It's going to rain (the native may be superstitious, and there may exist a belief that seeing a rabbit causes rain)

W.V.O. Quine claimed that translation is always "underdetermined by evidence"; that is, for any given utterance and context, there always exist multiple possible translations. He called this phenomenon "indeterminacy of translation".

The vast number of possible translations in this case may be reduced by asking the native speaker a series of questions to further establish the context. For example, we might ask, "Is this *gavagai* the same as that one?" (pointing at another rabbit). Whatever the native answers, this new information can be used to eliminate some of the possible translations.

However, here is a question: can we ever be certain that a translation is correct?

Obviously, as we get to know more and more about the context, we eliminate some of the possible translations and narrow down on the ones that fit better. But can we ever have enough knowledge about the context to narrow down on *the one*?

If you are interested...

As discussed, even when people speak the same language, their communication involves constant translation between what they say and what they mean. When things go wrong, funny stuff may happen, like in that humorous exchange between hotel management and a guest regarding his soap requirements that has gone viral on the Internet. Search for "The saga of hotel soap" and you will see what I mean. Originally, this conversation appeared in Shelley Berman's 1972 book *A Hotel is a Place*.

Take-away messages

Lesson 10. Language is a tool of thinking, but also a tool of communication. In order for communication to be successful, the message (thought, idea) must be coded, then sent, then decoded by the recipient to reconstruct the original message (thought, idea). The claim that I have made in this lesson is that any communication may be viewed as translation. Even in communication between people speaking the same language, it is still a case of translation from Mentalese to the language and back (reconstructing what people mean from what they say). A curious phenomenon that delineates the limits of communication is untranslatability – the inability of a structure from one language to be adequately translated into another language. Additionally, according to W.V.O. Quine, any translation is always underdetermined by the available context, so there always exist multiple possible translations (this is known as indeterminacy of translation).

Lesson 11 - Machine translation

Learning outcomes

a) [Knowledge and comprehension] What are the two perspectives on the ability of machines to translate successfully?
b) [Understanding and application] If we assume that machines can translate adequately, what does it mean for our understanding of human language and the human mind?
c) [Thinking in the abstract] How can we judge if a machine translation is of good quality?

Key concepts

Machine translation

Other concepts used

Bilingual text corpora, Turing test, rule-based approach to machine translation, statistical approach to machine translation

Themes and areas of knowledge

Themes: Knowledge and language
AOK: Natural Sciences, Human Sciences

Recap and plan

In the previous lesson, I suggested that communication using language may be viewed as a series of acts of translation (and this holds true even if the two people speak the same language). An indispensable part of translation is going between what people say (natural language) and what they mean (Mentalese). In this sense, there's no communication without thinking.

To what extent is every act of communication an act of translation? (#Scope)

Arguably, the best way to understand what makes us human is to try and build an android. Similarly, to figure out how exactly language-based communication happens, we can try and build a machine that will translate texts from one language into another. If we succeed, we may claim that we have taught the machine to think (to use Mentalese). If we fail, we can claim that the human mind is capable of understanding which cannot be captured by a computer algorithm.

In any case, developing algorithms of machine translation is a task that, depending on the outcome, has profound implications for our understanding of language, thought and communication.

Adequate machine translator = conscious machine?

You have probably already tried translating something from a language you don't know using an online translation tool (such as Google Translate), either out of necessity or just for fun. You have probably noticed how clumsy machine translation can be at times (to have the most fun, try translating something from your language into another, and then translate the output back into your language).

Although machines seem to be getting better at this, at the moment they cannot compete with human translators.

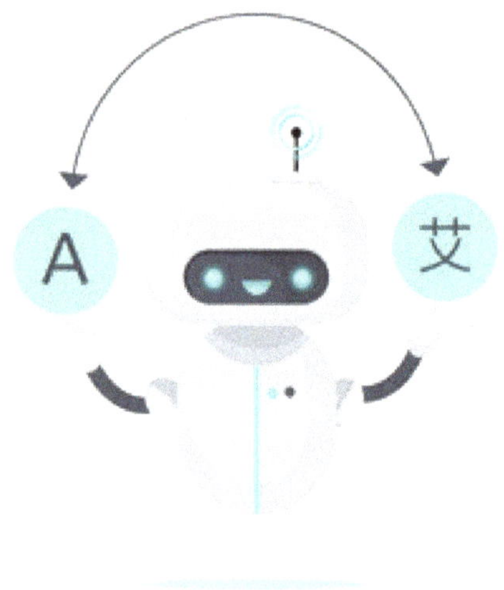

Image 44. Machine translation

But machine translation is so central to understanding language, communication and, indeed, human consciousness! This is why:

1) If we ever teach machines to translate successfully, it would mean that we have taught machines Mentalese. Because, as discussed, any act of translation actually involves two steps: from language A to ideas, from ideas to language B.
2) But we also agreed that the connection between a sentence and the thoughts corresponding to that sentence is the meaning of the sentence. If a machine can translate successfully, it means it successfully establishes this connection. Hence the machine understands the meaning of the sentence.
3) If a machine understands the meaning of language, can it speak the language? Does it mean it becomes conscious? Does it mean it becomes human? Does it mean that humans are just complex machines?

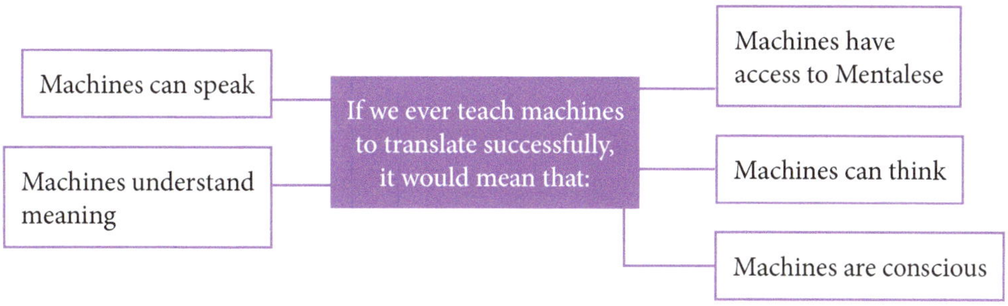

But before we can make far-reaching claims about conscious machines, we need to teach machines to translate from one language to another. How do we even do that?

Two camps: "It is a matter of time" versus "It is impossible"

As is often the case with important questions in life, researchers and philosophers have split into two camps (I sometimes feel like this is humanity's coping strategy: in any difficult situation, split into two camps!).

KEY IDEA: In any difficult situation, split into two camps!

Can machines be taught to use a language in the same way as humans do? (#Perspectives)

The first camp claims that *it is a matter of time* before machines will be able to make translation of good quality. New algorithms are emerging that could not be foreseen before. For example, many algorithms of machine translation these days are using large collections of natural language texts to analyze co-occurrence of words. This literally requires the whole capacity of the Internet to translate one sentence. Several decades ago, we could not even imagine that something like this would be possible. Is there a chance that in several decades from now we will invent something that will allow a next level of accuracy in machine translation engines?

The second camp claims that there are *in-principle obstacles* along the way and that machines will never be able to overcome them, no matter how far technology develops. They say that it this not a matter of technological progress, much like our inability to see inside a black hole. We cannot see inside a black hole not because our technology is not developed enough, but because nothing (not even light) escapes a black hole, so it is impossible to see it *in principle* no matter how great your technology is. The second camp in this debate believes that machine translation is like that.

No, there are in-principle obstacles — Will machines be able to equal humans in translation? — Yes, it is just a matter of time

Algorithms of machine translation

To what extent does machine translation enable fair access to knowledge for all language communities? (#Ethics)

The most basic algorithm of machine translation would be to simply take two dictionaries and establish a correspondence between words of two languages, then replace words of one language with words of another language. Obviously, this will not do. Some words only acquire their meaning in the context of the full sentence, so you need to understand the whole sentence in order to understand the word. For example, what does the word "charge" mean? And what does it mean in the sentence, "Don't provoke that bull, otherwise it may charge"?

A more complicated approach would be to teach the machine the rules of syntax and grammar. This is called a "*rule-based approach*". The drawback here is that the programmers need to be really explicit about everything. They need to sit down and write algorithms for the selection of the appropriate meaning for every case of ambiguity (for example, where the meaning of a word depends on the context). No human can possibly foresee all of the instances of ambiguity that may arise in language. And some decisions are really difficult to turn into an algorithm. For example, what algorithm do you use to decide that the word "conductor" in the sentence "a bare conductor runs under the tram" refers to a piece of wire?

An alternative approach is *statistical*. If you ever wondered, this is the approach that Google Translate uses. They started with rule-based, but switched over once their computational power increased and they had access to a tremendous amount of data. Statistical machine translation works by analyzing large bodies of text that have been translated by human translators – "*bilingual text corpora*". Looking through millions of documents, the algorithm detects patterns in translation and uses those patterns to make intelligent guesses about how to translate new texts. The larger the number of bilingual texts available to the algorithm, the more accurate the translations will be.

And here we go – we have engines such as Google Translate. They do a pretty decent job with translating typical texts in unambiguous contexts, but they fail to produce anything beyond rubbish in colloquial speech in unusual contexts or in language used figuratively. Will they ever improve to the extent where their translation will be indistinguishable from that of a human being? I am leaving this question open.

Critical thinking extension

What is a good quality machine translation?

How can we know if a translation is good? (#Methods and tools)

A "good quality" translation may be defined as one that sounds as if it has been written by a person.

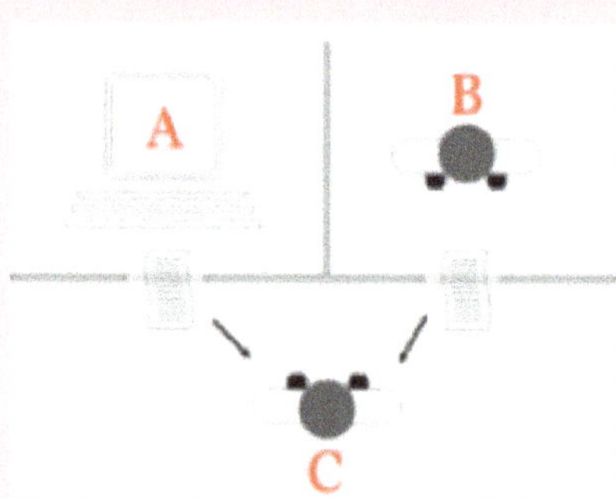

***Image 45**. Turing test*
(credit: Juan Alberto Sánchez Margallo, Wikimedia Commons)

Are you familiar with the Turing test? It was proposed by Alan Turing in 1950 as a method of establishing whether a computer is capable of thinking like a human being. Imagine three rooms – A, B and C. You are in room A. Rooms

B and C are occupied by another human and a computer, but you do not know which is where. You communicate to both of them by asking questions and receiving answers (for example, you can type your question and see the answer on your screen). After a certain time, you are required to say which of your two conversation partners is a human being and which one is a computer. If you cannot do that, then the computer has passed the Turing test, and we must admit that the machine is capable of thinking like a human.

The reverse of this test would be when a human being is trying to prove to a computer that they are indeed human. I bet you have already participated in this test many times – have you ever had to complete a CAPTCHA?

How can we use the Turing test in answering the question "What is a good quality machine translation?" Do you think this test would be sufficient?

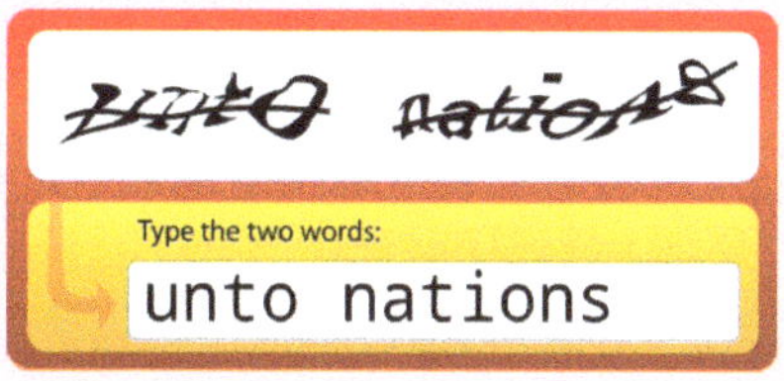

Image 46. CAPTCHA

If you are interested...

Interestingly, attempts to teach a computer human language have also resulted in computers becoming biased like humans. Artificial intelligent systems that learn a human language end up acquiring the same racial and gender biases as the people who speak this language. Isn't that a point in favor of the Sapir-Whorf hypothesis? Read more in Melissa Healy's article "What would make a computer biased? Learning language spoken by humans" (April 14, 2017) in the *Los Angeles Times*.

Take-away messages

Lesson 11. Machine translation is not just a curious engineering problem. A lot in our understanding of the nature of humans, thinking and language depends on whether or not this problem is solvable. If we manage to teach computers to successfully translate texts from one language into another, that would also mean that we have taught them to: (1) decipher the meaning of texts (that is, see the link between a natural language and Mentalese), (2) produce texts from meanings (that is, formulate a Mentalese thought in a natural language). Would this also mean that we have taught them to read? To understand? To think? There are two camps of scholars: one claims that technology will one day reach a point when machine translation will become adequate; the other one claims that this is impossible in principle. What is meant by an "adequate" machine translation is a separate question that is not easy to answer. One of the approaches is to use the Turing test, which claims that an adequate machine translation is one that is indistinguishable from a human-translated text.

Lesson 12 - Loaded language

Learning outcomes

a) [Knowledge and comprehension] What is loaded language?
b) [Understanding and application] How can loaded language be used to influence people's beliefs and behavior?
c) [Thinking in the abstract] To what extent is it problematic that language can convey additional meanings apart from the literal meaning? Is this a strength of language or its limitation?

Key concepts

Loaded language / emotive language, connotation

Other concepts used

Literal meaning

Themes and areas of knowledge

Themes: Knowledge and language, Knowledge and the knower
AOK: History, Human Sciences

Recap and plan

In the previous lessons, we considered what makes human language unique – the duplication of the real world in a system of signs. Signs serve as a bridge between things (existing in the world) and concepts (existing in the mind). We also looked at the Sapir-Whorf hypothesis – the idea that the structure of language determines (or at least influences) the structure of thought.

The Sapir-Whorf hypothesis looks at how language influences the way we think. But apart from being a tool of thinking, language is also a tool of communication.

In this lesson, we are considering how language can shape the way ideas are communicated.

Loaded language – the concept

Loaded language (also known as emotive language) refers to the practice of using language with the aim of producing a certain emotional response in the audience (or whoever receives the message).

KEY IDEA: Loaded language conveys a message beyond the literal meaning of words

Loaded language conveys a message beyond the literal meaning of words. Our language is very rich, and oftentimes there exist multiple ways to refer to the same thing. For example, a person who spends his Saturday afternoon participating in an anti-government demonstration is either a "rioter" or a "freedom fighter". Soldiers who are crossing the border of a sovereign state in response to its political instability are either "invaders" or "peacemakers". A man with no hair is either "bald" or "follicly challenged".

***Image 47**. Follicly challenged*

When can loaded language be useful in the acquisition of knowledge? (#Scope)

Curiously, there are many cases when a certain real-world object or phenomenon has a neutral sign as well as a positive and a negative sign associated with it. For example: a government official may be a "bureaucrat" or a "public servant"; a person who advocates for an abortion ban may be referred to as "anti-abortion" or "pro-life".

Example 1: Irrelevant associations influence big political decisions

Gilovich (1981) conducted a study with political science students at Stanford University. They were asked to assume the role of a high-ranking official in the U.S. government whose job is to analyze a foreign policy crisis and recommend a course of action to resolve it.

The hypothetical crisis described a small democratic country (Country B) that was threatened by its neighboring Country A which had a totalitarian regime. Country B obtained evidence that Country A was gathering troops on their border. Country B requested help from the United States.

This was followed by a description of both of the countries. Different groups of participants got identical descriptions except for several phrases. For example:

1) One of the groups got a description suggesting that oppressed minorities were fleeing from Country A in boxcars on freight trains. Another group's description suggested that minorities were fleeing from Country A in small boats. The first detail is a hint at Nazi Germany. The second detail is a hint at Vietnam War.
2) The description stated that in case of emergency the U.S. troops could be transported to Country B either in troop transports (group 1, hinting at World War II) or in Chinook helicopters (group 2, hinting at Vietnam War).

***Image 48**. A boxcar (credit: Slambo, Wikimedia Commons)*

***Image 49**. Boeing CH-47 Chinook helicopter (credit: Glenn Anderson, Wikimedia Commons)*

How can we know if our beliefs have been influenced by loaded language? (#Methods and tools)

These details were, of course, irrelevant to the scenario. They shouldn't have influenced the political decisions of persons responsible for deciding on the course of action. But *they* have influenced these decisions.

Participants in group 1 (with irrelevant details that created associations with World War II) recommended much more direct intervention of the U.S. including assisting Country B with pre-emptive strikes. Participants in group 2 (with irrelevant details hinting at the Vietnam War) were much more inclined to recommend a no-intervention policy and negotiations.

Indeed, World War II began as German expansion in Europe, but it quickly escalated to a larger scale and affected the whole world. Had there been some interference at earlier stages, the global conflict could have been prevented. On the contrary, American interference in the conflict in Vietnam arguably made the conflict worse, and American participation in the war was heavily condemned by many citizens at that time.

Obviously, the problem here is that such big decisions (whether or not to recommend a pre-emptive strike) are affected by such small irrelevant details (whether or not people are fleeing from the oppressed country in freight trains or in boats). Language loaded with these irrelevant associations affected people's decisions significantly. Curiously, "though subjects made recommendations consistent with specific historical episodes, they were unaware of the influence that these episodes apparently had on their decisions" (Gilovich, 1981, p. 806).

Example 2: Tiny differences in language have big consequences for students' behavior

Miller, Brickman and Bolen (1975) attempted to teach fifth graders not to litter (a really difficult task!). They split classes of fifth graders randomly into two groups. Group 1 was repeatedly told that they were neat and tidy kids (even if that wasn't the case). Group 2 was repeatedly told they should be neat and tidy.

In both Group 1 and Group 2, the intervention lasted for eight days. For example, on the first day in Group 1, the teacher commended the class for not throwing candy wrappers on the auditorium floor during school assembly. The teacher also passed on the comment of the janitor who (presumably) had said that their class was one of the cleanest in the building. On one of the days in Group 2, the teacher talked about garbage left by students in the lunch room and why garbage should be thrown away (looks terrible, attracts flies, presents a danger to health). On another occasion in Group 2, the teacher gave students a lecture on ecology and pollution.

Under what circumstances is it permissible to use loaded language to communicate knowledge? (#Ethics)

To measure the results, researchers invited an actor who played the role of a representative of a candy manufacturing company. The actor handed out candy for a tasting session five minutes before the break. In each classroom, the candy wrapping was a different color. After the tasting session, the students were dismissed and the researchers counted the number of candy wrappings left in the dustbin versus on the floor and in desks. This was done on the tenth day of the experiment and later on the 24th day when the experiment was discontinued.

Image 50. *It is not easy to convince fifth grades to throw away garbage*

Results showed that children in Group 1 littered much less. This was true even after the experiment stopped. By contrast, children in Group 2 started littering a little less when they were repeatedly told that they should be neat, but they quickly went back to normal levels of littering once the experiment ended. Apparently, if we simply tell fifth graders that they are neat and tidy, they actually become neat and tidy. Lecturing also works – but only a little bit and only if you lecture continuously. Once you stop lecturing, they go back to littering the same amount as they used to.

This shows how loaded language is a powerful tool that can influence our behavior, depending on how we use it.

Critical thinking extension

What makes it possible for language to be loaded and to convey, along with the "core" meaning, a bunch of additional meanings and associations? The existence of connotations.

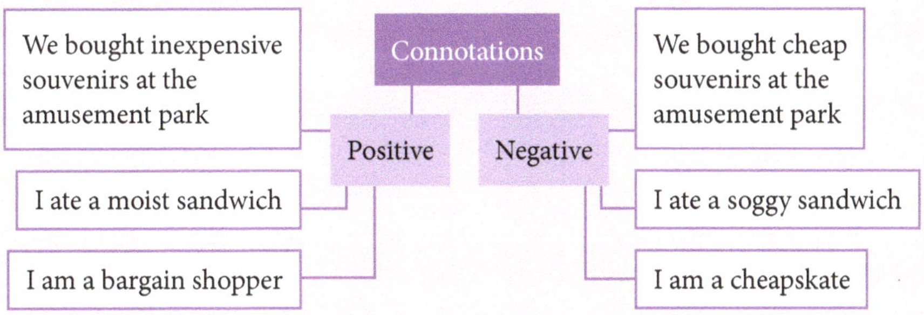

Connotations are a web of logical and emotional associations that a word creates in addition to its primary or literal meaning. Connotations may be roughly divided into positive and negative, depending on the overall emotional valence they carry. Perhaps these additional bits of meaning are precisely why we commonly have many words referring to the same thing. Take, for example, the word "to die". The meaning of this word is a fairly straightforward concept. However, there are various ways of expressing this same concept: to pass away, to cease to exist, to breathe one's last breath, to decease, to perish, to expire, to kick the bucket, to be no more, to meet one's maker, to bite the dust. If you're feeling adventurous, check out the list of 1,535 synonyms for the word "to die" on the website www.powerthesaurus.org.

Is the existence of connotations a strength of language or rather its limitation? (#Perspectives)

Each of these variants carries with it the core concept, and in addition to that a whole range of subtle associations and emotional hints.

Do you think the existence of connotations is problematic? Is it a strength of language that we have so many different ways to express the same concept, or is it more of a limitation?

If you are interested...

Using loaded language is a large part of propaganda and informational war. There are multiple techniques and tricks that have been discovered. If you are interested, here is a book that summarizes a huge number of such techniques and discoveries in a reader-friendly language but with lots of links to academic research published in peer-reviewed journals: Pratkanis, A., & Aronson, E. (2001). *Age of Propaganda: The Everyday Use and Abuse of Persuasion*. Holt Paperbacks.

Take-away messages

Lesson 12. Loaded language (or emotive language) refers to using language with the aim of producing a certain emotional response in the audience (or whoever receives the message). Loaded language conveys a message beyond the literal meaning of words. This becomes possible thanks to the existence of connotations – logical and emotional associations that a word creates in addition to its primary meaning. Language typically contains multiple words to refer to the same core concept, each bearing different connotations. There are many examples of using loaded language in propaganda and other fields to influence people. In this lesson we have looked at the use of language to manipulate political decision-making and the use of language to manipulate fifth graders into cleaning up after themselves.

6.4 - Language in the areas of knowledge

We have now looked at the key concepts and knowledge questions related to language. Explicitly or implicitly, we have been making connections to areas of knowledge along the way. However, it would be nice to make these links more pronounced and summarize them more formally. This is why the last part of this unit includes five lessons, each devoted to one of the areas of knowledge.

We will be discussing some key knowledge questions related to the role of language in each individual area of knowledge. The list is not exhaustive, of course. I merely selected some problems that are more in line with what has been discussed in this unit.

Some problems related to language are common for all areas of knowledge. For example, if a priori concepts shape our knowledge of things, it happens everywhere, no matter what area of knowledge we are talking about. However, some problems are more specific to particular areas of knowledge. It is these specific problems that I will try to focus on in the remaining lessons of the unit.

Lesson 13 - The role of language in Natural Sciences

Learning outcomes

a) [Knowledge and comprehension] What are some examples of language playing a role in natural sciences?
b) [Understanding and application] How is incommensurability of scientific theories similar to untranslatability?
c) [Thinking in the abstract] To what extent is our natural language responsible for some areas of science being so difficult to understand?

Key concepts

Incommensurability of scientific theories, untranslatability, scientific conventions

Other concepts used

The Steady State theory, the Big Bang theory, theory-laden facts, language as a tool of thought and a tool of communication, mole, Planck constant

Themes and areas of knowledge

Themes: Knowledge and language
AOK: Natural Sciences

Recap and plan

What role does language play in acquisition of knowledge in natural sciences? (#Scope)

We have spent quite a lot of time on the key concepts and debates surrounding language. We looked at language in its two most essential functions – language as a tool of thought and language as a tool of communication. Let's now apply what we know to areas of knowledge. What significance do these concepts and debates bear for Natural Sciences, Human Sciences, History, Mathematics and the Arts? Most of the things that will be discussed below have been already discussed in other lessons, but there's a good chance you haven't thought about them from the language perspective. Well, time to make connections.

Incommensurability as untranslatability

One phenomenon that we discussed as a key problem of scientific progress is incommensurability. It means that when one fundamental scientific theory replaces another fundamental scientific theory in the process of a paradigm shift, we can't really compare the two theories and make judgments as to which one is "better". This is because the two theories conceptualize the world differently and provide entirely different interpretations of the same empirical evidence. Arguably, since facts are *theory-laden* (which means that theory influences how observational facts are registered and perceived), even facts in these theories are different.

The problem of incommensurability can be viewed as a problem of language. Thomas Kuhn and Paul Feyerabend – the two classics who raised the issue – frequently referred to incommensurable scientific theories as theories that "speak different languages". Incommensurability in scientific theories is roughly equivalent to untranslatability in the study of language.

KEY IDEA: Incommensurability of scientific theories is a case of untranslatability

For example, the Steady State theory of the Universe claimed that the Universe always existed – it did not "evolve" from anything and did not have a "beginning". In the 1960s, this was replaced with the Big Bang theory, asserting that the Universe started with an explosion of an infinitely dense "singularity point" 13.8 billion years ago. Proponents of the Steady State theory were skeptical and they rightfully asked, "Well, then, what was before the Big Bang?" Since the Big Bang theory finds it difficult to answer this seemingly obvious question, they took it as a logical weakness of the theory.

But the thing is, if you accept the Big Bang model, the question "What was before the Big Bang?" does not make sense. Time is a physical property of our Universe, and our Universe started 13.8 billion years ago – together with time. There was no time before the Big Bang, and therefore there was no "before" before the Big Bang. The question only makes sense if it is asked in the language of the Steady State theory, which assumes that time is something absolute that has always existed and will always exist. The question cannot even be translated into the language of the new theory. It's untranslatable. The failure of the Big Bang model to answer the question is not a weakness of the model, it's an instance of incommensurability (and untranslatability).

***Image 51**. Does time have a beginning?*

Can it be claimed that different scientific theories "speak different languages", therefore a dialogue between them is impossible? (#Perspectives)

KEY IDEA: Questions formulated in one theory (language) may be unanswerable because they do not make sense in another theory (language)

To summarize: when two languages categorize the world differently, we run into the problem of untranslatability. That is why, if we view scientific theories as languages, incommensurability is a case of untranslatability.

Conventions

As we discussed, language performs two major functions: it is a tool of thought and it is a tool of communication. When it comes to communication, it is important in the scientific world to enable effective collaboration of researchers from around the globe. This means that, although scientists may speak different languages at home with their families, they must speak the same language when they communicate amongst themselves. An important component of this "common language" is the use of scientific conventions. For example, in chemistry and physics, a "mole" is a measure of quantity of a substance. The scientific community has agreed that a mole is 602,214,129,000,000,000,000,000 particles (usually written as 6.022×10^{23}). For example, a mole of water is 6.022×10^{23} water molecules. A mole of apples is 6.022×10^{23} apples.

But the point here is, scientists have agreed on a convention and invented a word, and it became easy for them to speak about quantities. Whatever language you speak, you know that a mole = 6.022×10^{23} particles.

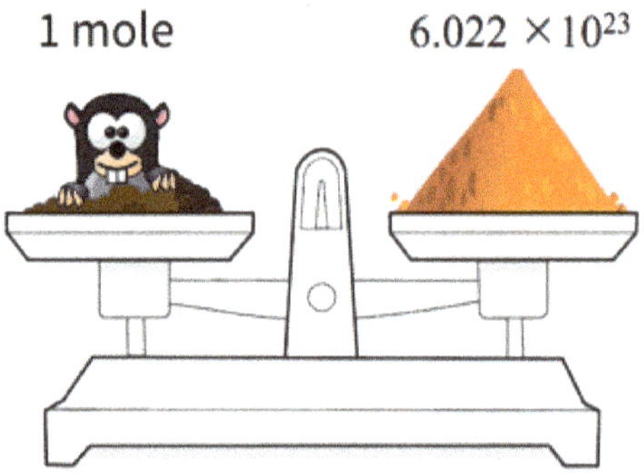

Image 52. A mole of moles

A kilogram, on the other hand, may be a lot more difficult to define. The only way to agree on how it is may be to say "a kilogram is a mass equivalent to the mass of this boulder". That is exactly what we've done. The "boulder" is a block of platinum-iridium alloy that has been housed at the International Bureau of Weights and Measures in France since 1889. It is sometimes referred to as the "Big K". Scientists just agreed that a kilogram is a mass equivalent to the mass of this object, and took great efforts to ensure that the mass of this prototype kilogram does not change.

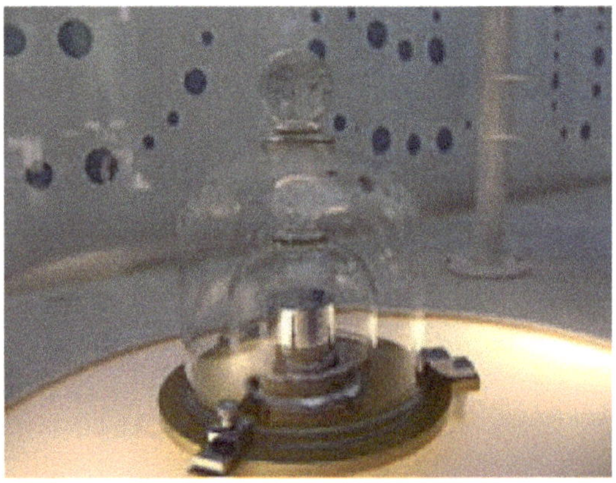
Image 53. A replica of the Big K under a protective double glass bell (credit: Japs 88, Wikimedia Commons)

Frustratingly, though, the mass of the Big K *has* changed since 1889. It has become approximately 50 micrograms lighter – that is the weight of an eyelash. Hence the definition of the kilogram has also been changing over the last century or so!

To what extent does our natural language limit our scientific knowledge? (#Methods and tools)

This is why scientists recently agreed to change the definition of the kilogram. The change became effective in 2019. At the General Conference of Weights and Measures in France, scientists voted to tie the definition of the kilogram to the Planck constant – one of the fundamental physical constants deeply ingrained into the fabric of reality. The Planck constant can never ever change, neither on the Earth nor on the other side of the Universe. If someone sneezes on the Big K, its mass will change and all measurements in the world would have to be adjusted. But you cannot sneeze on the Planck constant.

To summarize: language plays a huge role in natural sciences when it comes to conventions and definitions. Precise definitions allow scientists to communicate their ideas accurately.

KEY IDEA: Without conventions such as weights and measures, scientific collaboration would be impossible

Critical thinking extension

We often find it very difficult to wrap our heads around the latest discoveries in fields such as quantum physics, astrophysics and neuroscience. The deeper we get into the fabric of reality, the weirder it gets.

But could it be that we only find these findings and theories so weird because our natural language is not equipped to deal with these phenomena?

If a priori concepts exist, then all languages in the world reflect these concepts. For example, if time is an a priori concept, then we will all have the idea of time in our minds and the words to express this idea in our languages. But what if such a priori concepts are *incorrect* because they were formed in the limited minds of a certain biological species living in a remote corner of the galaxy? Our ancestors never had to deal with subatomic particles or stuff travelling at the speed of light, so no wonder we have no a priori concepts (or language) to reflect such phenomena.

So could it be that, in order to truly understand how the Universe works, we must somehow abandon our natural language because it creates a filter that does not allow us to see the world for what it actually is?

Is it permissible to encourage standardization of knowledge at the cost of diversity? (#Ethics)

If you are interested...

In September 1999, NASA lost control of its Mars Climate Orbiter, a $125 million spacecraft that was launched to Mars. On the day when NASA engineers were preparing to celebrate the spacecraft successfully reaching the orbit of Mars after 10 months of travel, the orbiter approached the planet's atmosphere too closely, burned and broke into pieces.

***Image 54**. Launch of Mars Climate Orbiter in 1998*

When NASA investigated the problem, they found that a piece of software that was designed to control the thrusters calculated the necessary force in pounds, while another piece of software that was reading this data assumed that the result was in metric units (newtons per square meter). This happened because the two pieces of software were written by two different labs (within the United States). You can read the full story on the Wikipedia page "Mars Climate Orbiter".

Take-away messages

Lesson 13. Language is deeply connected with knowledge in all areas, natural sciences are not an exception. We can find problems of knowledge in natural sciences for both functions of language – as a tool of thought and as a tool of communication. An example of a problem created in natural sciences by the use of language as a tool of thought is incommensurability of scientific theories. Incommensurability can be viewed as a special case of untranslatability. It may be difficult for scientific theories to communicate across the paradigm shift because questions asked by one theory make no sense in the "language" of the other theory. An example of the use of language as a tool of communication is creating conventions. Without conventions in fields such as weights and measures, scientific collaboration would be impossible.

Lesson 14 - The role of language in Human Sciences

Learning outcomes

a) [Knowledge and comprehension] What are some examples of language playing a role in human sciences?
b) [Understanding and application] What is the role of connotations and leading questions in studying human activity?
c) [Thinking in the abstract] To what extent can it be claimed that the object of research in human sciences is itself a product of language?

Key concepts

Connotation, leading question, social fact, brute fact

Other concepts used

Self-report, vocabulary, reconstructive memory, behaviorism, "black box"

Themes and areas of knowledge

Themes: Knowledge and language
AOK: Human Sciences

Recap and plan

As you remember, a distinguishing feature of human sciences is that, unlike natural sciences, they study objective phenomena (such as observable behavior) as well as subjective phenomena (such as people's intentions, experiences and values). To fully understand human activity, we must take into account both objective and subjective dimensions. But the only way to understand the subjective dimension of human existence is through subjective methods such as interpretation.

What is the role of language in knowledge acquisition in human sciences? (#Scope)

Language in human sciences plays a large role because interpretation is an integral part of knowledge and interpretation is impossible without language. We use language to report the results and, very often (as is the case with interviews, for example), we use language to collect data.

In this lesson, we will look at some common language-related aspects of human sciences.

Connotations in vocabulary of human sciences

If your ideal of science is something impartial and "objective", then your requirements to language used by this science are probably that:

1) Words have precise meanings that are interpreted identically irrespective of the context in which they are used.
2) Words have no connotations (they do not create a web of emotional associations) – how the researcher feels about an object or a phenomenon should not be part of the meaning of words denoting this object or phenomenon.

Words have no connotations — Ideal scientific language — Words have precise meaning

However, human sciences cannot achieve this ideal to the same extent as natural sciences. This is because we want to be able to describe subtle human experiences, which is not the same as describing the movement of rocks through space. Emotion-less and connotation-less words may not be suitable for capturing aspects of our inner worlds.

For example, how do you convey the idea that your research participant is angry in a way that is stripped of all connotations? You can try to express the idea of "angry" in terms of observable behavior:

- The participant banged the door when he left the room.
- The participant's voice was loud.
- The participant called other participants' names.

But this is not the same as saying "angry"! It is not as rich. It does not capture the essence of being angry. For this reason, words with emotional connotations are still used in human sciences.

The fact that many terms in human sciences coincide with words of everyday language may be problematic. For example, the word "violence" used as a term in psychology may be different from what we normally mean by violence when we use this word in everyday speech. Consider the word "depression". We commonly say "I'm depressed" when we are simply sad. That is not what depression means as a psychiatric diagnosis.

KEY IDEA: Vocabulary of human sciences cannot be free from connotations because it describes subtle human experiences

Leading questions

Is there such a thing as a neutral question? (#Perspectives)

In research with human participants, we often have to rely on their *self-report*. This is particularly true when we want to investigate how people experience something rather than observing their externally manifested behavior. Imagine you are interested in finding out how successful artists get inspiration for their work. You may agree that it is impossible to answer this question by observing the artists or even by measuring their brain activity. The only way is to ask them and listen to what they say. A large part of human sciences, when it comes to understanding human experiences, relies on these self-report narratives produced by research participants.

But if two interviewers conducted their interviews with the same participant, I bet their results would not be the same. Part of the reason is the use of leading questions. For example, compare these:

1) *How do you get inspired to create your work?*
2) *Where do you derive your inspiration from?*
3) *What inspires you to create your masterpieces?*
4) *When was the last time you felt inspired to work through the night?*

***Image 55**. Data collection in an interview*

All of these questions imply something. For example, the first one ("How do you get inspired to create your work?") implies that the artist is inspired. It assumes that there is no doubt that inspiration is there, and that the question is only about the *how*. Moreover, that question also implies that the artist *gets* inspired, that inspiration is a thing that comes and goes and that this process is controllable to some extent. Quite a few hidden assumptions in a seemingly innocent question!

Can you analyze the assumptions implicit in the other examples?

KEY IDEA: Leading questions may interfere with data collection in human sciences, but it is difficult (if not impossible) to formulate a neutral question

To what extent is it ethically problematic that in human sciences researchers can influence participants through the use of language? (#Ethics)

An influential researcher who demonstrated the true power of leading questions is Elizabeth Loftus, a psychologist who is famous for her *reconstructive memory* experiments. In a classic experiment (Loftus and Palmer, 1974), participants viewed videos of a car crash and were asked to estimate the speed of the moving car. The question that was used for this purpose had one word that was different in the five groups of participants: "About how fast were the cars going when they smashed / collided with / bumped into / hit / contacted each other?"

It was also shown that one week later, when asked if there was any broken glass in the video, participants in the "smashed" condition were more likely to remember seeing broken glass – even though there was none in the video. This suggested that the leading question actually changed their memory!

***Image 56**. Car crash*

The point is, since in human sciences we are often relying on asking participants questions and interpreting their answers, leading questions may create a problem. The answer may depend on the way the question was formulated. But is there such a thing as a neutral question? It seems like any question you could possibly ask, in one way or another, already suggests an answer to it.

Critical thinking extension

Social facts

Sometimes a distinction is made between brute facts and social facts. Brute facts exist even when there is no one around to observe them and interpret them. For example, asteroids moving through space are brute facts. Social facts are facts that are constructed by humans, and these facts cannot exist outside of our society or our interpretation. For example, the statement "London is the capital of the United Kingdom" is a social fact. We agreed to consider this city the capital of this country. Moreover, we agreed on where one country begins and another country ends, and we agreed that one of the cities should be the "capital".

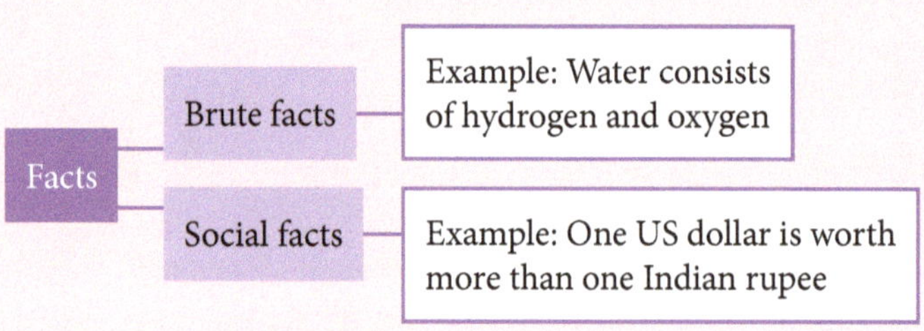

Imagine if our society disappeared (it's not difficult to imagine these days!). An alien civilization reached our planet and tries to reconstruct our history. They may be able to reconstruct brute facts, for example, to dig out our artefacts, to estimate how many people lived on the Earth, or to figure out how to drive our cars. But they will not have access to most of our social facts unless they understand the language. Social facts are *constructed* through language.

KEY IDEA: Social facts are constructed through language

Knowing this, to what extent can it be claimed that the object of research in human sciences is itself a product of language? That facts in human sciences are constructed through language? If we use language to study something that is a product of language, does it pose any problem for the quality of our knowledge?

If you are interested...

One interesting theory that dominated psychology at some point is behaviorism. Radical behaviorism had a notion of the "black box". "Black box" is what they called the human mind. They stated that various internal states for which we have words in our language (such as motivation, aim, satisfaction) are meaningless because we cannot observe them. To operate with unobservable constructs, according to them, means to be unscientific. So, they suggested that we eliminate all such words from the study of humans. Instead, we need to focus on observable behavior (hence the name).

You might be interested to learn more about the extent to which they succeeded, as well as the reasons why they had to give way to an alternative movement – cognitive psychology – that did recognize the content of the "black box" and returned these "meaningless terms" back to the realm of psychology. You might want to start with the video "Behaviorism: Pavlov, Watson, and Skinner" on the YouTube channel *Alana Snow*.

Take-away messages

To what extent can human activity be understood without language? (#Methods and tools)

Lesson 14. Human sciences are unique in that it is the study of two dimensions of human existence at the same time (the objective dimension such as observable behavior and the subjective dimension such as people's experiences). To understand the reasoning and motivations behind people's actions and the meanings they attach to their activities and events around them, we must use interpretation. Interpretation and interviews are sometimes the only window we have into subjective human experiences. These depend on language. Interviews and surveys may be affected by leading questions – participants' answers may depend on how the question was formulated. The vocabulary of human sciences is more dependent on context than that of natural sciences. Many words are borrowed from everyday language which may create some confusion (for example, "depressed" in everyday language is not the same as "depressed" as a psychiatric diagnosis). Moreover, facts investigated in human sciences are mostly "social facts" – they are constructed through language and, arguably, they only exist as long as language exists.

Lesson 15 - The role of language in History

Learning outcomes

a) [Knowledge and comprehension] What is propaganda?
b) [Understanding and application] How can propaganda affect history writing?
c) [Thinking in the abstract] How could a historian of the future separate facts from propaganda using social media as primary evidence?

Key concepts

Propaganda, Basic English, Newspeak

Other concepts used

Fake news, propaganda bots (political bots)

Themes and areas of knowledge

Themes: Knowledge and language
AOK: History

Recap and plan

We know history through language. There is simply no other way to know events of the past. You could argue that there are videos and pictures and material evidence (such as an ancient Greek vase). But what good are these artifacts if you cannot describe what is happening in the video (using language) or explain the function of the vase (again, using language)? As you remember, history is based on the process of historical interpretation. In its turn, historical interpretation cannot exist without language.

KEY IDEA: History is based on the process of historical interpretation, but historical interpretation cannot exist without language

What is the role of language in obtaining historical knowledge? (#Scope)

There is one aspect of language use that seems to be particularly important in history – historical propaganda. This is when a historian, while describing events of the past more or less accurately, simultaneously uses language to promote his or her political agenda.

Language and propaganda

When historians create an account of events of the past, their national and political identity may make them biased. They may portray the past in a light that presents their nation, culture, political party or religious group in a more favorable light. They may also present opposing groups in less favorable light. This can be done intentionally or unintentionally. Sometimes, they may be forced to do so.

***Image 57**. World War I propaganda*

When someone describes the past with the aim of influencing opinions of others and promoting one's political agenda, this is propaganda. It is fueled by mass media and censorship.

Even if you cannot tweak the facts, you can still play with language. Seemingly, you can describe events exactly as they happened, but through the use of language you can manipulate the impressions that your audience will be left with.

Here is one example from research into the use of language in propaganda – Wegner et al. (1981). Participants in this study read one of four headlines:

1) Bob Talbert Celebrates Birthday (neutral statement)
2) Bob Talbert Is Linked with Mafia (incriminating assertion)
3) Is Bob Talbert Linked with Mafia? (question)
4) Bob Talbert Is Not Linked with Mafia (denial)

The person in question was a fictitious city council candidate several weeks before the election. After reading the headline, participants were asked to rate their impressions of the candidate. Results showed that:

What role does loaded language play in history? How is it different from other areas of knowledge? (#Methods and tools)

1) Ratings based on neutral headings (such as "Bob Talbert Celebrates Birthday") were neutral and even slightly positive. This is probably good news. It means that by default we are of a moderately positive opinion about politicians.
2) Impressions after reading the incriminating assertions (such as "Bob Talbert Is Linked with Mafia") were quite negative.
3) But, most surprisingly, ratings in the other two groups (question and denial) were as negative as ratings in the group with incriminating assertions!

What the headline says	What the audience remembers
Bob Talbert Celebrates Birthday	Okay guy
Bob Talbert Is Linked with Mafia	Bad guy!
Is Bob Talbert Linked with Mafia?	Bad guy!
Bob Talbert Is Not Linked with Mafia	Bad guy!

In other words, it does not matter if you are directly accusing a politician or simply wondering out loud if the accusation is true, or even denying it – in the mass perception the outcome will be the same: an association will be created between the politician and the accusation.

This gives you almost infinite possibilities to manipulate mass consciousness through propaganda! You are welcome. Use it responsibly.

Basic English and Newspeak

Obviously, there are also more straightforward ways to manipulate mass consciousness through language and propaganda. You can just play around with the choice of words. The same group of people may be called "freedom fighters" or "rioters" or "terrorists" depending on your perception of what they do or why they do it. Language is so rich that it has multiple labels for the same thing, each label coming with a baggage of extra connotations and associations that it triggers. Plenty to choose from!

Should historians be allowed to express personal opinions? (#Ethics)

In the early 20th century, when the world was tormented by the first global war, many scholars were concerned with the use of language in propaganda. In 1923, the English scholars K. Ogden and I.A. Richards published a book entitled *The Meaning of Meaning* where they spoke about how meaning can be abused in language. They proposed to design a new international language that would make such manipulations impossible, a language where every word has a meaning that is precisely understood by everyone. It would be a language that peels the emotive content off of words denoting facts. For Ogden, this project culminated in designing what he called Basic English – a version of the English language restricted to a core vocabulary of around 800 words, designed to convey meaning without the extra bits (a sanitized English).

But not everyone agreed that a sanitized English would be a good idea. George Orwell – the author of the famous anti-utopian novel *1984* – started as a supporter of Basic English. He was in touch with Ogden by correspondence and he was even involved in promoting Basic English on mass media (BBC). However, over the course of time, his position drastically changed. In his novel, he describes Newspeak, a fictional language designed by a totalitarian society. The language was used to restrict thought and prevent people from questioning things and thinking critically. Clearly, opinions differ on whether or not creating a sanitized English would be a good idea.

***Image 58**. George Orwell*

Propaganda and history writing

You might ask, what significance does propaganda have for history? History is the study of the past. Surely well-educated historians can separate propaganda from facts?

Is it fair to say that an element of propaganda in history writing is inevitable? (#Perspectives)

But the difficulty here is that, even if a historian is well-trained to avoid the influence of propaganda, propaganda can affect primary evidence. This is how:

1) The person who is recording the events may intentionally record them in a way that would influence future historical interpretations in ways he or she desires. In other words, the primary source may be an agent of propaganda.
2) The person who is recording the events may be under the influence of propaganda of that time. His or her interpretation of the event may be influenced by propaganda. In other words, the primary source may be a victim of propaganda.

KEY IDEA: Propaganda can affect primary historical evidence. In the long run, this will make the work of a historian much more difficult.

That is why propaganda is not only a political problem. In the long term, it messes up primary evidence and makes the work of a historian harder and harder.

George Orwell famously said that history stopped in 1936 and, after that, there was only propaganda (Orwell, 1943). World War II witnessed ruthless media campaigns that created a large-scale informational war. Propaganda was mixed with facts, and historians found it difficult to tell which is which.

Critical thinking extension

Just imagine historians 100 years from now trying to create an account of events from 2020-2030. They will be confronted with loads of information – news footage, newspaper articles, tweets, Instagram photos. How do they determine which of the sources are trustworthy?

An interesting feature of the present time is also that many people get their news from social media. According to one poll (Gottfried and Shearer, 2016), 62 percent of U.S. adults turn to social media to get news. But news on social media are essentially "crowd sourced". They can be influenced and swayed by public comments. Recipients of the news may be more influenced, for example, by comments under a YouTube video than the video itself. This is why agents of propaganda often employ special people who write such comments! The war is very much on. It is a war over public opinion.

Image 59. Getting news from social media

But back to my question: if the public on social media messes up primary evidence so much (sometimes intentionally), how will historians of the future separate facts from propaganda?

If you are interested...

Fake news is a fabricated story (sometimes completely false, sometimes an exaggerated reality) that is disseminated over the Internet. Such news is usually sensational in character, causing people to share it on social media. When you read some sensational piece of news on Facebook and click "repost" without critically analyzing the sources and assessing the credibility of the piece, you may be falling victim to informational warfare.

A new phenomenon we are dealing with is "*propaganda bots*" (also known as "*political bots*"). If you are interested, you can read more in these articles:

1) "The bots that are changing politics" by Renee DiResta et al., published on *Vice* (November 2, 2017)
2) "YouTube's algorithm is hurting America far more than Russian trolls ever could" by Chris Taylor, published on *Mashable* (February 22, 2018)

Image 60. Political bots

Take-away messages

Lesson 15. As we discussed in the previous lesson, social facts are constructed through language. Therefore, language plays an essential role in history. One example of how language may distort our historical knowledge is the use of language in propaganda. The fact that language is so rich and emotive, and that it contains multiple words that refer to the same thing, gives lots of opportunities for propaganda to use language to influence public opinion. There has been research that showed, for example, that if you formulate an incriminating statement in the form of a question, technically you are not accusing anyone of anything, but the association is created in the mass consciousness anyway. There have been attempts to cleanse language of emotive content and make it precise in conveying meaning (Basic English) as well as criticism of such attempts (Newspeak). Propaganda may tremendously affect history writing because it interferes with primary sources.

Lesson 16 - The role of language in Mathematics

Learning outcomes

a) [Knowledge and comprehension] What is an imaginary number?
b) [Understanding and application] How justified would it be to claim that mathematical concepts have no referents in the real world?
c) [Thinking in the abstract] If a mathematical formula suggests something to be true, to what extent is this sufficient justification for us to accept it as true?

Key concepts

Signifier, referent, concept, abstraction

Other concepts used

Imaginary number, concept with no referent, "unreasonable effectiveness of mathematics"

Themes and areas of knowledge

Themes: Knowledge and language
AOK: Mathematics

Recap and plan

We are looking at the role of language in various areas of knowledge. So far, we have seen that the common problems of language (such as the relationship between language and thought or using language effectively as a tool of communication) are equally applicable to all individual areas of knowledge, but there are specific problems as well.

What role does language play in the acquisition of knowledge in mathematics? (#Scope)

For mathematics, this could be the problem of the connection between the signifiers and the referents. As you remember, a signifier is the material token of the sign (for example, the sequence of sounds in the word "elephant"). The referent is the thing in the real world that the sign represents (for example, an elephant, the animal).

Some claim that referents in the language of mathematics do not even exist. In other words, mathematical concepts do not point to anything in the real world.

Mathematics is a language that lost connection with reality

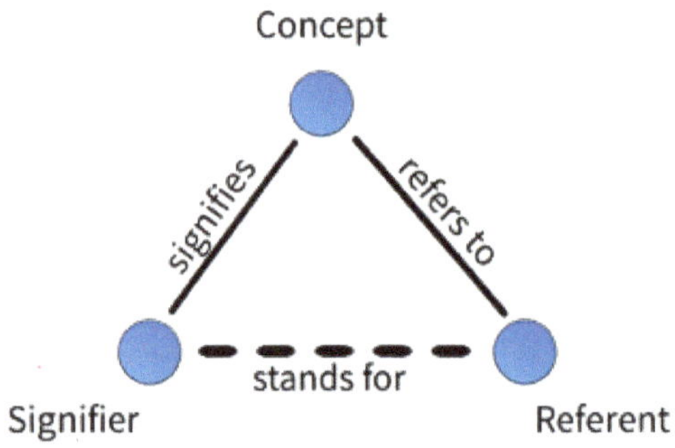

***Image 61**. The signifier, the referent, the signified*

There is no doubt that mathematical signs (the scribblings) are linked to mathematical concepts (the ideas), but are they also linked to anything in the real world? As you remember, there are three components of meaning – the signifier, the signified and the referent. So the question is, what counts as a referent in mathematical language, and does it even exist? Take, for example, *imaginary numbers*.

An imaginary number is any number that can be written in the form bi, where b is a real number and i is the imaginary unit. The imaginary unit i is defined by its property $i^2 = -1$.

To what extent can we claim that mathematical concepts are not linked to anything in the real world? (#Perspectives)

Let me decipher this a little. As you know, a positive number squared is a positive number, and a negative number squared is also a positive number. For example, $5^2 = 25$ and $(-5)^2 = 25$. So, the square of a number can never be negative.

An operation opposite to squaring is taking the square root of a number. For example, $5^2 = 25$; $\sqrt{25} = 5$. Since any number squared is a positive number, the square root of a negative number does not exist. In other words, $\sqrt{(-25)}$ has no solution. But sometimes mathematicians had to solve problems where they got a square root of a negative number in the result, and they could not continue because that was not allowed.

They were not happy. So, they *imagined* there exists a number which, when squared, results in -1.

$$i \times i = -1$$

or

$$i^2 = -1$$

which means that

$$\sqrt{(-1)} = i$$

Once they imagined this, they could continue with the previously unsolvable problems. For example, $\sqrt{(-25)}$ would be solved like this:

$$\sqrt{(-25)} = \sqrt{(-1 \times 25)} = \sqrt{(25)} \times \sqrt{(-1)} = 5 \times i = 5i$$

Now mathematicians could continue solving problems that used to be considered unsolvable! At first, some mathematicians used the word "imaginary" in a derogatory sense and refused to accept them as a real mathematical entity. But, gradually, imaginary numbers were proven to be useful. Currently, they are used in a whole range of practical applications. For example, without them we wouldn't have airplanes.

The point is, imaginary numbers are an example of a concept that has no correspondence in the real world. It has no referent.

Image 62. Imaginary number

But the connection is not entirely absent

However, we cannot simply claim that the language of mathematics has no relationship to the real world at all, can we? Simple mathematical concepts are more or less rooted in the real world. It is the complex concepts that we build upon them that become more and more abstract.

Image 63. Adding apples

We may start with counting objects: here are two apples, and here are three apples. Three apples are "more" than two apples. We may continue with abstracting the concept of "two-ness" from the concrete objects: here is two (of anything), and here is three (of anything). Three is larger than two. We can continue with addition: we can find a physical equivalent of it by putting two apples in a basket with three more apples. Then multiplication: we can trace it back to addition and the physical action of adding two apples to two apples to two apples: 2×3=2+2+2. Then squares: three squared = three multiplied by three = three plus three plus three (and at this point I can still think about the physical action of adding apples to a basket). Then square root: it's the opposite of squaring (at this point, it becomes harder to find an equivalent physical action, but I can think of it as un-doing the action). Then negative

Should scientists be paid to develop knowledge that does not have practical applications? (#Ethics)

numbers – it's the opposite of positive numbers. Then square roots from negative numbers… Here, the connection with reality has been seemingly lost, and these concepts only make sense in the system of other concepts, but not in a physical sense. However, there still exists a path (albeit overgrown and barely visible) to the original physical sense:

> *A square root of a negative number is an operation that is analogous to a square root of a positive number, which is an operation that is opposite to a square of a number, which is the same as multiplication of a number by the same number, which is the same as addition of that number to itself a "number" of times, and addition of a number to another number is like adding apples to more apples.*

See, apples do appear at the end of this sentence. Although mathematics is abstract, it does not mean that there is no connection to reality whatsoever.

KEY IDEA: Although it may seem that abstract mathematical concepts have no connection to reality (no referent), ultimately these abstract concepts are derived through mathematical transformations from the simplest, most basic mathematical operations that originally had a physical sense

Critical thinking extension

Many scholars that share the "mathematics is discovered" position think that mathematics has a profound connection to reality. These scholars would probably claim that mathematical concepts do have referents in the real world, but these things are so subtle that we cannot perceive them with our ordinary senses.

KEY IDEA: From the "mathematics is discovered" perspective, mathematical concepts have referents, but these referents are deeply hidden in the nature of things and inaccessible to our senses

The reason for such claims is that science and technology are all based on mathematics and they work so incredibly well. If there is no relation between mathematics and reality, why does technology work so well? Why do our spacecraft reach remote planets? Mathematics has to reflect some deep properties of reality. Eugene Wigner referred to this as the "*unreasonable effectiveness of mathematics*" (Wigner, 1960).

How is it possible that abstract mathematical entities (such as imaginary numbers) enable practical applications? (#Methods and tools)

In fact, in modern science some of our understanding of the world is based purely on mathematics, with no experimental evidence. Einstein's theories of relativity were a result of a purely mathematical exercise. He did not observe anything, nor did he conduct experiments. His formulas "told" him that his theories must be true. Admittedly, humanity later tested these theories and obtained experimental evidence corroborating them. But there exist theories – like the multiverse theory – that have not been corroborated by evidence, and we are not sure they will ever be. All of these talks about multiple dimensions are taking place because mathematically it is possible to construct a 4-dimensional, 10-dimensional, 123-dimensional space. If multiple dimensions are possible mathematically, why not assume that they actually exist in the real world? If mathematics reflects the properties of the real world, then what we can think of in mathematics must also be true of the world itself.

To what extent do you think mathematics can be used as a method of research in sciences, as opposed to merely a tool that analyzes data obtained by other methods? In other words, if a mathematical formula suggests something to be true (e.g. multiple dimensions), to what extent is this sufficient justification for us to accept it as true?

If you are interested...

An interesting (although indirect) piece of evidence for the claim that mathematics is a kind of language comes from research that is attempting to demonstrate that the development of linguistics and mathematical abilities in children is linked. The idea is that if learning mathematics helps children learn new languages (and vice versa), then these two areas probably use the same brain areas and the same skill set, so they are probably related.

There is an array of evidence for it. If you are interested, conduct a search for "mathematical and linguistic abilities" on Google Scholar.

Take-away messages

Lesson 16. Mathematics may be viewed as a language. It is a system of signs that exist in a certain relationship to one another. One problem specific to the language of mathematics may be its relationship with the referent. It seems to be the only language where the connection between signs and real-world objects has been lost (for example, what is the real-world referent of the imaginary number?). However, we also argued that the connection is not lost entirely. Every abstract mathematical concept can be traced back to more basic ones that are rooted in some physical reality. Moreover, scholars who share the "mathematics is discovered" position believe that mathematical concepts only appear to be abstract and "imaginary" when in fact they reflect deep properties of the world that are not accessible to us through our regular senses. How else can we explain the "unreasonable effectiveness of mathematics"?

Lesson 17 - The role of language in the Arts

Learning outcomes

a) [Knowledge and comprehension] What are the two camps of scholars regarding the role of language in art?
b) [Understanding and application] If we agree that a work of art conveys some message or meaning, must we also agree that art is a sign and hence art is language?
c) [Thinking in the abstract] To what extent is art translatable into a natural language (such as English)?

Key concepts

Sign, indeterminacy of translation, "beetle in a box" metaphor

Other concepts used

Essential property, shared meaning, mudra, "the unsayable", translatability of art

Themes and areas of knowledge

Themes: Knowledge and language
AOK: The Arts

Recap and plan

We have considered the role that language plays in various areas of knowledge – Natural and Human Sciences, History, Mathematics. In a nutshell, because language and thought are so closely related, it looks like language affects thought (and thought affects language) on a deep level in all of these areas of knowledge.

What is the role of language in the production of knowledge in the arts? (#Scope)

At first it may seem that language does not play any significant role in the arts, especially in art forms such as dance, painting, sculpture or music. Could it be that these forms of art are perhaps the only way for us humans to know something independently of the language we speak?

Many scholars believe that the answer is no. Such forms of art, they say, are also language. But some scholars believe that the answer is yes. These scholars say that art is a realm of the unsayable, that it affects our hearts directly without the need for, and the limitations of, labeling or categorization.

Objections to art being a language

Folks that object against considering art a language have their reasons.

Art lacks many features that are commonly associated with language. For example, language has a grammar. Grammar gives us rules of translating thoughts into sentences. If we want to express the idea that someone influenced something, we use the structure "Subject – verb in the past tense - object" (as in "The mouse stole the cheese"), but if we want to express the idea that something was influenced by someone, we use the structure "Object – auxiliary verb – verb in the past participle - subject" (as in "The cheese was stolen by the mouse"). Can we say that similar grammar-like rules exist in art (for example, something like "A combination of blue and green in depicting the Sun creates a feeling of despair")? It is debatable.

There are other differences, too. In language, signs are more or less arbitrary – we agreed to call a chipmunk a "chipmunk", but we could have called it something else. In art, signs are not arbitrary. We cannot replace a painting with some other arbitrary painting and claim that it conveys the same meaning.

KEY IDEA: In art, the link between the physical form of a sign and its meaning is not arbitrary. This makes art different from language.

Image 64. Mr. and Mrs. Andrews, by Thomas Gainsborough (1750). What does this painting have in common with language?

Art is a sign

Can it be said that language plays no role in knowledge conveyed by visual arts? (#Methods and tools)

But even these scholars often accept that art is symbolic of something. A work of art expresses an idea or a belief or an emotion. It is not just a canvas with paint on it – it stands for something. At least in this aspect, art bears a deep resemblance to language. Creating a work of art, according to this viewpoint, begins with an emotional experience or a thought, and then art becomes a form of expression, a sign for that experience or thought. Gary Hagberg describes the artist as a speaker who has thoughts but no language or vocabulary (Hagberg, 1995). Art is how the artist "names" their thoughts. It is the job of the audience to interpret it.

This is where it becomes tricky. If you agree that the essential feature of language is being a system of signs, and if you agree that art is used as a sign to convey some meaning, then you must also agree that art is a language! On the surface it may not resemble the language we use in our everyday lives, but essentially it meets the criteria.

KEY IDEA: If you agree that the essential feature of language is being a system of signs, and if you agree that art is used as a sign to convey some meaning, then you must also agree that art is language

Shared meaning

But this raises a question: if we see meaning of a sign as the connection between the signifier (the work of art) and the signified (the idea that is being expressed), is this meaning shared? In language, when two people hear the word "chipmunk", they (hopefully) have the same idea activated in their minds. Is the meaning of a work of art shared in the same sense? Probably not! The same piece of music may be interpreted differently by different listeners.

However, we can object that even in a natural language there are signs for which we cannot guarantee that their meaning is shared. Ludwig Wittgenstein in relation to this used the metaphor of a "beetle in a box".

Imagine everyone has a box, and inside that box is something that each person calls a "beetle". But only the person who has the box can look inside it. The contents of the box are not accessible to anyone else. So, although everyone has a certain "something" that they call a "beetle", it is possible that this "something" is actually different for different people (Wittgenstein, 1986, p. 100). Maybe mine is a spider?

Image 65. *Ludwig Wittgenstein (1889 – 1951)*

"Art is the realm of the unsayable". To what extent do you agree? (#Perspectives)

Now, when we speak about our subjective experiences or mental states that are not directly observable by others, aren't we essentially speaking about a beetle in a box? For example, I am telling you that I am anxious. I have a beetle in by box that I call "anxiousness". You have a similar box and you also have something in it that you call "anxiousness". When you hear that I'm anxious, you imagine that my beetle and your beetle are the same beetle. But, the thing is, you cannot be certain. Is what I call "anxiousness" and what you call "anxiousness" the same thing? It is relatively easier to agree on the meaning of words such as "chipmunk" because we can point at a chipmunk and agree that this thing over there is what we call a chipmunk. But with inner states and subjective experiences, it is much more difficult because we do not have an external object to point at.

Image 66. *Beetle in a box*

An artist's inner experiences that they are trying to express are the "beetle". We are looking at an artwork and it makes us think of our own beetle in our own box. Is it the same kind of beetle? We don't know for sure, but neither do we know when we use words such as "pain", "affection", or "shyness" in our natural language.

KEY IDEA: We cannot guarantee that the artist and the audience understand the meaning of a work of art in the same way, but neither can we make such a guarantee in our everyday use of language

Critical thinking extension

Translatability of art

If art is a language, can it be translated into another language? That is certainly what we are trying to do. Even now I am talking about art, in language! Therefore, I am trying to translate art into English. But is that even possible? If art cannot be put into words, why am I wasting time and energy trying to do it?

Do art critics have any special ethical obligations? (#Ethics)

You might remember W.V.O. Quine's concept of indeterminacy of translation? It stated that for any given utterance in a given context, there always exist multiple ways to translate this utterance into another language, and all these translations will be equally suitable to the context. Therefore, we can never be certain that our translation is correct. Do you think the idea of indeterminacy of translation applies to art?

Suppose an artwork is a "sentence" expressing some thought behind it. The sentence is a "sign" of this thought. According to the principle of indeterminacy of translation, there exist many ways to translate this sentence, but there doesn't exist a way to select the "best" translation. All translations could potentially be correct even if they are incompatible with each other. In other words, art is untranslatable.

On the other hand, if it is untranslatable and we know it, why do we stubbornly keep talking about art? We have a whole army of art critics whose job, essentially, is to translate works of art into a natural language. If art is untranslatable, why are we paying them?

If you are interested…

A distinguishing feature of Indian classical dance is the use of hand and finger gestures (mudras). Mudras create a sort of a vocabulary through which the dancer conveys both external events and inner experiences. Mudra is Sanskrit for "seal" or "mark". Much like words of a natural language, many of the mudras have multiple meanings that need to be decoded by the audience based on the context.

You can learn more about Mudras if you do an Internet search for "mudras in classical Indian dance". A good place to start would be the Wikipedia page "List of mudras (dance)".

Take-away messages

Lesson 17. Art conveys a meaning, it stands for something, and in this sense a work of art is a sign of the artist's inner experiences. The audience needs to decipher this sign much like we decipher language to understand what the speaker means. The meaning of this sign is not "shared", in the sense that different people will probably read different meanings into it. However, the same is true for much of our language (for example, words describing internal experiences, such as pain, anxiousness, happiness). A separate question is that of translatability: if art is a language, can it be translated into English? W.V.O. Quine thinks art is untranslatable. However, this raises the question of the role of art critics. Translating art into regular language is the essence of their job, and if we know that art is untranslatable, what are we paying them for?

Back to the exhibition

Pioneer plaque... Seventeen lessons later, I am looking at it again. There is one major question in my mind: should intelligent extraterrestrials intercept the plaque, will they understand the message?

We consciously avoided using any of our 7,000 currently existing natural languages. But the scribblings on the plaque are still symbols. They are signs that stand for something, they have a meaning. Doesn't this automatically make these scribblings a kind of language? By not writing the message in any of our natural languages, we have not avoided the use of language in principle. Our alien friends will still have to translate our message into a language of their own.

If Immanuel Kant was right (as well as other scholars who later supported his views), we humans have a number of concepts that are hard-wired into our brains. We are not sure what these concepts are (there have been various suggestions). Perhaps the concept of direction (forward, backwards), or the concept of quantity (many, few), or kinship (relative, non-relative), or even the concepts of space and time. These a priori concepts do not depend on our personal experiences, we are pretty much born with them. If this is so, such concepts may even determine a "universal grammar" that is common to all the variety of natural languages we speak. Perhaps this is why there is a set of symbols that we think will be intuitively obvious to everyone no matter what cultural background they come from. For example, if we draw an arrow to represent the direction in which something is moving, we can expect any other human being to understand what it means.

But will an alien understand it? Will an alien's a priori concepts be the same as our human ones? If our a priori concepts are similar, yes. But how can they be similar? They can – if we assume that a priori concepts are formed in an intelligent mind as a reflection of some fundamental properties of reality. For example, that quantity is something that is in the nature of this world, and hence any intelligent organism that evolves in this world must have some representation of quantity. If we continue this logic, we must also believe that mathematics is discovered (and not invented) and that alien mathematics will resemble our own.

Unfortunately, there is a chance that our a priori concepts do not reflect the world as it is. We humans evolved on a remote planet in the corner of the Universe, so our experiences are limited. Perhaps we only understand the arrow symbol for a direction so well because we evolved from a hunter-gatherer society, because in our genes we are all hunters? And even for such seemingly obvious concepts as space and time some modern discoveries in science suggest that they are not what they seem to us (and maybe they don't even exist!).

So, do our a priori concepts reflect the world as it is, or are they a product of our limited evolution in our limited circumstances in our corner of the galaxy? I wish we could know, but we can't (assuming, again, that Immanuel Kant is right). Unless we meet aliens. This is why I'm so eager to meet them!

The good news is, when (if?) extraterrestrial beings intercept one of the Pioneer plaques, they will understand it provided the following conditions are met:

1) Fundamental a priori concepts exist
2) These concepts reflect the fundamental properties of the world around us

If these conditions are met, then we (aliens and humans) already speak the same language: some part of our Mentalese is overlapping. If at least one of these conditions is not met, then the Mentalese we are speaking is different and hence there is no basis for translating from one language into another. Our languages become untranslatable.

Suppose that the first condition is not met. For example, that the strong version of the Sapir-Whorf hypothesis is true (the language we speak determines the way we think). If this is the case, aliens probably speak a very different language (maybe they communicate chemically?), and hence they think differently, and hence they will not be able to reconstruct the ideas that we tried to convey with the Pioneer plaques.

Suppose that the second condition is not met: a priori concepts exist, but they do not reflect the fundamental properties of reality. If this is the case, we have probably evolved in very different circumstances, and the a priori concepts that evolved with us are also fundamentally different. Therefore, we understand the world differently. Maybe even to the extent that we will not be able to recognize that we have encountered intelligent life when the encounter happens? Therefore – in all likelihood – our Pioneer plaques will be misunderstood.

Whichever is true, I know for sure that, if contact with extraterrestrial beings is established, I will volunteer to be on the team of researchers who try to translate communication between our species, much like Louise Banks from the movie *Arrival* who was described at the start of this unit. I will do this solely for the purpose of understanding if a priori concepts exist. There are few things I can think of that have more implications for our understanding of our own minds.

UNIT 7 - Assessment guidance

7.1 - Overview of assessment in TOK

Assessment in Theory of Knowledge is not like in other IB subjects. You are not required to study any prescribed material and recall it on the day of the exam. You will never be asked to reproduce something you studied in class or to define a term. There are no timed assessments, so there is no need to memorize anything. You will have plenty of time to gather your thoughts together and produce a good-quality result. This is good news.

Assessment in TOK consists of two components. Just like any other subject in the Diploma Programme, TOK has an internally assessed component and an externally assessed one.

Internally assessed means that your teacher marks it, but a sample of submissions from your school is then sent to external IB examiners who moderate the marks of your teacher. If they agree with the marks, everything remains as it is. If they disagree with the marks, they will change the marks in the sample and then will adjust the marks for the rest of the submissions from your school (there is some mathematics involved in this process). For the internally assessed component, you are required to produce a *TOK exhibition*.

Externally assessed means that your teacher will see the first draft of your work and give you feedback on it, but the final version is not assessed by your teacher. It goes straight to external IB examiners. The externally assessed component is the *TOK essay*.

In the final TOK grade, the two components are combined like this:

- 35 % internal assessment (TOK exhibition)
- 65 % external assessment (TOK essay)

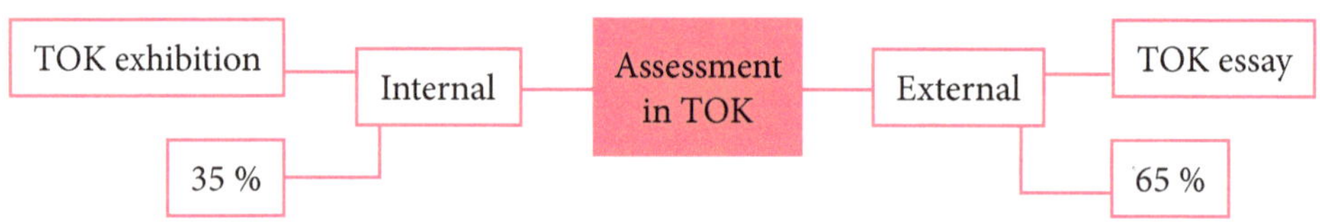

Together, with the Extended Essay, TOK is responsible for up to three marks in your IB Diploma. The mark you get is determined by the combination of your Extended Essay and TOK grades. The following matrix is used for this purpose:

		Theory of Knowledge				
		Grade A	Grade B	Grade C	Grade D	Grade E
Extended Essay	Grade A	3	3	2	2	Failing condition
	Grade B	3	2	2	1	Failing condition
	Grade C	2	2	1	0	Failing condition
	Grade D	2	1	0	0	Failing condition
	Grade E	Failing condition	Failing condition	Failing condition	Failing condition	Failing condition

7.2 - TOK exhibition

7.2.1 - Nature of the task

The TOK exhibition is designed to "explore how TOK manifests in the world around us" (IB TOK Guide).

Your task is to create an exhibition of three objects, or images of objects, that link to one of the 35 "IA prompts" provided in the TOK Guide. All three objects must be linked to the same IA prompt.

IA prompts
1) What counts as knowledge? 2) Are some types of knowledge more useful than others? 3) What features of knowledge have an impact on its reliability? 4) On what grounds might we doubt a claim? 5) What counts as good evidence for a claim? 6) How does the way that we organize or classify knowledge affect what we know? 7) What are the implications of having, or not having, knowledge? 8) To what extent is certainty attainable? 9) Are some types of knowledge less open to interpretation than others? 10) What challenges are raised by the dissemination and/or communication of knowledge? 11) Can new knowledge change established values or beliefs? 12) Is bias inevitable in the production of knowledge? 13) How can we know that current knowledge is an improvement upon past knowledge? 14) Does some knowledge belong only to particular communities of knowers? 15) What constraints are there on the pursuit of knowledge? 16) Should some knowledge not be sought on ethical grounds? 17) Why do we seek knowledge? 18) Are some things unknowable? 19) What counts as a good justification for a claim? 20) What is the relationship between personal experience and knowledge? 21) What is the relationship between knowledge and culture? 22) What role do experts play in influencing our consumption or acquisition of knowledge? 23) How important are material tools in the production or acquisition of knowledge? 24) How might the context in which knowledge is presented influence whether it is accepted or rejected? 25) How can we distinguish between knowledge, belief and opinion? 26) Does our knowledge depend on our interactions with other knowers? 27) Does all knowledge impose ethical obligations on those who know it? 28) To what extent is objectivity possible in the production or acquisition of knowledge? 29) Who owns knowledge? 30) What role does imagination play in producing knowledge about the world? 31) How can we judge when evidence is adequate? 32) What makes a good explanation? 33) How is current knowledge shaped by its historical development? 34) In what ways do our values affect our acquisition of knowledge? 35) In what ways do values affect the production of knowledge?

Each object must be accompanied by a written commentary that:
- Identifies the object and its specific real-world context
- Justifies its inclusion in the exhibition
- Explains the link to the IA prompt

There may or may not be an actual exhibition organized by your school. That will depend on your school context. In any case, the work you submit for assessment must be a single file containing a title clearly indicating the selected IA prompt, images of the three objects, a typed commentary for each of the objects, and appropriate citations and references. The maximum word count for the three commentaries combined is 950 words.

You are required to create an individual exhibition, so group work is not allowed. Multiple students in the same class are permitted to use the same IA prompt, but students in the same class are not allowed to use any of the same objects.

7.2.2 - What counts as an "object"?

There is a very wide variety of objects that can be used for the TOK exhibition. It is almost as wide as the world itself. The problem is not what to select, but how to select from such a wide range.

The objects may be something you came across in your academic studies or your life outside the classroom. It can be something that is of personal interest to you or something that you stumbled upon while looking for ideas online. It can be a physical object or a photograph of a physical object, in case the object itself cannot be obtained (no need to steal a mummy from British Museum – an image from the Internet would be sufficient, as long as you give proper references).

It can also be a digital object (for example, a tweet by a political leader or a news article from a website).

The only restriction is that the object must not be something that you created specifically for the purpose of the TOK exhibition. However, it may be a pre-existing object created by you (for example, a poem you wrote when you were younger, a painting that you created for an art class, a picture you took earlier, and so on).

Throughout this book in the boxes labelled "Exhibition" I tried to give you examples of various objects that could be used for this purpose.

7.2.3 - TOK exhibition assessment instrument

There is a single driving question underpinning the assessment of the TOK exhibition: *Does the exhibition successfully show how TOK manifests in the world around us?* This is the ultimate question that is placed above everything else. If the examiner's answer to this question after reading your written commentary is yes, they may very well ignore minor weaknesses and inconsistencies in your work.

The descriptor for the highest level of achievement (Excellent, 9-10 marks) is the following set of statements:
- *The exhibition clearly identifies three objects and their specific real-world contexts.*
- *Links between each of the three objects and the selected IA prompt are clearly made and well-explained.*

- *There is a strong justification of the particular contribution that each individual object makes to the exhibition.*
- *All, or nearly all, of the points are well-supported by appropriate evidence and explicit references to the selected IA prompt.*

We will unpack these statements in the following sections.

Does the exhibition successfully show how TOK manifests in the world around us?					
Excellent 9-10	Good 7-8	Satisfactory 5-6	Basic 3-4	Rudimentary 1-2	0
The exhibition clearly identifies three objects and their specific real-world contexts. Links between each of the three objects and the selected IA prompt are clearly made and well-explained. There is a strong justification of the particular contribution that each individual object makes to the exhibition. All, or nearly all, of the points are well-supported by appropriate evidence and explicit references to the selected IA prompt.	The exhibition identifies three objects and their real-world contexts. Links between each of the three objects and the selected IA prompt are explained, although this explanation may lack precision and clarity in parts. There is a justification of the contribution that each individual object makes to the exhibition. Many of the points are supported by appropriate evidence and references to the selected IA prompt.	The exhibition identifies three objects, although the real-world contexts of these objects may be vaguely or imprecisely stated. There is some explanation of the links between the three objects and the selected IA prompt. There is some justification for the inclusion of each object in the exhibition. Some of the points are supported by evidence and references to the selected IA prompt.	The exhibition identifies three objects, although the real-world contexts of the objects may be implied rather than explicitly stated. Basic links between the objects and the selected IA prompt are made, but the explanation of these links is unconvincing and/or unfocused. There is a superficial justification for the inclusion of each object in the exhibition. Reasons for the inclusion of the objects are offered, but these are not supported by appropriate evidence and/or lack relevance to the selected IA prompt. There may be significant repetition across the justifications of the different objects.	The exhibition presents three objects, but the real-world contexts of these objects are not stated, or the images presented may be highly generic images of types of object rather than of specific real-world objects. Links between the objects and the selected IA prompt are made, but these are minimal, tenuous, or it is not clear what the student is trying to convey. There is very little justification offered for the inclusion of each object in the exhibition. The commentary on the objects is highly descriptive or consists only of unsupported assertions.	The exhibition does not reach the standard described by the other levels or does not use one of the IA prompts provided.
Possible characteristics					
Convincing Lucid Precise	Focused Relevant Coherent	Adequate Competent Acceptable	Simplistic Limited Underdeveloped	Ineffective Descriptive Incoherent	

7.2.4 - What should be linked to what

There is some confusion among students regarding which elements of the exhibition should be linked and which should not, and also which links are assessed and which links are not assessed. In this section, I will try to provide more clarity.

What is required

1. Each object must be linked to the IA prompt

This is not negotiable. The link must be explicitly stated for each of the objects in turn. The IA prompts cannot be modified in any way. Stating the link between the object and the IA prompt means explicitly saying how (in what way) the object is an example of the prompt.

For instance, if your prompt is "*Are some things unknowable?*" (prompt 18) and your object is the recent black hole image taken by the Event Horizon Telescope, you might explain that the black hole is "unknowable" in the sense that we cannot see what is happening inside because not even light can escape its gravity. We think we know what a black hole is, but we cannot confirm our theories by observation. The black hole image taken by the Event Horizon Telescope is actually not an image of the black hole itself, but of the area surrounding it.

The important thing is, this link between the object and the prompt must be an explicit statement. Do not leave the examiner guessing what the connection is, just tell them directly.

2. You must explain the specific real-world context of each object

It has to be an object existing in a certain place at a certain time, not just a generic type. For example, a "bilingual dictionary" is not a specific object but a generic type. On the other hand, an English-Vietnamese dictionary that you used during your school trip to Vietnam is specific.

This requirement is there for a reason, not just to make your life as a student more miserable. The whole purpose of the TOK exhibition is to demonstrate how TOK can manifest in real life, and if your object does not have a specific context, you will not be able to do that.

Suppose the prompt you have selected is "*What is the relationship between knowledge and culture?*" (prompt 21). If your object is linked to a specific real world-context, you will be able to say, for example, that language contains certain concepts that cannot be adequately translated without a deep knowledge of the culture of the bearers of this language. You might be able to give an example of something you found particularly difficult to translate from English into Vietnamese during your school trip. This would be an effective demonstration of how lack of familiarity with the culture made it difficult for you to know what they meant by a certain concept or phrase. If you just used the generic "bilingual dictionary", such links would not be possible.

There is a mental exercise you can use to decide if the real-world context of your objects is sufficiently utilized in your written commentaries. After finishing your commentary, remove all of the explanations of the real-world context of your objects. If this did not impact the quality of the rest of the commentary, then your real-world context was underutilized and you need to review it. If you removed the real-world context and your commentary stopped making sense, then you've done a good job with the context.

3. You must justify the inclusion of each object in the exhibition

This is not the same as explaining the link between the object and the prompt. Each of your objects should contribute something to the overall message of your exhibition. It should highlight some unique aspect or dimension of the prompt. The three objects are not just examples illustrating the same point, they all make their own points.

Imagine I gave you a knowledge question (one of the IA prompts) and asked you to answer it in three simple sentences. You would not say the same sentence three times, would you? Each sentence would contribute something to the overall message and the three sentences together would convey a more complex idea than each of them individually. Each object in your exhibition is like a sentence; when you justify its inclusion in the exhibition, you explain why it is necessary to keep this sentence in your three-sentence-long answer.

What is not required

The three elements outlined above are required and assessed. Now, let me talk about elements that are *not* required and *not* assessed. There are some common misconceptions among students that lead them to think that the TOK exhibition task is more complicated than it actually is.

1. It is not required to link objects to "themes"

In the IB TOK syllabus, apart from the five areas of knowledge, there is one "core theme" (Knowledge and the knower) and five "optional themes" (Knowledge and technology, Knowledge and language, Knowledge and politics, Knowledge and religion, Knowledge and indigenous societies). Students are required to study the core theme and two of the five optional themes.

The IB TOK Guide states that it is "strongly recommended" that students base their exhibition on one of the themes (either the core theme or an optional theme). The reason for this recommendation is that it can be a useful way for students to "narrow down their choice of objects and give a focus to their exhibition".

Some students read this recommendation as a requirement to select one of the themes and ensure that all objects are connected to it, and even explain the connection in the written commentary. This is incorrect. No explanations regarding "themes" are necessary in the written commentary.

Your objects may come from any walk of life, be it within one of the IB "themes" or not. They may come from your academic life linked to one of the areas of knowledge. They may be related to your passionate desire to know whether or not aliens exist. You do not have to explain the link between your object and one of the "themes" in the written commentary, so I would not waste time doing so. Focus on important things: (1) links between each object and the prompt, (2) justifying the inclusion of each object, (3) real-world context of each object.

However, we must recognize that the reason the IB is making this recommendation is that the world of objects is very vast and it is easy to get overwhelmed with the variety of objects to choose from. So, it might be a good idea to narrow down your choice from the beginning.

Most commonly, the exhibition task will be undertaken by schools in the first year of the Diploma Programme. Depending on the approach you have taken in your school, you might have covered various amounts of material. Some of you might have studied one of the "themes", some of you might have started with one or more areas of knowledge, others might have started with key overarching concepts such as "doubt" or "bias". Let's just say that you have studied some TOK "topics", and narrowing your choice of object down to one or more topics that you feel most comfortable with would be a good option. See the section "Entry points" further in this unit for a more detailed discussion of the process of selecting the objects.

2. You do not have to explain how the objects are linked to each other, and in fact they do not have to be linked

It is not an assessment requirement, and linking objects to each other will not bring you more marks. On the contrary, it may take your focus off of the more important aspects, such as the link between each individual object and the prompt.

7.2.5 - Justifying the inclusion of objects in the exhibition

Earlier I compared each object in the TOK exhibition to a sentence which together make a three-sentence answer to the question in the IA prompt. In this section I will further unpack this metaphor and clarify it.

The situation you should try to avoid is when all three objects contribute to the exhibition in the same way. In other words, you do not want them all to make the same point. Suppose you have selected the prompt "*To what extent is objectivity possible in the production or acquisition of knowledge?*" (prompt 28). Then you said something along the lines of "objectivity is impossible". You then presented the following objects:

1) a journal article arguing that global warming is not a thing,
2) a history book claiming that Columbus did not discover America,
3) a website containing a conspiracy theory that Americans never landed on the Moon.

These are interesting examples, but they all seem to make the same point: that there may always exist an alternative opinion. You have illustrated this point with the first object; the second and the third object do not seem to add anything new, they are just additional illustrations of the same idea. This is an example of when the inclusion of objects in the exhibition is poorly justified.

As the examiner is reading your commentary, you want the story to unfold before their eyes. They have understood what you are trying to say with the first object. As you move on to the second object, say something new. Obviously, it should still be clearly focused on the IA prompt. For example:

***Image 1**. Three objects supporting the same idea*

1) Your first object is a journal article claiming that global warming is not a thing. The message you are sending with the inclusion of this object in the exhibition is that there always exists an alternative opinion. Alright, that's the first sentence in your three-sentence answer.

2) For the second object you take Franz Gall's map of skull regions. In the 19th century Franz Gall, the founder of phrenology, suggested that certain cognitive abilities correspond to certain areas of the brain and that by feeling the bumps on one's skull, he

could diagnose that person's abilities. Today this is widely used as an example of pseudoscience whose claims have been debunked in multiple research studies. Today we know objectively that this opinion is not correct. Therefore, the message you are sending with this object, and the second sentence in your three-sentence answer to the question, is that some opinions are provably wrong.

3) Finally, your third object is the cover of the *Skeptic* magazine published by the Skeptics Society – a particular issue, for example, the one where they debunk Scientology (Volume 17, number 1). The existence of such societies and publications is useful to the acquisition of knowledge because, through debunking misconceptions, it lets you know which opinions are wrong and in this way contributes to your knowledge. Therefore, the claim you are making with the inclusion of the third object in the exhibition is that, although complete objectivity may not be possible, it is still possible to make progress in the acquisition of knowledge by exercising healthy skepticism.

Note that all three objects above may be related to the theme "Knowledge and the knower" – they are all about the knowledge you acquire from the stuff you read, what you choose to believe in and what you choose to dismiss.

Let me just summarize. The IA prompt in this example was "*To what extent is objectivity possible in the production or acquisition of knowledge?*" The three-sentence answer that I suggested was the following:

1) There always exists an alternative opinion.
2) However, some opinions are provably wrong.
3) Although complete objectivity may be impossible, by exercising healthy skepticism we are still able to make progress in the acquisition of knowledge.

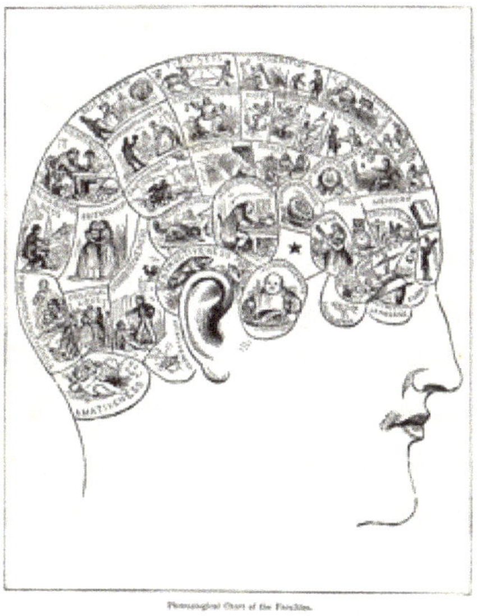

***Image 2**. Phrenology chart (1883)*

The three objects I used to illustrate these three points were a journal article that denies global warming, Gall's phrenological map of skull regions and the cover of a particular issue of the *Skeptic* magazine. Each of these objects supported one of the three points, and in this way each object made a unique contribution to the exhibition. To justify the inclusion of the object into the exhibition, then, would be to explain what unique point ("sentence") it makes in relation to the IA prompt.

I must also note that it is advisable to justify the inclusion of each object explicitly. Say "This object was included in the exhibition because..." or something similar, and then provide this justification. Examiners will be reading your commentary looking for signs of such justification. Make their job easier by simply telling them where to look.

***Image 3**. Three objects each making a unique contribution*

7.2.6 - Entry points

The TOK exhibition is a really broad task. Essentially, you are told to select three objects from the world around you and explain how TOK manifests in these objects. But the world is so big, and there are so many objects to select from. Moreover, all of the objects need to be linked to the same prompt, and their contributions to the prompt cannot just repeat each other. There are too many criteria to keep in mind while selecting from too many objects!

To make the task cognitively simpler and the exhibition more effective and focused, you may want to narrow down the search. There are multiple ways to do so, and these ways are sometimes called "*entry points*". An entry point is a point from which you start the process of narrowing down on the objects of your choice.

Below I discuss several possible entry points and highlight some of their advantages and disadvantages. The choice of entry point is totally up to you, and there is no such thing as a "better" entry point. Use your judgment and select the process that feels more natural to you.

Note that below I am only talking about choosing the first object, not the second and the third. This is because I believe the choice of the first object in many ways predetermines the choice of the other two. If you care about justifying the inclusion of each object in the exhibition, you will probably look for objects that do not make the same point as the first one, but make a slightly different point. This means that the first object, once it is included in the exhibition, seriously narrows down your search and gives you a much stricter sense of direction. On the other hand, this sense of direction is not there when you are choosing the first object. Hopefully, one of the three options presented below will help you make this important first step.

Option 1. Choose a topic, then choose a prompt, then choose the first object

When it is time for you to work on your TOK exhibition, you will have studied a number of topics in your TOK class, for example, knowledge and technology, bias in personal knowledge, the concepts of doubt, justification and truth, perhaps one or two areas of knowledge. You probably find some topics more engaging or easier to grasp. You can start by narrowing down on one of these topics.

For example, you may firmly decide that you want to explore something to do with technology. There you go, the world of objects has already become a lot smaller. With this in mind, look at the list of 35 prompts and select several that you think are related to the theme in an interesting way. Suppose, for example, that this one caught your eye: "*Are some types of knowledge less open to interpretation than others?*" (prompt 9).

You think: surely when technology is used to make measurements and register data, this is not open to interpretation? And you challenge yourself: can I find one example of when technology is used to obtain knowledge, but this knowledge is still open to interpretation? You conduct an internet search and you find, among other things, that CERN released 300 terabytes of data from the Large Hadron Collider experiments into public access. This is all "objective" data from particle experiments, but it makes no sense without human interpretation precisely because there is such a large amount of it. Opening public access to the full dataset was done precisely because new ways of looking at this data and reinterpretations of it can be precious in terms of obtaining new knowledge. You decide then to include the screenshot of the main page of the Open Data CERN project (http://opendata.cern.ch) as your first object.

Option 2. Choose a prompt, then choose a topic, then choose the first object

Suppose you are scrolling through the IA prompts and the following catches your eye: *Are some things unknowable?* (prompt 18). The question seems interesting to you. You decide to find some examples of things that are unknowable. The task is still not easily manageable, so you decide to limit the search to one of the topics that you have discussed in the TOK class. You choose language (for various reasons, perhaps simply because you feel slightly more comfortable with this topic). Immediately, you know that what you are looking for is an example of something that cannot be expressed in language (and hence cannot be known?).

You remember that several years ago you had an interesting conversation with your Portuguese friend who tried to explain some cultural concept to you, then gave up and said that some things are just untranslatable. You search the Internet for examples of "untranslatable" Portuguese words and find an article about the Portuguese word *saudade*. It means a melancholic longing for something or someone that is far away, a complex emotion of longing for something absent while knowing that you may never have it again, but at the same time being positive about the future. It is indeed not easy to translate, and it seems like only people with a specific cultural background can claim to know this emotion. You find a painting entitled "Saudade" (1899) by Almeida Júnior and decide to display this painting as your first object.

***Image 4**. Saudade (1899), by Almeida Júnior*

Option 3. Choose the first object, then choose a prompt most suitable to it

This entry point may be especially useful when you already have your eyes set on an object that might be interesting from the TOK point of view. As I am typing this, I'm looking at my keyboard and I'm wondering why the letters are arranged on it in such a weird way. They don't follow the alphabetical order. Do they have to be arranged like that?

A quick internet search brings me a personal discovery: the standard QWERTY is not the only existing keyboard layout. One of the alternatives is the Dvorak layout, named after its inventor August Dvorak. Apparently, a lot of research goes into this, and there are claims that Dvorak is more efficient than QWERTY because more keyboard strokes are made where the hands naturally rest, especially for right-handed people.

You decide to include a picture of the Dvorak layout as your first object. Is there a suitable IA prompt? One prompt catches your eye: "*How important are material tools in the production or acquisition of knowledge?*" (prompt 23). The argument you can make when explaining the link between the object and the prompt is that practically everything we do today we do with the help of a tool, and very often we are oblivious to the amount of work and research that generations before us invested into perfecting these tools. Even something as simple as writing a sentence depends to a large extent on the material tools we are using.

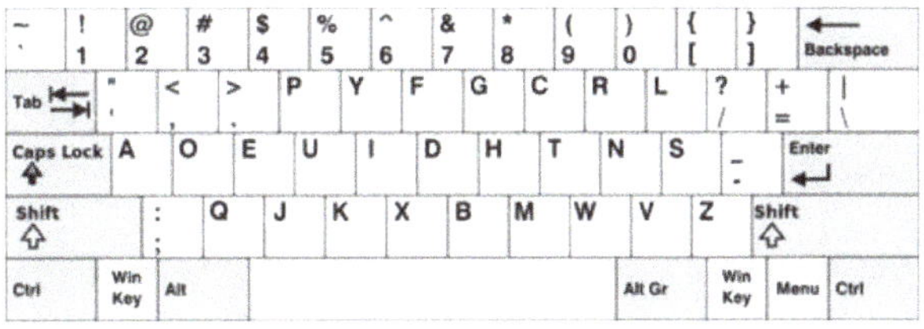

***Image 5**. The Dvorak keyboard layout*

7.2.7 - How to structure the written commentary

The IB does not have any specific requirements regarding formatting or the structure of the written commentary. However, I would recommend following this simple structure:

Element	Words
An opening paragraph explaining the overall purpose of your exhibition	50 words
A paragraph for the first object (clearly identify it, explain the real-world context, explain how it is linked to the prompt, justify its inclusion in the exhibition by outlining its unique contribution)	250 words
A paragraph for the second object (when you justify its inclusion in the exhibition, you can build upon the contribution of the first object)	250 words
A paragraph for the third object (when you justify its inclusion in the exhibition, you can build upon the contributions of the first two objects)	250 words
A concluding paragraph summarizing how the three objects in combination illustrate the IA prompt	100-150 words

In addition, you must also ensure that you have included all necessary references and acknowledged any work that is not your own. This is also true for the images. If the image is not your own, you should acknowledge the author and the source. References are not included in the word count.

7.2.8 - Concluding remarks

The TOK exhibition is designed to be an enjoyable task. Treat it this way. If you have a chance, make sure you attend the exhibition of the class above you to get a feel of what kinds of objects people select and how they justify their inclusion.

Give yourself sufficient time to brainstorm ideas (perhaps several months). But when the time comes, stick to your choice and cement it. It would be counterproductive to start changing your choice of objects a day before submission.

Choose one of the entry points, or use your own. Make sure to select objects with a specific context and explicitly describe this context. Clearly and explicitly explain the links between the IA prompt and each of your objects. Clearly and explicitly justify the inclusion of each object in the exhibition. Make sure there is a reasonable development in your three-sentence answer to the question.

Remember to properly cite all ideas and reference all sources, including the images if they are not your own. And, to reiterate, don't forget to enjoy the task.

7.2.9 - TOK exhibition checklist

In this section, you will find a checklist summarizing all of the guidance on the TOK exhibition task. You can use it to ensure that your work meets all necessary requirements. Tick the boxes that apply to your work and keep in mind your areas for improvement as you continue refining the final product.

Item	Check?
SELECTION OF OBJECTS	
I have selected one of the 35 IA prompts and I have not modified it in any way	☐
I have selected three objects, each linked to this IA prompt	☐
All of my objects are specific objects with a real-world context that I can explain	☐
Each of my three objects makes a unique contribution to the exhibition	☐
It *cannot* be said that all of my objects are examples illustrating the same point	☐
Nobody else in my class has selected the same objects	☐
COMMENTARY FOR EACH OBJECT	
I have explicitly explained the link between each of my objects and the prompt	☐
I have explained the specific real-world context of each object	☐
The real-world context of objects plays an important part in my commentary: if I remove it, the commentary will not make as much sense	☐
For each of my objects, I have explicitly formulated in one or more sentences how the object contributes to the exhibition (it has been included because…)	☐
For each of my objects, I can formulate in one sentence how it answers the IA prompt	☐
When I combine the three sentences (one for each object), they make sense as a coherent three-sentence answer to the prompt	☐
GENERIC COMMENTARY	
I have an opening statement describing my exhibition and explaining the overall message behind it	☐
I have a concluding remark that summarizes the contributions of the three individual objects and reflects on the way the exhibition as a whole answers the prompt	☐
FORMATTING	
I have included pictures of my objects in the same document with the written commentary	☐
I have included the necessary references and citations	☐
My written commentary is within 950 words	☐

7.3 - TOK essay

7.3.1 - Nature of the task

The TOK essay is an argumentative piece of writing. The focus in assessment is on your argumentation skills, your ability to apply knowledge concepts to specific situations, and the quality of your supporting examples. Above all that, the focus is on whether you understand how knowledge claims (and questions) are different from claims (and questions) about the world.

At the start of your second year of the Diploma Programme, the IB will release a list of 6 essay titles. For the May session the essay titles are released in the previous September, and for the November session the titles are released in the previous March. These titles will be formulated as knowledge questions that are focused on areas of knowledge. The chosen title must be used exactly as given; it is not allowed to be altered in any way.

The maximum length of the essay is 1,600 words.

7.3.2 - Typical mistakes

I will start with the most unfortunate typical mistakes that should be avoided at all costs. When these mistakes are made, the resulting work may be a great piece of writing, but it is not a TOK essay. This becomes the reason for a massive loss of marks by students every year. It is a real shame, because sometimes these essays are brilliant and highly convincing, it's just that they miss the point of TOK entirely.

1. Too much focus on personal knowledge

One of the prescribed essay titles that was released in the past (for the previous syllabus) read: *Do good explanations have to be true?*

Many students wrote essays suggesting that good explanations should be tailored to their recipient and therefore should not necessarily be true. According to one popular example, if a small child asks you to explain something complex such as "Why is the Sun hot?", it would be silly to give the accurate answer because the child will not understand astrophysics. Instead an explanation such as "The Sun is hot because it wants you to stay warm" would be satisfactory. Similarly, students could refer to their experience as school students – the way subjects are taught is very clearly a simplified truth and not the whole truth because the whole truth is too nuanced and complicated.

These are all wonderful examples, but they all miss the point because such answers interpret the essay title incorrectly. TOK essays have as their focus areas of *shared* knowledge. Therefore, the word "explanations" in the title doesn't mean the act of one person explaining something to another person. It means a shared explanation existing within a shared body of knowledge, such as a scientific theory, a school of art or a historical perspective. The Big Bang theory is an explanation of the origin of the Universe, and cubism is an explanation of what it means to be aesthetic in art.

By contrast, the act of one person explaining something to another person, as well as your experiences as a school student, all relate to personal knowledge. It will not be considered as something related to an area of knowledge, hence it is advisable to avoid arguments related to personal knowledge in a TOK essay (it is perfectly fine in the TOK exhibition, though!).

KEY IDEA: TOK essay titles are focused on areas of knowledge; therefore, your arguments should be focused on shared knowledge, not personal knowledge

2. Subject-specific arguments

There are five areas of knowledge in TOK, but TOK cannot be reduced to any one of them. TOK is "above" these areas of knowledge.

Sometimes the title of the essay may be formulated with reference to one particular AOK (for example History) but that does not mean you can simply discuss something you normally discuss in your History class.

Let me give you a more specific example.

Suppose the essay title is formulated as the following knowledge question: "*How significant are notable individuals in shaping Mathematics as an area of knowledge?*"

It might be tempting to remember great mathematicians and start explaining their contribution to the field. For example, you might write a whole page about Georg Cantor and how he invented a way to talk about mathematical infinity. You might say that this contribution was important because it provided mathematicians with the important concept of "sets" and a tool to describe any set, including an infinite one. You can mention that Cantor's theory led to some counter-intuitive discoveries, for example, the proof that some infinities are larger than others. Then you can keep talking about why the concept of infinity is important for mathematics. Perhaps you will even want to explain how exactly Cantor conceptualized infinity. This is all great as an example that supports a certain argument, but in itself this discussion is not a TOK discussion. It is much more suitable for a math class than a TOK class.

***Image 6**. Georg Cantor (1845 – 1918)*

The question above does not ask you about specific mathematicians and their specific contributions. It is a more generic question about the role of individual outstanding mathematicians in the development of knowledge. The debate that is implicit in this question can probably be reformulated like this: is knowledge in mathematics shaped by collective systematic effort, or is it shaped by outstanding individuals? It is probably the same kind of question that we ask when we wonder whether history is shaped by great leaders.

The two positions in this debate can probably be phrased like this:

1) Development of knowledge in mathematics is driven by collective effort. It is the result of systematic investigation where one person acts upon the achievements of others. If the work of any individual mathematician seems great or revolutionary, this is only because this particular individual happened to be in the right place at the right time. Efforts

of countless mathematicians made a discovery possible, and the "great mathematician" just happened to be the one who stumbled upon this discovery. From this perspective, we shouldn't overestimate the role of individuals in mathematics. If that mathematician failed to make the discovery, there would be some other mathematician who would not fail – it would only be a matter of time.

2) Development of knowledge in mathematics is driven by a few great individuals. If it were not for those individuals, mathematics would not have achieved what it has achieved. To further develop knowledge in mathematics, we need to patiently wait for the next genius to be born.

It is this generic argument that needs to be addressed in the essay, not specific mathematicians and their specific contributions (although, of course, specific mathematicians should be used as examples illustrating this argument).

Question: How significant are notable individuals in shaping mathematics as an area of knowledge?	
Answer 1 (not TOK)	**Answer 2 (TOK)**
Oh, let me give you some examples of great mathematicians and explain the contributions they made.	The question implies two opposing views on the driving force in the development of mathematics: notable individuals or collective effort. I can give you some examples of great mathematicians, but how significant can they be, in general, in shaping the area?

3. Examples from areas of knowledge that are not really related to knowledge

As follows from the point above, your key arguments in the essay should be generic arguments about knowledge. However, examples that support these generic arguments should be specific.

Using supporting examples is an important part of the TOK essay. If you have good abstract arguments supported by good specific examples, it is a clear demonstration that you have mastered the art of moving easily between the abstract and the specific, and that you see the TOK behind all the things you do in your regular classroom. Therefore, it is essential to make sure that your examples are good.

KEY IDEA: TOK essay = generic arguments about knowledge supported by subject-specific examples

Examples should be related to areas of knowledge. But there is a very tricky trap that many students fall into when they give an example that *they think* relates to an area of knowledge when in fact it doesn't.

Consider the following knowledge question: *How important are the opinions of experts in the search for knowledge?* Suppose you are arguing that opinions of experts *are* important, and you are looking for examples from various areas of knowledge to support this argument. This is what you come up with for History:

> Mikhail Kutuzov was the chief general commanding Russian troops at the time when Napoleon made a quick advance into Russian inland in 1812. They clashed in the famous and grandiose battle of Borodino near Moscow, with the outcome of the battle being

ambiguous and both sides suffering heavy casualties. After the battle, top commanders of the Russian army gathered for a conference where Kutuzov convinced everyone that their troops had to retreat and abandon Moscow. This was a difficult decision. The capital was evacuated and burned. The retreating army burned everything behind it. To many, this felt like losing the war. However, in the long run, the strategy proved effective. French troops were dragged deep inside the country and exhausted. Eventually Napoleon had to retreat, facing the severe Russian winter and lack of resources as everything had been burned along their route, and his forces were almost completely lost during this retreat. Kutuzov's decision was controversial and not universally supported, but his experience and expert vision allowed him to see the best course of action where others failed to see it.

It is a great story, but it doesn't work as an example for a TOK essay. It is a story from the past, a part of our history, but it is not related to the study of the past, to History as an area of knowledge. It is really important to know the difference. An example from History (as an area of knowledge) should involve historians and how they arrive at knowledge about the past. For example, the story of Kutuzov that I have just told you is something that I remember from my own History textbooks from back when I was a student. These History textbooks were written by experts, who based their writing on other books written by expert historians. It is the opinion of those historians that the decision to abandon Moscow was Kutuzov's cunning plan, but how can they be so sure? Is that a fact or is that their opinion? These and similar questions *are* related to History as an area of knowledge.

Image 7. *Portrait of Kutuzov, by R. Volkov (between 1812 and 1830)*

7.3.3 - Structuring the essay

A typical (incorrect) question

Students typically ask "How should I structure my TOK essay?" It is one of the most difficult questions I have ever had to answer in a teaching context. And yet I will give it a try.

The way I see it, you should be asking yourself a series of three questions, and these should come sequentially one after another:

1) What do I think about the question?
2) What argument will I make about the question?
3) And then: How should I structure my essay?

Image 8. *How should I structure my TOK essay?*

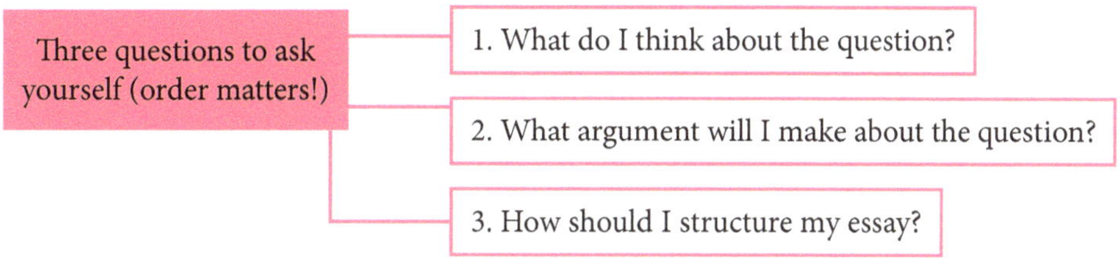

Step 1: What do I think about the question?

At Step 1, you explore the prescribed essay title and think about all arguments and examples that come to your mind in relation to it. For example, suppose the knowledge question you are attempting to answer is "*Can models be useful even when they are inaccurate?*"

As you keep thinking about this question, more and more examples, arguments and aspects will come to your mind. It will be just a collection of ideas and thoughts "around" the question – that's how our mind usually works! For example, among the multiple thoughts that occurred to you could be the following:

1) Oh, just recently in an Economics class we learned about the classical economic model that combines the law of supply and the law of demand. It predicts the point of equilibrium between price and quantity, all other things being equal. We spent quite a lot of time studying it, so it must be useful. But it does have a limitation in that it assumes that all the other factors are "equal", which is hard to imagine in real life.
2) I also remember from a Psychology class that we studied the "multi-store model of memory". This model assumes that memory consists of three stores (sensory memory, short-term memory and long-term memory), and that information flows in one direction from one store to the next. We criticized this model for being simplistic in that it does not explain some facts about memory.
3) I remember reading somewhere that there were several different models of the structure of the atom and that some of these models were discarded with the development of science. For example, the plum pudding model of the atom was proposed by J.J. Thomson in 1904; it suggested that the atom is a positively charged medium (a pudding) with negatively charged electrons (plums) placed inside. Later, with the discovery of the proton, this model was shown to be incorrect and now we accept a model in which there is a proton in the center and electrons are orbiting it.
4) So what can I say from all of these examples? Sometimes models are intentionally simplified, like the classic economic model of supply and demand. You can't really apply the "all other things being equal" logic to any specific real-life situation, but I guess the value of this model is that it brings out the abstract rule.
5) Sometimes models (like the one in my Psychology class example) are criticized for being too simple to explain the whole range of observed phenomena, but if that model was more complicated, it would become much more difficult to test it. So I guess there is some kind of a trade-off: complicated models are more accurate, but harder to test.
6) The plum pudding model was not just simplified, it was incorrect! But it was still useful as a stepping stone for further research. It inspired further inquiry in which it was tested and rejected, giving way to a more accurate model. So I guess even incorrect models can be useful precisely because they give scientists an impulse to design experiments to test them, and once incorrect models are rejected, we start understanding more about the world.

Step 1 may be finished here – this is what you think about the question. You would agree, however, that these six bullet points can hardly be called a coherent argument. These are just musings around the subject. Actually, a common mistake among students is to start writing the essay straight away, without planning it, and to submit these "musings" as the final product. There is no central argument here, and it is not clear what point is being made and what the conclusion is. Such a submission would resemble a "stream of consciousness" rather than a real essay.

***Image 9**. Musings around the subject*

Step 2: What argument will I make about the question?

Step 2 is where you look back at your musings and decide which ones to keep and which ones to ignore, and how to combine them into a single coherent argument. For the example above, you might end up with something like this:

> *Models are useful precisely because they are inaccurate. When they are inaccurate in the sense of "simplified", it allows researchers to more easily test them and gain knowledge about some common laws while ignoring the details of individual cases. When they are inaccurate in the sense of "incorrect", it inspires researchers to test them and replace them with better models, which fuels the development of knowledge.*

You understand at this point that there are some things from Step 1 that you will leave behind and not mention in your essay because they are not directly relevant to the argument that you formulated. You also understand, perhaps, that you need to look for additional supporting examples, claims and counterclaims to further develop the argument you have formulated. But the main outcome of this stage is that you finally know what you are going to say in your TOK essay.

***Image 10**. Get to the point*

Step 3: How should I structure my essay?

Step 3 is finally where you ask "How should I structure my essay?" Now that you know what it is that you are going to say in the essay, decisions on how to structure it become much more meaningful. Looking at the main argument and thinking about what could be an effective way to communicate it, you could come up with the following:

1) I need to start with the distinction between "simplified" and "incorrect", because in the context of my argument it is a very important distinction. I can start by saying that, in order to answer the question in the title, we need to first answer a subsidiary question - "What does it mean for a model to be inaccurate?" I can devote the first part of the essay to answering this question.
2) I can show different perspectives here. On the one hand, being inaccurate means not completely corresponding to the reality that the model represents. On the other hand, it seems impossible to completely correspond to reality. After all, the globe is not the Earth, but the only model of the Earth that is perfect in every way is the Earth itself. This brings me to say that any model is inherently inaccurate, and there is no such thing as an accurate model. But there do seem to exist degrees of inaccuracy. A milder degree is just being a "simplified" representation of reality, when the model reflects reality correctly but ignores certain properties (like how a globe ignores certain details of the Earth). A more serious degree of inaccuracy is when the model is incorrect, that is, misrepresents reality. Usefulness of the model may depend on which type of inaccuracy we are dealing with.
3) In the next paragraph I can focus on inaccuracy understood as simplification. Are simplified models useful? I can try to show both sides of the argument. On the one hand, simplification means that certain properties of real-life objects are ignored. This also means that a model is not fully applicable to real life. On the other hand, simplification means that what remains in the model are properties that are characteristic of many different objects, just like the classic economic model which is not really useful in every particular case but useful for capturing the essence of the relationship between supply and demand in general. I can conclude that simplified models are useful as long as they can serve as an idealization of the world.

4) Then in the next paragraph I can switch over to inaccuracy understood as an incorrect model. Again, I can try seeing pros and cons in that. From the negative side, such models may be misleading. From the positive side, they serve as a stepping stone for the development of science. In any case, when Thomson proposed the plum pudding model, he believed it was correct as there was no evidence to suggest otherwise. We do not know if our model is incorrect before it is shown to be incorrect. Perhaps we should assume all models to be incorrect and that they are just waiting for their time to be discarded. But that in itself is very useful, because once the old model is discarded, we will know what exactly was wrong with it, which is how our knowledge develops.
5) I will then add a conclusion summarizing all of my main arguments. Then I will go back to the beginning and add an effective introduction that formulates my thesis statement and explains to the reader how this statement is going to be unpacked.

At the end of this mental exercise, I have come to an essay structure that consists of an introduction, three paragraphs and a conclusion. Every paragraph in my example starts with a question, then presents two sides of the argument, then reconciles them in a sub-conclusion.

Image 11. *Writing an essay*

But note how the structure of the essay was the result of the thinking process behind it. If your thinking process is different, you may end up with a different structure.

7.3.4 - Tools of argumentation

Your essay needs to be a piece of argumentative writing. The argumentation needs to be good. So the question is, what makes your argumentation good?

In this section, I'm going to talk about "tools of argumentation" commonly used by students in the best essays I have seen. In fact, apart from being tools of argumentation, they are also tools of thinking! I have been doing my best in this book to model these tools of thinking through the way the lessons are structured and the information is presented.

Here they are:

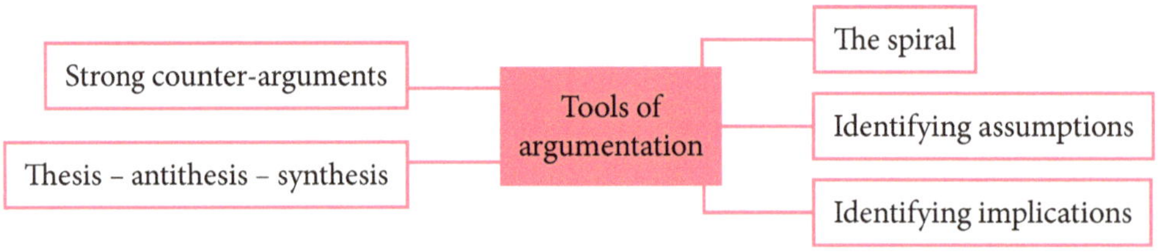

1. Strong counter-arguments

In many ways, this one is a litmus test for a good TOK essay. You know the quality of argumentation from the quality of counter-arguments. The overall idea is that, once you have put forward a thesis and supported it with an argument and an example, you need to think of potential counter-arguments to this thesis from those who don't agree with you. In other words: "*This is what I think and this is why. Now how would someone who disagrees with me object to this, and what would be their reasoning?*"

Counter-arguments presented in weak essays tend to be superficial and visibly flawed. It is usually obvious that the student has come up with the counter-argument because they knew they had to, but they haven't made the genuine attempt to step out of their own mind and take the perspective of someone who disagrees with them. Conversely, counter-arguments presented in strong essays are genuine, meaningful attacks on the weaknesses of the original thesis. Reading a good TOK essay is like watching a good sports match because you keep wondering who will win and you are never too certain.

***Image 12**. Strong counter-arguments*

For example, suppose you are answering the following knowledge question: "*Can a work of art have meaning of which the artist is unaware?*" and suppose the statement you are making is:

> *Yes, because beauty is in the eye of the beholder, and the meaning of a work of art will be different for different audiences.*

You might give an example to support this thesis: the way we read Shakespeare today is certainly different from the way he was perceived in his time, and the cultural and historical meaning of Shakespeare's works that we see today could not be seen by Shakespeare himself.

Now suppose two students were writing this essay and they both wanted to give a counter-argument to this statement. This is what they came up with:

Student A. On the other hand, sometimes without the knowledge of the artist's intention, the work of art can be misunderstood. For example, an illustration from a medieval Belgian manuscript of the *Roman de la Rose*, an allegorical poem popular at that time, depicts a woman raising a hammer over a baby lying on an anvil, with several other lifeless looking babies on the floor. To us it looks horrendous, and it's not easy to see anything else in this illustration apart from infanticide. However, the intention of the author was quite different, as obvious from the title of this illustration: *Nature Forging a Baby*. The picture was supposed to show the work of Mother Nature who is forging babies, like a blacksmith with an anvil and hammer.

***Image 13**. "Nature forging a baby", by Guillaume de Lorris and Jean de Meun, Roman de la Rose (1275)*

Student B. On the other hand, the idea that meaning of a work of art depends on the audience is a slippery slope leading to relativism in art. If meaning of art depends on the audience, then a work of art can have as many meanings as there are audiences, and these meanings can even contradict each other. But if that is the case, then there is no point in speaking about art as an area of knowledge at all. Knowing what a work of art means, in this case, is a job of a sociologist who studies various audiences and their perceptions. So if we accept that meaning in art depends on the audience, we must also accept that art is not an area of shared knowledge. For example, when Salvador Dali revealed his painting "*The Persistence of Memory*" in 1932, critics believed that the melting clocks were a representation of fluidity of space and time, and that this is how Dali artistically captures Einstein's theory of relativity. But when Dali was questioned, he said that he was simply inspired by the image of cheese melting in the sun. If we agree that the meaning of art depends on the audience, we must accept both these interpretations as true, which seems weird.

Student A's counter-argument is weak, and student B's counter-argument is strong.

Saying "sometimes without the knowledge of the artist's intention the work of art can be misunderstood" does not really contradict the statement that "the meaning of a work of art will be different for different audiences". In fact, it can be used as support: an audience that has seen the title "*Nature Forging a Baby*" and an audience that has not seen this title will interpret different meanings into this work of art. This is a weak counter-argument that will be easily rejected. It is there just for the sake of having a counter-argument.

By contrast, showing that the statement "the meaning of a work of art will be different for different audiences" leads to relativism in art is a strong counter-argument because it shows that the thesis runs itself into a problem. To reply to this counter-argument, you now need to say how you are going to solve the problem. Will you admit, for example, that art is not an area of knowledge?

2. Thesis – antithesis – synthesis

Good counter-arguments are an important building block of good argumentation, but they are not sufficient. You can't just present arguments and counter-arguments side by side and leave them be. The contradiction needs to be resolved, and some sort of conclusion needs to be made after considering both perspectives. In this section I will talk about a thinking tool that may be used to formulate such conclusions: thesis –antithesis – synthesis.

I'm sure you have witnessed situations where two people keep arguing with each other, each on diametrically opposite positions in the debate, firing arguments at each other and unable to find common ground. You might have wondered why they are so stubborn and why their debate is not moving anywhere out of the deadlock.

***Image 14**. Debate in a deadlock*

In 99 cases out of 100, the reason is that they are both right in their own way, but neither of the opponents understands it. They are both making certain assumptions and thinking within a certain framework, but they fail to see that the opponent's assumptions are different. Once they see that, the debate is likely to get resolved quickly and easily.

Let me first give you a non-TOK example to illustrate this.

Suppose Alice and Brianne are debating about allowing small children to play with digital devices. Alice says that giving children as young as 3 or 4 years old a smartphone is a good thing because it develops their fine motor skills and prepares them for the high-tech world that we live in today. Brianne says that smartphones are damaging to the young brain because they are addictive and don't present a cognitive challenge. Alice and Brianne can debate forever, and each of them can even find supporting research to back up their position. That is until Alice and Brianne realize that they are actually speaking about different things. Alice assumes that the child is exposed to moderate amounts of screen time and plays good educational games on the smartphone. Brianne assumes that the child has excessive amounts of screen time and plays flashy addictive video games. Once they understand this, they can easily agree that smartphones for small children may be harmful or beneficial, depending on amount of exposure and how they are used.

What happened here is that the two sides in the debate were implicitly making two opposite assumptions without realizing it. In a situation like this, simply firing arguments at each other and growing increasingly angry will not help. Within the assumptions that your opponent is making, your arguments won't make much sense, so they will not really reach the target. A constructive way to move the discussion forward would be to uncover the implicit assumptions and reconcile the two arguments by separating their "spheres of influence" (in such and such situations the argument is true, however, in such and such situations the counter-argument is true).

***Image 15**. Boy with a smartphone*

Now let me give you an example that is closer to TOK. Suppose Antony and Bryan are debating the following question: "*Can bias in knowledge be desirable?*"

Antony claims that it can because things like stereotypes have an adaptive function, they make our lives easier. A stereotype is useful because it saves us the mental energy that would be required if we had to analyze each and every situation of our lives with an open mind. For example, when you are selecting a dentist based on a friend's recommendation, you are likely to not be making the best choice. You could have found a better and cheaper dentist who is more competent to deal specifically with your problem if you conducted a thorough search online and systematically looked at reviews. However, by thinking "whatever is good for my friend is also good for me", you saved yourself a ton of mental energy. If we could not rely on stereotypes and other biases, we would find our everyday lives very challenging.

On the other hand, Bryan claims that bias in knowledge cannot be desirable. He says that overcoming bias is the whole point of acquisition of knowledge. Truth is the highest value that underlies all scientific endeavors. If the goal of science was not to find the truth, but to create a theory that is convenient to believe in, then science would be no different from propaganda. Considering bias in any way desirable goes against the very nature of science.

Antony and Bryan will find common ground once they realize that they are actually talking about different kinds of knowledge. Antony is talking about personal knowledge, and Bryan's argument assumes shared knowledge. Once they realize that, it is likely that they will quickly agree: bias may be okay in personal knowledge, but not in shared knowledge. Again, in this example, the debate was resolved by uncovering the implicit assumptions and reconciling the two arguments by separating their "spheres of influence".

***Image 16**. It is necessary to find a common ground to move on with the argument*

When you write a TOK essay – or, indeed, present any TOK argument – both sides exist within your own mind. They are the dialogue you have with yourself. Antony is your argument and Bryan is your counter-argument. I spoke in the previous section about how it is important to make your counter-arguments strong. But the presence of a strong counter-argument is not enough to move the analysis of a knowledge question forward. You need to somehow reconcile the argument and the counter-argument in a single conclusion. To achieve this, you usually need to uncover the implicit assumptions upon which both the argument and counter-argument are based.

KEY IDEA: Reconcile the argument and the counter-argument in a single conclusion by uncovering the implicit assumptions

Georg Hegel, a 19th century philosopher, spoke about the triad "thesis – antithesis - synthesis". He thought that this triad captures the essence of any process of development, so this also applies to the development of argumentation. The idea is that:

- Thesis is a statement that you make based on your best knowledge.
- Antithesis is a statement that rejects your thesis. It is a strong point, not just a weak counter-argument that can be easily dismissed.
- Synthesis is a modified thesis that takes into account the antithesis. Therefore, it is a better version of the thesis, and it takes argumentation to the next level.

Graphically speaking, the "thesis – antithesis - synthesis" process is a kind of spiral, because the synthesis returns back to the thesis, but on a whole new level. That is how argumentation develops instead of getting stuck in an infinite vicious circle of arguments and counter-arguments. Practice your synthesis!

3. The spiral

In the previous section, I spoke about the importance of a good synthesis. So far we have discussed two thinking tools for creating great TOK discussions: coming up with strong counter-arguments and making sure that the argument and the counter-argument are reconciled in a kind of "synthesis".

Thesis – antithesis – synthesis is a great way to describe the structure of argumentation in one paragraph of a TOK essay. But there is more than one paragraph. After you have presented your argument, offered a potentially strong counter-argument from someone who hypothetically disagrees with you, and reconciled both in a sub-conclusion, you might want to move on. You might look at your sub-conclusion and realize that the discussion is far from over, and the sub-conclusion just creates an impulse for further development of your analysis. Actually, this is exactly what tends to happen.

We now need to look at the process of argumentation in the essay in its entirety rather than focusing on one paragraph.

Another tool of argumentation that might be useful here is what I call "the spiral".

***Image 17**. Going up the spiral*

Essentially, "the spiral" is a sequence of several rounds of thesis – antithesis – synthesis, where the synthesis in the first round serves as a starting point for thesis in the next round, and so on. Let me take the non-TOK example mentioned above and demonstrate what a spiral argumentation might look like:

Should small children be allowed to play with digital devices? A demonstration of "spiral" argumentation	
Question:	Should small children be allowed to play with digital devices?
Thesis (person A):	Yes, they should, because it gives them the skills necessary for the modern digital world.
Antithesis (person B):	No, they should not, because it leads to addiction and deficits of cognitive development due to lack of cognitive challenge.
Synthesis:	Apparently, person A assumes that there is moderate exposure to digital devices, whereas person B assumes that the use of digital devices is excessive. We can agree that digital technology may have its benefits, but only when children are exposed to moderate amounts of it.
Implication:	But then the answer to the original question depends on whether or not it is possible to ensure that children will not be exposed to excessive amounts of digital technology. The synthesis implies that children should be allowed to use digital devices only if the amount of such use can be strictly controlled.
Thesis (person A):	It is possible to make a deal with small children that they will only have a certain amount of screen time per day, and this rule will become a part of their normal daily routine.
Antithesis (person B):	It is impossible to make such a deal with small children. The restrictive rule will only make smartphones more attractive to them, and you will have to tear them away from the device with a tantrum every single time.
Synthesis:	Apparently, person A assumes that inhibiting impulses can be easily taught at a young age, while person B assumes that inhibiting impulses at such a young age is difficult. We can agree that small children should be allowed to play with digital devices as long as it is used as a tool to teach them to control their impulses.
Implication:	The synthesis implies that we should only allow small children to play with smartphones if we use it as a lesson in moderation and self-control. But is that what really happens? Most parents seem to give their children a smartphone to distract them, not to teach them a lesson in self-control.
Conclusion:	Then the conclusion is that it is only in rare cases, as part of a well-planned educational strategy implemented by conscientious parents, that small children should be allowed to play with digital devices. If used correctly and strictly supervised, this could become an important life lesson in inhibiting one's impulses and contribute to the development of self-control along with some important digital skills. However, it can be extremely challenging with small children. Most parents give their children a smartphone simply to distract them with something, and such use is probably more harmful than beneficial. We should be aware of these dangers when we are making the decision, and the answer to the question "*Should small children be allowed to play with digital devices?*" depends on the maturity of parents as much as it depends on the maturity of kids.

In this example, argumentation follows a spiral structure. There are two rounds of thesis – antithesis – synthesis, and therefore two turns of the spiral. The second turn of the spiral uses the synthesis from the previous turn as the starting point. The way they are linked is through considering implications of the synthesis. Once you have reconciled the argument and the counter-argument in a synthesis statement, you look at the original question again and try to figure out what your synthesis suggests for an answer. What usually happens is that the synthesis takes you to a new level and you understand that the answer to the original question depends on how you resolve a related, but different, debate. In the example above, the answer to the original question ("*Should small children be allowed to play with digital devices?*") depends on whether or not we can strictly control the amount of exposure.

***Image 18**. Developing an argument through claims and counterclaims*

Visit our blog for more examples of spiral argumentation.

4. Identifying assumptions

I have already mentioned assumptions and implications several times. However, it would be useful to reiterate what they are because identifying assumptions and implications is a thinking tool in its own right. When I see that a student in a TOK essay explicitly identifies assumptions and discusses implications of an argument, it is usually a certain sign that I am dealing with a good essay written by a student with strong critical thinking skills.

We will start with assumptions.

What is an assumption?

An assumption of a statement is something that must be true for the statement also to be true. If X is your statement and A is the assumption, then X is true only if A is true. Assumptions are an answer to the question "What is this based on?"

For example, take the statement "We ran out of cornflakes, but I can go and get some from the grocery store in no time". One of the assumptions it rests upon is that the grocery store is open at this time of the day. X ("I can get some cornflakes from the grocery store in no time") is only true if A ("The grocery store is open") is also true.

It is possible for a statement to have more than one assumption, for example: X is true only if A, B and C are true.

Identifying assumptions is not easy because you have to think backwards from a given statement to the foundation upon which this statement was built. Moreover, assumptions are usually implicit, which is the whole problem. Two people debating about something may not realize that they are debating about different things because implicitly they are making different assumptions. This is why identifying assumptions, although not an easy task, is an important thinking tool to master.

Normally, school does not teach us to think backward and identify assumptions. Courses are usually taught in a bottom-up kind of way. For example, in Geometry, first you study the axioms and the key principles and then you are introduced theorems, gradually increasing the level of difficulty. But how often do you see a mathematical problem that gives you a theorem and asks you to name assumptions that must be true for this theorem to also be true? When I ask a group of students to name the Pythagorean theorem, I usually get quite a few knowledgeable people who are ready to give the answer. But when I ask the same students to name the assumptions that must be true for the Pythagorean theorem to also be true, I usually get puzzled looks. Our education does not reinforce this skill as much as it should.

On the other hand, all of the famous standardized tests used by universities in their selection process include tasks where you are required to identify assumptions of a given statement. There are such tasks in the GMAT, LSAT and ACT.

Below is an example mimicking a typical task on a standardized test:

Exercise: Identify the assumption
"I have put a lot of effort into writing this book, so it will be successful among TOK students". Which assumption is implicit in this statement? A. Every effort always translates into quality B. I know what TOK students will find useful C. This book will sell very well among students D. Students are the ones who decide which textbook to use E. I am a skillful writer

I believe that the correct answer is B. Here's why:

- **Option A** is a very broad. It does not have to be true for the statement to be true. There is no contradiction in believing that every effort does *not* necessarily translate into quality and at the same time believing that *my* effort does.
- **Option C** is not an assumption – it is an implication. Good sales are a consequence of the fact that students find a book useful, but not a condition for a book's success. In other words, you buy a book because you find it useful, but you do not find a book useful because you have bought it.
- **Option D** is irrelevant to the statement. It has nothing to do with the relationship between the effort I put in the book and its success among students. Moreover, if students are not the ones who decide which textbook to use, they can still find it helpful. In any case, I can easily imagine a situation where Option D is false and yet my statement remains true.
- **Option E**, I believe, is also a correct answer. If I am not a skillful writer, chances are that my book will not be successful among students no matter how much effort I invest into it.
- However, **Option B** is better suitable as a correct answer. If I am a skillful writer, but I do not know what will be useful to TOK students, I will end up writing a masterpiece that will be of little value. It is therefore essential for me to know what students will find useful. If this condition is not met, the statement will be false.

I would argue that both B and E are assumptions implicit in the statement, but in a forced-choice scenario like this one, I would prefer option B.

Thankfully, in a TOK essay you will not have to choose a correct answer from the given options, but this also means that you need to identify hidden assumptions all by yourself. Practice this skill in your TOK discussions and other subjects, and it will gradually become second nature.

As you have seen, the thinking tool thesis – antithesis – synthesis depends largely on your ability to identify hidden assumptions. You can make an effective synthesis once you uncover the (different) assumptions implicit in the argument and the counter-argument.

5. Identifying implications

In a sense, implications are logically opposite to assumptions.

What is an implication?
An implication is something that *follows* from your statement. If X is your statement and A is the implication, then, once you accept that X is true, you must also accept that A is true. Implications are an answer to the question "So what?" For example, take the statement "I was caught stealing a car". If this statement is true, then it must also be true that I am not coming home today for dinner. It is possible for a statement to have more than one implication, for example: if X is true, then A, B and C must also be true.

Identifying implications is another skill that is not sufficiently practiced in our education, yet it is widely required everywhere. Just like assumptions, implications are a common occurrence on standardized tests such as the GMAT, SAT, LSAT and ACT.

I must say that it is quite natural for people to stop in their thinking half-way, to not think things through. I sometimes use the following activity with my students: I tell them I will be reading out a series of statements, one by one, and I ask them to raise their hand if they agree with the statement. Then I give them the following statements:

1) It is OK to be homosexual.
2) If one of my friends turned out to be homosexual, I would not start thinking less of them.
3) I would not have any negative feelings if the president of my country turned out to be homosexual.
4) It is OK when a child has two same-sex parents (parent # 1 and parent # 2).
5) It is OK for nursery books to depict same-sex parents.

What typically happens is that the number of hands is reduced as I go from statement 1 to statement 5. Practically all students these days agree that "it is OK to be homosexual" but quite a few of them do not feel comfortable agreeing that nursery books can feature same-sex parents.

However, the thing is, statements 2, 3, 4 and 5 all follow from statement 1. They are all implications of the first statement. If you agree that it is OK to be homosexual, you must also agree with all of these other things. This is why we should not stop half-way and, once we have arrived at a certain conclusion, we should explore what implications it has.

Image 19. Implications

In the TOK context, exploring implications is often a useful tool when you feel stuck or when it seems to you that you have nothing more to say. Explore implications and you will immediately see a chance to deepen your argument.

In the spiral structure that I described previously, implications served as a link between two rounds of thesis – antithesis – synthesis. When I arrived at a synthesis (sub-conclusion), I explored its implications, and this became the starting point for new arguments.

7.3.5 - Communicating your ideas in a TOK essay

It is important to remember that what you think in your mind and what you say out loud are two different things. Examiners cannot assess what you think – they make a judgment based on what you say and how you say it. Therefore, it's not enough to have great arguments in response to the essay title – you need to be able to effectively communicate them.

Let me give you some suggestions on how to communicate your ideas in a TOK essay more clearly and how to get your point across.

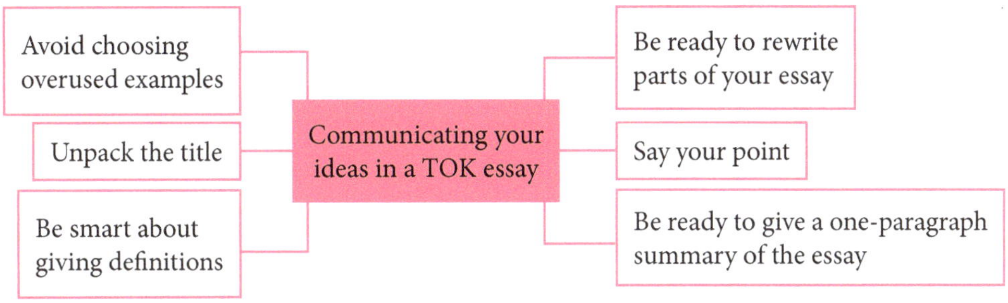

1. Be ready to rewrite parts of your essay

It is a common mistake among students to think about the task as "writing 1600 words". In all honesty, if you are aiming at a good result, you will most likely write much more than that, but *the final product* will be limited to 1600 words.

Looking at the knowledge question in the essay title, you might have some initial thoughts and decide that, once you start writing, you will be able to develop your argument further. And you will not be wrong; in the process of writing, your thoughts will take shape, more thoughts will occur to you, and finally you will reach the desirable threshold of 1600 words. However, what I just described is an example of *writing to think*. You are using writing to organize your thoughts.

This is very useful, but, unless you are a creature that is perfect in every single way, you cannot pass this writing for your final essay. As your thoughts shape, you will realize that some of the arguments made earlier are not very relevant, some of the examples are not well explained, some counter-arguments are not strong enough. Sometimes you will realize that your views on the problem have changed entirely, and, if you had a chance to start the essay again, you would now start it differently. These realizations are very important because now you have greater clarity on what you think about the title.

The next step is to decide which parts of this you want to communicate. You need to have another round of writing – *writing to communicate*.

Writing to communicate pursues purposes that are different from writing to think. Your potential reader is someone who is not necessarily familiar with your examples and someone who does not necessarily share your views. For some of your claims, you need to explain explicitly what they are based on. When you write to communicate, you will probably choose to leave some of your thoughts behind. Not everything that you wrote in the first round (writing to think) will be included in the second round.

After this round is finished, it is time to submit the essay draft for your teacher's feedback.

Image 20*. The rounds of writing and rewriting*

Note that a very common mistake among students is to write the first round ("writing to think") and submit the result to the teacher as the TOK essay draft. This is really unproductive. If you give your teacher a number of thoughts around the topic (rather than a clearly communicated argument), their feedback will be wasted. If they don't understand what you are trying to say or what point you are trying to make, they will not be able to give meaningful suggestions. Always submit your draft after you have completed both rounds of writing: writing to think *and* writing to communicate. This means that even at the draft stage, you will need to go back and rewrite considerable parts of your essay. Be prepared for that. Plan some time for that. It is a normal, healthy process of writing an analytical essay.

2. Say your point

Make sure to start every paragraph with a clearly articulated point you are making. In the paragraph itself, you will elaborate on the point and discuss some arguments and examples in relation to it, but readers need to understand at least roughly what you will be arguing about before they start reading your paragraph. It makes understanding a lot easier, and this way it is less likely that they will misinterpret what you are trying to say. It is also good practice to come back to the same point and reformulate it at the end of the paragraph, as a kind of a sub-conclusion or the main take-away message. This sub-conclusion will not be a mere repetition of what you said at the beginning of the paragraph. It will take into account all the development that happened in between. But the point is: say your point. Do not leave readers guessing what it was that you were trying to say.

Image 21*. Examiners figuring out what you are trying to say in the essay*

It would be a good idea to stick to the rule "one point – one paragraph".

Saying your point also applies to the introduction. The most clearly communicated essays that I have read provide a gist of the whole essay in the introduction. This way, after reading the first paragraph, I already have the big picture: I know what the student will argue about, what conclusion they will be trying to reach, what examples they will be using to support their statements. This is like a trailer for a movie, only the purpose is not to intrigue but to actually give spoilers.

3. Be ready to give a brief one-paragraph summary of the essay

You know you have presented a clear, effective argument when you can summarize it in one paragraph. This paragraph should capture the main idea of the essay with all the essential arguments, counter-arguments and conclusions. The paragraph should be such that, theoretically, someone does not have to read the whole essay to understand your point.

The rule is very simple. If you find it difficult to summarize the essay in one paragraph, then most probably one of the following is the case:

- You have many thoughts around the topic, but they are not structured and you are not sure what point you are trying to make. In other words, you haven't really thought through your essay.
- On the contrary, you don't have much to say on the topic, so you are trying to spend words talking about things that you think may be related to it.
- You have so many thoughts about this topic that you have confused yourself, and this confusion is reflected in your writing.

The summary paragraph is a great litmus test of the clarity that you have achieved as a result of your thinking process.

By the way, if you feel like you can summarize the whole essay in one sentence rather than one paragraph, then that is not a desirable situation. This might be a sign of a lack of cognitive complexity. You may want to consider some existing perspectives and come up with strong counter-arguments to show that the answer to the question is debatable. You will need more than one sentence to explain what the debatable aspects are and how you have dealt with them.

4. Unpack the title

TOK essay titles are formulated as knowledge questions focused on one or more areas of knowledge. As with all knowledge questions, you should expect them to be somewhat ambiguous. They will include knowledge concepts, and knowledge concepts by their very nature are broad. In a variety of different situations, they can sometimes be interpreted in a variety of different ways.

***Image 22**. Unpacking*

This means that every essay title will need to be "unpacked" before you are prepared to deal with it. You need to explain exactly how you understand it. This is also important because the way you understand the title may be different from the way the examiner understands it, and you want to explain your understanding for them to assess your work correctly. It is absolutely fine for you to interpret the title in your own way, but this should be clearly communicated.

To unpack the title, you should:

A) Clarify the meaning of the key concepts
B) Delineate the context in which you will consider the question (for example, areas of knowledge)
C) Explain the problem that is raised in the question

For example, consider the following title: *Is it inevitable that historians will be affected by their own cultural context?*

Unpacking the title: example 1

Is it inevitable that historians will be affected by their own cultural context?

A. Clarify the meaning of key concepts

It is not necessary to unpack the meaning of every single word in this question (which is something students sometimes try to do!). Everyone knows who a historian is, and even "cultural context" does not need clarification. But it may be necessary to clarify "inevitable" and "affected" in the context of this question, because for different people it may mean different things. Here is one way of doing it:

- For a historian to be affected by their own cultural context means that the way a historian interprets events of the past will be influenced by their cultural background. Influenced does not necessarily mean biased. They may emphasize certain details and ignore other details, see links between events where historians from a different culture do not see such links, and so on. In a nutshell, "affected" means "influenced" in a broad sense, but not necessarily distorted, flawed or incorrect.
- "Inevitable" means that there is not a single case where we can claim that a historian's interpretation of something was completely impartial. If we manage to find one counter-example, then we must accept that it is *not* inevitable for historians to be affected by their cultural context.

B. Delineate the context in which you will consider the question

The context in which we will consider the question is History, but we might also compare that to other areas of knowledge such as Human Sciences and the Arts to find out if being affected by your own cultural background is *as inevitable* in History as in these other areas of knowledge.

C. Explain the problem that is raised in the question

The problem raised in the question, then, is whether or not it is possible for a historian to avoid undesirable effects of their cultural background on their understanding of the past.

Let's also consider another example, the following essay title: Is there a single "*scientific method*"?

Unpacking the title: example 2

Is there a single "scientific method"?

A. Clarify the meaning of key concepts

Obviously, we need to unpack what is meant by the scientific method. For example, you can clarify that the scientific method is a very special method of gaining knowledge based on experiments. It requires a theory upon which you formulate certain predictions (hypotheses) that are tested in carefully organized experiments. You can also specify that for a method to be considered scientific, it has to be based on the logic of falsifiability.

B. Delineate the context in which you will consider the question

The context in which we consider this question seems to be up to us, but I would select, for example, natural and human sciences. This is the context where the question is debatable, because experimentation is not always possible in human sciences and the logic of falsifiability is not always applicable. In TOK, debatable = good.

C. Explain the problem that is raised in the question

The problem that is then raised in the question is whether or not knowledge can be considered "scientific" only if it satisfies the requirements of falsifiability and experimentation. What about those fields of knowledge where experiments are not possible? For example, we cannot conduct an experiment to confirm or refute the Big Bang theory. Similarly, in macroeconomics, we can only register variables as they occur in real life, but we cannot change them for the sake of experiment. Does it mean that such fields of knowledge are not scientific?

5. Be smart about giving definitions

In the previous point I spoke about "clarifying the meaning of key concepts", but I must also make a separate note on using definitions in the essay. A lot of students mistakenly think that they need to define all terms in the title, and unfortunately essay introductions are often just a list of definitions that makes things even more confusing.

Please don't use dictionary definitions. They define words as these words are used in everyday language, not as knowledge concepts. Moreover, dictionary definitions often "define" words through synonyms, so they simply introduce more words that need definitions and nothing at all gets clarified. On top of that, dictionary definitions will not be applicable to the context of your particular essay and your particular argument.

Instead of defining concepts, I would suggest you explain their meaning in the context of your essay. You may choose to explain descriptively, or through paraphrasing, or by giving examples and non-examples. In any case, such explanation should serve the sole purpose of ensuring that your readers and yourself have a common understanding of concepts.

It doesn't have to be a perfect definition. It just needs to make sense in your essay and prevent potential misunderstanding.

For example, consider the following knowledge question as a potential essay title: "*Is it possible to eliminate the effect of the observer in the pursuit of knowledge in the human sciences?*"

Obviously, it needs some explanation of what is meant by the effect of the observer. Note that it can be understood differently, and it is up to you which of the possible understandings to select – just communicate it clearly so that the examiner is on the same page as you.

***Image 23**. Definitions*

You might want to explain that the effect of the observer is any instance where the researcher (e.g. their expectations, beliefs, interests, cultural background) has had an influence on the results obtained in research. You might want to clarify that the observer effect is not limited to research studies where actual observation of human behavior is done. It can occur in research such as literature review or experimenting with rats running in a maze. The observer effect is *not* a problem when research findings are always the same no matter who conducts the study. In this paragraph I have defined – or rather explained – the observer effect, and this should be sufficient for the purposes of the essay.

Some students make it a point to define every single word, for example, they define "pursuit" and "human sciences". This is probably an unnecessary extreme. I'm pretty sure the examiner will understand "pursuit" in roughly the same way as you.

6. Avoid choosing overused examples

Finally, an essential component of the quality of your essay is the use of examples. As discussed, these should be examples illustrating knowledge. They should also be related to areas of knowledge (Human Sciences, Natural Sciences, Mathematics, History, the Arts).

But another piece of advice that must be given is to avoid examples that are overused. Remember that more than 150 thousand students are looking at the same 6 prescribed titles and deciding what examples they will be using. They are all doing that at approximately the same time in their IB Diploma Programme, so the same examples from their subjects are still fresh in memory. This means that some examples will be picked thousands of times, and examiners will genuinely get tired of reading the same paragraphs over and over again. Keynesian economics, schema theory in psychology, Galileo Galilei, and Flat Earth Society are all examples that are used by tens of thousands of students.

Just be mindful of that and ask yourself, how likely is it that many other students will use the same example? It often pays off to dig a little deeper and come up with something slightly more original. One of the examples I gave in this book is Hollow Earth theory, it can be used instead of Flat Earth. But obviously, when this book becomes super popular, students all over the world will start using this example, so that's wasted.

7.3.6 - TOK essay assessment instrument

In this section we will look at the TOK essay assessment instrument – the assessment criteria that examiners using when evaluating your work.

There is a single driving question underpinning the assessment of the TOK essay: *Does the student provide a clear, coherent and critical exploration of the essay title?* This is the ultimate question that is placed above everything else. If the examiner's answer to this question after reading your essay is yes, they may very well ignore minor weaknesses and inconsistencies in your work.

Does the student provide a clear, coherent and critical exploration of the essay title?					
Excellent 9-10	Good 7-8	Satisfactory 5-6	Basic 3-4	Rudimentary 1-2	0
The discussion has a sustained focus on the title and is linked effectively to areas of knowledge. Arguments are clear, coherent and effectively supported by specific examples. The implications of arguments are considered. There is clear awareness and evaluation of different points of view.	The discussion is focused on the title and is linked effectively to areas of knowledge. Arguments are clear, coherent and supported by examples. There is awareness and some evaluation of different points of view.	The discussion is focused on the title and is developed with some links to areas of knowledge. Arguments are offered and are supported by examples. There is some awareness of different points of view.	The discussion is connected to the title and makes superficial or limited links to areas of knowledge. The discussion is largely descriptive. Limited arguments are offered but they are unclear and are not supported by effective examples.	The discussion is weakly connected to the title. While there may be links to the areas of knowledge, any relevant points are descriptive or consist only of unsupported assertions.	The discussion does not reach the standard described by the other levels or is not a response to one of the prescribed titles for the correct examination session.
Possible characteristics					
Insightful Convincing Accomplished Lucid	Pertinent Relevant Analytical Organized	Acceptable Mainstream Adequate Competent	Underdeveloped Basic Superficial Limited	Ineffective Descriptive Incoherent Formless	

The descriptor for the highest level of achievement (Excellent, 9-10 marks) is the following set of statements:

- *The discussion has a sustained focus on the title and is linked effectively to areas of knowledge.*
- *Arguments are clear, coherent and effectively supported by specific examples. The implications of arguments are considered.*
- *There is clear awareness and evaluation of different points of view.*

To have a sustained focus on the title means to make sure that at any point of time it is absolutely clear to the reader how exactly your arguments contribute to answering the question in the title of the essay. It is very common for weak essays to stray away from the original question in the process of discussion. Be mindful also that the spiral argumentation is a powerful thinking tool, but you must make sure that each new turn of the spiral is actually contributing to answering the original question. Always ask yourself, how will discussing this help me answer the title? Do not include "interesting" arguments simply because they are interesting if they do not add anything to the question.

To link the discussion effectively to areas of knowledge means to focus your discussion on shared knowledge as opposed to personal knowledge. The essay should be about Natural Sciences, but not someone's understanding of natural sciences, Mathematics as a body of knowledge, but not the everyday difficulties of a student struggling to understand mathematics. "Typical mistakes" discussed previously in this unit are very relevant to this aspect of the assessment instrument.

To have clear and coherent arguments means to always be crystal clear about what point you are making and how you are justifying it. A good rule is one argument – one paragraph. Each paragraph should contain one key point that you are trying to communicate. Coherent arguments are ones that are logically linked to each other, so that it is clear what follows from what. This is opposed to simply presenting "thoughts inspired by the essay title".

To consider implications of arguments means, as we discussed above, to continue your arguments to their logical end and to explore what other statements must be accepted as true now that you arrived at a certain conclusion. Usually exploring implications is a good way to link arguments to each other, arranging them into a coherent whole (such as a spiral!).

Finally, your essay will demonstrate a clear awareness and evaluation of different points of view if you are serious about your counter-arguments and if you genuinely try to imagine how a hypothetical person who disagrees with you would defend their position. Good counter-arguments will come from a variety of perspectives.

It should be noted that this set of statements does not exhaust all the indicators that examiners are looking for in a good TOK essay. This is not a closed list, more like a set of examples for your reference. You might wonder, for instance, why considering implications of arguments is mentioned in the assessment instrument, but considering assumptions is not. This is not because identifying assumptions is not important in a TOK essay or because examiners don't mark this aspect of your work. Identifying assumptions is important, and examiners do consider it in marking as part of their general impression. All other tools of critical thinking are also important. The assessment instrument just gives examples of evidence of "good thinking". It should not be treated as a closed list.

7.3.7 - TOK essay checklist

In this section, you will find a checklist summarizing all of the guidance on the TOK essay. You can use it to ensure that your work meets all necessary requirements. Tick the boxes that apply to your work and keep in mind your areas for improvement as you continue refining the final draft.

Item	Check?
THE STRUCTURE	
The title	
The title of my essay is one of the six titles prescribed by the IB this year	☐
I have not modified the essay title in any way	☐
Introduction	
My introduction contains a clearly formulated thesis statement: what is it that I am going to say in my essay in response to the essay title?	☐
In my introduction, I clarify the meaning of key concepts	☐
In my introduction, I delineate the context in which I consider the question (for example, areas of knowledge)	☐
In my introduction, I explain the problem that is raised in the question	☐
My introduction provides a gist of the whole essay	☐
Body of the essay	
My essay can be divided into several logical parts – paragraphs	☐
Every major paragraph in my essay starts with a point that I am trying to make	☐
Every major paragraph in my essay ends with a clear sub-conclusion that comes back to the point made at the start of the paragraph	☐
I stick to the rule "one point – one paragraph"	☐
Conclusion	
I have included a conclusion that summarizes the main arguments I have made in the essay	☐
Reading my conclusion is like reading a condensed version of my whole essay	☐
My conclusion does not contain any new arguments or examples	☐
My conclusion is a concise argumentative answer to the question in the prescribed title	☐
My conclusion is formulated using the terminology of the prescribed title	☐
THE CONTENT	
Argumentation within each major paragraph	
The structure of argumentation in every major paragraph of my essay follows thesis – antithesis – synthesis	☐
I start every major paragraph with a thesis statement; this statement is formulated using the terminology of the prescribed title	☐
My thesis statements are supported by arguments and examples	☐
My essay contains strong counterclaims	☐
My counterclaims are also supported by arguments and examples	☐
In my essay, I identify implicit assumptions of claims and counterclaims	☐

In my essay, I identify implicit assumptions of claims and counterclaims	☐
I reconcile the claim and the counterclaim in a single sub-conclusion (synthesis)	☐
My sub-conclusions (syntheses) use the terminology of the prescribed title	☐
I explore implications of these sub-conclusions (syntheses)	☐
These implications become the starting point for further development of my argument	☐
Argumentation in the essay on the whole	
Argumentation in my essay follows the "spiral" structure	☐
The "synthesis" from the previous paragraph becomes the starting point for a thesis statement in the next paragraph	☐
From one paragraph to another, the argument in my essay is developing	☐
I have explored various perspectives; my essay demonstrates a clear awareness and evaluation of different points of view	☐
The examples I have used in my essay are related to areas of knowledge	☐
I have avoided choosing overused examples	☐
Focus	
The focus in my essay is on areas of knowledge (shared knowledge, not personal knowledge)	☐
The focus in my essay is on generic arguments about knowledge; when subject-specific knowledge is used, it is for the sake of supporting my arguments with examples	☐
At all times, my essay stays clearly focused on the prescribed title; it is clear to the reader how my discussion contributes to answering the question in the title	☐
Where I'm using additional knowledge questions, it is always clear how exactly answering these questions will contribute to answering the main question in the essay title	☐
Clarity of communication	
Throughout the essay, I say my point explicitly; I do not leave readers guessing what I meant	☐
If asked, I can summarize my essay in one paragraph that briefly outlines my arguments, counter-arguments and conclusions	☐
Where possible, I have avoided using dictionary definitions	☐
FORMATTING	
I have acknowledged all sources and included all necessary references	☐
My essay follows the required formatting: 12 type size, double spaced	☐
My essay is under 1600 words	☐

GLOSSARY

This glossary will help you remember the meaning of the key terms that appeared in the book. These are the concepts that formed the foundation of our discussions throughout the lessons. You don't have to know precise definitions, but you should be able to explain the meaning of these concepts and use them appropriately in relevant contexts. Whenever you have a doubt and want to double-check what a concept means, use the glossary. It will allow you to remind yourself of the key ideas and enhance your learning.

All of these concepts appear in the "Key concepts" section at the start of every lesson. They are also marked with red font. This is how you can keep track of which concepts are the focus of which lesson.

Concepts are the building blocks of thought, so clearly understanding the concepts is a major factor in developing your critical thinking.

A posteriori concepts – concepts that are formed in our minds as a result of our interaction with the world around us. "A posteriori" means "based on experience". We gain experience with objects of the real world and this allows us to perform a mental abstraction of certain properties of these objects. On the basis of this abstraction, we form concepts.

A priori concepts – concepts that exist in our minds even before we gain any sort of experience with the real world. "A priori" means "before experience". By definition, a priori concepts must be innate, which means that we must be born with them. If this is so, we can expect a priori concepts to shape our perception of reality. The existence of a priori concepts is debatable.

Abstraction – the process of "detaching" properties from real-world objects and generalizing them to ideas that exist in mental space and can be applied to multiple other objects. For example, I see seven trees – this is a fragment of reality. But the concept "seven" is an abstraction. It only exists in the mental space, but it can be applied to multiple other objects in the world (seven chairs, seven apples).

Aesthetic judgment – according to Immanuel Kant, a special type of judgment, a judgment about beauty or ugliness. Aesthetic judgments, according to Kant, are distinctly different from judgments of likes and dislikes because they are subjective, but nevertheless universal.

Aesthetic relativism – the belief that aesthetic properties (such as beauty) are merely characteristics of our perception, and that aesthetic judgments are no different from judgments of likes and dislikes. In other words, aesthetic relativism is the idea that "beauty is in the eye of the beholder".
Analogical reasoning – making a conclusion through the use of analogy.

Analogy – the reasoning that, if two objects or phenomena are similar in several important aspects, they should be similar in all other aspects as well. It is also possible to say that one of the two phenomena is an analogy for the other. For example, Darwinian evolution in this book has been used as an analogy for the development of personal knowledge.

Appearance – the way the world appears to us. This is in opposition to reality (the way the world actually is).

Areas of knowledge (AOKs) – large domains of knowledge universally shared by humans. IB TOK considers five areas of knowledge: Natural Sciences, Human Sciences, Mathematics, History, and the Arts.

Argument from awareness – the ethical argument stating that biases are blameworthy only when the individual is (or ought to be) consciously aware of them.

Argument from control – the ethical argument stating that we can only be morally responsible for actions that are within our control. For example, if we are aware of an implicit bias but can't control it, we should not be held responsible for its negative consequences.

Artificial consciousness – the ability of computers to have subjectively experienced mental states. We have agreed in this book that artificial intelligence means the ability of computers to act intelligently, while artificial consciousness means their ability to actually be intelligent. Some thinkers (such as Alan Turing) rejected the difference between acting intelligently and being intelligent.

Artificial general intelligence – the ability of computers to act intelligently in all areas (as opposed to specific areas of expertise). There is no doubt that computers can act intelligently in some areas, but the ability of computers to display general intelligence is debatable.

Artificial intelligence – a machine that exhibits properties of the human mind, such as learning and problem-solving. Artificial intelligence defined this way already exists. Sometimes the term is also used more broadly to refer to a machine that fully simulates human thinking. Whether or not machines will ever be capable of simulating human thinking completely is a debatable question. Artificial intelligence is different from artificial consciousness (see "artificial consciousness").

Artistic intention – the meaning and purpose of a work of art as perceived by the artist himself or herself. There are three perspectives on the source of knowledge in art. According to one of them, knowledge is contained in the artistic intention. The other two are perceptions of the audience and the artwork itself.

Artwork (work of art) – the product of the work of an artist, the creation itself, taken independently of both the artist's intentions and the perception of the audience. There are three perspectives on the source of knowledge in art. According to one of them, knowledge is contained in the artwork itself. The other two are perceptions of the audience and intentions of the artist.

Assumption – a statement that must be true for another statement to be true. Our beliefs are true only if their respective assumptions are true. For example, Newtonian physics assumes inertial space, Euclidean geometry assumes a perfectly flat surface, etc.

Authorship – in art, the question of who can be considered the creator of a work of art. The question of authorship is especially tricky if the work of art is completely or partially generated by a machine.

Automated theorem prover – a piece of software that can prove mathematical theorems by itself. This software is designed around formalized rules of logical reasoning of the human mind. After that, some starting parameters (for example, axioms in an axiomatic system) are fed into it and the algorithm is left to its own devices to apply rules of reasoning to the starting parameters and discover theorems.

Axiom – a statement that is accepted without proof as something that is obviously true or self-evident. Mathematics is an axiomatic system, which means that it is based on a set of axioms. All other statements in mathematics require proof by showing that they logically follow from the axioms, but axioms themselves do not require any proof.

Axiomatic system – a body of knowledge built upon a small number of self-evident statements (axioms) using deductive reasoning. Mathematics is an axiomatic system. In some sense, all knowledge in mathematics is already contained in the original set of axioms that just need to be gradually "unpacked".

Backward-looking scientific goals – the approach to defining the goal of scientific progress as gaining new knowledge that we did not have before. The criterion of progress here is placed in the past. This is opposed to forward-looking scientific goals.

Basic English – a version of the English language created by K. Ogden with the aim of stripping the words of all additional connotations and only conveying the literal, precise meaning. It was a sanitized version of English restricted to a core vocabulary of around 800 words.

"Beetle in a box" metaphor – the metaphor used by Ludwig Wittgenstein to argue that language cannot guarantee shared meaning. According to this metaphor, everyone has a box, and inside that box is something that each person calls a "beetle". But only the person who has the box can look inside it. Although everyone has a certain "something" they call a "beetle", there is no guarantee that they are all referring to the same thing. He applied the same reasoning to human language, especially when we use language as a sign for unobservable phenomena such as "pain" or "anxiousness".

Belief - an acceptance of something as true. The belief condition is one of the necessary conditions of knowledge in the classical "justified true belief" definition. A non-belief (for example, information written down in a book) is not knowledge.

Beyond a reasonable doubt – an expression that is sometimes used to replace "true" in the definition of knowledge as a justified true belief. When used this way, the definition addresses the fact that knowledge develops historically, so it is possible for us to justifiably believe that something is true, but later on realize that it's not the case.

Bias – a systematic deviation from the truth (or something that is currently accepted as the truth beyond a reasonable doubt).

Bias reduction – weakening or even eliminating either implicit biases themselves or their effects on our thinking and behavior.

Bias self-awareness – the ability of a person to be aware of their own implicit biases.

Big Data – the term used to characterize the newly emerged approach to collecting and processing data in human sciences. This has become possible due to a large increase in computational capacity. Big Data is characterized by four Vs: volume, variety, velocity and veracity. Samples are no longer used – the whole population is the sample. Big Data is not simply a large quantity of data – it is a different kind of data and a different logic of using it.

Brute fact – something that exists even when there is no one around to observe it or interpret it. For example, asteroids moving through space are brute facts. This is opposed to social facts that are constructed by humans and cannot exist outside of society.

Cartesian doubt – a form of skepticism proposed by René Descartes in the 17th century. The idea is to systematically doubt the truth of all statements in an attempt to find those few statements where the truth cannot be doubted. Systematic doubt is applied in order to find certainty.

Cause-effect inference – a conclusion of the type "A influences B". The only method that allows this kind of inference is an experiment, where the researcher manipulates A and measures how this manipulation affects B.

Certainty – the quality of being absolutely sure that something is true.

Circular dependence – in the definition of knowledge as a "justified true belief", the mutual dependence between truth and justification. Justification is a judgment about whether or not a belief is true. But the only way for us to know the truth of a belief is through justification.

Close reading – reading a text for its deep meaning. Close reading requires reading between the lines, for example, paying attention to how the author expresses the thought, what metaphors and stylistic devices are used, etc. Only humans, but not machines, can read texts closely. This is opposed to distant reading.

Cognitive bias – a systematic deviation of thinking from the patterns dictated by a normative model.

Coherence theory of truth – the approach suggesting that truth of a belief is established through its coherence with the previously accepted system of beliefs. In other words, a belief is true if it fits well into what we already know. Compare to: correspondence theory of truth, pragmatic theory of truth.

Communication – a process where one person sends a message and another person receives it. The sender codes an idea, sends the coded message across, and the receiver decodes the message. In doing so, both persons are using a language.

Complex system of dynamically interacting variables – any real-life phenomenon that is influenced in its development by multiple factors at once, where the factors also affect each other. Most real-life phenomena are complex systems of dynamically interacting variables, and this makes it hard for them to be investigated in artificial conditions of controlled experiments.

Compos mentis – the state of being aware and in control of one's thoughts and action. It is a Latin expression meaning "having full control of one's mind". The term is widely used in legal practice.

Computer simulation – a digital model of a real-life phenomenon designed to investigate how it works by changing some variables and seeing how this affects other variables. It is particularly useful with phenomena that are so complex that experimenting with them in real life would be unrealistic or unethical or too time-consuming.

Computer-generated knowledge – a discovery made by a computer on its own without human participation.

Concept – an abstract idea that exists in the mental space, a building block of thought. In the structure of the meaning of a sign, concepts are linked to the signified (a.k.a. the intension).

Conceptual hierarchy – the structural organization of concepts wherein high-level concepts include low-level concepts as their instances. For example, the concept "furniture" includes the lower-level concept "chair" as one of its instances. To correctly define a concept, we need to name the higher-level concept (category) and name the properties that differentiate our concept from other instances in the same category.

Conceptual properties of a work of art – the symbolic content of a work of art that cannot be reduced to physical properties.

Confirmation bias – the tendency to focus on evidence that supports your expectation or theory and ignore evidence that contradicts it.

Conjecture – in mathematics, a rule that is hypothesized to be true but that does not have a formal proof. It is an observed regularity that is not proven with certainty.

Connotation – a logical or emotional association that a word creates in addition to its literal meaning. Every language usually has multiple words denoting the same thing or idea, and although the literal meaning is the same, connotations may be very different (for example, compare "to die" and "to kick the bucket").

Consistency (of an axiomatic system) – the property of an axiomatic system being free from internal contradictions. A consistent axiomatic system does not generate any statements that contradict each other.

Context – background information that may be helpful to enhance our understanding of something. In hermeneutics, understanding is a continuous movement between the text and the context.

Continuity hypothesis – the idea that child language may differ from local adult language only in ways that adult languages differ from each other. This idea was put forward by linguistic nativists. According to their observations, the illegal grammar structures that children produce when they are still learning their native language are usually legal in one of the other existing languages. This means that children never use incorrect grammar – they just speak one the other naturally existing languages.

Continuum – something that changes gradually without any clear cut-off points. In this book, we considered objectivity–subjectivity as a continuum rather than a binary opposition, which means that there is no sharp line between the two.

Core Mentalese – the part of the language of thought that consists of concepts and structures that are a priori and innate. All people have these concepts and all people think this way. Compare this to "peripheral Mentalese". Core Mentalese and peripheral Mentalese are two terms invented in this book to reconcile linguistic nativism and the Sapir-Whorf hypothesis.

Correspondence theory of truth – the approach suggesting that truth of a belief is established through its correspondence to reality. In other words, a belief is true if it is supported by observation or other empirical evidence. Compare to: coherence theory of truth, pragmatic theory of truth.

Counter-stereotypical information – any information that contradicts an existing stereotype. Exposure to counter-stereotypical information may be an effective method of bias reduction.

Culturally specific experiences (cultural experiences) – experiences that one is exposed to due to belonging to a particular culture.

Darwinian evolution – the idea that biological species develop through a process of adaptation to the demands of the environment. This idea is based on four main principles: natural variation, differential fitness, survival of the fittest, and natural selection.

Data ethics – a field of technoethics that explores the issues of using data in a morally acceptable way. It is especially pertinent in Big Data research projects that may massively collect users' personal data.

Deductive reasoning – the form of reasoning from the general to the specific. For example: All men are mortal, Socrates is a man, hence, Socrates is mortal. All mathematics is based on deductive reasoning where the starting axioms are the premises and the theorems are conclusions that deductively follow from them.

Deep human response – subjective experiences that we all share on a deep level simply because we are all human beings. Examples include our feelings about death, our attitude to solitude, our feelings of guilt, and so on.

Deep self argument – the ethical argument stating that individuals can be held morally accountable for all actions they perform, whether or not these actions are within their conscious control or awareness.

Demarcation criterion – a criterion that draws a line between science and non-science. Many demarcation criteria have been proposed in history. Examples are the verification criterion and the falsification criterion.

Demarcation problem – the problem of distinguishing between science and non-science.

Descriptive models of thinking – in psychology, models of intuitive, automatic (System 1) thinking. These include various heuristics.

Determinism – the idea that all things in the Universe can be completely explained by causes that acted upon them in the past. According to determinism, if we have complete knowledge about the state of the Universe at a particular time, we can completely recreate its past and exactly predict its future.

Digital art – the practice of using digital technology as part of either creating or displaying the work of art. Examples of digital art include generative art, interactive art, internet art, and many others.

Distant reading – reading for superficial characteristics of the text without necessarily understanding its meaning. Examples include counting words and their combinations, calculating probabilities of word occurrence and co-occurrence, categorizing parts of speech. Machines are capable of distant reading. This is opposed to close reading.

Dogmatism – one of the perspectives on the role of doubt in knowledge (dogmatism, skepticism, fallibilism). It claims that we can reach certain truths, and further questioning of such truths is undesirable. Doubt may be detrimental for the advancement of knowledge. Dogmas are ideas that we do not question.

Dualism –the belief that consciousness exists and it cannot be fully explained by the physical properties of the brain. Dualism is one of the responses to the hard problem of consciousness. The other two responses are physicalism and eliminative materialism.

Duplication of the world – the phenomenon wherein human language creates a replica of the world in a system of signs that denote objects of the real world, but are understood in the absence of those objects. For example, the word "chair" denotes chairs existing in the real world, but it is also understood even if no chairs are present in the immediate environment. In this sense, language creates a replica of the world.

Educated interpretation – an explanation which, although subjective, is based on thorough knowledge of contextual details. It is different from an uneducated interpretation which simply provides a subjective explanation, filling gaps in knowledge with guesses.

Eliminative materialism – the belief that consciousness is a physical process, and consciousness as we experience it is an illusion. Eliminative materialism is one of the responses to the hard problem of consciousness. The other two responses are dualism and physicalism.

Emotive language – see "loaded language".

Empirical evidence – evidence based on observation and experience with the real world. Empirical is the opposite of theoretical.

Enculturation – internalizing norms of culture as one is growing up.

Epistemologically objective knowledge (also referred to simply as objective knowledge) – knowledge gained through methods of precise registration and measurement. These methods eliminate the influence of the observer as much as possible, so the results of the observation do not depend on who the observer is.

Epistemologically subjective knowledge (also referred to simply as subjective knowledge) – knowledge obtained through interpretation. It may be deeper than objective measurement, but results will differ from one knower to another.

Epistemology – the theory of knowledge. It answers questions of the type "How do we know that…?" It is opposed to ontology.

Ethics (element of the knowledge framework) – an element of the knowledge framework that explores ethical issues that arise in the process of obtaining knowledge. The focus is not on the ethical issues themselves, but on the wider understanding of the relationship between knowledge and ethics.

Ethics of artificial intelligence – a field of technoethics that explores ethical problems associated with building a thinking machine.

Ethics of history writing – the set of moral principles guiding the work of a historian. According to one approach, ethics of history writing may be used to define historical objectivity.

Experience sample – aspects of the world that someone has had personal experience with. Our experience sample is always tiny in comparison to the world itself or the experiences we could potentially have.

Experiment – the method of research where the researcher manipulates one variable (A), keeps all other variables constant and measures the resulting changes in another variable (B). An experiment is the only method that allows researchers to make cause-effect inferences.

Experimental mathematics – the field of knowledge that emerged as a result of attempts to incorporate computers into the process of mathematical discovery. It includes such sub-fields as proof-by-exhaustion, automated theorem provers, proof assistants, conjecture discoveries, and others.

Explicit attitude – a conscious attitude toward something that we are aware of.

Explicit thinking – a kind of thinking that can be formalized in a set of symbols and a set of rules. Products of explicit thinking can be written down and taught to others. Explicit thinking is in opposition to implicit thinking.

Extension (of a sign) – the same as the referent. It is called this way because the referent is the collection of the objects and phenomena of the world so it is external (extends into the real world).

Extrapolation – a kind of logical inference based on observing current trends of development and assuming that they will continue in the future.

Fallibilism – one of the perspectives on the role of doubt in knowledge (dogmatism, skepticism, fallibilism). It claims that our knowledge, in principle, can be mistaken, but it is not a reason to abandon such knowledge. Even mistaken knowledge can be useful. Knowledge claims may be accepted temporarily.

False analogy – a logical fallacy in analogical reasoning; it occurs when the analogy is based on inessential, superficial characteristics while ignoring crucial differences.

Falsifiability – the ability of a statement or theory to be proven wrong. A theory is falsifiable if it is possible (in principle) to conduct a study that will disprove it. Falsifiability is the main parameter of the falsification criterion.

Falsification criterion – a demarcation criterion that is based on finding contradictory evidence. It states that a theory is scientific if it attempts to find refuting evidence for its claims. A theory is not scientific if its claims are not falsifiable. We accept scientific knowledge as provisionally true if we try to refute it but fail.

Forward-looking scientific goals – the approach to defining the goal of scientific progress as finding out the truth. The criterion of progress here is placed in the future. This is in contrast to backward-looking scientific goals.

Functions of science – the goals of scientific understanding of the world. It is believed that science has four functions: description, explanation, prediction, control. All of these functions are based on the idea of determinism.

Futurism – the field of knowledge that tries to predict the future of human civilization based on a rational analysis of its past. Forecasts are made based on extrapolating the rates of development of technology that have been observed in the past.

Futurist – a specialist in futurism.

General intelligence – see "artificial general intelligence".

Generative art – art that is produced partially or completely by a computer algorithm.

Gettier-style counter-examples – hypothetical scenarios suggested by Edmund Gettier to demonstrate the problems with defining knowledge as a justified true belief. These are situations when someone has a belief, this belief is both reasonably justified and true and, yet, from the common sense perspective, it is difficult to say that the person in question "knows".

Gödel's second incompleteness theorem – the theorem stating that "a consistent axiomatic system cannot prove its own consistency". Kurt Gödel published the proof of this theorem in 1931 as a response to Hilbert's second problem.

Hard problem of consciousness – explaining how and why some organisms have subjective experiences. The problem was introduced by David Chalmers. Both the "why" and the "how" are important aspects of the problem. The "why" asks about the advantage we get from the existence of subjective experiences. The "how" asks about the exact processes through which a material thing - the brain - produces subjective experiences.

Hermeneutic circle – in hermeneutics, the process of interpreting a text. It is a constant movement between the whole and the parts: (a) to understand a text, one needs to understand every separate element of it, (b) but complete understanding of a separate element is only possible if one understands the whole text.

Hermeneutics – the art and science of understanding, or the "theory of understanding". Hermeneutics was formulated as an alternative to the "theory of knowledge".

Heteroglossia – the creative co-existence of varying and often conflicting historical perspectives. The word translates from Latin as "different languages". Heteroglossia is also an approach to defining historical objectivity according to which we should allow multiple perspectives to co-exist instead of selecting one of them. Importantly, even incommensurable (incompatible) perspectives should be included in this co-existence, as this only adds to the depth of our understanding of history.

Heuristics – "cognitive shortcuts", simplified thinking strategies that people use under lack of time, incomplete information or similar restraints.

Hilbert's second problem – the second from a list of 23 problems posed in 1900 by the mathematician David Hilbert. The formulation of the problem is: "Can we prove that an axiomatic system is consistent?"

Historical context (of a work of art) – information about the trends of art existing at the time the artist was creating his or her work. This information could be useful for interpreting the work of art.

Historical development of knowledge – the changes that the body of shared knowledge goes through over the course of the advancement of human civilization.

Historical fact – something that actually happened in the past. Theoretically, historical facts should not be dependent on viewpoints, opinions and interpretations of historians - they should be "objective". However, it is debatable that historical facts understood this way even exist. Every fact in history already contains an element if interpretation in it.

Historical interpretation – a historian's judgment about an event in the past, including its significance, factors that might have caused it, its role in the subsequent events. Like with any subjective judgment, historical interpretation is influenced by factors such as the historian's own cultural background, so the element of subjectivity may be inevitable. However, it may be argued that subjective judgments are the only way to understand the subjective dimension of human activity such as human experiences, intentions, goals or values. These aspects of human activity cannot be measured objectively.

Historical objectivity (objective historical knowledge) – knowledge about the past that accurately reflects what actually happened and is not influenced by subjective interpretations and viewpoints of historians. It is debatable whether or not historical objectivity is in principle achievable.

Historical perspective – a way of looking at events of the past that is determined by a particular standpoint of a historian, for example, their cultural background, theoretical orientation or political beliefs.

Human activity – in a broad sense, any activity performed by human beings as well as products of this activity. Human activities are the main focus of investigation in human sciences. Human activities, unlike the behavior of material things, are meaningful and purposeful.

Human condition – the experience of existence as a human being. This term is closely linked to the concept "deep human response".

Human-verifiable proof – in mathematics, a computer-assisted proof that can be manually verified by a human.

Idiographic approach to research – in human sciences, the approach that sees the purpose of research as in-depth understanding of unique people, groups or phenomena. According to this approach, universal applicability of results is not the goal of research. It is opposed to the nomothetic approach.

Implication – a statement that must be true if the statement you previously accepted is true. For example, if you accept that it is raining outside, you must also accept that streets will be wet and that you need to have appropriate footwear.

Implicit bias – a special kind of cognitive bias that stays below the level of conscious awareness. Implicit biases affect our thinking and decision-making, but we do not realize it.

Implicit thinking – a kind of thinking that is unconscious and difficult to formalize (for example, riding a bicycle, hunting a wild boar). Implicit thinking is linked to intuition. It may be impossible to express implicit thinking in a set of symbols. Implicit thinking is in opposition to explicit thinking.

Incommensurability – the property of fundamental scientific theories which makes it impossible for one theory to be understood through the perspective (or terminology) of another, meaning that rival theories cannot be directly compared. Comparing incommensurable theories is like comparing apples and oranges. This applies both to rival theories existing at the same time and to theories replacing each other in the process of scientific development.

Inconsistency (of an axiomatic system) – the property of being logically incoherent. An inconsistent axiomatic system is the one in which two contradictory statements can both be proven from the same set of axioms.

Indeterminacy of translation – the idea that translation is always underdetermined by evidence, and that for any given utterance and context there always exist multiple possible translations. This leads to a problem: how can we ever be certain that a translation is correct? The term was suggested by W.V.O. Quine.

Indeterminism – the idea that not all events in the Universe occur due to preceding causes; some events are a product of true chance. Therefore, we cannot understand these events by identifying their causes.

Inductive reasoning – reasoning from particular examples to a general rule. It is commonly used in areas of knowledge where conclusions are based on empirical observations. If we observe something to be true many times, at some point we make a leap of generalization from "it is true in many instances" to "it is true in all instances". This is an inductive generalization.

Information bubble – pre-selected information that we are surrounded by due to modern digital technology. This includes, for example, information pre-selected and pre-ranked by a search engine based on activity of other users and our own search history.

Information processing – cognitive processes such as sense perception, thinking and decision-making.
Intelligence explosion – a hypothetical point in the future when the exponential development of artificial intelligence will result in a very rapid increase of computational power within a very short time.

Intension (of a sign) – the same as the signified. It is called this way because the signified is the mental concept that is internal (exists in your mind).

Intentions of the artist – see "artistic intention".

Interactive art – the result of a designed interaction between the viewer and the artwork. The input of the viewer is transformed into an aspect of the artwork itself. It often results in an output that is unique and unrepeatable.

Interactive theorem prover – a piece of software that a human mathematician uses as a tool when developing a formal proof. It does not prove the theorem for you, but it simplifies the task. This is opposed to automated theorem provers.

Internet art – forms of art that make use of the collaborative capacity of the Internet, for example, an installation that feeds random tweets on multiple screens in real time.

Interpretation – the process of obtaining knowledge about something (usually some aspect of human activity) by trying to understand its meaning and significance. Interpretation is a subjective method of obtaining knowledge. The interpreter uses their own world of subjective experiences to understand someone else's world of subjective experiences. Interpretation is often opposed to precise scientific measurement.

Intersubjectivity – convergence between subjective beliefs. In other words, it is when different people have subjective beliefs about something, but these beliefs match. If we look at subjectivity–objectivity as a continuum rather than a binary opposition, intersubjectivity is the middle point between two extremes.

Intra-mathematical criterion of truth – in mathematics, this is the approach that defines the truth of a mathematical system in relation to the system itself. Most commonly, a statement is considered to be true if it is coherent with the other statements in the system (see "coherence theory of truth"). The intra-mathematical criterion does not require mathematics to relate in any way to the real world around us. In the debate "Is mathematics invented or discovered?" the "invented" position assumes the intra-mathematical criterion of truth.

Judgments of likes and dislikes – judgments of taste and personal preference, for example, "dumplings are tasty". Immanuel Kant insisted that aesthetic judgments are distinctly different from judgments of likes and dislikes.

Justification – providing reasons to demonstrate that a knowledge claim is true. There are various forms of justification (for example, based on observational evidence, logical reasoning, faith in authorities).

Knower – a person who knows. This is IB TOK terminology to refer to, very generally, any sentient creature that is a bearer of knowledge.

Knowledge – the very idea of a definition of knowledge is disputed. A definition that is widely accepted in epistemology is "justified true belief". According to this definition, justification and truth are necessary and sufficient conditions for a belief to be accepted as knowledge. However, this definition is problematic because there is a circular relationship between justification and truth (vicious circle of truth). For this and other reasons, some people reject any definitions of knowledge whatsoever. For example, the IB suggests that we instead use a metaphor in which knowledge of something is like a "map to a territory".

Knowledge claim – a statement conveying something about knowledge (as opposed to something about the world). For example, "Justifications based on observation are more reliable than logical proofs".

Knowledge concepts – abstract concepts that relate to various aspects of obtaining knowledge. Examples include certainty, bias, responsibility, justification and many others. Knowledge concepts are the main focus of this book.

Knowledge framework – four groups that knowledge questions are organized into in IB TOK. The groups are: scope, methods and tools, perspectives, ethics.

Knowledge question – a general, contestable question about knowledge that draws upon abstract concepts. Knowledge questions are questions about knowledge, in contrast to questions about the world. Knowledge questions are contestable, in contrast to regular questions that may have a correct answer. Knowledge questions are general, in contrast to regular questions that are subject-specific or situation-specific. Since they are general, they draw upon abstract concepts about knowledge (such as truth, justification, certainty, evidence, and so on).

Kuhn loss – a period in scientific development when the old paradigm has been replaced and this has led to a temporary decrease in puzzle-solving ability. Since there is now a new paradigm, there are more things we do not know and have to investigate anew from the fresh perspective. According to Kuhn, this regress is temporary, and the new paradigm catches up with the old one and ends up outperforming it in the puzzle-solving ability.

Language of thought (Mentalese) – the hypothetical system of constructing meanings from concepts that exists behind the language that we speak. When we construct a sentence in a spoken language, this is the product of translation from the language of thought into this spoken language. Proponents of the idea of language of thought believe that concepts (thoughts) can exist without language. This position is attractive to linguistic nativists and those who support the existence of universal grammar.

Language-A – language in a generic sense, a system of meaningful signs. For example, the following questions are questions about language-A: "When did humans acquire language?", "What role does language play in the acquisition of knowledge?". Language-A, language-B and language-C are terms suggested in this book to illustrate various aspects of language and its development.

Language-B – a naturally existing language, such as English, Mandarin or Italian. Language-B is a specific manifestation of language-A. Language-A, language-B and language-C are terms suggested in this book to illustrate various aspects of language and its development.

Language-C – language as it is used by a particular individual. An example would be a young child's version of his or her native tongue. They would not speak the "grown-up" version of the language. Language-C is a specific manifestation of language-B. Language-A, language-B and language-C are terms suggested in this book to illustrate various aspects of language and its development.

Leading question – a question that already implicitly suggests an answer to it. For example, the question addressed to an artist "How do you get inspired to create your work?" suggests that the artist is indeed inspired. One of the problems with human sciences is that it is difficult to avoid the use of leading questions in data collection.

Levels of knowledge questions – the division of knowledge questions based on how general they are. In the terminology we accepted in this book, level 0 are non-knowledge questions about the world; level 1 are knowledge questions that are specific to a particular situation or problem within an area of knowledge; level 2 are knowledge questions that are applicable to a range of situations or an area of knowledge on the whole; level 3 are knowledge questions that are very general, going beyond the boundaries of areas of knowledge.

Linguistic empiricism – the school of thought that claims that all language is learned, that is, acquired through experience. Children are born with no knowledge of language and gradually acquire it through trial and error. This is opposed to linguistic nativism.

Linguistic nativism – the school of thought that children are already born with some understanding of language (more precisely, principles of grammar). In other words, some language is innate. This position is opposed to linguistic empiricism.

Loaded language (emotive language) – the practice of using language with the aim of producing a certain emotional response in the audience (or whoever receives the message). Loaded language conveys a message beyond the literal meaning of words. It is possible due to the existence of connotations.

Machine translation – the process of using a computer algorithm to automatically convert a text in one language into another language. Various algorithms of machine translation exist, for example, the rule-based approach and the statistical approach. Machine translation is much larger than simply an engineering task. Arguably, if we build a machine that can successfully translate from one language into another, this machine may also understand the language, and therefore be able to think.

Mary's room – a thought experiment proposed by Frank Jackson in 1982. In this experiment, Mary, the color scientist, knows all there is to know about color in the physical sense (including the reaction of the human brain to the perception of color). However, her entire life she spends in a black-and-white room. Then one day she goes outside and experiences color for the first time. The question is, does she learn anything new? If you say yes, you believe in the existence of qualia.

Mathematical anti-realism – the position opposite to mathematical realism. According to mathematical anti-realism, there is no sense in which mathematical entities "exist" in the real world. Mathematical anti-realism supports the view that mathematics is invented rather than discovered.

Mathematical intuition – the ability of a mathematician to successfully find elegant solutions to mathematical problems without sifting through all possible combinations. It is a kind of a "hunch", but it is difficult to say what it is exactly and where it comes from. Mathematical intuition is often opposed to the brute-force approach used by automated theorem provers.

Mathematical proof – the process of reasoning in mathematics where the truth of a statement is deduced from the truth of other statements that were earlier accepted as true. In turn, the truth of these earlier statements is deduced from other statements and eventually from axioms.

Mathematical realism – the position according to which mathematical structures are intrinsic to nature. Mathematical realism claims that mathematical entities exist in reality in some form, so it supports the view that mathematics is discovered rather than invented. Their main argument is that the fit between mathematics and reality is too miraculous for something that was invented.

Meaning (of a sign) – something that a sign stands for or points at. There are various views on what exactly comprises the meaning of a sign. According to one position, the meaning of a sign is its relation to the referent. According to another position, the meaning of a sign is its relation to the concept (mental idea) that it expresses.

Meaningful doubt – skepticism regarding the certainty of knowledge on the basis of identifying its essential limitations. Unlike superficial doubt, meaningful doubt identifies the weakest aspects of knowledge and in that sense encourages further inquiry.

Meme – a unit of culture that bears a certain meaning (for example, a catchy tune, the idea of God, a ritual, a greeting sign).

Memeplex – a complex of memes (for example, religions, languages, works of art).

Memetics – a study of memes. It provides an application of Universal Darwinism to the development of personal knowledge.

Mentalese – see "language of thought".

Metaphor – an analogy where something is regarded as representative or symbolic of something else. For example, a map has often been used as a metaphor for knowledge. A metaphor may be an alternative to using a definition, but it is debatable whether metaphors are better than definitions.

Methods and tools – an element of the knowledge framework. It explores how knowledge is produced. This is not limited to formal methodologies (for example, the experimental method) and also includes cognitive tools (for example, assumptions, reasoning, language).

Mistake – a false belief. Mistakes should be separated from biases because biases are systematic mistakes.

Multiperspectivity (in history teaching) – the idea of using different historical perspectives to help students embrace history more holistically. As a concept, multiperspectivity is broader than heteroglossia. Heteroglossia is a combination of fundamentally incompatible perspectives that engage in a dialogue, transforming each other. Multiperspectivity is simply the presence of various perspectives.

Naïve theory – a system of beliefs about the world that people share despite the fact that it is inaccurate or outdated. Naïve theories are usually the result of misunderstanding of shared knowledge due to the influence of personal experiences.

Necessary and sufficient conditions – logical conditions defining the truth of a statement. If A and B are necessary conditions for a statement to be true, it means that the statement will be false even if one of these conditions is not met. If A and B are sufficient conditions for a statement to be true, it means that no other condition is needed for us to accept this statement. In the definition of knowledge as a "justified true belief" justification and truth are necessary and sufficient conditions for a belief to be accepted as knowledge.

Newspeak – a fictional language described by George Orwell in his anti-utopian novel 1984. In the novel, Newspeak was designed by a totalitarian society to restrict thought and prevent people from questioning things and thinking critically.

Nomothetic approach to research – in human sciences, the approach that sees the purpose of research in deriving universally applicable generalizations (laws). It is opposed to the idiographic approach.

Non compos mentis – the opposite of compos mentis (see "compos mentis").

Non-propositional knowledge – knowledge that cannot be expressed verbally. Examples include "how to" knowledge (I know how to ride a bicycle) and knowledge by acquaintance (I recognize my brother when I see him).

Normal science – a period in scientific development when a predominant paradigm is established and scientists widely agree on this paradigm. During these periods, science takes the form of puzzle-solving - trying to fit results of experiments into the existing paradigm, like pieces that fit into a puzzle.

Normative models of thinking – in psychology, models describing rational, analytical (System 2) thinking. Examples include logic and probability theory.

Noumenon (plural: noumena) – according to Immanuel Kant, an object or an event that exists independently of human perception. It is real, but unknowable. This is opposite to phenomenon.

Objective knowledge of objectively existing phenomena – this is when you use scientific methods and precise measurement to study something that exists objectively and independently of the observer.

Objective knowledge of subjectively existing phenomena – this is when you are trying to use precise measurement to understand someone else's subjective experiences.

Objectively existing phenomena – see "ontologically objective phenomena".

Observation – in the broad sense, the process of gathering observational evidence, for example, astronomical observations or a scientific experiment.

Observational evidence – evidence provided on the basis of empirical methods, for example, an experiment. Any evidence where you can get real-world data. This is often opposed to purely theoretical justification.

Observer – in a broad sense, a knower who is obtaining knowledge about the real world. A scientist, a fiction writer, a historian are all examples of observers. In natural sciences, the observer is removed as much as possible from the process of observation, but in other areas of knowledge (such as human sciences) removing the observer may be impossible or even undesirable.

Ontologically objective phenomena (objectively existing phenomena) – things and events that exist in the world around us independently from our perception. For example, when nobody is observing an asteroid moving through space, it still exists.

Ontologically subjective phenomena (subjectively existing phenomena) – parts of an individual's subjective experiences, for example, the feeling of grief. By definition, they exist subjectively, and another person cannot "objectively" perceive them.

Ontology – the study of being. It answers questions like "Does God exist?" or "Is the Universe infinite?". It is opposed to epistemology.

Opinion – a person's judgment about something (not necessarily justified).

Originality – in art, the quality of being fresh in its form and content, not derivative from previous work.

Paradigm – a system of agreed-upon views that informs activities of the scientific community at any given point of time in the process of scientific development. According to Thomas Kuhn, paradigms are necessary for the scientific community to work successfully. At the same time, there is no attempt to test the agreed-upon views. When paradigms are no longer productive in solving scientific problems ("puzzles"), they are replaced by other paradigms in the process of a scientific revolution.

Paradigm shift – the process of replacing one paradigm by another during a scientific revolution. Paradigm shifts are fundamental changes in the principles and beliefs that define the whole system of scientific knowledge at a given time. The concept was introduced by Thomas Kuhn.

Perception of the audience – the way recipients of a work of art understand it. There are three perspectives on the source of knowledge in art. According to one of them, knowledge is contained in the perception of the audience (beauty is in the eye of the beholder). The other two perspectives are intentions of the artist and the artwork itself.

Peripheral Mentalese – the part of the language of thought that consists of concepts and structures that are learned through experience. It may be different for different people and cultures. Compare this to "core Mentalese". Core Mentalese and peripheral Mentalese are two terms invented in this book to reconcile linguistic nativism and the Sapir-Whorf hypothesis.

Personal context of a work of art – details about the personal life of the artist that might be important to fully understand the artwork.

Personal experience – the sum of all instances of interaction of a person with various aspects of the world. This is a broad definition that includes any type of interaction, both practical and theoretical. For example, if you have seen a zebra on a safari trip, you have some personal experience with zebras. If you watched a documentary about zebras, you also have experience with them.

Personal knowledge – knowledge that belongs to an individual and is not necessarily shared by other individuals.

Perspective – a viewpoint, a way of looking at something determined by one's vantage point. Perspectives are always defined by two aspects: what you see and where you are looking from. If the vantage point (where you are looking from) is not specified, that's an opinion but not a perspective. Perspectives may be similar to biases in some situations, but not always. For example, it is probably not reasonable to call historical perspectives "biases".

Perspectives (element of the knowledge framework) – an element of the knowledge framework that explores various interpretations or points of view regarding knowledge. These may be various interpretations co-existing at the same time or perspectives that replace each other historically.

Phenomenon (plural: phenomena) – (1) according to Immanuel Kant, an object or an event that is given to us through our perception. This is opposite to noumenon. (2) In a broad sense (used throughout this book), any object or event.

Philosophical zombie – a thought experiment about qualia. The philosophical zombie is a hypothetical creature who is indistinguishable from a normal human being on the outside but has no subjective experiences.

Physical properties of a work of art – things like color, shape, composition, symmetry. Everything about a work of art that has a physical nature. Physical properties in a work of art are combined with its conceptual properties.

Physicalism – one of the responses to the hard problem of consciousness; the belief that consciousness exists, but it can be fully explained by the physical properties of the brain. Physicalists assert that everything in the world, including mental states and consciousness, is physical in nature. The other two responses are dualism and eliminative materialism.

Physics envy – the term describing the belief of some thinkers that human sciences should try to resemble natural sciences as much as possible.

Poverty of the stimulus (POS) – the observation that children's linguistic competence cannot be explained by their linguistic experience. According to the POS argument, children are exposed to minimal grammar and vocabulary, and theoretically from this experience they can infer a whole variety of grammars, but they don't. Somehow, they quickly figure out the correct rules. According to Noam Chomsky and other linguistic nativists, this means that some of the grammar is innate.

Pragmatic theory of truth – the approach suggesting that truth of a belief is established through its usefulness in the current state of development of knowledge. In other words, if a belief makes sense in the currently accepted system of knowledge and if it allows to develop this system further, then it makes sense to provisionally accept it as true. Compare to: coherence theory of truth, correspondence theory of truth.

Pre-interpretation – in hermeneutics, a form of initial interpretation or belief that is further refined when we obtain more information about something. It is a starting point of understanding.

Principles of universal grammar – the deep rules that are common to every language and cannot be violated. According to Noam Chomsky (and other linguistic nativists), when children are born, they already understand these principles.

Proof assistant – see "interactive theorem prover".

Proof-by-exhaustion – a special kind of proof in mathematics when the computer checks all possible permutations and exhausts all possibilities. It is not traditional deductive proof, because the truth of a statement is not deduced from other statements, but rather established "experimentally". For this reason, many mathematicians refused to accept proof-by-exhaustion as "proper mathematics".

Propaganda – information used to promote a political cause or point of view. In history writing, propaganda is when someone describes the past with the aim of influencing opinions of others and promoting one's own political agenda. Language is an important tool of propaganda.

Propositional knowledge – any knowledge that can be expressed in the form of a statement. For example, "Atoms consist of electrons and protons".

Pseudo-science – a non-science that disguises itself as a science. "Pseudo" means "false". Examples include ufology, astrology, phrenology, homeopathy and many others.

Purposes (what for?) – the driving goals of human activities, the meaning behind these activities. This is to be distinguished from reasons. As Daniel Dennett points out, there are two meanings of the question "why?" in the English language – "how come?" and "what for?". When we ask about purposes of human activity, we are asking the "what for?" question.

Puzzle-solving – the scientific activity of solving problems generated by a theory (such as observations that do not fit, aspects of reality that the theory cannot explain, prior knowledge that the theory contradicts). The puzzle-solving approach was proposed by Thomas Kuhn as an alternative to the realist view on scientific progress. We cannot know if in the process of scientific progress we are getting closer to the truth, but we can know if our theories are becoming better at solving puzzles.

Qualia (singular: quale) – instances of subjective experience. This term captures the "what it's like to" phenomenon, for example, what it feels like to have the first sip of coffee after a long night's sleep. The big questions are: "Do qualia exist?", "Are they knowable?"

Questions and claims about the world – subject-specific or situation-specific questions and claims about some aspect of reality (for example, today's weather, Pythagorean theorem, history of the Roman empire). Questions and claims about the world are contrasted to questions and claims about knowledge (of the world).

Radical skepticism – the school of thought promoting the idea that we must not accept as knowledge anything that is less than absolutely certain.

Random assignment of parameters – the starting point of a simulation. Parameters are assigned to components of the model randomly, but within certain constraints. Then the simulation is launched, components of the model dynamically interact with each other, and parameters are updated.

Randomness – the quality of lacking a pattern, unpredictability. According to indeterminism, randomness rather than causality is intrinsic in the fabric of nature.

Realist approach to scientific progress – the view that theories may have a truth value (that is, there are true scientific theories and there are false ones). Scientific progress is then defined as gradually replacing false scientific theories with true ones.

Reality – the objectively existing world around us. In Immanuel Kant's opinion, the world as it really is (noumena) should be clearly distinguished from the world as it appears to us (phenomena). Hence, the distinction between reality and appearance.

Reasons (how come?) – the causes of human activities, the factors in the past that influenced these activities. This is to be distinguished from purposes. As Daniel Dennett points out, there are two meanings of the question "why?" in the English language – "how come?" and "what for?". When we ask about reasons of human activity, we are asking the "how come?" question.

Redefinition of art – periodic changes in what is understood to be the nature and the purpose of art. In this book we have made the claim that art develops by redefining itself in response to challenges such as photography or photocopying, therefore redefinition of art is the driving force of its development.

Referent – one of the three components of a sign according to structural linguistics (the signifier, the signified, the referent). The referent is the class of objects or phenomena of the material world to which the sign applies. For example, the referent of the word "elephant" is the collection of all elephants in the world.

Reflexive control – consciously controlling one's behavior to anticipate and reduce the influence of implicit bias.

Reflexivity – the process of considering how the researcher's own mental processes may have influenced results of the research. The term comes from human sciences.

Research ethics – a field of ethics that explores the issues of conducting research in a morally acceptable way, honestly and without doing harm.

Rival interpretations – in history, different, sometimes conflicting accounts of the same events of the past. Rival interpretations exist due to the fact that historians construct their accounts on the basis of their perspectives. Perspective-less accounts of the past, arguably, are impossible.

Sapir-Whorf hypothesis – the suggestion that the way people think is strongly affected by the language they speak. The hypothesis was proposed by linguist Edward Sapir and his student Benjamin Whorf in 1929. There are two versions of the hypothesis. The strong version claims that "language determines thought", the weak version merely claims that "language influences thought".

Scientific convention – an agreed and generally accepted standard of naming and defining a scientific property or parameter. For example, it is conventional to define the unit of amount of substance as a "mole", which is any amount of matter containing exactly 6.02214076×1023 particles.

Scientific progress – development of scientific knowledge over the course of time. The word "progress" implies that some sort of improvement occurs during the development (in other words, that scientific knowledge is getting closer to meeting the goals of science).

Scientific revolution – a period in scientific development when some fundamental assumptions of the predominant paradigm are challenged and the unsolved puzzles become so critical that the old paradigm has to be replaced by another one. A scientific revolution is a very significant change where old knowledge is being rejected as something based on initially faulty assumptions.

Scientific worldview – a coherent global description of the world currently accepted by the scientific community. Fitting new knowledge into the scientific worldview is a necessary condition of understanding in natural sciences.

Scope – an element of the knowledge framework. It explores the nature of the problems that are investigated in each theme or area of knowledge. It also shows the place of the theme or area of knowledge within human knowledge in general.

Selection bias – in the work of a historian, refers to giving more weight to evidence supporting one perspective and less weight to evidence associated with conflicting perspectives. The historian may give a balanced coverage of selected sources, but the selection itself maybe biased.

Shared knowledge – knowledge that is jointly produced by large groups of people. Areas of knowledge are examples of shared knowledge.

Sign – a sound or any other material token (such as a gesture or a knot tied on a rope) that denotes some aspect of the environment. Unlike signals, signs may be used in the absence of the actual stimulus that they denote. As a consequence, signs (unlike signals) do not have to be linked to a biological need and can be taught from one person to another.

Signal – a sound or other material token (such as a smell or a gesture) that points to an aspect of the environment that has an immediate significance. Signals are different from signs. Signals cannot occur in the absence of the aspect of the environment that they are linked to. Non-human animals cannot teach them to each other. Signals are linked to a biological need (such as hunger or survival).

Signified – one of the three components of a sign according to structural linguistics (the signifier, the signified, the referent). The signified is the idea or a mental image that is evoked by the signifier. For example, when I say "elephant", there is a mental image formed in your head – this mental image is the signified.

Signifier – one of the three components of a sign according to structural linguistics (the signifier, the signified, the referent). The signifier is the material token, for example, the sequence of sounds in a word or a gesture in a sign language.

Skepticism – one of the perspectives on the role of doubt in knowledge (dogmatism, skepticism, fallibilism). It is a radical perspective asserting that, if knowledge claims are not absolutely certain, they must be rejected. Skepticism accepts either certain knowledge or nothing.

Small Data – the term used to characterize the typical approach to collecting and processing data in human sciences. The researcher has a plan of data collection informed by theory. On the basis of this plan, data is collected in a standardized way from a limited sample of participants. Results are then generalized to wider groups based on the belief that the sample is representative of the target population. There is not a lot of data, it is homogeneous and static.

Social fact – a fact that is constructed by humans. Social facts cannot exist outside of our society or our interpretation. For example, the statement "London is the capital of the United Kingdom" is a social fact. Social facts are constructed through language. This is in contrast to brute facts.

Source of bias – a factor or a group of factors that cause a bias to occur. For example, a historian's cultural identity may be a source of bias in their interpretation of events of the past.

Space – according to Immanuel Kant, one of the a priori concepts that are innate in the human mind and influence our perception of the world. Due to this a priori concept, we perceive things to be close together or far apart, although in reality that may not necessarily be true. Also see "time".

Spacetime – a model of space and time in which they are not separate from each other, but time is the fourth dimension of space. This model was proposed by Hermann Minkowski, who was building upon Einstein's relativity theory.

Standards of justification – commonly accepted views on what counts as a good justification within a particular area of knowledge. Standards of justification differ from one area of knowledge to another. This means that if something is accepted as good justification in one area, it may not be accepted in another area.

Subject-specific terminology – terms used within a certain specialized subject area, for example, "circumference", "acceleration", "dictatorship". Subject-specific terminology is contrasted to knowledge concepts. The former describes the world, the latter describes our knowledge of the world.

Subjective experiences – felt mental states, such as being disappointed with an incorrect decision or experiencing pain after touching a hot surface.

Subjective knowledge of objectively existing phenomena – this is when something exists objectively, but you are studying it through subjective interpretation rather than measurement.

Subjective knowledge of subjectively existing phenomena – this when you are using your subjective interpretation to understand someone else's subjective experiences.

Subjectively existing phenomena – see "ontologically subjective phenomena".

Subjectivity and universality of aesthetic judgment – according to Immanuel Kant, two key properties of aesthetic judgments. Aesthetic judgments are subjective in the sense that they are based on a complex subjective response that we experience when engaging with a work of art. But aesthetic judgments are universal because when we say that a painting is beautiful, we speak as if beauty was a property of the painting itself, not merely a property of our perception of it.

Super-mathematical criterion of truth – in mathematics, this is the approach that defines the truth of a mathematical system in relation to the real world. Most commonly a mathematical system in this approach is considered to be "true" if it enables successful practical applications, for example, in science and engineering. The super-mathematical criterion assumes that mathematical entities exist in one way or another in the real world, and it is consistent with the "discovered" position in the debate "Is mathematics invented or discovered?".

Superficial doubt – groundless skepticism, blind rejection of knowledge on the grounds that "nothing is certain". This is opposite to meaningful doubt.

System 1 thinking – the hypothetical system of thinking and decision-making that is responsible for quick, automatic, intuitive decisions. It developed earlier in the process of evolution, and humans are not the only species that have it.

System 2 thinking – the hypothetical system of thinking and decision-making that is deliberate, logical, rational and analytical. It developed later in the process of evolution, and humans are the only species that have it.

Technoethics – a sub-field of ethics that explores the new questions of morality that emerged in the age of technology. Examples include ethics of artificial intelligence (robotics), data ethics, cyber ethics, etc.

Technological singularity – a hypothetical point in the future when technological development will result in changes so dramatic that everything human will lose significance and give way to the machines.

Teleology – the study of purposes, or an explanation of a phenomenon with reference to its purposes. This is opposite to determinism (the belief that everything can be completely explained by preceding causes).

Tests for truth – the application of three theories of truth (correspondence, coherence, pragmatic) to a knowledge claim in order to establish its truth value. It is possible that a knowledge claim passes some but not all tests for truth.

Text – in hermeneutics, anything the knower interacts with to understand it better. It is a very broad term because hermeneutics suggests that "everything is a text".

Text mining – digitalizing texts and using computer algorithms to derive numerical information from them. Text mining is used in various fields of human sciences and history. It is an example of how technology plays a role in obtaining knowledge in these fields.

Themes – elements of the IB TOK course that look into various aspects of knowledge. There is one core theme (Knowledge and the knower) and five optional themes (Knowledge and language, Knowledge and technology, Knowledge and politics, Knowledge and religion, Knowledge and indigenous societies). IB students are required to study two of the five optional themes.

Theorem – in mathematics, a proven statement. To prove a theorem means to demonstrate that it follows deductively from other statements that are already known to be true.

Theories of truth – approaches to defining the truth. There are three theories: the correspondence theory of truth, the coherence theory of truth, and the pragmatic theory of truth.

Theory – in science, a coherent explanation given to observable data, bringing all observational evidence together in a single explanatory framework.

Theory-laden fact – an observational fact that already bears the influence of the background theory. The problem is that observational facts are inevitably theory-laden, and there is no such thing as a "pure" fact or observational statement.

Time – according to Immanuel Kant, one of the a priori concepts that are innate in the human mind and influence our perception of the world. Due to this a priori concept, we perceive events as existing on a linear scale from "before" to "after", although this is not necessarily a property of reality itself. Also see "space".

Translation – the process of expressing a thought coded in one language in another language. Translation requires first understanding the thought behind the utterance in one language (also called the source language) and then expressing the same or equivalent thought in another language (also called the target language).

Truth – the property of "correctness" of a belief. It is not easy to give a single definition, as it is much better characterized through the various theories of truth.

Turing test – a thought experiment proposed in 1950 by Alan Turing to determine if a machine is intelligent.

Underdetermination of theory by data (evidence) – the idea that a scientific theory can never be fully reduced to supporting evidence. Because of this, it is usually the case that more than one theory can fit equally well into the available body of evidence.

Understanding – an insight that becomes possible when we combine fragmented knowledge about various parts or aspects of something into one meaningful whole. Unlike knowledge, understanding: (1) is holistic, (2) covers all essential aspects of a phenomenon, (3) is rooted in context, (4) applies to individual cases.

Universal Darwinism – the idea that Darwinian evolution applies not only to the development of biological species, but also in other contexts, including the development of non-living things. For example, Darwinian evolution has been applied to the development of the physical Universe. The three necessary and sufficient conditions of evolution, according to Universal Darwinism, are replication, variation and differential fitness.

Universal grammar – rules of language that are hypothetically innate to the human mind, that is, babies are born with an understanding of universal grammar. It is common for all existing languages. The idea of universal grammar was the response Noam Chomsky (and other linguistic nativists) gave to the poverty of the stimulus (POS) argument.

Universally applicable law – a law that is equally applicable to all objects or people at all times. Newton's law of universal gravitation is an example: it applies to all objects in the Universe. In human sciences, the nomothetic approach to research attempts to derive similar universally applicable laws of human activities. Examples are laws of economics or laws of behavior in psychology.

Untranslatability – the inability of something from one language to be adequately translated into another language.

Verification criterion – a demarcation criterion that is based on supporting evidence. It states that scientific knowledge is true if there exists empirical evidence supporting it. A theory is scientific if its claims are verifiable by evidence. Compare this to the falsification criterion.

Verisimilitude – "truthlikeliness" of a scientific theory. This is a concept introduced by Karl Popper in response to the argument that we can never know the truth directly and therefore we cannot say if in the process of scientific development theories are getting closer to the truth or not. According to Popper, we can still infer their closeness to truth indirectly. It is possible for one false theory to have higher verisimilitude than another false theory, and scientific progress is a gradual increase in verisimilitude. The main indicator of verisimilitude is the number of informative true predictions made by the theory.

Verstehen position – the idea that in order to achieve full understanding of meaningful human behavior, you need to study it from within. For example, to understand the culture of an indigenous community, you need to spend some time living among these people. Verstehen is a German word that means "understanding".

Vicious circle of truth – the idea describing the logically problematic relationship between truth and knowledge: knowledge is defined through the truth, but the truth can only be accessed through knowledge.

What-if thought experiment – a hypothetical scenario where you imagine that one aspect of this world is different from what it is, and then you logically derive how other aspects would be different. For example, think about the following scenario: what if all people were bias-free?

REFERENCES

Albers, D.J., Reid, C., and Dantzig, G.B. (1986). An Interview with George B. Dantzig: The Father of Linear Programming. *The College Mathematics Journal, 17(4),* p.292-314.

Appel, K.I., & Haken, W. (1989). *Every planar map is four colorable.* Providence, R.I.: American Mathematical Society.

Assis, A.A. (2016). Objectivity and the first law of history writing. *Journal of the Philosophy of History (2016)*, 1-23.

Ayres, I. (2007). *Super Crunchers: Why thinking-by-numbers is the new way to be smart*. New York: Bantam Books.

Barnhardt, R. & Angayuqaq, O.K. (2008). Indigenous Knowledge Systems and Education. In: *Why Do We Educate?: Renewing the Conversation.* Eds Coulter, D.L., Wiens J.R., Fenstermacher, G.D.

Bernstein, J. (1984). *Three Degrees Above Zero: Bell Labs in the Information Age.* New York: Charles Scribner's Sons

Bevir, M. (1994). Objectivity in History. *History and Theory, 33(3)*, 328-244.

Blackmore, S. (2000). *The Meme Machine.* Oxford University Press.

Boolos, G. (1994). Gödel's Second Incompleteness Theorem Explained in Words of One Syllable. *Mind*, 103 (409), p. 1 – 3. doi.org/10.1093/mind/ 103.409.1

Bostrom, N. (2003). Are you Living in a computer simulation? *Philosophical Quarterly, 53 (211)*, 243–255.

Briley, D, Morris, M.W & Simonson, I. (2005). Cultural chameleons: Biculturals, conformity motives, and decision making. *Journal of Consumer Psychology, 15(4)*, 351–362.

Carr, N. (2011). *The shallows: What the Internet is doing to our brains.* New York: W.W.Norton & Company Inc.

Chalmers, D. (1995). Facing up to the problem of consciousness. *Journal of Consciousness Studies, 2(3)*, 200 – 219.

Chiu, L.H. (1972). A cross-cultural comparison of cognitive styles in Chinese and American children. *International Journal of Psychology, 17(4)*, 235–242.

Clement, J. (1983). A conceptual model discussed by Galileo and used intuitively by physics students. In D. Gentner & A. L. Stevens (Eds.), Mental models (pp. 325–340). Hillsdale, NJ: Erlbaum.

Cohen, M. (1999). *101 Philosophy Problems.* Routledge Taylor Francis.

Cohen, M., & Gonzalez, R. (2008). *Philosophical Tales: Being an Alternative History Revealing the Characters, the Plots, and the Hidden Scenes That Make Up the True Story of Philosophy.* Wiley-Blackwell.

Columb, C., & Plant, E.A. (2010). Revisiting the Obama effect: Exposure to Obama reduces implicit prejudice. *Journal of Experimental Social Psychology, 47*, 499-501.

Correll, J., Park, B., Judd, C.M., & Wittenbrink, B. (2007). The influence of stereotypes on decisions to shoot. *European Journal of Social Psychology, 37*, 1102-1117

Costa, A., Foucart, A., Hayakawa, S., Aparici, M., Apesteguia, J., Heafner, J., & Keysar, B. (2014). Your morals depend on language. *PLoS ONE, 9(4)*, e94842. doi:10.1371/journal.pone.0094842

Crain, S., & Thornton, R. (2006). *Acquisition of syntax and semantics.* In M. J. Traxler, & M. A. Gernsbacher (Eds.), Handbook of Psycholinguistics, Second Edition (pp. 1073-1110). Amsterdam ; Boston: Elsevier. https://doi.org/10.1016/B978-012369374-7/50029-8

Danson, E. (2006). *Weighing the World.* Oxford University Press.

Dastin, J. (2018, October 10). Amazon scraps secret AI recruiting tool that showed bias against women. *Reuters.* Retrieved from https://www.reuters.com

Davidson, D. (1975). *Inquiries into Truth and Interpretation.* Oxford: Oxford University Press.

Davisson, C. J. & Germer, L. H. (1928). Reflection of Electrons by a Crystal of Nickel. *Proceedings of the National Academy of Sciences of the United States of America, 14 (4)*, 317–322.

Dawkins, R. (1974). *The Selfish Gene.* Oxford University Press.

Debenedictis, A. (2014). *Evolution or creation? A comparison of the arguments.* Bloomington: Xlibris LLC.

Dennett, D.C. (2018). *From Bacteria to Bach and Back. The Evolution of Minds.* Penguin Books.

Deregowski, J.B. (1998). *W H R Rivers (1864 – 1922): the founder of research in cross-cultural perception.* Perception, Vol. 27, p. 1393–1406.

Dowding-Green, R. (2018, April 23). An evaluation of the interpretations of Vincent Van Gogh's Starry Night. *Medium.* Retrieved from https://medium.com/@raphaeladowdinggreen/an-evaluation-of-the-interpretations-of-vincent-van-goghs-starry-night-cf1352edd589

Du Sautoy, M. (2017). *What We Cannot Know. From Consciousness to the Cosmos, the Cutting Edge of Science Explained.* London: 4th Estate.

Eibenberger, S. et al. (2013). Matter-wave interference with particles selected from a molecular library with masses exceeding 10000 amu. *Physical Chemistry Chemical Physics, 15* (35), 14696–14700.

Einstein, A. (2005). Geometry and Experience (1921). Lecture before the Prussian academy of sciences. *Scientiae Studia, 3(4),* 665-675.

Englich, B., Mussweiler, T., & Strack, F. (2006). Playing dice with criminal sentences: The influence of irrelevant anchors on experts' judicial decision making. *Personality and Social Psychology Bulletin, 32(2)*, 188-200.

Feyerabend, P. (1975). *Against Method.* Verso Books.

Fisher, H., Aron, A., & Brown, L. (2005) Romantic Love: An fMRI Study of a Neural Mechanism for Mate Choice. *The Journal of Comparative Neurology,* 493, 58-62.

Flanagan, M. (1998). The perpetual bed. Retrieved January 10, 2020, from https://studio.maryflanagan.com/the-perpetual-bed/.

Gamow, G. (1964). *Mr. Tompkins in Wonderland.* Cambridge University Press. (First published 1939).

Gardner, M.B. (1920). *A Journey to the Earth's Interior.* Aurora, Illinois. Retrieved from https://www.sacred-texts.com/earth/jei/index.htm

George, J., Meyers, A., & Chasalow, B. (2012, June 2012). How it works: Chris Milk's The Treachery of Sanctuary. *Vice: Entertainment.* Retrieved from https://www.vice.com/en_us/article/3dpg9v/how-it-works-chris-milks-ithe-treachery-of-sanctuaryi

Gettier, E. (1963). Is Justified True Belief Knowledge? *Analysis, 23(6)*, 121–123.

Gewirtz, D. (2018, May 7). Google Duplex beat the Turing test: Are we doomed? *ZDNet.* Retrieved from https://www.zdnet.com/article/google-duplex-beat-the-turing-test-are-we-doomed/

Gibney, E. (2014, May 7). Model Universe recreates evolution of the Cosmos. *Nature: News.* Retrieved from: https://www.nature.com/news/model-universe-recreates-evolution-of-the-cosmos-1.15178

Gilovich, T. (1981). Seeing the past in the present: The effect of associations to familiar events on judgments and decisions. *Journal of Personality and Social Psychology, 40(5)*, 797-808.

Glanzberg, M. (2018). Truth. In E. N. Zalta (Ed.), The Stanford encyclopedia of philosophy (Fall 2018 ed.). Retrieved from http:// plato.stanford.edu/archives/fall2018/entries/truth/

Gonthier, G. (2008). Formal proof – the four-color theorem. *Notices of the American Mathematical Society, 55(11)*, 1382 – 1393.

Gordon, P. (2004). Numerical cognition without words: evidence from Amazonia. *Science, 306(5695)*, 496-499.

Gottfried, J., & Shearer, E. (2016, May 26). *News use across social media platforms.* Pew Research Center. Retrieved from http://www.journalism.org/2016/05/26/news-use-acrosssocial-media-platforms-2016/

Gugerty, L. (2006). Newell and Simon's Logic Theorist: historical background and impact on cognitive modelling. *Human Factors in Ergonomics Society Annual Meeting Proceedings, 50(9)*, 880 – 884.

Hagberg, G. L. (1995). *Art as Language: Wittgenstein, Meaning and Aesthetic Theory.* Ithaca: Cornell University Press.

Harris, R. (2019). *Pi record now at 31.4 trillion digits in 2019 thanks to Google Compute.* Retrieved from https://appdevelopermagazine.com/pi-record-now-at-31.4-trillion-digits-in-2019-thanks-to-google-compute/

Hock, R.R. (2015). *Forty Studies That Changed Psychology. Explorations into the History of Psychological Research. 7th edition.* Pearson Education Limited.

Hodge, M. (2018, January 5). Indonesian villagers dig up their dead relatives and dress them up in eerie ritual. *The Sun.* Retrieved from www.thesun.co.uk.

Hodson, H. (2014, August 27). Supercomputers make discoveries that scientists can't. *New Scientist:* Technology. Retrieved from: https://www.newscientist.com/article/mg22329844-000-supercomputers-make-discoveries-that-scientists-cant/

Hoffmann, D. (2015, March). *Do we see reality as it is?* [Video file]. Retrieved from https://www.ted.com/talks/donald_hoffman_do_we_see_reality_as_it_is?referrer=playlist-how_your_brain_constructs_real

Jackson, F. (1982). Epiphenomenal Qualia. *The Philosophical Quarterly*, 32 (127), 127-136.

Jung, C.G. (1979). *Flying Saucers: A Modern Myth of Things Seen in the Sky.* Princeton University Press.

Kahneman, D. (2011). *Thinking Fast and Slow.* Farrar, Straus and Giroux.

Kaspersky Lab (2016). From Digital Amnesia to Augmented Mind. Retrieved from: https://media.kaspersky.com/pdf/Kaspersky-Digital-Amnesia-Evolution-report-17-08-16.pdf

Kay, P. & Kempton, W. (1984). What is the Sapir-Whorf hypothesis? *American Anthropologist*, 86(1), 65-79.

Klein, C. (2018). *7 Things You May Not Know about the Battle of Waterloo.* Retrieved from: https://www.history.com/news/7-things-you-may-not-know-about-the-battle-of-waterloo

Kobie, N. (2019, June 7). The complicated truth about China's social credit system. *Wired.* Retrieved from: https://www.wired.co.uk/article/china-social-credit-system-explained

Kuhn, T.S. (1962). *The Structure of Scientific Revolutions.* Chicago: University of Chicago Press.

Kuhn, T.S. (1977). *The Essential Tension.* Chicago: The University of Chicago Press.

Kurzweil, R. (2005). *The Singularity is Near.* New York: Penguin Group.

Lang, S. (2007). *British History for Dummies. 2nd edition.* John Wiley & Sons, Ltd.

Langer, E., Blank, A., & Chanowitz, B. (1978). The mindlessness of ostensibly thoughtful action: The role of "placebic" information in interpersonal interaction. *Journal of Personality and Social Psychology, 36(6)*, 635-642.

Laplace, P.S. (1951). *A Philosophical Essay on Probabilities*, translated into English from the original French 6th ed. by Truscott, F.W. and Emory, F.L. New York: Dover Publications

Lazer, D., & Kennedy, R. (2015, January 10). What we can learn from the epic fail of Google Flu Trends. *Wired.* Retrieved from: https://www.wired.com/2015/10/can-learn-epic-failure-google-flu-trends/

Lenat, D. B., & Brown, J. S. (1984). Why AM and EURISKO appear to work. *Artificial Intelligence, 23(3)*, 269—294.

Lessel, M. (2016). About the origin: Is mathematics discovered or invented? *The Lehigh Review, Volume 24-2016*, 78-85.

Letter from Vincent van Gogh To: Theo van Gogh Date: Arles, Monday, 9 or Tuesday, 10 July 1888. Retrieved from http://www.vangoghletters.org/vg/letters/let638/letter.html

Letter from Vincent van Gogh To: Willemien van Gogh Date: Arles, Sunday, 26 August 1888. Retrieved from http://vangoghletters.org/vg/letters/let670/letter.html

Li, X., & Chen, X. (2018). Airport simulation technology in airport planning, design and operating management. *Applied and Computational Mathematics, 7(3)*, 130-138.

Loftus, E.F., & Palmer, J.C. (1974). Reconstruction of automobile destruction: An example of the interaction between language and memory. *Journal of Verbal Learning and Verbal Behavior, 13(5)*, 585-589.

MacGregor, S. (2019). *The Three Battles of Waterloo: Same Conflict – Different Perspectives.* Retrieved from: https://www.warhistoryonline.com/napoleon/three-battles-of-waterloo-same.html

Machine Intelligence Research Institute (2013). Intelligence explosion FAQ. Retrieved from: https://intelligence.org/ie-faq/

Manjoo, F. (2011, December 29). Will robots steal your job? *Slate.* Retrieved from: http://www.slate.com/articles/technology/robot_invasion/2011/09/will_robots_steal_your_job.html

McCullagh, C.B. (2000). Bias in historical description, interpretation, and explanation. *History and Theory, 39(1)*, 39-66

Mendoza, S.A., Gollwitzer, P.M., & Amodio, D.M. (2010). Reducing the expression of implicit stereotypes: Reflexive control through implementation intentions. *Personality and Social Psychology Bulletin, 36(4)*, 512-523.

Miller, R.L., Brickman, P., & Bolen, D. (1975). Attribution versus persuasion as a means for modifying behavior. *Journal of Personality and Social Psychology, 31(3)*, 430-441.

Munroe, R. (2014). *What If?: Serious Scientific Answers to Absurd Hypothetical Questions.* Xkcd.Inc.

Niiniluoto, Ilkka, "Scientific Progress", The Stanford Encyclopedia of Philosophy (Summer 2015 Edition), Edward N. Zalta (ed.), URL = <https://plato.stanford.edu/archives/sum2015/entries/scientific-progress/>.

Oberheim, Eric and Hoyningen-Huene, Paul, "The Incommensurability of Scientific Theories", The Stanford Encyclopedia of Philosophy (Fall 2018 Edition), Edward N. Zalta (ed.), URL = <https://plato.stanford.edu/archives/fall2018/entries/incommensurability/>.

Orwell, G. (1943). *Looking back on the Spanish war. In England, New England and Other Essays* (1953). London: Secker and Warburg. Retrieved from http://orwell.ru/library/essays/Spanish_War/english/esw_1

Park, D.C., and Huang, C.-M. (2010). Culture wires the brain: A cognitive neuroscience perspective. *Perspectives on Psychological Science, 5(4)*, 391-400.

Pinker, S. (2005, July). *What our language habits reveal.* [Video file]. Retrieved from https://www.ted.com/talks/steven_pinker_on_language_and_thought?language=en

Popkin, G. (2014). Slow, cold start to Universe suggested. Idea provides alternative to Big Bang theory of cosmic origin. *Science News.* Retrieved from https://www.sciencenews.org/article/slow-cold-start-universe-suggested

Popper, K. (1963). *Conjectures and Refutations: The Growth of Scientific Knowledge.* Routledge and Kegan Paul.

Quine, W.V.O. (2013). *Word and Object. New edition.* The MIT Press.

Rivers, W H R. (1901). Vision, in *Reports of the Cambridge Anthropological Expedition to Torres Straits*, vol.2. Ed. A.C.Haddon. Cambridge: Cambridge University Press, p. 1-132.

Robertson, C. (2016, April 11). The true difference between knowledge and understanding. *Medium.* Retrieved from https://medium.com/better-humans/the-true-difference-between-knowledge-and-understanding-282f8a99b1a7

Robinson, A. (2011). *In Theory Bakhtin: Dialogism, Polyphony and Heteroglossia*. Retrieved from https://ceasefiremagazine.co.uk/in-theory-bakhtin-1/

Rocca, F.J. (2015, September 21). The Collapse of American Morality and the Dangers of Aesthetic Relativism. *The Washington Sentinel*. Retrieved from www.thewashingtonsentinel.com.

Roncato, S. & Rumiati, R. (1986). Naive statics: Current misconceptions on equilibrium. *Journal of Experimental Psychology: learning, memory, and Cognition*, 12(3), 361-377.

Searle, J.R. (1980). Minds, brains, and programs. *Behavioral and Bran Sciences, 3(3)*, 417 – 457.

Snibbe, S. (1998). Boundary Functions. Retrieved from: https://www.snibbe.com/projects/interactive/boundaryfunctions

Steinberg, M.S., Brown, D.E., & Clement, J. (2007). Genius is not immune to persistent misconceptions: conceptual difficulties impeding Isaac Newton and contemporary physics students. I*nternational Journal of Science Education, 12(3)*, 265-273.

Stinson, L. (2014, July 23). A wacky device that turns polluted air into glitch art. *Wired: Design*. Retrieved from: https://www.wired.com/2014/07/a-clever-device-that-turns-polluted-air-into-art/

Strack, F., & Mussweiler, T. (1997). Explaining the enigmatic anchoring effect: Mechanisms of selective accessibility. *Journal of Personality and Social Psychology, 73(3)*, 437-446.

Sullivan, D. (2007, April 26). What is Google PageRank? A guide for searchers & webmasters. *Search Engine Land*. Retrieved from: https://searchengineland.com/what-is-google-pagerank-a-guide-for-searchers-webmasters-11068

Tait, W.W. (2001). Beyond the axioms: The question of objectivity in Mathematics. *Philosophia Mathematica, 9(1)*, 21-36.

Thiselton, A.C. (2009). *Hermeneutics: An Introduction*. Cambridge: Eerdmans.

Thomas, M. (2011, July 15). Monday's medical myth: you can catch a cold by getting cold. *The Conversation*. Retrieved from: http://theconversation.com/mondays-medical-myth-you-can-catch-a-cold-by-getting-cold-2488

Thomas, S.D. (2009). *The Last Navigator: A Young Man, an Ancient Mariner, the Secrets of the Sea*. Booksurge Publishing.

Thornton, R. 2004. Why continuity. In A. Brugos, L. Micciulla and C.E. Smith (Eds.), Proceedings of the 28th Boston University Conference on Language Development, 620-632. Somerville, MA: Cascadilla Press.

Tolman, E. C. (1948). Cognitive maps in rats and men. Psychological Review, 55(4), 189-208.

Turing, A. (1950). Computing machinery and intelligence. *Mind, 49*, 433 - 460.

Turnbull, C.M. (1961). *The Forest People. A Study of the Pygmies of the Congo*. Simon & Schuster.

Tversky, A., & Kahneman, D. (1974). Judgment under uncertainty: Heuristics and biases. *Science, 185*, 1124-1131.

Unkelbach, C., Forgas, J.P., & Denson, T.F. (2008). The turban effect: The influence of Muslim headgear and induced affect on aggressive responses in the shooter bias paradigm. *Journal of Experimental Social Psychology, 44(5)*, 1409-1413.

Veselov, V. (2014, June 9). Computer AI passes Turing test in "world first". *BBC News: Technology*. Retrieved from: https://www.bbc.com/

Voiskunsky, E., & Lukodyanov, I. (1974). *The Crew of the Mekong*. Moscow: Mir Publishers.

Von Bredow, R. (2006). *Brazil's Pirahã tribe*. Living without numbers or time. Spiegel Online. Retrieved from https://www.spiegel.de/international/spiegel/brazil-s-Pirahã-tribe-living-without-numbers-or-time-a-414291.html

Wansink, B., Akkerman, S., Zuiker, I., & Wubbels, S. (2018). Where does teaching multiperspectivity in History education begin and end? An analysis of the uses of temporality. *Theory and Research in Social Education, 46(4)*, 495-527.

Wason, P. C. (1968). Reasoning about a rule. *Quarterly Journal of Experimental Psychology*, 20, 273–281.

Wegner, D.M., Wenzlaff, R., Kerker, R.M., & Beatiie, A.E. (1981). Incrimination through innuendo: Can media questions become public answers? *Journal of Personality and Social Psychology, 40(5)*, 822-832.

Wigner, E. (1960). The unreasonable effectiveness of mathematics in the natural sciences. *Communications in Pure and Applied Mathematics, 13*, 1-14.

Wilson, M. (2012, may 23). An ant ballet, choreographed by pheromones and robots. *Fast Company*. Retrieved from: https://www.fastcompany.com/1669858/an-ant-ballet-choreographed-by-pheromones-and-robots

Wittgenstein, L. (1986). *Philosophical Investigations. 3rd edition*. Basic Blackwell Ltd.

Wolchover, N. (2013, February 22). In computers we trust? *Quanta Magazine*. Retrieved from: https://www.quantamagazine.org/in-computers-we-trust-20130222/

Young, T. (1802). The Bakerian Lecture: On the Theory of Light and Colours. *Philosophical Transactions of the Royal Society of London, 92*, 12–48.

Zandwill, N. (2019). Aesthetic Judgment. In E. N. Zalta (Ed.), *The Stanford encyclopedia of philosophy* (Spring 2019 ed.). Retrieved from https://plato.stanford.edu/entries/aesthetic-judgment/

Milton Keynes UK
Ingram Content Group UK Ltd.
UKHW050941080823
426501UK00005B/20

9 780995 139008